2017-2018
SEPTEMBER–AUGUST
KJV ▶

Standard LESSON COMMENTARY®

KING JAMES VERSION

EDITORIAL TEAM
in alphabetical order

Jim Eichenberger

Ronald L. Nickelson

Douglas Redford

Andrew Sloan

Jonathan Underwood

Margaret K. Williams

Volume 65

Standard®
PUBLISHING
part of the David C Cook family

IN THIS VOLUME

Standard Lesson Commentary is published annually by Standard Publishing, www.standardpub.com. Copyright © 2017 by Standard Publishing, part of the David C Cook family, Colorado Springs, Colorado 80918. All rights reserved. Printed in the United States of America. Scripture taken from the *King James Version*. Lessons and/or readings based on *International Sunday School Lessons for Christian Teaching*; copyright © 2014, by the Committee on the Uniform Series.

INDEX OF PRINTED TEXTS

The printed texts for 2017–2018 are arranged here in the order in which they appear in the Bible.

✝

DON'T FORGET THE VISUALS!

The visuals pictured in the lessons are small reproductions of 18" x 24" full-color posters that are included in the *Adult Resources* packet for each quarter. These visuals include maps, charts, Bible art, photography, and calligraphy that will engage the visual learners in your class. Also included in *Adult Resources* are digital images of all the printed posters, PowerPoint® presentations for the lessons, and reproducible student activity pages.

From your supplier, order numbers 1629117 (fall 2017), 2629118 (winter 2017–2018), 3629118 (spring 2018), and 4629118 (summer 2018). Call 1-800-323-7543 or go to www.standardlesson.com/standard-lesson-resources/.

CUMULATIVE INDEX

A cumulative index for Scripture passages used in the STANDARD LESSON COMMENTARY
for September 2016–August 2018 (of the 2016–2022 cycle) is provided below.

NOTES:

_____

_____

_____

_____

_____

_____

STANDARD LESSON COMMENTARY

An effective study tool for ANY type of group!

FOR MORE THAN six decades, *Standard Lesson Commentary* (SLC) has been a trusted resource for Bible teachers. Those decades have seen new educational structures and technologies emerge. During that time, Standard Lesson products have been developed to help teachers in nearly any Bible teaching environment.

Classic Midweek Study

"Our congregation has a vibrant Wednesday night study. About 50 of us gather in the church auditorium for a lecture-oriented lesson. How do I use Standard Lesson Commentary *in this pulpit-to-pew setting?"*

What you need:

- *Standard Lesson Commentary*
- *Adult Resources*

The Lesson Outline on the second page of each SLC lesson is designed to structure a lecture presentation. Use the two verbal illustrations in the lesson at the appropriate points, as shown in the outline. Close with the Thought to Remember and Prayer from the next-to-last page of the lesson.

A word of caution: Don't think that a traditional setting cannot benefit from modern technology! *Adult Resources* contains a PowerPoint presentation for each session. For this environment, remove all slides except for the teaching outline, the Thought to Remember, and the visual for the lesson. As you teach, click through the slides to keep your group on task and engaged.

Mobile Mania

"My group could not be more different than the preceding example! We are a small class of twenty-somethings who are serious about Bible study. But everyone in the group uses a mobile device to access the Bible. How can Standard Lesson Commentary *help me with my mobile maniacs?"*

What you need:

- *Standard Lesson Commentary*
- *Free memberships to StandardLesson.com*

Mobile devices have changed the way we access information. This technology can be a great asset to serious Bible study.

Have students access www.standardlesson.com during your next class. Then have them click on the Members tab on the right-hand side of their menu bars and sign up for a free membership. A few clicks and they're connected!

Your copy of the SLC will still be your go-to resource, but your students will participate through the resources they now have access to as members of StandardLesson.com.

Start class by having members download the latest edition of In the World. This is a current-events discussion activity to introduce the lesson of the week. Have them read the article and discuss the accompanying questions.

Your lesson structure will come from the last page of the lesson, titled Involvement Learning.

Note the sections of that lesson plan that refer to using the reproducible pages. Your students have access to those free pages with their memberships to StandardLesson.com. Have them open the page for the lesson as directed on the Involvement Learning page. You are leading the class from the wealth of resources in your SLC, and your group is participating with the free resources accessible with their mobile devices.

Traditional Classroom Setting

"I teach in a very typical Sunday school setting. We have a classroom, tables, and chairs. What tools do I need to use Standard Lesson Commentary *most effectively in this setting?"*

What you need:

- ***Standard Lesson Commentary***
- ***Adult Resources***
- **Student books (*KJV & NIV* only)**

Display the full-color posters from *Adult Resources* in your classroom to pique interest in each lesson. There is one poster designed for each session. The caption under the thumbnail-size depictions of the visuals in the SLC will tell you how and when to refer to them.

You will use your copy of the SLC to structure the lesson. Your students will have copies of the Bible text and an abbreviated version of the commentary in their student books. This will aid in presentation and understanding of the main points of the lesson.

Your students will be able to analyze and apply the content with the activities in their student books. The activities will help students gain a deeper understanding the day's Bible lesson and motivate them to apply it.

Deep Thinkers, Big Talkers

"My group not only loves to study the Bible; they can't stop talking about it! How can the Standard Lesson Commentary *help me lead discussion-oriented classes effectively?"*

What you need:

- ***Standard Lesson Commentary***
- **Free memberships to StandardLesson.com**

Bible study is not complete without a commitment to apply what has been studied. Certainly strong, informed discussion is a great way to do just that.

A free membership to StandardLesson.com will give you access to In the World, a perfect way to open a discussion-oriented class. Each week our writer examines a news item or human-interest story in light of the Bible passage being studied. Before class, download this article with accompanying discussion questions and make a copy for each member of your group. Begin the session by distributing this activity and discussing it.

The commentary in the SLC will help you unpack the Bible content, verse by verse. Note that interspersed in the Bible commentary are What Do You Think? discussion questions. As you encounter these questions during your lesson presentation, open discussion by posing them. This will prompt your students to think deeply about the Bible content and how to apply it.

Note that the questions do not have pat answers! They are meant to *get* your group to think, not *tell* them what to think. These challenging questions are just what your group of deep thinkers and big talkers need for engaging, meaningful Bible study!

(continued on next page)

Getting Down to Business

"My class is filled with business professionals. I can't help but think that they feel more at home in the company boardroom than in the church's classroom! How can the **Standard Lesson Commentary** *help me help them?"*

What you need:

- *Standard Lesson Commentary*
- *Adult Resources*

Few things are more common in the business world than PowerPoint slide presentations. This method of communication is sure to be familiar to a class such as yours.

Adult Resources contains a PowerPoint presentation for every lesson. Each presentation includes the Lesson Outline, the visual for that lesson, What Do You Think? discussion questions, and learning activities that will help the group discover and apply lesson content.

A great advantage of PowerPoint is that students are engaged visually while you control the pace of the lesson as you present the lesson's Bible content.

For Personal Growth

"I am in a group that uses curriculum other than the **Standard Lesson Commentary.** *How can I best use the SLC on my own during my daily quiet times?"*

What you need:

- *Standard Lesson Commentary*
- *Devotions*

The *Standard Lesson Commentary* is designed specifically to help teachers of the Bible. But there is nothing stopping you from being both the teacher and a classroom of one!

The daily thoughts in *Devotions* are coordinated with topics in the SLC. The devotional readings begin with the topic for the week on Monday, then build daily to a climax on Sunday, when *Devotions* uses Scripture for the week's SLC lesson.

A good approach is to study part of the SLC lesson daily and end each private time with *Devotions*. There are many ways to divide up the lesson commentary throughout the week. Here is one:

Mon: the lesson's Introduction
Tue–Thu: verse-by-verse commentary
Fri: two verbal illustrations
Sat: discussion questions
Sun: Conclusion, Prayer, Thought to Remember

For more than six decades, *Standard Lesson Commentary* has been "that Sunday school book"—a trusted resource for adult Bible education in the church.

But Standard Lesson adds to this resource with helps for a wide variety of Bible study contexts. You can find them all at www.standardlesson.com!

COVENANT WITH GOD

Special Features

Lessons

Unit 1: Signs of God's Covenants

Unit 2: Called into Covenant with God

Unit 3: An Everlasting Covenant

QUARTERLY QUIZ

Use these questions as a pretest or as a review. The answers are on page iv of This Quarter in the Word.

Lesson 1

1. God affirmed to Noah that seedtime and _____ would never cease. *Genesis 8:22*

2. God told Noah of the need to destroy the earth a second time with water. T/F. *Genesis 9:11*

Lesson 2

1. Abraham was given his name because he would be _____ of many nations. *Genesis 17:5*

2. The covenant sign Abraham and his male descendants were to bear was _____. *Genesis 17:11*

Lesson 3

1. The penalty for working on the Sabbath was what? (death, 40 lashes, prison?) *Exodus 31:14, 15*

2. The Lord's words to be obeyed were written on two tablets of wood. T/F. *Exodus 31:18*

Lesson 4

1. God's rescue of His captive people was for the sake of God's holy _____. *Ezekiel 36:22*

2. God promised to give His people a new what? (pick two: land, heart, spirit, stone, name?) *Ezekiel 36:26*

Lesson 5

1. Abram's (Abraham's) belief was counted to him for _____. *Genesis 15:6*

2. Which people group is not mentioned as occupying the land promised to Abram's seed? (Moabites, Jebusites, Kenites?) *Genesis 15:18-21*

Lesson 6

1. The Lord's descent on Sinai was accompanied by what? (hail, wind, fire?) *Exodus 19:18*

2. Only Moses was allowed to approach God on Mount Sinai. T/F. *Exodus 19:24*

Lesson 7

1. Having the fear of God is a personal deterrent to _____. *Exodus 20:20*

2. At the heart of Israel's worship was to be an altar of what? (gold, silver, earth?) *Exodus 20:24*

Lesson 8

1. The Lord granted permission to David to build a "house" for God. T/F. *2 Samuel 7:5, 12, 13*

2. David's predecessor as king was who? (Saul, Samuel, Solomon?) *2 Samuel 7:15*

Lesson 9

1. The returned exiles traced their difficulties back to the time of the kings of which country? (Babylon, Assyria, Greece?) *Nehemiah 9:32*

2. The people's commitment to the law of God included a curse and an oath. T/F. *Nehemiah 10:29*

Lesson 10

1. God granted Phinehas, priest and grandson of Aaron, a covenant of _____. *Numbers 25:10-12*

2. God said that a different Phinehas would die on the same day as his brother. T/F. *1 Samuel 2:34*

Lesson 11

1. God revealed to Jeremiah that the new covenant would be made with the houses of _____ and _____. *Jeremiah 31:31*

2. A key feature of the new covenant is that God forgives sin but does not forget it. T/F. *Jeremiah 31:34*

Lesson 12

1. The experience at Sinai was so intense that even Moses was fearful. T/F. *Hebrews 12:21*

2. The writer of Hebrews affirms that God is a consuming _____. *Hebrews 12:29*

Lesson 13

1. The two physical elements of the Lord's Supper are _____ and cup. *1 Corinthians 11:26-28*

2. Self-examination should precede observing the Lord's Supper. T/F. *1 Corinthians 11:27-29*

QUARTER AT A GLANCE

by Douglas Redford

THE CONCEPT of a covenant-making deity was virtually unknown to pagan religions of the ancient Near East (see Get the Setting, page 4). The impersonal nature of their fictitious gods contrasts starkly with the personal nature of the true God, the one who declares, "I have loved thee with an everlasting love" (Jeremiah 31:3). He demonstrates that love through the covenants He makes with humanity.

Signs from God

A characteristic of God's covenants is His provision of signs to accompany them. Such signs, or symbols, serve as reminders or visual aids. As such, they keep people aware of both their privileges and their responsibilities under the covenant at issue. This is necessary; for while God has a spotless record as a covenant keeper, humans are just as consistent in being covenant breakers. God knows all too well our tendency to forget or to be distracted from pursuing His desires for us.

The covenant signs highlighted in our first unit of study are the rainbow, circumcision, Sabbath observance, and the presence of the Spirit. The presence of the rainbow (lesson 1) and the Spirit (lesson 4) point to obligations God has placed on himself. On the other hand, the signs of circumcision (lesson 2) and observance of the Sabbath (lesson 3) point to obligations that God placed on humans. An interesting difference!

Servants of God

Our second unit of study highlights God's partnership with the obedient. Under particular consideration in that regard are Abraham (lesson 5), Moses (lessons 6 and 7), and David (lesson 8). They are key figures in the history of Israel, history that included a return from exile that only God could have orchestrated (lesson 9).

Sometimes the making of a covenant is accompanied by non-enduring signs—visual aids intended only for the original audience. For example, God's covenant with Abraham featured a rather mysterious procedure in which God had him participate. This assured the patriarch that God would keep His promises.

Offering more examples are the two lessons concerning Moses as they note the sights and sounds of thunder, lightning, thick cloud, loud trumpet, smoke, fire, earthquake, thick darkness, and even the voice of God himself! All were meant to have a lasting impression on the Israelites in deterring sin (Exodus 20:20). But history reveals Israel's failure in this regard, and the Jews of Nehemiah's day had their personal experience of return from exile as a reminder to obey God.

Son of God

Our third unit of study touches on some distinctive qualities of the new covenant in Jesus. The prophet Jeremiah (lesson 11) foresaw this covenant as he looked ahead to God's intentions to "remember their sin no more" (Jeremiah 31:34). The study from Hebrews 12 (lesson 12) notes how Jesus is the mediator of the new covenant. Fittingly, that

> **God has a spotless record as a covenant keeper.**

lesson is followed by instructions on observing the Lord's Supper. Christ instituted this visual aid as a way for us to remind ourselves of the basis of the new covenant under which we live.

When *New* Means *Better*

Personal experience teaches us that something advertised as new does not always mean it is better than what is being replaced. But Hebrews 8:6 is our assured reminder that the new covenant in Christ is infinitely better than the old. How privileged we are to live under the better!

GET THE SETTING

by Lloyd Pelfrey

BINDING AGREEMENTS, or covenants, were known and used in ancient times. A more familiar term today is *contracts*. We can hardly imagine how any society, ancient or modern, could function without them!

The Bible's first use of the word *covenant* is in Genesis 6:18 regarding Noah (compare 9:8-17, lesson 1). But a passage often overlooked concerning an even earlier covenant is Hosea 6:7. The majority interpretation affirms that not only had Israel ("they") broken covenants, Adam had done so as well—although the word *covenant* is not used in Genesis 1–3. (The Hebrew word *adam* can refer to the first human, to people in general [compare Job 31:33 on these two], or to a place [Joshua 3:16].)

If the very first human can be said to have been associated with a covenant, then it is reasonable to assume that covenants became widespread among humanity in general. Indeed, solid evidence exists to establish that this is the case. At least four types of covenants have been identified.

Parity Agreements

These occur when two or more individuals enter freely into a pact of some kind. Archaeologists have discovered an abundance of documentation, with records dated before the time of Abraham (2000 BC), describing business agreements, marriages, etc. The rituals varied. In one case, a clay tablet describes a ceremony in which a she-goat and a dog were brought as sacrificial animals. A participant insisted that he wanted a young donkey instead. That was done, and the covenant was established. The patriarchs Abraham, Isaac, and Jacob each entered into parity agreements (see Genesis 14:13; 26:28-31; 31:44, respectively).

Suzerain or Vassal Covenants

A king who conquered a nation was considered the suzerain (pronounced *soo*-zer-in), and the suzerain dictated terms to the vassal. The Hittites of Asia Minor are given the credit for developing a suzerain covenant that was used as a model by many throughout the second millennium BC.

Some scholars have discerned that the outline of a Hittite suzerain treaty is used for the book of Deuteronomy and the last chapter of Joshua. This factor helps date the writing of these books.

A compilation from different treaty tablets demonstrates the parts of a suzerain document: a preamble with the name and titles of the suzerain, a prologue describing previous deeds, the actual terms for the parties, the deposit of the document in a specific place (often a temple), a listing of witnesses, and the curses or blessings on the parties of the covenant. The listing of witnesses often includes the names of gods and goddesses.

Divine Covenants

Deity is not merely a witness in this type of covenant; He establishes its terms. This is the type of covenant found most frequently in the Bible. It is virtually unknown in pagan religions, since their gods do not speak. We say "virtually" because scholars have found what appears to be a record of one such covenant: a clay tablet from about 680 BC. The tablet lists the pagan god Asshur promising future battle victories to King Esarhaddon of Assyria (mentioned in 2 Kings 19:37; Isaiah 37:38; and Ezra 4:2).

Covenant Renewals

Found only in the Bible, these feature rededication to an existing covenant. Joshua 24:25 summarizes one such.

Conclusion

In His wisdom, God stated His relationship with people through an instrument familiar to everyone: the covenant. The Son of God came to establish a new covenant so all peoples might have the opportunity to enter it—and to keep it.

THIS QUARTER IN THE WORD

Answers to the Quarterly Quiz on page 2

Lesson 1—1. harvest. 2. false. **Lesson 2**—1. father. 2. circumcision. **Lesson 3**—1. death. 2. false. **Lesson 4**—1. name. 2. heart, spirit. **Lesson 5**—1. righteousness. 2. Moabites. **Lesson 6**—1. fire. 2. false. **Lesson 7**—1. sin. 2. earth. **Lesson 8**—1. false. 2. Saul. **Lesson 9**—1. Assyria. 2. true. **Lesson 10**—1. peace. 2. true. **Lesson 11**—1. Israel, Judah. 2. false. **Lesson 12**—1. true. 2. fire. **Lesson 13**—1. bread. 2. true.

LESSON CYCLE CHART

International Sunday School Lesson Cycle, September 2016–August 2022

Year	Fall Quarter (Sep, Oct, Nov)	Winter Quarter (Dec, Jan, Feb)	Spring Quarter (Mar, Apr, May)	Summer Quarter (Jun, Jul, Aug)
2016–2017	**The Sovereignty of God** (Isaiah, Matthew, Hebrews, Revelation)	**Creation: A Divine Cycle** (Psalms, Luke, Galatians)	**God Loves Us** (Psalms, Joel, Jonah, John, Romans, Ephesians, 1 Peter, 1 John)	**God's Urgent Call** (Exodus, Judges, Prophets, Acts)
2017–2018	**Covenant with God** (Pentateuch, 1 & 2 Samuel, Nehemiah, Jeremiah, Ezekiel, 1 Corinthians, Hebrews)	**Faith in Action** (Daniel, Matthew, Acts, Ephesians, 1 Timothy, James)	**Acknowledging God** (Pentateuch, 2 Chronicles, Psalms, Luke, John, 2 Corinthians, Hebrews, Revelation)	**Justice in the New Testament** (Matthew, Luke, Romans, 2 Corinthians, Colossians)
2018–2019	**God's World and God's People** (Genesis)	**Our Love for God** (Exodus, Deuteronomy, Joshua, Psalms, Matthew, Luke, Epistles)	**Discipleship and Mission** (Matthew, Luke, Acts, Romans)	**Covenant in God** (Ruth, 1 Samuel, Matthew, Mark, Ephesians, Colossians, Hebrews)
2019–2020	**Responding to God's Grace** (Pentateuch, 1 Samuel, 1 Kings, Luke, Epistles)	**Honoring God** (1 Kings, 1 Chronicles, Matthew, Luke)	**Justice and the Prophets** (Esther, Prophets, 1 Corinthians)	**Many Faces of Wisdom** (Proverbs, Ecclesiastes, Gospels, James)
2020–2021	**Love for One Another** (Genesis, 1 Samuel, Luke, John, Acts, Epistles)	**Call in the New Testament** (Isaiah, Gospels, Acts, Romans, 1 Corinthians, Hebrews)	**Prophets Faithful to God's Covenant** (Exodus, Joshua, 1 & 2 Kings, Ezra, Nehemiah, Lamentations, Prophets)	**Confident Hope** (Leviticus, Matthew, Luke, Romans, 2 Corinthians, Hebrews, 1 John)
2021–2022	**Celebrating God** (Exodus, 2 Samuel, Psalms, Mark, Acts, Revelation)	**Justice, Law, History** (Pentateuch, 2 Samuel, Ezra, Job, Isaiah, Nahum)	**God Frees and Redeems** (Deuteronomy, Ezra, Matthew, John, Romans, Galatians)	**Partners in a New Creation** (Isaiah, John, Revelation)

God	Creation	Love	Call	Covenant	Faith	Worship	Justice

OBJECTS OR PARTNERS?

Teacher Tips by Jon Weatherly

"I TAUGHT WELL; they learned poorly." As a teacher of the Bible, I have wanted to use that excuse. I have worked to be well prepared and to have thoughtful learning objectives and engaging lesson plans. So how do I respond when things do not go well? Blame the students!

New Outlook

Lately I have revised my view. In the past I thought of class members as the objects of my teaching, those who received what I gave. Now I try to think of them as partners in the quest to know God and His Word.

As objects, class members are the things moved by my efforts. I stimulate their interest. I deliver content to their minds. I touch sensitive places in their hearts. I induce them to follow the path that I have laid out. Sometimes I get that just right. Sometimes I fail. It's up to me.

But partners are different. Partners participate as equals. Every partner contributes. In a teaching/learning partnership, everyone is teaching and everyone is learning in a committed, long-term relationship. Teaching partners rather than teaching objects makes me acknowledge this unchanging truth: *each individual brings a distinct perspective.*

New Approach

As a teacher of objects, I aim the lesson at class members, with their differences, as best I can. As a teacher of partners, I rely on those differences to help everyone understand aspects of truth that we would otherwise miss. I remain the senior partner: I take responsibility to lead the conversation and assure full engagement. But I approach the class expecting everyone to contribute uniquely.

Differences of gender, ethnicity, education, culture, and economic class can either divide or enrich a group of people. As I think of my students as partners, I realize that their differences are an asset. As a man, I hear other men's perspectives on the Bible in ways that resonate with my own. But I need to hear women's perspectives as they read the Bible, to balance and even correct mine. The same is true for me as a person with a graduate-school education, as I listen to people with different backgrounds and experiences.

Common Ground

Our common ground and irreducible standard is, of course, the sacred text of Scripture. The text means what the original writers intended it to mean, not what we want it to mean. The Bible challenges all of our experiences with its declaration of God's truth. It corrects our faulty conclusions. But to do that, it needs to be heard for what it truly is. As we study the language, history, and literary art of the Bible, the clash of our differing perspectives helps us distinguish mere opinion from genuinely biblical teaching.

But what if the personal experiences of one of our class partners has resulted in a deeply flawed view of the biblical text? In a partnering classroom, truth is still truth. Within the errors of others may lie kernels of truth that can inform everyone in the partnership.

Imagine a class member who cannot affirm the Bible's teaching that God is "Father." Does that person have a troubled past with a human father? How can Scripture redirect that person to an important part of the human birthright? Can every class member learn from the conversation?

Better Together

Together we can contribute to a more mature understanding of the God of the Bible as we listen to and respect each other's perspectives. Partnerships are not easy or tidy. But over time they can be powerful. See how your class performs differently when members become partners instead of objects!

THE
RAINBOW

DEVOTIONAL READING: Isaiah 54:1-10
BACKGROUND SCRIPTURE: Genesis 8:20–9:17

GENESIS 8:20-22

20 And Noah builded an altar unto the LORD; and took of every clean beast, and of every clean fowl, and offered burnt offerings on the altar.

21 And the LORD smelled a sweet savour; and the LORD said in his heart, I will not again curse the ground any more for man's sake; for the imagination of man's heart is evil from his youth; neither will I again smite any more every thing living, as I have done.

22 While the earth remaineth, seedtime and harvest, and cold and heat, and summer and winter, and day and night shall not cease.

GENESIS 9:8-17

8 And God spake unto Noah, and to his sons with him, saying,

9 And I, behold, I establish my covenant with you, and with your seed after you;

10 And with every living creature that is with you, of the fowl, of the cattle, and of every beast of the earth with you; from all that go out of the ark, to every beast of the earth.

11 And I will establish my covenant with you; neither shall all flesh be cut off any more by the waters of a flood; neither shall there any more be a flood to destroy the earth.

12 And God said, This is the token of the covenant which I make between me and you and every living creature that is with you, for perpetual generations:

13 I do set my bow in the cloud, and it shall be for a token of a covenant between me and the earth.

14 And it shall come to pass, when I bring a cloud over the earth, that the bow shall be seen in the cloud:

15 And I will remember my covenant, which is between me and you and every living creature of all flesh; and the waters shall no more become a flood to destroy all flesh.

16 And the bow shall be in the cloud; and I will look upon it, that I may remember the everlasting covenant between God and every living creature of all flesh that is upon the earth.

17 And God said unto Noah, This is the token of the covenant, which I have established between me and all flesh that is upon the earth.

KEY VERSE

I will establish my covenant with you; neither shall all flesh be cut off any more by the waters of a flood; neither shall there any more be a flood to destroy the earth. —**Genesis 9:11**

COVENANT WITH GOD

Unit 1: Signs of God's Covenants
LESSONS 1–4

LESSON AIMS

After participating in this lesson, each learner will be able to:

1. List elements of the covenant God made with Noah and all living creatures on the earth after the flood.

2. Compare and contrast the Noahic covenant with other covenants God made.

3. Write a statement of commitment to honor the covenant relationship he or she enjoys as a believer in Christ.

LESSON OUTLINE

Introduction

A. It's a Sign!

A quick glance at an object, image, or document can give us information in an instant. When we see a diamond on the ring finger of a woman's left hand, we immediately know that a proposal for marriage has been accepted. The presence of a license plate on an automobile indicates that the vehicle is allowed to operate on public roads. That framed diploma in our doctor's office assures us that he or she has completed a course of study in preparation for treating our ailments.

By these and many other visual devices we communicate. It should not surprise us, then, that God does the same. Today we will look at a sign from God that communicates not only an important promise but also a fact of history.

B. Lesson Background

The biblical account of the great flood is but one of at least five ancient flood stories. The existence of the latter leads some to believe that the biblical account used them as sources, and that the flood is a legendary myth of an ancient and ignorant people. But if there truly was a great flood in ancient times, then stories of the event would be passed down from generation to generation.

As people spread over the earth and formed distinct cultures, these stories would take on the characteristics of those cultures. It would be strange indeed if accounts of the actual great flood were absent altogether from ancient writings! So the existence of the nonbiblical stories actually serves to confirm that there was indeed a great flood at some point in history. The Bible's account of this flood is the accurate one. The Bible's unerring track record on other historical matters and the divine inspiration of Scripture (2 Timothy 3:16) assure us of this fact.

The biblical account of the great flood is detailed in giving specifics for the beginning of the flood, the length of time the rain fell, how long the floodwaters covered the earth, and how long it took for the waters to recede. The total amount of time adds up to a little more than a year (Genesis 7:11; 8:14).

I. Noah Worships

(Genesis 8:20-22)

One can only imagine the joy and relief that Noah and his family experience on leaving the ark and stepping once again on solid ground. Noah's first act thereafter is to worship, to give thanks to the Lord for His providential care in bringing his family safely through this experience.

A. First Altar (v. 20)

20. And Noah builded an altar unto the LORD; and took of every clean beast, and of every clean fowl, and offered burnt offerings on the altar.

This is the first altar mentioned in Scripture—though it is not the first blood sacrifice (see Genesis 4:4). When Noah was commanded to save pairs of animals in the ark, more clean animals were spared than unclean ones (Genesis 6:19, 20; 7:2, 3). Perhaps the act of sacrifice noted in the verse before us has been intended from the beginning, provision for it having been made by keeping more of the appropriate animals alive. We are not told what differentiates clean animals from unclean ones at this point in history, but Noah somehow knows the difference.

> *What Do You Think?*
> What are some ways to express thanks to God for a deliverance or other special blessing?
> *Talking Points for Your Discussion*
> - In acts of private worship
> - In acts of corporate worship
> - In acts of worship that witness to unbelievers
> - Other

B. Final Curse (v. 21)

21. And the LORD smelled a sweet savour; and the LORD said in his heart, I will not again curse the ground any more for man's sake; for the imagination of man's heart is evil from his youth; neither will I again smite any more every thing living, as I have done.

The writer (Moses) uses figurative language to describe God's response to the sacrifice. Since "God is a Spirit" (John 4:24), we need not assume that God smells things the same way we do or has a literal, physical heart. Nevertheless, we understand such language. The same manner of figurative language is used when Scripture speaks of the "hand" and "arm" of the Lord (Deuteronomy 4:34; 5:15; 7:19; etc.). This kind of figurative language is known as *anthropomorphic*.

The point being made is that God accepts the offering. Moses will use the same kind of language later to describe the sacrifices and burnt offerings that the new nation of Israel will be commanded to present to the Lord (see Exodus 29:18, 25, 41; compare Philippians 4:18; contrast Leviticus 26:31; Amos 5:21).

But we may wonder to what end God accepts Noah's offerings. In later times, burnt offerings will atone for sin (Leviticus 1:1-9) and to ordain the Aaronic priesthood (Exodus 29). Some suggest that Noah's offerings are for atonement for the sins of all who perished in the flood, but that is not likely. Ordinarily an offering of atonement is made in lieu of punishment, but those who have perished have already been punished.

More likely, Noah's sacrifice is to purify the earth. Aaron and his sons will offer burnt offerings to purify themselves for the new priesthood centuries later; similarly, Noah offers sacrifices to cleanse the earth as home to new generations.

Up to this point in the Bible, the ground has been spoken of as being under a curse only twice. The ground was cursed in Genesis 3:17 because of sin. Only with difficulty would humanity be able to make a living from it (3:18, 19). Much later, Noah's father, Lamech, prophesied Noah to be the one to bring relief from the burdensome toil because of the ground "which the Lord hath cursed" (5:29). The question that arises, then, is whether the statement *I will not again curse the ground* here in 8:21 refers to the flood itself or to the original curse of 3:17. If the latter, then the prophecy of 5:29 is fulfilled—but then we have to ask why thorns and thistles still interfere (3:18) and why agriculture still involves sweat-producing labor (3:19). If the reference is to the punishment of the flood, then the promise to *not again curse the ground* is another way of stating the promise never again to flood the earth (see 9:11, below).

The reason given, because *the imagination of man's heart is evil from his youth,* fits better with the concept that the flood itself was the curse of the ground that will not be repeated. Time will reveal that the flood is not the permanent solution to sin, so repeating it will serve no purpose. The sacrifice of Christ will be needed to address the heart need and sin guilt of people.

C. Continual Seasons (v. 22)

22. While the earth remaineth, seedtime and harvest, and cold and heat, and summer and winter, and day and night shall not cease.

Days and years and seasons come about by the rotation of the earth and the tilt of its axis as the planet moves around the sun. These are constant and unchanging. But sometimes weather can block awareness of those constants. In a strong storm, the sun can be obscured to such an extent that daytime seems like night. One can imagine that the 40 days of rain Noah experienced were difficult to count. The cloud cover needed to produce such rain probably blocked sunlight almost totally during much of that time.

In addition, the months that passed with water high enough to cover the mountains (Genesis 7:20, 24) surely resulted in climate change. Evaporation of the floodwaters would have caused significant cloud cover once again. The earth would have cooled during this time. Perhaps Noah and his family were able to discern a significant change in climate by the end of their time on the ark. This could have caused concern about where such climate change would lead.

This promise in the verse before us allays any such fears. Even when storms are strong enough to obscure the sun for a time, *day and night shall not cease.* Climate change may occur, but there will still be *summer and winter.* In one area the winter may bring snow, but in others the winter is more of a rainy season. Still the seasons change with regularity as the earth continues on its course around the sun.

Even so, the Lord does allow for cataclysmic change—even outright destruction. The constant change of seasons that allows *seedtime and harvest* will continue only as long as the earth itself does so. Peter refers to the Noahic flood as an illustration that God is able to judge the world and that there is coming another destruction, one by fire (2 Peter 3:6, 7). But until that time of judgment, the cycles of the seasons will continue. Perhaps we should spend more time warning of the coming judgment because of sin rather than worrying about predictions of climate change because of carbon dioxide in the atmosphere!

What Do You Think?
How can we use Genesis 8:22 to comfort someone after a disastrous weather event?
Talking Points for Your Discussion
- Considering the person's familiarity with and/or acceptance of Scripture
- Regarding the danger of trivializing a situation
- Other

II. God Promises
(GENESIS 9:8-11)

Genesis 9:1-7 (not in today's text) begins with God's instruction for Noah and his family to increase the population. Humanity is to multiply anew over the face of the earth. Hand in hand with this instruction is a covenant that God expresses between himself and the earth.

A. Covenant Participants (vv. 8-10)

8, 9. And God spake unto Noah, and to his sons with him, saying, And I, behold, I establish my covenant with you, and with your seed after you.

This is the fifth time the biblical record reports on God's speaking to Noah. God spoke to him alone on the first three occasions (Genesis 6:13; 7:1; 8:15). Beginning at 9:1, Noah's sons are addressed as well. There is no explanation for the

HOW TO SAY IT

Aaronic	Air-*ahn*-ik.
anthropomorphic	*an*-thruh-puh-**more**-fik.
Lamech	*Lay*-mek.
Noah	*No*-uh.
Noahic	No-*ay*-ik.

change, and it would be reading too much into the text to suggest the sons were not true believers before the flood and only afterward were proper candidates for inclusion in the covenant.

Even before the flood, God indicated His intent to make the covenant that is now under discussion (Genesis 6:18). All those who came through the flood, as well as their descendants (*your seed after you*), are included. Therefore all people for all time who live after the flood are part of the covenant.

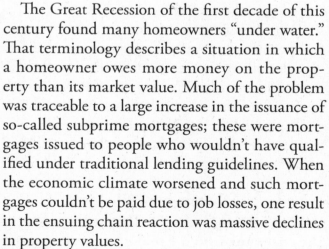

What Do You Think?
How can the fact that we are included in a covenant God made first with Noah encourage us?
Talking Points for Your Discussion
- When we are spiritually or emotionally "down"
- When we are spiritually or emotionally "up"

10. And with every living creature that is with you, of the fowl, of the cattle, and of every beast of the earth with you; from all that go out of the ark, to every beast of the earth.

The covenant includes animals as well. This is not to be understood that animals have equal value in God's sight. Jesus specifically rejects that notion (Matthew 10:31; Luke 12:7). The fact that animals are permitted as food for humans (Genesis 9:3) further reinforces that humans are of greater value than animals.

Even so, *every living creature* shares in the covenant. They have their place in God's creation, and even those permitted as food are not to be eaten with their blood still in them, which is their life (Genesis 9:4). Animal life has value and is entitled to a certain measure of respect. Human superiority is not a license to abuse animals (see Proverbs 12:10).

B. Covenant Promises (v. 11)

11a. And I will establish my covenant with you; neither shall all flesh be cut off any more by the waters of a flood.

As important as what the covenant promises is what it does not promise. It does not promise there will never be another flood of any magnitude, nor does it promise that there will never again be loss of life by means of flooding.

Floods have occurred many times since the days of Noah. The covenant promises instead not to repeat a flood like the one just experienced. From now on, floods will never be so severe as to leave only eight survivors (1 Peter 3:20).

11b. Neither shall there any more be a flood to destroy the earth.

The second part of the covenant promise reinforces the first part. Any understanding of the Noahic flood to have been merely localized must deal with this promise. If the promise is never to repeat a local flood, then the promise cannot be believed because there have been many local floods since the promise was given.

What Do You Think?
How would you respond to someone who says that floods today prove that God has not kept His promise?
Talking Points for Your Discussion
- Answering a new believer who is uncertain about the authority of Scripture
- Answering an unbeliever who is seeking answers sincerely
- Answering a hardened atheist

◆ On Being "Under Water" ◆

The Great Recession of the first decade of this century found many homeowners "under water." That terminology describes a situation in which a homeowner owes more money on the property than its market value. Much of the problem was traceable to a large increase in the issuance of so-called subprime mortgages; these were mortgages issued to people who wouldn't have qualified under traditional lending guidelines. When the economic climate worsened and such mortgages couldn't be paid due to job losses, one result in the ensuing chain reaction was massive declines in property values.

Governmental agencies responded with laws and regulations designed to prevent recurrence of such a crisis. Whether these efforts will be successful, who knows? On the other hand, God's promise never again to destroy the earth by flood is 100 percent certain. The God who makes the promise to

Visual for Lesson 1. *Start a discussion by pointing to this visual as you ask, "In what ways have you found this statement to be true in your own life?"*

all humanity also wants to help us personally. We all end up "under water" in various ways at various times—sometimes due to our own foolishness or sin, sometimes through no fault of our own. Either way, the solution begins with looking to the God who restores. No matter how far "under water" our lives seem to be, He stands ready to help. Think of how much He already has done so by giving His Son to die for our sins!

—C. R. B.

III. Bow Confirms
(Genesis 9:12-17)

Promises backed with a confirmation are especially powerful. An example from real estate transactions is earnest money. This is a deposit that confirms a buyer's intent to follow through on an offer to purchase (compare 2 Corinthians 5:5; Ephesians 1:14). The confirmation of God's promise in today's text is of a different kind but no less strong.

A. Symbol (vv. 12, 13)

12, 13. And God said, This is the token of the covenant which I make between me and you and every living creature that is with you, for perpetual generations: I do set my bow in the cloud, and it shall be for a token of a covenant between me and the earth.

God offers the rainbow as the visual symbol (*token*) that guarantees He will keep His promise.

Some Bible students believe that this is the first appearance of a rainbow ever; others believe that God simply adds significance to the phenomenon that already exists.

The word used to refer to the rainbow here is the same word in both English and Hebrew as the bow that is a weapon of war (examples: Genesis 48:22; 1 Samuel 18:4). This overlap may simply be a reference to the shape they have in common, the long arc typifying both the rainbow and the archer's bow. Some suggest a greater significance in proposing that God is laying aside His *bow* (weapon) and will not again exercise the kind of wrath the world has just experienced.

B. Significance (vv. 14, 15)

14. And it shall come to pass, when I bring a cloud over the earth, that the bow shall be seen in the cloud.

The rainbow's spectrum of color is created as sunlight passes through atmospheric moisture. We generally do not see a rainbow during a storm, when sunlight is blocked by clouds. So this symbol of the covenant is not seen each and every time there are rain clouds *over the earth*, but when the sunlight is not obscured by clouds.

> *What Do You Think?*
> How does knowing the science of a rainbow affect your appreciation of it as a covenant symbol from God?
>
> *Talking Points for Your Discussion*
> - What it suggests about divine and human knowledge
> - What it suggests about why God uses symbols in the first place
> - Other

15. And I will remember my covenant, which is between me and you and every living creature of all flesh; and the waters shall no more become a flood to destroy all flesh.

Note that the Lord does not say we should see the rainbow and remember His covenant; rather, He says *I will remember my covenant*. We may find it odd that the all-knowing God needs to be reminded of anything. Once again the text uses figurative language. While we need reminders, God does not; but we understand that a reminder is assurance that something important will not be forgotten. God is giving assurance that He will not forget or forsake His covenant. And in that regard the rainbow is a symbol for us as well.

C. Summary (vv. 16, 17)

16, 17. And the bow shall be in the cloud; and I will look upon it, that I may remember the everlasting covenant between God and every living creature of all flesh that is upon the earth. And God said unto Noah, This is the token of the covenant, which I have established between me and all flesh that is upon the earth.

These two verses essentially repeat what has already been said. In so doing, they summarize the covenant. The phrase *everlasting covenant* repeats a concept from verse 12, where God says this covenant is "for perpetual generations." But neither the word *everlasting* nor the word *perpetual* should be taken to mean that the covenant extends into eternity. The time limitation of Genesis 8:22 is that the covenant is in force "while the earth remaineth."

That observation is not to be taken as a warning of possible flooding in our eternal abode! Rather, it sheds light on the significance of the word *everlasting* as it is occurs in other contexts regarding God's covenants (examples: Genesis 17:13, 19; Leviticus 24:8; 2 Samuel 23:5; 1 Chronicles 16:17).

◆ *PREPAREDNESS* ◆

One of the most famous photos of a rainbow is that of nature photographer Galen Rowell (1940–2002). His photo shows a rainbow with one end appearing to rest on a palace in Tibet. When Rowell first saw the rainbow, it wasn't near the palace. But his artistic sense could "see" that it could be. So he ran more than a mile to get the building and rainbow lined up properly. His physical and aesthetic preparedness resulted in an artistic triumph.

We recall that "faith is the substance of things hoped for, the evidence of things not seen" (Hebrews 11:1). In that regard, "by faith Noah . . . became heir of the righteousness which is by faith" (11:7). He did not need to foresee a covenant that would result in being symbolized by a rainbow.

What Noah needed—and had—was prepared faith. It was a faith that trusted God for the future. It was a faith that led Noah to obedient action. The blessing signified by the rainbow resulted.

For Noah, it was all about preparedness. Building the ark was vital, of course. But the basis of God's choosing him to do so was spiritual in nature (Genesis 6:9). And so it is with us. If we do not sense God's calling for a task, perhaps the issue is our own spiritual unpreparedness to receive such a calling.   —C. R. B.

Conclusion

A. I Promise

Being something of a grammar purist, I chafe when I hear people say "I promise" when they really mean "I assure you." Sometimes the two are interchangeable, but sometimes they are not. An example of the latter is when someone says "I promise you, I was not the one who did that." A promise always looks to the future. I can make assurances about the past, but I can promise only for the future, as in "I promise I will never do such a thing again!" God promised that "the waters shall no more become a flood to destroy all flesh" (Genesis 9:15). The rainbow assures us that He will keep His promise.

B. Prayer

Father, as the rainbow comforts us with Your promise never again to destroy the earth by flood, may we also be moved to action by the coming destruction by fire. Empower us to share Jesus as the way of escape. We pray in His name. Amen.

C. Thought to Remember

Nothing is more certain than a promise
from the God who cannot lie!

VISUALS FOR THESE LESSONS

The visual pictured in each lesson (example: page 14) is a small reproduction of a large, full-color poster included in the *Adult Resources* packet for the Fall Quarter. That packet also contains the very useful *Presentation Tools* CD for teacher use. Order No. 1629117 from your supplier.

INVOLVEMENT LEARNING

Enhance your lesson with KJV Bible Student *(from your curriculum supplier) and the reproducible activity page (at www.standardlesson.com or in the back of the* KJV Standard Lesson Commentary Deluxe Edition*).*

Into the Lesson

Before class, write each of the following words or phrases on separate index cards. (Each word or phrase is followed by a suggested gesture that you will not write on the card.)

It's OK (touching thumb with forefinger)

Come here (flexing pointing forefinger)

Great job (fist bump or high five)

Be quiet (forefinger to lips)

Good-bye (wave hand)

Get out (extended arm and forefinger or point-ing thumb over shoulder)

I didn't like it (thumb pointed down)

Peace (forming a V with index and middle fingers)

It's a deal (handshake)

Start class by having a class member take an index card and communicate the word or phrase with a simple gesture. The class members who will make the *great job* and *it's a deal* gestures will need to do so with another person.

Alternative. Distribute copies of the "Sign Scramble" activity from the reproducible page, which you can download. Have students work individually or in pairs.

After either activity, lead into Bible study by saying, "We use different symbols, gestures, and signs to communicate without words. Today we will look at a sign from God that communicates an important promise."

Into the Word

Divide your class into three groups, giving each one paper and pens. Each group should be assigned a section of the lesson text. Each group should try to summarize the lesson text with a couplet, two rhyming lines of poetry.

Scripture assignments and sample couplets follow:

Group 1—Never Again (Genesis 8:20-22)

Though humankind is prone to sin,

God won't destroy all life again.

Group 2—I Establish (Genesis 9:8-11)

God's solemn promise has been made

From Noah's time up till this day.

Group 3—My Token (Genesis 9:12-17)

When seeing a rainbow, everyone should

Remember that God's promise is good.

Allow time for groups to share their couplets and summarize their Scripture assignments.

Option. Write both the Scripture assignments and the sample couplets on the board. Read each section of the text together as a class. Then discuss the content of each section, referring to the cou-plet and to the commentary.

Into Life

On the top of the board or on two large posters, write these two headings: *Ways I Show Dependence on God's Promises* and *Ways I Show I Doubt God's Promises.* Take time to brainstorm items to add under either heading. Sample ideas follow:

Dependence: prayer, regular church attendance, personal devotional Bible reading, participation in a small group, a disciplined plan for giving to support the work of the church, volunteering for ministry such as a short-term mission trip, finding an accountability partner.

Doubt: workaholism, substance abuse, worry, fixation on entertainment and escapism, unhealthy focus on money and possessions, neglecting church attendance and prayer and Bible study, behaving differently around believers than around unbelievers, dishonesty

Alternative. Distribute copies of the "Pre-scribed Promises" activity from the reproducible page. Have students choose the need they have today and memorize the corresponding prescribed promise from the Bible this week.

CIRCUMCISION

DEVOTIONAL READING: Psalm 105:1-11
BACKGROUND SCRIPTURE: Genesis 17

GENESIS 17:1-14

1 And when Abram was ninety years old and nine, the LORD appeared to Abram, and said unto him, I am the Almighty God; walk before me, and be thou perfect.

2 And I will make my covenant between me and thee, and will multiply thee exceedingly.

3 And Abram fell on his face: and God talked with him, saying,

4 As for me, behold, my covenant is with thee, and thou shalt be a father of many nations.

5 Neither shall thy name any more be called Abram, but thy name shall be Abraham; for a father of many nations have I made thee.

6 And I will make thee exceeding fruitful, and I will make nations of thee, and kings shall come out of thee.

7 And I will establish my covenant between me and thee and thy seed after thee in their generations for an everlasting covenant, to be a God unto thee, and to thy seed after thee.

8 And I will give unto thee, and to thy seed after thee, the land wherein thou art a stranger, all the land of Canaan, for an everlasting possession; and I will be their God.

9 And God said unto Abraham, Thou shalt keep my covenant therefore, thou, and thy seed after thee in their generations.

10 This is my covenant, which ye shall keep, between me and you and thy seed after thee; Every man child among you shall be circumcised.

11 And ye shall circumcise the flesh of your foreskin; and it shall be a token of the covenant betwixt me and you.

12 And he that is eight days old shall be circumcised among you, every man child in your generations, he that is born in the house, or bought with money of any stranger, which is not of thy seed.

13 He that is born in thy house, and he that is bought with thy money, must needs be circumcised: and my covenant shall be in your flesh for an everlasting covenant.

14 And the uncircumcised man child whose flesh of his foreskin is not circumcised, that soul shall be cut off from his people; he hath broken my covenant.

KEY VERSE

I will make my covenant between me and thee, and will multiply thee exceedingly. —Genesis 17:2

COVENANT WITH GOD

Unit 1: Signs of God's Covenants
LESSONS 1–4

LESSON AIMS

After participating in this lesson, each learner will be able to:

1. Tell what God promised to Abraham and his descendants in the covenant of Genesis 17.

2. Explain the symbolic value of circumcision.

3. Write a prayer of praise to God for His covenant-making nature.

LESSON OUTLINE

Introduction

A. Marked for Life

German immigrant Martin Hildebrandt is said to have been the first professional tattoo artist in the United States. He traveled from camp to camp during the American Civil War, tattooing both Union and Confederate soldiers. The tradition of getting a tattoo to signify service in the American military continues to this day.

The permanent nature of a tattoo as well as the pain associated with getting one makes it a rite of passage in some sense for many today. Ancient Israelites were forbidden to "print any marks" (tattoos) on their skin (Leviticus 19:28), but tattoos are mainstream in modern Western culture. One in three Americans between the ages of 18 and 50 has at least one tattoo.

Regardless of what one may think of this practice, such a permanent and visible mark is recognized as one of association. God gave Abraham and his descendants a permanent mark to show that they belonged to Him. But the mark of circumcision was more personal and less visible.

B. Lesson Background

Abraham, as we see him renamed in Genesis 17:5, first appears in the biblical record as Abram in 11:26. There his birth to Terah is noted, and the remainder of Genesis 11 records the family's move from Ur of the Chaldees (in modern Iraq) to Haran (in modern Syria).

God called Abram to leave his family (or most of it) and to go to a land that God would show him (Genesis 12:1). Scholars are divided on whether the call in chapter 12 is a repeat of an earlier call, in Ur, or is actually a record of the earlier call. In Stephen's defense to the Sanhedrin, he affirmed that God called Abram "when he was in Mesopotamia, before he dwelt in Charran [Haran]" (Acts 7:2). God promised to make of Abram a great nation, to bless him, and to make his name great (Genesis 12:2). He was age 75 when he left Haran for the land of Canaan (12:4).

God repeated His promise in Genesis 13. Abram had separated from nephew Lot because the land could not support the livestock of both groups (13:5-12). Lot had taken the lush Jordan valley toward Sodom, so Abram was left with land that had lesser pasture. It seemed he got the worse part of the deal, but God reassured him of his future (13:16, 17). The promises are stated a third time in Genesis 15. Abram "believed in the Lord; and he counted it to him for righteousness" (15:6).

The promises depended on Abram's having an heir, but we see him childless through Genesis 15. Sarai, Abram's wife, proposed a solution: "Behold now, the Lord hath restrained me from bearing: I pray thee, go in unto my maid; it may be that I may obtain children by her" (16:2). Abram agreed, and so he became the father of Ishmael by Sarai's servant, Hagar. But Ishmael, born to Abram at age 86 (16:16), was not the child of promise.

I. Great Promise
(Genesis 17:1, 2)
A. Passage of Time (v. 1)

1. And when Abram was ninety years old and nine, the Lord appeared to Abram, and said unto him, I am the Almighty God; walk before me, and be thou perfect.

Thirteen years pass without notice in the divine record between Genesis 16:16 and 17:1, given mentions of Abram's age. Whether the Lord appears or otherwise speaks to him during these 13 years, we cannot say. Some suggest that 13 years of silence is some kind of punishment for Abram because he went along with the idea of breaking sexual faithfulness to his wife, Sarai, in

HOW TO SAY IT

Canaan	*Kay*-nun.
Chaldees	*Kal*-deez.
Charran	*Kar*-an.
El-Shaddai *(Hebrew)*	El-*Shad*-eye.
Haran	*Hair*-un.
Ishmael	*Ish*-may-el.
Keturah	Keh-*too*-ruh.
Mesopotamia	*Mes*-uh-puh-***tay***-me-uh.
Terah	*Tair*-uh.
Ur	Er.

order to have a child. But like most all arguments from silence, this is mere conjecture.

The name by which *the Lord* identifies himself is *the Almighty God,* the first of dozens of times He is designated as such (sometimes rendered simply as "the Almighty"). The Almighty God is *El Shaddai* in Hebrew, a term we hear in Christian songs today. The significance of this designation seems to be that God is unlimited in His ability to act for the good of His people; nothing can thwart His plans.

> *What Do You Think?*
> How does the description of God as Almighty affect you personally? How should it?
> *Talking Points for Your Discussion*
> - In terms of courage
> - In terms of confidence
> - Other

That does not mean God's promises are unconditional, however. Here He puts the condition on Abram to *walk before me* (that is, to live to meet with God's approval) and *be . . . perfect.* The two may seem to be one and the same, and from a God-centered perspective that is reasonable. But Abram's pagan culture is not centered on God; hardly anyone lives with the desire to please Him. The emphasis here is on *before me.* In effect, God is saying "Make me, not your culture, your standard of conduct."

The word translated *perfect* is the same word used of Noah in Genesis 6:9. It need not be understood as "absolute perfection," but more as "living with integrity in not being open to charges of wrongdoing." Putting the two together, we might see the conditions as living by God's standards (first) and also living in such a way that is respected by the people around him as well.

B. Increase of Numbers (v. 2)

2. And I will make my covenant between me and thee, and will multiply thee exceedingly.

This is the third time God has promised to bless Abram (see Genesis 12:1-3; 15:1-21). In the second blessing, God specifically told him that a son of Abram's own flesh and blood would be his heir

(15:4). The record then notes the implications of Abram's belief (15:6).

In spite of that faith, Abram had come to believe that he needed to take matters in his own hands. When Sarai, his wife, suggests he take her servant Hagar as a surrogate wife, he agrees; Ishmael is born as a result. But the covenant of which God speaks does not involve Ishmael. God will multiply Abram through another son, one yet to be born to Abram and Sarai.

II. New Status
(Genesis 17:3-8)
A. Father of Nations (vv. 3-7)

3. And Abram fell on his face: and God talked with him, saying.

Abram is properly awed by this appearance of the Lord. Whether falling *on his face* means lying prostrate before God or dropping to his knees and bowing forward is not specified. In either case, Abram shows the respect due to the Lord.

> **What Do You Think?**
> How can we worship in the spirit Abram exhibited without literally falling on our faces?
> *Talking Points for Your Discussion*
> - Regarding postures of humility
> - Regarding attitudes of submission
> - Regarding evidence of sincerity
> - Other

4. As for me, behold, my covenant is with thee, and thou shalt be a father of many nations.

Earlier God had promised to make of Abram "a great nation" (Genesis 12:2). Now the promise is that he will be *a father of many nations*. It is easy to read this and to see the fulfillment in Israel (through Isaac and his son Jacob), Edom (through Isaac and his son Esau), the nations that descend from Ishmael, and also the nations that descend from Abraham via Keturah (the woman he marries after Sarah's death; Genesis 25:1-6).

But there is more to the covenant than political nations, since Paul makes clear that Isaac alone is the heir of promise (Romans 9:7). Thus the nations primarily in view, the ones included in this promise, must come from Isaac, whom Abram will father.

5. Neither shall thy name any more be called Abram, but thy name shall be Abraham; for a father of many nations have I made thee.

God gives two symbols of the covenant. The second symbol is described in Genesis 17:10-14, below. The first is the name change we see here. Abram, whose name means "exalted father," is henceforth to be known as Abraham, which probably means *father of many*. As God repeats the promise of making Abraham such a father, He speaks as if it is already the case.

6. And I will make thee exceeding fruitful, and I will make nations of thee, and kings shall come out of thee.

Abraham has one son at this point: Ishmael, whose mother is Hagar. God promises a greater fruitfulness to come. It will be seen in the birth of Isaac and, later, in the birth of six sons to Keturah (Genesis 25:1, 2). However, the key to the covenant promise is Isaac, so the fruitfulness God promises is Abraham's through his descendants. Grandson Jacob will have 12 sons and a daughter. The nation of Israel will come from these sons, with many kings born to them.

These kings will make their entrance some 900 years later with Saul. He will be a descendant of Abraham's great-grandson Benjamin. Greater far than the kings of Israel will be the King of kings and Lord of lords: Jesus (see Matthew 1:1-16).

7. And I will establish my covenant between me and thee and thy seed after thee in their generations for an everlasting covenant, to be a God unto thee, and to thy seed after thee.

The language of *everlasting covenant* is the same as that used in Genesis 9:16 (see lesson 1) and Exodus 31:16 (see lesson 3). Insofar as it finds its fulfillment in Christ, it is an enduring covenant in the fullest sense of the term *everlasting*. Paul makes clear that Christ is the fulfillment; see Galatians 3:16, where the apostle distinguishes between the singular seed as opposed to the plural seeds. This indicates the fulfillment is in the one person, Jesus Christ.

Even so, there appears to be a dual fulfillment, as it is to *thy seed after thee in their generations*.

So the fulfillment is in the generations of Abraham's seed until the ultimate fulfillment is seen in Christ himself.

B. Possession of Land (v. 8)

8a. And I will give unto thee, and to thy seed after thee, the land wherein thou art a stranger, all the land of Canaan, for an everlasting possession.

Abraham has been in Canaan for more than two decades at this point, and still he owns none of it. Further, God has already said his descendants will be oppressed in a foreign land for 400 years (Genesis 15:13). Even so, God assures Abraham that his descendants will indeed be given *all the land of Canaan, for an everlasting possession.*

◆ *EVERLASTING POSSESSION* ◆

In 1831, Joseph Smith and his followers moved west to establish a communal society. They tried settling in various places, but strife seemed to follow them everywhere they went, often prompted by their nonbiblical doctrine.

The Mormons, as they came to be called, eventually began a colony in Nauvoo, Illinois. Smith was jailed in 1844 in nearby Carthage on a charge of riot (the charge was upgraded to treason). While incarcerated, he was killed by mob action on July 27, 1844.

Brigham Young succeeded Smith as leader. Young sought a promised land where his people would be free from the kind of strife that had dogged them. When in 1847 the travelers reached the valley of the Great Salt Lake in what is now Utah, Young said, "This is the place." The rest, as they say, is history.

Speaking of history, much of the teaching of Smith and Young is erroneous in that regard. One error was their supposition that a "promised land" could be found on earth. The opposite is true: we are "strangers and pilgrims" on earth (1 Peter 2:11), where we "pass the time . . . sojourning . . . in fear" (1:17). Our promised land is not a geographical location. Ultimately, neither was Abraham's. Even though "by faith he sojourned in the land of promise, . . . he looked for a city which hath foundations, whose builder and maker is God" (Hebrews 11:9, 10). May we do so as well.

—C. R. B.

8b. And I will be their God.

Even more important than the land promise is the relationship promise we see here. This promise is repeated in texts such as Exodus 29:45 and is included in the new covenant that is promised in Jeremiah 31:33. Humans have sought deities for centuries. When the search is insincere, the result is invented, fictitious gods. But when one seeks God wholeheartedly, He's not hard to find because He reveals himself (Psalm 19:1; Jeremiah 29:13; Acts 17:27). The God of Abraham's descendants is the living God.

III. Personal Mark
(GENESIS 17:9-14)

A. Significance of Obedience (vv. 9-13)

9. And God said unto Abraham, Thou shalt keep my covenant therefore, thou, and thy seed after thee in their generations.

In exchange for the blessings to be accorded, Abraham and his descendants are to keep God's covenant. This means to submit to Him as their God and obey His commandments. One of the first items requiring obedience is set forth in the next two verses.

10, 11. This is my covenant, which ye shall keep, between me and you and thy seed after thee; Every man child among you shall be circumcised. And ye shall circumcise the flesh of your foreskin; and it shall be a token of the covenant betwixt me and you.

The *token of the covenant* is the circumcision of each male. This token (symbol) is so important that it is spoken of as if it were the covenant in and of itself: *this is my covenant*. Circumcision will be the mark of God's people for generations.

When Jesus inaugurates the new covenant, physical circumcision will no longer play a part (1 Corinthians 7:19). But circumcision will still be of significant figurative importance. Circumcision —cutting off a small piece of flesh—becomes a symbol of putting off the sins of the flesh in the new covenant (Colossians 2:11-13). This circumcision is not done with hands; thus it is a spiritual event. Colossians 2:12 connects it with baptism, a physical act and yet one in which God is working spiritually as well: "wherein also ye are risen with him through the faith of the operation of God."

What Do You Think?
What can we do to cooperate with the Holy
    Spirit in circumcising our hearts? Explain.
Talking Points for Your Discussion
- Regarding use of spiritual gifts
- Regarding management of finances
- Regarding how we pray
- Other

---

12. And he that is eight days old shall be circumcised among you, every man child in your generations, he that is born in the house, or bought with money of any stranger, which is not of thy seed.

Circumcision is to be done on the eighth day after a male child is born in the covenant family (compare Leviticus 12:3; Philippians 3:5). This will become part of a ceremony that includes bestowing a name on the child (compare Luke 1:59; 2:21). The law applies both to natural-born sons and sons *not of thy seed* (see also Genesis 17:27; Exodus 12:48).

13. He that is born in thy house, and he that is bought with thy money, must needs be circumcised: and my covenant shall be in your flesh for an everlasting covenant.

The sign of the covenant is on the physical bodies of the covenant people, specifically on the sex organ of the males. One might wonder how a mark in a part of the body that is kept covered (1 Corinthians 12:23) can be a symbol of anything. Symbols are meant to be seen. In this case, the symbol of the covenant is not to be seen by others, but is a reminder to the covenant-keeper himself. As he dedicates the most personal part of his body to the Lord, so also he dedicates his whole life. And through marriage and marital relations, the wife of the covenant keeper is included in this sacred covenant.

B. Penalty for Disobedience (v. 14)

14. And the uncircumcised man child whose flesh of his foreskin is not circumcised, that soul shall be cut off from his people; he hath broken my covenant.

Disobedience to the covenant leads to exclusion from the covenant community. There is a play on words here. To circumcise someone is to cut off a small piece of flesh; refusal to submit to the procedure results in the man's being *cut off from his people*.

It is not clear what that penalty involves, whether capital punishment or banishment, or whether it is done by God or by a human agent. When Moses started toward Egypt in obedience to God's call, "the Lord met him, and sought to kill him"; Moses' wife quickly circumcised their son, and the Lord "let him go" (Exodus 4:24-26). This may suggest that it is God who cuts off the one who fails to keep the covenant. However, no deaths are noted when the entire nation of Israel later fails to circumcise the next generation until after crossing the Jordan (Joshua 5:2-8). Apparently the cutting off of the covenant breaker is to be a human responsibility.

◆ RECOMMENDED BUT OPTIONAL? ◆

Muslims consider themselves to be the purest of those who trace their spiritual history to Abraham. They claim lineage through Ishmael, Abraham's son who was born to Hagar after Abraham and Sarah took it upon themselves to push God's plan along.

However, Islam (the religion of Muslims) does not view circumcision as mandatory. Instead it is a recommended but optional ritual that is seen to show a Muslim male's closeness to Abraham as spiritual ancestor and physical forefather.

The Old and New Testaments reveal no such middle-of-the-road stance. Submission to circumcision in the Old Testament was mandatory if one wanted to remain part of the covenant people. The opposite is seen in the New Testament: physical circumcision is strongly advised against (with an exception for practical reasons at Acts 16:3), since it is part of the old law that is no longer in force.

Instead, the New Testament advocates Jesus' emphasis on purity of the inner person (Matthew 15:18; etc.). But that brings us full circle back to the Old Testament, where the same emphasis is found. See Leviticus 26:41; Jeremiah 6:10; compare Acts 7:51. —C. R. B.

Conclusion
A. Deal Breaker

In any negotiation, certain factors are known as deal breakers. These are matters that must be satisfied or there is no transaction. In buying a house or car, not having a clear title is a deal breaker. If the seller cannot produce a title without encumbrances (liens, etc.) on the item for sale, then the wise buyer will walk away. The buyer will not accept promises such as, "I'll send you the title later, once I clear up the tax lien on the property." Failure to have a clear title in hand is a deal breaker.

Other situations don't have the same legal concern as a clear title, but they are deal breakers nonetheless. In warm, humid climates, lack of

Visual for Lesson 2. *Point to this visual as you ask, "Which part of life might a new Christian most try to declare 'off-limits' to God? Why?"*

air-conditioning is a deal breaker to many home buyers. For parents, a home in an inferior school district is a deal breaker. These kinds of deal breakers vary from buyer to buyer, but we all have them.

For Israel's covenant with the Lord, to not be circumcised was a deal breaker. Refusal of circumcision meant exclusion. The precise reason circumcision was so important is never stated. But it was indeed critically important—and *that* fact *was* stated. No Israelite had an excuse for failure in this matter.

Perhaps the reason it was so important was because it had significance beyond itself, beyond even the covenant to which it witnessed. The New Testament calls features of the old covenant "a shadow" of something more substantial to come (Colossians 2:17; Hebrews 10:1). "In Jesus Christ neither circumcision availeth any thing, nor uncircumcision; but faith which worketh by love" (Galatians 5:6; compare 6:15).

B. Prayer

Father, we thank You for the spiritual circumcision that is done to all Christians by Your Spirit—the circumcision of the heart. Help us to live in the manner Your Word would have us. We pray in Jesus' name. Amen.

C. Thought to Remember

Our connection with God can result in intimacy greater than any other relationship.

INVOLVEMENT LEARNING

Enhance your lesson with KJV Bible Student *(from your curriculum supplier) and the reproducible activity page (at www.standardlesson.com or in the back of the* KJV Standard Lesson Commentary Deluxe Edition).

Into the Lesson

Before class, write the following phrases on separate index cards: *is a permanent mark / can show affiliation / involves a painful process / is always with a person / can be a constant reminder of a decision made / affirms a commitment.*

To begin class, give six volunteers one of these cards each. Have those holding a card read it aloud, pausing to have the class try to guess what the card refers to. Continue until all clues are read or until someone guesses that the cards refer to tattoos. For extra impact, purchase a pair of false tattoo sleeves, readily available this time of year from party supply stores. Wear them under a jacket and take off the jacket to reveal the answer. Be prepared to respond if someone mentions Leviticus 19:28.

Alternative. Distribute copies of the "Vanity Plates" activity from the reproducible page, which you can download. Have students work individually or in pairs.

After either activity, ask the class to list other ways people show loyalties, interests, and affiliations. Some possibilities include sports team T-shirts, bumper stickers, displaying a flag, etc. Lead into Bible study by saying, "A person may wave a flag, sport a tattoo, take a pledge, wear a T-shirt, purchase vanity license plates, or show loyalty in any number of other ways. Today we will look at a sign God gave Abraham and his descendants to show their loyalty to God."

Into the Word

Divide the class into three groups, giving each group a portion of the Bible text and the opening line that goes with it. Each group should read its portion of the text and create a dramatic monologue that starts with its given opening line.

Great Promise (Genesis 17:1, 2)—*I was afraid we really blew it with God. But . . .*

New Name (Genesis 17:3-8)—*Talk about a fresh start! We even have new, meaningful names!*

Personal Mark (Genesis 17:9-14)—*Aren't signs meant to be seen? But then I understood what God was telling us.*

Allow time for groups to share their monologues and summarize their Scripture assignments.

Alternative. Distribute copies of the "God's Property" activity from the reproducible page. You can do this as a whole-class activity, or assign small groups one of the three sections of text and questions on the sheet.

Into Life

Say, "God gave the people of Israel a mark that showed that He was keeping His promises to them and that they accepted an intimate relationship with Him. What is the equivalent mark for a Christ follower?"

Have a volunteer read aloud Colossians 2:11-15 for your class. After the whole passage is read, have your reader repeat verses 11, 12 slowly. Discuss the connection between spiritual circumcision and physical baptism.

Say, "Pause for a moment and consider your own heart. Christ began this cutting away process when you accepted Him as Savior. Thank God for already cutting away certain sins from your life. Then think of one specific sinful act or attitude He still needs to remove from you. During this week pray regularly that God will continue to mark your life with obedience to Him in that regard."

Before class, obtain small heart stickers or temporary tattoos from a party supply or school supply store. Give each class member a sticker or temporary tattoo to take home as a prayer reminder. Challenge your learners to wear it hidden underneath clothing sometime in the week ahead as a personal sign of being in a covenant relationship with Christ. Stress that this is only a devotional memory aid, and not a substitute for biblical directives.

SABBATH OBSERVANCE

DEVOTIONAL READING: Psalm 92
BACKGROUND SCRIPTURE: Genesis 2:1-3; Exodus 31:12-18; Isaiah 56:1-8

EXODUS 31:12-18

12 And the LORD spake unto Moses, saying,

13 Speak thou also unto the children of Israel, saying, Verily my sabbaths ye shall keep: for it is a sign between me and you throughout your generations; that ye may know that I am the LORD that doth sanctify you.

14 Ye shall keep the sabbath therefore; for it is holy unto you: every one that defileth it shall surely be put to death: for whosoever doeth any work therein, that soul shall be cut off from among his people.

15 Six days may work be done; but in the seventh is the sabbath of rest, holy to the LORD: whosoever doeth any work in the sabbath day, he shall surely be put to death.

16 Wherefore the children of Israel shall keep the sabbath, to observe the sabbath throughout their generations, for a perpetual covenant.

17 It is a sign between me and the children of Israel for ever: for in six days the LORD made heaven and earth, and on the seventh day he rested, and was refreshed.

18 And he gave unto Moses, when he had made an end of communing with him upon mount Sinai, two tables of testimony, tables of stone, written with the finger of God.

KEY VERSES

Verily my sabbaths ye shall keep: for it is a sign between me and you throughout your generations; that ye may know that I am the LORD that doth sanctify you. Ye shall keep the sabbath therefore; for it is holy unto you. —**Exodus 31:13b, 14a**

Graphic: Enterline Design Services LLC / iStock / Thinkstock

COVENANT WITH GOD

Unit 1: Signs of God's Covenants

Lessons 1–4

LESSON AIMS

After participating in this lesson, each learner will be able to:

1. Summarize the Sabbath regulations of the Mosaic covenant.

2. Explain Jesus' statement in Mark 2:27.

3. Explain to a fellow believer why Sabbath observance does not apply in the New Testament era.

LESSON OUTLINE

Introduction

A. The Dark Side of Achievement

The term *burnout* was popularized in the 1970s by American psychologist Herbert Freudenberger. In working with those who devoted themselves to serving others in free clinics, Freudenberger found that many clinic workers became exhausted, listless, and unable to cope over time. Doctors, nurses, and social workers exhibited burnout when their idealism gave way to cynicism as they felt increasingly ineffective and helpless. Today the word *burnout* is applied to those who are stressed-out in many other professions as well.

The negative effects of burnout at work spill over into home and social life. When that happens, relationships do not get the full focus they deserve, prioritizing becomes difficult, and busyness replaces true accomplishment. Over the long run, burnout can make people vulnerable to illness.

Our bodies have limitations. Overwork paired with insufficient rest is a poisonous recipe for burnout. Today we will look at God's antidote.

B. Lesson Background

The subject of our lesson is early instruction to the Israelites regarding the Sabbath. But this instruction was not the first on this subject. The first mention of the word *Sabbath* as a noun was when God provided manna as the Israelites sojourned toward Mount Sinai. Two days' worth was to be gathered on the sixth day of the week so the people could rest on the seventh—the Sabbath (Exodus 16:21-30). On any other day, gathering more than one day's worth resulted in spoilage (16:20). But manna gathered on the sixth day and saved for the Sabbath did not spoil (16:24).

In the third month after leaving Egypt, the Israelites assembled in front of Mount Sinai (Exodus 19:1). There God spoke to them and gave them the Ten Commandments (20:1-17). The requirement to keep the Sabbath was the fourth of those and was the longest (20:8-11). Further instructions regarding the Sabbath followed. These required land to be left fallow one year in seven; a weekly Sabbath rest for every person and beast of burden was mandatory (23:10-12).

Moses confirmed the covenant with the people in Exodus 24; then God called him again to the top of the mountain to receive more instructions (24:12). A break of sorts occurs with Exodus 24:18 as "Moses was in the mount forty days and forty nights." The section that follows (Exodus 25–31) records God's commands about the construction of the tabernacle and how to furnish it. Today's text comes at the conclusion of this section.

I. Sacred Sabbath
(Exodus 31:12-15)
A. Special Sign (vv. 12-14a)

12. And the LORD spake unto Moses, saying.

This is the seventh time in the section Exodus 25–31 that the Lord is recorded as speaking to Moses (the other six are Exodus 25:1; 30:11, 17, 22, 34; 31:1). Parallels have been drawn between this feature and the seven days of creation in Genesis 1:1–2:3. We may observe that the seventh day in Genesis is the original Sabbath; the seventh time the Lord speaks in Exodus 25–31, the subject is the Sabbath (a Hebrew word transliterated into English).

13a. Speak thou also unto the children of Israel, saying, Verily my sabbaths ye shall keep.

This is not the first mention of Sabbath in our Bibles. The first occurs in Exodus 16:23 (see the Lesson Background). Going back further, when Genesis 2:2 says that "God . . . rested on the seventh day from all his work," the Hebrew word underneath the translation "rested" is *Sabbath*; but there it is a verb, not a noun as in Exodus 16:23. Genesis 2:3 also features the verb form of this word: "God blessed the seventh day, and sanctified it: because that in it he had rested from all his work." There is no mention, however, of how the seventh day was sanctified (made holy) or how (or whether) God's people observe it as such.

13b. For it is a sign between me and you throughout your generations; that ye may know that I am the LORD that doth sanctify you.

Circumcision is considered a covenant sign between God and His people (Genesis 17:9-11, last week's lesson), but that rite is limited to males. Keeping the Sabbath, by contrast, applies to all Israelites. Exodus 20:8 speaks of keeping the Sabbath holy; in the verse before us, however, the emphasis is on the holiness of the Sabbath keeper: *I am the Lord that doth sanctify you.* The word *sanctify* means to be set apart or made holy. Prior to giving Israel the Ten Commandments, God had called His people "a kingdom of priests, and an holy nation" (Exodus 19:6; compare Revelation 1:6; 5:10; 20:6).

14a. Ye shall keep the sabbath therefore; for it is holy unto you.

We just learned that the Sabbath is to be kept because it is a sign that God's people are holy. Now we are back to a reflection of Exodus 20:8, where the day itself is holy. This matches what we just observed about Genesis 2:3.

B. Severe Penalty (vv. 14b, 15)

14b. Every one that defileth it shall surely be put to death: for whosoever doeth any work therein, that soul shall be cut off from among his people.

The primary means of observing or keeping the Sabbath is refraining from work. Rest—which is what the word *Sabbath* means—is the key to keeping the day as God intends. Another feature of Sabbath observance is found in Numbers 28:9, 10, where the daily offerings are to be doubled on that day (compare 2 Chronicles 2:4; 8:13). Leviticus 23:3 indicates the Sabbath is a day for a "holy convocation." That seems to be an umbrella term that includes not only the Sabbath but also the first day of the week (Exodus 12:16), feasts (Leviticus 23:4), and the Day of Atonement (23:27).

While bodily rest is not the only means of Sabbath observance, it is the aspect that carries the stiffest penalty if not observed. Anyone who does *any work* on the Sabbath is to *be put to death*. Numbers 15:32-36 records the one time we know of when this penalty was carried out. It happened during the wilderness experience of Israel when a man was found gathering sticks, presumably firewood (building a fire is also prohibited on the Sabbath; see Exodus 35:2, 3).

When the offender is brought before Moses and Aaron, there is uncertainty regarding what to do. Such uncertainty seems strange in light of the clear command in this text, but perhaps the issue in question is the means of execution. The Lord declares that the offender is to be stoned, and that is what happens. Stoning is also the punishment for blasphemy, and that is no doubt what the Lord intends for Israel to understand regarding the gravity of defiling the Sabbath. It is holy, as God is holy, so to defile the Sabbath is an act of blasphemy.

15. Six days may work be done; but in the seventh is the sabbath of rest, holy to the LORD: whosoever doeth any work in the sabbath day, he shall surely be put to death.

There is no new information here; the repetition is for emphasis. Only *six days* of a week are for work; then Sabbath rest is prescribed in the Mosaic law—in several places (examples: Exodus 20:9-11; 23:12; 34:21; Leviticus 23:3; Deuteronomy 5:13-15). The sanctity of the Sabbath is paramount. No work may be done on that day. This explains the intensity of the Jewish leaders' opposition of what they considered "work" by Jesus on the Sabbath (Luke 13:14).

Yet there are practical exceptions to this law, and Jesus cites one example in answer to the synagogue ruler's complaint: those who own livestock do the work required to give the animal water on the Sabbath (Luke 13:15). Elsewhere Jesus points out that priests work on the Sabbath and are yet "blameless" (Matthew 12:5; compare Numbers 28:9, 19). In an emergency, the owner of a sheep might work on the Sabbath without incurring guilt (Matthew 12:11). And any parent whose son turns eight days old on the Sabbath will have the child circumcised on that day so "that the law of Moses should not be broken" (John 7:22, 23).

Jesus summarizes the nature of the Sabbath this way: "The sabbath was made for man, and not man for the sabbath" (Mark 2:27). The Sabbath was instituted to provide relief from labor. There is no eight-hour workday in either Moses' day or in Jesus'. For six days people labor for 12 hours (John 11:9; compare Matthew 20:1-12). A day of rest is needed to recharge the body. It's hard to keep one's spiritual defenses up when the body is continually exhausted.

II. Continual Covenant
(EXODUS 31:16, 17)

A. Throughout the Generations (v. 16)

16. Wherefore the children of Israel shall keep the sabbath, to observe the sabbath throughout their generations, for a perpetual covenant.

The word translated *perpetual* is the same one translated "everlasting" of the rainbow in Genesis 9:16 (lesson 1) and of circumcision in 17:7 (lesson 2). Until the old covenant is replaced by the new, the endurance of Sabbath regulations is *perpetual* throughout the generations of Israel.

Some believers honor the Sabbath in various ways even today, with practices varying widely. Some groups insist that Saturday, the seventh day of the week and the Sabbath, is the proper day of worship for the church. They hold services and restrict activity on Saturday. Others simply import Sabbath regulations from the old covenant into their understanding of the church's responsibility; some of these folks even use the word *Sabbath* to refer to Sunday, the first day of the week. According to these believers, only those who respond to emergencies (fire, police, hospital staff, etc.) should engage in work on Sunday. Still others take a more temperate view, holding a personal preference for refraining from work on Sunday but not insisting on the practice by others (compare Romans 14:5).

The New Testament practice overall seems most like the temperate view. Jewish believers of the first century AD continue to observe the Sabbath and many other aspects of the Law of Moses. Even Paul, "the apostle of the Gentiles" (Romans 11:13), practices certain ceremonial portions of the law (Acts 18:18; 21:20-24; 24:17).

But Paul also notes that pressure to conform to Sabbath rules must be resisted (Colossians 2:16, 17). Sabbath observance is not to be imposed on the church. As the new covenant comes into force, the old covenant "decayeth and waxeth old" and "is ready to vanish away" (Hebrews 8:13).

> ### What Do You Think?
> How would you respond to a fellow believer who insists that worship, rest, and essential functions are the only allowable activities for Christians on Sunday?
> *Talking Points for Your Discussion*
> - Regarding the basis of his or her belief
> - Regarding the original-creation basis of Sabbath regulations as contrasted with the new-creation emphasis of the new covenant
> - Considering Romans 14:5; 1 Corinthians 8:9-13; Colossians 2:16-19; Hebrews 4:9

B. Imitating the Lord (v. 17)

17. It is a sign between me and the children of Israel for ever: for in six days the Lord made heaven and earth, and on the seventh day he rested, and was refreshed.

Also like circumcision, Sabbath observance serves as *a sign* of God's covenant with Israel. The tribes of Israel will be in constant contact with pagan groups during and after taking the promised land. Such groups will either influence Israel to serve the Baals or will be influenced by Israel to serve Yahweh. The pagans' observance of how the Israelites rest on the Sabbath can serve as a witness

that the Israelites are a separate people who are faithful to the one, true God. This God is the Creator of Heaven and earth. The identity of Yahweh as the Creator and the observance of the Sabbath as the day He rested from His work of creation are linked as one reminder of the uniqueness of the God the Israelites serve. Another reminder that observance of the Sabbath provides is that the God the Israelites serve is the one who delivered them from Egyptian bondage (Deuteronomy 5:12-15).

> ### What Do You Think?
> How have you seen Christian observance of a day off influence culture?
> *Talking Points for Your Discussion*
> - Regarding business practices (Chick-fil-A, Hobby Lobby)
> - Regarding practices of high-profile individuals
> - Other

◆ TILL . . . WHAT? ◆

In the ceremony that was long a part of the Christian covenant of marriage, the bride and groom vowed "to have and to hold from this day forward, for better for worse, for richer for poorer, in sickness and in health, to love and to cherish, till death us do part." Those promises go all the way back to the 1549 Anglican Book of Common Prayer.

But times have changed. Couples are now more likely to promise to love each other "through fat and skinny" or "until you become a Cubs fan." Yes, those are actual vows spoken in real weddings! The trend these days seems to be to play down the "till death do us part" idea and take the whole marriage idea more lightly. Perhaps there is something to be said for making wedding ceremonies less somber than they used to be. But the levity may also reflect the fact that marriage itself seems to be taken less seriously these days than many of us think it should.

When God told the Hebrews to keep the Sabbath, it was a "till death do us part" sign of His covenant with them, and then some! A regular day of rest was to be kept sacrosanct throughout their

Visual for Lesson 3. *Point to this visual as you challenge the class to name tasks that are "work" to some but relaxing "rest" to others.*

generations. The principle, though not the legalistic imposition of it, is still a good idea for all of us! See the lesson's concluding thoughts. —C. R. B.

III. Tables of Testimony

(Exodus 31:18)

18. And he gave unto Moses, when he had made an end of communing with him upon mount Sinai, two tables of testimony, tables of stone, written with the finger of God.

The entire monologue of Exodus 25–31 takes place on Mount Sinai. God had called Moses up to the mountain, promising to meet Moses and to give him "tables of stone, and a law, and commandments which I have written; that thou mayest teach them" (Exodus 24:12).

What is written on the stones that Moses receives is probably not the entire message of these chapters, however, but the Ten Commandments. Moses is given additional instruction, which he himself writes along with the historical narrative that accompanies it here in the book of Exodus. Moses is the author of this book as well as the rest of the books of Law, commonly referred to as the Pentateuch (Genesis–Deuteronomy).

The *two . . . tables of stone* do not last long. When Moses comes down from the mountain, he finds the people of Israel worshiping a golden calf idol. God has already told Moses about it (Exodus 32:7, 8), so it's not a surprise to him when he

sees what is going on. But the actual sight of it is apparently worse than Moses imagined. When he sees "the calf, and the dancing," Moses loses his temper. He throws "the tables out of his hands, and [breaks] them beneath the mount" (32:19). These are later replaced, and the new tables are specifically said to contain "the words of the covenant, the ten commandments" (34:28).

These new tables will be kept in the ark of the covenant for many generations (Hebrews 9:4). They will still be there when Solomon installs the ark in the temple that he will build around 965 BC (1 Kings 8:9). They will probably remain there until the Babylonians destroy the temple and plunder its contents in 586 BC.

◆ *In Stone and From Stone* ◆

Country music seems dedicated to sadness. Heartbreak, nostalgia for better times, and job loss are recurring themes. Also recurring are laments about attempts to escape from trouble by means of trucks, trains, and alcohol. One example of such pathos is the song "Chiseled in Stone." A couple has a spat. She runs in tears from the bedroom; he heads for the bar to drown his troubles. There he meets an old man who tells him to go home to his wife while he still has her. The old man's wife is dead, and he has no one waiting for him at home. Her name is chiseled in stone in the cemetery.

HOW TO SAY IT

Aaron	*Air*-un.
baals	*bay*-ulz.
Colossians	Kuh-*losh*-unz.
Deuteronomy	Due-ter-*ahn*-uh-me.
Hebrews	*Hee*-brews.
Israelites	*Iz*-ray-el-ites.
Leviticus	Leh-*vit*-ih-kus.
manna	*ma*-nuh (*a* as in *mat*).
Mosaic	Mo-*zay*-ik.
Moses	*Mo*-zes or *Mo*-zez.
Pentateuch	*Pen*-ta-teuk.
Sabbath	*Sa*-buth (*a* as in *mat*).
sanctified	***sank***-tuh-*fide*.
Sinai	*Sigh*-nye or *Sigh*-nay-eye.
Yahweh (Hebrew)	*Yah*-weh.

The words inscribed on stone tablets that God entrusted to Moses resulted in death when disobeyed. "The motions of sins, which were by the law, did work in our members to bring forth fruit unto death" (Romans 7:5). The law reminds us of our sin, the consequent separation from God, and our need for Christ (Galatians 3:23, 24; Colossians 1:21).

The glory of God's plan is that Christ allowed himself to be killed to pay the penalty of our law-breaking. He was placed in a tomb where His body lay stone-cold dead for three days. His emergence from the stone tomb established that the reign of death was over. Jesus, "the stone which the builders disallowed" (1 Peter 2:7), is the one who promises "to him that overcometh will I give . . . a white stone, and in the stone a new name written" (Revelation 2:17). Jesus is the "living stone" (1 Peter 2:4) who brings us life.   —C. R. B.

Conclusion

A. Why Sabbath Observance Is Obsolete

Examining the Ten Commandments alongside Christian practice, we reach a conclusion that is uncomfortable to many: it seems that nine of the Ten Commandments still apply, but one—the command to keep the Sabbath (Saturday)—does not. A close look at each of the Ten Commandments in light of other Scripture reveals why this conclusion is valid. Nine of the commandments are based on the nature of God; and since His nature never changes (Malachi 3:6; James 1:17), neither does the application of those nine. The Sabbath commandment, however, is based on works of God. His works of the old creation (Genesis 2:2, 3) and deliverance under the old covenant (Deuteronomy 5:15) are now superseded by His work of deliverance under the new covenant that results in new creation (Romans 8:19-23; 2 Corinthians 5:17).

Since the new covenant is bound intrinsically with Christ's resurrection from the dead, we honor Him on the day He won that victory (Matthew 28:1; Mark 16:1, 2; Luke 24:1; John 20:1). This is the first day of the week (Acts 20:7), the Lord's Day (Revelation 1:10), the day we call Sunday.

B. Why the Sabbath Principle Still Stands

Although Sabbath requirements are no longer in force, are there benefits in the Sabbath principle of regular, periodic rest? Matthew Sleeth thinks so. A former emergency room doctor, Sleeth is the author of *24/6: A Prescription for a Healthier, Happier Life.* The book calls for making one day a week a work-free day. In an interview with CNN, he said, "I don't try to define what rest is for a person, but I ask you to figure out what work is for you, and don't do it one day out of the week."

Taking a day off has been associated with a variety of health benefits, including stress management. No doubt, that is one reason God gave the Sabbath to His old covenant people—to provide rest and relief. But even if keeping the Sabbath principle as a day of rest is legitimate for one's personal health and devotion, it is not something to be demanded of others or made a test of fellowship (again, Romans 14:5, 6; Colossians 2:16).

The Sabbath was made for man (Mark 2:27), and each man (and woman) is free to apply the principle of Sabbath rest as seems best. But the fulfillment, the substance, is Christ (compare Hebrews 4:1-13).

What Do You Think?
  What features of church life can we improve to serve better as signs to point the world to Christ?
Talking Points for Your Discussion
- Regarding practices taken from New Testament command and/or precedent
- Regarding practices developed for expediency
- Regarding the degree to which such improvements are enforced on others
- Other

C. Prayer

Father, thank You for the eternal rest promised to Your people. May we live faithful to Your Son, Jesus, using our time, our work, and our rest to honor Him. We pray in His name. Amen.

D. Thought to Remember

God did not design us to be 24/7/365 machines!

INVOLVEMENT LEARNING

Enhance your lesson with KJV Bible Student *(from your curriculum supplier) and the reproducible activity page (at www.standardlesson.com or in the back of the* KJV Standard Lesson Commentary Deluxe Edition*).*

Into the Lesson

Before class, set up one to three stations. Each station should have (1) a flashlight with no batteries inserted, (2) just enough fully charged batteries as needed to power the flashlight, and (3) one dead battery.

As learners arrive, direct them to a station, asking them to get the flashlight at that station to work. This will take some trial and error, because the one dead battery among the charged batteries will keep the flashlight from working.

After all class members have arrived, review what this exercise teaches: one dead battery can keep a flashlight from working. Likewise, for any group to function well, everyone must be "fully charged."

Alternative. Distribute copies of the "Candle Meltdown" activity from the reproducible page, which you can download. Have students work individually on this for a few minutes before asking the entire class to share their opinions.

After either activity, lead into Bible study by saying, "Our bodies have limitations. Too much work paired with insufficient rest is a recipe for burnout. Having our energy depleted can hurt us and those around us. Today we will look at God's prescription for avoiding burnout."

Into the Word

Explain that while the Sabbath was a command only for the Jews, the principles found in the Sabbath are important for us today.

Prepare for this activity by writing the phrases in each assignment on separate index cards. Divide your class into three groups, giving each group one of the following assignments and a set of index cards. They are to put their cards in order to reveal a Sabbath principle and be prepared to tell how their assigned Scripture verses applied to the Jewish Sabbath and to Christian practice today. (Our suggestions are in italics.)

Assignment 1—A day set apart / for God / reminds us that / God is holy / and calls us / to be set apart / from this world.

Exodus 31:12-15; 1 Peter 1:14-16

God gave the Jews a special day different from others, which they recognized as set apart for God. God wants us to recognize His holiness by living lives that are set apart from the sins of this world.

Assignment 2—A day set apart / for God / can be celebrated / with others who / share a / covenant relationship / with Him.

Exodus 31:16; Hebrews 10:24, 25

The Sabbath was to be observed by all Israelites of the Old Testament era. Christians meet together to recognize their special relationship with each other and with God.

Assignment 3—A day set apart / for God / demonstrates that / our work / can wait / as we take time / to be refreshed.

Exodus 31:17, 18; Mark 2:27

The Sabbath recognized that even God stopped His work to rest. Christians today still benefit when we set apart time for renewal.

After work is complete, have groups share their research.

Into Life

Write, *I need to rest when . . .* across the top of the board. Brainstorm with the group about times when a Sabbath rest is needed. Your learners may mention the following: *when I find myself being a workaholic; when I feel emotionally weary; when I think I don't have time to rest; when I realize I have overcommitted myself to trivial matters; when I join an assembly of believers for worship and study.*

Alternative. Distribute copies of the "Time Peace" activity from the reproducible page. Have students evaluate themselves with these timepiece comparisons.

Close either activity with prayer.

SPIRIT-FILLED HEART

DEVOTIONAL READING: Isaiah 43:14-21
BACKGROUND SCRIPTURE: Ezekiel 36, 37; Titus 3:1-11

EZEKIEL 36:22-32

22 Therefore say unto the house of Israel, Thus saith the Lord GOD; I do not this for your sakes, O house of Israel, but for mine holy name's sake, which ye have profaned among the heathen, whither ye went.

23 And I will sanctify my great name, which was profaned among the heathen, which ye have profaned in the midst of them; and the heathen shall know that I am the LORD, saith the Lord GOD, when I shall be sanctified in you before their eyes.

24 For I will take you from among the heathen, and gather you out of all countries, and will bring you into your own land.

25 Then will I sprinkle clean water upon you, and ye shall be clean: from all your filthiness, and from all your idols, will I cleanse you.

26 A new heart also will I give you, and a new spirit will I put within you: and I will take away the stony heart out of your flesh, and I will give you an heart of flesh.

27 And I will put my spirit within you, and cause you to walk in my statutes, and ye shall keep my judgments, and do them.

28 And ye shall dwell in the land that I gave to your fathers; and ye shall be my people, and I will be your God.

29 I will also save you from all your uncleannesses: and I will call for the corn, and will increase it, and lay no famine upon you.

30 And I will multiply the fruit of the tree, and the increase of the field, that ye shall receive no more reproach of famine among the heathen.

31 Then shall ye remember your own evil ways, and your doings that were not good, and shall lothe yourselves in your own sight for your iniquities and for your abominations.

32 Not for your sakes do I this, saith the Lord GOD, be it known unto you: be ashamed and confounded for your own ways, O house of Israel.

KEY VERSE

A new heart also will I give you, and a new spirit will I put within you: and I will take away the stony heart out of your flesh, and I will give you an heart of flesh. —**Ezekiel 36:26**

Graphic: Kristina Vingelevskaya / Hemera / Thinkstock

COVENANT WITH GOD

LESSON AIMS

After participating in this lesson, each learner will be able to:

1. Summarize Ezekiel's message of hope for the exiles in Babylon.

2. Explain how feeling shame for one's sins can help the forgiven to lead lives of purity.

3. Identify one improvement to be made that will better exemplify the presence of God's indwelling Spirit in his or her life and make a plan for change.

LESSON OUTLINE

Introduction

A. It Just Sounds Better

Some words and phrases are meant to hinder communication. It is not uncommon for those in government or business to use euphemisms—nice-sounding words or phrases instead of their less attractive counterparts. Such a practice is so common that we may barely notice. We understand that a "previously acquired vehicle" is really just a used car. Those who are "economically disadvantaged" live in poverty. To end up in "correctional custody" is to be in prison.

Some euphemisms are more insidious than others. Admitting that a military attack resulted in "collateral damage" obscures the fact that innocent civilians died. A politician who "committed terminological inexactitude" has lied. And cries for "equal rights" may in some (but not all) circumstances be code words for an attempt to legalize immoral behavior.

Sadly, experience has taught us not to take people at face value. Too often people conduct themselves with hidden agendas as they hide behind obscure communication. But God is very clear about wanting new hearts in His people.

B. Lesson Background

Ezekiel prophesied from Babylon, where he had been taken captive along with the king of Judah and 10,000 others in 597 BC (2 Kings 24:12-14). In the fifth year of their captivity (592 BC), the word of the Lord came to Ezekiel, and his prophetic ministry began (Ezekiel 1:3).

Ezekiel was a contemporary of the prophet Jeremiah. Both prophesied the end of the nation of Judah. Jerusalem would be destroyed and the temple defiled. Jeremiah preached this message in Jerusalem, where he was in danger of being executed for treason. But Jeremiah persisted and even wrote a letter to the exiles in Babylon, telling them to prepare for a lengthy captivity (Jeremiah 29:1-23).

Ezekiel echoed the same message while in Babylon. As a captive himself, he encouraged his fellow Israelites not to believe the false rumors of an early return from exile. The first 30 chapters of the book that bears his name predict the dire consequences of sin on Judah and surrounding nations.

Word came of the prophecy's fulfillment—Jerusalem had indeed fallen (Ezekiel 33:21). From that point on, the prophet's tone became softer, more comforting. He provided a foundation for faith and hope. Though the city had fallen, God had not forgotten His people. Relief would come.

I. Holy Name
(Ezekiel 36:22-24)
A. Profaned (v. 22)

22. Therefore say unto the house of Israel, Thus saith the Lord God; I do not this for your sakes, O house of Israel, but for mine holy name's sake, which ye have profaned among the heathen, whither ye went.

The phrase *the house of Israel* refers to Ezekiel's fellow exiles in Babylon (see the Lesson Background). It is to them that the current message from *the Lord God* is directed.

In the time between the arrival of news that Jerusalem had fallen and the declarations that begin in the verse before us, the Lord makes about three dozen pronouncements regarding actions He intends to implement personally. Slightly more than half are statements of positive intent regarding the future status of His true "sheep" (example: Ezekiel 34:11), elsewhere referred to as "a remnant" (example: Ezra 9:8). The statements of negative intent are directed against various groups that oppress and/or mislead His sheep.

But God will not take the positive actions because the people are righteous or entitled to such a blessing. Quite the contrary! As Joshua led Israel into the promised land some eight centuries before, God had already warned the Israelites not to defile themselves and the land by imitating the religious practices of the previous inhabitants. To do so would result in removal from the land (Leviticus 18:24-30).

That is exactly what had happened, however. As a result, the people earned God's judgment and were driven from the land into exile. Israel, the northern kingdom, was conquered by Assyria in 722 BC. Judah, the southern kingdom, was taken to Babylon in a series of deportations that began in about 605 BC.

So Ezekiel speaks to people who are guilty of defiling their land. They have received God's just judgment. But the Babylonians, with very few exceptions (Jeremiah 40:1-3), do not see it that way. They see a people conquered by their own armies and gods. This is one way the Israelites have profaned God's name, since it allows the Babylonians to see Him as inferior to worthless idols.

God will not tolerate this forever. So for His *holy name's sake*, He will show himself greater than the gods of Babylon (compare Exodus 12:12).

B. Sanctified (vv. 23, 24)

23. And I will sanctify my great name, which was profaned among the heathen, which ye have profaned in the midst of them; and the heathen shall know that I am the Lord, saith the Lord God, when I shall be sanctified in you before their eyes.

The solution to (or prevention of) the profaning of God's name is to make it holy—to sanctify it. The pagan Gentiles (*the heathen*) believe their gods to be greater than the Lord; they think this has been proven because they have taken the Lord's people captive. But the Lord will do something that will reverse such thinking. Exactly what that will be is the subject of the next verse.

Before we go there, however, we should consider the designation *the Lord God*. The prefaces to many editions of the Bible explain that the English rendering *Lord* with capital letters indicates that the divine name YHWH is being translated. By comparison, the rendering *Lord* with small letters

HOW TO SAY IT

Assyria	Uh-*sear*-ee-uh.
Babylon	*Bab*-uh-lun.
Babylonian	Bab-ih-*low*-nee-un.
Canaan	*Kay*-nun.
Ezekiel	Ee-*zeek*-ee-ul or Ee-*zeek*-yul.
Gentiles	*Jen*-tiles.
heathen	*hee*-thun.
Judeans	Joo-*dee*-unz.
Leviticus	Leh-*vit*-ih-kus.

indicates translation of a different word. When the two Hebrew words are adjacent (as they are about 300 times in the Old Testament) the translation in the *King James Version* is *the Lord GOD*, as we see here.

◆ SANCTIFYING HIS NAME ◆

Jewish people of biblical times grew into the practice of not vocalizing God's name. They didn't want to be guilty of speaking it lightly or irreverently. How different from today, when many people use His name merely as a filler expression! Some try to avoid a problem by substituting words such as *golly, gosh,* or *geez* in place of the holy names of God and Jesus.

One wonders if misuse of God's name is tied somehow to the larger issue of religious terminology as used in profane or even just flippant ways. The Bible words *hell* and *holy* seem to be particular favorites in this regard. Is a person who unthinkingly exclaims "Holy cow!" thereby more prone to misuse God's name as well?

Perhaps the old axiom "when in doubt, throw it out" will serve us well here. Rather than seeing how close we can get to a fire without being burned, we are better served by keeping our distance. But beware: attempts to change speech patterns by mere force of will won't work since unholy utterances spring from an unholy heart (Matthew 15:8, 18). —C. R. B.

24. For I will take you from among the heathen, and gather you out of all countries, and will bring you into your own land.

The most obvious defeat of the fictitious gods of the Gentiles will be in the return of God's people to their homeland. The defeat of God's people and their deportation to Babylon has created the impression that the Babylonian gods are greater than the Lord; that defeat has caused His name to be profaned. The Lord's reversing of that condition will prove He is, after all, superior to them; His name will be sanctified (compare Exodus 12:12). God's sanctifying of His name and His holiness is connected with correcting misperceptions of *the heathen* in several places in this book (see Ezekiel 20:9, 14, 22, 41; 37:28; 39:7, 21, 23).

II. Holy People
(EZEKIEL 36:25-27)
A. From Filthy to Clean (v. 25)

25. Then will I sprinkle clean water upon you, and ye shall be clean: from all your filthiness, and from all your idols, will I cleanse you.

Not only will the people be returned to their homeland, they also will be cleansed or purified. To *sprinkle clean water* on people is the language of ritual purification (Leviticus 14:1-7, 49-52; Numbers 8:5-7; 19:11-13, 16-20; compare Hebrews 10:22). This is more than ritual, however. The cleansing from idolatry will be effective; after the exile, Judah will never again be led into the worship of idols. Some students think the reference to water in this verse and to spirit in the next verse form the background of Jesus' statement in John 3:5.

B. From Stone to Flesh (v. 26)

26. A new heart also will I give you, and a new spirit will I put within you: and I will take away the stony heart out of your flesh, and I will give you an heart of flesh.

Dr. Christiaan Barnard is credited with performing the first successful human heart transplant (December 3, 1967). But centuries before, God promises not only *a new heart* for the exiles of Judah, but also *a new spirit* (compare Ezekiel 18:31). In many texts, the words *spirit* (or *Spirit*) and *flesh* signify different spheres that may be opposed to one another (examples: John 3:6; Romans 7; Galatians 5). But here God's promise of a new spirit goes hand in hand with the promise of a new *heart of flesh* for the people. Their old hearts of stone (Ezekiel 11:19) must be replaced.

No mention is made of the old spirit in the people, but it must be a mind-set that is opposed to God and His will. Another prophet speaks of "the spirit of whoredoms" in describing fascination with idolatry (Hosea 4:12; 5:4). The people's spirit of rebellion needs to be replaced (next verse).

C. From Disobedience to Obedience (v. 27)

27. And I will put my spirit within you, and cause you to walk in my statutes, and ye shall keep my judgments, and do them.

Ezekiel 11:19, mentioned above, was the first time the prophet relayed God's promise of a new heart and a new spirit for the people. That was spoken a few years before Jerusalem had fallen. At that time the people still there were saying that the exiles were separated from the Lord, but they themselves were not. They were claiming that God had disinherited the Judeans taken into exile, and ownership of the land belonged to those in Jerusalem (11:15). This thinking amounted to casting all blame onto those already in captivity and claiming God's favor for themselves.

But that is not God's point of view! Those who had been deported to Babylon earlier had actually found "sanctuary" (Ezekiel 11:16). God intends to return the exiles to Judah as He puts a new heart and new spirit in them at that time (11:17-20). The obstinate and unrepentant people who were not taken in an earlier deportation ultimately suffer the greater punishment (2 Kings 25:1-21; 2 Chronicles 36:15-20). The message in the verse before us, coming after the fall of Jerusalem, is a reminder of the earlier promise. The city's fall is not cause for despair; rather, it is evidence that the promise in Ezekiel 11 is still valid. With the spirit of rebellion removed and a new spirit from the Lord implanted, the people will indeed turn from their former disobedience.

What Do You Think?

What are some proper and improper ways to help fellow Christians exhibit behavior that conforms to the expectations of the Holy Spirit, who lives within us?

Talking Points for Your Discussion

- In light of "don't judge" passages such as Matthew 7:1-5; Luke 6:37, 41, 42; John 8:7; and James 4:11, 12
- In light of "do judge" passages such as Matthew 7:15-20; Luke 6:43-45; 1 Corinthians 5:12, 13; and 1 John 4:1-3

III. Fertile Land
(Ezekiel 36:28-30)
A. Land of Fathers (v. 28)

28. And ye shall dwell in the land that I gave to your fathers; and ye shall be my people, and I will be your God.

Those left behind in Judah after 597 BC, "the poorest sort of the people" (2 Kings 24:14), had been claiming that the land of Canaan no longer belonged to those taken into exile. But God is the one who gave the land to the *fathers* (patriarchs Abraham, Isaac, and Jacob) in the first place, through the leadership of Joshua (about 1400 BC). And God reserves for himself the decision regarding present and future ownership of the land of promise. All the tribes of divided Israel have forfeited this gift (see on Ezekiel 36:22, above). Even so, God promises to bring back the exiled Judeans —not merely to the land, but to a relationship with Him (compare Jeremiah 30:22).

B. Absence of Famine (vv. 29, 30)

29. I will also save you from all your uncleannesses: and I will call for the corn, and will increase it, and lay no famine upon you.

The people's impurity is due to idol worship (Ezekiel 36:25, above). By turning to the Lord, the people will be pure once again. Famine, often a discipline of the Lord for unfaithfulness (examples: Deuteronomy 32:19-24; 1 Kings 17:1), will no longer be a problem. To the contrary, the crops will be abundant; the Lord himself will cause the bounty. (The word *corn* in the *King James Version* does not refer to maize, which is unknown in the time and place of the text, but to grains or kernels in general; compare John 12:24.)

30. And I will multiply the fruit of the tree, and the increase of the field, that ye shall receive no more reproach of famine among the heathen.

The abundance will extend to all agriculture, whether *the fruit of the tree* or the crops *of the field*. Agriculture in Israel includes grapes, olives, figs, and grains such as wheat and barley.

Famine brings not just physical suffering but also shame, especially when marked as an act of divine punishment. Bountiful crops, the opposite of famine, remove that reproach and disgrace. *The heathen* nations will no longer look at the Lord's people as abandoned by Him.

> ### What Do You Think?
> How would you respond to a believer who uses Ezekiel 36:29, 30 to assert that those who are truly cleansed by God will never face economic reversals or hardships?
> ### Talking Points for Your Discussion
> - Considering the context of the passage
> - Considering Matthew 19:23, 24; John 15:20; 2 Corinthians 6:3-10; Revelation 2:9; etc.
> - Other

IV. Repentant People
(Ezekiel 36:31, 32)
A. Ashamed (v. 31)

31. Then shall ye remember your own evil ways, and your doings that were not good, and shall lothe yourselves in your own sight for your iniquities and for your abominations.

Having been blessed by the grace of God, the Israelites will come to see clearly how disgraceful their former behavior has been. They will repent of their former ways, coming to loathe their past unfaithfulness (compare Ezekiel 6:9).

The *iniquities* and *abominations* of the exiles are grounded in idol worship. The Israelites were told hundreds of years earlier that they were neither to worship the fictitious gods of the pagans nor worship the Lord God in the manner that the pagans worshipped their gods (Exodus 23:24; Deuteronomy 12:30, 31). But the people are guilty of both, having engaged in grossly immoral practices in the process. They will do well to loathe such behavior.

◆ LOATHING ... WHAT? ◆

The term *self-loathing* has come into vogue in recent years. It commonly refers to a person who is uncomfortable with his or her identity. Self-loathing may result from being identified as part of a certain demographic segment of humanity, inclusion in which the individual has no control over. Self-hate (a sometime synonym) may also be traced to voluntary choices that have resulted in destructive and/or shameful behavior. Self-hatred is understandable in many contexts. But it is better to focus hatred on the behavior that breaks relationship with God: the behavior of sin.

The nation of Israel as a whole had sinned against God in serious ways. Prophets had called for repentance, but the nation had refused. The people had every reason to hate their shameful, sinful behavior (a first step toward repentance), but many or most did not. Failure of leadership to set the proper example played a large part (Ezekiel 8:9-12; 13:1-7; 14:1-3). Ezekiel's message was rejected by the people who should have been most aware of their sin, namely those with whom he shared exile. But they thought little of him and his message (33:30-32).

Being created in the image of God is the best reason for not hating ourselves (Genesis 1:26, 27). But that is also the best reason to hate sin, a vital step toward repentance and forgiveness. That doesn't mean having a "holier than thou" attitude. It *does* mean having a desire to be holy as God is holy (1 Peter 1:15, 16). —C. R. B.

> ### What Do You Think?
> To what extent is it appropriate for Christians to engage in self-loathing? Why?
> ### Talking Points for Your Discussion
> - Regarding voluntary choices
> - Regarding involuntary circumstances

B. Confounded (v. 32)

32. Not for your sakes do I this, saith the Lord GOD, be it known unto you: be ashamed and confounded for your own ways, O house of Israel.

Once again God confirms that the people have not earned any consideration. He does not intend to act for their sake, but for His own. He does not reward any merit on their part. They have no merit. Their deeds deserve only rejection.

God wants the exiles to understand this, so He takes care to explain it and repeat the explanation. The people are to be ashamed of their former conduct. The grace He will grant them is not to mislead them into thinking that His favor is due to anything on their part. He wants them to see their former behavior for what it is.

That is the only sure deterrent to repeating bad behavior. The law can impose penalties, but that by itself does not prevent a repetition of the unlawful behavior. The person who has sinned has to come to see the sinfulness of his or her own behavior. That is what God challenges the people to do. Once they come to see their own sin's shamefulness, its disgrace, they will be cured of repeating it.

Ever since the time of the judges, which began about 1380 BC, the people have wavered between faithfulness to God and the worship of idols. Elijah had offered the people this challenge on Mount Carmel: "How long halt ye between two opinions? if the Lord be God, follow him: but if Baal, then follow him" (1 Kings 18:21). The wavering must stop!

Conclusion

A. Learning to Blush

Everyone has had the experience of saying something embarrassing. Perhaps it was as innocent as simply getting our words tangled so that what came out of our mouths was not at all what we intended. Or maybe it was not so innocent, and we said something unkind about an individual whom we thought was not within earshot. Then we realized the person overheard us after all. The combination of words and circumstance caused us to

Visual for Lesson 4. *Start a discussion by pointing to this visual as you ask, "In what ways has a Spirit-filled heart changed your outlook on life?"*

embarrass ourselves. And we blushed. It's a natural reaction.

But Jeremiah spoke of a time in Israelite history when the people did not know how to blush. They sinned against God and, when they learned of their sin, still felt no shame. "Were they ashamed when they had committed abomination? nay, they were not at all ashamed, neither could they blush" (Jeremiah 6:15; 8:12).

When Ezekiel told the people to be "ashamed and confounded," he used a Hebrew word very closely associated with the one translated "blush" in Jeremiah. Both men lived in a culture where shame seemed to be a lost concept. The same was true in Paul's day (1 Corinthians 5:1, 2). The same is true in ours.

And what a great loss it is! Until we can be ashamed of our sin, we will not be able to see things as God does.

B. Prayer

Heavenly Father, may a keen sense of our unworthiness bring forth the sense of shame that leads to repentance. May we never treat sin lightly or assume that it is anything less than detestable. May that attitude lead us to abandon sin and walk in holiness. We pray in Jesus' name. Amen.

C. Thought to Remember

For hearts to be changed, they must be receptive to change.

INVOLVEMENT LEARNING

Enhance your lesson with KJV Bible Student *(from your curriculum supplier) and the reproducible activity page (at www.standardlesson.com or in the back of the* KJV Standard Lesson Commentary Deluxe Edition*).*

Into the Lesson

Write on the board some familiar euphemisms —phrases used to obscure the meanings of more negative terms. Some examples (with their harsher meanings, which you won't write) are *workforce imbalance correction* (layoffs), *economically disadvantaged* (poor), *culturally deprived environment* (slums), *courtesy call* (telemarketing), *negative patient outcome* (death), *commit terminological inexactitude* (lie), *pre-enjoyed vehicle* (used car); *correctional facility* (prison).

Ask learners to identify the intended meanings behind these carefully worded terms. Spend a few minutes discussing ways people try to hide their true feelings, motives, and agendas from others.

Lead into Bible study by saying, "Sadly, experience has taught us not to take people at face value. Too often there are motives in human hearts that are hidden behind various fronts of euphemisms. God, however, is very clear about His motives. He wants a different type of heart in His people. Let's learn about that."

Into the Word

Divide the class into three groups. Supply each group with pen and paper and one of the following research assignments.

Group 1—For the sake of God's name

1. Read Ezekiel 36:22, 23 and underline the words *name/name's* and *sake* every time they appear. What is God saying about the sake of His name?

2. Read the following passages and list what God does for His name's sake: 1 Samuel 12:22; Psalm 23:3; 31:3; Isaiah 48:9; Jeremiah 14:21.

Group 2—Renewal of a people by give and take

1. Read Ezekiel 36:24-30.

2. Make a list of what God will take away from His people and another list of what He will give to His people. Compare and contrast the lists.

Group 3—Reminder of unworthiness

1. Agree or disagree with the statement: "God wants us to feel good about ourselves." Compare and contrast your answers with Ezekiel 36:31, 32.

2. Read Psalm 51 (focusing on vv. 3-7, 11, 17). Tell how David agrees with Ezekiel about feeling good about oneself.

Alternative. Distribute copies of the "The Divine Agenda" activity from the reproducible page, which you can download. Have students work individually or in pairs to match items on God's agenda for Israel to the verses in which they are promised.

Into Life

Distribute to each learner a paper heart (homemade or purchased). Give these directions: "On this heart, write, with a ballpoint pen, 'My New Heart.' Keep this heart somewhere nearby this week. Keep a simple lead pencil with it." (You may want to provide little pencils with erasers for the class.)

Continue: "When you are struck that there is something amiss in your behavior and spiritual life, write it on the back side of the heart. Remember, though, that lead pencil writing is quite erasable . . . if the writer commits to eliminating it. That is our challenge from Ezekiel: let God erase our sin!"

Alternative. Distribute copies of the reproducible page activity "From Disgrace by Grace." This exercise will foster both group discussion and personal examination for life application as it reviews and reinforces the following key ideas of the lesson text:

1. God's name has been disgraced among the nations.

2. The way God's honor can be restored is by the humble repentance and changed behavior of His people.

God's Covenant with Abraham

Devotional Reading: Psalm 33:1-9
Background Scripture: Genesis 15

Genesis 15:1-6, 17-21

1 After these things the word of the Lord came unto Abram in a vision, saying, Fear not, Abram: I am thy shield, and thy exceeding great reward.

2 And Abram said, Lord God, what wilt thou give me, seeing I go childless, and the steward of my house is this Eliezer of Damascus?

3 And Abram said, Behold, to me thou hast given no seed: and, lo, one born in my house is mine heir.

4 And, behold, the word of the Lord came unto him, saying, This shall not be thine heir; but he that shall come forth out of thine own bowels shall be thine heir.

5 And he brought him forth abroad, and said, Look now toward heaven, and tell the stars, if thou be able to number them: and he said unto him, So shall thy seed be.

6 And he believed in the Lord; and he counted it to him for righteousness.

. . . .

17 And it came to pass, that, when the sun went down, and it was dark, behold a smoking furnace, and a burning lamp that passed between those pieces.

18 In the same day the Lord made a covenant with Abram, saying, Unto thy seed have I given this land, from the river of Egypt unto the great river, the river Euphrates:

19 The Kenites, and the Kenizzites, and the Kadmonites,

20 And the Hittites, and the Perizzites, and the Rephaims,

21 And the Amorites, and the Canaanites, and the Girgashites, and the Jebusites.

Key Verse

In the same day the Lord made a covenant with Abram, saying, Unto thy seed have I given this land, from the river of Egypt unto the great river, the river Euphrates. —**Genesis 15:18**

COVENANT WITH GOD

LESSON AIMS

After participating in this lesson, each learner will be able to:

1. List key elements of Abraham's vision.

2. Explain the relationship between belief and righteousness.

3. Write a prayer of commitment to produce spiritual offspring for Christ.

LESSON OUTLINE

Introduction

A. Such a Deal

In 1984, the Kansas City Royals wanted to keep star third baseman George Brett on the team. To do so, they negotiated a rather odd contract. First, the Royals agreed to give Brett the bat he used in the infamous 1983 "pine tar game," when his go-ahead home run was ruled an out (a decision later reversed) because he allegedly had too much pine tar on his bat. Second, the contract also gave Brett part ownership of an apartment complex in Memphis!

While we may never sign an agreement giving us a baseball bat and buildings, we are familiar with contracts. Whether we call an agreement a contract, a pledge, or a covenant, the sealing of promises has always been an essential element of society. This lesson looks at a covenant, not between people, but between a person and God.

B. Lesson Background

God's covenant with Abraham began when the Lord called him (at the time known as Abram) to leave his homeland and move to unfamiliar surroundings (Genesis 12:1). Abraham "obeyed; and he went out, not knowing whither he went" (Hebrews 11:8). The year was about 2000 BC.

Though Abraham's initial obedience was exemplary, his faith journey was not without bumps. By the end of the same chapter in which Abraham left his homeland in response to God's call, he had passed off his wife Sarah (known as Sarai at that stage) as his sister in order to gain favorable treatment from Pharaoh in Egypt (Genesis 12:10-13).

Abraham also had to deal with certain problems involving his nephew Lot, who had chosen to live in the vicinity of Sodom (Genesis 13:5-13). When Sodom became entangled in a regional war between coalitions of kings, Lot was captured (14:1-12). Abraham had to lead a commando raid to defeat a coalition and rescue Lot (14:13-16).

Following this victory, Abraham was met by Melchizedek, who was "king of Salem" and "the priest of the most high God" (14:18). He blessed Abraham, and in return Abraham gave him a tenth of the spoils taken in battle (14:19, 20).

I. Apprehension

(GENESIS 15:1-3)

As Genesis 15 opens, the scene has shifted from Abraham's interactions with earthly kings to an encounter with the ultimate king, God himself.

A. God's Protection (v. 1)

1a. After these things the word of the LORD came unto Abram in a vision, saying, Fear not, Abram.

Fear not is one of the most common commands in Scripture. Usually the speaker is God or an angel, and Abraham is addressed by his original name before it is changed (Genesis 17:5). If he feared the Egyptians enough to lie about his relationship with his wife (see the Lesson Background), how much more likely is he to be terrified of God! The Bible uses the word *vision* more than a hundred times, and this is the first. God communicates in various ways before the coming of Christ (Hebrews 1:1), and visions are one method.

1b. I am thy shield.

The word picture of the Lord as a *shield* is not uncommon in the Old Testament (see Deuteronomy 33:29; Psalms 3:3; 28:7; 84:11; 115:9-11; etc.). Similar metaphors, such as rock, fortress, and tower, highlight the Lord to be a trustworthy, steadfast source of strength (compare 2 Samuel 22:3; Psalms 18:2; 31:3; 71:3; etc.).

1c. And thy exceeding great reward.

Of greater interest may be why the Lord describes himself as Abraham's *exceeding great reward*. After the successful night attack in Genesis 14:15, 16, the king of Sodom, who had benefited from Abraham's victory, offered him all the plunder seized from the enemy. But Abraham declined because he did not want the king to be able to claim he had "made Abram rich" (14:23). Following this refusal of a reward, the Lord now comes to Abraham and says, in effect, "Although you have turned down a reward, I can give you a far greater one; in fact, I am your greatest reward."

◆ *REGARDING RISK AND REWARD* ◆

After teaching him how to use the special keyboard, I watched Musa (name changed) type the first words of Scripture ever written in his language. Musa's easy smile belied the difficult and risky decision he had made.

He is one of very few Christians among his people. Years before, the secret police caught him talking about Jesus; they pulled out his toenails and threw him into a pit. He moved to a neighboring country with his family but returned to translate the Bible for his people. He had left comfortable living conditions for an uncomfortable and dangerous environment far from his family. Why would he take such a risk?

We could ask the same question of Abraham. Their two answers would be similar: they left home in obedience to God. We understand that we are not guaranteed safety in this world. But when we yield to God's call, we reap the eternal rewards of His blessing—what a promise!

Are God's call and promise compelling you to go to risky and uncomfortable places? If so, when will you get started? —D. & L. G.

B. Abraham's Protest (vv. 2, 3)

2a. And Abram said, Lord GOD, what wilt thou give me, seeing I go childless.

Abraham's response indicates that he is wrestling with how to reconcile God's grand declaration with the current circumstances. His words reflect continuing awareness of the Lord's promise to make of Abraham "a great nation" (Genesis 12:2). But that requires descendants (compare 12:7). Yet at this point Abraham remains childless, and his wife is past the age of childbearing (compare 12:4 with 17:17). How can God truly be Abraham's "exceeding great reward" under these circumstances?

What Do You Think?

Other than proper use of Romans 8:28, what are some ways to encourage fellow believers to maintain hope in difficult circumstances?

Talking Points for Your Discussion

- In the face of personal tragedy or loss
- In the face of financial pressure
- In the face of family problems
- Other

2b. And the steward of my house is this Eliezer of Damascus?

Abraham reasons the likely outcome. His concern stems from a practice of the time, confirmed by archaeological finds at Nuzi in the 1920s. According to custom, a childless couple can adopt a household servant or steward, who cares for them and provides proper burial when they die. Then the servant inherits the family property. Abraham can see no outcome but this one.

Abraham's servant Eliezer may have been acquired during travel from Haran to Canaan (Genesis 12:4, 5), since Damascus is located between the two. Assuming he is still living at the time, Eliezer is likely the "eldest servant" in 24:2, who is dispatched to find a wife for Isaac.

3. And Abram said, Behold, to me thou hast given no seed: and, lo, one born in my house is mine heir.

Abraham now states as a fact what he presented as a question in the previous verse. The custom, if not prevailing law, is quite clear.

What Do You Think?

How should Christians admit to uncertainties regarding God's promises, if ever?

Talking Points for Your Discussion
- In congregational gatherings
- In midsize groups
- In small groups
- In one-on-one counseling
- In private times with God

II. Assurance
(GENESIS 15:4-6)

God later declares Abraham to be "a prophet" (Genesis 20:7). But perhaps Abraham isn't quite there yet. Hearing and believing prophecies from God, the ultimate prophet, is a vital prerequisite.

A. God Blesses (vv. 4, 5)

4. And, behold, the word of the LORD came unto him, saying, This shall not be thine heir; but he that shall come forth out of thine own bowels shall be thine heir.

God responds to Abraham's statement in Genesis 15:3 with the assurance we see here. Abraham is to father a child who will be the heir, but when that will occur is not stated. As comforting as *the word of the Lord* is at this time, it will not be fulfilled until Abraham is age 100 and his wife is 90 (17:17). As the years drag on, that unknown timing will be a continual challenge to Abraham's faith, even as he considers "not his own body now dead" (Romans 4:19).

5. And he brought him forth abroad, and said, Look now toward heaven, and tell the stars, if thou be able to number them: and he said unto him, So shall thy seed be.

Now the Lord provides a visual aid to show Abraham the magnitude of what lies ahead. Being challenged to *tell the stars* would seem to indicate that this communication from God occurs at night. (To *tell* means to count; think of what a bank teller does in counting out money.) But caution reminds us that Genesis 15:1, above, speaks of a vision. Therefore we do not know if night has actually fallen by this time or if the command to look at the stars is part of what Abraham witnesses in his vision. It's also possible that the vision of 15:1 and the word of the Lord of 15:4 occur at different times.

Later, in Genesis 22:17, we find the added imagery of seashore sand that further illustrates how innumerable Abraham's descendants will be. Hebrews 11:12 also uses both comparisons.

What Do You Think?

What cues can you begin using to remind yourself daily of the certainty of God's promises?

Talking Points for Your Discussion
- Cues involving the sense of sight
- Cues involving the sense of sound
- Cues involving the sense of touch
- Cues involving the sense of taste
- Cues involving the sense of smell

We know from the New Testament that God's promise to Abraham refers not only to the great nation that comes from his natural descendants (Genesis 46:2, 3; 47:27) but also to the spiritual descendants who will respond to Jesus in faith, as

Abraham did to God. Galatians 3:26-29 establishes this link, especially verse 29: "And if ye be Christ's, then are ye Abraham's seed, and heirs according to the promise."

Paul makes a similar connection in Romans 4:16-18. Note that the conclusion of that segment is the same as the concluding line of the verse before us.

B. Abraham Believes (v. 6)

6. And he believed in the LORD; and he counted it to him for righteousness.

This declaration is so important that the New Testament quotes or refers to it five times (see Romans 4:3, 9, 22; Galatians 3:6; and James 2:23). Faith is what God has always asked of people, whether in Old or New Testament times. We today are not called to respond to the same covenant Abraham was offered in this passage; but we are called to respond to God's covenant at present, which requires us to believe in the name of His Son, Jesus Christ (John 3:16; 20:30, 31).

The verb behind the translation *counted* occurs about 150 times in the Old Testament, and this is the first. The idea in contexts similar to this one is to regard something or someone as having a certain characteristic, although that thing or person may not actually have that characteristic (compare Genesis 31:15; Numbers 18:27; Job 18:3; Proverbs 17:28; etc.). The translations in the five New Testament passages noted above are "counted" (Romans 4:3), "reckoned" (Romans 4:9), "imputed" (Romans 4:22; James 2:23), and "accounted" (Galatians 3:6); all of these capture the idea of the same Greek word used in all instances.

And what a marvelous concept it is! Because of our sin, "there is none righteous, no, not one" (Romans 3:10). But if we come to God on the basis of faith in Jesus rather than on the basis of our own works, then God will count us as righteous. He can do so because the death Jesus suffered paid the penalty for our sins (2 Corinthians 5:21).

◆ *TAKING THE PLUNGE* ◆

A thin wire trailed high above a muddy river. Our friends waited on the opposite shore for me to entrust my safety to the ramshackle zip line.

No amount of praying and pleading, whining and wheedling changed the situation. I just had to take the plunge and jump.

That experience has proved helpful many times since. There comes a point when we've done enough thinking and talking. Then it's time to trust God and step out in faith. Marriage. Having children. Working in an African refugee camp. God has lists for us.

Abraham is a hero and model in taking the plunge of faith. He began by obeying God's command to leave his homeland, and so he "went out, not knowing whither he went" (Hebrews 11:8). What a leap of faith! But he didn't stop there. When God asked him to believe the impossible, that even in his childless old age he would have more descendants than he could count, Abraham chose to let go of his fears and believe. As a result, God "counted it to him for righteousness" (Genesis 15:6).

Is there anything that God wants you to do but you are putting it off? If so, why?   —D. & L. G.

III. Affirmation
(GENESIS 15:17-21)

In the intervening verses not addressed in today's lesson (Genesis 15:7-16), the Lord speaks of granting to Abraham the land of Canaan. Abraham requests and receives assurance in this regard. The response begins with the Lord's directive that

HOW TO SAY IT

Amorites	*Am*-uh-rites.
Canaanites	*Kay*-nun-ites.
Eliezer	El-ih-*ee*-zer.
Euphrates	You-*fray*-teez.
Girgashites	*Gur*-guh-shites.
Hittites	*Hit*-ites or *Hit*-tites.
Jebusites	*Jeb*-yuh-sites.
Kadmonites	*Kadd*-mun-ites.
Kenizzites	*Ken*-ez-zites or *Ken*-uh-zites.
Melchizedek	Mel-*kiz*-eh-dek.
Nuzi	*New*-zee.
Perizzites	*Pair*-ih-zites.
Pharaoh	*Fair*-o or *Fay*-roe.
Rephaims	*Ref*-a-ims.

Abraham arrange for a sacrifice of livestock and birds in a certain way.

At sunset Abraham falls into a deep sleep. Then God speaks and gives Abraham what may be called a future history of the man's descendants. The land in which Abraham now resides will indeed become the home of his descendants, but only after a period of 400 years in bondage in another land. Ironically Abraham has already been in that land, Egypt (Genesis 12:10-20).

A. Concluding a Ceremony (v. 17)

17a. And it came to pass, that, when the sun went down, and it was dark.

Here we are given the conclusion of what Abraham sees during his deep sleep that begins in Genesis 15:12. What happens there occurs "when the sun was going down"; what happens now occurs *when the sun went down*. So now the sun has fully set, and it is dark. The fact that another night is falling (that is, in addition to the night of Genesis 15:5) is not problematic given the visionary nature of what Abraham is seeing. A vision, like a dream, can occur outside of normal time limitations.

17b. Behold a smoking furnace, and a burning lamp that passed between those pieces.

The presence of smoke and/or fire signifies at times in Scripture the presence of God (Exodus 3:1, 2; Psalm 18:8). This will be especially true at Mount Sinai (Exodus 19:18) when God will establish a covenant with the descendants of Abraham, the children of Israel (next week's lesson). *Those pieces* to which the verse before us refers are parts of the animals sacrificed in Genesis 15:10.

B. Confirming a Covenant (vv. 18-21)

18a. In the same day the LORD made a covenant with Abram, saying, Unto thy seed have I given this land.

To us, the actions of Genesis 15:9-17 may seem rather bizarre as a backdrop to the making of the covenant now mentioned. An explanation will help us connect the dots.

In the ancient world, animals were often used as visual aids in the process of making or ratifying treaties or covenants. For example, the ruler of a certain nation might say to a conquered peo-

ple, "Here is what will happen to you if you dare to rebel against me"; and he would then break the leg or the neck of a sheep or other animal.

Similar, but reversing the direction, are cases when a person takes a certain vow and says something like "May this happen to me if I fail to keep my promise"—and then proceeds to break the animal's leg or neck. These are called self-maledictory oaths: the maker invokes harm on self should he fail to carry through.

This latter is the type of covenant God seems to be making with Abraham. Essentially, God's promise is this: "May what has happened to these animals [that have been cut in pieces] happen to me if I do not keep my promise of land to you." Of course, God cannot be "cut up" since He has no physical body (John 4:24). But the Lord is speaking to Abraham in terms that the man understands in his time and place. As Abraham gets the message, he will see clearly how committed God is to keeping His promise.

> **What Do You Think?**
> In light of your own experiences of delayed answers to prayer, in what ways can you help others trust God?
> *Talking Points for Your Discussion*
> - Regarding spiritually mature believers
> - Regarding new believers
> - Regarding unbelievers

18b. From the river of Egypt unto the great river, the river Euphrates.

The Lord establishes the future boundaries of the promised land. Many assume that *the river of Egypt* refers to the Nile River because of its prominence. However, the Wadi el-Arish, which separates Palestine and Egypt, is more likely. The distance between these two rivers is some 400 miles at their closest points. Boundaries such as outlined here will be realized as a result of King David's battle conquests centuries later.

19-21. The Kenites, and the Kenizzites, and the Kadmonites, and the Hittites, and the Perizzites, and the Rephaims, and the Amorites, and the Canaanites, and the Girgashites, and the Jebusites.

Our lesson text concludes with a listing of various peoples whom the Israelites will confront when they enter Canaan after 400 years in bondage (Genesis 15:13). In other references, only one such group may be mentioned in order to highlight some especially offensive behavior on its part (example: "the iniquity of the Amorites" in 15:16). Also, some passages include groups not listed here (example: the Hivites in Exodus 3:8, 17; 13:5; etc.). See overlapping lists in Exodus 3:8, 17; 23:23; 33:2; 34:11; Deuteronomy 20:17; Joshua 3:10; 9:1; 11:3; 12:8; 24:11; Judges 3:5; 1 Kings 9:20; 2 Chronicles 8:7; Ezra 9:1; and Nehemiah 9:8.

Old Testament history makes clear that none of these "-ites" end up being the most serious threat to God's people. Rather, the Israelites themselves become their own worst enemy. That happens when they fail to follow the Lord, when they do not live as descendants of Abraham should.

What Do You Think?

How do we deal with situations of greater difficulties as we try to follow God's leading?

Talking Points for Your Discussion

- Considering how Bible people reacted in God-honoring ways (Acts 4:19; 2 Corinthians 6:3-10; 2 Timothy 3:10-13; 4:6-8; Hebrews 11; etc.)
- Considering how Bible people reacted in ineffective or sinful ways (Genesis 16:1-4; Jonah 1:1-3; Mark 14:66-72; Galatians 2:11-13; etc.)

Conclusion

A. Join the Club

Most Bible students are aware of how Abraham is highlighted in Scripture because of his faith. Abraham's faith takes up more verses in Hebrews 11 (commonly called "the faith chapter") than anyone else's. Yet Abraham's faith clearly was not perfect. In addition to problems noted in the Lesson Background, today's lesson reveals the man expressing concerns as to whether God will keep His promise of offspring. Abraham then voiced a desire for some kind of guarantee that God would fulfill the promise of land. So where is this man's exemplary faith?

The Bible does not hide the weaknesses or failures of even its staunchest heroes and heroines of faith. As Abraham had his struggles, so did Moses (Numbers 11:10-15), Miriam (Numbers 12), Elijah (1 Kings 19:1-4, 14), John the Baptist (Matthew 11:1-6), and Peter (Matthew 26:69-75). Such examples can be a source of encouragement when our faith walk is more of a limp. At such times we are in good company.

These individuals did not stagnate. The Abraham who stumbled at times eventually became the Abraham willing to place his son on the sacrificial altar in obedience to God's command; the Peter who denied Jesus eventually became the Peter who died a martyr's death; etc.

Abraham was not a man of perfect faith. Yet never is the statement of Genesis 15:6 revoked: "He believed in the Lord; and he counted it to him for righteousness."

B. Prayer

Father, the challenges to faith in our time can be intimidating. We find ourselves pleading with the disciples of Jesus, "Increase our faith!" Use our daily contacts and circumstances to shape us into people who model true faith to a skeptical world. We pray this in Jesus' name. Amen.

C. Thought to Remember

Faith keeps one focused on
the faithfulness of God.

Some Bible Covenants

NAME		SCRIPTURE	SUBSTANCE OF COVENANT	SIGN OF COVENANT
	The Covenant in Eden	Genesis 2:9, 15-17	Adam and Eve would live forever in paradise if they did not eat of the tree of the knowledge of good and evil	The covenant was signified by access to the tree of life
	The Covenant with Noah	Genesis 8:20–9:17	God would never again destroy the earth by flood	The covenant was signified by the rainbow
	The Covenant with Abraham	Genesis 12:1-3	Abraham would have a multitude of descendants, would have a land in which to live, and would be a blessing to all the earth	The covenant was signified by circumcision
	The Old (Mosaic) Covenant	Exodus 31:12-18	God gave Israel laws for all aspects of life	The covenant was signified most notably by Sabbath observance
	The Covenant with David	2 Samuel 7:4-17; Luke 1:30-33; 2:12	God promised that the rule of David's line would never end	The covenant was signified by the birth of the King of kings, Jesus
	The New Covenant	Hebrews 8:7-13; Jeremiah 31:27-34	Salvation is available through Jesus	The covenant was signified by the resurrection of Jesus and is celebrated in baptism and the Lord's Supper

Visual for Lesson 5. *Use this chart as a starting point to compare and contrast the new covenant with various Old Testament covenants.*

INVOLVEMENT LEARNING

Enhance your lesson with KJV Bible Student (from your curriculum supplier) and the reproducible activity page (at www.standardlesson.com or in the back of the KJV Standard Lesson Commentary Deluxe Edition).

Into the Lesson

To begin class, write this definition on the board: "a voluntary, deliberate, and legally binding agreement between two or more competent parties."

Ask class members to identify the term defined by that description. Of course, it is a *contract.* Briefly discuss the types of contracts your learners have entered into.

Alternative. Distribute copies of the "Document Needed" activity from the reproducible page, which you can download. Have students work individually or in pairs to identify items and services that usually have a contract associated with them.

After either activity, lead into Bible study by saying, "We sign contracts to buy houses, obtain jobs, finance cars, purchase insurance, and for a host of other reasons. Today we will look at a covenant or contract that God entered into with Abraham."

Into the Word

Divide the class into three groups, giving each group pen and paper and a portion of the Bible text. Say, "Twitter used to be unique among social media websites because at one time it limited the length of messages sent on it. Each message (or 'tweet') could contain no more than 140 characters. Let's see if you can summarize or explain a portion of today's text as a tweet of no more than 140 characters."

Assign Scripture to be summarized as follows. Examples are in italics.

Group 1—Abram expressing his concern about God's promise (Genesis 15:1-3)

God promises me protection and wealth. But what good is it if I cannot pass it along to my descendants? My estate will go to someone outside of my family after I die! (134 characters)

Group 2—God assuring Abram that the promise will be kept (Genesis 15:4-6)

I promised Abram a descendant and he will get one. In fact, no one will be able to count the number of his descendants. And all he has to do to get this gift is to trust in me! (138 characters)

Group 3—A reporter telling about the sealing of the covenant (Genesis 15:17-21)

After sunset, God affirmed his covenant by passing as fire and smoke through Abram's sacrifice. God set the boundaries of the land Abram's descendants would inherit. (140 characters)

After group work is complete, have groups share their tweets and summarize their Scripture assignments.

Into Life

Say, "Abram was assured that God's promises to him would be handed down from generation to generation. This included parents teaching their own children, but it also included the entire community of Israel coming together to pass God's truth to succeeding generations. What does that mean for us today?"

Close this session by brainstorming a list of ways they can ensure that future generations are not denied access to the covenant promises of God. Some ideas would include volunteering in the church nursery, assisting with the church's children's programs, participating in intergenerational service projects, organizing an adopt-a-grandparent ministry, offering to help a single parent, etc.

When the list is complete, have students consider accepting one or more tasks.

Alternative. Distribute copies of the "Transfer of Ownership" activity from the reproducible page. Have students look up the Scriptures referred to in the activity and match them with a way to pass faith to the next generation.

Close either activity with prayer that the Lord's church remain strong from generation to generation.

GOD'S COVENANT WITH ISRAEL

DEVOTIONAL READING: Psalm 135:1-9, 19-21
BACKGROUND SCRIPTURE: Exodus 19; Isaiah 60:3

EXODUS 19:16-25

16 And it came to pass on the third day in the morning, that there were thunders and lightnings, and a thick cloud upon the mount, and the voice of the trumpet exceeding loud; so that all the people that was in the camp trembled.

17 And Moses brought forth the people out of the camp to meet with God; and they stood at the nether part of the mount.

18 And mount Sinai was altogether on a smoke, because the LORD descended upon it in fire: and the smoke thereof ascended as the smoke of a furnace, and the whole mount quaked greatly.

19 And when the voice of the trumpet sounded long, and waxed louder and louder, Moses spake, and God answered him by a voice.

20 And the LORD came down upon mount Sinai, on the top of the mount: and the LORD called Moses up to the top of the mount; and Moses went up.

21 And the LORD said unto Moses, Go down, charge the people, lest they break through unto the LORD to gaze, and many of them perish.

22 And let the priests also, which come near to the LORD, sanctify themselves, lest the LORD break forth upon them.

23 And Moses said unto the LORD, The people cannot come up to mount Sinai: for thou chargedst us, saying, Set bounds about the mount, and sanctify it.

24 And the LORD said unto him, Away, get thee down, and thou shalt come up, thou, and Aaron with thee: but let not the priests and the people break through to come up unto the LORD, lest he break forth upon them.

25 So Moses went down unto the people, and spake unto them.

KEY VERSE

Moses brought forth the people out of the camp to meet with God; and they stood at the nether part of the mount. —**Exodus 19:17**

Photo: panaramka / iStock / Thinkstock

COVENANT WITH GOD

Unit 2: Called into Covenant with God

LESSONS 5–9

LESSON AIMS

After participating in this lesson, each learner will be able to:

1. Summarize what the Israelites were to do and not do at Sinai.

2. Explain why it was necessary for the Israelites to meet God on His terms.

3. Recruit an accountability partner to help him or her identify and eliminate a weakness in respecting a spiritual boundary.

LESSON OUTLINE

Introduction

A. High Price of Doubt

Tommie Woodward moved from St. Louis to Texas in 2015. Shortly after arriving, the 28-year-old saw signs warning that alligators were in the waters of Burkart's Marina. He was more than a little skeptical. A marina employee warned him to stay out of the water. Woodward scoffed.

A justice of the peace summarized the ensuing incident this way: "He removed his shirt, removed his billfold, . . . jumped in to the water and almost immediately yelled for help." As a result of his disbelief, Woodward became the first person killed by an alligator in Texas in almost 180 years.

We have seen warning signs many times and in many places. God himself expresses His desires via warnings. He has warned His people frequently about the conditions regarding admission into His presence. Today's lesson considers an example.

B. Lesson Background

As noted in last week's study of Abraham, part of the Lord's message in the covenant-making ceremony with that man was that Abraham's descendants would be in "a land that is not theirs" for 400 years (Genesis 15:13). After that they would "come out with great substance" (15:14). That coming out was the exodus, which occurred under the leadership of Moses.

Today's lesson takes us to "the third month" following the exodus (Exodus 19:1). Acting ungrateful along the way (15:24; 16:2; 17:3), the Israelites came to the "desert of Sinai" and "camped before the mount," which was Mount Sinai (19:2). There they prepared themselves to hear from God. He had delivered them from hard bondage in Egypt and was about to initiate a covenant relationship with them.

The forthcoming covenant required preparation. Having called to Moses "out of the mountain" (Exodus 19:3), the Lord instructed him to convey a message to the Israelites that focused on (1) what God had done for them, delivering them "on eagles' wings," and (2) what God intended to do for them in making them "a peculiar treasure unto me above all people . . . a kingdom of priests, and an holy nation" (19:4-6). When Moses relayed the Lord's words to the Israelites, they voiced their willingness to obey (19:8). Such a profession of commitment is admirable. But did the people really understand the challenges and responsibilities being placed before them?

Moses informed the people that the Lord would come down upon Mount Sinai to speak to them. But limits or boundaries around the mountain meant the people weren't to get too close. Only when they heard the sound of the trumpet were they allowed to approach (Exodus 19:13).

The people were also told to wash their clothes before meeting with God (Exodus 19:14); this symbolized cleanliness. The command to abstain from marital relations (19:15) was given so the people would avoid ceremonial uncleanliness (see Leviticus 15:18). They were to be as fully prepared as possible when He descended on the mountain.

I. Sacred Mountain
(Exodus 19:16-19)
A. The People Fear (v. 16)

16a. And it came to pass on the third day in the morning, that there were thunders and lightnings, and a thick cloud upon the mount.

The previous instructions to the people have stressed preparation for *the third day* (Exodus 19:11, 15). That pivotal day has now arrived, and an awe-inspiring series of sounds and sights begin *in the morning*.

Normal thunder, lightning, and cloud cover are familiar. But this situation is anything but normal! "A pillar of a cloud" had guided the people during their departure from Egypt (Exodus 13:21) and

HOW TO SAY IT

Abihu	Uh-*bye*-hew.
Deuteronomy	Due-ter-*ahn*-uh-me.
Israelites	*Iz*-ray-el-ites.
Nadab	*Nay*-dab.
Sinai	*Sigh*-nye or *Sigh*-nay-eye.
Thessalonians	*Thess*-uh-**lo**-nee-unz (*th* as in *thin*).
Zacchaeus	Zack-*key*-us.

protected them when the Egyptian army pursued (14:19, 20). On other occasions, the Lord speaks to individuals from a cloud (Numbers 12:5-8; Deuteronomy 31:15, 16). Something similar also occurs in the New Testament (see Matthew 17:5). Further, a cloud "received" Jesus at His ascension (Acts 1:9), and He will return "with clouds" (Revelation 1:7; compare Daniel 7:13).

16b. And the voice of the trumpet exceeding loud; so that all the people that was in the camp trembled.

This is the first time a particular Hebrew word translated *trumpet* occurs in the Bible. (The word translated "trumpet" in Exodus 19:13 is different.) In common usage, these will be fashioned from rams' horns in the years ahead (see Joshua 6:4; contrast Numbers 10:2). As such, these instruments will become familiar to the people as devices for signaling (Joshua 6:20; 2 Samuel 15:10; etc.). Indeed, that is the function of the trumpet in the verse before us, but its nature and *voice . . . exceeding loud* are anything but common! This trumpet's sounding is God's signal for the people to draw near to the mountain (see the Lesson Background).

The overwhelming nature of the visual and audible elements terrify the people; Moses is no exception (see Hebrews 12:21). The people fear death, should they approach close enough for God to speak to them directly (Exodus 20:19, next week's lesson).

◆ On Fearing God ◆

When a volcano erupts, volcanic lightning may result. The display is also called "dirty lightning" because it occurs in the midst of the ash being expelled. Someone has called it "the fusion of flash with ash." Scientists know that it takes a powerful eruption to create electrical energy strong enough to allow study of volcanic lightning, given all the smoke and ash obscuring the view.

Scientific discoveries with regard to volcanic lightning might allow skeptics to explain away the miraculous element of what happened at Mount Sinai. But the survival of Moses in the midst of all the phenomena disallows this (see Exodus 19:20, below). The thunder and lightning on Mount

Sinai can be explained only as a supernatural act of God. All this brought the appropriate reaction from the Israelites: fear of God.

We should not expect to have such an experience today. Even so, when was the last time that a display of a force of nature caused you to tremble before the Creator of all such forces?   —C. R. B.

B. The People Approach (vv. 17-19)

17. And Moses brought forth the people out of the camp to meet with God; and they stood at the nether part of the mount.

Moses has had his own experience of approaching the holy God. At the burning bush, God required him to remove his footwear because he was standing on holy ground (Exodus 3:1-6). No such act is required of the people here. They have been commanded to prepare in other ways to meet God (see the Lesson Background). Unlike Moses' experience at the burning bush, the people have had time to prepare for this meeting. Ultimately, God is the one who determines what is an acceptable way to come into His presence (compare Hebrews 12:22-24 [lesson 12]; contrast 2 Thessalonians 1:8-10).

Moses takes the lead in bringing *the people out of the camp to meet with God.* But they go no farther than *the nether part of the mount,* which refers to Mount Sinai's base. Previous instruction pronounced the death penalty for anyone approaching the mountain prematurely (Exodus 19:12, 13). That penalty is now lifted, since the trumpet has indeed sounded. The penalty seems to be still in force regarding physical contact with the mountain (19:24).

18. And mount Sinai was altogether on a smoke, because the LORD descended upon it in fire: and the smoke thereof ascended as the smoke of a furnace, and the whole mount quaked greatly.

The scene intensifies as thickening smoke accompanies quaking. Centuries later, the prophet Isaiah will encounter the Lord amidst smoke and shaking (Isaiah 6:4). Given that the people are already trembling (Exodus 19:16), how will they react now as the Lord descends *in fire?*

All of the phenomena associated with this experience are mentioned in the book of Revelation. These occur in descriptions of God's dwelling place (Revelation 8:4, 5; 11:19; 15:8) and His judgment (16:17, 18; 20:10, 14, 15; 21:8). The phrasing *as the smoke of a furnace* is similar to that in Revelation 9:2, another terrifying scene.

19. And when the voice of the trumpet sounded long, and waxed louder and louder, Moses spake, and God answered him by a voice.

The ever-louder *voice of the trumpet* seems to be a prelude to a conversation between Moses and God. The form that God's response takes is a bit uncertain, since the Hebrew word translated *voice* can also be translated "thunder," as it is in Exodus 9:23, 28, 29; etc.

II. Solemn Message
(EXODUS 19:20-25)
A. Calling for Moses (v. 20)

20. And the LORD came down upon mount Sinai, on the top of the mount: and the LORD

called Moses up to the top of the mount; and Moses went up.

The general statement of Exodus 19:18 that the Lord "descended upon it [Mount Sinai] in fire" is intensified and perhaps made more personal by the description here. Moses does not take the initiative to approach the Lord, but waits until invited to do so.

For Moses to climb *up to the top of the mount* is a hike of several thousand feet—and Moses is 80 years old (Exodus 7:7)! But when the invitation comes, Moses simply obeys. There is no arguing as in Exodus 3:11–4:13.

B. Cautioning the People (vv. 21-23)

21. And the Lord said unto Moses, Go down, charge the people, lest they break through unto the Lord to gaze, and many of them perish.

After reaching the top of Mount Sinai, Moses is told to *go down*! This command seems to occur immediately after Moses completes his ascent, given the urgency of the message he is to convey to *the people*.

The command itself seems to repeat the warning in Exodus 19:12, 13. Here, however, the warning goes beyond the issue of touching the mountain to the further possibility that the people might *break through unto the Lord to gaze* upon Him, thus violating the set boundaries. The temptation to look upon the Lord will naturally be very great. But the boundaries set earlier must be maintained and respected.

◆ OF GAPERS AND CURIOSITY ◆

Drivers in urban areas confront the frustration of heavy traffic on a daily basis. Accidents may bring traffic to a standstill until the wreckage is cleared and the injured attended to properly. Delays may be experienced not only by uninvolved drivers in the lane(s) where the accident occurred but also by drivers on the other side of the median of divided highways. Although no accident has occurred on the other side, traffic there may move slowly as well because of "gapers." These are curious drivers who slow down to catch a glimpse of the wreckage. The slowdown is known as "gapers' delay" or "rubbernecking."

Curiosity is a double-edged sword. On the positive side, curiosity leads to new inventions that make life better. Negatively, curiosity creates literal and figurative gapers' delays; and fascination with the macabre can lead to further tragedy. We all can give examples of times when the maxim "curiosity killed the cat" proved to be true in one sense or another.

Curiosity proved to be a positive thing for Zacchaeus, who wanted to see Jesus (Luke 19). Herod also wanted to see Jesus (Luke 23:8, 9), but the outcome was negative because of his motives. Curiosity could have resulted in death for the Israelites at Mount Sinai. They were not to be gapers of God's glory.

The double-edged sword of curiosity should cause us to examine ourselves. What things should we and should we not be curious about? See 1 Timothy 1:3-7; etc.   —C. R. B.

> **What Do You Think?**
> How would you go about explaining to an unbeliever the spiritual importance of various boundaries that God has set?
> *Talking Points for Your Discussion*
> - Regarding sex
> - Regarding the sanctity of life
> - Regarding business ethics
> - Other

22. And let the priests also, which come near to the Lord, sanctify themselves, lest the Lord break forth upon them.

The priests are singled out for a specific warning. The office of priest will be highly significant in the religious life of Israel in the years ahead. The requirements and sanctified functions of the office have not yet been specified, but they might be in practice by this point nonetheless. God has already called the people to be a "kingdom of priests" (Exodus 19:6).

Perhaps the priests referred to here are the elders who fulfill a priestly role in various settings and circumstances. For example, "the elders of Israel" were commanded to prepare the Passover lambs in Exodus 12:21.

However this group is constituted, it is clear that the Israelites understand who the priests are; those having such a title must consider themselves duly warned. They must not presume themselves to be exempt from having to respect prescribed limits.

Exactly how they are to *sanctify themselves* is not specified. Apparently it involves some kind of ritual or ceremony of which the priests themselves are aware. To fail in this regard is to invite the Lord's wrath to *break forth upon them*. This brings to mind the image of a dam that holds back a huge amount of water; if the dam gives way, a furious torrent is released. Such is the wrath of God upon those who trifle with His holiness, as tragically learned by Nadab and Abihu (Leviticus 10:1, 2) and others.

What Do You Think?
How can Christians do a better job of sanctifying themselves in preparing to meet God in worship?
Talking Points for Your Discussion
- Regarding things to start doing
- Regarding things to stop doing

23. And Moses said unto the LORD, The people cannot come up to mount Sinai: for thou chargedst us, saying, Set bounds about the mount, and sanctify it.

The reference here is Exodus 19:11, 12, as Moses recounts the Lord's clear instructions. People, places, animals, and things are all subject to being sanctified (set apart as holy) in one way or another (examples: Exodus 13:2; 29:36). Mount Sinai is among these in the current context.

C. Calling for Aaron (v. 24a)

24a. And the LORD said unto him, Away, get thee down, and thou shalt come up, thou, and Aaron with thee.

The Lord has a new set of instructions: Moses is to depart and bring back his brother Aaron. Aaron will be the first to serve in the role later known as "high priest" (Numbers 35:25; etc.; compare Exodus 28:1), so this mountaintop experience undoubtedly serves as part of his preparation for that office.

What Do You Think?
What positives and negatives are there in having a close relative as a partner in ministry? Why?
Talking Points for Your Discussion
- In terms of accountability
- In terms of shared values
- In terms of supervision
- Other

D. Conveying the Warning (vv. 24b, 25)

24b, 25. But let not the priests and the people break through to come up unto the LORD, lest he break forth upon them. So Moses went down unto the people, and spake unto them.

The Lord repeats the warning of Exodus 19:21, 22, and once more Moses' simple obedience is highlighted.

Conclusion

A. Two Testaments—One God

Passages such as the one studied in this lesson have led some to see the God of the Old Testament as remote and aloof; by contrast, the God of the New Testament is one of mercy and love. The New Testament presents Jesus, who came in love to save the world (John 3:16). To this viewpoint, the foreboding, threatening God-of-law has given way to the welcoming God-of-grace. One result of this faulty viewpoint is that some people minimize or ignore the Old Testament.

But are the presentations of God in the two testaments really all that different? No. A close look reveals many references to God's love and compassion in the Old Testament and many references to judgment and wrath in the New. Within the book of Exodus, source of today's lesson, we may consider the words of the Lord when Moses ascended Mount Sinai to receive again the law on tables (tablets) of stone: "The Lord, The Lord God, merciful and gracious, longsuffering, and abundant in goodness and truth" (Exodus 34:6).

The Old Testament prophets, who are sometimes characterized as little more than harbingers of gloom and doom, are just as passionate about declaring the depths of God's love. "I have loved thee with an everlasting love," says God through His prophet (Jeremiah 31:3). God is the one who "pardoneth iniquity" and "delighteth in mercy" (Micah 7:18). He is the one who casts all our sins "into the depths of the sea" (7:19). The picture of God's compassion is just as pronounced in the Old Testament as it is in the New.

As for God's wrath and judgment in the latter, one need only flip through the book of Revelation to be convinced. That book affirms existence of the "lake which burneth with fire and brimstone: which is the second death" (Revelation 21:8). Hebrews 12:29 tells us that "our God is a consuming fire," and 2 Thessalonians 1:7-9 pictures Jesus' return as a day when He will "in flaming fire [take] vengeance on them that know not God, and that obey not the gospel."

The Scriptures clearly and consistently teach both the mercy and the wrath of the Lord in both testaments. A passage such as today's should not result in viewing God as unloving. And the fact that He has come to us lovingly in the person of His Son, Jesus, should not lessen our sense of fear (in the sense of reverence) toward God. If anything, grace should enhance our reverence for the God who put strict limitations on the Israelites at Mount Sinai, yet removed such limitations when He broke forth into our world through a human mother's womb.

B. Preparing to Meet God

When I was growing up in rural south central Indiana, it was not uncommon to see signs (sometimes rather crudely constructed) along country roads with the message "Prepare to Meet Thy God" (from Amos 4:12). The Israelites in today's text were told to prepare very diligently and specifically to meet God at Mount Sinai. Today we do not meet with God under the same circumstances as the Israelites did. Nevertheless, we can draw lessons from their experience regarding our own preparation for worship.

Many times we get so busy during the week, crowding our days with activities, that we find ourselves having little time to prepare properly for Sunday worship. As a result, Sunday morning finds us scrambling to get to Sunday school or worship—and perhaps arriving late at that. Our bodies may be seated and stationary, but our minds are racing in a hundred different directions. We are not really prepared to meet God.

A well-organized preparation for worship can seem impossible at times, especially in households with small children. But we can and should do better. We may simply need to become more intentional and deliberate about our preparation, formulating a plan for addressing distractions.

As with other areas of our lives, it is all too easy to lapse into less than ideal patterns of behavior and then become content to leave those behaviors unchallenged and unchanged. The ancient Israelites had a three-day warning to prepare to meet God. What would happen if we committed ourselves weekly to even a three-*hour* time during which we prepared to meet God in worship?

C. Prayer

Father in Heaven, help us not to lose our sense of reverence even in—or especially in—this era of grace. May we allow the Scriptures to be our primary source of truth about You, rather than being swayed by the world's tainted and often irreverent perspective. We pray in Jesus' name. Amen.

D. Thought to Remember

We must come to God on His terms, not ours.

Holy, Holy, Holy!

Holy, holy, holy!
Tho' the darkness hide Thee,
Tho' the eye of sinful man
Thy glory may not see;
Only Thou art holy;
there is none beside Thee,
Perfect in power, in love,
and purity.

Visual for Lessons 6 & 7. *Start a discussion by pointing to this hymn and asking learners to describe how God's holiness and love interrelate.*

INVOLVEMENT LEARNING

Enhance your lesson with KJV Bible Student *(from your curriculum supplier) and the reproducible activity page (at www.standardlesson.com or in the back of the* KJV Standard Lesson Commentary Deluxe Edition*).*

Into the Lesson

Before class, write each of the following on a separate index card:

Keep Off the Grass	Crime Scene
No Trespassing	High Voltage
Do Not Enter	Beware of Dog
Restricted Area	Employees Only
Private Property	Quarantine

To begin class, ask for four volunteers and divide them into teams of two people each. One person on each team will give clues to his or her teammate about what is written on each card, without using any of the words on the card.

Send one team out of the room while the first team plays. Allow that team 30 seconds to give as many correct answers as they can. Then bring the other team in and repeat the process to determine the winner.

Alternative. Distribute copies of the "Silly Signs" activity from the reproducible page, which you can download. Use this as a small-group or whole-class activity. Students choose a warning sign on the page and give it a silly, incorrect meaning.

After either activity, lead into Bible study by saying, "We have experienced warning signs, real and symbolic, on many occasions. God also warned His people that there were very serious limits when entering His domain. Let's learn more."

Into the Word

Divide your class into three groups. Each group is to create a brief role play in which a Christian is responding to a non-Christian friend's idea about approaching God. The main talking points, for teacher use, follow in italics.

Group 1—The presence of God can best be described as a place of peace and acceptance.

Respond with ideas from Exodus 19:1-19a; Romans 1:18; Revelation 11:19.

God's holiness and power are anything but comforting and peaceful to sinful humans. His presence is not described as a peaceful meadow, but more like a volcanic explosion.

Group 2—Some people, being holier than others, have the right to come into God's presence.

Respond with ideas from Exodus 19:21-23; Romans 3:10-12.

No human being is holy enough to approach God. Even those in the Old Testament appointed to be priests had to be purified before coming before Him.

Group 3—There are many paths to God; we come to Him in our own way.

Respond with ideas from Exodus 19:20, 24, 25; John 14:6.

Moses could not go up to God without God first coming down. Aaron, the ancestor of all high priests, could not approach God without an invitation. Today, Jesus is that ultimate intercessor who came down so we can enter God's presence through Him.

Alternative. Distribute copies of the "Serious Signs" activity from the reproducible page to be used as a group activity.

After either group activity is complete, have groups share their work. Comment as necessary, referring to the commentary.

Into Life

Divide the class into small groups, giving each group pens and paper. Make sure Bibles and concordances are available for all groups.

Using the principles of today's study and supporting Scriptures they can find, groups should create a brief tract called "How to Meet God." The basic outline should be:

1. God is holy.
2. Humans are sinful.
3. Jesus intercedes for us.

After a few minutes of group work, allow groups to share their tracts.

OBEYING GOD'S LAW

DEVOTIONAL READING: Psalm 119:49-64
BACKGROUND SCRIPTURE: Exodus 20

EXODUS 20:18-26

18 And all the people saw the thunderings, and the lightnings, and the noise of the trumpet, and the mountain smoking: and when the people saw it, they removed, and stood afar off.

19 And they said unto Moses, Speak thou with us, and we will hear: but let not God speak with us, lest we die.

20 And Moses said unto the people, Fear not: for God is come to prove you, and that his fear may be before your faces, that ye sin not.

21 And the people stood afar off, and Moses drew near unto the thick darkness where God was.

22 And the LORD said unto Moses, Thus thou shalt say unto the children of Israel, Ye have seen that I have talked with you from heaven.

23 Ye shall not make with me gods of silver, neither shall ye make unto you gods of gold.

24 An altar of earth thou shalt make unto me, and shalt sacrifice thereon thy burnt offerings, and thy peace offerings, thy sheep, and thine oxen: in all places where I record my name I will come unto thee, and I will bless thee.

25 And if thou wilt make me an altar of stone, thou shalt not build it of hewn stone: for if thou lift up thy tool upon it, thou hast polluted it.

26 Neither shalt thou go up by steps unto mine altar, that thy nakedness be not discovered thereon.

KEY VERSE

In all places where I record my name I will come unto thee, and I will bless thee. —**Exodus 20:24**

COVENANT WITH GOD

LESSON AIMS

After participating in this lesson, each learner will be able to:

1. Describe the Israelites' reaction to God's presence at Sinai.

2. Explain what a proper fear of the Lord signifies.

3. Write a prayer that confesses disobedience to God and asks Him for strength to resist the temptation that leads to such disobedience.

LESSON OUTLINE

Introduction

A. Unwelcome Guest

On September 19, 2014, Omar J. Gonzalez, an Iraq War veteran with post-traumatic stress disorder, jumped over the White House's fence and entered the building's front door. He was quickly stopped by security officers and arrested. Gonzalez was carrying a knife, and he had two hatchets, a machete, and 800 rounds of ammunition in his vehicle nearby. In June 2015, when he was sentenced to 17 months in prison, Gonzalez said, "I never meant to harm anyone." At the time of his arrest, he said he wanted to warn the president that the atmosphere was collapsing.

We would never presume to barge into the presence of a world leader in such a way. We would want our meeting to communicate the respect the office deserves. The same is true with God.

B. Lesson Background

Our lesson text today covers the Israelites' response to God's declaring the Ten Commandments in Exodus 20:1-17. (You may also have heard the Ten Commandments called The Decalogue, meaning "ten words.") Our passage is part of the record of God's covenant with the Israelites. He had told them previously through Moses, "Now therefore, if ye will obey my voice indeed, and keep my covenant, then ye shall be a peculiar treasure unto me above all people: for all the earth is mine: and ye shall be unto me a kingdom of priests, and an holy nation" (Exodus 19:5, 6).

Within the Ten Commandments are the fundamentals concerning how the people of God were to obey Him. Obedience is required of God's covenant people; in fact, a disobedient covenant people is a contradiction in terms—now as then.

I. Fearing the Lord
(EXODUS 20:18-21)

A. Appealing to Moses (vv. 18, 19)

18. And all the people saw the thunderings, and the lightnings, and the noise of the trumpet, and the mountain smoking: and when the people saw it, they removed, and stood afar off.

The printed text for today begins the same way last week's text from Exodus 19 began—with an impressive display of sounds and sights including *thunderings* and *lightnings* and the sound *of the trumpet*. The presence of smoke on Mount Sinai was also a part of that description. The people's reaction here is similar to what it was then; they "trembled" earlier (compare Exodus 19:16), and here they move away from where they have been standing and stand *afar off*.

Having just heard the Lord's voice followed by the manifestation of His power on the mountain, they are terrified. We are not told exactly how far the people move, but it must be enough that they feel less threatened.

What Do You Think?

In what ways have you seen dramatic presentations of the gospel to be most effective?

Talking Points for Your Discussion

- Regarding Good Friday programs
- Regarding Easter programs
- Regarding Christmas programs
- Other

---

19. And they said unto Moses, Speak thou with us, and we will hear: but let not God speak with us, lest we die.

One gets the impression that the people's tone at this point is one of pleading with Moses that he become their intercessor or mediator. They cannot handle the intensity of hearing God speak so directly with them; they fear for their lives if He should do so. Of course, they have already heard that voice—and survived. But the experience has overwhelmed them with a feeling of absolute dread.

HOW TO SAY IT

◆ *"JOHN THOMAS SMITH . . ."* ◆

"Once upon a time," as stories go, two-parent families represented the norm. Typically, fathers would go off to work in the morning and come home at night, while mothers stayed home to care for the house and the children. Many fathers found that their after-work tasks included administering discipline to the children for whatever trouble they had been into during the day. During the day, if a child misbehaved, he might hear his mother say, "Johnny, just wait until your father gets home!" If the misdeed was moderately serious, the child's middle name might be added: "John Thomas . . ."

If the misbehavior was very serious, or if the mother had become exasperated by a series of minor misdeeds, Johnny might hear, "John Thomas Smith, you just wait till your father gets home, and *then* you will be in *real* trouble!" The child would have time to contemplate what that threat could entail. The child's fear of the father's wrath could be a sign of respect, if the father was a just father. It could also be a sign of terror, if the father was prone to excessive discipline.

The Israelites who stood before Moses at the base of the mountain seem to have thought of God as a terror-inducing tyrant. Perhaps, like errant children, they realized their behavior did not measure up to the divine standards that had so recently been set before them. Fear was an appropriate response for them. —C. R. B.

B. Answering the People (v. 20)

20. And Moses said unto the people, Fear not: for God is come to prove you, and that his fear may be before your faces, that ye sin not.

There is a practical reason for God's speaking so directly to the people, as Moses notes. They should not *fear* in the sense of thinking that God has come to destroy them. Whatever fear has been engendered by this experience at the mountain is *to prove,* or test, the people so that they have the proper attitude toward the God who is entering into a covenant with them. A healthy or proper fear of God will motivate them so that they *sin not.*

Even in the New Testament, Christians are told to maintain fear or reverence toward God in a way that impacts their daily conduct. The writer of Hebrews encourages us to "serve God acceptably with reverence and godly fear: for our God is a consuming fire" (Hebrews 12:28, 29 [lesson 12]). Paul tells the Corinthians to work on "perfecting holiness in the fear of God" (2 Corinthians 7:1).

Ironically, and tragically, this experience will not keep the people from sinning. By the time we come to Exodus 32, the people become convinced that Moses (who has gone back up the mountain to meet with God) is not returning. They build a golden calf and worship it, giving it credit for what the Lord has done (Exodus 20:1, 2; 32:1-4). At the point recorded in our text, the people are terrified at God's voice and presence; but that fear does not sustain them enough to affect their behavior when another type of "testing" occurs with Moses' absence.

What Do You Think?

What should be the outcome when we incorporate respect for God's holiness with gratitude for His grace?

Talking Points for Your Discussion

- Effect on use of the tongue
- Effect on behavior
- Effect on prayer life
- Other

C. Approaching the Lord (v. 21)

21. And the people stood afar off, and Moses drew near unto the thick darkness where God was.

The presence of a *thick darkness* has not yet been mentioned as part of what the people have witnessed. One gets the impression that, since thunder and lightning are also mentioned (v. 18), something like a storm is present on the mountain. Such a scene is associated with the Lord's presence in Isaiah 28:2; 29:6; and Nahum 1:3.

For the Israelites, the darkness is part of what frightens them about drawing near to the Lord. They remain afar off, hesitant to come any closer. Moses, however, sees beyond the darkness to God himself. He understands that the Lord, who has just given His commandments by which His peo-

ple are to live and has called them to be His covenant people, has only their best interests at heart.

II. Hearing the Lord
(Exodus 20:22-26)
A. False Gods (vv. 22, 23)

22. And the LORD said unto Moses, Thus thou shalt say unto the children of Israel, Ye have seen that I have talked with you from heaven.

After Moses draws near, the Lord conveys to him a message to pass on to His people. The message is couched in terms of what they *have seen,* but just as crucial to their understanding of God is what they have *not* seen.

The people have not seen any visible form of God. He has simply spoken to them. This spotlights His distinctiveness from other deities, those worshipped by other peoples. Their gods have visible forms (idols, images)—but they cannot speak or do anything (Psalm 135:15-17). Israel's God speaks and reveals to His people His will for them and His desire to make them His covenant people. This is what no other god can do.

Later, in the book of Deuteronomy, Moses will address the second generation of Israelites to prepare them to enter the promised land. At that time he will recall the significance of the Sinai encounter: "And ye came near and stood under the mountain; and the mountain burned with fire unto the midst of heaven, with darkness, clouds, and thick darkness. And the Lord spake unto you out of the midst of the fire: ye heard the voice of the words, but saw no similitude; only ye heard a voice. And he declared unto you his covenant, which he commanded you to perform, even ten commandments; and he wrote them upon two tables of stone" (Deuteronomy 4:11-13).

As Christians we recognize the importance of the Word of God since we have the complete Scriptures. But even for these Israelites, who are just beginning a new relationship with God, it is vital that they understand what it means to hear His words spoken to them—specifically the words that comprise the Ten Commandments. This leads to the prohibition against images and idols that follows.

23. Ye shall not make with me gods of silver, neither shall ye make unto you gods of gold.

Essentially God is repeating the contents of the first two commandments: have no other gods before Him and make no graven images (Exodus 20:3, 4). But here the focus is on the importance of heeding God's law, or God's voice from Heaven, and not being seduced into making and worshipping gods that can be seen and touched. Yes, they may look impressive, and the images representing them may be quite costly since they are made of silver or gold—but they say and do absolutely nothing. What is their true worth?

One of the supreme tragedies in Old Testament history is how often God's covenant people stray from the first two commandments and embrace idol worship. Warnings and declarations against this sin saturate the words of the prophets and the psalms in particular. Consider Isaiah's challenge to the false gods of his day: "Shew the things that are to come hereafter, that we may know that ye are gods: yea, do good, or do evil, that we may be dismayed, and behold it together. Behold, ye are of nothing, and your work of nought: an abomination is he that chooseth you" (Isaiah 41:23, 24).

The psalmist's words in Psalm 115:4-8 are equally as contemptuous: "Their idols are silver and gold, the work of men's hands. They have mouths, but they speak not: eyes have they, but they see not: they have ears, but they hear not: noses have they, but they smell not: they have hands, but they handle not: feet have they, but they walk not: neither speak they through their throat. They that make them are like unto them; so is every one that trusteth in them." As one writer puts it, the fact that God is *I Am* means that idols *are not.*

◆ NO OTHER GODS? ◆

Christians of different traditions have long debated whether the Ten Commandments prohibit using statues or pictures in worship. The early church discouraged making portraits of Christ and other biblical figures. During the eighth and ninth centuries, the Eastern (Byzantine) church wavered in its practice, sometimes allowing such icons, sometimes not. The veneration of images and pictures later became common throughout the Western (Roman Catholic) church.

The Protestant Reformation brought the issue to life again. Some reformers, such as Martin Luther, saw nothing wrong with using images as "helps to devotion." They viewed the commandments "Thou shalt have no other gods before me" and "Thou shalt not make unto thee any graven image" as a single commandment. (They split the commandment on coveting into two, thus maintaining a total of ten.) Others, such as John Calvin, saw the prohibition against image-making as a separate commandment, forbidding the creation of images.

Some of us who have no tradition of icons, either painted or sculpted, may be tempted to look down on those who do, accusing them of getting close to worshipping idols. However, our pride may be misplaced. Various forms of idolatry abound, including valuing our pleasure, our possessions, or other things above God. —C. R. B.

What Do You Think?
What are some ways to guard against the influence of cultural idols?
Talking Points for Your Discussion
- Regarding celebrities
- Regarding things
- Regarding philosophies
- Other

B. True Worship (vv. 24-26)

24. An altar of earth thou shalt make unto me, and shalt sacrifice thereon thy burnt offerings, and thy peace offerings, thy sheep, and thine oxen: in all places where I record my name I will come unto thee, and I will bless thee.

God proceeds to instruct His people as to how proper worship of Him is to be carried out. He will later give specific instructions about *burnt offerings* and *peace offerings,* found within the book of Leviticus (Leviticus 1, 3). The people already know something about offerings and altars since these are part of their history (Genesis 8:20; 12:7, 8; 13:18; 22:7). Now God will direct them as to how to conduct these in a manner pleasing to Him.

Some altars from this period of history are made of mud bricks. That may be what the command to make *an altar of earth* describes. Some suggest that making such an altar is meant to remind the people of God's creation of man from the dust of the earth (Genesis 2:7). This appears to be how altars should be prepared until the time when the tabernacle is constructed and set up. The altar of burnt offering for that structure is to be made of wood (Exodus 27:1).

God also instructs Moses about the places of sacrifice. Offerings are not to be done in a random, haphazard fashion. God states that *in all places where I record my name I will come unto thee, and I will bless thee.* Later, in his instructions to the people, Moses will specify that at "the place which the Lord your God shall choose out of all your tribes to put his name there," the people must bring their offerings, sacrifices, and tithes (Deuteronomy 12:5-7). Worship carried out according to God's instructions will bring His blessings to His people.

Again, consider the contrast: idol worshippers can fashion their idols and worship them however they desire, but their gods have no power to bless them as the Lord does. God's promise in this verse also addresses the earlier fears of the people. They have been hesitant to come near Him, but here He promises to come to them to show His favor. But they must come on His terms, not theirs.

> *What Do You Think?*
> How do we recognize the warning signs that indicate attempts to relate with God on terms other than His?
> *Talking Points for Your Discussion*
> - Regarding the form and content of prayers
> - Regarding the form and content of worship
> - Other

25. And if thou wilt make me an altar of stone, thou shalt not build it of hewn stone: for if thou lift up thy tool upon it, thou hast polluted it.

Some altars in the Old Testament are made of stones (example: the one that Elijah set up on Mount Carmel in 1 Kings 18:31, 32). Here God states that if the people desire to make for Him *an altar of stone,* it is not to be made *of hewn,* or cut, *stone.* The use of any tool in shaping the stones pollutes the altar, making it unfit for ceremonial use.

Exactly why this is the case is not explained; perhaps a certain pagan practice (such as one linked to the religion of Egypt, from which the people have recently come) is involved with this prohibition. By the time of Solomon, "hewed stones" were used in laying the foundation of the temple in Jerusalem (1 Kings 5:17, 18).

26. Neither shalt thou go up by steps unto mine altar, that thy nakedness be not discovered thereon.

Whether earthen or stone, the altar is not to have steps in order to approach it. Otherwise, the worshippers below might see under the officiating priest's robe. Ritual nudity was often a part of pagan worship; here God indicates His desire to preserve modesty. Prohibiting steps seems also to have been temporary, similar to the requirement of uncut stones. It appears the brass altar for Solomon's temple must have had steps, since it was 10 cubits (15 feet) high (2 Chronicles 4:1). By then God had prescribed certain undergarments, for the priest to wear (Exodus 28:42, 43), which was another way to maintain modesty.

> *What Do You Think?*
> What are some ways to encourage modesty without using legalistic dress codes?
> *Talking Points for Your Discussion*
> - In the church
> - In the home
> - In the example we set
> - Other

Some Bible students have suggested symbolic meanings behind the stipulations we read in this passage. For example, the fact that the altar is to be made of uncut stones is believed to signify that no human effort can achieve forgiveness of sin; this can be granted by God alone. The possibility of indecent exposure when going up the altar to make a sacrifice would counter the message of the sacrifice, which provides a covering for man's sin. But such interpretations are not really grounded in the Scripture itself, so one must exercise caution in presenting or accepting them.

Conclusion

A. Words That Still Ring True

When I was growing up, revivals were an important part of church life. My home church in Indiana usually held two revivals, one in the spring and one in the fall, and for a number of years each of those revivals consisted of two weeks of nightly services, Monday through Friday.

It was at one of those services in the spring of 1964 that I went forward at the preacher's invitation and voiced my desire to become a Christian. The invitation hymn that was sung that night was "Trust and Obey." The words of that song, particularly the chorus, came to mind while preparing these lessons on the subject of obeying God's voice: "Trust and obey, for there's no other way to be happy in Jesus, but to trust and obey."

Those words remain as true today as they were over 50 years ago when I decided that I would become a follower of Jesus. They were also true for the Israelites who stood at the foot of Mount Sinai and heard God's voice amidst all the overpowering sights and sounds that were a part of that unforgettable experience. Of course, being "happy in Jesus" was not an issue for those Israelites at Sinai. But in order to fulfill their responsibilities as God's covenant people, to "trust and obey" was essential.

Obedience—that is what God has always required of His people, in both Old and New Testaments. To foolish, disobedient King Saul, the prophet Samuel gave this rebuke: "To obey is better than sacrifice, and to hearken than the fat of rams" (1 Samuel 15:22). The northern kingdom fell to the Assyrians "because they obeyed not the voice of the Lord their God" (2 Kings 18:12).

Jeremiah confronted the people of the southern kingdom of Judah with a review of their history and of what God had demanded of their forefathers: "Obey my voice, and I will be your God, and ye shall be my people" (Jeremiah 7:23). The present reality facing Jeremiah was a far different story: "But thou shalt say unto them, This is a

Visual for Lessons 6 & 7. *Point to the third and fourth lines of this hymn as you simply ask "Why?" in discussing Exodus 20:22.*

nation that obeyeth not the voice of the Lord their God, nor receiveth correction: truth is perished, and is cut off from their mouth" (Jeremiah 7:28).

Christians are of the new covenant. With that new covenant, God has not come with all the phenomena that we have seen displayed at Mount Sinai in today's lesson text. Instead He has come to be with us in Jesus, or Emmanuel, meaning "God with us" (Matthew 1:22, 23).

We do not deal with issues such as preparing burnt offerings and constructing altars on which to sacrifice them—matters covered in today's text. However, what God requires of us remains exactly what was required of the Israelites. That requirement is captured in one word: obedience. "Why call ye me, Lord, Lord," asks Jesus, "and do not the things which I say?" (Luke 6:46). He also tells us, "If ye love me, keep my commandments" (John 14:15).

In other words, trust and obey.

B. Prayer

Father, forgive our halfhearted obedience and the times we create excuses and dodge our responsibilities as covenant people. So often we fail to give our best for You and Your kingdom. Restore our sense of passion and purpose so that a broken world can see Christ in us. In His name, amen.

C. Thought to Remember

Obedience to God brings true freedom.

INVOLVEMENT LEARNING

Enhance your lesson with KJV Bible Student (from your curriculum supplier) and the reproducible activity page (at www.standardlesson.com or in the back of the KJV Standard Lesson Commentary Deluxe Edition).

Into the Lesson

To begin class, have your group imagine that the president or some other prominent figure has promised to be in class in two weeks. Discuss what preparations would need to be made for that visit. Your discussion might include:

What classroom changes need to be made?

What should we wear?

What should we offer our guest in terms of special refreshments, a commemorative gift, etc.?

What security precautions do we need to take?

What special lesson or program should we present, if any?

Alternative. Distribute copies of the "Properly Addressed" activity from the reproducible page, which you can download. Use this as an individual, small-group, or whole-class activity. Students match a dignitary's title with the accepted address.

After either activity, lead into Bible study by saying, "Most of us would not prepare for a meeting with a head of state casually or haphazardly. We would want our meeting to communicate respect due the position. The same is true with God. Let's learn about how we are to approach Him."

Into the Word

Divide the class into two groups, giving each group paper and pens. Each group should read its assigned text as a basis for making the requested contrast. Anticipated responses are in italics; do not distribute those.

Group 1—Contrast godly fear with ungodly fear (Exodus 20:18-21).

Godly Fear=Respect and Awe
Seeks God's approval (v. 20)
Wants to meet God's standards (v. 20)
Draws nearer to God (v. 21)

Ungodly Fear=Terror and Panic
Withdraws from God (v. 18)
Dreads what God would say (v. 19)
Keeps distance from God (vv. 18, 21)

Group 2—Contrast godly worship with ungodly worship (Exodus 20:22-26).

Godly Worship=Reverence
Recognizes that God reveals His will for us (v. 22)
Admits sin with sacrifice (v. 24)
Approaches God with simplicity (v. 23)

Ungodly Worship=Ritual
Tries to make God manageable by making images of Him (v. 23)
Tries to make sin prettier with decorated altars (v. 25)
Symbolic degradation, such as exposing oneself (v. 26)

Allow groups to share their research. Comment using the suggested responses and content from the commentary as needed.

Into Life

Draw these three scales on the board:

How often I study God's Word

<——————————————————————>

Sunday Only   Daily

How I apply God's Word

<——————————————————————>

Seeing Sins of Others   Testing Myself

Nature of my prayers

<——————————————————————>

Formal and Repetitive   Earnest and Personal

Allow students some time to evaluate themselves on each scale. Then have them gather in groups of two or three to share their evaluations and to pray for one another.

Alternative. Distribute the "Less Like . . . More Like" activity from the reproducible page. Allow students to use it individually for a closing prayer time or as a take-home activity.

GOD'S COVENANT WITH DAVID

DEVOTIONAL READING: Psalm 89:1-15

BACKGROUND SCRIPTURE: 2 Samuel 7:1-16; Psalm 89; 1 Chronicles 22:6-8

2 SAMUEL 7:1-6, 8-10, 12-16

1 And it came to pass, when the king sat in his house, and the LORD had given him rest round about from all his enemies;

2 That the king said unto Nathan the prophet, See now, I dwell in an house of cedar, but the ark of God dwelleth within curtains.

3 And Nathan said to the king, Go, do all that is in thine heart; for the LORD is with thee.

4 And it came to pass that night, that the word of the LORD came unto Nathan, saying,

5 Go and tell my servant David, Thus saith the LORD, Shalt thou build me an house for me to dwell in?

6 Whereas I have not dwelt in any house since the time that I brought up the children of Israel out of Egypt, even to this day, but have walked in a tent and in a tabernacle.

. . . .

8 Now therefore so shalt thou say unto my servant David, Thus saith the LORD of hosts, I took thee from the sheepcote, from following the sheep, to be ruler over my people, over Israel:

9 And I was with thee whithersoever thou wentest, and have cut off all thine enemies out of thy sight, and have made thee a great name, like unto the name of the great men that are in the earth.

10 Moreover I will appoint a place for my people Israel, and will plant them, that they may dwell in a place of their own, and move no more; neither shall the children of wickedness afflict them any more, as beforetime.

. . . .

12 And when thy days be fulfilled, and thou shalt sleep with thy fathers, I will set up thy seed after thee, which shall proceed out of thy bowels, and I will establish his kingdom.

13 He shall build an house for my name, and I will stablish the throne of his kingdom for ever.

14 I will be his father, and he shall be my son. If he commit iniquity, I will chasten him with the rod of men, and with the stripes of the children of men:

15 But my mercy shall not depart away from him, as I took it from Saul, whom I put away before thee.

16 And thine house and thy kingdom shall be established for ever before thee: thy throne shall be established for ever.

KEY VERSE

Thine house and thy kingdom shall be established for ever before thee: thy throne shall be established for ever.
—2 Samuel 7:16

COVENANT WITH GOD

Unit 2: Called into Covenant with God

LESSON AIMS

After participating in this lesson, each learner will be able to:

1. Summarize the key points in God's covenantal promise to David.

2. Explain how Jesus brings that promise to its ultimate fulfillment.

3. Write a prayer that expresses a personal desire to serve God in a particular way and openness to a bigger plan God may have.

LESSON OUTLINE

Introduction

A. Lasting Legacies

Presidents of the United States have many avenues for leaving legacies. One such is by means of the Presidential Libraries Act of 1955. This act established a system of libraries operated and maintained by the National Archives and Records Administration (NARA). At the beginning of 2016, the 13 presidential libraries that are maintained by the NARA contained over 400 million pages of printed materials, about 10 million photographs, over 15 million feet of motion-picture film, and nearly 100,000 hours of audio and video recordings.

It's natural to want to leave our mark on earth in some lasting way. King David himself had a plan as to how he would do that. But the fact that he had "shed blood abundantly" as a "man of war" (1 Chronicles 22:8; 28:3) meant that God had a different idea.

B. Lesson Background

The previous two lessons examined Scriptures dealing with God's covenant with the nation of Israel. Today we move forward to the time of King David to consider another covenant God made—this one with the "man after [God's] own heart" (Acts 13:22).

David was in very ordinary surroundings when Samuel came to Bethlehem to anoint a replacement for King Saul. The youngest of eight brothers, David's viability as a candidate to be king was not seriously considered by his father, so Samuel pushed the issue: after none of David's seven brothers proved to be God's chosen, David was sent for and anointed as Israel's next king (1 Samuel 16:1-13).

After Saul's death, David became king of only the tribe of Judah, which he ruled for seven and a half years. When Saul's son Ishbosheth was murdered, the way became clear for David to become king over the entire nation (2 Samuel 5:1-5). David proceeded to conquer the city of Jerusalem and bring the ark of the covenant there (5:6-10; 6:12-23). He also defeated the Philistines who had been a thorn in Israel's side for some time (5:17-25).

While the above achievements were steps David took to solidify his reign, today's lesson text records what God did to solidify that reign in a way David never could have imagined.

I. Plan Denied
(2 SAMUEL 7:1-6)
A. David's Ambition (vv. 1, 2)

1a. And it came to pass, when the king sat in his house.

The Hebrew word translated *house* is used of a common dwelling place (Judges 11:30, 31). It can also describe the dwelling of a king or of a god; in fact, the word is used of both Solomon's residence and the Lord's temple in 1 Kings 9:1. King Hiram of Tyre sent workers and materials to build a house (same Hebrew word) for David (2 Samuel 5:11). One gets the impression that this was a very well-designed, attractive structure.

1b. And the LORD had given him rest round about from all his enemies.

We should note that the military victories recorded in 2 Samuel 8 may well have occurred prior to the events in chapter 7. The material of this book may be arranged topically rather than chronologically, with the focus in chapters 6 and 7 on David's faithfulness and God's blessing in response to that.

2. That the king said unto Nathan the prophet, See now, I dwell in an house of cedar, but the ark of God dwelleth within curtains.

This is the first time *Nathan the prophet* is mentioned in Scripture. He will appear later as the

bearer of bad news after David commits adultery with Bathsheba (2 Samuel 11:1-27).

Here David voices to Nathan his concern: he himself has a fine home in which to reside, *but the ark of God dwelleth within curtains*—that is, in a tent or tabernacle (2 Samuel 6:17; 1 Chronicles 16:1). To David, this is just not right! The ark of the covenant represents the presence of Israel's true king, the Lord God Almighty, with His people. David realizes that the Lord deserves better than this.

> *What Do You Think?*
> What should a genuine concern for things of God look like today?
> *Talking Points for Your Discussion*
> - During corporate worship
> - In small groups
> - In our private lives

B. Nathan's Approval (v. 3)

3. And Nathan said to the king, Go, do all that is in thine heart; for the LORD is with thee.

Nathan's initial reaction is to agree wholeheartedly with David. One gets the impression that Nathan does not consult the Lord at all. He seems to assume that the idea is a good one; what could be wrong with building such a structure for the Lord?

C. The Lord's Alternative (vv. 4-6)

4, 5. And it came to pass that night, that the word of the LORD came unto Nathan, saying, Go and tell my servant David, Thus saith the LORD, Shalt thou build me an house for me to dwell in?

Nathan has spoken in haste. His earlier words of approval were his own, not the Lord's.

Years later at the dedication of the temple, King Solomon will recall what the Lord had told David about his desire to build a house for the ark: "Forasmuch as it was in thine heart to build an house for my name, thou didst well in that it was in thine heart" (2 Chronicles 6:8). David's intentions are good, but it is not God's desire that he should be the one to carry out this noble task.

HOW TO SAY IT

Ahaz	*Ay*-haz.
Assyria	Uh-*sear*-ee-uh.
Babylon	*Bab*-uh-lun.
Bathsheba	Bath-*she*-buh.
Ephesians	Ee-*fee*-zhunz.
Hiram	*High*-rum.
Manasseh	Muh-*nass*-uh.
Pentecost	*Pent*-ih-kost.
Philistines	Fuh-*liss*-teenz or *Fill*-us-teenz.
Tyre	Tire.

6. Whereas I have not dwelt in any house since the time that I brought up the children of Israel out of Egypt, even to this day, but have walked in a tent and in a tabernacle.

For God to have the kind of house that David desires to build has never really been high on God's list of priorities. To this point the tabernacle and the tent that covered it, as prescribed by God to Moses centuries earlier (Exodus 26), have sufficed.

At the dedication of the temple, Solomon, David's son, will cite the words of the verse before us (see 1 Kings 8:16). He then will note in the same verse that while God was not concerned about choosing a city in which to dwell, He was concerned about choosing a person. This is what the Lord addresses in the next part of His message given through Nathan.

◆ *HOUSE PLANS* ◆

I looked out the window of our mud hut in Africa to admire the piles of wood and cement that had just arrived. Soon we would build our own cement-block house! Then we would learn the local language, get to know people, and help them translate the Bible into their own language. But two months after we moved into our new home, we had to evacuate the country because of political instability. What a loss it seemed! And now medi-cal issues are further delaying our return. Why did God take us away from the house and the ministry in Africa that we had planned for His kingdom?

In 2 Samuel 7:1-6, King David also had great plans of constructing a building. But God essen-tially said, "No, I have other plans." And God's plans were much greater than David's! David would have erected a building that time would soon destroy, but God established the house and king-

Even though we haven't been able to return to our house in Africa yet, we are already starting to see how God's plans are greater than ours. Two national Bible translators have been able to use the house we built as an office, and another dislocated missionary family has found a home there, from which they can continue their ministry for now.

Has the Lord said no to any of your great plans? If so, take heart. His plans are infinitely greater!

—D. & L. G.

II. Past Described
(2 SAMUEL 7:8-10)
A. Blessings to David (vv. 8, 9)

8. Now therefore so shalt thou say unto my servant David, Thus saith the LORD of hosts, I took thee from the sheepcote, from follow-ing the sheep, to be ruler over my people, over Israel.

The Lord calls attention to what He has done for David. David did not work himself up from the position of shepherd to become king of Israel. Rather, it was God who took him from *following the sheep* and set him apart to become an infinitely greater kind of shepherd: *ruler over my people, over Israel* (compare Psalm 78:70, 71).

9. And I was with thee whithersoever thou wentest, and have cut off all thine enemies out of thy sight, and have made thee a great name, like unto the name of the great men that are in the earth.

When Samuel anointed David to be king of Israel, "the Spirit of the Lord came upon David from that day forward" (1 Samuel 16:13). Not long afterward one of Saul's servants said of David, "the Lord is with him" (16:18). That became the key to David's greatness (2 Samuel 5:10).

The Lord goes on to list specific blessings that have resulted from His being with David. The first is the defeat of David's enemies. Second, the Lord has given David *a great name, like unto the name of the great men that are in the earth.* This is reminiscent of what God had promised to Abraham (Genesis 12:2). First Chronicles 14:17 states, "And the fame of David went out into all lands; and the Lord brought the fear of him upon all nations."

B. Blessings to Israel (v. 10)

10. Moreover I will appoint a place for my people Israel, and will plant them, that they may dwell in a place of their own, and move no more; neither shall the children of wickedness afflict them any more, as beforetime.

The greatness God has granted to David was not for David's benefit alone. The Lord is concerned for His *people Israel.* God desires not only to give David "rest" (2 Samuel 7:1, above) but also to give His people *a place of their own* and relief from those who have afflicted them in the past (as, for example, during the time of the judges as noted in 7:11, not in today's text). God did indeed desire a place—not for himself but for His people.

But that was only the beginning of God's intentions. At the end of 2 Samuel 7:11, the Lord elaborates on His desires for David: "The Lord telleth thee that he will make thee an house." God has asked David, "Shalt thou build me an house for me to dwell in?" (7:5). The Lord's answer is, "No, you are not going to build me a house. I am going to build you a house!" (paraphrase of 7:11).

III. Promise Defined
(2 SAMUEL 7:12-16)
A. Special Descendant (v. 12)

12. And when thy days be fulfilled, and thou shalt sleep with thy fathers, I will set up thy seed after thee, which shall proceed out of thy bowels, and I will establish his kingdom.

Here the Lord sketches the "when" and "through whom" regarding the promised house and kingdom. The first two phrases of the verse before us establish the when: it will happen after David's death (another kind of "rest"). After that becomes reality, God will work through David's *seed,* or offspring, to fulfill the promise. But to whom does the word *seed* refer?

B. Special Duty (v. 13)

13. He shall build an house for my name, and I will stablish the throne of his kingdom for ever.

The first phrase in this verse and history as it unfolds seem at first to indicate that David's son Solomon is the one to build a house for the Lord. But the second phrase must give us pause since our knowledge of history reveals that the promise is not limited to fulfillment via Solomon. Rather, Jesus Christ is the ultimate seed of David through whom God's *for ever* promise comes to pass.

This fact begins to be established in the New Testament when the angel Gabriel tells Mary that "the Lord God shall give unto [Jesus] the throne of his father David: and he shall reign over the house of Jacob for ever; and of his kingdom there shall be no end" (Luke 1:32, 33). On the Day of Pentecost, Peter ties the fulfillment of the promise to the resurrection of Jesus (Acts 2:29-32; compare Acts 13:23; Galatians 3:16-19).

Though many in Jesus' time thought of the kingdom primarily in political terms, Jesus' kingdom is a spiritual one (John 18:36). It is the church, comprised of those who have come out of the "darkness" of sin (Colossians 1:13) into His "marvellous light" (1 Peter 2:9).

What Do You Think?

What strategies can we use to ensure we stay focused on the spiritual nature of God's kingdom?

Talking Points for Your Discussion

- Regarding techniques that invite interaction with culture
- Regarding techniques that resist interaction with culture

C. Special Discipline (vv. 14, 15)

14, 15. I will be his father, and he shall be my son. If he commit iniquity, I will chasten him with the rod of men, and with the stripes of the children of men: but my mercy shall not depart away from him, as I took it from Saul, whom I put away before thee.

The first statement in verse 14 is quoted in Hebrews 1:5, which clearly affirms its fulfillment in Jesus. This portion of the promise raises questions, especially since we have already proposed a fulfillment in Jesus. But how can sinless Jesus be the fulfillment when it is possible for this son of David to *commit iniquity*? If the promise refers to Solomon, how can God say that *my mercy shall not depart away from him*? We recall that God judged Solomon for his foolish acceptance of the gods of his many wives who turned his heart away from the Lord (1 Kings 11:4, 9-13, 31-33).

It is clear from a study of Old Testament history that not all the kings who descended from David were men after God's own heart as David was. Some of them, such as Ahaz and Manasseh, were guilty of great wickedness against God (2 Kings 16:1-18; 21:1-16). Those kings who behaved in this manner were disciplined by the Lord. He used *the rod of men*—the nations and armies of Assyria and Babylon—to bring judgment upon the kings who failed to trust and obey the true king of God's people.

None of these instances of rebellion by kings who were descendants of David nullified the covenant promises to David recorded in our text. The promise "I will stablish the throne of his kingdom for ever" remains intact.

Regarding God's word to David, Psalm 89:30-34 states this: "If his children forsake my law, and walk not in my judgments; if they break my statutes, and keep not my commandments; then will I visit their transgression with the rod, and their iniquity with stripes. Nevertheless my lovingkindness will I not utterly take from him, nor suffer my faithfulness to fail. My covenant will I not break, nor alter the thing that is gone out of my lips."

Concerning Jesus, one could say that He was treated as though He had committed iniquity. He took *the stripes* inflicted by *the rod of men* along with various other abuses, climaxed by the crucifixion (Isaiah 53:4, 5). But that suffering at the cross was not the consequence of personal guilt; rather, He took upon himself the punishment that guilty sinners (every human) deserves.

All of what God has in store for David is quite a contrast with the Lord's treatment of Saul, David's predecessor. Given David's knowledge of God's treatment of Saul, David can offer personal testimony regarding both God's stern judgment (toward Saul) and steadfast mercy (toward David).

D. Special Dominion (v. 16)

16. And thine house and thy kingdom shall be established for ever before thee: thy throne shall be established for ever.

This verse summarizes the essence of the covenant God has made with David. The house that God will build for David will be far more wonderful and enduring than any house David could ever build for God. Even when Solomon's magnificent temple falls to ruins before the Babylonian army, God's promise to David remains unshakable. That house, that kingdom, is the church of Jesus. And what Jesus said of his church remains as true today as on the day He said it: "The gates of hell shall not prevail against it" (Matthew 16:18).

◆ THE ETERNAL KINGDOM ◆

My family lives and works with refugees who have fled their country in Africa. Their president and military are dropping bombs and sending soldiers against their homes. There have been many stories about horrific abuses of civilians.

About a year after most of them fled to a refugee camp across the border, the country in which they were seeking safety fell into civil war between that country's government and anti-government forces. Again many terrible stories of abuse have emerged from both factions. Meanwhile, our friends in the refugee camp have faced food and water rationing and constant fear of violence.

Caught between so many warring "kingdoms," imagine how they must feel when they encounter God's promise to David, fulfilled in Christ: "And thine house and thy kingdom shall be established for ever before thee: thy throne shall be established for ever" (2 Samuel 7:16).

How blessed we are to be under the ultimate rule of one who is just, merciful, and eternal! So many injustices have been done and so little mercy has been shown to our refugee friends, but they can take hope in the eternal king who will make things right and show mercy to them forever.

If you are facing difficulties or persecution because of earthly leaders or "kingdoms," take comfort in the promise that in Christ's kingdom we will be under the leadership and protection of one who loved us so much that He gave His own life for us, and that He will rule forever.

—D. & L. G.

What Do You Think?
   How should citizenship in God's eternal kingdom affect how we interact with the various authority structures of the world?
Talking Points for Your Discussion
   ▪ Regarding political structures
   ▪ Regarding business structures
   ▪ Considering Luke 20:25; John 18:36; Acts 4:19; 5:29; Romans 13:1-7; 1 Peter 2:13-17

Conclusion
A. We Are David

On November 14, 1970, the Marshall University football team was returning from a game in North Carolina to the Marshall campus in Huntington, West Virginia. The charter plane they were on crashed, killing all 75 individuals on board. Those who perished included 37 players, head coach Rick Tolley, members of his coaching staff and the school's athletic director, and 25 athletic boosters. In 2006 a movie was made to tell the story of that team and that tragedy. Its title was brief but compelling: *We Are Marshall.*

In a sense all Christians can say, "We are David." True, few of us have had any experience watching sheep or fighting wild animals in defense of sheep. But what the Lord said to David in 1 Samuel 7:8, 9 could be applied to His treatment of any of us. God took us from what we were (lost, sinful) and made us part of His family. We did nothing to deserve such a status; what we deserved was condemnation. But Jesus, who had done nothing to deserve death, gave His life for us at the cross.

Paul states the contrast first by describing humanity's sorry status: "dead in trespasses and sins . . . fulfilling the desires of the flesh and of the mind" (Ephesians 2:1, 3). Then comes the welcome remedy: "But God, who is rich in mercy, . . . hath quickened us together with Christ" (2:4, 5). This is the same mercy that took David from the humble task of watching sheep to become Israel's greatest king and the recipient of a very special covenant indeed.

While few of us have had any experience *watching* sheep, we have all had experience *acting* like sheep by "going astray" (1 Peter 2:25). And we have all been rescued by the good shepherd.

B. Prayer

Father, thank You for the mercy You have shown us in Christ Jesus. We are so unworthy of such treatment; Your faithfulness is such a stark contrast to our unfaithfulness. May our lives each day reflect our awareness that we are not our own; we have been "bought with a price" (1 Corinthians 6:19, 20). In Jesus' name, amen.

C. Thought to Remember
What God builds with us endures.
What we build without Him does not.

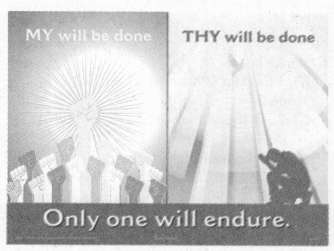

Visual for Lesson 8. *Point to this visual as you invite learners to give examples of times God's will superseded their own.*

INVOLVEMENT LEARNING

Enhance your lesson with KJV Bible Student *(from your curriculum supplier) and the reproducible activity page (at www.standardlesson.com or in the back of the* KJV Standard Lesson Commentary Deluxe Edition*).*

Into the Lesson

Display at the front of the classroom a trophy, plaque, ribbon, medal, or the image of one of these items. When learners arrive, say, "There are many ways to define success. Sometimes we may seek out rewards for our achievements, and other times the achievements themselves are the rewards."

Ask volunteers to share their greatest accomplishments. (Be prepared to give your own example to get things started.) After several class members have shared, ask for volunteers to share a not yet accomplished goal or ambition.

Alternative. Distribute copies of the "Lasting Legacy" activity from the reproducible page, which you can download. Set a timer for 90 seconds and have learners compete to see either who finishes first or who finds the most matches in the allotted time.

After either activity, lead into Bible study by saying, "Human life does not last forever, so we desire to leave our mark on earth in some real way. David had a plan as to how he would do that, but we will see that God had a different idea."

Into the Word

Divide learners into three groups, giving each group an index card labeled in one of the following ways:

Group 1—
David's Plan (2 Samuel 7:1-6)
Group 2—
God's Fulfilled Plans (2 Samuel 7:8, 9)
Group 3—
God's Promised Plans (2 Samuel 7:10, 12-16)

Have the groups read their assigned verses and discuss (a) the motive behind their assigned plan, (b) the details of the plan, and (c) in what specific ways the plan was or wasn't fulfilled.

Allow several minutes for groups to work. As needed you may wish to prompt groups with these suggested responses:

Group 1—*(a) To honor and thank the Lord and to elevate His position over David's; (b) To build a permanent home to replace the ark's tent; (c) At first Nathan approved because of David's good intentions, but Nathan found the Lord's will was different.*

Group 2—*(a) To make David ruler over the Lord's people; (b) The Lord took David out of the fields, was with him, protected him from his enemies, and lifted his name; (c) David became king.*

Group 3—*(a) To build a permanent home for God's people ultimately through Jesus; (b) To plant God's people in a permanent dwelling place, to protect them from wickedness, to bless David's line and establish a kingdom through it, to build a house for the Lord's people through David's lineage; (c) Fulfilled by the birth, death, and resurrection of Jesus, who came from David's line and established the kingdom of God on earth for all God's followers.*

Allow groups to report. As they do so, jot responses on the board. Use the commentary to correct misconceptions or fill in any gaps.

Into Life

Have learners discuss this question in pairs: "What are some of your short- and long-term goals and how can we, like David and Nathan, check whether those align with God's plans?"

Then ask volunteers to share thoughts with the class. (Possible responses: pray, regular Bible study, guidance from a friend, give God greater control over our time and resources, etc.)

Alternative: Have students individually fill out the "God's Plans First" activity from the reproducible page. Or you may wish to send it home to be used throughout the week.

Use either activity to note that the motive for our plans may be God-honoring, but God may have plans that are better still. Encourage learners to spend time throughout the week bringing their short- and long-term plans to God.

God's Covenant with the Returned Exiles

DEVOTIONAL READING: Psalm 103:1-14
BACKGROUND SCRIPTURE: Nehemiah 9, 10

Nehemiah 9:32-38

32 Now therefore, our God, the great, the mighty, and the terrible God, who keepest covenant and mercy, let not all the trouble seem little before thee, that hath come upon us, on our kings, on our princes, and on our priests, and on our prophets, and on our fathers, and on all thy people, since the time of the kings of Assyria unto this day.

33 Howbeit thou art just in all that is brought upon us; for thou hast done right, but we have done wickedly:

34 Neither have our kings, our princes, our priests, nor our fathers, kept thy law, nor hearkened unto thy commandments and thy testimonies, wherewith thou didst testify against them.

35 For they have not served thee in their kingdom, and in thy great goodness that thou gavest them, and in the large and fat land which thou gavest before them, neither turned they from their wicked works.

36 Behold, we are servants this day, and for the land that thou gavest unto our fathers to eat the fruit thereof and the good thereof, behold, we are servants in it:

37 And it yieldeth much increase unto the kings whom thou hast set over us because of our sins: also they have dominion over our bodies, and over our cattle, at their pleasure, and we are in great distress.

38 And because of all this we make a sure covenant, and write it; and our princes, Levites, and priests, seal unto it.

Nehemiah 10:28, 29

28 And the rest of the people, the priests, the Levites, the porters, the singers, the Nethinims, and all they that had separated themselves from the people of the lands unto the law of God, their wives, their sons, and their daughters, every one having knowledge, and having understanding;

29 They clave to their brethren, their nobles, and entered into a curse, and into an oath, to walk in God's law, which was given by Moses the servant of God, and to observe and do all the commandments of the LORD our Lord, and his judgments and his statutes.

KEY VERSE

Howbeit thou art just in all that is brought upon us; for thou hast done right, but we have done wickedly.
—**Nehemiah 9:33**

Covenant with God

LESSON AIMS

After participating in this lesson, each learner will be able to:

1. Recount the main themes of the prayer offered by God's people.

2. Give an example of God's faithfulness in contrast with the ancient Israelites' faithlessness.

3. Make a plan to correct the problem of (or resulting from) one unkept commitment.

LESSON OUTLINE

Introduction

A. Never Forget

September 11, 2001, lives long in American memory, the terrorist attacks of that day claiming about 3,000 lives. On every anniversary, the names of the victims who died in New York City are read aloud there against a background of somber music. Memorial services are also held at the Pentagon and in Shanksville, Pennsylvania.

Lessons of the past, even very painful ones, can help us prepare for the future. The exile to Babylon was a painful experience for the people of God. Upon returning, the exiles took time to reflect on their past and seek guidance for their future.

B. Lesson Background

Today's study comes from a Scripture text taken from the time near the conclusion of Old Testament history. God's people in the northern kingdom of Israel had been conquered by the Assyrians in 722 BC. To the south, the kingdom of Judah fell to Babylon in 586 BC. But the time of captivity in Babylon that followed was not a period (in grammatical terms), as though it marked the end for God's people. It was a comma, a pause during which God disciplined His wayward people with the intent to bring them back home. Isaiah, writing some 150 years before that homecoming occurred, prophesied that it would happen and even gave the name of the ruler (Cyrus) who was to issue the decree that permitted the captives to do so (Isaiah 44:24–45:1; 2 Chronicles 36:22, 23).

There were three return trips to Judah after Cyrus's decree. The first was in 538 BC, led by Zerubbabel, Sheshbazzar, and Jeshua. About 50,000 made the trip (see Ezra 1–6). The second journey came in 458 BC when Ezra traveled to Judah with fewer that fellow returnees 2,000 (Ezra 8); the reason was to provide needed spiritual guidance (7:6-10). The third journey was led by Nehemiah in 444 BC.

Nehemiah was the cupbearer to the king of Persia when he learned the distressing news that the walls around Jerusalem still lay in ruins (Nehemiah 1). That was nearly 100 years after the first return to Judah! He felt compelled to rectify this situation personally so the city could properly defend itself from attack. Thanks to Nehemiah's steady, courageous, and prayerful leadership, the wall was completed in less than two months (6:15).

Nehemiah, working with Ezra, understood that while protecting the city physically was vital, maintaining the spiritual defenses of the people was even more critical. Nehemiah 8 records a time of concentrated teaching from God's law. Later that month (the seventh month), God's people observed the Feast of Booths, or Tabernacles, as prescribed in the law (8:13-18).

Later that same month, the people began a time of intense prayer and reading of the law. The prayer is recorded in Nehemiah 9:5-37; a special focus of the prayer was confession of sin. Our printed text is taken from the conclusion of this prayer. Indicators of the intense earnestness of the prayer are seen in how the people dress, in their disassociation from others, and in the amount of time spent reading God's law, confessing sin, and worshipping (9:1-3).

I. Pleading with God

(NEHEMIAH 9:32-37)

A. Faithful God (v. 32a)

32a. Now therefore, our God, the great, the mighty, and the terrible God, who keepest covenant and mercy.

HOW TO SAY IT

Assyria	Uh-*sear*-ee-uh.
Babylon	*Bab*-uh-lun.
Babylonians	Bab-ih-*low*-nee-unz.
Cyrus	*Sigh*-russ.
Deuteronomy	Due-ter-*ahn*-uh-me.
Israelites	*Iz*-ray-el-ites.
Jeshua	*Jeh*-shoo-uh.
Levites	*Lee*-vites.
Nehemiah	*Nee*-huh-**my**-uh.
Nethinims	*Neth*-ih-nimz.
Samaria	Suh-*mare*-ee-uh.
Sheshbazzar	Shesh-*bayz*-er.
Sinai	*Sigh*-nye or *Sigh*-nay-eye.
Zerubbabel	Zeh-*rub*-uh-bul.

God's steadfast character is highlighted throughout this prayer (Nehemiah 9:6, 8, 17, 27, 28, 31). He has remained faithful in spite of the unfaithfulness of His covenant people. The verse before us continues this theme as God is addressed as *the great, the mighty, and the terrible God, who keepest covenant and mercy*. The word *terrible* is used here in its older sense of the terror, or fear, that should grip us when we contrast who God is (holy and righteous) with who we are (sinners deserving only His judgment). This prayer is making just such a contrast.

This should also bring to mind how God revealed himself to the Israelites in the passages studied previously for lessons 6 and 7. There we saw how He spoke from Mount Sinai in such a display of sounds and sights that the Israelites trembled with fear (Exodus 19:16). They begged Moses to speak with them rather than having them hear the voice of God (20:18, 19).

The references to God's keeping *covenant and mercy* may reflect an awareness of the language that is found in Moses' address to the Israelites in the book of Deuteronomy, particularly in its latter chapters. There Moses describes a series of curses or punishments that the people of Israel will experience if they turn away from the Lord. These are explained in detail in Deuteronomy 28:15-68.

But then comes the promise of compassionate restoration should the people repent (Deuteronomy 30:1-10). Those who lift up the prayer in our lesson text for today repeatedly call attention to the Lord's *mercy* (Nehemiah 9:17, 27, 28, 31). These wise leaders know there is no hope for them apart from God's mercy. Their prayer imparts this same reality to those in attendance.

What Do You Think?
What steps should we take if we discover that our prayers are intensely "deep" only when we are in need or distress?
Talking Points for Your Discussion
- Considering preparation to pray
- Considering location of prayer
- Considering our view of God
- Other

{Remember}

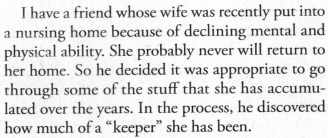

Visual for Lesson 9. *Point to these images (or comparable ones of other nations) as you ask your class how the words* memorial *and* memory *relate.*

◆ *KEEPING* ◆

I have a friend whose wife was recently put into a nursing home because of declining mental and physical ability. She probably never will return to her home. So he decided it was appropriate to go through some of the stuff that she has accumulated over the years. In the process, he discovered how much of a "keeper" she has been.

He was not surprised to discover pictures their children drew when they were preschoolers (they are now in their 40s). There were file folders full of copies of letters she had written to her children and programs of youth musicals the children had been in. What did surprise him was the discovery of Christmas cards they had received in the 1970s. There were four groups of unused Christmas cards, some of them accompanied by books of unused stamps. (And since these are from before the days of "forever" stamps, they will need additional postage.)

As a mother and a wife in charge of the household, she kept many things—some useful, some not. Some had nostalgic value, others valueless in every sense. Perhaps we can identify with some of her accumulation, but the fact remains she was a "keeper" (in the sense of "hoarder," but much less extreme). Nehemiah reminds us that God is also a "keeper." The covenants God makes are valuable and worth keeping. How unfortunate and disastrous that the Israelites did not keep their side of the covenant! Lesson learned? —J. B. N.

B. Unfaithful People (vv. 32b-37)

32b. Let not all the trouble seem little before thee, that hath come upon us, on our kings, on our princes, and on our priests, and on our prophets, and on our fathers, and on all thy people, since the time of the kings of Assyria unto this day.

From greatest to least, everyone has been affected by the Lord's discipline. No one has been immune or exempt. Everyone has suffered *since the time of the kings of Assyria unto this day;* this is a period of about 278 years from the viewpoint of those present. (See the Lesson Background for more chronology.) As the prayer is uttered, the Persian Empire has the upper hand over God's people.

The phrase *let not all the trouble seem little before thee* may seem puzzling. Would the afflictions of God's covenant people ever seem "little" to Him? Why would such a plea need to be offered? Such language is not meant to remind God of something He might forget. Rather, it is a way for the praying person or persons to voice dependency on God for His mercy. If the people think He views their woes as trivial and ignores their cries, to whom will they go for help?

33. Howbeit thou art just in all that is brought upon us; for thou hast done right, but we have done wickedly.

Those praying are also quick to note that all they have experienced in the form of the Lord's discipline is completely deserved. God is *just;* He has *done right* in all His dealings. His people have no one to blame for their sorry condition but themselves, as confessed throughout the prayer (Nehemiah 9:16-31).

> ### What Do You Think?
> What place should affirmations of God's justice have in prayers of new-covenant believers?
> *Talking Points for Your Discussion*
> - Considering the evil present in the world
> - Considering cultural definitions and redefinitions of right and wrong
> - Other

34. Neither have our kings, our princes, our priests, nor our fathers, kept thy law, nor hear-

kened unto thy commandments and thy testimonies, wherewith thou didst testify against them.

For leaders to act with a callous disregard for God's *law,* His *commandments,* and His *testimonies* does not bode well for the people as a whole. The *testimonies, wherewith thou didst testify against them* most likely are the warnings stated by God in His law. Those warnings are that sin brings consequences. When the people failed to heed the warnings, the resulting divine punishment testifies that they got what they deserved.

35. For they have not served thee in their kingdom, and in thy great goodness that thou gavest them, and in the large and fat land which thou gavest before them, neither turned they from their wicked works.

Once more the Lord's great goodness and abundant provisions are contrasted with the people's abundant instances of rebellion. The word *fat* implies great size and often signifies prosperity or blessing (compare Isaiah 30:23). The promised land was God's gift to the people, but that gift had to be received according to the giver's terms. That did not happen.

> **What Do You Think?**
> How would you describe the relationship between a person's "gratefulness index" and his or her dedication to God?
> *Talking Points for Your Discussion*
> - In terms of speech patterns
> - In terms of behavior
> - In terms of prayer life
> - Other

36. Behold, we are servants this day, and for the land that thou gavest unto our fathers to eat the fruit thereof and the good thereof, behold, we are servants in it.

The people are *servants* in that they are slaves in what was meant to be their home. Even though they are now back in the land that God had given them, they are under the control of the Persians.

37. And it yieldeth much increase unto the kings whom thou hast set over us because of our sins: also they have dominion over our bodies, and over our cattle, at their pleasure, and we are in great distress.

The yield of the promised land was originally intended to benefit God's people. Now much of it is given to *the kings* who have *dominion over* the people. This goes back to the days of the Assyrians, to whom the kings of both Israel and Judah had paid tribute. Once more those who pray this prayer acknowledge that this has all happened, not because of the superior strength or military might of these kings. It is *because of our sins.* The real problem confronting the nation is not any foreign rule; it is the bondage of sin—and this has always been the case.

The concluding statement of this verse captures well the condition of the people: *we are in great distress.* Their only hope is to call upon the Lord in humble repentance.

◆ *IT'S THEIR FAULT?* ◆

It seems like a law of human nature to blame others for our failures. Eve blamed her disobedience on the serpent. Adam blamed his on Eve. He even blamed God (since God had given Eve to him). I read once of a woman whose husband was prone to blaming her for everything. After he got into an argument with his own mother on the telephone, he hung up, turned to his wife, and said, "Well, it's *your* mother-in-law!"

It's so easy to blame our government for all that is wrong in the country. Yet we are the ones who elected the officials to office. It is easy to blame the producers of television shows for "all the garbage" that appears on our TV screens. Yet if people did not buy the products of companies that advertise on such programs, the programs would disappear. To place the blame, we often need to look at ourselves.

As the prayer looked at the problems of Judah, it acknowledged that the problem was not "someone else" but "us." Although the prayer refers to various individuals of the past who got the downhill slide started, it is also quick to affirm that the problem of foreign domination is "because of our sins." As my favorite comic strip character, Pogo, once said, "We have met the enemy and he is us."

—J. B. N.

II. Pledging to God
(NEHEMIAH 9:38; 10:28, 29)
A. Stated Commitment (9:38)

38. And because of all this we make a sure covenant, and write it; and our princes, Levites, and priests, seal unto it.

Normally we think of God as the one who initiates covenants. But here those who pray so earnestly demonstrate their desire to take action. The fact that the word *covenant* is italicized in the *King James Version* means that it does not appear in the Hebrew text. But the intent of the people and their leaders to obligate themselves to God is clear nonetheless.

The *seal* likely refers to the manner in which documents of the time are made official. This is done by means of a signet ring (Genesis 41:41-43; Esther 3:10-12). Those in positions of authority—namely, the *princes, Levites,* and *priests*—set the example. This time they lead the way not in wickedness but in pledges of obedience. Nehemiah 10:1-27 (not in today's text) goes on to list the names of dozens of these leaders who put their seal on the prepared document. Thereafter follows a description of a further act of dedication.

B. Solemn Ceremony (10:28, 29)

28a. And the rest of the people, the priests, the Levites, the porters, the singers, the Nethinims.

The rest of the people follow the example set by the leaders cited in Nehemiah 9:38. The additional *priests* and *Levites* are perhaps those who have not taken part in leading the time of reading and teaching God's law and of repentance described in chapters 8 and 9. But they desire to be part of this pivotal moment of renewed commitment to the Lord.

The porters are the temple's gatekeepers (compare 1 Chronicles 9:21). They may also include those who guard the new gates to the city (Nehemiah 7:1-3), but the offices mentioned in the verse before us are associated more with temple service. David had designated individuals to serve in this capacity as part of his efforts to help prepare Solomon for the building of the temple (1 Chronicles 26:1-18). David also organized those "over the service of song" (1 Chronicles 6:31) and *the singers* mentioned likely serve a similar function.

The term *Nethinims* is a Hebrew transliteration. Translated, it means something like "given ones" to refer to those given over to serve in some capacity in the temple. Their specific function is not clear to us. (Compare 1 Chronicles 9:2; Ezra 2:43, 58, 70; Nehemiah 3:26, 3; etc.)

28b. And all they that had separated themselves from the people of the lands unto the law of God, their wives, their sons, and their daughters, every one having knowledge, and having understanding.

Part of preparing for this service of rededication involved the people who are "the seed of Israel" separating themselves "from all strangers" (Nehemiah 9:2). This separation may refer to Israelites who had married outside the covenant (compare Deuteronomy 7:3), but now divorce their pagan spouses. Ezra had dealt with similar forbidden arrangements previously (Ezra 9:1–10:8), and Nehemiah will have to deal with it later (Nehemiah 13:23-28). The separation could also describe the putting away of foreign gods.

What Do You Think?

What techniques can we use to separate ourselves from the world while still engaging it with the gospel?

Talking Points for Your Discussion

- Considering "separation texts" such as 2 Corinthians 6:14-18; Colossians 2:8; 1 Timothy 4:7; 1 John 2:15
- Considering "engagement texts" such as Matthew 5:13-16; 28:19, 20; Acts 17:22-31

Those who take the bold step of separation join others in the act of commitment (see the next verse). This group includes *every one having knowledge, and having understanding.* Similar language is used in Nehemiah 8:2, 3 to describe those who received the teaching of the Law of Moses as spearheaded by Ezra. Perhaps those who could not understand (infants and small children, for example) were gathered in another location where they could receive teaching presented on their level.

29. They clave to their brethren, their nobles, and entered into a curse, and into an oath, to walk in God's law, which was given by Moses the servant of God, and to observe and do all the commandments of the LORD our Lord, and his judgments and his statutes.

The next action taken by those listed in the previous verse is outlined here. There is no mention of their sealing the prepared document of Nehemiah 9:38 as do those whose names are listed in 10:1-27. But they indicate their agreement with that document by placing themselves under *a curse* and *an oath* to *walk in God's law* in its entirety.

We do not know the exact contents of this curse and oath, but the terms themselves indicate sincere intent. Perhaps the curse is something similar to the self-maledictory oath discussed in lesson 5 (page 46).

When we read the action steps that are promised in the rest of Nehemiah 10, we see how seriously the people are taking this covenant. This is no mere lip service. A general promise to live a holier life is one thing; to list specific actions of genuine repentance is another.

What Do You Think?
In what ways can we model submissiveness to God without appearing sanctimonious?
Talking Points for Your Discussion
- In terms of speech patterns
- In terms of behavior
- Considering the difference between the words *submissive* and *passive*

Conclusion
A. The Greater Work

One of the most noteworthy characteristics of Nehemiah (both the book and the man) is the priority of prayer. Most of the prayers mentioned in the book are quite brief (Nehemiah 4:4, 5; 5:19; 6:9, 14; 13:14, 22, 29, 31). In two cases praying is referred to, but nothing is said of the contents (2:4; 4:9). A longer prayer comes at the beginning of the book after Nehemiah learns the distressing news about the city walls (1:5-11). By far the longest prayer is found in the passage from which today's lesson text is drawn (9:5-37).

The title of today's lesson (and the theme for this unit of studies) highlights God's part in making covenants with various individuals and groups in the Old Testament. Even so, the importance of prayer as part of the covenant renewal ceremony in today's study must not be bypassed. We live in a time (in Western society) when the resources for studying the Bible and planning various church programs are incredibly numerous. Just a few seconds with a computer provides us with access to scores of such materials.

While consulting all these resources, it's easy to forget to consult our most important and needed resource: earnest prayer. In fact it is an insult to count prayer as just another "resource" to aid us in getting our work done. As Oswald Chambers put it, "Prayer does not fit us for the greater work; prayer is the greater work."

Many churches used to schedule "prayer meetings" for the middle of the week. True, sometimes these gatherings focused on physical or personal needs more than larger spiritual concerns; but nowadays prayer meetings seem to have gone the way of revivals and community youth rallies.

The perceived needs of church members have resulted in some churches adding staff to meet those needs. Thus we have ministers of visitation, ministers of education, ministers of missions, etc. There are even "ministers" of technology and sports on some church staffs! Is it time to consider creating a staff person designated as a "minister of prayer"? Can you think of someone in your congregation who would be able to fulfill such a role? If you can't think of anyone, what does that say?

B. Prayer

Father, forgive us for our prayerlessness. Help us to give prayer the priority Your Son and the first-century church gave it. Let us not view prayer as just another tool; may we seek to be Your instruments who pray and serve only to bring glory to You. We pray this in Jesus' name. Amen.

C. Thought to Remember
Reflect on the past, but pray for the future.

INVOLVEMENT LEARNING

Enhance your lesson with KJV Bible Student *(from your curriculum supplier) and the reproducible activity page (at www.standardlesson.com or in the back of the* KJV Standard Lesson Commentary Deluxe Edition*).*

Into the Lesson

As class begins, have learners give examples of the ways people remember daily commitments and obligations. *(Possible responses: calendars, sticky notes, schedules, alarms, etc.)*

Then ask volunteers to identify some ways we honor and remember specific events or people from history. *(Possible responses: national memorial structures, certain days of the year, etc.)*

Alternative. Before learners arrive, place in chairs copies of the "Remember This?" activity from the reproducible page, which you can download. Have class members work on this as others arrive. After everyone has had at least 90 seconds to work, continue.

After either activity, dig deeper by asking the following questions: (1) What happens when we don't use daily reminders to keep us on track? (2) What might happen if we didn't remember and reflect on events from the past?

To transition into Bible study, say, "Lessons of the past can help us prepare for the future. That is the purpose of some holidays, memorials, and monuments. The returning exiles took time to reflect on their past for that same reason. Let's learn about that."

Into the Word

Say, "In the chapters preceding today's lesson text, Nehemiah discovered that Jerusalem was in spiritual and physical ruins. After addressing these needs, he reviewed past actions that led to these situations, examined current conditions, and set a course for the people's future."

Write these headings across the top of the board:
Past (Nehemiah 9:32-35)
Present (Nehemiah 9:36, 37)
Future (Nehemiah 9:38; 10:28, 29)

Have volunteers read each section of the text. After a section is read, ask the class to give information from those verses that describes the past, present, and future of Israel. Write their answers under the appropriate headings as they are called. Use the following possible responses as prompts when necessary:

Past—*God kept His covenants and promises; Israel's kings, princes, priests, prophets, fathers, and everyone else have been afflicted since the Assyrians conquered them; God has exacted justice on the Israelites for their wicked behavior; none of the Israelites have kept the law or obeyed the Lord, and their sin has brought God's punishment; God gave the Israelites the bountiful land they live in, and the Israelites continued to ignore God and His law.*

Present—*The Israelites are servants in the land God had given them; the foreign kings who rule over the Israelites make a great profit from the Israelites' land; the Israelites' bodies, livestock, and land all belong to their foreign overlords.*

Future—*Certain priests, Levites, and rulers initiate and seal a covenant with God; the rest of the Israelites follow this example and set themselves apart for the Lord; they all agree to follow God's law, binding themselves with a curse for failure to do so; the Israelites realign themselves with God and His will and resolve to turn away from their sin.*

Say, "Like the Israelites, we all have made mistakes, but by remembering our pasts, we can keep ourselves on the path that God has set out for us."

Into Life

Have learners pair off to discuss this question: "Are there one or more people in your world who need their relationship with God restored as Israel's was?" Give pairs the opportunity to spend a few minutes praying together for the person or people.

Alternative. Distribute copies of the "Daily Bread" activity from the reproducible page. Have learners spend several minutes completing the activity on their own, or send it home to be used throughout the week.

FAITHFUL GOD, UNFAITHFUL PEOPLE

DEVOTIONAL READING: Psalm 44:1-8, 13-19, 26
BACKGROUND SCRIPTURE: Numbers 25; 1 Samuel 2:27-36

NUMBERS 25:10-13

10 And the LORD spake unto Moses, saying,

11 Phinehas, the son of Eleazar, the son of Aaron the priest, hath turned my wrath away from the children of Israel, while he was zealous for my sake among them, that I consumed not the children of Israel in my jealousy.

12 Wherefore say, Behold, I give unto him my covenant of peace:

13 And he shall have it, and his seed after him, even the covenant of an everlasting priesthood; because he was zealous for his God, and made an atonement for the children of Israel.

1 SAMUEL 2:30-36

30 Wherefore the LORD God of Israel saith, I said indeed that thy house, and the house of thy father, should walk before me for ever: but now the LORD saith, Be it far from me; for them that honour me I will honour, and they that despise me shall be lightly esteemed.

31 Behold, the days come, that I will cut off thine arm, and the arm of thy father's house, that there shall not be an old man in thine house.

32 And thou shalt see an enemy in my habitation, in all the wealth which God shall give Israel: and there shall not be an old man in thine house for ever.

33 And the man of thine, whom I shall not cut off from mine altar, shall be to consume thine eyes, and to grieve thine heart: and all the increase of thine house shall die in the flower of their age.

34 And this shall be a sign unto thee, that shall come upon thy two sons, on Hophni and Phinehas; in one day they shall die both of them.

35 And I will raise me up a faithful priest, that shall do according to that which is in mine heart and in my mind: and I will build him a sure house; and he shall walk before mine anointed for ever.

36 And it shall come to pass, that every one that is left in thine house shall come and crouch to him for a piece of silver and a morsel of bread, and shall say, Put me, I pray thee, into one of the priests' offices, that I may eat a piece of bread.

KEY VERSE

I will raise me up a faithful priest, that shall do according to that which is in mine heart and in my mind.
—1 Samuel 2:35

Covenant with God

LESSON AIMS

After participating in this lesson, each learner will be able to:

1. Retell God's responses to the priestly ministries of the son of Eleazar and the sons of Eli.

2. Explain the consequences of unfaithfulness.

3. Identify and correct one unkept commitment.

LESSON OUTLINE

Introduction
  A. A Matter of Trust
  B. Lesson Background: Phinehas #1
  C. Lesson Background: Phinehas #2
I. God Rewards Zeal (NUMBERS 25:10-13)
  A. God Speaks (v. 10)
  B. Phinehas Commended (v. 11)
  C. Covenant Established (v. 12)
  D. Permanence Promised (v. 13)
II. God Punishes Sins (1 SAMUEL 2:30-36)
  A. Consequences of Unfaithfulness
    (vv. 30-34)
    Honor
  B. Rewards for Faithfulness (vv. 35, 36)
    A Faithful Priest
Conclusion
  A. Unfaithful to Commitments
  B. Prayer
  C. Thought to Remember

Introduction

A. A Matter of Trust

Since 1977, Gallup has been asking people to rate the trustworthiness of various professions. Clergy have usually ranked near the top in these polls. For example, in the 1980s about two of every three Americans agreed that ministers have "high" or "very high" moral standards. In 2013, however, fewer than half of those polled responded in that way. "The Catholic priest abuse stories from the early 2000s helped lead to a sharp drop in Americans' ratings of clergy, a decline from which the profession has yet to fully recover," wrote one analyst.

There are some people we instinctively trust and others we do not. When those in vocational ministry misuse their authority, it is not only they who suffer. There is collateral damage when trust is violated. The Bible shows that some of God's priests were trustworthy, while others were not. As is true today, this made difference in lives other than their own.

B. Lesson Background: Phinehas #1

Numbers 25:1-9 gives the background to the story of a certain man's zeal for God and commitment to the covenant of Mount Sinai (the law). The Israelites were camped at Shittim, the final place stopping place before crossing the Jordan (Joshua 2:1; 3:1) and before Moses' death on Mount Nebo (Deuteronomy 32:48-52). Shittim was about 10 miles east of Jericho.

But tragedy struck when a plague killed 24,000 Israelites because of disobedience to God's covenant laws (Numbers 25:9). The idolatrous worship of Baal, the main fertility cult of Canaanites at the time, was the context. The vicinity was probably the foot of the mountain of Peor (23:28).

Such worship was an attempt to influence a pagan god and goddess to have sexual encounters so that the land and its inhabitants would be productive. The accompanying sacrifices and feasts (Numbers 25:2) were an abomination to God in combining what today would be considered forms of pornography, idolatry, sexual immorality, and worship of nature. Of the Ten Commandments broken, that episode violated at least the first (no other gods), the second (no idols), and the seventh (no adultery). No wonder God's wrath was poured out against the leaders who encouraged God's people to yoke themselves to Baal of Peor! (See Numbers 25:4, 5; Deuteronomy 4:3; Hosea 9:10). God's wrath was withdrawn only when Phinehas intervened in a deadly way.

That background has its own background in the form of Balaam's oracles in Numbers 22–24. Having failed at cursing the Israelites—blessing them instead in four oracles—Balaam advised Balak on how to entice the Israelites to sin (Numbers 31:16; Revelation 2:14). The year was about 1407 BC.

C. Lesson Background: Phinehas #2

The second part of the lesson jumps ahead about 340 years to consider another man by the name of Phinehas. He, his brother Hophni, and their father Eli were priests (1 Samuel 1:3). The brothers were corrupt, and they are called "Belial" (2:12), a Hebrew word that means "wicked" (see that translation of Belial in Deuteronomy 15:9).

Their actions in taking advantage of worshippers was a great sin in God's sight (1 Samuel 2:17). They added to their sin by seducing women who served at the entrance to the tent of meeting and by ignoring their father's rebuke (2:22-25); they therefore knowingly broke at least the fifth, seventh, and eighth of the Ten Commandments, probably others as well (Exodus 20:1-17; Deuteronomy 5:7-21).

The life of godly Samuel sharply contrasts with theirs (see 1 Samuel 1–4). At some point during young Samuel's formative years, an unnamed "man of God" came to Eli and condemned the unpriestly way that man and his two sons were conducting themselves (2:27-29). The zeal of Phinehas #2 was certainly not like that of Phinehas #1!

I. God Rewards Zeal
(NUMBERS 25:10-13)

Two things are clear from Numbers 25:7-9: (1) the first Phinehas of today's study had just killed two people for blatant disobedience to God and (2) his initiative in that respect halted further Israelite deaths. Even so, 24,000 were already dead by plague—capital punishment from the Lord.

A. God Speaks (v. 10)

10. And the LORD spake unto Moses, saying.

The use of *LORD* (small capital letters) represents God's personal name "Yahweh." The unique relationship that Moses has with Yahweh has already been seen in the incident of the jealousy of Aaron and Miriam (Numbers 12). Yahweh reprimanded those two by reminding them that He usually gives prophets visions or dreams, but with Moses He speaks "mouth to mouth . . . and not in dark speeches; and the similitude of the Lord shall he behold" (Numbers 12:8; compare Exodus 33:11). That last phrase reminds us of the occasion when Moses was able to see the "back" of Yahweh as He passed by (Exodus 33:19-23). Thus we should understand that Yahweh is communicating with Moses in a direct way.

B. Phinehas Commended (v. 11)

11. Phinehas, the son of Eleazar, the son of Aaron the priest, hath turned my wrath away from the children of Israel, while he was zealous for my sake among them, that I consumed not the children of Israel in my jealousy.

HOW TO SAY IT

Abiathar	Ah-*bye*-uh-thar.
Adonijah	Ad-owe-*nye*-juh.
Azariah	Az-uh-*rye*-uh.
Baal	Bay-al.
Balaam	*Bay*-lum.
Balak	*Bay*-lack.
Canaanites	*Kay*-nun-ites.
Eleazar	El-ih-*a*-zar or E-lih-*a*-zar.
Gibeah	*Gib*-ee-uh (*G* as in *get*).
Hophni	*Hoff*-nye.
Levitical	Leh-*vit*-ih-kul.
Peor	*Pea*-or.
Phinehas	*Fin*-ee-us.
Shittim	Shih-*teem*.
Yahweh (Hebrew)	*Yah*-weh.
Zadok	*Zay*-dok.

This is the Lord's recap of what is narrated in Numbers 25:6-9. What *Phinehas,* grandson of the first high priest, did with so much zeal was to kill an Israelite man and a Midianite woman while they engaged in an immoral act. The sinful nature of that act was compounded by the idol worship that accompanied it (25:1-3).

We may be shocked that a priest has committed such an act! But we must remember a couple of things. First, those sins amounted to religious and political treason. Second, the death toll would have been much higher than 24,000 (Numbers 25:9) if Phinehas had not acted. As it stands, God commends him for being *zealous for my sake.* The result of this man's actions was a great point of rescue: God *consumed not the children of Israel in . . . jealousy.*

The words *zealous* and *jealous* are closely related. This is seen where a word in the original language is translated "jealous" or "jealousy" in one passage but "zealous" or "zeal" in another. For example, the Hebrew noun translated "jealousy" in Ezekiel 8:3, 5 and Zechariah 8:2 is rendered "zeal" in Isaiah 9:7; 37:32; 59:17; 63:15. In the New Testament, the Greek noun translated "jealousy" in 2 Corinthians 11:2 is the same one translated "zeal" in Philippians 3:6.

The common idea is one of fervency. We usually think of jealousy as a negative thing, but it can be positive when the fervency (zeal) is properly motivated and informed. We see the positive side in John 2:17 (quoting Psalm 69:9); we see the opposite in Philippians 3:6. Thus we should take care to understand what it means for the Lord to be jealous. The biblical concept of jealousy when applied to God indicates a profound sense of caring and commitment. God's "name is Jealous" (Exodus 34:14).

> **What Do You Think?**
> What are some ways to be fervent for God today?
> *Talking Points for Your Discussion*
> ▪ Before believers
> ▪ Before unbelievers
> ▪ Before no one but God himself

C. Covenant Established (v. 12)

12. Wherefore say, Behold, I give unto him my covenant of peace.

God's *covenant of peace* is attested in the Old Testament only here and in Isaiah 54:10; Ezekiel 34:25; 37:26; and Malachi 2:5. The latter is part of a stinging rebuke of priests who were not obeying the Word of God in contrast with forefather Levi. "My covenant was with him of life and peace. . . . The law of truth was in his mouth, and iniquity was not found in his lips: he walked with me . . . and did turn many away from iniquity" (2:5, 6). One could say the same of Phinehas.

Peace (*shalom*) is more than the absence of hostilities. It means wholeness, health, well-being, and blessing. Further implications of this *covenant of peace* are given in the next verse.

> **What Do You Think?**
> What are some ways your church can promote peace without getting political?
> *Talking Points for Your Discussion*
> ▪ Racially
> ▪ Economically
> ▪ Socially
> ▪ Other

D. Permanence Promised (v. 13)

13. And he shall have it, and his seed after him, even the covenant of an everlasting priesthood; because he was zealous for his God, and made an atonement for the children of Israel.

The scope of the covenant of peace is now explained: it is *the covenant of an everlasting priesthood.* Phinehas is assured that his descendants will enjoy God's blessing and security. Phinehas himself will become famous for his righteous indignation, an act that is considered to be *an atonement* for the Israelites (compare Psalm 106:28-31).

Later, Phinehas will have a role in the destruction of these same Midianites as well as Balaam, who had instigated the sordid affair (Numbers 25:16-18; 31:1-8). He becomes noted as a defender of God's honor (see Joshua 22:11-20; Judges 20:24-28) and as a ruler over the gatekeepers of the tabernacle (1 Chronicles 6:4, 50; 9:20).

II. God Punishes Sins

(1 Samuel 2:30-36)

A second Phinehas is now a part of our lesson. He and brother Hophni are the sons of Eli, a priest (1 Samuel 2:12-17, 22-25). Eli seems to have seldom, if ever, disciplined his sons for their malicious acts (2:29). God had chosen Aaron, son Eleazar, and grandson Phinehas for the honorable and holy task of priesthood. But Eli and his sons have brought dishonor and unholiness to the role.

A. Consequences of Unfaithfulness (vv. 30-34)

30. Wherefore the Lord God of Israel saith, I said indeed that thy house, and the house of thy father, should walk before me for ever: but now the Lord saith, Be it far from me; for them that honour me I will honour, and they that despise me shall be lightly esteemed.

The Lord God of Israel is speaking through an unnamed "man of God unto Eli" (1 Samuel 2:27). *Be it far from me* is an idiomatic statement that denies to Eli the positive content of the rhetorical questions of 1 Samuel 2:28. Thus God is revoking a promise because that promise is taken for granted and even despised—thus despising God himself, who made the promise.

◆ HONOR ◆

In medieval Europe, honor was usually associated with members of the nobility and what was perceived as their rights. To take land away from a nobleman, to malign his reputation, or to offend him in some way was to disparage his honor, requiring him to do battle to restore that honor.

In early America, duels were fought to avenge men's honor; one instance was the killing of Alexander Hamilton by Aaron Burr, Vice President of the United States. Similar duels were fought over offensive comments about a woman's reputation.

Honor codes live on. Military academies have them. Universities have them. And college instructors may give take-home exams on the "honor system," which assumes that a student will not cheat. Our society may not have the same honor code as medieval Europe or even our own country's early days, but ancient Israel real-

ized that God's honor was not something to be trifled with. For God's people to act immorally was to denigrate God's honor. Have we learned this lesson?   —J. B. N.

31. Behold, the days come, that I will cut off thine arm, and the arm of thy father's house, that there shall not be an old man in thine house.

Behold reflects a Hebrew expression meant to get the attention of the one listening—in this case, Eli. The word *arm* in Hebrew thought suggests "strength." Indeed, God will *cut off* the *arm* (strength) of the house of Eli to the point that all shall die young. The days are coming, and sooner than one thinks, when these curses will begin to unfold. The sin of Hophni and Phinehas will have repercussions that reach beyond their own lives and times.

32. And thou shalt see an enemy in my habitation, in all the wealth which God shall give Israel: and there shall not be an old man in thine house for ever.

The Hebrew word translated *enemy* can be understood in the general sense of "distress" (as it is translated in Judges 11:7). Indeed, an enemy creates distress! This is a word of judgment against Eli and his sons. Those three live and conduct their unholy ministry at Shiloh (1 Samuel 1:3), the place of the tabernacle (Joshua 18:1). By the time of the prophet Jeremiah some four centuries later, Shiloh is no more (Jeremiah 7:12, 14; 26:6, 9; Psalm 78:59, 60).

The prophecy that *there shall not be an old man in thine house for ever* continues the judgment against Eli and his lineage. Their fate is discussed below.

33. And the man of thine, whom I shall not cut off from mine altar, shall be to consume thine eyes, and to grieve thine heart: and all the increase of thine house shall die in the flower of their age.

The thought of the last phrase of 1 Samuel 2:32 is repeated in different words in the last phrase of the verse now before us. The shortened life expectancy for Eli's line means that he will be the last one to live to be "an old man" (1 Samuel 4:18).

For God to *cut off* Eli's descendants *from mine altar* means an end to their tenure as priests. A fulfillment happens several generations later regarding Abiathar. The texts 1 Samuel 4:18-21; 14:3; and 22:9, 20 establish him to be a descendant of Eli. Following the destruction of Shiloh, the sanctuary ends up about 16 miles due south, in Nob (between Gibeah and Jerusalem). The priests who serve at Nob during the reign of King Saul pay with their lives for welcoming David (21:1-10; 22:9-19). Abiathar alone escapes and joins David (22:20-23). Ultimately, however, the prophecy against Eli's descendants is fulfilled when Solomon removes Abiathar from the priesthood because of the man's complicity in a rebellion (1 Kings 1:7, 8, 19, 25; 2:26, 27).

34. And this shall be a sign unto thee, that shall come upon thy two sons, on Hophni and Phinehas; in one day they shall die both of them.

The Israelites' superstitious use of the ark of the covenant as a good-luck charm in battle (1 Samuel 4:3, 4) ironically has the opposite effect: its presence causes such fear among the enemy troops that they fight even harder (4:6-9). The result is total

defeat for the Israelites. On that *one day* both sons of Eli die, being among the 30,000 slain (4:10, 11). Eli himself dies when told the news (4:18).

B. Rewards for Faithfulness (vv. 35, 36)

35. And I will raise me up a faithful priest, that shall do according to that which is in mine heart and in my mind: and I will build him a sure house; and he shall walk before mine anointed for ever.

The *faithful priest* refers to Zadok, a priest during David's reign (2 Samuel 8:17; 15:24-29, 35; 20:25). Zadok will replace Abiathar as high priest after the latter conspires with Adonijah against Solomon (1 Kings 2:35).

God firmly establishes the *house* (dynasty) of Zadok so that his family flourishes for many years, beginning with his son Azariah (1 Kings 4:2), continuing through the return of the exiles (1 Chronicles 6:12-15; Ezra 3:2). *Mine anointed* refers to all the Davidic kings under which the descendants of Zadok serve as priests.

◆ A FAITHFUL PRIEST ◆

Martin Luther (1483–1546) was studying to be a lawyer when he had a scary encounter with a thunderbolt. The experience led him to become a monk instead.

Because Luther was already well educated, the monastery decided to further his training and have him become a priest. Five years later, he was awarded the doctor's degree and a position on the faculty at the University of Wittenberg. While teaching, he also served as the parish priest for St. Mary's Church in town. It was during his studies there that he came to a new understanding of salvation. Contrary to prevailing Roman Catholic interpretation, Luther concluded that the apostle Paul taught salvation by God's grace, not by works of merit or by purchase of indulgences.

For years he was badgered to recant and submit to the authority of the church. On trial, Luther was again told to recant his writings. He responded that some of his writings were commentaries on Scripture; to recant them would be to deny the Word of God. Ultimately he declared, "Here I stand, I can do no other." Luther remained faithful to his calling in the best way he knew how. He could do nothing else.

Peter says all believers are being "built up a spiritual house, an holy priesthood, to offer up spiritual sacrifices, acceptable to God by Jesus Christ" (1 Peter 2:5). What more can you do to be faithful to your priestly calling? —J. B. N.

> **What Do You Think?**
> Which spiritual disciplines are most helpful to you for remaining faithful? Why?
> *Talking Points for Your Discussion*
> - Regarding disciplines of service
> - Regarding disciplines of worship
> - Regarding disciplines of prayer
> - Regarding disciplines of Bible reading
> - Considering 2 Peter 1:5-8

36. And it shall come to pass, that every one that is left in thine house shall come and crouch to him for a piece of silver and a morsel of bread, and shall say, Put me, I pray thee, into one of the priests' offices, that I may eat a piece of bread.

Often God's judgment reveals irony in the process. To this point Eli's sons have exercised their greed and gluttony by extracting more sacrificial meat than they should have (1 Samuel 2:12-17). But in the future Eli's descendants will have to beg *for a piece of silver and a morsel of bread.*

Conclusion

A. Unfaithful to Commitments

In the Old Testament, every Israelite was obligated to keep the covenant. Likewise, Christians everywhere are obligated to keep the new covenant. But keeping commitments can be difficult. The apostle Paul used Israel's experience in the wilderness as a warning against failure in this regard (see 1 Corinthians 10:1-10). He exhorts his readers to "not lust after evil things, as they also lusted" (10:6). In other words, Christians are to avoid idolatry, sexual immorality, grumbling against God's will, etc. When we commit such sin, we are in danger of losing it all! Since we are the ones "upon

whom the ends of the world are come" (10:11), the stakes could not be higher.

The third and fourth chapters of the book of Hebrews make a similar point as the author repeatedly quotes from and otherwise alludes to Psalm 95:7-11.

> Today if ye will hear his voice, harden not your heart, as in the provocation, and as in the day of temptation in the wilderness: when your fathers tempted me, proved me, and saw my work. Forty years long was I grieved with this generation, and said, It is a people that do err in their heart, and they have not known my ways: unto whom I sware in my wrath that they should not enter into my rest.

God rewards those who are faithful to His covenant, and He punishes those who are unfaithful. Let us be aware of our continuing need to examine ourselves in this regard and repent when necessary.

B. Prayer

Father, forgive us the sin of unfaithfulness to our priestly covenant responsibilities! Grant us hearts for keeping our commitments to You. May we by Your grace continue to be counted in the community of the committed. In Jesus' name, amen.

C. Thought to Remember

Others see God's faithfulness when we are proven to be faithful.

Visual for Lesson 10. *Start a discussion by pointing to this visual as you ask, "What techniques can help us keep our commitments to God?"*

INVOLVEMENT LEARNING

Enhance your lesson with KJV Bible Student *(from your curriculum supplier) and the reproducible activity page (at www.standardlesson.com or in the back of the* KJV Standard Lesson Commentary Deluxe Edition*).*

Into the Lesson

To begin class, divide the class into two teams, asking each to pick a spokesperson. Say, "A recent poll asked people what category of professionals they considered most and least trustworthy. Let's see if you can guess the top five in each category."

Starting with the "most trusted" category, alternate asking teams to guess a profession in that category. Score a point for each correct answer. Continue until all are guessed or until both teams give two wrong answers in a row. Move on to the next category. This is what the poll found:

Most trusted:
1=nurses
2=pharmacists
3=medical doctors
4=engineers
5=dentists

Least trusted:
1=car salespeople
2=members of Congress
3=advertising executives
4=stockbrokers
5=HMO managers

Did your students find any surprises? What occupations would they add to either list?

Lead into Bible study by saying, "There are some people we instinctively trust and others we do not. Some pollsters find that priests and other clergy can be considered either highly trustworthy or highly untrustworthy, depending on a person's past experiences. The Bible shows that some of God's priests were trustworthy, while some were not. As is true today, this made a big difference."

Into the Word

Divide the class into groups of two or three, giving each group a pen and a copy of the lesson text from page 81. Allow a few minutes to complete the following Scripture marking activity:

1. Circle characteristics God wants His priests to have.
2. Underline rewards given to faithful priests.
3. Draw a line through punishments for unfaithful priests.

Alternative. Download and distribute copies of the "Good Phinehas, Bad Phinehas" activity from the reproducible page. You may wish to have both Scriptures read aloud before working through the answers as a class.

After either activity, lead a class discussion with the following questions:

• How could the character of priests have shaped people's understanding of the nature of God?

• What are some results when priests misuse their position in order to obtain power over others?

• Read 1 Peter 2:9 and Revelation 1:6. If all Christians are priests, what does our text say to us?

Move to the Into Life section by saying, "The perception of God that people have is greatly influenced by their perception of those who claim to represent Him. If we want others to know that they can trust God, they need to know they can trust us. Let's see how we can be more faithful priests."

Into Life

Give an index card to each student. Tell them, "Think about a promise you have made to someone in the past month that you failed to do or have not yet followed through on. Write that on your index card. Underneath write either one way you will make up for your failure or a plan to do what you promised."

Encourage your students to complete the cards in class or take them home to complete.

Alternative. Pass out copies of the "Good Riddance!" activity from the reproducible page. Have students work alone or in pairs to complete it. Ask for volunteers to share their conclusions.

PROMISE OF A NEW COVENANT

DEVOTIONAL READING: Psalm 87
BACKGROUND SCRIPTURE: Jeremiah 31

JEREMIAH 31:27-34

27 Behold, the days come, saith the LORD, that I will sow the house of Israel and the house of Judah with the seed of man, and with the seed of beast.

28 And it shall come to pass, that like as I have watched over them, to pluck up, and to break down, and to throw down, and to destroy, and to afflict; so will I watch over them, to build, and to plant, saith the LORD.

29 In those days they shall say no more, The fathers have eaten a sour grape, and the children's teeth are set on edge.

30 But every one shall die for his own iniquity: every man that eateth the sour grape, his teeth shall be set on edge.

31 Behold, the days come, saith the LORD, that I will make a new covenant with the house of Israel, and with the house of Judah:

32 Not according to the covenant that I made with their fathers in the day that I took them by the hand to bring them out of the land of Egypt; which my covenant they brake, although I was an husband unto them, saith the LORD:

33 But this shall be the covenant that I will make with the house of Israel; After those days, saith the LORD, I will put my law in their inward parts, and write it in their hearts; and will be their God, and they shall be my people.

34 And they shall teach no more every man his neighbour, and every man his brother, saying, Know the LORD: for they shall all know me, from the least of them unto the greatest of them, saith the LORD: for I will forgive their iniquity, and I will remember their sin no more.

KEY VERSE

I will put my law in their inward parts, and write it in their hearts; and will be their God, and they shall be my people. —**Jeremiah 31:33**

Graphic: Angel _ 1978 / iStock / Thinkstock

COVENANT WITH GOD

Unit 3: An Everlasting Covenant

LESSON AIMS

After participating in this lesson, each learner will be able to:

1. List salient features of the new covenant.

2. Explain the significance of the new covenant's being written on the heart rather than on tablets of stone.

3. Identify an area of "head knowledge" of God's will in his or her life that has not become "heart obedience," and make a plan for correction.

LESSON OUTLINE

Introduction

A. In Need of a Do-Over

My college alma mater used to hold a golf tournament during homecoming festivities. Sponsoring the tournament was my favorite Old Testament professor, and he went strictly by the rules. As a duffer, I hardly knew the rules, much less played by them. On one of my big swings off the tee, my ball landed up against a tree halfway down the fairway. The professor told me to take a penalty stroke and place the ball a club's length from the tree.

But that would hurt my score! My golfing partner was much more lenient in the face of my frustration. He said, "Just take a do-over! Just kick it out from the tree and hit it! No penalty as far as I'm concerned." Well, you can guess which voice I wanted to listen to!

While this experience is trivial by comparison, ancient Israel was given a do-over by God. Israel had to suffer exile for her sins, but God reversed the exile, restored the Israelites to their land, and granted the promise of a new covenant. There would be a new people of God in a day to come. They would know Him in the fullest sense, would have His law written on their hearts, and would experience complete and total forgiveness for sin.

B. Lesson Background

Jeremiah's ministry may have begun about 627 BC; many scholars believe he influenced the law reforms enacted by King Josiah (640–609 BC). Jeremiah lived to see the death of Josiah and the collapse of his reforms. Ultimately Jeremiah encouraged the people of Judah to capitulate to the new superpower, the Babylonians, because Babylon was the instrument of God's judgment against their sins. Jeremiah's ministry ended sometime after the Babylonian-appointed governor of Judah (Gedaliah) was assassinated in about 585 BC. The prophet was forced to flee to Egypt, where tradition says he died.

The book of Jeremiah is complicated, and its episodes are often difficult to date. Most of Jeremiah's oracles are judgments against the Judeans, the people of the southern kingdom of divided

Israel (the tribes of the northern kingdom having been taken into exile by the Assyrians decades before). Those oracles lament the apostasy of the people. The only hope Jeremiah gives is found in a section known as the Book of Consolation, which is Jeremiah 30:1–33:26.

But what a hope it is! God promised to make the exiles His people once again (Jeremiah 30:22), to "make a new covenant" with them (31:31-34), to return them to their land (32:41), and to establish once and for all time the Davidic dynasty as originally promised (33:15-26; 30:9). The theme of the Book of Consolation is restated often: "I will cause their captivity to return" (32:44; see 30:3, 18; 31:23; 33:7, 26). The covenant theme of "Ye shall be my people, and I will be your God" is also repeated (30:22; also 31:1, 33; 32:38).

I. Reversal of Judgment
(Jeremiah 31:27-30)
A. Sowing Seed (v. 27)

27. Behold, the days come, saith the Lord, that I will sow the house of Israel and the house of Judah with the seed of man, and with the seed of beast.

This verse begins, as does Jeremiah 31:31 (below), with a Hebrew word that means "Pay attention! This is important!" The word is translated *Behold* in the *King James Version* but is bypassed in other versions of the Bible.

The phrase *the days come* occurs numerous times in this book (Jeremiah 7:32; 9:25; 16:14;

HOW TO SAY IT

Assyrians	Uh-*sear*-e-unz.
Babylonians	Bab-ih-*low*-nee-unz.
Deuteronomy	Due-ter-*ahn*-uh-me.
Ezekiel	Ee-*zeek*-ee-ul or Ee-*zeek*-yul.
Gedaliah	Ged-uh-**lye**-uh (*G* as in *get*).
Jeremiah	Jair-uh-*my*-uh.
Josiah	Jo-*sigh*-uh.
Pentecost	*Pent*-ih-kost.
Philippians	Fih-*lip*-ee-unz.
Sinai	*Sigh*-nye or *Sigh*-nay-eye.
Yahweh (*Hebrew*)	*Yah*-weh.

19:6; 23:5, 7; 30:3; 31:27, 31, 38; 33:14; 48:12; 49:2; 51:47, 52). Sometimes the phrase introduces a prediction of wrath and punishment. Those cases are entirely consistent with God's warning, through Moses, that if the Israelites broke the covenant He made with them at Mount Sinai, then serious consequences would ensue (Deuteronomy 28:15-68). The bitterness of the forthcoming exile will be so profound that Jeremiah describes it with an image of Rachel "weeping for her children" (Jeremiah 31:15; compare Genesis 30:22; Matthew 2:18).

In the case at hand, however, the phrase *the days come* introduces a prediction of blessing and restoration. The depopulation of the Judean homeland that results from exile (Jeremiah 33:10) will be reversed, since God promises to *sow the house of Israel and the house of Judah with the seed of man, and with the seed of beast* when the exile is over (compare 33:12, 13).

We note that the promise includes the northern kingdom of Israel as well as the southern kingdom of Judah. The northern kingdom was destroyed in 722 BC by the Assyrians. For all that we can perceive today, the northern tribes never recovered and never returned. Some Christians today look for that yet to happen. Others, however, interpret the return of "Israel" as the ingathering of Gentiles into the church (compare Acts 15:12-21).

> **What Do You Think?**
> What are some ways our lives should demonstrate trust in God to fulfill His promises?
> *Talking Points for Your Discussion*
> - As the church corporate
> - In family life
> - As individuals

B. Rebuilding (v. 28)

28. And it shall come to pass, that like as I have watched over them, to pluck up, and to break down, and to throw down, and to destroy, and to afflict; so will I watch over them, to build, and to plant, saith the Lord.

In an obvious and a nonobvious way, this verse echoes Jeremiah 1:10-12, which describes the call of Jeremiah, God's plan for him, and God's intended actions regarding Judah and Jerusalem. The obvious parallel consists of the words and phrases that are identical in the two places (*break down, destroy, build, plant,* etc.).

The nonobvious parallel is a play on words in the Hebrew that isn't apparent in English. The wordplay is set up when Jeremiah says, "I see a rod of an almond tree" (Jeremiah 1:11). God's reply "Thou hast well seen: for I will hasten my word to perform it" (1:12) then completes the wordplay because the noun translated "almond" and verb translated "hasten" are virtually identical in the original Hebrew. This connects with 31:28 in the fact that the same Hebrew verb occurs here twice, being translated *have watched* and *will I watch* (compare 44:27).

In essence, these two segments reflect the two-fold purpose of Jeremiah's prophetic ministry to Judah: (1) pronouncement of judgment upon the nation because of their sins and (2) the subsequent restoration after the people have "gotten the message" regarding who is behind both—none other than God himself. This theme occurs repeatedly throughout the book (compare Jeremiah 18:7; 24:6; 31:40; 32:41, 42; 44:27; 45:4, 5).

◆ *GROW AS YOU GO* ◆

One summer I found a packet of mixed flower seeds and decided to plant them. It was a simplistic effort on my part: not much soil prepara-

Visual for Lesson 11. *Point to this visual as you ask, "In what sense is it now 10 minutes to midnight? In what sense is it 10 minutes to high noon? Why?"*

tion other than digging up some weeds, scattering the seeds, and covering them over. Amazingly, one by one, here and there, tiny little shoots began to emerge. Some grew quickly, others slowly, but eventually there was a hodgepodge of flowers of various heights, sizes, and vibrant colors. A later attempt to repeat this success brought only dismay. My neglect in the second effort was apparent —as was my silly assumption that a garden would reinstate itself without nurture.

There are times when we treat the spiritual garden of our walk with God the same way. Planting with deliberation and intent yields spiritual results (1 Corinthians 3:6; etc.). This includes planting the Word of God in our hearts. To fail to do so is to stagnate spiritually. Stagnation eventually becomes regression as worldly philosophies seep in and persuade us to trust our own strengths and abilities (compare Colossians 2:8). Before we realize it, the pressures to succeed and guarantee our futures in this world have come to dominate our thoughts and actions (compare Luke 12:16-21).

The Bible is the light for our way (Psalm 119:105; compare 2 Timothy 3:16). In Christ we have within us "a well of water springing up into everlasting life" (John 4:14). To neglect the things of God is to invite Him to neglect us. But to embrace His way fully is to invite His blessing. Have we learned anything from the history of Israel? See 1 Corinthians 10:1-13. —C. M. W.

C. An Old Proverb (v. 29)

29. In those days they shall say no more, The fathers have eaten a sour grape, and the children's teeth are set on edge.

When the future exiles wallow in the misery of their situation, they naturally will try to come to grips with the reason for it. In so doing, many will latch on to a proverb that becomes popular, the one we see in the verse before us (compare Ezekiel 18:2). This proverb is a "Why me?" complaint. The effect is to blame God for being unjust in punishing the wrong people (compare Ezekiel 18:25-29; 33:17-20).

But lest we be too quick to dismiss this proverb as mere blame-shifting, we should recognize precedent for it in Exodus 34:7. That passages affirms that God visits "the iniquity of the fathers upon the children unto the third and fourth generation" (also Exodus 20:5). Today we readily observe the intergenerational consequences of parents sent to jail for committing crimes. Children often do suffer for the sins of their fathers (compare Lamentations 5:7; Jeremiah 32:18, 19).

The fact that the sins of one generation have consequences for another is not the same as saying that God punishes an innocent group for the sins of a guilty group. Even so, Israelite history does indeed record instances of children dying as a consequence of the sins of their parents (see Numbers 16:23-33; Joshua 7:24, 25; 2 Samuel 11:1–12:19; 21:1-9). Although there are times when the all-knowing and sovereign God deems this to be fitting, it is rare and certainly not the norm. The problem in today's text is that when exile comes, the people will apply the proverb to disavow any culpability for their situation.

> **What Do You Think?**
> How would you counsel a fellow believer who blames distressing circumstances on the actions of others?
> *Talking Points for Your Discussion*
> - When the claim is true
> - When the claim is false

D. A New Proverb (v. 30)

30. But every one shall die for his own iniquity: every man that eateth the sour grape, his teeth shall be set on edge.

The old proverb will not do! People will be punished for their own sins, not the sins of others (compare Ezekiel 18:3, 4).

Scholars often emphasize the element of "corporate responsibility" in Hebrew thinking to the point that a concept of "personal responsibility" seems almost nonexistent. That is not accurate! Both levels of responsibility are part of Hebrew thought. For example, Moses tried three times to blame the people for his not being allowed to enter the promised land (Deuteronomy 1:37; 3:26; 4:21), but God put the blame squarely on Moses himself (32:51, 52). Other examples could be given.

All of us have enough sin in our lives to justify any punishment from God. To blame someone else will not do. Not only is the old proverb thrown out, a new one replaces it: *every man that eateth the sour grape, his teeth shall be set on edge.*

◆ *"Did You Do That?"* ◆

We see the humor in videos that show dog owners accusing their pets of having committed some catastrophe in the home. The accusatory "Did you do that?" results in sad expressive eyes and slumped body on the part of the dog, giving the sense that he realizes he has been caught in a wrongdoing. With circumstantial evidence stacked against the creature, he looks guilty whether he actually is or not.

A little toddler might react the same way as a parent pretends to appear serious because of some mishap—a spilled bowl of cereal, food covering the toddler's face and hair, etc. But all the while the parent tries to hide his own laughter at the child's surprise at being caught. The retelling of the tale to others and the ensuing chuckles validate the less-than-serious nature of the misdeed.

However, the age and culpability of the accused and the nature of a crime can affect our humor, or lack of it, at some offenses. We are likely to consider these quite differently—with sadness of heart for bad choices, or maybe with demands for justice to be swift and severe for the horrendous actions.

If we are honest and discerning, though, a sense of fairness will sometimes point its finger back at ourselves. If we judge our wrongdoings to be less reprehensible than those of others, Romans 3:23 is a pointed reminder otherwise. Even so, we do not forget the eternal judge whose love and mercy far surpasses the transgressions anyone commits (Romans 4:7, 8). All of us can be glad for that.

—C. M. W.

II. Restoration of Relationship
(Jeremiah 31:31-34)
A. A New Covenant (v. 31)

31. Behold, the days come, saith the LORD, that I will make a new covenant with the house of Israel, and with the house of Judah.

The phrase *the days come* refers to "the last days" of prophetic utterance (Isaiah 2:2; Micah 4:1) when the Messiah comes to establish God's reign. In addition to places in today's lesson text, similar words are found in Jeremiah 30:7, 8, 24; 31:38; 33:14, 15, all of which are located within the Book of Consolation (see the Lesson Background).

Various passages speak of something new to be done or established for people of God (examples: Ezekiel 11:19; Malachi 3:16–4:1-6). But the verse before us is the only place in the Old Testament where the term *new covenant* is used. Some have proposed that if we could pick the single most important verse in the Old Testament, Jeremiah 31:31 would be it.

Hebrews 8:8-12 indicates the vital importance of Jeremiah 31:31-34 by quoting it in its entirety —the longest quotation of an Old Testament passage in the New Testament. Much of what follows Hebrews 8:8-12 is commentary on this Jeremiah passage. We note that the Greek words translated "new covenant" in Hebrews 8:8; 12:24 are the same ones translated "new testament" elsewhere. Jesus referred to this when he instituted the Lord's Supper (Luke 22:20; 1 Corinthians 11:25).

As noted in comments on Jeremiah 31:27, above, interpretations vary on the meaning of the word *Israel* in the sense intended in this passage. Some students propose that the historical northern kingdom of Israel was so sinful that it was or should be considered Gentile or heathen (compare 2 Kings 17:15; etc.). Thus to unite Israel and Judah would be like adding Gentiles to the people of God (see Romans 15:8-13). Others think that Jeremiah 3:11 calls the basis of this viewpoint into question: "backsliding Israel hath justified herself more than treacherous Judah" (see also Ezekiel 16:51, 52). Even so, Gentiles are promised a blessing through Abraham (Genesis 12:3; 22:18; etc.).

B. The Old Covenant (v. 32)

32. Not according to the covenant that I made with their fathers in the day that I took them by the hand to bring them out of the land of Egypt; which my covenant they brake, although I was an husband unto them, saith the LORD.

The old covenant was received at Mount Sinai by the generation that God rescued *out of the land of Egypt* in the exodus (Exodus 19–24). Tragically, the Israelites repeatedly broke that covenant (see Exodus 32; Jeremiah 7:21-26; 11:1-17). The relationship between God and His people is therefore analogous to that of a faithful husband who has an unfaithful wife (compare Hosea 2). Israelite unfaithfulness is frequently described in terms of adultery (Jeremiah 3:6-10; 5:7; etc.).

C. Written on the Heart (v. 33)

33. But this shall be the covenant that I will make with the house of Israel; After those days, saith the LORD, I will put my law in their inward parts, and write it in their hearts; and will be their God, and they shall be my people.

The not-that-but-this format of Jeremiah 31:32, 33 signifies that contrasting elements of the two covenants are to be noted. The old covenant has been written on stone (Exodus 24:12; 31:18; 34:1), and the people of the era are to internalize its laws (Deuteronomy 6:4-9). The new covenant, by contrast, is written on *inward parts* and *hearts*, and God is the one who puts it there (compare Hebrews 10:16). It is through the Holy Spirit, who indwells each and every Christian, that God does so, as suggested by Romans 8:5-11.

The contrasts invite examination of similarities as well. We see one such similarity in the verse before us: *[I] will be their God, and they shall be my people* (compare Jeremiah 24:7; 30:22; 31:1; 32:38; Ezekiel 11:20; 14:11; 36:28; 37:23, 27; Zechariah 8:8). This is also the typical phrase for creating covenants of the Old Testament era (see Exodus

29:45; Leviticus 26:12; Jeremiah 7:23; 11:4). We note that this similarity speaks to the intended result, while the contrasts speak to differing methods for achieving that result. Those living under the old covenant could have lived under God's desired outcome, but their law breaking made that impossible.

So a new method was needed. That new method is not explained fully in our lesson text. But our historical perspective affirms that the new covenant is founded on the life, death, and resurrection of Christ.

> **What Do You Think?**
> How can you make your heart more receptive to having God's Word written on it?
> *Talking Points for Your Discussion*
> - Regarding things to do more of
> - Regarding things to do less of
> - Regarding things to abandon altogether

D. No More Sin (v. 34)

34. And they shall teach no more every man his neighbour, and every man his brother, saying, Know the LORD: for they shall all know me, from the least of them unto the greatest of them, saith the LORD: for I will forgive their iniquity, and I will remember their sin no more.

This verse predicts a perfect state of affairs: no one is needed to teach about the Lord because everyone already has the knowledge. This seems puzzling, since we understand that a teaching function does indeed exist under the new covenant (Matthew 28:19, 20; Romans 12:7; etc.).

One interpretation proposes that the verse before us looks to the time after Jesus' second coming, when our presence with God in Heaven yields our fullest knowledge of Him. Another interpretation proposes that Jeremiah's prediction contrasts the need for human mediators under the old covenant (priests of the tribe of Levi) with the direct access to God that people have under the new covenant (1 Thessalonians 4:9; Hebrews 4:16; 10:19-22; 1 John 2:27).

Either way, the time of the new covenant will be an era when the people of God include more than the peoples of ancient Israel and Judah. Knowledge of God will spread to peoples of all nations and languages (Revelation 7:9).

> **What Do You Think?**
> In what ways should forgiveness change one's behavior?
> *Talking Points for Your Discussion*
> - Toward God
> - Toward fellow believers
> - Toward unbelievers

Conclusion

A. The Power of the New Covenant

The restoration promised in today's text began with the return of exiles and the rebuilding of the temple. But the promised restoration was not fully inaugurated until the coming of Jesus in the first century AD. Hebrews 8 establishes that the promises of Jeremiah 31:31-34 are fulfilled in Jesus, our high priest.

When we put today's text alongside Romans 4:16; 9:6-8, we see the old covenant being replaced by a new one—a covenant based not on law and physical ancestry but on faith in the one whose death paid the price for our sins: Jesus Christ. This expands the covenant people to include potentially every person regardless of ancestry, nationality, etc. It was possible for "a stranger" to be included under the old covenant (Exodus 12:48, 49; Numbers 15:13-16; etc.), but the division between Israelite and non-Israelite was still there. A power of the new covenant is to tear down that barrier (Ephesians 2:14). All are welcome!

B. Prayer

Father, thank You for the new covenant we have in Christ! By His sacrifice we experience daily forgiveness. You have transformed our wills and minds to Yours, and we are grateful. May we love You with the entirety of our being. We pray in Christ's name, amen.

C. Thought to Remember

May God's law be written on our hearts.

INVOLVEMENT LEARNING

Enhance your lesson with KJV Bible Student *(from your curriculum supplier) and the reproducible activity page (at www.standardlesson.com or in the back of the* KJV Standard Lesson Commentary Deluxe Edition*).*

Into the Lesson

On the board write the following in large letters:

CTRL-Z

Ask the class if those letters look familiar. Have someone explain what they mean.

Say, "Those familiar with computers will know that the letters stand for a computer shortcut for an 'undo' command. When the Control and Z keys are pressed at the same time, the last change a user made is reversed. A typo disappears. An accidentally deleted address is restored. An altered photograph is changed to its original state." After discussing the value of an "undo" command on a computer, ask learners to tell of a time they wished they had had an "undo" command for a life situation.

Alternative. Download and distribute copies of the "Out with the Old" activity. Ask students to complete it individually or in pairs.

After either activity, lead into Bible study by saying, "We all have experienced times when we wished we could do something over again or take back words spoken in haste. Although we cannot undo the past, the prophet Jeremiah spoke of a 'do-over' that God would grant His people."

Into the Word

Divide the class into an equal number of pairs or small groups. Instruct each group to read what Jeremiah said in today's text and write a brief summary as though they were TV news reporters. Half of the groups are to focus on the bad news in his words, and the other half are to focus on the good news. The bad news groups should mention the coming exile and why it will happen. The good news groups should talk about God's promise to sow seeds and replant after the exile, along with His promise of a new covenant.

Below are some possible contents of the reports. Use parts of these as hints for groups that have a hard time getting started.

Bad News Report—*In his speech today, the prophet Jeremiah had more gloomy predictions about what God is going to do to this nation. Using images of God's plucking up, tearing down, destroying, and bringing disaster, Jeremiah let the audience know that they could expect terrible times ahead. He reminded them of how they had broken the covenant. Using some proverbs, Jeremiah said that the people had no one to blame but themselves.*

Good News Report—*In his speech today, Jeremiah seemed determined to lift everyone's spirits with his encouraging words about a hopeful future. Even though God will punish the nation and tear it down, there is a day coming when He will rebuild and replant. God will also replace the old covenant written on stones with a covenant written on hearts. It will be a time when God's people will be just that in the fullest sense.*

Ask for volunteers to read their reports as a TV news reporter would.

Into Life

Lead a discussion on the new covenant by asking these questions: (1) What is it about us humans that just knowing what we should do to please God is not enough to help us do it? (2) Why is the new covenant more helpful than the old? (3) How does God's gift of the Holy Spirit make a difference? (4) In what ways was your life changed for the better since you became a Christian?

Distribute tiny heart-stickers and suggest that class members affix them in places where they will serve as frequent reminders of having been given a new heart; such places may include a mirror used daily, the edge of a computer screen, the case of a smartphone, etc.

Alternative. Distribute copies of the reproducible page activity "In with the New." This can serve as a homework assignment to help class members review the differences between the old and new covenants.

MEDIATOR OF THE NEW COVENANT

DEVOTIONAL READING: Psalm 66
BACKGROUND SCRIPTURE: Hebrews 12:14, 15, 18-29; Psalm 66

HEBREWS 12:14, 15, 18-29

14 Follow peace with all men, and holiness, without which no man shall see the Lord:

15 Looking diligently lest any man fail of the grace of God; lest any root of bitterness springing up trouble you, and thereby many be defiled.

. . . .

18 For ye are not come unto the mount that might be touched, and that burned with fire, nor unto blackness, and darkness, and tempest,

19 And the sound of a trumpet, and the voice of words; which voice they that heard intreated that the word should not be spoken to them any more:

20 (For they could not endure that which was commanded, And if so much as a beast touch the mountain, it shall be stoned, or thrust through with a dart:

21 And so terrible was the sight, that Moses said, I exceedingly fear and quake:)

22 But ye are come unto mount Sion, and unto the city of the living God, the heavenly Jerusalem, and to an innumerable company of angels,

23 To the general assembly and church of the firstborn, which are written in heaven, and to God the Judge of all, and to the spirits of just men made perfect,

24 And to Jesus the mediator of the new covenant, and to the blood of sprinkling, that speaketh better things than that of Abel.

25 See that ye refuse not him that speaketh. For if they escaped not who refused him that spake on earth, much more shall not we escape, if we turn away from him that speaketh from heaven:

26 Whose voice then shook the earth: but now he hath promised, saying, Yet once more I shake not the earth only, but also heaven.

27 And this word, Yet once more, signifieth the removing of those things that are shaken, as of things that are made, that those things which cannot be shaken may remain.

28 Wherefore we receiving a kingdom which cannot be moved, let us have grace, whereby we may serve God acceptably with reverence and godly fear:

29 For our God is a consuming fire.

KEY VERSES

Wherefore we receiving a kingdom which cannot be moved, let us have grace, whereby we may serve God acceptably with reverence and godly fear: for our God is a consuming fire. —**Hebrews 12:28, 29**

COVENANT WITH GOD

Unit 3: An Everlasting Covenant

LESSONS 10–13

LESSON AIMS

After participating in this lesson, each learner will be able to:

1. State the meaning and significance of the word *mediator*.

2. Explain how and why the believers' approach to God in the Old Testament era differs from the believers' approach to Him in the New.

3. Explain Jesus' role as mediator to one unbeliever in the week ahead.

LESSON OUTLINE

Introduction

A. In the Presence of Greatness

At one time or another, we wonder what it would be like to meet a great figure of the past. What would it be like to have breakfast with Abraham Lincoln during America's Civil War? How would we react in the presence of Winston Churchill or Catherine the Great?

Chances are, such meetings would not be as pleasant as we would like them to be! After all, why would such leaders even acknowledge us? The only way such a meeting could happen (aside from solving the issue of time travel!) is if someone were to take us into the presence of such greatness.

At Mount Sinai to approach God was forbidden (see lesson 6). To that scenario we contrast the era of the new heaven and earth, when believers are welcomed into God's presence. Even now, we are encouraged to "come boldly unto the throne of grace" (Hebrews 4:16). Something significant has changed that allows us into God's presence.

B. Lesson Background

We do not know who wrote the book of Hebrews. One reason for this uncertainty is that the book, unlike most biblical letters, does not begin by identifying the author. Some Bible students think Paul wrote Hebrews. Various similarities between Hebrews and Galatians, one of Paul's letters, are seen to lend support to this proposal. One such similarity is the subject of this lesson: the contrast of Mount Sinai with the heavenly Jerusalem (see Galatians 4:24-26).

There is less uncertainty regarding the original intended audience of the book of Hebrews: Christians of Jewish background who, in the face of persecution and doubt, wanted to abandon the church and return to the synagogue. By the time we get to the text of today's lesson, the author of Hebrews has painted the consequences for such a decision in stark terms: there is no escape for those who reject the Christian message of salvation (Hebrews 2:3). Forsaking the blessings of the Christian life (such as the Holy Spirit) leaves one with no options for repentance and restoration to God (6:4-6).

The bottom line is not that the old covenant is bad; rather, it is that the old covenant is obsolete, having been superseded by a better covenant (Hebrews 8:13). And this new covenant did not arise from thin air. The Christian covenant was prophesied in the Old Testament (Hebrews 8:7-12, which quotes Jeremiah 31:31-34; see lesson 11).

The author of Hebrews uses vivid word pictures to support his points. The function of the Word of God is compared with that of a sword (Hebrews 4:12). Christian teachings are likened to categories of milk and meat (5:12-14). The Christian life is compared with a foot race (12:1). Worship is described as a "sacrifice of praise" (13:15). Our lesson today relies on the imagination of the reader to picture Mount Sinai at the time of the reception of the law. It was a place of terrifying thunder and lightning and of a supernatural trumpet blast that caused the people to tremble. The mountain was filled with smoke and fire, and it shook violently (Exodus 19:16-19; lesson 6). This filled the hearts of the people with fear. We must keep this unique, awe-inspiring event from Israel's past in mind as we engage our lesson this week.

I. The Terrifying Mountain
(Hebrews 12:14, 15, 18-21)
A. Peace and Holiness (vv. 14, 15)

14. Follow peace with all men, and holiness, without which no man shall see the Lord.

The context of Hebrews shines clearly here, for *peace* is a reference to the Jewish concept of *shalom*, a peace that results in personal well-being. The original readers of the book, having come from a Jewish background, are well acquainted with this idea. This is not a peace in which hostilities are merely paused. Rather, differences and disputes have been resolved and laid aside for good.

The Old Testament teaches that this kind of peace ultimately comes from God (Numbers 6:26; Psalm 29:11). But the author knows that our behavior influences that of others; therefore, he couples the admonition for *peace with all men* to a call for *holiness*. This means we are to live lives that are above reproach so that we represent our holy God faithfully to our family and neighbors.

> **What Do You Think?**
> What are some things you can do to foster peace with others?
> *Talking Points for Your Discussion*
> - To repair a broken peace
> - To maintain an existing peace
> - Considering Matthew 10:34-36

If the context of Hebrews is that of Jewish Christians leaving the church to return to the synagogue, then we can understand the urgency of these words. There has been a church split. It is likely that bitter words and accusations have been traded. The author reminds everyone that peace and holiness are central teachings in both old and new covenants. Without holiness, one cannot *see the Lord* (compare Matthew 5:8; 1 Peter 1:15, 16, quoting Leviticus 11:44, 45; 19:2). There is no justification for ungodly actions.

> **What Do You Think?**
> How will God see holiness in you daily?
> *Talking Points for Your Discussion*
> - At times when only He can see you
> - At times when others are watching as well

15. Looking diligently lest any man fail of the grace of God; lest any root of bitterness springing up trouble you, and thereby many be defiled.

The author's concern, is reinforced by a warning. It is embarrassing to witness callous and angry behavior within the church. When attitudes and actions of Christians are founded on *bitterness* rather than holiness, the method and mission of the church is damaged. When we think we are upholding godly standards in a strong and confident manner, we actually may be hindering the church's message of *the grace of God*.

◆ Peace with Others ◆

I met a new believer who had experienced a huge life transformation when she came to know the Lord. Her newfound faith grew, and she became involved in the children's program at her church. Her enthusiasm spread to other members of the congregation.

Somewhere along the way, she began having conflicts with the minister. He had different ideas about ministry, and the new believer's ideas and enthusiasm clashed with his. One afternoon she vented her frustrations to me regarding how he wouldn't allow innovation and change.

I empathized with her. I was young and enthusiastic myself and understood the frustration of feeling stifled in my excitement for service. However, I also understood that the conflict was simply a matter of perspective.

At one point in the conversation, the woman confided that she might leave that church and attend another one. "That might be a good idea, but you'll need to come to some peace with him eventually since you'll be spending eternity together in Heaven," I replied. "You don't want to be stuck around someone you didn't get along with here on earth!"

I was half joking, but I could see that my point hit home. She smiled as she realized that though they had differing opinions about how to serve Jesus, they still loved the same God, who wants His children to get along.　　　—L. M. W.

B. Burning and Blasting (vv. 18, 19)

18a. For ye are not come unto the mount that might be touched.

The author now turns to one of his last major illustrations from the Old Testament: the setting of the giving of the law at Mount Sinai. That event is burned into the collective memories of his readers of Jewish background, since the giving of the law marked the nation of Israel distinct from all other nations. There is no event more cherished in the heart of a devout Jew than this one.

The author of Hebrews describes Mount Sinai in ways that parallel Old Testament depictions in Exodus 19 and Deuteronomy 5. For one thing, the mountain *might be touched* (Exodus 19:12). That indicates the mountain was real, not a mythical creation. Scholars today debate the location of Mount Sinai, but most recognize Jebel Musa (Arabic for "Mount Moses") in the Egyptian Sinai Peninsula as the site.

18b. And that burned with fire, nor unto blackness, and darkness, and tempest.

The author also recalls atmospheric phenomena: darkness, dense cloud cover, and storminess, including thunder and lightning, characterized the day (Exodus 19:16a). The stormy darkness was pierced by the descent of the Lord in fire accompanied by thick smoke that covered the mountain (19:18).

19. And the sound of a trumpet, and the voice of words; which voice they that heard intreated that the word should not be spoken to them any more.

The sound of a trumpet signaled the descent of the Lord to the top of Mount Sinai. That blast of sound was not a fanfare from a human trumpeter hiding in the rocks. Exodus 19:19 describes it as a single long blast that grew louder and louder. We are left to imagine that this was from the horn of an angelic trumpeter having inexhaustible lung capacity (see Revelation 8:6).

The trumpet blast was accompanied by *the voice* of the Lord (Exodus 19:19; compare Revelation 1:10). What this sounded like is not described. But it struck terror into the hearts of the people, so much so that they begged for it to stop (see Deuteronomy 5:23-27).

C. Fear and Quaking (vv. 20, 21)

20, 21. (For they could not endure that which was commanded, and if so much as a beast touch the mountain, it shall be stoned, or thrust through with a dart: And so terrible was the sight, that Moses said, I exceedingly fear and quake:).

The author elaborates on the terror that beset the people of Israel at Mount Sinai. First, there was a fear of physical well being, because to *touch the mountain* meant death. The consequence extended even to livestock. If a cow or lamb wandered too close and made contact with Mount Sinai, the people had to kill it. That represented a loss of high value to the owner, given the remote location in the desert of Sinai.

Second, *Moses* himself was cowed by what he witnessed. We should not forget that Moses was called to ascend this mountain of terror in short order (Exodus 19:20). We honor him for his fortitude in various situations as leader of the Israelites.

Yet even Moses, among the greatest of the Jewish heroes, was afraid on this occasion.

II. The Blessed Mountain
(HEBREWS 12:22-29)
A. Heavenly Jerusalem (vv. 22-24)

22. But ye are come unto mount Sion, and unto the city of the living God, the heavenly Jerusalem, and to an innumerable company of angels.

The author turns to another mountain, a metaphorical peak that represents the realities of the Christian life and system: *mount Sion* (usually spelled Zion). It is not a remote desert crag. Rather, it is a *city,* a place where people live. As the location *of the living God,* it is the Lord's permanent presence, not a place of temporary visitation as was Sinai. It is a *heavenly* place, not found on the earth at the end of any highway or sea voyage. It is *Jerusalem,* the site of God's perfect temple. It is populated by *an innumerable company of angels,* heavenly beings we would expect to find there.

The book of Revelation elaborates on the idea of a *heavenly Jerusalem,* there called "new Jerusalem" (Revelation 3:12; 21:2). The city descends onto a mountain, much like the Lord's descent to Mount Sinai (21:10). The presence of the Lord results in a perfect temple for worship (21:22). Heaven is full of the hosts of God's angels offering worship to the Lord (5:11).

23. To the general assembly and church of the firstborn, which are written in heaven, and to God the Judge of all, and to the spirits of just men made perfect.

This is no dreamworld in the sky, but a reality for the author and his readers. His blessed mountain is seen in the *church,* a community made up

HOW TO SAY IT

Deuteronomy	Due-ter-*ahn*-uh-me.
Galatians	Guh-*lay*-shunz.
Haggai	*Hag*-eye or *Hag*-ay-eye.
Jebel Musa	*Jeh*-buhl *Moo*-suh.
Sinai	*Sigh*-nye or *Sigh*-nay-eye.
synagogue	*sin*-uh-gog.

of those whose names are *written in heaven,* in the book of life (Philippians 4:3; Revelation 21:27). *God the Judge of all* controls this book. His judgments are absolute and final; therefore, a name in this book is the assurance of salvation (compare Revelation 3:5; 13:8; 17:8).

Jesus Christ, *the firstborn,* is the preeminent person in God's plans (Colossians 1:15, 18). Since Christians are made holy by His atonement (Hebrews 2:11), we are *the church of the firstborn.* Our names are in the book, for we are judged *just,* even *perfect,* through the sacrificial work of Christ (see Hebrews 10:14; 11:40).

What Do You Think?
Of the images in verses 22, 23 contrasting the Christian's destination with Mount Sinai, which is most significant to you? Why?

Talking Points for Your Discussion
- City of the living God, heavenly Jerusalem
- Company of angels
- The firstborn
- Spirits made perfect

24. And to Jesus the mediator of the new covenant, and to the blood of sprinkling, that speaketh better things than that of Abel.

Jesus must be the central focus of this spiritual mountain of the church because he has mediated *the new covenant.* Without His atoning sacrifice, there would be no new covenant, and the Jewish Christians might as well return to the synagogue.

The author leaves the Sinai illustration momentarily to reconsider Abel (Genesis 4:10), already mentioned in Hebrews 11, the book's Faith Hall of Fame chapter. There it is said of righteous Abel that "being dead yet speaketh," his offering having been declared "more excellent" (Hebrews 11:4). Even so, this voice from the old covenant cannot compare with the once-for-all sacrifice of Christ (Hebrews 9:26; compare 1 Peter 3:18).

Both Jesus and Abel lost their lives at the hands of those who had evil intent (Luke 24:7; 1 John 3:12). But the shedding of Jesus' blood is infinitely more valuable than that of Abel or of all animals ever sacrificed (see Hebrews 9:11–10:18).

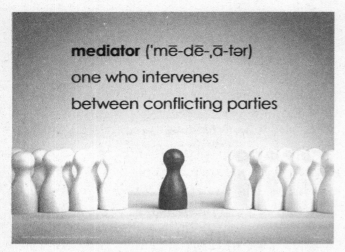

mediator (ˈmē-dē-ˌā-tər)
one who intervenes
between conflicting parties

Visual for Lesson 12. *Start a discussion by pointing to this visual as you ask your learners to give synonyms for the word* mediator.

◆ A MEDIATOR MAKES A DIFFERENCE ◆

While living overseas, I sometimes had trouble understanding the language in the community where I lived. This became painfully evident one day when I received a notice that a package awaited me at the post office. I went there and handed the notice to the clerk. She pushed a form back at me and muttered something incomprehensible. I asked her to repeat it. She sighed impatiently and did so. I finally understood she wanted me to write something. I did my best to transcribe her words while she became frustrated. She eventually gave me my package and sent me on my way.

The next time I received notice of a package, my trip to the post office was made with more reluctance. When I opened the door, the same clerk caught sight of me and yelled for me to go away! I did so but returned with an interpreter.

That encounter went smoothly. The clerk, if not kind, was at least polite. The presence of a mediator made a huge difference in her attitude toward me. Christians can approach God without fear of being told to go away! And we don't have to go in search of a mediator—He's right here. See 1 Timothy 2:5.   —L. M. W.

B. Inescapable God (vv. 25-27)

25. See that ye refuse not him that speaketh. For if they escaped not who refused him that spake on earth, much more shall not we escape,

if we turn away from him that speaketh from heaven.

The author's plea takes on a heightened urgency as he moves toward a conclusion. Don't be stubborn, he warns. There was no escape from the terrifying voice of God at Mount Sinai; there can be no escape for those who reject the message of salvation through Jesus (see Hebrews 2:2-4). This is the current and eternal voice *from heaven*. To leave the church and turn back to the synagogue is a foolish choice with eternally grave consequences.

> *What Do You Think?*
> How can we guard against becoming resistant to God's Word?
> *Talking Points for Your Discussion*
> - During times of triumph
> - During times of distress

26a. Whose voice then shook the earth: but now he hath promised, saying.

The author recalls the Sinai experience a final time, now focusing on the quaking of the mountain (Exodus 19:18). Those who witnessed the event had confirmation of God's powerful visitation to the earth. The shaking of the earth is used frequently in the Bible as a confirmation of the Lord's presence (examples: Judges 5:4, 5; Psalm 18:7).

26b. Yet once more I shake not the earth only, but also heaven.

The quaking at Sinai serves as the writer's launching point for quoting Haggai 2:6. This is a prophetic promise that, unlike at Sinai, a future shaking will include *heaven* as well as *the earth*. The setting of the book of Haggai is 520 BC, the year the rebuilding of the Jerusalem temple was completed. The author of Hebrews uses the promised shaking to confirm the superiority of the Christian claims since the shaking is associated with "the desire of all nations" coming and filling "this house with glory" (Haggai 2:7). In Christ, we are not dealing with a mere system of laws directed at a single people group of the earth, but with an eternal system that encompasses *not the earth only, but also heaven* (compare Revelation 6:14).

27. And this word, Yet once more, signifieth the removing of those things that are shaken,

as of things that are made, that those things which cannot be shaken may remain.

Hebrews uses the full prophetic import of Haggai's words to arrive at the conclusion of this argument. The prophet's words indicate yet again a finality to God's visitations. The Jewish system is built on things that can be shaken, meaning they are temporary (compare Matthew 27:51). The old system is obsolete, and its elements are no longer valid. Christians, by contrast, have a system that *cannot be shaken* because its constituent parts are eternal. The centerpiece is the eternal, perfect, "once for all" sacrifice of Christ (Hebrews 10:10). This is the visitation of God that marks "the end of the world" (9:26) and starts the countdown to the future return of Christ in glory.

C. Godly Fear (vv. 28, 29)

28, 29. Wherefore we receiving a kingdom which cannot be moved, let us have grace, whereby we may serve God acceptably with reverence and godly fear: For our God is a consuming fire.

Having concluded his resounding argument that only Christians are in a right relationship with God, the author moves to application. Since our kingdom, the church, is impervious to any quaking or disruption, we should appreciate our situation with *grace.* We can learn something from the people of Israel who were overwhelmed by the majesty of the Lord's presence: that "something" is to come before Him *acceptably with reverence* as we commit to serve Him. The Greek word behind the word *serve* is translated "worship" elsewhere (example: Acts 24:14), and both senses are here. We worship God when we serve Him.

For Hebrews, serving God must be done with the proper attitude. He describes this as *reverence and godly fear.* This is reinforced by a dire warning: *God is a consuming fire.* This warning is borrowed from Moses himself (Deuteronomy 4:24) and serves to remind the readers that Christians worship the same God who visited Israel at Mount Sinai. Christians are the beneficiary of a superior relationship to God based on the mediating work of Christ (Hebrews 9:15; 12:24), but they do not serve a different God.

Therefore, he ends where he began this section, the picture of the Bible's fiery, powerful, awe-inspiring God (see Hebrews 12:18). We should never take God's grace as a sign of weakness. He is still "Judge of all" (Hebrews 12:23), and when He judges, His verdicts are swift and sure.

What Do You Think?
How should the fact that "God is a consuming fire" affect the way we live?
Talking Points for Your Discussion
- Given that God is merciful (Deuteronomy 4:31)
- Given that God is a shield (Psalm 84:11)
- Given that God is love (1 John 4:16)

Conclusion
A. Two Mountains

Isaiah 2:2 looks forward to the day when "the mountain of the Lord's house shall be established . . . and all nations shall flow unto it." What a glorious promise! There will be a single place of worship that will unite believers of all nations in their service to the one true God.

But which mountain is this? Is it Mount Sinai, the place of terror, the place of law? Or is it the mountain John sees in Revelation 21, a great high peak that has new Jerusalem dropped onto its top (Revelation 21:10)?

Hebrews points us to this second mountain and does not require us to wait for it. It is available now. God shook the earth when He gave the law. When Jesus died and then broke the bonds of death, God shook earth and Heaven. The old is passed away, for God has made all things new (Revelation 21:5). Let us go to the new mountain, the kingdom that will not be shaken.

B. Prayer

Lord of fire and earthquakes, Lord of light and truth, may we never forget Your power or Your grace. May we serve You with holiness and reverence. We pray in the name of Jesus; amen.

C. Thought to Remember

God's grace is not an absence of holiness.

INVOLVEMENT LEARNING

Enhance your lesson with KJV Bible Student *(from your curriculum supplier) and the reproducible activity page (at www.standardlesson.com or in the back of the* KJV Standard Lesson Commentary Deluxe Edition*).*

Into the Lesson

Before class, write this on the board: *I would love to meet [name of famous person of the past or present], but I don't know if I could handle it.*

As students arrive, point to this statement and ask them to think of how they would complete it.

After everyone has arrived and had a chance to consider the statement, ask for responses. Ask each respondent to give reasons for wanting to meet that famous person, but focus on why he or she would be nervous to do so. Encourage responders to identify feelings of awe, inadequacy, intimidation, etc. After a few responses, ask if anything could be done to make the encounter less frightening.

Alternative. Download and distribute copies of the "Awesome Kings" activity from the reproducible page. Have students work individually or in pairs.

After either activity, lead into Bible study by saying, "There have been great and powerful figures in history. We know of impressive people in our own time. But being in the presence of such a person will pale in comparison to what it will be like to meet the Lord face-to-face. How can we expect to do that?"

Into the Word

Say, "The Bible often speaks of mountains and associates certain ones with great acts of God. When we think about it, the size and majesty of mountains make them logical places to associate with God's greatness and power. In our Bible text today, two very different mountain experiences are described."

On the board write these two headings:

Terrible Mountain   Blessed Mountain

Divide the class into two teams, assigning each team one of the two mountains. Ask each team to choose a recorder to write on the board.

When recorders are ready at the board, the other members of both teams should read Hebrews 12:18-29 silently. Each group should work with its recorder to list as many descriptions of its mountain that are mentioned or implied in the text. Possible lists may contain descriptions such as these:

Terrible Mountain—*burning with fire, darkness, death, earthshaking, quaking fear, tempest, terrifying voice, untouchable*

Blessed Mountain—*church of the firstborn, city of the living God, grace, heavenly Jerusalem, innumerable angels, names written in Heaven, reverence and godly fear, people made perfect, unmovable kingdom*

After group work is complete, note that both mountains describe the presence of God. Ask the class to find a single word in verse 24 that explains the blessed difference. If no one says "mediator," be sure to steer them in that direction. Have learners find synonyms to construct a definition of that word. They may think of words such as *arbiter, fixer, broker, moderator, conciliator, go-between, intercessor,* etc. The constructed definition should be along the lines of "someone who brings conflicting parties together."

Into Life

Have someone read 1 Timothy 2:5 aloud. Then ask, "How is Jesus especially qualified to represent you before God?" If learners are slow to respond, give a hint to think in terms of Jesus' *person* (who He is in His being) and *work* (what He did). After some discussion have students pair off and role-play how one of them as a believer would share with the other, an unbeliever, about the benefits of having Jesus as our mediator.

Alternative. Pass out copies of the "Awesome Mediator" activity from the reproducible page. Ask students to pair off and discuss what approach they would use with each individual.

REMEMBERING THE COVENANT

DEVOTIONAL READING: Colossians 1:9-20
BACKGROUND SCRIPTURE: 1 Corinthians 11; Jude 3

1 CORINTHIANS 11:23-34

23 For I have received of the Lord that which also I delivered unto you, That the Lord Jesus the same night in which he was betrayed took bread:

24 And when he had given thanks, he brake it, and said, Take, eat: this is my body, which is broken for you: this do in remembrance of me.

25 After the same manner also he took the cup, when he had supped, saying, This cup is the new testament in my blood: this do ye, as oft as ye drink it, in remembrance of me.

26 For as often as ye eat this bread, and drink this cup, ye do shew the Lord's death till he come.

27 Wherefore whosoever shall eat this bread, and drink this cup of the Lord, unworthily, shall be guilty of the body and blood of the Lord.

28 But let a man examine himself, and so let him eat of that bread, and drink of that cup.

29 For he that eateth and drinketh unworthily, eateth and drinketh damnation to himself, not discerning the Lord's body.

30 For this cause many are weak and sickly among you, and many sleep.

31 For if we would judge ourselves, we should not be judged.

32 But when we are judged, we are chastened of the Lord, that we should not be condemned with the world.

33 Wherefore, my brethren, when ye come together to eat, tarry one for another.

34 And if any man hunger, let him eat at home; that ye come not together unto condemnation. And the rest will I set in order when I come.

KEY VERSE

This cup is the new testament in my blood: this do ye, as oft as ye drink it, in remembrance of me.

—1 Corinthians 11:25

Covenant with God

Unit 3: An Everlasting Covenant

LESSONS 10–13

LESSON AIMS

After participating in this lesson, each learner will be able to:

1. Identify what is to be remembered when observing the Lord's Supper.

2. Explain Jesus' identification of His body and blood with the bread and cup, respectively.

3. Create and implement a personal strategy for self-examination during the Lord's Supper.

LESSON OUTLINE

Introduction

A. Sights, Sounds, Smells

The tang of hot apple cider, the crunch of leaves under our feet, and the sight of a pumpkin may instantly transport us back to our childhood. The scent of pine needles and peppermints, the sounds of sleigh bells, and a cold wind on our faces communicate a season of the year to us without a word's being spoken. The sound of surf and the feeling of sand between our toes are all we need to think about summer. Earthy smells of freshly tilled gardens and the sound of bird songs bring us into springtime. We may not remember the exact same events that another might when having those senses teased, but we remember.

Memories are triggered by our senses. So that we never forget what Jesus has done, He has given us a sensory experience that helps us remember.

B. Lesson Background

The church in Corinth was started by Paul on his second missionary journey in the early AD 50s, barely 20 years after the death and resurrection of Christ. Corinth was not a center of renowned culture like Athens, but a city of hard-working folks from many backgrounds. It had a Jewish community, and it is here that Paul met Aquila and Priscilla (Prisca), Jews who had come from Rome and were running a tent-making business (Acts 18:2, 3). Paul, Aquila, and Priscilla worked together in other venues (see Acts 18:18; compare Romans 16:3; 1 Corinthians 16:19; 2 Timothy 4:19).

The Corinthian church was a rambunctious and troubled group. It had problems with factionalism, immorality, rivalry, divorce, and false doctrine. Despite its troubles, though, the church in Corinth had a throbbing vibrancy and dynamism that shone through its mistakes. It had a large place in Paul's heart. He started the congregation and saw it through its birth pains, left and returned for at least one visit, and wrote two substantial letters to help it sort out problems (1 and 2 Corinthians). The trials of the Corinthians that caused Paul to write become a blessing to us, for we are able to see how the great apostle dealt with difficult issues in a godly and inspired way.

At the heart of the problems in Corinth was a disrespect that some members had for other members. This lack of concern caused a crisis in the way they practiced the Lord's Supper. Understanding the way the Corinthians met for worship will give context to today's lesson text.

First, the weekly meeting of the Corinthian church was likely on what we would call Saturday evening. In Jewish reckoning, one day ended and a new day began when the sun went down. The first day of the week, Sunday, therefore began on our Saturday night. The Corinthian church probably chose to meet in the evening because many of its members worked (some were slaves) and could not gather during the day.

Second, the Corinthians observed the Lord's Supper each week as part of their worship service. It would not be overstatement to say that this was the central part of their time together. Churches today celebrate the Lord's Supper with differing frequency and importance, but for these ancient Christians it was central and weekly. This makes Paul's comments about the Lord's Supper very important, and this centrality causes it to be a reflection of deeper spiritual and social currents within the congregation.

Third, the Corinthian Lord's Supper was in the context of a fellowship meal. They did not have the option of tiny plastic cups or individual wafers purchased from the Christian supply house in Corinth. Rather, they used bread and wine that was a normal part of meals. How this worked, exactly, we do not know, but it created problems. Apparently the meal began before everyone arrived, and sometimes there was no food left by the time they did arrive (1 Corinthians 11:17-22). This produced an awkward atmosphere of disrespect that belied the message of unity that should have been at the core of remembering Christ in community.

HOW TO SAY IT

Aquila	*Ack*-wih-luh.
Corinthians	Ko-*rin*-thee-unz (*th* as in *thin*).
Galatians	Guh-*lay*-shunz.
Jeremiah	Jair-uh-*my*-uh.
Pilate	*Pie*-lut.

I. The Meal of Remembrance
(1 CORINTHIANS 11:23-26)
A. The Broken Bread (vv. 23, 24)

23. For I have received of the Lord that which also I delivered unto you, That the Lord Jesus the same night in which he was betrayed took bread.

At the Jerusalem Conference (Acts 15) Paul had contact with most of the original apostles, so any of them could have told Paul about what happened the *night in which* Jesus *was betrayed*. However, Paul notes that he received his information *of the Lord*. This agrees with what Paul tells the Galatians about having received his message by direct revelation from Jesus Christ (Galatians 1:12).

Paul frames the last supper in an unexpected way. He does not say it takes place the night before Jesus' crucifixion, but on the night he was betrayed. The memory of Judas's betrayal is strong (see Mark 3:19). That was an epic night, a night remembered for many things. It was Jesus' last night on earth before His death, and it set in motion a chain of events that changed the course of history.

Paul's recounting of the last supper begins with a simple loaf of bread. It is likely that this was unleavened Passover bread (Luke 22:15), something like the matzo bread used by Jewish people today.

24. And when he had given thanks, he brake it, and said, Take, eat: this is my body, which is broken for you: this do in remembrance of me.

Paul relates that Jesus gave *thanks* over the bread. The Greek word for "give thanks" is *eucharisteo,* and this is why some Christian traditions refer to the Lord's Supper as the Eucharist. It is appropriate that when we observe the Lord's Supper, we remember to give thanks to God for the sacrifice of Christ that the symbolic meal represents.

The traditional Passover meal features a time when bread is shared. We do not know how closely modern Passover observances reflect practices from the time of Jesus, but the use of unleavened bread is significant because of its connection with the original Passover meal. The exodus from Egypt was a hurried undertaking, so much so that it did not allow for the making of bread that had time to rise from its yeast (Exodus 12:39). Eating unleavened bread is a way for Jewish people to remember their hasty escape from the land of slavery. Jesus transformed this ancient symbol into a new focus of *remembrance*.

> **What Do You Think?**
> Other than *In Remembrance of Me*, what would be some good inscriptions for Communion tables? Why?
>
> *Talking Points for Your Discussion*
> - Inscriptions that focus on Jesus
> - Inscriptions that focus on the participants
> - Other

Jesus himself used the analogy of bread as a representation of His physical body (John 6:51). Using a loaf that can be broken for the Lord's Supper adds to our appreciation of His sacrifice. Jesus was cruelly whipped, was crowned with thorn branches, and had nails driven through His hands and feet. His body was abused. He died after hours of physical agony, and we should not forget this.

B. The Shared Cup (vv. 25, 26)

25. After the same manner also he took the cup, when he had supped, saying, This cup is the new testament in my blood: this do ye, as oft as ye drink it, in remembrance of me.

The modern Passover service has four cups that are shared, each with an important symbolic function. Luke's account of the last supper includes two cups, one that is given thanks over (Luke 22:17) and one that Jesus uses to symbolize the new covenant (22:20). Paul teaches the Corinthians to follow the example of drinking of *the cup* that comes after the breaking of the bread.

This symbol from the last supper is designed to remind us of *blood*. Blood is associated with sacrifice in the Old Testament (Leviticus 9:18). Blood removed from the animal is a sign of death and is associated with making a testament, a binding agreement between two parties. The covenant between God and the Israelites was sealed with a bloody ceremony. The blood used in this was called "the blood of the covenant" (Exodus 24:8).

Jesus' words show His intention to move beyond this earlier agreement at Sinai and inaugurate a new, superior agreement. This is the new covenant prophesied in Jeremiah 31:31. A new relationship is to be established where laws are a matter of the heart (31:33) and where sins are forgiven forever (31:34). Paul teaches that the shedding of Christ's blood is "a propitiation" (Romans 3:25), an acceptable substitute to God for the punishment for sins that we deserve. When we drink the cup of the Lord's Supper, we should remember that Christ's death makes our forgiveness possible. We are not simply remembering our Savior and His death. We are remembering that we are forgiven people, saved by His blood. This is the essence of *the new testament*, meaning the new covenant.

◆ AN EVERLASTING CONNECTION ◆

A traveling replica of the Hebrew tabernacle came to a nearby city. Thinking it would help my children understand the Bible stories they know, I took them to tour the tabernacle.

We donned headphones and listened to a narrator describe the parts of the tabernacle as we walked to the different stations. We saw the altar and threw wood chips on the fire, representing the sacrifice of our lives to God. We lit a lamp to symbolize the light of God in our lives and carried burning sticks of incense representing our prayers.

My youngest daughter and I toured the tabernacle together. I watched her dip matzo bread into the cup and eat it, hearing how the bread that the Hebrews ate symbolized the future sacrifice of Jesus on the cross. Later that night, my little girl told me how she felt close to God when she was in the tabernacle and how listening to the description of the symbols made her feel like she was there in the desert with the Hebrews.

When the Israelites ate the Passover, they remembered their deliverance from Egypt (Deuteronomy 16:2, 3). When we take Communion, we remember our deliverance from sin.—L. M. W.

26. For as often as ye eat this bread, and drink this cup, ye do shew the Lord's death till he come.

We are accustomed to remembering this sacrificial *death* of Christ when we *eat* and *drink* the elements of the Lord's Supper, but Paul adds something more. The meal of remembrance indicates a waiting period. It is necessary until Christ comes again. As we wait, the celebration of the Lord's Supper is a way of showing the central truth of the gospel, which is Jesus' sacrificial death.

The elements of the Lord's Supper speak through actions in powerful and beautiful ways. Rather than just hear words, when we take of the loaf and cup we see, touch, smell, and taste. We share in a way that is visible to all onlookers. The celebration is intended to be done in community, therefore serving as a witness to the unity of the church. Paul knows this is important for the Corinthians. But they seem more focused on divisions than harmony.

What Do You Think?
What can churches do to enhance the sensory impact of the Lord's Supper?
Talking Points for Your Discussion
- Regarding the sense of sight
- Regarding the sense of sound
- Regarding the sense of hearing
- Regarding the sense of taste
- Regarding the sense of touch

II. The Implications of the Meal
(1 CORINTHIANS 11:27-34)
A. Unworthy Participation (v. 27)

27. Wherefore whosoever shall eat this bread, and drink this cup of the Lord, unworthily, shall be guilty of the body and blood of the Lord.

Having rehearsed the origin of the Lord's Supper and explained its meaning, Paul now gives some implications for the participants and the church that hosts it. These serve as warnings for the Corinthians. They have badly distorted the practice (1 Corinthians 11:17-22), and these distortions have serious consequences.

First, Paul warns that those who participate in observing the Lord's Supper must do so in a worthy manner. To participate unworthily is to become guilty of the same type of disrespect for Jesus that fueled the angry mob at His crucifixion. Jesus' self-sacrifice was met with abuse and ridicule. Pilate allowed His death, knowing He was innocent (Luke 23:4; John 19:4). Herod and the soldiers mocked Jesus by dressing him in a royal robe and jamming a crown of thorns on his head (Luke 23:11; John 19:2). The chief priests and the crowd countered Pilate's verdict of innocence with demands to kill Jesus (Luke 23:13-21). The way the Corinthians are observing the Lord's Supper is a mockery in the spirit of those who conspired to kill Jesus. Such unworthy participants do not leave the meal of remembrance with blessings, but with symbolic blood on their hands.

◆ LIFE-GIVING BLOOD ◆

My daughter's fourth-grade teacher uses pet lizards to teach the students about caring for living creatures. Each table in the classroom has its own lizard; my daughter's table has two. One Monday morning, my little girl went into the classroom and headed straight for the lizard cage to check on them after the weekend. She leaned down to inspect him and saw blood smeared on the clear plastic side of the cage! Horrified, she alerted the teacher, who determined that the lizards had been fighting and one was injured.

My daughter was upset. The presence of the blood made the situation even more dangerous than just two arguing lizards. Blood meant a real battle had taken place, and someone had lost! Happily, both lizards survived the ordeal; but whenever I tell that story, someone gasps in horror. The thought of a little girl finding blood, a fight so violent that it drew that blood . . . it all seems more appalling than we are used to hearing about in a fourth-grader's classroom.

The Bible repeatedly uses blood as a symbol of life. Without blood, there is no life, so anything to do with blood evokes a strong reaction in us. And for Christians, blood is a reminder of the importance of the sacrifice of Jesus. The human situation was so dire that it required a sacrifice of blood to redeem it. But there is just one sacrifice, just one battle for our salvation—"through the offering of

the body of Jesus Christ once for all" (Hebrews 10:10).
—L. M. W.

What Do You Think?
What steps can we take to avoid observing the Lord's Supper in an unworthy way?
Talking Points for Your Discussion
- Regarding motives
- Regarding means (time, place, etc.)
- Regarding spiritual preparation

B. Self-Examination (vv. 28, 29)

28, 29. But let a man examine himself, and so let him eat of that bread, and drink of that cup. For he that eateth and drinketh unworthily, eateth and drinketh damnation to himself, not discerning the Lord's body.

How do we properly heed Paul's dire warning? The key is one of self-examination before the time of observing the Lord's Supper arrives. Are we coming with an attitude of humility and thankfulness? Have we looked into our hearts to root out hidden and persistent sin that damages our relationships with the Lord and others?

Failure in self-examination results in failure to discern *the Lord's body.* These words anticipate 1 Corinthians 12:12, where Paul uses the metaphor of a human body to represent the church, Christ's body. This calls the Corinthians to pay attention to the others who are observing in the Lord's Supper with them—their fellow church members. The self-examination Paul demands involves correcting attitudes toward others. The Lord's Supper should remind us of reconciliation. We are all sinners in need of a Savior. We are all forgiven as a result of the same sacrificial death of our Lord. There are no privileged diners at the Lord's table.

What Do You Think?
What are some ways to become more discerning, as that word is used in this context?
Talking Points for Your Discussion
- Prior to corporate worship
- During corporate worship

C. Judging Ourselves (vv. 30-32)

30. For this cause many are weak and sickly among you, and many sleep.

Paul is not speaking here of some magical properties of the elements of the Lord's Supper, as if improper attitudes cause them to become poison that sickens us and brings *sleep* (death). Paul is saying that the entire atmosphere of hostility and disrespect that has overtaken the Corinthians is causing spiritual numbness and alienation. Even more, the stress of this spiritual sickness may be causing physical illness, even premature death. This speaks to the deep dysfunction of this congregation, who were even bringing lawsuits against one another (1 Corinthians 6:7). This must be corrected at the core, at the hostile heart. This is why self-examination must be honest, even brutal.

31, 32. For if we would judge ourselves, we should not be judged. But when we are judged, we are chastened of the Lord, that we should not be condemned with the world.

If we all practice sincere self-judgment, focusing on our own areas that need correction, we are less likely to judge others. Paul says that if such self-judgment leads to self-correction, we avoid the need for Christ to chasten us. Furthermore, such self-judgment will protect us from the eventual judgment of condemnation that Christ will make on the unbelieving world. The time of the Lord's Supper is an ideal opportunity for self-examination and self-judgment in light of the sacrifice of Christ.

What Do You Think?
What self-correction procedures do you find especially noteworthy?
Talking Points for Your Discussion
- In a spiritual sense
- In a physical sense
- In a mental sense

D. Caring for Others (vv. 33, 34)

33, 34. Wherefore, my brethren, when ye come together to eat, tarry one for another. And if any man hunger, let him eat at home; that ye come not together unto condemnation. And the rest will I set in order when I come.

Paul finishes the section with two simple directives to help solve the Corinthians' problems with the Lord's Supper. First, they should *tarry* (wait) until everyone arrives before beginning. This is a matter of mutual respect and concern. Some Corinthians who work on Saturday are not free to come until their work is done. Being impatient with them for that is not a sign of respect.

Second, the expectations of a meal are causing problems, so Paul advises that everyone *eat at home*. We do not know how many people are involved in the Corinthian church, perhaps a couple hundred. For such a group, the logistics of staging a weekly meal are outweighing the benefits. They need to focus on the essentials of the Lord's Supper in order to be able to relish its meaning and power. To be distracted from this risks *condemnation*, a result no one wants.

There seem to be other issues to resolve concerning the Lord's Supper, given Paul's concluding statement that *the rest will I set in order when I come*. But Paul's two directives are the most important correctives for the time being.

The way the Lord's Supper is observed in congregations today varies widely. But the principles behind Paul's directives to the Corinthians are still authoritative: remember what the loaf and cup signify, and respect your fellow participants.

Conclusion

A. Celebrating

I had the honor of sharing the Lord's Supper with an African village congregation a few years ago. This was a very poor community. The church building was a thatched-roof hut with a dirt floor. There were no modern facilities, padded chairs, or technical enhancements as I was accustomed to at home. The worship service was much longer, with energetic singing, multiple sermons, and performances by joyous children's choirs.

At the end, we celebrated the Lord's Supper. It was a little different, with an assortment of glasses and a freshly baked loaf of bread. We took turns coming in an unhurried manner to the little table where the elements sat. The number of glasses for the red juice was insufficient for the people, so

Visual for Lesson 13. *When you arrive at 1 Corinthians 11:24, pose the discussion question associated with it as you point to this visual.*

they were refilled and reused as the service proceeded. People came to the table in groups, often holding hands. Expressions of praise and prayer peppered this time. It took about 30 minutes, much longer than the efficient five-minute celebrations at my church back home!

Yet I felt I was at home. The culture shock for me of being in an African village was great, but the comfort of meeting with fellow believers around the Lord's table outweighed this. Jesus' presence was there too, and I could not help but remember Him and the sacrifice He made for me and for my fellow believers.

The Lord's Supper is a time to remember our new covenant with God, founded on the fact that Christ's death makes forgiveness possible. It is also a time to remember that He did not die for me alone, but for all who come to Him as the New Testament directs. I still see their faces when I come to the table.

B. Prayer

Father, before celebrating the Lord's Supper, may we examine our hearts to clear them of unworthy distractions and disrespect for those with us as we remember the new life we have because of Christ's death. We pray in Jesus' name, amen.

C. Thought to Remember

The Lord's Supper connects us with God and fellow believers.

INVOLVEMENT LEARNING

Enhance your lesson with KJV Bible Student *(from your curriculum supplier) and the reproducible activity page (at www.standardlesson.com or in the back of the* KJV Standard Lesson Commentary Deluxe Edition*).*

Into the Lesson

Before class place the following items in separate sandwich bags: half a lemon; cut onions; paper towel dampened with vinegar; paper towel dampened with ammonia; and paper towel dampened with perfume (or other strong scents of your choice). To begin class, pass the bags around, asking students to sample their aromas. As they do, have them think of any memories a particular scent triggers for them.

Then ask for specific responses. For example, the ammonia might bring back memories of doing household chores as a child. The onions might trigger memories of cookouts. Perfume might bring a specific person to mind.

Say, "Researchers have found that smell is very powerful for triggering memories. Other senses are all memory aids also, especially when combined."

Alternative. Download and distribute copies of the "Getting the Sense of It" reproducible page. Have students work on it in small groups.

After either activity, lead into Bible study by saying, "We are so forgetful sometimes! But our memories are often triggered by our senses—a certain scent, taste, sound, touch, or visual cue. We are never to forget what Jesus has done, so we are given a way to remember Him regularly."

Into the Word

Divide the class into three groups. Each group should act as mentors to a new believer. Using the assigned texts below, each group will answer its person's questions about the Lord's Supper.

Group 1—1 Corinthians 11:23-26

"I'm really new to church, so taking Communion is unfamiliar to me. Why do you do it? How can I be sure I'm doing it the right way?"

Group 2—1 Corinthians 11:27-30

"Last Sunday I heard a verse about not taking Communion in a way that brings condemnation.

What does that mean? How can I make sure I don't do that?"

Group 3—1 Corinthians 11:28, 31-34

"I'm not sure what I'm supposed to be thinking about during the Communion service. I get distracted by the people around me and how they're acting. What do you focus on during that time?"

Encourage groups to prepare a person to ask the question and another to present the group's answers. Possible responses are as follows:

Group 1—*Jesus wants us to remember His death on the cross for us, so He gave us the bread to remind us of His body that was beaten, abused, and pierced. The fruit of the vine reminds us of the blood that flowed from His wounds. Because He took the punishment we deserved, we have been saved by His death and cleansed of our sins. The Lord's Supper is a time to focus your thoughts on Jesus and all He has done for you.*

Group 2—*One way we can be unworthy is if we come to the table with bitterness or ill feeling toward other Christians. That's why we are told to make sure our hearts are right with God. If you are focusing on Jesus and His death on the cross and confess any sinful attitudes toward others, then you will please God.*

Group 3—*I focus on the bread and cup in order to meditate on how much I love Jesus because of His death on the cross for me. I try not to notice other people and what they are doing, as it's more important that I focus on myself and whether or not I am living up to God's expectations.*

Into Life

Set some time aside to plan a special Communion service just for your class. Talk about a time and place for this special remembrance.

Alternative. Distribute copies of the "Getting the Gist of It" activity from the reproducible page. Read through the themes and ask students to share other ways they meditate during Communion time.

FAITH IN ACTION

Special Features

Lessons

Unit 1: The Early Church Proclaims Faith in Christ

Unit 2: A Living Faith in God

Unit 3: Self-Controlled, Upright, and Godly Faith

QUARTERLY QUIZ

Use these questions as a pretest or as a review. The answers are on page iv of This Quarter in the Word.

Lesson 1

1. Which two apostles were present at the healing of the man who couldn't walk? *Acts 3:11*
2. An apostle told the people that they had denied Jesus in the presence of _____. *Acts 3:13*

Lesson 2

1. Sergius Paulus is described as wanting to hear the Word of God. T/F. *Acts 13:7*
2. What punishment did Elymas receive for his actions? (blindness, leprosy, death?) *Acts 13:8, 11*

Lesson 3

1. The man healed at Lystra had never walked. T/F. *Acts 14:8*
2. To what town did Paul go after being stoned in Lystra? (Berea, Derbe, Philippi?) *Acts 14:20*

Lesson 4

1. The wise men asked about the "King of the Jews," for they had seen His _____. (angel, star, miracles?) *Matthew 2:2*
2. The wise men were warned in a dream not to return to King Herod. T/F. *Matthew 2:12*

Lesson 5

1. Paul described himself to the Ephesians as a soldier of the Lord. T/F. *Ephesians 4:1*
2. Paul exhorted the Ephesians to keep the ____ of the Spirit in the bond of peace. *Ephesians 4:3*

Lesson 6

1. Daniel asked that he and his friends be given food other than the king's for _____ days. (7, 10, 12?) *Daniel 1:12*
2. Before what king were Daniel and his friends brought? *Daniel 1:18*

Lesson 7

1. King Darius commanded the furnace be heated hotter than usual. T/F. *Daniel 3:19*

2. The king declared that God had sent His _____ to rescue the three Israelites. *Daniel 3:28*

Lesson 8

1. Daniel confessed that God's people had not listened to His servants the _____. *Daniel 9:6*
2. Daniel prayed that God's anger be turned away from the city of _____. *Daniel 9:16*

Lesson 9

1. The messenger told Daniel that the prince of the kingdom of Persia had withstood the messenger for how many days? (7, 14, 21?) *Daniel 10:13*
2. Who helped the messenger overcome the problem noted above? (Gabriel, Michael, Elijah?) *Daniel 10:13*

Lesson 10

1. In James, which of Abraham's actions illustrate that faith without works is dead? (left home, circumcised, offered Isaac?) *James 2:20, 21*
2. What other example of faith and works does James use? (Joshua, Rahab, Ruth?) *James 2:25*

Lesson 11

1. What does James describe as small yet capable of making great boasts? *James 3:5*
2. James uses both fire and poison to describe the tongue. T/F. *James 3:6, 8*

Lesson 12

1. In what city did Tabitha (or Dorcas) live? (Caesarea, Damascus, Joppa?) *Acts 9:36*
2. Peter stayed in Joppa with Simon, who was a _____. (tanner, tentmaker, weaver?) *Acts 9:43*

Lesson 13

1. Paul told Timothy to fight the good fight of _____. (faith, hope, love?) *1 Timothy 6:12*
2. Before whom was Jesus' "good confession" made? (Herod, Pilate, Cyrus?) *1 Timothy 6:13*

QUARTER AT A GLANCE

by Douglas Redford

MANY COMMON expressions consist of noun pairs that seem to go together naturally. Think of *salt and pepper, cause and effect,* and *macaroni and cheese.* In the Bible, *faith and works* form just such a pair. The lessons for this quarter emphasize how important this combination is for any follower of the Lord. Faith and works go hand in hand in both Old and New Testaments.

Committed Faith

Within the first unit of study is the Christmas story (lesson 4). There we consider anew the account of the wise men, whose faith prompted them to leave home and follow a star to a distant land. Faith in action is also evident in the healing of a man who couldn't walk (lesson 1), in the sending forth of Barnabas and Saul on the first missionary journey (lesson 2), and in the devotion of those same two men in proclaiming the gospel in spite of hardship (lesson 3).

The final lesson of the unit challenges Christians to "keep the unity of the Spirit in the bond of peace" (Ephesians 4:3). Only in an atmosphere of unity can faith result in the action that the head of the church desires.

Courageous Faith

The four lessons of the second unit, all from the book of Daniel, depict bold exercise of faith in the one true God while in a culture hostile to that faith. Whether the issue was objecting to certain food (lesson 6) or refusing to bow down to an idol (lesson 7), the steadfast faith demonstrated by Daniel, Shadrach, Meshach, and Abednego is timeless, relevant for Christians of every place and century. Since our real home is in Heaven, we too are in exile until we arrive there (Philippians 3:20; 1 Peter 1:1; 2:11).

While in exile, we pray. And lesson 8 provides something of a model in that regard. Disciplined,

earnest prayer is foundational to a faith that works. Daniel's confession of sin and plea for mercy speak powerfully to our own situation of exile.

Lesson 9 concludes the unit by examining a rather mysterious vision experienced by Daniel. While some of the vision's details may spark questions, the message is plain: Daniel was to draw strength and hope from believing that God remained in control. So must we.

Consistent Faith

The final unit of studies takes us back to the New Testament. Lessons 10 and 11 are drawn from the especially convicting book of James. This book is small but mighty, an observation that James makes regarding the tongue. The studies from James also call attention to the close link between faith and faithfulness. The author's illustrations undergird his affirmation that "faith without works is dead" (James 2:26). This affirmation also involves a study in contrasts between Abraham (father of the Israelite nation) and Rahab (the prostitute from Jericho).

Also included is the example of Dorcas, who was renowned for her acts of selfless service (lesson 12). The exhortation of Paul to fight the good fight of faith (lesson 13) is pointed at one particu-

> *Only in an atmosphere of unity can faith result in the action that the head of the church desires.*

lar church leader (Timothy), but it also has something to say to all Christians. Cultural animosity has the potential of silencing the church into inaction, but followers of Jesus must resolve to put their faith *in action.* As we affirm that we are justified by faith and not by works (Galatians 2:16), we also acknowledge in the same breath that a faith that does not result in works is a dead faith (James 2:26). So it was and is!

GET THE SETTING

by Mark S. Krause

FAITH: there is nothing more central to being a Christian. We hold that faith is essential to salvation (Hebrews 11:6). Without faith, Christianity would be hollow and strange to us. But what did the first ones to hear the message of the gospel understand by the word *faith*? To what did they compare it in their first-century world?

In the Greco-Roman World

For early Christians who were familiar with Greek literature, *faith* was not necessarily a religious concept. Homer spoke of "oaths of faith," using the word in the sense of loyalty among warriors. Aristotle warned his students to put "no faith in arguments designed to trick the people," using the word in the sense of "depend upon" or "have confidence in"; thus, "don't depend upon tricky arguments." Herodotus warned that barbarians are neither faithful nor true in anything, meaning they were not to be trusted. In the Greek commercial world, one could even use the word *faith* in the sense of "credit."

In the religious sphere, the relationship between people and the deities they worshipped was not based on faith. The pagan gods and goddesses were fickle and untrustworthy, often yielding to selfish desires. Their followers tried to appease them in order to gain some benefit. In order to get a divine boon, it was assumed that the god would have to receive something in return: a pledge, a service, an offering, etc.

In effect, the interaction between mortal and god was one of bargaining rather than that of faith as Christians understand the latter. The relationship was also one of fear, as pagans understood gods and goddesses to be both powerful and capricious. Indeed, some entreaties were for protection by one god from the anger of another god. Any faith involved was in one's own ability to bend the god's will to one's advantage or trust in a priest or priestess who was skilled in such work.

In the Old Testament Era

In the Old Testament, faith is grounded in the fact that God is the faithful one, the one who always keeps His promises and never abandons His covenants. We find many statements like this one: "Know therefore that the Lord thy God, he is God, the *faithful* God, which keepeth covenant and mercy with them that love him and keep his commandments to a thousand generations" (Deuteronomy 7:9).

The importance of the Hebrew word translated *faithful* in that passage is signaled by the fact that it occurs dozens of times in the Old Testament. The fact that it is applied to God as well as people means that God expected faithful behavior and trust from His people because He himself is always faithful. In fact, the Old Testament's first use of this word (translated "believed") is applied to none other than the great hero of faith Abraham, who "believed in the Lord; and he counted it to him for righteousness" (Genesis 15:6).

This statement is so important that it is quoted five times in the New Testament (see Romans 4:3, 9, 22; Galatians 3:6; James 2:23 [lesson 10]). For Abraham to have believed in God meant that that man firmly trusted that God's promises would come about. Hebrews 11 offers a litany of Old Testament faith examples, but the greatest is Abraham, the ultimate ancestor of the Jewish nation.

In the New Testament Era

The Greco-Roman (pagan) bargaining mentality regarding their fictitious deities is easy to dismiss. Yet how many times have we ourselves slipped into this kind of thinking? We find ourselves in a troubling situation, but instead of approaching God in faith, we try to bargain: "O Lord, if You will just get me out of this situation, I promise that I will . . ." God may or may not honor attempts to bargain with Him (compare Numbers 21:1-3). But He always honors faith.

This Quarter in the Word

Mon, Feb. 12	Widow's Son Restored to Life	1 Kings 17:17-24
Tue, Feb. 13	Jesus Raises Widow's Son	Luke 7:11-17
Wed, Feb. 14	Care for Widows and Orphans	James 1:22-27
Thu, Feb. 15	Peter's Healing Ministry	Acts 5:12-16
Fri, Feb. 16	Philip's Preaching Ministry	Acts 8:4-8
Sat, Feb. 17	Aeneas Healed, Residents Turn to God	Acts 9:32-35
Sun, Feb. 18	Calling the Church to Active Service	Acts 9:36-43
Mon, Feb. 19	Timothy Joins Paul's Team	Acts 16:1-5
Tue, Feb. 20	Timothy, an Active Teacher	1 Corinthians 4:14-21
Wed, Feb. 21	Epaphroditus, Paul's Coworker	Philippians 2:25-30
Thu, Feb. 22	Timothy, Paul's Envoy	1 Thessalonians 3:1-10
Fri, Feb. 23	Teach the Sound Words of Christ	1 Timothy 6:2b-8
Sat, Feb. 24	Money, Root of Many Evils	1 Timothy 6:9, 10
Sun, Feb. 25	The Good Fight of Faith	1 Timothy 6:11-21

Mon, Nov. 27	Take Refuge in the Lord	Psalm 118:1-9
Tue, Nov. 28	The Lord, My Strength and Salvation	Psalm 118:10-14
Wed, Nov. 29	A Blessing Promised to All Peoples	Acts 3:22-26
Thu, Nov. 30	Your Faith Saved You	Luke 7:44-50
Fri, Dec. 1	Contrasting Responses	Acts 13:44-49
Sat, Dec. 2	Crippled Beggar Requests Alms	Acts 3:1-10
Sun, Dec. 3	Repent and Believe in Jesus	Acts 3:11-21
Mon, Dec. 4	Joshua Discerned as New Leader	
		Deuteronomy 31:14, 15, 23; 34:9
Tue, Dec. 5	Eli Senses God's Call to Samuel	1 Samuel 3:1-9
Wed, Dec. 6	Test the Spirits	1 John 4:1-6
Thu, Dec. 7	Blind Man Discerns Jesus as Prophet	John 9:13-17
Fri, Dec. 8	Jews First, Then Greeks	Romans 1:8-12, 16, 17
Sat, Dec. 9	Door of Faith Opened to Gentiles	Acts 14:21-28
Sun, Dec. 10	Spirit-Filled Leadership Discernment	Acts 13:1-12
Mon, Dec. 11	Rejoicing While Suffering	Colossians 1:24—2:5
Tue, Dec. 12	Jews and Gentiles Called to Repent	Acts 17:22-33
Wed, Dec. 13	Believing and Suffering in Christ	Philippians 1:27-30
Thu, Dec. 14	Suffering So Others May Be Saved	2 Timothy 2:1-10
Fri, Dec. 15	Consolation When Afflicted	2 Corinthians 1:3-11
Sat, Dec. 16	Speaking Boldly, Forced to Flee	Acts 14:1-7
Sun, Dec. 17	Proclaiming Christ Faithfully	Acts 14:8-11, 19-23

Answers to the Quarterly Quiz on page 114

Lesson 1—1. Peter and John. 2. Pilate. **Lesson 2**—1. true. 2. blindness. **Lesson 3**—1. true. 2. Derbe. **Lesson 4**—1. star. 2. true. **Lesson 5**—1. false. 2. unity. **Lesson 6**—1. 10. 2. Nebuchadnezzar. **Lesson 7**—1. false. 2. angel. **Lesson 8**—1. prophets. 2. Jerusalem. **Lesson 9**—1. 21. 2. Michael. **Lesson 10**—1. offered Isaac. 2. Rahab. **Lesson 11**—1. the tongue. 2. true. **Lesson 12**—1. Joppa. 2. tanner. **Lesson 13**—1. faith. 2. Pilate.

ii

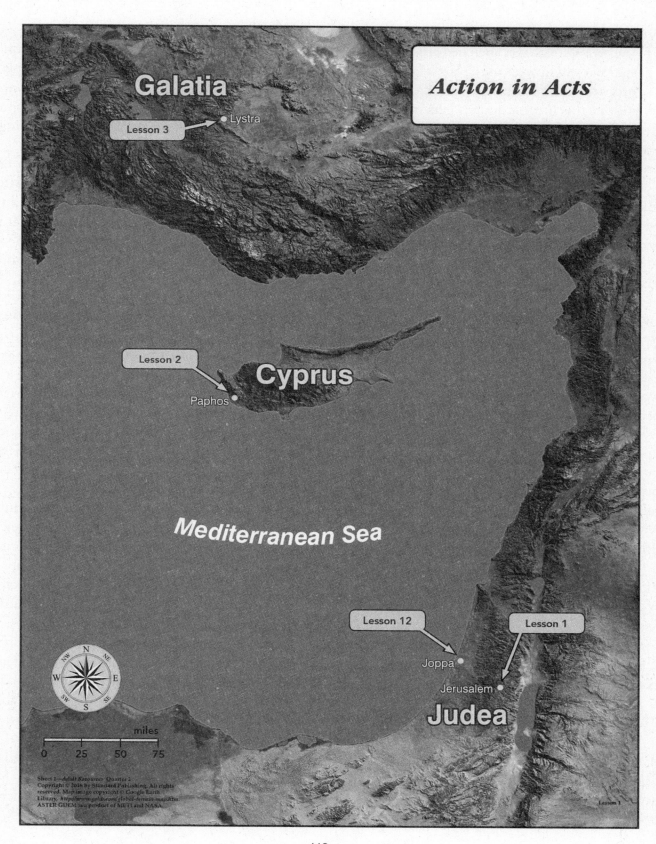

Galatia

Action in Acts

Lesson 3 → Lystra

Lesson 2 → Cyprus

Paphos

Mediterranean Sea

Lesson 12 → Joppa

Lesson 1 → Jerusalem

Judea

miles

0   25   50   75

Lesson 1

INTRODUCING THE LESSON

Teacher Tips by Jim Eichenberger

IMAGINE A LIFEGUARD perched atop his seaside station— swimwear of the latest fashion, skin bronzed but not burned, and hair perfectly styled. But this lifeguard never gets in the water! After all, the salt water will fade the new trunks, waves will wash off the sunblock, and the whole process will destroy his styled locks.

One cannot imagine a less effective lifeguard! His is not a task to be accomplished from water's edge! Yet it is tempting to teach Bible lessons with such an attitude. Our learners are struggling in the deep waters of life. Do we shout out Bible instructions from our perch? Or do we dive in?

Accept Reality: We Are Drowning!

A Christian musician opened concerts by saying "It's *nice* to be in this *nice* place for this *nice* event with such *nice* people. It's just so *nice*!" He would then recite Jeremiah 17:9—"The heart is deceitful above all things, and desperately wicked: who can know it?"

Point made. We gather for Bible instruction— be it from a concert, a sermon, or a lesson—not because we are nice. We do so because we need help in fighting the waves of wickedness from within ourselves and from our culture. We are drowning and need a lifeguard to rescue us!

A good lesson introduction does not immediately open to the Scripture lesson text. The remainder of the lesson will deal with Bible content and application. Rather, the first step of a lesson must show your willingness to understand the kind of waves that are battering your class members. Give them the opportunity to tell you.

Identify Yourself: In This Together!

Your lesson introduction should demonstrate that you live in the same world as your students. The weekly free download "In the World" will help you do just that for each Sunday's lesson (standardlesson.com). Further help is found in the introduction to each lesson in this commentary, in the Involvement Learning lesson plans, and in the PowerPoint® slides in *Adult Resources*. Use these to help your students meet you on the common ground of everyday life before moving to the higher ground of Bible truth.

When you use references to pop culture, facts from a variety of disciplines, and quotations from famous people to introduce a lesson, you send two powerful messages: (1) "Yes, I too know that the world has something to say about this topic" and (2) "The Bible, although centuries old, has something to say about this topic as well."

Evaluate Learners: How Deep Are They?

Underwater rescue teams must not return to the surface too quickly. A too rapid change in pressure can cause a painful and even deadly condition called *the bends*. Students may experience the bends emotionally when a teacher tries to pull them from culture into Bible study too rapidly. Therefore, the amount of time spent on the lesson introduction should be based on how deeply class members are immersed in their culture.

For example, a study of the Bible account of the friendship of David and Jonathan might be preceded by only a brief introduction for a group that is close and has solid Christian friendships. In such a case, a simple discussion question such as, "Who is the first person in your life you identified as your best friend?" might be sufficient. But when introducing the same text to a group that struggles with making solid friendships, you may need a longer activity. For example, matching a collection of quotes (both positive and negative) about friends with the famous person who said it would ease the class into the topic more slowly.

Effective lifeguards and teachers have this in common: both enter the environment of those who are drowning. A proper lesson introduction helps the teacher do just that.

FAITH IN JESUS

DEVOTIONAL READING: Psalm 118:1-14
BACKGROUND SCRIPTURE: Acts 3

ACTS 3:11-21

11 And as the lame man which was healed held Peter and John, all the people ran together unto them in the porch that is called Solomon's, greatly wondering.

12 And when Peter saw it, he answered unto the people, Ye men of Israel, why marvel ye at this? or why look ye so earnestly on us, as though by our own power or holiness we had made this man to walk?

13 The God of Abraham, and of Isaac, and of Jacob, the God of our fathers, hath glorified his Son Jesus; whom ye delivered up, and denied him in the presence of Pilate, when he was determined to let him go.

14 But ye denied the Holy One and the Just, and desired a murderer to be granted unto you;

15 And killed the Prince of life, whom God hath raised from the dead; whereof we are witnesses.

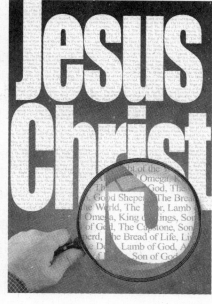

16 And his name through faith in his name hath made this man strong, whom ye see and know: yea, the faith which is by him hath given him this perfect soundness in the presence of you all.

17 And now, brethren, I wot that through ignorance ye did it, as did also your rulers.

18 But those things, which God before had shewed by the mouth of all his prophets, that Christ should suffer, he hath so fulfilled.

19 Repent ye therefore, and be converted, that your sins may be blotted out, when the times of refreshing shall come from the presence of the Lord;

20 And he shall send Jesus Christ, which before was preached unto you:

21 Whom the heaven must receive until the times of restitution of all things, which God hath spoken by the mouth of all his holy prophets since the world began.

KEY VERSE

His name through faith in his name hath made this man strong, whom ye see and know: yea, the faith which is by him hath given him this perfect soundness in the presence of you all. —**Acts 3:16**

AFaith in Action

Unit 1: The Early Church Proclaims Faith in Christ

LESSONS 1–5

LESSON AIMS

After participating in this lesson, each learner will be able to:

1. Recall key points from Peter's speech in the temple.

2. Explain how saving faith relates to committed trust in the risen Jesus.

3. Demonstrate such faith by affirming God's blessing of spiritual wholeness.

LESSON OUTLINE

Introduction
  A. Five-Tool Players
  B. Lesson Background
I. Wholeness—From Where? (Acts 3:11-15)
  A. Looking for Human Saviors (vv. 11, 12)
  B. Rejecting the Divine Savior (vv. 13-15)
    The Servant Leader
II. Wholeness—From Whom? (Acts 3:16-18)
  A. Jesus' Name, Our Faith (v. 16)
  B. Jesus' Payment, Our Debt (vv. 17, 18)
III. Wholeness—When? (Acts 3:19-21)
  A. Beginning with Repentance (vv. 19, 20)
    Restorative Justice?
  B. Finished at the End of the Age (v. 21)
Conclusion
  A. Finding Genuine Wholeness
  B. Prayer
  C. Thought to Remember

Introduction

A. Five-Tool Players

When looking for a future superstar, most baseball scouts seek players that excel in five facets of the game. Those five are hitting for average, hitting for power, base running, throwing, and fielding.

Such "five-tool players" are rare, however. In the history of the game, only a handful merit that designation. Willie Mays was one. A lifetime .302 hitter, he had 660 career home runs and collected 3,283 hits along the way. Mays was also a great base runner, stealing 338 bases. "Hammerin' Hank" Aaron slugged 755 home runs, drove in 2,297 runs, and stole 240 bases while posting a career .305 batting average during his career. Ken Griffey Jr. was named to his league's all-star team 13 times and won seven Silver Sluggers awards. Other players fall into the five-tool category, but the list is short.

As scouts look for five-tool players, employers look to hire someone who is the "complete package," and we admire a person who seems to "have it all together." But the Bible tells us that there is only one way to be perfectly whole.

B. Lesson Background

The book of Acts narrates the history of Jesus' followers in the first generation following His death and resurrection. Written as a companion volume to the Gospel of Luke, Acts portrays the church as the continuation of God's work, in Jesus, to reclaim a people for himself from all nations (Acts 1:1, 8). God accomplishes this purpose as Christians testify to what they have seen and heard: that in fulfillment of God's promises, Jesus willingly surrendered to death and was raised to life again by God. The resurrected and ascended Jesus remained active through the words and deeds of His followers as they were empowered by the Holy Spirit.

The conflict between the Jewish council (also known as the Sanhedrin) and Jesus continued as persecution of Jesus' followers. The council consisted of the high priest and 70 leaders appointed by him. Under the watchful eye of the Roman overlords, the council supervised operations of the temple of Jerusalem and served as something of a combination legislature and judiciary. Members of the council had seen in Jesus a rival to council authority and vested interest (John 11:48). Thus council members had fomented the movement to put Him to death, although the decision was not unanimous (Luke 20:19; 22:66–23:1, 50, 51). The people feared the council (John 7:13; etc.), but the council also feared the people (Mark 11:18, 32; Luke 20:19; 22:2; etc.).

The center of the council's power was the temple. The temple was not merely a building; it was a 35-acre complex that included courtyards and semi-enclosed areas where people could gather. Jesus had taught in these environs (John 7:14, 28; etc.), and there His followers continued to teach and pray after His ascension (Acts 2:44–3:1).

Immediately before today's text begins, the apostles Peter and John had come to the temple. As they did, they crossed paths with a man who was disabled and begging. Rather than give him money, Peter declared "In the name of Jesus Christ of Nazareth rise up and walk" (Acts 3:6). The man's instantaneous healing was reminiscent of Jesus' own healing miracles (compare Luke 5:17-26; 6:6-11). The man then entered the temple courts on restored legs and praised God, by whose power he had been made whole (Acts 3:8). Today's text picks up as people reacted.

I. Wholeness—From Where?
(ACTS 3:11-15)

A. Looking for Human Saviors (vv. 11, 12)

11. And as the lame man which was healed held Peter and John, all the people ran together unto them in the porch that is called Solomon's, greatly wondering.

Having received an unimaginable blessing from *Peter and John*, the formerly disabled man vigorously grabs the two apostles in joy and gratitude. No one who witnesses the scene can doubt that he believes that these two have played a key role in his being granted wholeness of body. The man familiar to everyone as the beggar who "sat for alms at the Beautiful gate of the temple" is now

seen by all "walking and praising God" (Acts 3:9, 10). We can imagine a crowd of hundreds *greatly wondering* over this miracle. They are more than ready for the explanation!

12. And when Peter saw it, he answered unto the people, Ye men of Israel, why marvel ye at this? or why look ye so earnestly on us, as though by our own power or holiness we had made this man to walk?

Peter addresses the crowd as fellow members of the nation of Israel who share a common knowledge of God's actions and promises. Their common background of being covenant people is the context for understanding this miracle. That context should remind them that Peter and John have no *power or holiness* of their own by which to have made *this man to walk*. They, like all humans, are imperfect, subject to frequent failures of judgment and action (examples: Luke 9:51-56; 22:31-34). The people should know that the power to bring the miraculous wholeness now evident belongs to God alone.

What Do You Think?
How can we ensure that people can see that it is God's power that undergirds our accomplishments?
Talking Points for Your Discussion
- Regarding our reaction to compliments and criticism
- Regarding the scale of our undertakings
- Other

B. Rejecting the Divine Savior (vv. 13-15)

13. The God of Abraham, and of Isaac, and of Jacob, the God of our fathers, hath glorified his Son Jesus; whom ye delivered up, and denied him in the presence of Pilate, when he was determined to let him go.

Peter has explicitly called on the authority and power of Jesus in commanding the man to stand and walk (Acts 3:6). Now Peter gives credit where credit is due, meaning that he and John are only instruments of the miracle (compare 14:8-15).

Peter stresses that it is none other than *the God of Abraham, and of Isaac, and of Jacob* who is due the credit. This phrasing condenses much of the storyline of Scripture; knowing that storyline is the key to understanding the healing miracle just performed. The storyline is further condensed in the phrase *the God of our fathers.* Those *fathers* include the three patriarchs mentioned by name here (compare Hebrews 7:4).

Those men were the first to receive the promise that God would reclaim His rebellious world by blessing all nations (Genesis 12:3; 22:18; 26:4). That reclamation is underway, and the miracle points unmistakably to the *Son Jesus* as the one with the power to have made it happen. Thus Peter joins the story of Jesus with that of the ancient patriarchs.

The Greek word translated *Son* can also be translated "child" (examples: Luke 2:43; 9:42) or "servant" (examples: Luke 1:54, 69; 7:7; 12:45; 15:26). If Peter is thinking in terms of the latter, then he is remembering that God's servant is a key figure in the book of Isaiah. The song of God's servant in Isaiah 52:13–53:12 predicts that exalted servant's debasement and rejection by His people. Even so, He is willing to be punished and killed for the wrongdoing of others. But in the end God gives Him the place of victory and strength. Isaiah says that God will absolve guilt and restore wholeness through one in whom all rejection and suffering will climax.

That is the story of Jesus' life. His rejection and crucifixion fulfill promises God made through

Visual for
Lesson 1

This visual will help your learners keep a geographical perspective during the lessons from Acts.

Isaiah. Jesus willingly took the lowliest of positions to serve others; in so doing, He fully expressed the glory of God before the world. That glory continues to be displayed as a man with a severe disability is healed by the power of Jesus, the once lowly, crucified servant who now sits at the right hand of God (compare Hebrews 8:1; 10:12; 12:2; 1 Peter 3:22).

> ### What Do You Think?
> What are some ways that our personal limitations can serve as a basis for bringing glory to God?
> *Talking Points for Your Discussion*
> - Regarding what other see in us
> - Regarding what we alone see in ourselves

14a. But ye denied the Holy One and the Just.

Peter now underlines and personalizes the tragedy of underestimating Jesus. He is *the Holy One* in a way like no other. He is *the Just,* meaning righteous in all His ways. The concepts of being just and right (or righteous) are frequently interchangeable in Scripture, and that is the case here (compare Deuteronomy 32:4; Nehemiah 9:33; Ezekiel 18:5; Romans 3:26).

14b. And desired a murderer to be granted unto you.

When Pilate offered to release Jesus, the crowd called instead for the release of Barabbas, a man imprisoned for sedition and murder (Luke 23:13-25). Thus the long story of human rebellion against God reached its lowest point. But the Son of God, supremely innocent, did not stop the process. The innocent gives His life willingly for the guilty as a guilty man was set free.

In this way members of the crowd now present had denied Jesus. Peter knew of this all too well since the climate of that moment had led to his own denial (Luke 22:34, 57-61). He therefore speaks not as a pure example but as an impure but forgiven messenger of the one who forgives.

15a. And killed the Prince of life, whom God hath raised from the dead.

The word translated *Prince* brings with it the idea of "author," as it is translated in Hebrews 12:2. Peter therefore may be referring to Jesus both as the divine Creator (compare John 1:3; Colossians 1:15, 16) as well as the one whose death restores life. The spiral of irony boggles the mind: without realizing it, the angry crowd had sent to death the one who came to restore life to humanity trapped in the grip of death. Yet it is by Jesus' death that life is restored because His death paid sin's price (Isaiah 53:5; Romans 3:21-26; 1 Peter 2:24).

By raising Jesus, God reaffirmed the Son's identity, brought Him to the heavenly throne as divine king, and fulfilled ancient promises to restore humanity to wholeness. Jesus' resurrection is the definitive proof that in Him God's gift of eternal life will triumph.

Reading this text today, we must listen carefully. In centuries following the writing of the New Testament, many misread this text and others as saying that all Jewish people bore responsibility for the death of Jesus. But Peter makes the statements we see here only about the people of Jerusalem, some of whom were in the crowd that called for Jesus' death (Acts 13:27).

15b. Whereof we are witnesses.

The concept of witness is vital to the establishment of fact (Deuteronomy 19:15-21; Matthew 18:16; 2 Corinthians 13:1; etc.), and the word appears dozens of times in the Bible in that regard. Pharisees tried and failed to discredit Jesus on the basis of inadequate witness (John 8:12-18). Peter's stress on *whereof we are witnesses* should be understood in this light (see also Acts 2:32; 5:32; 10:39, 41; 13:31).

◆ *THE SERVANT LEADER* ◆

Victor Herman (1915–1985) accompanied his father to Russia in 1931 to help build a car manufacturing plant. When Victor became an adult, he refused to become a Russian citizen and was imprisoned for 18 years. His memoir *Coming Out of the Ice* tells the story. He and 15 other prisoners were locked in a small cell 24 hours a day, forbidden to move or speak. At night they slept jammed together on the cold concrete floor.

One man, "the Elder," voluntarily took a place near the door. The spot was closest to the stench of the latrine. This position also made him the first to be beaten by sadistic guards. The Elder made sure that each man got his daily bowl of soup. Herman says the Elder's example of servant leadership in that horrible setting taught him that "only the one who is most exposed to the blows of the system can claim authority to lead and serve."

Peter informed his audience that Jesus placed himself in the greatest jeopardy in order to bring salvation. He served in a way no other can so that we would be servants of sin no more (John 8:34; Romans 6:6-18; etc.). What should we learn from Jesus' example?
                                                        —C. R. B.

II. Wholeness—From Whom?
(ACTS 3:16-18)

A. Jesus' Name, Our Faith (v. 16)

16. And his name through faith in his name hath made this man strong, whom ye see and know: yea, the faith which is by him hath given him this perfect soundness in the presence of you all.

No human power has made the man whole. Only God could do so. It happened by the power of Jesus (Acts 3:6). The miracle done *in his name* demonstrates the truth of all Peter's claims.

HOW TO SAY IT

Barabbas	Buh-*rab*-us.
Deuteronomy	Due-ter-*ahn*-uh-me.
Ezekiel	Ee-*zeek*-ee-ul or Ee-*zeek*-yul.
Nazareth	*Naz*-uh-reth.
Nehemiah	Nee-huh-**my**-uh.
patriarchs	*pay*-tree-arks.
Pilate	*Pie*-lut.
Sanhedrin	*San*-huh-drun or San-*heed*-run.

> *What Do You Think?*
> What steps can we take to stay mindful of the ways God has shown His power in our lives?
> *Talking Points for Your Discussion*
> - In our worship
> - In our families
> - In our private devotions

As the righteous, divine king, Jesus acts on behalf of His people—people who, like Peter and

John, have faith in Him. They have confessed Him as king and have sought His mercy, mercy that He always gives to those who seek it. Jesus' self-sacrificial death and God's raising Him from the dead give the basis for this faith. The man's healing is a visible manifestation of the invisible but no less real wholeness that King Jesus grants to His faith-filled subjects.

B. Jesus' Payment, Our Debt (vv. 17, 18)

17. And now, brethren, I wot that through ignorance ye did it, as did also your rulers.

Those who had called for Jesus' death had no idea of the gravity of their deed (Luke 23:34). Even Jesus' closest followers did not understand what was unfolding before their eyes (18:31-34). God's purpose, though revealed in Israel's Scriptures, remained hidden until He had accomplished it. Only with Jesus' resurrection could others understand who He truly was and how He had fulfilled God's promises (24:25-27, 30-32, 36-48). Now Peter passes the truth along. Ignorance is now ended, and the people are without excuse. They must seek the king's mercy urgently.

> *What Do You Think?*
> How can we help each other get past blind spots in understanding Jesus properly?
> *Talking Points for Your Discussion*
> - Regarding methods used by Jesus himself
> - Regarding methods used by the apostle Paul
> - Other

18. But those things, which God before had shewed by the mouth of all his prophets, that Christ should suffer, he hath so fulfilled.

Peter affirms, as Jesus did also (Luke 24:27, 44), that the suffering and death of the Christ was the event to which all the words of the prophets pointed. The divine drama of Jesus' death, resurrection, and heavenly enthronement were not just predicted by a few prophets in a few texts such as Isaiah 52:13–53:12. Rather, it is the outcome of everything that God said through *all his prophets,* whether the subject was that of people's sin and its judgment, God's mercy and grace, His people's suffering and oppression, or humanity's long-ing for true justice and goodness to be realized. Jesus' death brings all prophetic declarations to their focal point, resolving human need by means of divine self-sacrifice.

III. Wholeness—When?
(Acts 3:19-21)

A. Beginning with Repentance (vv. 19, 20)

19. Repent ye therefore, and be converted, that your sins may be blotted out, when the times of refreshing shall come from the presence of the Lord.

Those who have rebelled against the true king must abandon their rebellion and seek the king's mercy. This is the meaning of *repent,* a turning away from evil—first of all the evil of having revolted against the rule of the divine king.

To *be converted,* or turned back, is the step that complements the first. Thus we do not just abandon rebellion and seek the king's mercy; we further commit as loyal subjects, obediently to trust the king to provide, protect, and rule.

> *What Do You Think?*
> What should others see in us as evidence of genuine repentance?
> *Talking Points for Your Discussion*
> - Regarding changed speech patterns
> - Regarding changed behavior
> - Regarding changed goals
> - Regarding changed attitudes

The phrase *times of refreshing* refers to the promise of God from the first instance of human rebellion forward, the promise to break the destructive cycle of human rebellion. This revives humanity to the state of blessed life that God intends.

These times of refreshing are the hopes expressed by the prophets: of the gathering of scattered Israel, the establishment of God's true temple, the turning of the nations to the true God, and the reign of God as king to the farthest reaches of the earth. The fulfillment of those promises has begun with Jesus' death, resurrection, and ascension. Peter's audience can receive the benefit if they embrace the truth (compare Acts 2:38).

Conor McBride walked into a Tallahassee police station on March 28, 2010, and said, "You need to arrest me; I just shot my fiancée in the head." He was telling the truth. He and Ann Margaret Grosmaire had argued for 38 hours. Then he shot her. In the hospital, Ann was unconscious when her father was sure she said "forgive him" before she died.

Conor was charged with first-degree murder, but Ann's parents didn't want him to spend his life in prison. A prison chaplain told them about the concept of restorative justice. It's an approach to sentencing in which the prisoner, his family, officials, and the family of the victim try to agree on a lesser sentence than the law requires. It happened; Conor's sentence for murder was only 20 years.

God's system of restorative justice works differently. We are offered a restored, right relationship with Him only on the basis of Christ's payment for the penalty of our sins. A more appropriate designation for God's system of restorative justice is *grace*. This system requires no gathering of various parties to agree to a reduced sentence. God's grace means there is *no* sentence! Why would anyone reject such an offer?   —C. R. B.

20. And he shall send Jesus Christ, which before was preached unto you.

The promised times of refreshing will climax with Jesus' return. His life, death, and resurrection show that He is the Christ, God's promised king. Christ's rule as king would seem to be a disaster for those who had called for Jesus' death. But the king offers mercy. He invites repentant rebels to be restored as His subjects by their faith in Him and His offer of grace. Those who respond to that offer anticipate Jesus' future return as king as do faithful servants when their absent master returns (Luke 19:11-27).

B. Finished at the End of the Age (v. 21)

21. Whom the heaven must receive until the times of restitution of all things, which God hath spoken by the mouth of all his holy prophets since the world began.

As Peter announced previously, Jesus is enthroned at God's right hand until His victory is complete (Acts 2:34-36; compare Psalm 110:1). That period of heavenly enthronement grants His enemies the opportunity to turn from their rebellion and seek His mercy. But it is not an unlimited opportunity. The king is determined to see His kingdom come in its fullness. He will indeed renew the world to His design. To wait is foolish. Now is the time to put faith in Him, acknowledging Him as the king that He is.

Peter's message to the gathered crowd prompts many to do exactly what he says, and the company of Christians grows from about 3,000 to 5,000 (Acts 2:41; 4:4). But not all the rebels turn. The same Sanhedrin that condemned Jesus to death goes on to arrest Peter and John (Acts 4:1-3) and orders them not to preach (4:17, 18), an order boldly defied (4:19, 20). No earthly authority can silence the faithful witnesses of the true king!

Conclusion

A. Finding Genuine Wholeness

The challenge of trust confronts every generation. Will we continue to put our trust in ourselves, with our miserable record of failure and our evident brokenness? Or will we find genuine wholeness as we faithfully commit to the risen King Jesus?

B. Prayer

Father, we submit to Your Son Jesus as King, our Sovereign Lord. We trust in His merciful forgiveness. Strengthen us to live out Your gracious gift of wholeness in lives that reflect Your renewal of creation, already begun. We pray this in the name of Jesus. Amen.

C. Thought to Remember
Only Jesus fills the God-shaped hole
to make us whole.

VISUALS FOR THESE LESSONS

The visual pictured in each lesson (example: page 124) is a small reproduction of a large, full-color poster included in the *Adult Resources* packet for the Winter Quarter. That packet also contains the very useful *Presentation Tools* CD for teacher use. Order No. 2629118 from your supplier.

INVOLVEMENT LEARNING

Enhance your lesson with KJV Bible Student *(from your curriculum supplier) and the reproducible activity page (at www.standardlesson.com or in the back of the* KJV Standard Lesson Commentary Deluxe Edition*).*

Into the Lesson

Bring to class several things that are incomplete in some way. Possibilities are a remote control with no batteries (cover to the battery compartment missing), one chopstick, a single sock, a doll with one shoe, etc. Pass the items around and ask students what the items have in common. Talk about which items are still functional as they are, and which are useless at this time. Discuss what each item needs in order to be whole or complete.

As a variation of this activity, provide a jigsaw puzzle that contains fewer than 100 pieces. Keep a handful of pieces hidden away. Ask the class to assemble the puzzle. When they realize the puzzle is incomplete, talk about how they feel about the process and the result.

Alternative. Distribute copies of the "What's Missing?" activity from the reproducible page, which you can download. Have students work individually or in small groups.

Lead into Bible study by saying, "That which is whole or complete is more useful, more valuable. The same is true with people. Employers look to hire someone who is 'the complete package.' Secular psychologists advise how to become 'self-actualized,' and we admire a person who 'has it all together.' But the Bible tells us that there is only one way to be perfectly whole. Let's talk about that today."

Into the Word

Divide the class into two groups. Have groups read Acts 3:11-21 together and then complete the following research assignments. Anticipated responses are in italics.

Group 1—Why were the people looking to Peter and John for answers? *They thought Peter and John had healed the beggar by their own power or holiness.*

According to Peter, why was the beggar's infirmity reversed? *It was by faith in Jesus' name.*

How did Peter urge people to respond to what they had seen and heard? *They needed to repent.*

Group 2—To whom did Peter tell the people that they should look for answers? *Jesus/God.*

What was the stated purpose of Christ's suffering? *It was to fulfill what the prophets had foretold.*

How had God promised to respond to their repentance? *He would wipe away their sins, refresh them, send Christ, and restore everything when the time comes.*

Allow groups to share their responses. After the key facts of the healing are recalled, ask how saving faith relates to committed trust in the risen Jesus. Refer to the commentary as needed. After discussion say, "People who are broken want to be made whole—not just those who are broken physically, like the beggar, but also those who are spiritually broken. But we often search for wholeness in the wrong places, through the wrong people, at the wrong times, and in the wrong ways. Peter proclaimed that only Jesus can restore us to wholeness. It was true then, and it holds true today."

Close the activity by reading aloud Acts 3:16. Then give each person the opportunity to read the verse, inserting his or her own name in place of each reference to the man. Remind students that it is still our faith in Jesus that makes us strong and heals us from the infirmity of our sins.

Into Life

As a group, choose a person or family going through a period of brokenness. Brainstorm possible ways to help and, as a group, choose an option to implement in coming weeks.

Alternative. Distribute copies of "Helping the Hurting" from the reproducible page. Have students complete the activity individually.

After either activity, say, "We are all broken. And as we strive to remain faithful in this life, we have the responsibility to care for each other until that time when all is restored."

FAITH TO DISCERN

DEVOTIONAL READING: Psalm 146
BACKGROUND SCRIPTURE: Acts 13:1-12

ACTS 13:1-12

1 Now there were in the church that was at Antioch certain prophets and teachers; as Barnabas, and Simeon that was called Niger, and Lucius of Cyrene, and Manaen, which had been brought up with Herod the tetrarch, and Saul.

2 As they ministered to the Lord, and fasted, the Holy Ghost said, Separate me Barnabas and Saul for the work whereunto I have called them.

3 And when they had fasted and prayed, and laid their hands on them, they sent them away.

4 So they, being sent forth by the Holy Ghost, departed unto Seleucia; and from thence they sailed to Cyprus.

5 And when they were at Salamis, they preached the word of God in the synagogues of the Jews: and they had also John to their minister.

6 And when they had gone through the isle unto Paphos, they found a certain sorcerer, a false prophet, a Jew, whose name was Barjesus:

7 Which was with the deputy of the country, Sergius Paulus, a prudent man; who called for Barnabas and Saul, and desired to hear the word of God.

8 But Elymas the sorcerer (for so is his name by interpretation) withstood them, seeking to turn away the deputy from the faith.

9 Then Saul, (who also is called Paul,) filled with the Holy Ghost, set his eyes on him,

10 And said, O full of all subtilty and all mischief, thou child of the devil, thou enemy of all righteousness, wilt thou not cease to pervert the right ways of the Lord?

11 And now, behold, the hand of the Lord is upon thee, and thou shalt be blind, not seeing the sun for a season. And immediately there fell on him a mist and a darkness; and he went about seeking some to lead him by the hand.

12 Then the deputy, when he saw what was done, believed, being astonished at the doctrine of the Lord.

KEY VERSE

The deputy, when he saw what was done, believed, being astonished at the doctrine of the Lord.

—Acts 13:12

Faith in Action

Unit 1: The Early Church Proclaims Faith in Christ

Lessons 1–5

Lesson Aims

After participating in this lesson, each learner will be able to:

1. Recall the events from the beginning of Paul's first missionary journey.

2. Identify the work of the Holy Spirit as empowering Christ's followers to accomplish His mission in a way that reflects Christ's saving work.

3. Write a prayer asking for the Holy Spirit's empowerment for bold witness in the week ahead.

Lesson Outline

Introduction

A. Plot Twists

A mark of a memorable movie is the unexpected plot twist. The story of the film seems to be heading in an expected direction until it takes an unanticipated turn that keeps moviegoers thinking about it long after. In *The Empire Strikes Back* (1980), Luke Skywalker battles Darth Vader, whom Skywalker believes murdered his father. But in a surprising plot twist, he learns that Darth Vader *is* his father! Astronaut George Taylor believes he is on an alien world in *Planet of the Apes* (1968). He (and the audience) is shocked to discover that he is actually on a future Earth nearly destroyed by humans and overthrown by apes. And who can forget the film *Psycho* (1960) in which the murderous mother turns out to be none other than Norman Bates himself!

Real life has its share of the unexpected as well —plot twists. We can react to those moments with surprise, with despair, or in any number of other ways. The apostle Paul was successful because his reactions to the unexpected were based on knowing God, who stands above all plot twists.

B. Lesson Background

In Acts 8–12 Christians began to move out from Jerusalem as persecution and other circumstances scattered them. Acts 13–21 is a bit different as it identifies three distinctive missionary journeys of the apostle Paul and his companions. By the time of the episode in today's text, Paul (known as Saul at the time) was linked with Barnabas by the need to assure the Jerusalem Christians that their former persecutor had become a faithful believer in Jesus (Acts 9:26, 27). Barnabas was already notable in the Jerusalem church for his generosity (4:36, 37).

After the gospel spread to Antioch, Barnabas invited Paul to join him there as a teacher in the church (Acts 11:19-26). Antioch, where our text begins, was a major city in Syria; we take care not to confuse it with a different Antioch of Acts 13:14. Syrian Antioch featured a multiethnic population and was one of the largest cities of the Roman Empire.

As the gospel spread to the city, both Jews and Gentiles became believers. This multicultural group found itself living in fellowship. As a famine approached, they generously provided relief for their fellow believers in distant Jerusalem (Acts 11:27-30). Such a background prepared the church at Antioch well as the first to send missionaries to share the gospel with people in other places.

I. Accept the Assignment
(ACTS 13:1-5)

A. Direction from Leadership (vv. 1-3)

1a. Now there were in the church that was at Antioch certain prophets and teachers.

We are introduced to a group of leaders *in the church . . . at Antioch*. The term *prophets* indicates those inspired by God to speak for Him. Modern readers of the Bible often associate prediction of the future with prophets. But the biblical prophet is less a "foreteller" than a "forthteller"—someone who proclaims God's truth, though sometimes that truth does deal with the future. *Teachers* are those who instruct others in the Christian message.

The text does not clearly identify some as prophets and others as teachers. The two terms may overlap, indicating prophets who teach or teachers who prophesy (compare Ephesians 4:11). In any case, the book of Acts understands their work to be empowered by the Holy Spirit, who enables the church to prophesy (Acts 2:17-21), to speak the message of God truly and boldly.

1b. As Barnabas, and Simeon that was called Niger, and Lucius of Cyrene, and Manaen, which had been brought up with Herod the tetrarch, and Saul.

The first and last names on the five-person list are already familiar in the story; they are about to become the focus of the narrative. In between are three names that demonstrate the diversity of the multicultural Antioch church. *Simeon* is an Aramaic name, likely indicating birth and upbringing as a Jew in the Jewish homeland. He is *called Niger*, a Latin (that is, Roman) word meaning "black." While the modern notion of race did not exist in the biblical world, peoples from Africa south of the Sahara commonly migrate to the Mediterranean region and are well known in the world of the Bible. Simeon may be such a person.

Lucius is a Greek name, and he is said to come from *Cyrene* (compare Luke 23:26; Acts 2:10), a region of North Africa to the west of Egypt (approximately where modern Libya is). So two of the leaders of the church in Antioch are likely from Africa (compare Acts 11:20).

Manaen is described as having *been brought up with Herod the tetrarch*, also known in nonbiblical sources as Herod Antipas. A tetrarch is someone who rules a fourth part of an area, and this particular Herod rules Galilee and Perea from 4 BC to AD 39 (Luke 3:1). He was the son of so-called Herod the Great (reigned 37–4 BC; see Matthew 2:1-19). Herod the tetrarch is known for beheading John the Baptist (Matthew 14:1-12). Having been a childhood companion of Herod Antipas, Manaen clearly comes from the upper echelon of wealth and power. His presence shows that the gospel is penetrating all segments of the population.

> ### What Do You Think?
> What can we do to achieve more diversity in church leadership?
> *Talking Points for Your Discussion*
> - Regarding racial diversity
> - Regarding socioeconomic diversity
> - Other

2. As they ministered to the Lord, and fasted, the Holy Ghost said, Separate me Barnabas and Saul for the work whereunto I have called them.

The scene is that of church leaders joined in focused worship with fasting. Fasting is associated with seeking God's will in some texts (examples: 2 Chronicles 20:3; Luke 4:1, 2) and with mourning in others (examples: Esther 4:3; Matthew 9:15).

Either or both reasons for fasting may hold true here. A mournful fasting is appropriate given the church leaders' realization of the lost state of Jews and Gentiles who do not know of the salvation that is now available from God through fulfilled promises in Jesus. If this is a fasting to focus on discerning God's will, those gathered may be startled in receiving direct communication from *the Holy Ghost*. The content of that communication is a summons for two of their number to be shared with the world at large. The others are to ratify and support God's summons. The purpose is clear: to push forward God's program of witness to Christ to the ends of the earth (Acts 1:8).

3. And when they had fasted and prayed, and laid their hands on them, they sent them away.

Exactly how God reveals His message to the teachers and prophets is not explained. But how the leaders respond is emphasized: they obey fully. Continuing their prayer and fasting, they place hands on Barnabas and Saul in a way that shows that they pray for God's blessing and power to be with them (compare Acts 6:6; 1 Timothy 4:14; 2 Timothy 1:6; Hebrews 6:2). With that, the two missionaries depart, not knowing what lies ahead.

> *What Do You Think?*
> How can the church do better in the area of prayerful decision making?
> *Talking Points for Your Discussion*
> - At the leadership level
> - At the level of the midsize group
> - At the small-group level
> - At the level of the individual

B. Following a Plan (vv. 4, 5)

4. So they, being sent forth by the Holy Ghost, departed unto Seleucia; and from thence they sailed to Cyprus.

Underlining the Holy Spirit's calling, the text now describes the movements of Barnabas and Saul. *Seleucia* is the harbor city on the Mediterranean coastline that serves Antioch, which lies a dozen or so miles inland. From Seleucia the missionaries sail southwest about 130 miles to a harbor on *Cyprus*, a large, well-populated island. Barnabas is on his home territory here (Acts 4:36), a fact that may provide the reason for traveling there first.

◆ AFFINITY EVANGELISM ◆

Motorcyclists, quilters, volleyball players—all have been known to use their recreational interests to introduce Christ to others who enjoy the same activities. *Affinity evangelism* is the current term for this practice.

In affinity evangelism, Christians take the gospel with them to celebrations, events, and activities that unbelievers will attend as well. Such occasions may be designed by Christians, with evangelistic intent built in. Or such circumstances may merely be part of the fabric of the local culture. The gospel receives a better hearing when communicated to those known to have something in common with the messenger.

Since Barnabas was a native of Cyprus, he knew the people and their culture. He and Saul were Jews, so they took the gospel message to Jewish synagogues (see next verse below). Both cultural and spiritual affinity contributed to the success of their evangelistic efforts. The same approach, if done with integrity, still works.   —C. R. B.

5. And when they were at Salamis, they preached the word of God in the synagogues of the Jews: and they had also John to their minister.

Salamis is the easternmost harbor city on Cyprus, closest to the point from which the two have sailed. To begin their preaching ministry *in the synagogues of the Jews* will become Paul's standard practice in the years ahead. Synagogues are the perfect places for preaching the gospel. Faithful Jews gather there on the Sabbath for worship. Those gathered already believe in the God of Israel, and they are waiting for God's promises to be fulfilled.

> *What Do You Think?*
> What principles of and places for successful evangelism can we draw for today from the actions of Barnabas and Saul?
> *Talking Points for Your Discussion*
> - Considering also Acts 13:42; 14:1; 17:1-4, 10-12; 19:8
> - Contrasting Acts 14:8-18; 17:16-34; 19:9, 10

The person named *John* who accompanies the two is John Mark (see Acts 12:12, 25; 15:37). Like many Jews of the day, the man has both a Jewish name and a Greco-Roman name. His Jewish name John (meaning "the Lord is gracious") is from the Hebrew; the Roman name Mark (meaning "a large hammer") is from Latin. He is a cousin of Barnabas (Colossians 4:10).

II. Recognize Roadblocks
(Acts 13:6-8)
A. Spiritual Counterfeit (v. 6)

6. And when they had gone through the isle unto Paphos, they found a certain sorcerer, a false prophet, a Jew, whose name was Barjesus.

Paphos is located on the western end of Cyprus. The straight-line distance between Salamis and Paphos is about 88 miles. But curving, hilly roads make the travel distance more like 115 miles. After a preaching journey of unknown duration, the team encounters a figure common to the Greco-Roman world: *a sorcerer* (compare Acts 8:9).

Sorcerers present themselves as having the ability to manipulate unseen beings and forces of the spirit world. Reciting long incantations, using potions, performing strange tasks—such are their stock-in-trade. Sorcery is witchcraft, forbidden to the people of Israel (Leviticus 19:31; Malachi 3:5; etc.).

Like John Mark just mentioned, this man goes by two names. We see his Jewish name here: *Barjesus*. From Aramaic, it means "son of Jesus." This does not refer to Jesus of Nazareth, of course, as the name Jesus (derived from the name Joshua) is common. The man's Greek name is given in verse 8, below. Jesus' warnings regarding false prophets apply (Matthew 7:15-20).

B. Powerful Detractor (vv. 7, 8)

7. Which was with the deputy of the country, Sergius Paulus, a prudent man; who called for Barnabas and Saul, and desired to hear the word of God.

Barjesus is an attendant of the court of a Roman official. The provinces of the Roman Empire are governed by local rulers who have pledged loyalty to Rome or by those appointed by the emperor or senate. As a senate-appointed governor, *Sergius Paulus* is politically the most powerful man on Cyprus. The missionaries apparently are having such an impact on Cyprus that they come to this official's attention. So he seeks *to hear the word of God* from them firsthand.

8. But Elymas the sorcerer (for so is his name by interpretation) withstood them, seeking to turn away the deputy from the faith.

The gospel represents a threat to the sorcerer, whose Greek name we now see as *Elymas*. If Sergius Paulus is to be persuaded by the message brought by the missionaries, Elymas will have to lose influence and position. The power behind the gospel leaves no need for any competitors.

So Elymas resists the message that Barnabas and Saul bring, perhaps by interrupting and challenging them as they speak with the governor. As is so often the case in the New Testament narratives, resistance to the gospel arises from attempts to hold on to power (examples: John 11:48; Acts 19:23-27).

III. Counter Conclusively
(Acts 13:9-12)
A. Defining Differences (vv. 9, 10)

9. Then Saul, (who also is called Paul,) filled with the Holy Ghost, set his eyes on him.

This is the point in Acts where *Saul* begins to be known by his Greek name, which is *Paul*. Along with this change in designation comes a switch

HOW TO SAY IT

Antioch	*An*-tee-ock.
Aramaic	*Air*-uh-**may**-ik.
Barnabas	*Bar*-nuh-bus.
Cyprus	*Sigh*-prus.
Cyrene	Sigh-*ree*-nee.
Elymas	*El*-ih-mass.
Herod Antipas	*Hair*-ud *An*-tih-pus.
Lucius	*Lew*-shus.
Manaen	*Man*-uh-en.
Niger	*Nye*-jer.
Paphos	*Pay*-fus.
Salamis	*Sal*-uh-miss.
Seleucia	Sih-*lew*-shuh.
Sergius Paulus	*Ser*-jih-us *Paul*-us.
synagogue	*sin*-uh-gog.
tetrarch	*teh*-trark or *tee*-trark.

in the order of names: henceforth "Barnabas and Saul" (Acts 11:30; 12:25; 13:1, 2, 7) becomes "Paul and Barnabas" (in Greek, Acts 13:43, 46, 50; 15:2 [twice], 22, 35, 36; exceptions: 14:12, 14; 15:12, 25). This likely indicates a change in leadership as Paul becomes viewed as "the chief speaker" (14:12). And in the verse at hand, it is Paul who confronts the antagonist. *Filled with the Holy Ghost* is an expression the author uses to indicate that a bold act of speech is pending (Luke 1:41, 67; Acts 2:4; 4:8, 31). With eyes focused on the sorcerer, Paul is set to deliver to Elymas a stark message from God.

10a. And said, O full of all subtilty and all mischief, thou child of the devil, thou enemy of all righteousness.

Paul addresses the man with terms that accuse him of dishonesty and deception. The sorcerer's claims are a shallow fraud. Any power that he exercises other than mere sleight of hand involves the power *of the devil*, the deceitful adversary of God and humanity. To be an *enemy of all righteousness* is to oppose God's plan to make the world right, a plan coming to its fulfillment in Jesus. The sorcerer twists with his charades the straight, true paths that God has created.

10b. Wilt thou not cease to pervert the right ways of the Lord?

This expression is especially ironic. The word translated *ways* appears earlier in Acts to refer spiritually to the way of Christ (Acts 9:2; compare John 14:6) as well as to the physical roadway to Damascus, where Jesus appeared to Paul (Acts 9:17b). As a persecutor of Christians, Paul himself had been one who perverted *the right ways of the Lord*. Having seen the risen Lord Jesus and come to faith in Him, Paul now accuses another of making the same terrible mistake.

> ### What Do You Think?
> What circumstances today call for strong confrontation rather than a gentler approach, if any? Why?
>
> *Talking Points for Your Discussion*
> - Regarding tensions between church and culture
> - Regarding tensions within the church

B. Providing Evidence (vv. 11, 12)

11. And now, behold, the hand of the Lord is upon thee, and thou shalt be blind, not seeing the sun for a season. And immediately there fell on him a mist and a darkness; and he went about seeking some to lead him by the hand.

After the Lord Jesus appeared to him on the road to Damascus, Paul was blind until a follower of Jesus came to lay hands on him in prayer and to baptize him (Acts 9:8-18). The physical blindness was an apt expression of Paul's spiritual condition as a persecutor of Christians. Now Paul pronounces the same sign on Elymas.

The *mist and a darkness* that surround the man may be either a way of describing the sorcerer's own experience of blindness or an indication that the man's blindness is accompanied by a miraculous sign that is visible to others. Having to be led *by the hand* also happened to Paul (Acts 9:8), an ironic repeat of the "time out" imposed on each for misleading others in opposing the gospel. Paul makes clear that this act is the Lord's, whose hand is upon Elymas in judgment.

But this judgment is not final: the blindness is temporary (*for a season*). God's purpose in this event is to demonstrate to Elymas and those around him how wrongheaded is his opposition to the gospel. As it was for Paul on the road to Damascus, the act of judgment has repentance and faith as its goal, even if the outcome is different in each case.

◆ FALSE SPIRITUALITY ◆

The Force is a familiar concept to anyone who has seen the *Star Wars* movies. The idea plays on a change in culture in which a vague spirituality is displacing Christianity. Various occult practices have increased their presence in recent years. The fascination many people have with Eastern religions plays a part as well.

Some Christians refer to horoscopes as if they are relevant. Others arrange their homes according to the ideas of Feng shui to protect themselves from "bad qi." Good qi is supposedly encouraged if, among other things, the furniture arrangement does not block its movement. And what about incorporating "sacred" words, rituals, and objects borrowed from pagan religions into Christian practice?

Sorcery is still around, and it presents itself to us in various pleasing forms (compare 2 Corinthians 11:12-15). But before we can confront it, we have to recognize it. Can we do so, or are we blind to its dangers?　—C. R. B.

12. Then the deputy, when he saw what was done, believed, being astonished at the doctrine of the Lord.

Whether Elymas changes in his opposition to the gospel, the book of Acts does not say. We simply know that each time in Acts where messengers of the gospel encounter those who engage in witchcraft, the gospel prevails.

Whatever the case with Elymas, the Roman governor Sergius Paulus does indeed come to faith. As the text describes it, his faith follows his witnessing the power of Christ over the sorcerer. But it is not simply the miracle that impresses him: Paul's teaching about Jesus fills him with astonishment that drives him to faith. The greatest work of God is not vanquishing the magician opponent, but raising Jesus from the dead.

> *What Do You Think?*
> What are some ways to present the gospel that will cause unbelievers to take notice?
> *Talking Points for Your Discussion*
> - Regarding unbelieving acquaintances
> - Regarding unbelieving family members
> - Regarding unbelieving strangers

Conclusion

A. God's Surprises

How has your life been different from what you expected a year ago? 10 years ago? How has your life been different from what you expected when you came to faith in Jesus?

When we ask ourselves such questions, we may feel disappointment that we did not follow through in pursuing goals and dreams. Some of us may feel disappointment with God, that He did not deliver in the way we had hoped.

Visual for Lessons 2 & 13. *Use this visual as a backdrop during class consideration of the question that is associated with Acts 13:10b.*

But if we ask the question differently, perhaps our feelings will change. How has God worked in your life to accomplish His purpose in the last year, or 10 years, or since you came to faith in Jesus? While He may not have done with us what He did with Paul, through the Holy Spirit God is shaping us and using us to reclaim rebellious humanity. As He does so, He usually surprises us.

How can we respond to such surprises? Like the leaders in the Antioch church, we need to share God's perspective on our broken world, ready to be His instruments by the Spirit's power in the next surprising situation. We need to accept each situation that lies before us as filled with potential for service in Christ's name. We need to trust the power of God's Holy Spirit to work in us when we know we are inadequate for the task. We need to act by a faith that sees God at work in even the most surprising circumstances.

B. Prayer

Heavenly Father, may we trust in the Spirit's guidance rather than our own planning as we serve as Your instruments in the various moments of life. Teach us to follow Your Son as we live in uncertainty. We pray this in Jesus' name. Amen.

C. Thought to Remember

Success depends not on knowing what comes next, but rather in knowing the author of our story.

INVOLVEMENT LEARNING

Enhance your lesson with KJV Bible Student *(from your curriculum supplier) and the reproducible activity page (at www.standardlesson.com or in the back of the* KJV Standard Lesson Commentary Deluxe Edition).

Into the Lesson

Give each person a sheet of paper and a pen. At your signal, each person should begin writing a fictional story beginning with the sentence, "It was a dark and stormy night." After 2–3 minutes say, "Plot twist!" and have everyone pass his or her paper to the left. Writers should pick up the new story where it left off, adding an unexpected turn of events. In another 2–3 minutes, repeat the "Plot twist!" and pass papers again.

Repeat as time allows, letting everyone know when the final plot twist is taking place, so writers can wrap up the action. Invite volunteers to read the finished stories, but don't let this drag out.

After the activity say, "Life is filled with unexpected circumstances—plot twists. We can react to those moments with anger, with despair, or in any number of other ways. The apostle Paul succeeded in ministry because of how he responded when things did not go according to plan. Let's look at some examples."

Into the Word

Invite someone to read aloud Acts 13:1-5. Then say, "Paul had come a long way since the days when he persecuted Christians. Now he was not only one of them, but chosen among them for special ministry. How do you think Paul and Barnabas felt about the assignment they had been given? How did they prepare? What do you think they expected?" Note: don't ask all three questions at once; allow time between them for discussion.

After a time of discussion say, "Things seemed to be going well for a time. Paul and Barnabas were preaching in the synagogues, spreading the gospel—it was all going according to plan. Then . . . plot twist!"

Choose someone to read aloud Acts 13:6-8. Ask, "Why do you think Elymas was determined to keep the deputy of the country (the proconsul) from hearing Paul and Barnabas? What did

Elymas likely fear?" After discussion say, "Elymas probably thought he had things under control. He was keeping a very powerful man right where he wanted him. Then . . . plot twist!"

Ask someone to read aloud Acts 13:9-11. After reminding students how and why God blinded Saul in Acts 9, ask, "How were Saul and Elymas similar? How were they different? What had Paul learned about God from his own experience that enabled him to speak with such conviction?" Again, allow time for responses to a question before posing the next one. Make a transition by saying "Paul and Barnabas didn't back down when confronted by Elymas. The sorcerer became blind as Paul declared he would. And then . . . plot twist!" Read aloud verse 12 together.

Alternative: Distribute copies of the "Proconsul's Perspective" activity from the reproducible page, which you can download. Have students work individually or in small groups.

Close either activity by saying, "Things didn't turn out as Paul and Barnabas expected. But their faith in Jesus empowered them to keep preaching despite a false prophet's efforts to deter them. We don't know whether Elymas chose to believe in Christ, but we know the official did. Paul and Barnabas succeeded through plot twists."

Into Life

Say, "We all know someone who is facing a plot twist. It can be hard to see God's plan or His hand during those times." Invite the class to share examples, but caution about using real names. Challenge students to encourage those people by showing faith, speaking truth, and petitioning God. Challenge them to pray daily for others this week, asking God to hold and strengthen those people as they strive to walk in faith.

Alternative. Distribute copies of "The Power of Prayer" from the reproducible page. Have students complete the activity individually.

FAITH TO PERSEVERE

DEVOTIONAL READING: 2 Corinthians 1:3-11
BACKGROUND SCRIPTURE: Acts 14; Colossians 2:6, 7

ACTS 14:8-11, 19-23

8 And there sat a certain man at Lystra, impotent in his feet, being a cripple from his mother's womb, who never had walked:

9 The same heard Paul speak: who stedfastly beholding him, and perceiving that he had faith to be healed,

10 Said with a loud voice, Stand upright on thy feet. And he leaped and walked.

11 And when the people saw what Paul had done, they lifted up their voices, saying in the speech of Lycaonia, The gods are come down to us in the likeness of men.

. . . .

19 And there came thither certain Jews from Antioch and Iconium, who persuaded the people, and, having stoned Paul, drew him out of the city, supposing he had been dead.

20 Howbeit, as the disciples stood round about him, he rose up, and came into the city: and the next day he departed with Barnabas to Derbe.

21 And when they had preached the gospel to that city, and had taught many, they returned again to Lystra, and to Iconium, and Antioch,

22 Confirming the souls of the disciples, and exhorting them to continue in the faith, and that we must through much tribulation enter into the kingdom of God.

23 And when they had ordained them elders in every church, and had prayed with fasting, they commended them to the Lord, on whom they believed.

KEY VERSES

When [Paul and Barnabas] had preached the gospel to that city, and had taught many, they returned again to Lystra, and to Iconium, and Antioch, confirming the souls of the disciples, and exhorting them to continue in the faith, and that we must through much tribulation enter into the kingdom of God. —**Acts 14:21, 22**

Faith in Action

Unit 1: The Early Church Proclaims Faith in Christ

LESSONS 1–5

LESSON AIMS

After participating in this lesson, each learner will be able to:

1. Describe the experiences of Paul and Barnabas in Lystra and nearby cities.

2. Compare the experiences of Paul and Barnabas with those of Christians experiencing opposition in the present.

3. Choose attitudes and behaviors that express faithful persistence in challenging circumstances.

LESSON OUTLINE

Introduction

A. Misheard Lyrics

Sometimes singers and songwriters make their lyrics deliberately vague, leaving interpretation to the listener. Quite often, however, lyrics to famous pop songs are misheard. Those who sing along to a favorite song may be singing words that were never intended! For example, in the song "Purple Haze" Jimi Hendrix did not sing "'scuse me while I kiss this guy," but rather "'scuse me while I kiss the sky." Credence Clearwater Revival did not give directions to a "bathroom on the right," but warned of a "bad moon on the rise." The Rolling Stones vowed that they would "never be your beast of burden," not counseling cooks to "never leave your pizza burnin'"!

We all want to be heard. We do not like to be misunderstood. It's bad enough when it happens unintentionally, but problems multiply when it happens with malicious intent. Paul's experience with regard to the latter has something to teach us.

B. Lesson Background

Our text continues the story of Paul's first missionary journey of about AD 47–49. After traveling across the island of Cyprus, Paul, Barnabas, and John Mark sailed northward to Asia Minor (modern Turkey). From its south coast they traveled inland first to Perga, where John Mark called it quits (Acts 13:5, 13; 15:37, 38). It was then on to Antioch of Pisidia, a straight-line distance of about 75 miles; walking distance was much farther due to terrain. There Paul preached in the synagogue; his message led many to faith but provoked bitter opposition from others (13:13-52). This pattern was to repeat itself throughout Paul's missionary travels. Wherever the gospel went in Acts, it met with opposition as well as faith.

I. Miracle and Misidentification

(Acts 14:8-11)

From Antioch of Pisidia, the missionaries traveled eastward to smaller towns. The first was Iconium, where again preaching led to division and controversy (Acts 14:1-7). The team of Paul and

Barnabas then moved on to Lystra, the setting of today's text. Lystra was a modest-sized town on a secondary highway and thus somewhat isolated from contact with the wider world. A local language was used commonly there even after the Greek language had spread through the region centuries before the New Testament. Archaeologists have recovered inscriptions from the area showing the persistence of belief in traditional pagan gods and goddesses.

A. Result of Faith (vv. 8-10)

8. And there sat a certain man at Lystra, impotent in his feet, being a cripple from his mother's womb, who never had walked.

A man with a lifelong disability comes to the forefront of the account. Perhaps like so many in his condition, there is little he can do except beg for money to survive. He reminds us of the man encountered by Peter and John at the gate to the temple, also lame from his birth (Acts 3:2). Both unnamed men were living in deep need, never having encountered anything that could change their condition.

9. The same heard Paul speak: who stedfastly beholding him, and perceiving that he had faith to be healed.

Now the man with a disability hears the preaching of Paul about Jesus. Perhaps that preaching includes accounts of miraculous healings on the part of the Son of God (Luke 5:17-26; 7:22). The man's response to this message is the beginning of faith. The text describes Paul looking closely at him, as Peter had done with the lame man at the temple (Acts 3:4). From what Paul sees, perhaps by various expressions of body language, the apostle understands that the man has *faith to be healed*. The man is convinced that the Jesus whom Paul preaches can change his life as no other can (compare Matthew 9:27-30).

10. Said with a loud voice, Stand upright on thy feet. And he leaped and walked.

Perceiving the man's faith, Paul boldly commands him to do what he has never done before: stand on his heretofore powerless legs. The man does that and more, like the man Peter had healed (Acts 3:8). If the power of Jesus can accomplish this miracle, then surely it can bring the fullness of God's blessings to the people of Lystra!

B. Conclusion of Crowd (v. 11)

11. And when the people saw what Paul had done, they lifted up their voices, saying in the speech of Lycaonia, The gods are come down to us in the likeness of men.

Absent any devout Jews in Lystra, it's safe to assume that everyone there worships pagan deities. So naturally the people try to comprehend the miracle just witnessed within the framework of stories about those gods. The conclusion: Paul and Barnabas must be two of those very gods.

As we read the reaction *the gods are come down to us in the likeness of men*, we naturally recall that that's what Jesus did. There is a critical difference, however. The stories of pagan gods in human form involve masquerades to promote self-serving agendas. The fictitious god acts for his or her own benefit. The New Testament affirms, however, that Jesus "was made in the likeness of men," He concurrently took upon himself "the form of a servant" (Philippians 2:7). Though always retaining His divine nature, Jesus never used His divine prerogatives for His own advantage. He willingly suffered death for the sake of humanity, choosing not

Visual for Lesson 3. *Start a discussion as you point to this visual while asking, "What interferes with our hearing God's call on our lives?"*

to save himself so that He could save others. Sadly, the New Testament witnesses to the fact that people at times seem quite willing to bestow the status of "god" on mere humans (Acts 12:22), while being most unwilling to believe that Jesus is the Son of God (John 1:11; 9:1-34).

II. Attack and Aid
(ACTS 14:19, 20a)

Paul and Barnabas attempt to correct the false impression in the intervening verses that are not part of today's lesson text. The fickleness of the crowd is seen in what comes next.

A. Opposition (v. 19)

19a. And there came thither certain Jews from Antioch and Iconium, who persuaded the people.

The miracle has made an enormous impact on the people of Lystra. But this does not ensure a favorable hearing from everyone! The preaching of Paul and Barnabas had stirred up opposition in places previously visited—Antioch of Pisidia and Iconium (Acts 13:13–14:7). Jewish opponents from those two towns now seek to suppress the gospel in Lystra. Their determination is seen in their willingness to travel many miles. Their opposition is so persuasive that a mob action results.

The amount of time that elapses until these opponents arrive on the scene is unspecified. It may take several days for word to travel from Lystra back to Antioch and Iconium, and for opponents in those two cities to coordinate their plans.

19b. And, having stoned Paul, drew him out of the city, supposing he had been dead.

Stoning is one means of execution in the ancient world, employed to engage members of the entire community in the judgment against the accused (example: Leviticus 24:14). In many cases the victim is first cast into a pit, then large stones are dropped or thrown on him or her. We cannot know the specific means of Paul's stoning. But it is certainly a horrific experience as a crowd of people overtakes Paul, utterly convinced that he deserves to die. The fact that those who stone Paul do not stop until they believe him to be dead implies that he suffers visibly severe injuries.

Paul himself had participated in the stoning of Stephen (Acts 7:58; 8:1). Later, he will note a stoning to be among other episodes of violent persecution (2 Corinthians 11:23-27). In his letter to the Galatians, thought by many scholars to have been written to the churches in this region just after his first missionary journey, he will remark that he bears on his body "the marks" of Jesus (Galatians 6:17). Perhaps he refers to the scars of the violent incident under consideration here.

◆ *WHAT GOES AROUND COMES AROUND?* ◆

Most of us have heard others use the word *karma*. By this they typically mean that someone who has done wrong is now being repaid by a negative circumstance. The popular karmic sentiment "What goes around comes around" is appealing at first glance since it seems to say the same thing as the Bibles regarding reaping what one sows (Proverbs 11:18; 22:8; etc.).

But karma is a pagan concept. The notion that karma determines one's future (reincarnated) lives should cause us to recognize the idea as unbiblical. Another red flag is that karma is a rigid, unyielding cause-and-effect system. Paul, as a Christian of Jewish background, knew that God had forgiven his sins, with no future punishment in store.

Even so, Paul came to experience the kind of persecution he had inflicted on others (Acts 8:1-3; 9:1, 2; Galatians 1:13; Philippians 3:6). It could make him even more grateful that the Lord had forgiven him and saved him from such a sinful life. What about you? —C. R. B.

B. Support (v. 20a)

20a. Howbeit, as the disciples stood round about him, he rose up, and came into the city.

The narrative does not tell us whether Paul actually dies and God miraculously raises him, or whether he comes close to death but God restores him to strength. What we are told is that *the disciples*—probably residents of Lystra recently brought to faith in Jesus—are not prevented from gathering round about Paul and witnessing the result of God's protection. They are certainly able to affirm that God has rescued Paul.

III. Departure and Return
(Acts 14:20b-23)

Paul and Barnabas must make a decision: stay in Lystra or leave town. There is no record of God's revealing a divine decision in this regard (contrast Acts 16:6-10; 18:9-11).

A. To Derbe (v. 20b)

20b. And the next day he departed with Barnabas to Derbe.

Paul is strong enough to set out for Derbe *the next day*, a walking trip of at least 60 miles. This is not what we would expect of a man left for dead the day before! Clearly God's power has protected and preserved Paul just as much as His power made the lame man whole.

The trip to Derbe takes the travelers to the southeast. This means they will not be crossing paths with the agitators who are returning home to Antioch (to the northwest) or Iconium (to the north).

B. In and from Derbe (vv. 21, 22)

21. And when they had preached the gospel to that city, and had taught many, they returned again to Lystra, and to Iconium, and Antioch.

Prior to reaching Derbe, Paul and Barnabas had met serious opposition in every city in which they preached in the Galatian region. As we read about their continuing travels and ministry, we are amazed that they continue in the face of such serious resistance. Yet they do indeed preach in Derbe, with influence on many people there.

Even more surprising is the missionaries' following move: returning to each of the cities where they experienced persecution! A different route is certainly possible. It's possible to press to the east, through Paul's hometown of Tarsus (Acts 21:39), and finally back to Antioch of Syria. Instead they retrace their steps, going back to the sites of their suffering.

> **What Do You Think?**
> When was a time God called you to minister in a hostile environment? How did things turn out?
> *Talking Points for Your Discussion*
> - Regarding ministry to a fellow believer
> - Regarding ministry to an unbeliever

22a. Confirming the souls of the disciples, and exhorting them to continue in the faith.

The missionaries' purpose in retracing their steps is so that they can continue to teach the new followers of Jesus. Such ongoing teaching is always important, but it is especially vital when those new to the faith live in an environment that is hostile to that faith.

The Greek underneath the translation *confirming* is also translated "strengthening" in Acts 18:23, and that is the sense here. The strengthening is that of urging the new disciples to embrace attitudes and behaviors consistent with their new faith. Christians in every era have realized the importance of grounding new converts in their faith with ongoing teaching. The Christians of the first generation are our model.

22b. And that we must through much tribulation enter into the kingdom of God.

The text emphasizes a particular aspect of the missionaries' ongoing teaching: the significance of suffering for the followers of Jesus. The gospel focuses on Jesus' suffering, His willing death for the sake of sinners. The book of Acts and the volume that precedes it, the Gospel of Luke, emphasize that Jesus' suffering is the culmination of all the suffering of God's people in history (Luke 11:49-51). Indeed, the story of God's people in the Bible is repeatedly a story of hardship and suffering.

The new disciples are entering just such a life. What they had seen happen to Paul and Barnabas will happen to them, as it likely has already. Being God's person does not mean an end to suffering. Rather, it means suffering as others suffer. Even more than that, it means distinctly suffering because of belonging to God and so not conforming to the pattern of the world.

But this suffering is not pointless. By His suffering Christ brought the kingdom of God, God's promised rule, into the world. Because of His suffering, Christ is exalted at God's right hand and extends His rule ultimately to embrace all the earth (Acts 1:6-8). Acts shows that by living in step with Jesus' teaching, the followers of Jesus encounter hardships and persecution as He did (John 15:20). As Paul and Barnabas continue to experience this truth, so will the new believers. God's kingdom is always shaped like a cross; yet God's Spirit empowers us to carry the cross.

◆ *BACK TO THE FRONT LINES* ◆

Wars result in horrific injuries for many soldiers. Yet sophisticated prosthetics allow some who have lost limbs to return to duty. But there is another force at work in allowing recovered soldiers to do so. That factor is drive, says John Fergason, chief prosthetist at the Center for the Intrepid, San Antonio Military Medical Center. Drive is a soldier's desire to continue the mission in spite of personal cost. For such personnel, loyalty to one's comrades seems to be the most powerful factor at work.

In spite of having been stoned and left for dead, Paul returned to the places where he had been attacked. He could have said "mission accomplished, let's go home." But he didn't. His return demonstrated that the power of the gospel was greater than the evil in the world. That return had something important to say not only to the people of the area but also to his traveling companion Barnabas (compare John 11:8-10). What is your level of boldness saying to others? —C. R. B.

C. Selection (v. 23)

23a. And when they had ordained them elders in every church.

The new believers will need leadership after the missionaries depart, so Paul and Barnabas select leaders for them. The Greek underneath the word *ordained* is also translated "chosen" in 2 Corinthians 8:19, and that is the idea here.

Elders is the term used here and elsewhere in the New Testament for these leaders (Acts 11:30; 15:2-6, 22, 23; 16:4; 20:17; Titus 1:5; 1 Peter 5:1). This term is commonly used in Judaism to refer to those who lead because of their maturity (examples: Jeremiah 26:17-19; Acts 25:15). Christians adopt this as one of the terms for their own leaders (see 1 Timothy 5:17; 1 Peter 5:5; other designations are found in Acts 20:28; 1 Timothy 3:2; and Titus 1:7).

These leaders are to look out for the welfare of those in their charge, with analogy to shepherds who feed and protect their flock of sheep (Acts 20:28-30; 1 Peter 5:1-4; compare Hebrews 13:17). The leadership designations in Ephesians 4:11 remind us of the New Testament's plural use of leadership terms (see also Philippians 1:1; 1 Timothy 4:14; Titus 2:2). The responsibility to nurture and lead the church never falls to one person alone. It is always a shared duty, part of the church's fellowship in the love of Christ, who is the "chief Shepherd" (1 Peter 5:4).

The context implies clearly enough a certain level of spiritual maturity to serve as one of the leaders who shepherd God's people. If much trouble marks the way of God's kingdom, then those who lead others on that way must know what it is to suffer faithfully as Christ's followers. That experience in turn will enable them to guide others who encounter their own suffering.

23b. And had prayed with fasting, they commended them to the Lord, on whom they believed.

Paul and Barnabas began their missionary travels with a calling delivered while they and other church leaders were fasting and praying (Acts 13:1-5). Now the two missionaries use the same procedure with the new leaders. See comments on Acts 13:2 in lesson 2.

To pray to God is to acknowledge that one's fate does not lie within oneself. To be *commended . . . to the Lord* recognizes dedication of one's life to His care and protection. The converts had come to believe in Him through the preaching of Christ's death and resurrection. Now they trust the God who raised Jesus from the dead to carry them through every circumstance. Even death itself will not separate them from God's love (Romans 8:35-39).

> *What Do You Think?*
> What specific situations call for prayer and fasting today? Why?
> *Talking Points for Your Discussion*
> ▪ Among fellow Christians
> ▪ By Christians in the presence of unbelievers

Conclusion

A. Power Seen in Suffering

Stories and experiences of opposition to the Christian faith can be very discouraging to us. Sometimes we look to the past and think that there was a time when the Christian faith was warmly and widely received. That selective memory contrasts with our view of the present, when it seems that hostility to Christian faith is common in all quarters.

We do well in such instances to remember that suffering is the means by which we experience God's kingdom. None of the biblical exemplars of our faith escaped suffering, and Jesus himself suffered supremely at the hands of His enemies.

Hostility to the faith should not surprise us. But neither should those experiences of persecution blind us to the other things that God is doing. As He did with Paul and Barnabas, God is bringing people to saving faith through the faithful witness of His suffering people.

Today, even as we see persecution coming from every direction, we also see faith in Christ taking root in the lives of people whom we thought far from God's truth. The power of Christ that healed the lame man continues to transform lives around us in amazing ways. In fact, we realize that the power of Christ is often most clearly demonstrated among His people when they suffer.

Are we ready to accept and act on both of these realities? Can we demonstrate firm faith in Christ when our faith is tested by suffering and persecution? Are we ready to acknowledge and celebrate the work of God that is happening all around us? Will we revere Christ in our hearts and serve in His name with our hands, despite the hardships and with expectation of His victory? Do we desire to see the victory of God enough that we are willing to see it in our own suffering?

B. Prayer

God Almighty, as Paul and Barnabas committed the new believers to Your care, so we likewise commit ourselves. Teach us faithfulness in every situation, a faithfulness that praises You in hardship as in triumph. We pray in Jesus' name. Amen.

C. Thought to Remember

Speak up; speak out; speak clearly!

HOW TO SAY IT

Antioch	*An*-tee-ock.
Barnabas	*Bar*-nuh-bus.
Corinthians	Ko-*rin*-thee-unz (*th* as in *thin*).
Cyprus	*Sigh*-prus.
Derbe	*Der*-be.
Galatians	Guh-*lay*-shunz.
Iconium	Eye-*ko*-nee-um.
Lycaonia	*Lik*-uh-*o*-ni-uh.
Lystra	*Liss*-truh.
Pisidia	Pih-*sid*-ee-uh.
synagogue	*sin*-uh-gog.
Syria	*Sear*-ee-uh.
Tarsus	*Tar*-sus.

INVOLVEMENT LEARNING

Enhance your lesson with KJV Bible Student *(from your curriculum supplier) and the reproducible activity page (at www.standardlesson.com or in the back of the* KJV Standard Lesson Commentary Deluxe Edition*).*

Into the Lesson

Do an online search for the "Who's on First?" comedy routine by Abbott and Costello. You can either show a video of the original routine to the class or print out a script and invite two volunteers to act it out.

Alternative. Distribute pens and copies of the "Say What?" activity from the reproducible page, which you can download. Students will be reading complicated directives and matching them with more simplified versions. Have students work individually or in small groups. When students are finished, review the correct answers together.

After either activity, say, "We all want to be heard. We do not like to be misunderstood, ignored, or misquoted. But it happens! Let's look at how Paul responded during times when others suffered from spiritual deafness."

Into the Word

Divide the class into three groups. Give each group one of these research assignments about confronting spiritual deafness.

Group 1—Deafness of pagan ideas
Case studies of culturally caused spiritual deafness: Acts 14:8-13; 17:16-18
Paul's prescription: Acts 14:15-17; 17:22-28

Group 2—Deafness of anger and jealousy
Case studies of jealousy-caused spiritual deafness: Acts 14:19; 17:5-7
Paul's prescription: Acts 14:20; 17:10

Group 3—Deafness of forgetfulness
Case studies of spiritual deafness caused by forgetting what was taught: Acts 14:21, 22; Titus 1:10
Paul's prescription: Acts 14:23; Titus 1:5-9

Allow groups time to report. Here are some points you may wish to make:

Group 1—In Lystra, the crowd interpreted Paul's miracle as coming from their pagan gods. Later, a very educated group in Athens interpreted Paul's words as adding to the list of gods and goddesses they already acknowledged. In both cases, Paul responded with a more detailed explanation, correcting their misconceptions.

Group 2—In Lystra, jealous Jews stoned Paul and left him for dead. In Thessalonica, jealous Jews hired a mob to cause a riot. In both cases, Paul was supported by other believers. They gathered around him in Lystra. In Thessalonica, they protected him from a mob.

Group 3—In Antioch of Syria, Paul found it necessary to remind the church about what he had already taught them. Paul sent Titus to the church in Crete to remind them of the truth.

In both cases, Paul determined the need to appoint leaders to remind believers of the truth, even when he was absent.

Into Life

Say, "We all have a story to tell. God has written our stories of faith, using hardships and struggles to bring about something beautiful. Our stories can help others see what God has done in our lives and can give them hope that He can do something meaningful in theirs."

Have students write or tell their stories thus far. Suggest that they include the following points:
My life before I accepted Jesus.
How I came to faith in Jesus.
Blessings after I became a Christian.
Struggles after I became a Christian.

Discuss how they can more effectively share the good news of Jesus through those stories. (Note: be aware of how much time this will require!)

Alternative. Distribute pens and copies of the "Rooted and Built Up" activity from the reproducible page. Have students work individually to complete the activity.

FAITHFUL SEEKERS
OF THE KING

DEVOTIONAL READING: Isaiah 49:1-7
BACKGROUND SCRIPTURE: Matthew 2:1-12

MATTHEW 2:1-12

1 Now when Jesus was born in Bethlehem of Judaea in the days of Herod the king, behold, there came wise men from the east to Jerusalem,

2 Saying, Where is he that is born King of the Jews? for we have seen his star in the east, and are come to worship him.

3 When Herod the king had heard these things, he was troubled, and all Jerusalem with him.

4 And when he had gathered all the chief priests and scribes of the people together, he demanded of them where Christ should be born.

5 And they said unto him, In Bethlehem of Judaea: for thus it is written by the prophet,

6 And thou Bethlehem, in the land of Juda, art not the least among the princes of Juda: for out of thee shall come a Governor, that shall rule my people Israel.

7 Then Herod, when he had privily called the wise men, enquired of them diligently what time the star appeared.

8 And he sent them to Bethlehem, and said, Go and search diligently for the young child; and when ye have found him, bring me word again, that I may come and worship him also.

9 When they had heard the king, they departed; and, lo, the star, which they saw in the east, went before them, till it came and stood over where the young child was.

10 When they saw the star, they rejoiced with exceeding great joy.

11 And when they were come into the house, they saw the young child with Mary his mother, and fell down, and worshipped him: and when they had opened their treasures, they presented unto him gifts; gold, and frankincense, and myrrh.

12 And being warned of God in a dream that they should not return to Herod, they departed into their own country another way.

KEY VERSE

When they were come into the house, they saw the young child with Mary his mother, and fell down, and worshipped him: and when they had opened their treasures, they presented unto him gifts; gold, and frankincense, and myrrh. —**Matthew 2:11**

FAITH IN ACTION

LESSON AIMS

After participating in this lesson, each learner will be able to:

1. Describe the historical setting of the encounter between Herod and the wise men.

2. Contrast God's guidance of the wise men on their mission with His guidance of Christians today.

3. Identify one area of ministry where God is leading him or her and discuss with a church leader the best way to follow that path faithfully.

LESSON OUTLINE

Introduction
 A. Thanks, but No Thanks!
 B. Lesson Background
I. Making the Effort (MATTHEW 2:1, 2)
 A. Long Trip (v. 1)
 B. Clear Goal (v. 2)
  The Trip of a Lifetime
II. Probing for Information (MATTHEW 2:3-8)
 A. Knowing Whom to Ask (vv. 3-6)
 B. Knowing Whom to Trust (vv. 7, 8)
III. Worshipping the King (MATTHEW 2:9-12)
 A. Right Place, Right Time (vv. 9, 10)
 B. Good Attitude, Great Gifts (v. 11)
  An Unexpected Gift
 C. Spiritual Insight, Wise Choice (v. 12)
Conclusion
 A. Speaking Our Language
 B. Prayer
 C. Thought to Remember

Introduction

A. Thanks, but No Thanks!

It's often very hard to find the perfect Christmas gift! Even so, the worst Christmas gifts are relatively well established in cultural tradition. For example, such tradition tells us that fruitcake is the proverbial unwanted holiday present. Not far behind is the so-called ugly Christmas sweater. It is probably best not to give food that will never be eaten or clothes that will never be worn!

Common sense also can spot a bad gift idea. Does a loved one really need to be reminded of neglected housework by the gift of a vacuum cleaner? Does a friend need a hint to lose weight by the gift of a gym membership? Would a gift of deodorant be the best way to tell a coworker that he or she has a problem in that area? An insult wrapped up in a festive box and adorned with a ribbon is still an insult!

When we give gifts, we want to give something that is appreciated. That is all the more true in this season of giving and receiving gifts. Today's text examines noteworthy gift givers of history. We can get some tips about giving—especially giving to God—from them.

B. Lesson Background

Herod the Great (ruled 37–4 BC) was the first Roman puppet king of Judea. Although ruler of the Jews, Herod was of Arabic and Idumean descent. (The latter are descended from the Edomites of Genesis 36:9; etc.) While Herod professed a commitment to Judaism, his racial background, wildly excessive lifestyle, and absolute loyalty to Rome led many Jews to question his true beliefs.

Herod is perhaps most famous for his massive public building projects, including a renovation and expansion of the Jerusalem temple complex (compare John 2:20). Profoundly paranoid, Herod maintained a large personal bodyguard who also functioned as a secret police. Through this force Herod eliminated enemies real and perceived (including members of his own family) and otherwise squelched dissent. It is in such a setting of paranoia that the events of today's lesson take place.

I. Making the Effort

(Matthew 2:1, 2)

A. Long Trip (v. 1)

1a. Now when Jesus was born in Bethlehem of Judaea in the days of Herod the king.

Bethlehem, a country village some six miles south of Jerusalem, is well known as the hometown of the great king David (1 Samuel 17:12). The designation *Bethlehem of Judaea* distinguishes this town from a different Bethlehem in Joshua 19:15. Matthew clarifies the location not for the sake of geographical precision, however, but to stress the connection between Jesus and His ancestor David, who had been promised that his descendants would reign forever (2 Samuel 7).

Ten centuries after David's death, God is working to fulfill this ancient prophecy in an unexpected way. Regarding the nature of *Herod the king*, see the Lesson Background.

1b. Behold, there came wise men from the east to Jerusalem.

One day near the end of Herod's reign, certain *wise men* show up in the capital city. The Greek underneath the translation *wise men* is *magi*, and this helps us understand their nature. The same word is used in the old Greek version of Daniel 1:20; 2:2, 10, 27; 4:7; 5:7, 15, where it is usually translated "magicians." They are not like the sleight-of-hand magicians of today, but are of a caste of mysterious holy men. They are experts in astrology, medicine, history, and politics. They serve as counselors in royal courts and are revered as experts on the unseen worlds of nature and the gods.

The fact that these men come *from the east* indicates that they are not emissaries of the Roman Empire, since Rome is located to the west. A point of origin in the area of Babylon and Mesopotamia would explain their familiarity with Judaism, since they would have had contact with communities of Jews whose ancestors had remained in that area since the days of Nehemiah and Ezra. Because wise men, as the designation is used here, are often attached to royal courts, it is reasonable to assume that they have been sent as a delegation to welcome the birth of a new Jewish king; this theory may explain their lavish gifts, noted below.

B. Clear Goal (v. 2)

2. Saying, Where is he that is born King of the Jews? for we have seen his star in the east, and are come to worship him.

Since the wise men are seeking *he that is born King of the Jews,* they naturally come looking in Jerusalem, the center of Jewish faith and culture. Exactly how and why *his star in the east* has directed the quest is something of a mystery. If the nature of the travelers' wisdom includes astrology, then they are accustomed to seeking signs of impending world events in the heavenly bodies. It seems most likely that something unusual has transpired that involves a celestial body associated with the Jewish people. Comparing these observations with the wise men's religious research, they conclude that a new Jewish king has been born.

But have they concluded that this recently born child is the Messiah, promised to come through the Jewish people? If so, has it been their contact with Jews living in the Persian Empire to the east that has made them aware of Daniel's prophecies of a divine kingdom that will last forever (Daniel 2:44, 45; etc.)?

These are tantalizing questions with uncertain answers. In any case, the wise men seek *to worship* the new king. Tradition says that the men are three in number, but the text does not say that.

HOW TO SAY IT

Babylon	*Bab*-uh-lun.
Bethlehem	*Beth*-lih-hem.
Edomites	*Ee*-dum-ites.
frankincense	*frank*-in-sense.
Galilee	*Gal*-uh-lee.
Gentiles	*Jen*-tiles.
Herod	*Hair*-ud.
Idumaean	Id-you-*me*-un.
magi	*may*-jye or *madge*-eye.
Mesopotamia	*Mes*-uh-puh-***tay***-me-uh.
Messiah	Meh-*sigh*-uh.
messianic	mess-ee-*an*-ick.
myrrh	mur.
Nehemiah	*Nee*-huh-***my***-uh.
Persia	*Per*-zhuh.

THE TRIP OF A LIFETIME

Jules Verne gained fame in 1873 with his novel *Around the World in Eighty Days.* The main character is Phileas Fogg, a British bachelor whose life is governed by an obsession for precision. The stuffy, meticulous gentleman wagers that he can travel around the world in exactly 80 days. His friends believe it's impossible, and the story unfolds with difficulties that force Fogg to change plans frequently.

The changes delay him, and he is despondent in his belief that he is arriving home a day late. Yet despite his perfectionism, he had forgotten that he had crossed the International Date Line. He had succeeded in his quest after all!

Many of us imagine a "trip of a lifetime" we'd like to take. It might be an African safari, a motorcycle trip to Alaska, or a visit to every state in America. The wise men probably had not been sitting around dreaming of a quest when one said, "Hey, guys, let's go check out Jerusalem and see if a new king has been born!" No, it was a celestial sign that impelled them on their journey, pulling them westward. If you think about it, their trip of a lifetime can be ours as well: every time we come to worship Jesus, we are taking just such a trip.

—C. R. B.

II. Probing for Information
(MATTHEW 2:3-8)

A. Knowing Whom to Ask (vv. 3-6)

3. When Herod the king had heard these things, he was troubled, and all Jerusalem with him.

As the wise men naturally look for the new "King of the Jews" in the city of the current king, little can they know the effect their visit will have on that paranoid ruler *and all Jerusalem with him.* People who have vested interests in maintaining the status quo do not want that status quo disturbed (compare John 11:48)!

4. And when he had gathered all the chief priests and scribes of the people together, he demanded of them where Christ should be born.

Herod's logic in consulting the religious leaders of the Jews is unclear. Why does he assume that the appearance of the wise men has anything to do with a *Christ*, real or fake? Perhaps the wise men themselves have suggested that the star has something to do with the coming of a Messiah, although Matthew does portray them as fully aware of the implications of the sign of the star they had seen.

Does Herod make the association between these strange visitors and ancient prophecies of a coming Christ himself? If so, does he really believe he can undermine God's plan? Perhaps he doubts the integrity of the wise men, believing that they are in league with rebels who seek to foment insurrection by stirring up the religious sentiments of the masses; or, more likely, he fears that the sensation created by the appearance of the wise men may be capitalized on by his political enemies, real or imagined.

5, 6. And they said unto him, In Bethlehem of Judaea: for thus it is written by the prophet, And thou Bethlehem, in the land of Juda, art not the least among the princes of Juda: for out of thee shall come a Governor, that shall rule my people Israel.

The priests and scribes refer Herod to Micah 5:2. This passage predicts the appearance of a ruler of Israel who will come from Bethlehem. The ruling of Israel in 5:2 and providing for Israel in 5:4 (not quoted here) strongly resembles what was said of David in 2 Samuel 5:2; 1 Chronicles 11:2. Although Micah prophesied more than seven centuries before the birth of Jesus, first-century Jews still hold the prophecy dear. The prevailing interpretation of Micah 5:2 and other prophecies is that the Messiah will take the lead in purging the land of foreign influences and restore devotion to Israel's God (compare Acts 1:6).

> *What Do You Think?*
> What steps should you take to gain greater *understanding* of Scripture, not just greater *knowledge* of it?
> *Talking Points for Your Discussion*
> ▪ Considering Satan's ability to quote Scripture (Matthew 4:6)
> ▪ Considering culture's misuse of Scripture

B. Knowing Whom to Trust (vv. 7, 8)

7. Then Herod, when he had privily called the wise men, enquired of them diligently what time the star appeared.

Realizing the possible political implications of the wise men's disturbing report, paranoid Herod begins his own search for the Messiah. His inquiry regarding *what time the star appeared* is an issue of year and month, not time of day. Even without reading the rest of the account, at a minimum the question seems designed to calculate the age of the new "King of the Jews." Knowledge is power, and with knowledge of the location (Bethlehem) and age of the Messiah (time the star appeared), Herod will have the upper hand, or so he must think.

8. And he sent them to Bethlehem, and said, Go and search diligently for the young child; and when ye have found him, bring me word again, that I may come and worship him also.

There is no indication that the wise men fail to answer Herod's question in the previous verse truthfully; the unrecorded answer to the query about the time of the star's appearance leads Herod to conclude that the person the wise men seek is a *young child*. The wise men apparently see no reason to doubt Herod's motives in his questioning and his declared intent to *come and worship him also*.

But all this must be evaluated in light of Herod's political cunning, his murderous track record, and his paranoia. Even with no knowledge of Herod's murderous actions in Matthew 2:13, 16-18, history tells us of his evil character. In that light, his self-preservation instincts must be in overdrive. If political enemies are hatching a scheme involving a baby from Bethlehem to put forward as a challenger to his throne, any show of force could alert the rebels and allow them to move the child elsewhere.

Herod therefore decides to let the wise men locate the child for him. The assumption may be that their efforts will not arouse the suspicions of the imagined rebels. Herod's stated desire to worship serves to reinforce the wise men's understanding that the one they seek must be more than the heir-apparent son of an ordinary political king.

III. Worshipping the King
(MATTHEW 2:9-12)

A. Right Place, Right Time (vv. 9, 10)

9. When they had heard the king, they departed; and, lo, the star, which they saw in the east, went before them, till it came and stood over where the young child was.

The wording of this verse in the original Greek text is difficult and has given rise to much speculation about the exact nature of "the star of Bethlehem." Matthew seems to imply that as the wise men depart Jerusalem they suddenly see the same star they had earlier seen in their eastern homeland, the one that had led them to travel to Israel. But ordinary stars do not move through the sky and linger over specific geographical locations. This fact has led many scholars to speculate that the wise men actually view a planet or comet. Scientific explanations, however, miss the point of the story: whether a star, a planet, or something else, God continues to lead the wise men in their long journey to find the true King of the Jews.

Visual for Lesson 4. *Point to this visual as you ask your learners what they have heard about these three roles as they relate to Jesus.*

10. When they saw the star, they rejoiced with exceeding great joy.

We note that the *exceeding great joy* the wise men experience is not over seeing Jesus, but rather over seeing *the star*. Perhaps their experiences with Herod, his officials, and the Jewish religious leaders has unsettled them. Doubtless they are confused to discover that no King of the Jews has been born in the palace. Perhaps they have begun to doubt whether they have correctly interpreted the signs, wondering if their long journey is at a dead end. The sudden reappearance of the star renews their hopes.

B. Good Attitude, Great Gifts (v. 11)

11. And when they were come into the house, they saw the young child with Mary his mother, and fell down, and worshipped him: and when they had opened their treasures, they presented unto him gifts; gold, and frankincense, and myrrh.

Modern nativity sets often include figurines of the wise men presenting gifts to Jesus as he lies in the manger. This suggests that the wise men are there with the shepherds who come after the angel announces the birth to them (Luke 2:7-20). But Matthew indicates that the wise men meet Mary in a *house,* with no reference to the manger.

This fact, plus the note in Matthew 2:16 that Herod massacres all the male children in Bethlehem age two years and under, has led many

scholars to suggest that the wise men arrive in Bethlehem several months after Jesus' birth. On the other hand, Luke's reference to a manger allows the possibility that Jesus was taken into a house soon after being born. Therefore the timeframe of the wise men's visit can be anywhere from a day or two after Jesus' birth up to a dozen or more months later.

In any case, the actions of the wise men create a striking and deliberate contrast with the earlier scenes in the story. On one hand, Herod, the King of the Jews, is now on the alert to a possible rival, and the Jewish priests and scribes cannot be bothered to travel from Jerusalem to see their new Messiah, their new Christ.

On the other hand, pagan travelers from another country—men with comparatively little understanding of Israel's God or His requirements—have completed a long, dangerous journey to bow before Jesus and present Him with lavish gifts. *Frankincense* and *myrrh* are exotic and expensive spices used as key ingredients in ancient perfumes and ointments; the *gold* the travelers bring likely represents more money than a peasant couple such as Joseph and Mary will see in a lifetime. The actions of the wise men reflect a prominent theme in Old Testament messianic prophecies, the theme of Gentiles (like the wise men) coming to Jerusalem to worship the Christ (see Isaiah 11:10; 14:1; 49:6; 60:1-3; etc.).

What Do You Think?
  What questions could we ask ourselves to help ensure that generosity accompanies worship?
Talking Points for Your Discussion
  - Regarding what links generosity with worship
  - Regarding what drives a wedge between generosity and worship

◆ AN UNEXPECTED GIFT ◆

Since 1880, many of America's presidents have sat behind the same desk. The desk is an unusual piece of furniture, in part because it was given to President Rutherford B. Hayes by Queen Victoria. Perhaps a more interesting fact is that the desk was carved out of lumber taken from the British ship HMS *Resolute*. The *Resolute* was involved in a several-year Arctic rescue expedition by the British Royal Navy. The ship itself was abandoned by its crew and locked in ice for over a year. In 1855 it was found by an American whaling ship, freed from the ice, and brought to harbor in New England, where it was restored and then returned to England. When the British Navy decommissioned the ship years later, some of its timbers were used to make the desk.

Presidents have received many unusual gifts from foreign leaders: Teddy Roosevelt was given a zebra and lion from Ethiopia; Richard Nixon received a panda from China. Gifts vary widely, from raw meat to ceremonial daggers to paintings, but they all become United States property, ending up in the national archives.

The gifts the wise men brought to the king of the Jews show that such giving is a tradition of long standing. The difference in this case is that the king they came to honor was the God of Heaven in human form, who gives the blessing of salvation to all who worship Him. What gifts do you bring Him this season?   —C. R. B.

C. Spiritual Insight, Wise Choice (v. 12)

12. And being warned of God in a dream that they should not return to Herod, they departed into their own country another way.

God has not only helped the wise men on their way, leading them to the object of their quest, He also makes provisions for their safe return home. Although Herod has instructed them to return with news of the child's location, they instead make their exit toward *their own country* by *another way*.

The wise men seem to have had no warning or inkling of the danger posed by Herod until they are *warned of God in a dream*. Herod is likely aware (or becomes aware) that that Micah 5 passage also predicts that the Messiah from Bethlehem will go forth to destroy the invaders and their pagan religious customs. To Herod, this can mean only a challenge to his own pro-Roman policies. Periodic insurrections are not unknown in this time and place (compare Acts 5:36, 37), and Herod is infamous for eliminating opposition.

What Do You Think?
When was a time you sensed God's leading through something other than His Word? What did that experience teach you?
Talking Points for Your Discussion
- Positive lessons
- Negative lessons

Conclusion
A. Speaking Our Language

Missionaries and Bible translators often stress the importance of speaking God's truth in the native language, or "heart language," of people who do not know Christ. Today's story is a remarkable illustration of how far God will go to communicate to those who seek to know Him.

The Old Testament condemns undue attention to stars (Deuteronomy 4:19; etc.) and takes an unfavorable view of those who do (Isaiah 47:13; etc.). Yet Matthew's account of the birth of Jesus features both a star as a sign and stargazers who interpret it as such! Although God prefers to reveal himself through spokespersons whose messages become Scripture, the wise men seemed not to have had access to the book of Micah. So God spoke to them in a "language" they could understand.

The wise men seem the least likely category of people to play a part in the story of Jesus' birth. Yet their willingness to follow God's lead in the face of great peril made them spectators to the greatest event in history: the entry of the Son of God into the world. God knows hearts, and He perceived that these men would seek Him faithfully despite danger if given an opportunity. They did. Do you?

B. Prayer

Heavenly Father, guide our steps as You did those of the wise men! May those steps lead us ever faithfully toward Jesus. We pray in His name. Amen.

C. Thought to Remember
God will light the way for those
who seek to bring Him glory.

Involvement Learning

Enhance your lesson with KJV Bible Student (from your curriculum supplier) and the reproducible activity page (at www.standardlesson.com or in the back of the KJV Standard Lesson Commentary Deluxe Edition).

Into the Lesson

Invite students to talk briefly about the best gift they ever received and what made it so special. Then ask students to think about the worst gift they ever received and what made it so disappointing. Share an example of your own. (Calculate in advance how much time this will require, depending on class size; don't let this segment drag out.) *Option*: After obtaining copyright permission, show the clip of Ralphie wearing his gift of a bunny suit from his aunt in the classic Christmas movie *A Christmas Story*.

Alternative. Distribute pens and copies of "The Good, the Bad, the Ugly" activity from the reproducible page, which you can download. Have students work individually.

After either activity, say, "This is a season of giving and receiving gifts. When we give gifts, we want to give something that is appreciated. Today we will get some tips from some of the most famous gift-givers in history."

Into the Word

Say, "Twitter is unique among social media in that it limits the length of messages. As of the time of this writing, each message (called a 'tweet') can contain no more than 140 characters."

Divide the class into three groups, giving each group pen and paper and a portion of the Bible text noted below. Each group should read its portion of the text and summarize it as a tweet that reflects the possible thoughts of the wise men in that portion of the text. (Sample tweets are in italics; don't include those.)

Group 1—On the long journey to Jerusalem (Matthew 2:1, 2) *We ask ourselves whether or not this trip is worth it. But even though the trip is hard, we know what lies at the end of it. We are going to meet a king like no other in history.* [140 characters]

Group 2—After meeting with Herod (Matthew 2:3-8). *The palace seems like a logical place to find the new, great king. And the king there was inquisitive. He sent us to a small town close by and wants us to report back.* [134 characters]

Group 3—After finding the one sought (Matthew 2:9-12). *We found him and offered gifts worthy of a prophet, priest, and king. Wow! But God warned us in a dream to stay clear of evil king Herod, who is nothing like Jesus!* [132 characters]

After work is complete, have groups share their tweets and summarize their Scripture assignments. Refer to the commentary to make sure all main points are made clearly and completely.

Say, "Everyone involved in these marvelous events had questions. Nothing like this had ever happened before—or since! But one thing was without question: the baby born in Bethlehem was changing things, and the wise men had traveled a great distance in order to honor Him. They put forth effort, they asked the right questions, and they experienced the joy of worshipping the Messiah."

Into Life

Give each person a pen and a sheet of paper. Ask students to list three people closest to them; then ask students to list the non-monetary gift he or she would most like to be able to give to each person on the list. Be alert to any mention or non-mention of giving the gift of the gospel. Discuss.

Alternative. Distribute pens and copies of "Better to Give" activity from the reproducible page. Have students work individually or in small groups to complete the listed Scriptures. Remind them to consider these Scriptures as they give and receive gifts this Christmas.

FAITH TO UNITE

DEVOTIONAL READING: Psalm 68:1-6, 15-20, 32-35
BACKGROUND SCRIPTURE: Ephesians 4

EPHESIANS 4:1-16

1 I therefore, the prisoner of the Lord, beseech you that ye walk worthy of the vocation wherewith ye are called,

2 With all lowliness and meekness, with longsuffering, forbearing one another in love;

3 Endeavouring to keep the unity of the Spirit in the bond of peace.

4 There is one body, and one Spirit, even as ye are called in one hope of your calling;

5 One Lord, one faith, one baptism,

6 One God and Father of all, who is above all, and through all, and in you all.

7 But unto every one of us is given grace according to the measure of the gift of Christ.

8 Wherefore he saith, When he ascended up on high, he led captivity captive, and gave gifts unto men.

9 (Now that he ascended, what is it but that he also descended first into the lower parts of the earth?

10 He that descended is the same also that ascended up far above all heavens, that he might fill all things.)

11 And he gave some, apostles; and some, prophets; and some, evangelists; and some, pastors and teachers;

12 For the perfecting of the saints, for the work of the ministry, for the edifying of the body of Christ:

13 Till we all come in the unity of the faith, and of the knowledge of the Son of God, unto a perfect man, unto the measure of the stature of the fulness of Christ:

14 That we henceforth be no more children, tossed to and fro, and carried about with every wind of doctrine, by the sleight of men, and cunning craftiness, whereby they lie in wait to deceive;

15 But speaking the truth in love, may grow up into him in all things, which is the head, even Christ:

16 From whom the whole body fitly joined together and compacted by that which every joint supplieth, according to the effectual working in the measure of every part, maketh increase of the body unto the edifying of itself in love.

KEY VERSES

I therefore, the prisoner of the Lord, beseech you that ye walk worthy of the vocation wherewith ye are called, with all lowliness and meekness, with longsuffering, forbearing one another in love; endeavouring to keep the unity of the Spirit in the bond of peace. —**Ephesians 4:1-3**

Faith in Action

LESSON AIMS

After participating in this lesson, each learner will be able to:

1. Discuss the significance of unity to the identity and mission of the church.

2. Explain why appreciation of the diversity of individual gifts is critical to unity in the church.

3. Identify and use his or her spiritual gifts to advance the church's mission.

LESSON OUTLINE

Introduction
  A. A House Divided
  B. Lesson Background
I. Reason for Unity (EPHESIANS 4:1-6)
  A. Worthy of the Calling (vv. 1-3)
  B. Nature of Our Faith (vv. 4-6)
    United We Stand, Pridefully We Fall
II. Means to Attain Unity (EPHESIANS 4:7-11)
  A. Through Differences (vv. 7-10)
  B. Through Leadership (v. 11)
III. Results of Unity (EPHESIANS 4:12-16)
  A. Mature to Serve (vv. 12, 13)
    What's on Your List of Sins?
  B. Grounded to Stand (v. 14)
  C. Truthful to Love (vv. 15, 16)
Conclusion
  A. Growth and Health
  B. Prayer
  C. Thought to Remember

Introduction

A. A House Divided

Abraham Lincoln's statement that "a house divided against itself cannot stand" remains one of the most famous quotes from American political history. But how many Americans today realize that Lincoln was quoting Jesus (Matthew 12:25; Mark 3:25)?

Jesus' statement was in response to accusations that He himself cast out demons by the power of Satan. But it would make no sense for the devil to empower Jesus to cast demons out of people. Satan's house would be divided against itself.

In today's passage, Paul applies a similar logic to the mission of the church: it would make no sense for God's people to divide themselves and work against one another, especially in view of the fact that Christ is working in each of us individually to accomplish His purposes. No house, no kingdom, and no church can stand if its people do not work together.

B. Lesson Background

Ephesus was one of the most significant centers of first-century Christianity. With many thousands of residents and serving as a shipping hub for the Lycus River Valley and the Aegean Sea, Ephesus was one of the largest and richest cities in the Roman world. The city's magnificent temple to its patron goddess, Artemis, was revered as one of the seven wonders of the ancient world and was a major tourist attraction. As a cosmopolitan commercial and religious center, Ephesus was widely known for its religious diversity: Jews lived side-by-side with pagans of all stripes, and occult practices and their accompanying superstitions were prevalent (see Acts 19).

Small wonder that the apostle Paul chose Ephesus as a base for evangelistic efforts in western Asia Minor. He spent almost three years in the city (Acts 19:8-10; 20:31) preaching to Jews and Gentiles and sending his own disciples to plant churches in nearby cities like Colosse and Laodicea. Acts 19 and 20 are dedicated largely to the history of the founding of the church in Ephesus. Unable to visit personally (see first verse of the lesson), Paul wrote.

Even though the Ephesian Christians enjoyed strong apostolic leadership, they struggled to live faithfully in a world driven by possessions, pride, and false conceptions of God and His will. In Acts 20, some three years before Ephesians was written, Paul warned the elders of the Ephesian church that self-serving leaders would create factions, splitting the body to serve their own purposes.

I. Reason for Unity
(Ephesians 4:1-6)
A. Worthy of the Calling (vv. 1-3)

1. I therefore, the prisoner of the Lord, beseech you that ye walk worthy of the vocation wherewith ye are called.

The word *therefore* marks an important transition in Ephesians. As *the prisoner of the Lord* under arrest in Rome, Paul has time on his hands—so he writes letters. To this point in this letter, he has been addressing profound concepts relating to adoption as God's chosen children (Ephesians 1:4-14), the relationship between Jews and Gentiles in the plan of salvation (2:11-22), and his own calling as an apostle (3:1-13). Building on these themes, the apostle turns to the practical implications of one's calling in Christ: God expects His chosen people to use what He has given them to work together in advancing the mission of the church.

2. With all lowliness and meekness, with longsuffering, forbearing one another in love.

HOW TO SAY IT

Aegean	A-*jee*-un.
Artemis	*Ar*-teh-miss.
Colosse	Ko-*lahss*-ee.
Colossians	Kuh-*losh*-unz.
Corinthians	Ko-*rin*-thee-unz (*th* as in *thin*).
Ephesians	Ee-*fee*-zhunz.
Ephesus	*Ef*-uh-sus.
Gentiles	*Jen*-tiles.
Laodicea	Lay-*odd*-uh-*see*-uh.
Philemon	Fih-*lee*-mun or Fye-*lee*-mun.
Philippians	Fih-*lip*-ee-unz.
Tychicus	*Tick*-ih-cuss.

This verse defines what it means to live a life worthy of God's calling as it emphasizes virtues that promote unity. To embrace *all lowliness* is to recognize that everything we have comes from God. Such humility in turn influences how we treat others. Character traits of meekness, longsuffering, and forbearance are to replace traits of harshness, tendencies to quarrel, and impatience. We as God's adopted children are to imitate our heavenly Father in loving one another.

3. Endeavouring to keep the unity of the Spirit in the bond of peace.

The Holy Spirit, working in each person, produces a spirit of unity within the church. Absence of unity, therefore, means that some are not following the Spirit's lead. Galatians 5:22-25, Paul's famous discussion of the "fruit of the Spirit," also characterizes the Holy Spirit as producing qualities in us that tend to unity, as opposed to the sinful desires of the flesh that selfishly divide us (5:19-21).

Paul's reference to *the bond of peace* may play on his reference to himself as the Lord's "prisoner" in verse 1: like the chains that bind a convict, the Spirit ties believers together in a web of peace.

> *What Do You Think?*
> How might the characteristics listed in verse 2 reveal themselves as we work in unity?
> *Talking Points for Your Discussion*
> - Examples of things said and not said
> - Examples of things done and not done
> - Examples of nonverbal body language

B. Nature of Our Faith (vv. 4-6)

4. There is one body, and one Spirit, even as ye are called in one hope of your calling.

The verse begins the recitation of Paul's famous "seven ones," which he uses to illustrate the vital nature of unity among Christians. *One body* draws on the human body as a metaphor for the church, which Paul elsewhere characterizes as "the body of Christ" (1 Corinthians 12:12-27). In this analogy, the parts of the body, each with its own unique function, represent individual Christians with their varied spiritual gifts. While the heart cannot do what the lungs can do and vice versa, both are absolutely vital to life. And so it is in the church.

With the reference to *one Spirit,* Paul begins to use the unity of God as an analogy for the kind of unity He expects to see in the church. Also, this verse with the next two present one of the few places in the Bible that address what later becomes known as the doctrine of the Trinity. God the Father, God the Son (Christ), and God the Holy Spirit are distinct in their work yet fully united in their purpose. Since God is one and since there is only one God, there is no room for Christians, as God's children, to divide from one another.

One hope relates the principle of unity to our salvation. We fulfill our hope of Heaven as we unite and work together.

5. One Lord, one faith, one baptism.

The New Testament authors often use *Lord* in reference to Christ. There is only one Christ and only one true *faith* in Him that provides salvation. As Paul reminds the Corinthians (1 Corinthians 1:11-17), no one is baptized in the name of a Christian leader; all believers of all personality types, ages, races, and gifts experience the same baptism reflecting the same faith in the same Christ that takes us to the same Heaven. This being true, how can we not be united in our work?

What Do You Think?

What reminders of common ground in Jesus have helped you defuse conflict?

Talking Points for Your Discussion

- Concerning silent reminders to ourselves
- Concerning audible or visible reminders to ourselves
- Concerning reminders to others

---

6. One God and Father of all, who is above all, and through all, and in you all.

Although God the Father is in some sense distinct from Christ, they are completely united as one, and there is only one God. That God is *above all* as Creator and Ruler, and that He is *through all* in the sense that He is everywhere and sustains everything, cannot be disputed. It therefore must be true that God is working in all of us individually to bring us together for a common purpose.

◆ *UNITED WE STAND, PRIDEFULLY WE FALL* ◆

El Chapo was his nickname. It means "Shorty," but Joaquín Guzmán Loera stood tall in the world of drug trafficking. He was Mexico's drug kingpin. His organization smuggled tons of drugs through tunnels dug under the border between the U.S. and Mexico.

In 2001, friends helped El Chapo escape from prison. He was recaptured in 2014 and sent to a maximum-security prison. He escaped again a year later. The escape route was a tunnel accessed through a hole in the floor of his cell's shower. The notorious criminal organization embarrassed the Mexican government with the sophisticated escape.

Pride led to El Chapo's re-recapture, however: word of his whereabouts leaked out when he was trying to arrange a deal for a movie of his life story. The organizational unity that had led to "success" in El Chapo's illegal activities was thereby undone.

The church has the noblest of missions: making disciples (Matthew 28:19, 20). But evil people like El Chapo aren't the only ones whose pride causes stumbling. When *our* way becomes more important than *Christ's* way, the world will be sure to see it.   —C. R. B.

II. Means to Attain Unity
(EPHESIANS 4:7-11)

A. Through Differences (vv. 7-10)

7. But unto every one of us is given grace according to the measure of the gift of Christ.

Grace is used here in a more nuanced fashion than in earlier chapters. In the contexts of Ephesians 1:6 and 2:5-8, *grace* refers to God's unmerited favor and love—a love so strong that it called unworthy people to be children and heirs. Here *grace* still refers to God's favor, but with a focus on what He does after we are saved: Christ shows favor by granting each of us gifts and abilities that can be used to serve the church.

Every one of us emphasizes that no one is left out. God views all spiritual gifts, and all the people who have them, as equally important to the work of the church. It is therefore critical that they/we all work together to get the job done.

8. Wherefore he saith, When he ascended up on high, he led captivity captive, and gave gifts unto men.

This is a loose quotation of Psalm 68:18, cited here in support of the fact that Christ, the one who *ascended upon high*, is the source of our gifts. In the psalm, God the conquering king takes His enemies as captives and receives tribute (*gifts*) from them as spoils of war. Paul is apparently drawing on an ancient reading of the psalm that proposes that God is not receiving gifts but giving them to His people—gifts plundered from His enemies (the original Hebrew of the psalm can be interpreted in either sense).

The phrase *he led captivity captive* is difficult. Some students think it refers to believers who have been captured from sin's clutches (2 Corinthians 2:14); others propose it refers to spiritual enemies (Colossians 2:15).

9, 10. (Now that he ascended, what is it but that he also descended first into the lower parts of the earth? He that descended is the same also that ascended up far above all heavens, that he might fill all things.)

Paul views the psalm as a prophecy of Christ. The Jesus who was powerful enough to ascend *up far above all heavens* (Acts 1:9-11) and was willing to make himself of "no reputation" (Philippians 2:7) in descending *into the lower parts of the earth* in human form is certainly able and willing to gift us to serve His church!

B. Through Leadership (v. 11)

11. And he gave some, apostles; and some, prophets; and some, evangelists; and some, pastors and teachers.

Paul has just stressed that Christ has graciously given gifts, and we normally think of these spiritual gifts as abilities that individual Christians receive to fulfill a particular service or calling. By analogy with 1 Corinthians 12:4-11 and Romans 12:6-8, one might conclude that each believer "owns" a gift that God has given him or her—as in, "this ability is mine to use for God." Such a posture readily lends itself to a sense of pride in one's accomplishments.

Here, however, the gifts are not abilities and talents that individuals have received, but rather are people whom God has put into the church to accomplish its mission. These people, exercising their God-given talents, belong to the church as essential equipment. This being the case, Christ must have intended for all these individuals (all of us) to work together toward one unified purpose.

All types of service are important, and Paul lists several service positions that illustrate the diversity of abilities with which Christ endows us. *Apostles* is likely used in the narrow sense of those who, like Peter and Paul, witnessed the resurrected Christ personally; thus they are authorities on Jesus' teachings.

Prophets are empowered not only to predict the future (foretelling) but also to speak God's truth (forthtelling); the latter is similar to the role of the modern preacher. At the risk of oversimplification, *evangelists* can be viewed as comparable with modern missionaries (see Acts 21:8).

The verse before us is the only place in the New Testament where the word *pastors* occurs. The Greek word behind it is elsewhere translated "shepherd(s)" (example: Matthew 9:36). Their function is to provide pastoral care. Some students see the phrase *pastors and teachers* as designating one kind of gifted person: a "pastor-teacher."

III. Results of Unity
(EPHESIANS 4:12-16)

A. Mature to Serve (vv. 12, 13)

12. For the perfecting of the saints, for the work of the ministry, for the edifying of the body of Christ.

The opening word of this verse indicates the purpose, or intended result, of Christ's act of giving the individuals of verse 11 to the church.

FOR THE MOST PERFECT UNION . . .

One body, Spirit, hope, Lord, faith, baptism, one God and Father of all.

Visual for Lesson 5. *Start a discussion by pointing to one entry on the list as you ask, "What if we lacked this one but had the other six?"*

Paul mentions what Christ intended for individual believers as well as what He intended for the church as a whole in this giving. When God's gifted people work together for the common good, individual believers become better equipped to serve. As we each grow, the church as a whole is built up and made stronger, better able to fulfill its purpose of reaching a lost world. It should go without saying that Christ did not give us gifts to serve ourselves or to divide us from others.

What Do You Think?
What are some appropriate ways to respond after being blessed by another's faithful use of spiritual gifts?
Talking Points for Your Discussion
- In private discussion with him or her
- In public

13. Till we all come in the unity of the faith, and of the knowledge of the Son of God, unto a perfect man, unto the measure of the stature of the fulness of Christ.

The mature believer, and churches composed of mature believers, will be characterized by unity, knowledge of Christ, and imitation of Christ. *Unity of the faith* likely refers not to saving faith in Christ but rather to the established orthodox truth of the gospel (compare 1 Timothy 1:19, 20; 3:9; 4:1, 6; 6:20, 21; 2 Timothy 4:7; Jude 3). Paul does not suggest that unity comes at the expense of truth, but rather that commitment to the truth will lead to unity. The Greek noun translated *knowledge* occurs more than a dozen times in Paul's writings, frequently in contexts of comprehending something about God (Romans 1:28; 10:2; Ephesians 1:17; Colossians 1:9). What could be more important than studying to gain an ever-better *knowledge of the Son of God*?

Such knowledge reaches its pinnacle when we achieve *the fulness of Christ*. We move toward that goal as we put away our own desires in order better to think and act as Jesus did. Attaining Christ's fullness will include every aspect of what we today call discipleship: knowing who Jesus was and what He did and taught as we try to live daily by His teachings and example. Even though we can never perfectly achieve this in this life, it remains the goal of those on the path to spiritual maturity.

◆ *WHAT'S ON YOUR LIST OF SINS?* ◆

Tom was a 50-something elder in his church, and he was rather pleased with his maturity in the faith. One Sunday, a visiting preacher spoke at the church, and Tom and his wife invited him over for dinner. The visit was pleasant until Tom began to complain about the spiritual immaturity of many church members, compared with the high level of Tom's own spiritual achievement.

Tom asserted that he had reached the point of no longer sinning. The standard of judgment he used was a list of practices that were not a part of his lifestyle. It included adultery, gambling, the use of alcohol and tobacco, etc. Missing from the list were sins of the heart: a critical spirit, a divisive attitude, etc. Tom's approach to spiritual maturity was to glory in the vices he *didn't* practice rather than the virtues that *did* characterize his life.

Paul's exhortation focuses on love that builds each other up rather than on man-made rules that eventually tear the church apart. Paul was not soft on sin, but he knew that a prideful spirit was just as un-Christlike as the habits of the flesh Tom was so pleased to say he had outgrown. (Well, Tom did acknowledge that he would *occasionally* make a "mistake"!) Do a lack of love and the absence of a unifying spirit make it onto our list of sins as we seek maturity in Christ?   —C. R. B.

B. Grounded to Stand (v. 14)

14. That we henceforth be no more children, tossed to and fro, and carried about with every wind of doctrine, by the sleight of men, and cunning craftiness, whereby they lie in wait to deceive.

Paul sometimes compares the church with a human who is (or should be) growing in intellectual and emotional maturity from life as a child into adulthood. In the most famous of these maturing passages, 1 Corinthians 13, Paul says that the mature church composed of mature believers will be characterized by love and full knowledge of God. Regarding the passage at hand, Paul extends the reference to "knowledge" in verse 13 to stress that the mature church will be doctrinally sound. Such a church is able to discern falsehood and protect itself from those who seek to divide. When the church is united as all its individual parts work together, it will be much more difficult for self-seeking people to promote their own agendas.

The metaphor of a boat tossed by the waves and wind—analogous to the child who cannot discern truth from falsehood—illustrates the dangers of immaturity and divisiveness. Unity in truth is the proper anchor for the church and its message.

C. Truthful to Love (vv. 15, 16)

15, 16. But speaking the truth in love, may grow up into him in all things, which is the head, even Christ: from whom the whole body fitly joined together and compacted by that which every joint supplieth, according to the effectual working in the measure of every part, maketh increase of the body unto the edifying of itself in love.

Paul again stresses that unity comes through truth, not at the expense of truth. The focus here is clearly on how believers within the church interact with one another. Those who are mature will converse truthfully, guided by a spirit of love that unites. Such love neither gives nor takes offense when the truth is spoken.

Continuing with the analogy of the church as a human body, Christ as *the head* is the center of thought, reason, and motivation (see Colossians 1:15-20). The mature church will be united in purpose and guided by Christ. Each member of the church may be compared with a *joint*. Just as each joint and muscle in the human body fulfills a distinct function, each Christian is gifted by the Spirit to fulfill a distinct calling. When this happens—as each individual part matures and develops—the entire body becomes mature and strong. The result is, again, love, so that unity is both the driver of the church's growth and the goal of its growth.

> ### What Do You Think?
> What are some practical ways to keep truth and love balanced in our interactions?
> *Talking Points for Your Discussion*
> - Identifying times when truth is expressed in unloving ways
> - Identifying times when love is expressed in such a way that truth is eclipsed

Conclusion

A. Growth and Health

Parents know of many trips to the pediatrician during the first two years of life. Doctors pay close attention to the age when a child begins to stand, to take her first steps, and to speak. While each person is different, growth statistics are important because they are primary indicators of a child's health. Similarly, farmers measure the quality of soil and seed by crop yields. Whether plants, animals, or people, growth is a sign of health.

Paul would say that the same is true of the church. As we grow as individuals, the church collectively grows in maturity and numbers. When we find that we and/or our church isn't growing, it may be time for a spiritual checkup to determine whether something is amiss.

B. Prayer

Lord, we fall prey to pride at times. Help us appreciate one another and work together to fulfill the work of Christ. In his name we pray. Amen.

C. Thought to Remember

"United we stand, divided we fall."

INVOLVEMENT LEARNING

Enhance your lesson with KJV Bible Student *(from your curriculum supplier) and the reproducible activity page (at www.standardlesson.com or in the back of the* KJV Standard Lesson Commentary Deluxe Edition*).*

Into the Lesson

Play a group game such as Charades, in which team members must communicate well and work together in order to succeed. After a few rounds, lead into Bible study, saying, "They say there is no *I* in *team*. The best teams work because they are unified in reaching for a shared goal. Paul wrote to the church in Ephesus about that type of unity. Let's see what he had to say."

Into the Word

Divide the class into three groups. Supply each group with pen and paper and one of the following research assignments on handouts you create. They will read portions of today's text and compare them with parallel portions of Scripture. Partial suggested responses are in italics; do not include those on handouts.

Group 1—Reason for Unity

1. What characteristics of our lifestyle demonstrate that we seek the unity worthy of the name "Christian"? Compare Ephesians 4:1-3; Philippians 1:27; 2:1-4.

We show we are one in Jesus by showing that the humble nature of Jesus rules us.

2. How does unity among believers demonstrate key truths of our faith? Compare Ephesians 4:4-6 and John 17:20-23.

We share one faith because we worship the one and only God. When we are one, we show that the Father, the Son, and the Spirit are one and that Jesus was sent by God.

Group 2—Means of Attaining Unity

1. What is the difference between expectations of unity and expectations of uniformity in the church? Compare Ephesians 4:7-10; Romans 12:6a; 1 Corinthians 12:11.

Christian unity is not achieved by being the same, but by allowing God to make us different!

2. What role does leadership play in attaining unity? Compare Ephesians 4:11; Romans 12:6b-8.

Those differing gifts allow us both to serve one another and to lead one another in our shared faith.

Group 3—Results of Unity

1. How does unity fight evil? Compare Ephesians 4:12-14; Romans 12:21.

When we are taught the truth, we are no longer divided by the evil one. Knowing what is right and good overcomes that which is evil.

2. Why is love crucial for Christian unity? Compare Ephesians 4:15, 16; 1 Corinthians 12:27-31; 13:13.

Love builds us up. It is what unifies all of God's gifts, making love the greatest gift of all.

Allow groups to report after they have completed their research.

Alternative. Distribute copies of the "Circles of Unity" activity from the reproducible page, which you can download. Have students work individually or in small groups. Allow them to share their findings.

Into Life

Invite students to give examples of times when they've seen unity among Christians. In contrast, have them list times when they have seen a lack of unity among believers (caution against using real names of churches and people). Encourage students to talk about the impact those events had on their lives and their community.

Ask, "Based on these kinds of interactions, what conclusions would an unbeliever draw about Jesus?" Remind students that the way we treat each other as Christians not only affects us, but it is a witness to others about Christ.

Ask students to think about things in their own lives that keep them from "the unity of the Spirit" and "the bond of peace."

Alternative. Distribute copies of the "Roadblocks to Unity" activity from the reproducible page, which you can download. Have students work individually.

A SINCERE FAITH

DEVOTIONAL READING: Psalm 56
BACKGROUND SCRIPTURE: Daniel 1

DANIEL 1:8-21

8 But Daniel purposed in his heart that he would not defile himself with the portion of the king's meat, nor with the wine which he drank: therefore he requested of the prince of the eunuchs that he might not defile himself.

9 Now God had brought Daniel into favour and tender love with the prince of the eunuchs.

10 And the prince of the eunuchs said unto Daniel, I fear my lord the king, who hath appointed your meat and your drink: for why should he see your faces worse liking than the children which are of your sort? then shall ye make me endanger my head to the king.

11 Then said Daniel to Melzar, whom the prince of the eunuchs had set over Daniel, Hananiah, Mishael, and Azariah,

12 Prove thy servants, I beseech thee, ten days; and let them give us pulse to eat, and water to drink.

13 Then let our countenances be looked upon before thee, and the countenance of the children that eat of the portion of the king's meat: and as thou seest, deal with thy servants.

14 So he consented to them in this matter, and proved them ten days.

15 And at the end of ten days their countenances appeared fairer and fatter in flesh than all the children which did eat the portion of the king's meat.

16 Thus Melzar took away the portion of their meat, and the wine that they should drink; and gave them pulse.

17 As for these four children, God gave them knowledge and skill in all learning and wisdom: and Daniel had understanding in all visions and dreams.

18 Now at the end of the days that the king had said he should bring them in, then the prince of the eunuchs brought them in before Nebuchadnezzar.

19 And the king communed with them; and among them all was found none like Daniel, Hananiah, Mishael, and Azariah: therefore stood they before the king.

20 And in all matters of wisdom and understanding, that the king enquired of them, he found them ten times better than all the magicians and astrologers that were in all his realm.

21 And Daniel continued even unto the first year of king Cyrus.

KEY VERSE

Daniel purposed in his heart that he would not defile himself with the portion of the king's meat, nor with the wine which he drank: therefore he requested of the prince of the eunuchs that he might not defile himself.
—**Daniel 1:8**

AFAITH IN ACTION

Unit 2: A Living Faith in God
LESSONS 6–9

LESSON AIMS

After participating in this lesson, each learner will be able to:

1. Recount the details of the first test that Daniel and his friends faced as captives in Babylon and how they responded to it.

2. Give examples of modern workplace situations that parallel those of the text.

3. Form a plan for responding to a workplace challenge that the model of the text addresses.

LESSON OUTLINE

Introduction

A. Worst-Case Scenarios

In 1999, Joshua Piven and David Borgenicht authored *The Worst-Case Scenario Survival Handbook,* a guide to surviving the worst of all imaginable catastrophes. The book has sold over 10 million copies and inspired a series of related books, games, and even a television show.

While strategic planners regularly discuss how to react in extreme circumstances, they usually do not consider situations as extreme as those Piven and Borgenicht describe. Their book provides instructions for situations such as landing a plane when the pilot is incapacitated, defusing a bomb, escaping from quicksand, and surviving a shark attack.

Bad things do happen to good people. True, we may not have had to survive a shark attack or defuse a bomb, but we have all experienced crisis: the loss of a job, conflict with a family member, etc. There is much to learn from how an Old Testament prophet dealt with a crisis in his life.

B. Lesson Background

The focus of this quarter's lessons is the two-fold nature of faith as encompassing both belief and action. The unit of four lessons that begins with today's study is drawn from the Old Testament book of Daniel.

Daniel and his three friends lived in perilous times for Judah and its capital of Jerusalem. The "third year of the reign of Jehoiakim king of Judah," mentioned in Daniel 1:1, was 605 BC. This was also the year when King Nebuchadnezzar came to power in Babylon. He ruled for 43 years.

The siege of Jerusalem by Nebuchadnezzar noted in Daniel 1:1 was the first of a series of excursions by Babylon into Judah, climaxed by the fall of Jerusalem and the destruction of Solomon's temple in 586 BC. (Note that the land of Babylon or Babylonia is also referred to as Chaldea, and the residents are called Chaldeans.)

Of course, it is vital to read what follows the account in Daniel 1:1: "And the Lord gave Jehoiakim king of Judah into [Nebuchadnezzar's] hand, with part of the vessels of the house of God" (1:2).

This makes clear what all of Scripture proclaims: kings such as Nebuchadnezzar, as great as they may be or consider themselves to be, are ultimately under the reign of the truly "great King," the Lord (Psalm 48:2).

Part of the Babylonians' strategy in conquering territories such as Judah was to select individuals from those territories who showed significant potential for being schooled in the culture of the Babylonians. In the words of Daniel 1:4, they were looking for individuals

> in whom was no blemish, but well favoured, and skilful in all wisdom, and cunning in knowledge, and understanding science, and such as had ability in them to stand in the king's palace, and whom they might teach the learning and the tongue of the Chaldeans.

This practice was intended to replace the captives' cultural identity with that of the Babylonians'. Among those taken from Jerusalem for this purpose were Daniel and his friends Hananiah, Mishael, and Azariah (Daniel 1:6). Daniel 1:3 notes that these young men were drawn from the royal family and nobility of Judah.

One component of the reeducation of captives was that of changing their given names. In a culture where names were of great significance, such an action was intended to show the captives that their very identity had been changed. Thus Daniel, Hananiah, Mishael, and Azariah became Belteshazzar, Shadrach, Meshach, and Abednego, respectively (Daniel 1:7). The new names included references to fictitious Babylonian gods (compare 4:8); they no longer reflect the name of the God of Judah.

It is interesting that while Daniel's three friends are referred to by their new names exclusively after Daniel 2:17, Daniel himself, whose Hebrew name means "God is judge," is identified by both his old and new names together six times (see Daniel 1:7; 2:26; 4:8, 19; 5:12; 10:1). Some propose this to be a way of recognizing that Daniel's God remained in control in a pagan setting; but this theory does not explain why the same is not noted of Daniel's three friends, who serve the same God. Our lesson text begins with the first of a series of tests that Daniel and his friends faced regarding their loyalty to the true God—*their* God.

I. Maintain Values
(DANIEL 1:8-10)
A. Request Made (v. 8)

8a. But Daniel purposed in his heart that he would not defile himself with the portion of the king's meat, nor with the wine which he drank.

Daniel 1:5 tells us that King Nebuchadnezzar "appointed [Daniel and his friends] a daily provision of the king's meat, and of the wine which he drank: so nourishing them three years, that at the end thereof they might stand before the king." However, Daniel has determined *in his heart* not to *defile himself with* such provisions. Most likely there are one or two reasons that lead to Daniel's decision not to eat and drink what the king offers. First, the food may have been presented to Babylonian gods as part of a pagan ceremony (compare 1 Corinthians 8). Second, the food may violate the regulations on clean and unclean foods given in the law of Moses (Leviticus 11).

The reference to Daniel's *heart* is noteworthy for indicating his steadfast devotion to his God. Daniel's captors can change his surroundings and

HOW TO SAY IT

Abednego	Uh-*bed*-nee-go.
Azariah	Az-uh-*rye*-uh.
Babylon	*Bab*-uh-lun.
Babylonian	Bab-ih-*low*-nee-un.
Belteshazzar	Bel-tih-*shazz*-er.
Chaldeans	Kal-*dee*-unz.
Cyrus	*Sigh*-russ.
eunuchs	*you*-nicks.
Gentiles	*Jen*-tiles.
Hananiah	Han-uh-*nye*-uh.
Jehoiakim	Jeh-*hoy*-uh-kim.
Judean	Joo-*dee*-un.
Melzar	*Mel*-zar.
Meshach	*Me*-shack.
Mishael	*Mish*-a-el.
Nebuchadnezzar	*Neb*-yuh-kud-**nez**-er.
Persian	*Per*-zhunz.
Shadrach	*Shay*-drack or *Shad*-rack.

his name, but they cannot touch his heart. That belongs to God alone.

◆ **"When in Rome, Do as the Romans"** ◆

The above axiom is so familiar that we usually shorten it to just "When in Rome." This saying has its origin in antiquity, being a short paraphrase of advice to Augustine (AD 354–430) from Ambrose (AD 337–397). The longer, more precise version is this:

> When I go to Rome, I fast on Saturday, but here [in Milan] I do not fast. On the same principle . . . observe the custom prevailing in whatever church you come to attend, if you desire neither to give offense by your conduct, nor to find cause of offense in another's.

The advice is to be understood in the context of how Christians saw fit to practice their faith with regard to matters of opinion in various locations (compare Romans 14:5, 6).

Modern culture has hijacked the axiom to justify accommodating oneself to whatever secular customs are practiced in a given location. So, for example, the "what happens in Vegas stays in Vegas" mind-set is taken to justify immoral behavior while visiting that city. But we are careful to note that Daniel didn't adopt an unthinking "when in Babylon, do as the Babylonians do" outlook when interacting with that pagan culture.

The issue that confronted Daniel also confronts us: Which of society's customs are appropriate to practice, and which are not? This is a question that must be asked and answered on a daily basis.

—C. R. B.

What Do You Think?

When was a time you honored a boundary to stay true to God's will? What did you learn from that experience that could help others?

Talking Points for Your Discussion

- Regarding tactfulness (example: Judges 8:1-3) vs. directness (example: Judges 12:1-6)
- Considering boundaries that you model for others to honor as well (Ephesians 5:3-7; etc.) vs. boundaries of private conscience (Romans 14:22; etc.)

8b. Therefore he requested of the prince of the eunuchs that he might not defile himself.

It is also to Daniel's credit that he goes through the proper channels to voice his concerns about his diet. He does not become obnoxious or defiant in his behavior; rather, he brings his concerns to *the prince of the eunuchs*. For Daniel to take his request to someone with such a title may indicate that Daniel and his friends were made eunuchs when brought to Babylon (compare Isaiah 39:7). Such was a common practice in ancient times. Adding to the uncertainty is the fact that the Hebrew word translated *eunuch(s)* is also translated "officer(s)" (example: 1 Samuel 8:15) and "chamberlain(s)" (example: 2 Kings 23:11).

B. Request Granted (vv. 9, 10)

9. Now God had brought Daniel into favour and tender love with the prince of the eunuchs.

Here is additional evidence of the Lord's control (compare Daniel 1:2) as God honors the faithfulness of Daniel. This man's experience in a foreign land is thus very similar to Joseph's in Egypt (Genesis 39:2-4, 20-23).

10. And the prince of the eunuchs said unto Daniel, I fear my lord the king, who hath appointed your meat and your drink: for why should he see your faces worse liking than the children which are of your sort? then shall ye make me endanger my head to the king.

The official is sensitive to the fact that he answers to King Nebuchadnezzar for his conduct. The pronouns *your* and *ye* are plural in the Hebrew text, thus the official recognizes that Daniel speaks for his three friends. If these four do not eat from the king's table, their appearance may suffer—and so will the one in charge! (Note: the Hebrew behind the word *children* here and vv. 13 and 17 is translated "young men" elsewhere [example: 1 Kings 12:8-14], and that is the sense here.)

II. Offer Solutions
(Daniel 1:11-16)
A. Limited Trial (vv. 11-14)

11, 12. Then said Daniel to Melzar, whom the prince of the eunuchs had set over Dan-

iel, Hananiah, Mishael, and Azariah, Prove thy servants, I beseech thee, ten days; and let them give us pulse to eat, and water to drink.

To the individual *whom the prince of the eunuchs* has put in charge of Daniel and his friends, Daniel suggests an alternative diet for him and his friends. They are to be given *pulse to eat, and water to drink.* The word *pulse* renders a Hebrew word that means "things that are sown." In other words, Daniel is requesting that he and his friends be offered a diet of vegetables and water for a period of *ten days.* Since the time of training that Daniel and his friends are undergoing is three years (Daniel 1:5), a 10-day "trial run" will not interfere with the overall program.

We can also note in passing that the word *Melzar* (also in Daniel 1:16) is a transliteration, not a translation. We don't really know if that's a man's name or is a title of some kind.

> ### What Do You Think?
> How should a Christian go about appealing an employer's policy that goes against his or her Christian convictions?
>
> *Talking Points for Your Discussion*
> - Considering how to pray about the appeal
> - Considering the medium of the appeal (personal discussion, e-mail, etc.)
> - Considering the tone of the appeal
> - Considering the basis of the appeal
> - Other

13. Then let our countenances be looked upon before thee, and the countenance of the children that eat of the portion of the king's meat: and as thou seest, deal with thy servants.

At the end of the 10 days, the person in charge can examine the results, specifically the *countenances,* or appearance, of the four young men, comparing their appearance with those who have eaten of *the king's* fare. He can *deal with* the four men as the results dictate. If their appearance is inferior to that of the others, that will be sufficient evidence to end the experiment.

14. So he consented to them in this matter, and proved them ten days.

Daniel's tactful, polite approach is persuasive, so the test commences. Tactfulness seems to be an important personality characteristic of Daniel (compare Daniel 2:14).

B. Exemplary Results (vv. 15, 16)

15. And at the end of ten days their countenances appeared fairer and fatter in flesh than all the children which did eat the portion of the king's meat.

It may seem odd that Daniel and his friends could have looked *fatter,* following a 10-day diet of nothing but vegetables and water, than those who have eaten *the portion of the king's meat.* However, the term *fat* in the Old Testament often implies being well nourished. The term thus speaks favorably of the four men's overall appearance without suggesting that they gained weight.

16. Thus Melzar took away the portion of their meat, and the wine that they should drink; and gave them pulse.

God has already caused the foreign officials to look with favor on Daniel and his friends (Daniel 1:9), and it seems that He has done so again. Melzar honors his promise and allows the four men to continue with their nutrition plan.

> ### What Do You Think?
> What did you learn from an experience when you saw an attempt to honor God backfire?
>
> *Talking Points for Your Discussion*
> - Regarding a "holier than thou" witness
> - Regarding misunderstanding of God's desires
> - Regarding an inconsistent witness
> - Other

III. Work Diligently
(Daniel 1:17-21)

A. Empowered by God (vv. 17, 18)

17a. As for these four children, God gave them knowledge and skill in all learning and wisdom.

Here is another sign of God's special blessing and care for the four young men from Judah. Daniel 1:4 says that the Babylonians' intention is to teach the young captives "the learning and the tongue of the Chaldeans." But Daniel and his three friends have an additional teacher: God.

◆ JONAH, ESTHER, OR DANIEL? ◆

Someone observed that the fundamental question of theology has always been how the church can present the gospel in the thought-forms of its surrounding culture as winsomely as possible without giving up the central core of the gospel. Modern answers to the question have been "all over the map," as they say. But we also see wide variety in the Bible as various devout people react differently to cultural influences.

At one extreme was Jonah. He wanted absolutely nothing to do with the culture into which God sent him to preach. And Jonah did his best (or his worst) to avoid his mission. He goes down in history as the only preacher disappointed that his preaching was successful (see Jonah 3:6–4:3)! At the other extreme was Esther, who came close to allowing the context of her new culture to blind her to her obligation to her own people (Esther 2:7-18; 4:9-14).

Daniel and his friends stand between these extremes. They were willing to be instructed in the language and ways of their captors (Daniel 1:4). But to be instructed about something does not necessarily imply personally adopting the values that stand behind cultural practices. The fact that these men ended up with the approval of both God and King

BEING A PERSON OF FAITH IN A HOSTILE CULTURE

COOPERATION
PROPOSE CONSTRUCTIVE SOLUTIONS
DANIEL 1

Visual for Lesson 6. *Ask learners if they see the problem with this visual (the gears are locked). Then ask for constructive solutions to the problem.*

Nebuchadnezzar indicates that the four walked this tightrope perfectly. So . . . how are your tightrope-walking skills these days? —C. R. B.

> **What Do You Think?**
> How would you use Daniel 1:17a, 20, if at all, to counsel a student who is worried about being corrupted by secular higher education?
> *Talking Points for Your Discussion*
> - Regarding the role of humility
> - Regarding the role of discernment
> - Regarding the role of academic excellence
> - Comparing and contrasting with other opportunities to engage culture

17b. And Daniel had understanding in all visions and dreams.

Daniel demonstrates *his understanding in all visions and dreams* on two occasions for King Nebuchadnezzar (see Daniel 2:31-45; 4:19-27). Daniel will also experience visions that will leave him deeply shaken, even sickened (7:15, 28; 8:27; 10:8, 16, 17). In one instance, the Lord withholds understanding (8:26, 27).

18. Now at the end of the days that the king had said he should bring them in, then the prince of the eunuchs brought them in before Nebuchadnezzar.

The note that *the end of the days that the king had said* is at hand means that the Hebrew men have completed the three-year training and education regimen of Daniel 1:5. This is the time when the king will grant his approval; however, Daniel and his friends already have approval from one who has greater authority than Nebuchadnezzar, that being the approval of God himself (Daniel 1:9, 17). On the identity of *the prince of the eunuchs,* see commentary on 1:8b, above.

B. Outperforming the Godless (vv. 19-21)

19. And the king communed with them; and among them all was found none like Daniel, Hananiah, Mishael, and Azariah: therefore stood they before the king.

The king interacts with all of those who have gone through the training program. No individual or group is more distinguished than *Dan-*

iel, Hananiah, Mishael, and Azariah. Perhaps the continued use of their Hebrew names, after being given new names in Daniel 1:7, is meant to highlight the fact that the God whose name is a part of their given names is the source of the wisdom that has caused them to excel in a pagan environment. The king can change their names, but he can do nothing to hinder the power and influence of their God.

That these four men stand *before the king* means that they now enter his service. A similar expression is used of David's service to King Saul (1 Samuel 16:21, 22). The ultimate service of the four still belongs to the King of kings, however.

> *What Do You Think?*
> What have you seen Christians do to improve work relationships? Which of those actions are models for to emulate?
> *Talking Points for Your Discussion*
> ▪ In contexts of paid employment
> ▪ In contexts of volunteer work

20. And in all matters of wisdom and understanding, that the king enquired of them, he found them ten times better than all the magicians and astrologers that were in all his realm.

The four Judean captives distinguish themselves from their peers. The expression *ten times* is a way of saying that they are far more competent than any of the other men who come before the king. Pagan *magicians and astrologers* possess their own methods (compare Exodus 7:11, 22; 8:7, 18; Acts 8:9-12). But as verse 17 has already informed us, God has given Daniel, Hananiah, Mishael, and Azariah the edge over everyone else.

Consider again the parallel with Joseph in the book of Genesis. He too was taken to a foreign land (against his will) and there demonstrated a wisdom in interpreting dreams that the Egyptian magicians and wise men did not possess (Genesis 41:8, 15, 16).

21. And Daniel continued even unto the first year of king Cyrus.

This final verse in our text calls attention to the duration of Daniel's service on foreign soil. He will outlast not only the great King Nebuchadnezzar

but the Babylonian Empire itself, which will fall to the Persians in 539 BC. Daniel will then continue his exemplary service under *Cyrus,* the ruler who will issue during his *first year* the decree allowing those Jews who wish to do so to go back home to Judah (2 Chronicles 36:22, 23).

Daniel's three friends are mentioned again when they are promoted to higher positions "over the affairs of the province of Babylon" (Daniel 2:49) and in chapter 3 in the account of the "fiery furnace," the subject of next week's study.

Conclusion

A. Strategy for Exiles

A change of setting became very real and intense for Daniel and friends. Their status changed from being part of a majority in Judah to being a clear minority in Babylon. These four young men could have viewed their new status from a primarily negative perspective in never again being able to serve God as they once did. But they chose instead to see their circumstances more in terms of an open door to honor God before pagans.

That more positive perspective produced within Daniel and his companions a strategy that we as exiles who serve Jesus in alien territory (compare 1 Peter 2:11) can apply. Daniel, while expressing his dislike for the foods offered by the king, used the proper channels to present his objections. Daniel was not disrespectful toward those in authority, and neither should we be (Romans 13:1-5; 1 Peter 2:12-19). Our intention to "obey God rather than men" (Acts 5:29) does not mean that we must set out to create hostility.

B. Prayer

Our Father, guide us in following the example of Daniel as we exhibit tact and grace under pressure. May we emulate our ultimate example, Jesus, who was filled with grace and truth. Grant us your Spirit's power in our spheres of influence. We pray in Jesus' name. Amen.

C. Thought to Remember

Godly conviction combined with diplomacy
can overcome many crises.

INVOLVEMENT LEARNING

Enhance your lesson with KJV Bible Student *(from your curriculum supplier) and the reproducible activity page (at www.standardlesson.com or in the back of the* KJV Standard Lesson Commentary Deluxe Edition*).*

Into the Lesson

As a class, browse through news headlines (either from newspapers or online) to find 10–12 examples of different types of crises. Examples can range from financial crises to political crises to medical crises to safety crises, and so on. Write the headlines in a place where everyone can see them. Then, as a class, discuss the crises and whom they effect. Then work together to number the headlines in order from most disastrous to least.

Alternative. Distribute pens or pencils and copies of the "In Case of Emergency" activity from the reproducible page, which you can download. Have students work individually or in small groups to match emergency situations with the best responses.

After either activity, transition to the Bible study by saying, "Bad things happen to good people. We have all experienced a crisis in our lives—loss of a job, conflict with a family member, or an unexpected move. Let's learn how an Old Testament prophet dealt with a crisis in his life."

Into the Word

Prior to class, prepare grocery bags with the items described below. If you can't gather the actual items, replace them with pictures or written descriptions. Read Daniel 1:8-21 as a class. Then divide students into three groups, giving each group one of the bags. Have groups unpack the bags and follow the instructions on the index cards you've prepared as described below. After several minutes, let groups share the questions they've been given and report to the class. Allow further discussion.

Group 1—Give this group a bag containing a bag of sugar and a box of sugar substitute/artificial sweetener. The card should say, "Read Daniel 1:8-10 and discuss: If Daniel had decided to SUBSTITUTE his diet for the one offered by the king,

what other things might he have been tempted to embrace while at the palace?"

Group 2—Give this group a grocery bag containing some type of cleaning solution. The card should say, "Read Daniel 1:11-16 and discuss: Rather than defiantly refusing what was offered him, Daniel suggested a SOLUTION. Why was this so important?"

Group 3—Give this group a grocery bag containing women's cosmetic foundation. The card should say, "Read Daniel 1:17-21 and discuss: Because of their faithfulness, God blessed Daniel and his three companions with remarkable wisdom and knowledge. How did these things lay a FOUNDATION for David as he faced future trials?"

Alternative. Distribute pens or pencils, paper, and copies of the "Rearview Mirror" activity from the reproducible page. Have students work individually or in small groups to prepare a monologue from Daniel's perspective. Invite volunteers to share the monologues with the class.

After either activity, say, "People often find themselves confronted by contradictory requirements from different sources of authority. How do we resolve such conflicts? Daniel's active faith combined with tact helped him resolve his conflict and remain obedient to God."

Into Life

Say, "Daniel saw God's faithfulness throughout his life, and it strengthened him. As adults, we have a perspective and a foundation that younger believers may not yet have." Give examples of crises that young believers might be facing (parents divorcing, trouble at school, uncertain future, injury or illness, etc.). Discuss ways that mature Christians could offer encouragement and support. Challenge students to commit to impacting the lives of young believers through their own knowledge, experience, and faith.

A BOLD FAITH

DEVOTIONAL READING: Romans 12:9-21
BACKGROUND SCRIPTURE: Daniel 3

DANIEL 3:19-23, 26-28

19 Then was Nebuchadnezzar full of fury, and the form of his visage was changed against Shadrach, Meshach, and Abednego: therefore he spake, and commanded that they should heat the furnace one seven times more than it was wont to be heated.

20 And he commanded the most mighty men that were in his army to bind Shadrach, Meshach, and Abednego, and to cast them into the burning fiery furnace.

21 Then these men were bound in their coats, their hosen, and their hats, and their other garments, and were cast into the midst of the burning fiery furnace.

22 Therefore because the king's commandment was urgent, and the furnace exceeding hot, the flame of the fire slew those men that took up Shadrach, Meshach, and Abednego.

23 And these three men, Shadrach, Meshach, and Abednego, fell down bound into the midst of the burning fiery furnace.

. . . .

26 Then Nebuchadnezzar came near to the mouth of the burning fiery furnace, and spake, and said, Shadrach, Meshach, and Abednego, ye servants of the most high God, come forth, and come hither. Then Shadrach, Meshach, and Abednego, came forth of the midst of the fire.

27 And the princes, governors, and captains, and the king's counsellors, being gathered together, saw these men, upon whose bodies the fire had no power, nor was an hair of their head singed, neither were their coats changed, nor the smell of fire had passed on them.

28 Then Nebuchadnezzar spake, and said, Blessed be the God of Shadrach, Meshach, and Abednego, who hath sent his angel, and delivered his servants that trusted in him, and have changed the king's word, and yielded their bodies, that they might not serve nor worship any god, except their own God.

KEY VERSE

Nebuchadnezzar spake, and said, Blessed be the God of Shadrach, Meshach, and Abednego, who hath sent his angel, and delivered his servants that trusted in him, and have changed the king's word, and yielded their bodies, that they might not serve nor worship any god, except their own God. —**Daniel 3:28**

Faith in Action

Unit 2: A Living Faith in God
Lessons 6–9

Lesson Aims

After participating in this lesson, each learner will be able to:

1. Summarize the deliverance of Shadrach, Meshach, and Abednego from death, and relate Nebuchadnezzar's reaction to that deliverance.

2. Identify circumstances or issues in today's world that require a response of bold faith from Christians.

3. Write a message of encouragement to a Christian who is imprisoned because of his or her faith.

Lesson Outline

Introduction
 A. No Compromise
 B. Lesson Background
 I. Fury of the King (Daniel 3:19-23)
 A. Attitude Change (v. 19a)
 B. Draconian Response (vv. 19b-21)
 C. Collateral Damage (vv. 22, 23)
  Reacting to "Error"
 II. Work of All-Powerful God (Daniel 3:26-28)
 A. Different Attitude (v. 26)
 B. Thorough Inspection (v. 27)
 C. Proper Credit (v. 28)
  Surprised by . . .
Conclusion
 A. The Flames of Fellowship
 B. Prayer
 C. Thought to Remember

Introduction
A. No Compromise

No Compromise is the title of an album by Keith Green (1953–1982), a Christian musician. But it is also a description of his life. Green's confrontational lyrics and spoken messages put him at odds with believers and unbelievers alike at times.

Probably the greatest controversy he stirred was decrying commercialism in producing Christian resources, including his own music! In 1979, Green began refusing to charge money for concerts or albums. He and his wife mortgaged their home to finance his music personally. By May 1982, Green had shipped out more than 200,000 copies, 61,000 for free. He refused to compromise his principles, accepting the consequences.

We all struggle with doing the right thing—when to speak up and when to shut up. Sometimes we don't even know what the "right" thing is! It can be the same when it comes to our faith. Because we love God, there will be times when we may face derision, isolation, or worse for standing up for Him. Three captives in a foreign land give us a great example of refusing to compromise in the face of deadly consequences.

B. Lesson Background

Last week's study focused primarily on the young man Daniel, although his three friends in captivity were involved in everything that occurred (Daniel 1:11-20). All four of them had been taken into exile in Babylon in about 605 BC.

Daniel is described as having "understanding in all visions and dreams" (Daniel 1:17). He was able to relate to King Nebuchadnezzar the content of his dream when no one else could, then provide the interpretation. Daniel left no doubt as to the accuracy of his words when he concluded by telling the king, "The dream is certain, and the interpretation thereof sure" (2:45).

In response the grateful king acknowledged Daniel's God as "a God of gods, and a Lord of kings, and a revealer of secrets" (Daniel 2:47). He also made Daniel "ruler over the whole province of Babylon, and chief of the governors over all the wise men of Babylon" (2:48). Daniel then requested that his fellow countrymen Shadrach, Meshach, and Abednego be placed "over the affairs of the province of Babylon" (2:49). But their new positions of authority did not make them exempt from tests of their faith.

Today's lesson text finds Shadrach, Meshach, and Abednego on "the plain of Dura" (Daniel 3:1). Its location is not known; some suggest it was a few miles south of the city of Babylon. There King Nebuchadnezzar built an image of gold. Some scholars propose that the image depicted the king himself (based on 2:38). But another possibility is that the image represented the king's patron god, Nabu (or Nebo in Isaiah 46:1), which the first part of Nebuchadnezzar's name refers to.

Anyone who refused to bow to the image faced death (Daniel 3:6). Obedience to such a command clearly violated the first two of the Ten Commandments (Exodus 20:3-6), so the young Hebrew men refused to worship the image. Their disobedience was reported to King Nebuchadnezzar, who had the three brought before him.

The king offered them a chance to change their minds (Daniel 3:15), but the three restated their determination not to bow to the king's image. They affirmed that their God was able to deliver them from the furnace, but whether He would choose to do so or not made no difference in their devotion to Him. They would not yield to the king's demand (3:16-18).

We note that this test was quite different from the one recorded in last week's text from Daniel 1. There Daniel was in a position to suggest an alternative concerning the diet that he and his friends were to eat. But in Daniel 3 no alternatives were available. The choice was clear: bow and live, or refuse and die.

I. Fury of the King
(DANIEL 3:19-23)

We may wonder why Daniel himself plays no part in the account of the fiery furnace of Daniel 3. No fewer than six proposals have been offered to explain Daniel's absence from this account: (1) he was away on government business, (2) he was busy in a cabinet meeting, (3) he was too ill to attend,

(4) his governmental status was so high (2:48) that although he was present he was not expected to bow to the image, (5) he was not present at the ceremony because the categories of invited officials (3:2, 3) did not include him, and (6) his reputation was so highly established that jealous opponents dared not call his actions into question.

The bottom line is that we simply don't know why Daniel himself isn't a participant in the incident of today's lesson. It is likely in any case that Daniel and his three friends pray continually and fervently for one another.

A. Attitude Change (v. 19a)

19a. Then was Nebuchadnezzar full of fury, and the form of his visage was changed against Shadrach, Meshach, and Abednego.

Kings do not like to hear the word *no* or see their commands disobeyed. The half-verse before us describes the intensity of Nebuchadnezzar's anger in this regard. That the three men dare to defy his edict, especially after being given a second chance to obey, results in the king's being *full of fury*. He is seething; he is ready to explode.

What the king undergoes on the inside is visible in his body language as his *visage* changes. This refers to his facial expression. Perhaps the king's face turns red or he clenches his teeth in his rage.

> *What Do You Think?*
> What are some appropriate ways to respond to anger directed at Christianity by secular culture?
> *Talking Points for Your Discussion*
> - When the anger is justified
> - When the anger is unjustified
> - Considering biblical examples

B. Draconian Response (vv. 19b-21)

19b. Therefore he spake, and commanded that they should heat the furnace one seven times more than it was wont to be heated.

The king's rage quickly turns into action. The furnace mentioned may be a type used for firing bricks. Or it may be used solely for executions, since burning people alive is often used by the

Babylonians for capital punishment. The phrasing *one seven times more* is a different way of saying "seven-fold." The king seems to demand that the intensity of the flames match the intensity of his anger.

20. And he commanded the most mighty men that were in his army to bind Shadrach, Meshach, and Abednego, and to cast them into the burning fiery furnace.

To bind Shadrach, Meshach, and Abednego does not require extraordinary strength—anyone can do it. But *to cast them into the burning fiery furnace* will mean having to get very close to the intense fire. This will require top-notch physical fitness; thus the summons to *the most mighty men*.

21. Then these men were bound in their coats, their hosen, and their hats, and their other garments, and were cast into the midst of the burning fiery furnace.

The three men are not prepared in any special manner for what appears to be certain death. And why should they be? Whatever they are wearing is about to be consumed by the fire, so any change of clothing would be unnecessary and a waste of time. Their sentence is to be carried out immediately with no delay whatsoever. Not a minute is therefore spent on removing a stitch of clothing—not their *coats*, not their *hosen* (trousers or "leggings" of some kind), not headgear, nor any *other garments* they happen to have on.

The fact that the king desires the men to be bound may seem curious. If their execution is so urgent, why not save a couple of minutes and throw them into the furnace unbound? The importance of the details will be seen later.

What Do You Think?

How can we prepare for religious persecution, or is such preparation even possible? Explain.

Talking Points for Your Discussion

- Regarding attitude
- Regarding spiritual disciplines
- Considering Psalm 119:157; Matthew 5:10-12, 43-45; John 15:20; 2 Corinthians 12:10; 2 Timothy 3:10-12; Hebrews 10:32-39; Revelation 2:10

C. Collateral Damage (vv. 22, 23)

22. Therefore because the king's commandment was urgent, and the furnace exceeding hot, the flame of the fire slew those men that took up Shadrach, Meshach, and Abednego.

Two things we see here are startling indeed. The first is the fact that the fire is so intense that the executioners cannot get close enough to the furnace to throw in *Shadrach, Meshach, and Abednego*—the three condemned men—without incurring their own deaths.

The second is the fact that those who die are the ones most physically able to survive their task: "the most mighty men" of verse 20! Perhaps they did not have time to take adequate precautions against the searing heat *because the king's commandment was urgent*. The nature of the furnace's design may also play a part (see below).

What Do You Think?

In what ways can we show solidarity with persecuted Christians across the globe?

Talking Points for Your Discussion

- In tangible ways
- In intangible ways

---

23. And these three men, Shadrach, Meshach, and Abednego, fell down bound into the midst of the burning fiery furnace.

Most commentators believe the furnace involved is of an upright design, perhaps built into an embankment. This theory is consistent with the description of *Shadrach, Meshach, and Abednego* falling into it since such a design could require stairs be climbed first. The need to climb stairs would expose the executioners to the fiery heat for a longer period of time, perhaps causing them to faint and fall to their own deaths.

Even so, this is all rather speculative since (1) the "cast into" of verse 21 does not require interpretation of a vertical drop from a height (compare Matthew 7:19) and (2) the wording in the verse before us of falling *down* can also be used to describe the final part of any kind of toss of a person whose feet are *bound*. A problem with this kind of theory is that a furnace designed this way might not allow the king to see in (Daniel 3:24).

Michael Servetus (1511–1553) was a Spanish theologian. He was also what is sometimes referred to as a polymath—a person with expertise in numerous areas of learning. For Servetus, this included medicine, law, mathematics, astronomy, and literature. A prodigious writer, he authored books in many fields of learning. Among those was *On the Errors of the Trinity,* in which he challenged orthodox views.

Ideas deemed to be heretical frequently resulted in capital punishment in those days, and with the same fury shown by Nebuchadnezzar centuries before. For his views, Servetus was burned at the stake in Geneva, Switzerland, where the Protestant reformer John Calvin held great sway. Calvin wholeheartedly approved the death sentence for Servetus. The heretical writings of Servetus are seen by some to have led to the creation of the Unitarian churches in Europe.

Unpopular stances have been suppressed with violence for centuries. Nebuchadnezzar took this route, as did the Romans in the time of Christ, etc. This raises the question for Christians: How do we treat others who disagree with us, whether in religion, politics, or other areas of life?   —C. R. B.

II. Work of All-Powerful God
(DANIEL 3:26-28)

Daniel 3:24, 25, not part of our lesson text, records what occurs after the three men are cast into the furnace. No doubt Nebuchadnezzar expects to hear cries of agony from the three rebels, but instead observes "four men loose, walking in the midst of the fire . . . and the form of the

HOW TO SAY IT

Abednego	Uh-*bed*-nee-go.
Babylon	*Bab*-uh-lun.
Babylonian	Bab-ih-*low*-nee-un.
Meshach	*Me*-shack.
Nabu	*Nah*-boo.
Nebo	*Nee*-bo.
Nebuchadnezzar	*Neb*-yuh-kud-***nez***-er.
Shadrach	*Shay*-drack or *Shad*-rack.

fourth is like the Son of God" (3:25). Some speculate this person to be a pre-incarnate appearance of Jesus. Later the king will state that the God of the three men "sent his angel" to protect them (3:28).

Either way, a miracle has occurred as the previously bound men (Daniel 3:20, 21, 23, 24) are now "unbound" and moving with apparent ease within the "burning fiery furnace" (a phrase used eight times in chapter 3). Even more astounding is the fact that the men are unhurt.

A. Different Attitude (v. 26)

26. Then Nebuchadnezzar came near to the mouth of the burning fiery furnace, and spake, and said, Shadrach, Meshach, and Abednego, ye servants of the most high God, come forth, and come hither. Then Shadrach, Meshach, and Abednego, came forth of the midst of the fire.

Nebuchadnezzar had asked rhetorically about the ability of any god to deliver *Shadrach, Meshach, and Abednego* from the fire (Daniel 3:15). But having just witnessed what happens (or doesn't happen) to the three men, the king's attitude changes dramatically.

Gone is the arrogant and contemptuous spirit as Nebuchadnezzar acknowledges the God of these men to be *the most high God.* In calling the three to *come forth,* he refers to them as *servants* of that same God. We note that, having disobeyed the king's previous command, they *do* obey this one! This command is that of a humbler, gentler man than the one who was raging at them a few minutes earlier. That the three are able to walk out says something about the design characteristics of the furnace.

The king does not address the fourth individual. Perhaps he is no longer present, or this may reflect Nebuchadnezzar's uncertainty as to his identity.

B. Thorough Inspection (v. 27)

27. And the princes, governors, and captains, and the king's counsellors, being gathered together, saw these men, upon whose bodies the fire had no power, nor was an hair of their head singed, neither were their coats changed, nor the smell of fire had passed on them.

All the king's officials gather around the three men, amazed at what they are seeing. These three men have just emerged from a blazing furnace, with flames too intense for some of the king's strongest men. Yet the Hebrew men show no evidence whatsoever of exposure to fire. They do not even smell of smoke! They have emerged from the furnace just as they were when they were cast into it except for one thing: their bindings are gone (Daniel 3:25).

> **What Do You Think?**
> ▶ How can you use a personal experience of God's deliverance as a witness to others?
> *Talking Points for Your Discussion*
> - As a witness to fellow believers
> - As a witness to unbelievers

C. Proper Credit (v. 28)

28a. Then Nebuchadnezzar spake, and said, Blessed be the God of Shadrach, Meshach, and Abednego, who hath sent his angel, and delivered his servants.

We do not know how much time passes as the three young men are inspected by the king and his officials. In offering homage to *the God of Shadrach, Meshach, and Abednego,* the king recalls the appearance of an *angel.* Babylonian religion includes belief in many angelic spirits; it is impossible to know specifically which Nebuchadnezzar has in mind, if any. He acknowledges once more (as in Daniel 3:25) that whoever appeared with the three men in the flames was not an ordinary human. We note irony in the fact that the king praises the God of these men, yet continues to speak of them using their Babylonian names.

28b. That trusted in him, and have changed the king's word, and yielded their bodies, that they might not serve nor worship any god, except their own God.

Nebuchadnezzar goes on to pay tribute to the three men who have dared to defy his earlier command to bow to the image. The basis of their courageous stand is their unshakable trust in their God. Because of this *the king's word* is changed. Nebuchadnezzar's demand was negated by the faith of Shadrach, Meshach, and Abednego. Faced

with the choice of obeying either an earthly king or the heavenly one, they chose the latter. They have honored a much more authoritative word than King Nebuchadnezzar's.

> **What Do You Think?**
> ▶ How do we know when we should defy rather than obey earthly authority?
> *Talking Points for Your Discussion*
> - Considering defiance passages such as Acts 4:18-20; 5:27-29
> - Considering obedience passages such as Romans 13:1, 2; 1 Peter 2:13-17
> - Considering the potential result of martyrdom

Nebuchadnezzar also notes that the three men have *yielded their bodies* in service to their God. They have not merely professed loyalty to God; they have backed up their profession with a willingness to die for Him. They have declared that even if God chose not to come to their aid and spare them from the furnace, they would never compromise their trust in Him (Daniel 3:17, 18). Nebuchadnezzar later admits that "there is no other God that can deliver after this sort" (3:29).

Does this mean Nebuchadnezzar converted to the faith of Shadrach, Meshach, and Abednego? His words in response to their deliverance may make us think so. The king uttered similar words in Daniel 2:47 after Daniel interpreted his dream. Even so, the king refers to "my gods" (plural) in Daniel 3:14. Nebuchadnezzar will be disciplined severely by the Lord because of his arrogance (4:1-33). That experience will be followed by another tribute of praise to God (4:34-37). Nebuchadnezzar may view the Lord as the highest of many gods. There is room for doubt that he embraces true monotheism (the worship of one God alone).

◆ SURPRISED BY . . . ◆

C. S. Lewis (1898–1963), probably the most-read Christian apologist of the twentieth century, was a very reluctant convert to Christianity. Following what he called a "blandly Christian childhood," Lewis turned to atheism to satisfy his heart's spiritual longings. Eventually, it was his appreciation for beauty and art—and the joy these gifts of God bring—that caught him by surprise and led to his conversion. The conversion came, in part, because of the influence of some fellow intellectuals who had become Christians, including J. R. R. Tolkien, author of *Lord of the Rings.* Lewis found joy in turning to Christ, an experience he later wrote about in *Surprised by Joy,* published in 1955.

Nebuchadnezzar's realization that no other god was like the God of the Hebrew people caught him by surprise. It did not come through intellectual conversations or exposure to beauty. It came, rather, through incontrovertible evidence of God's power. Such surprising evidence resulted not in terror (contrast Mark 4:41) but in praise on the part of the king.

The God who surprised Nebuchadnezzar hundreds of years before Christ is the same God who surprised the residents of Jerusalem in the first century AD (Acts 2:5-12; 3:11-16; etc.). He surprises us yet today at various times and in various ways. How we react will reveal our hearts.   —C. R. B.

Conclusion

A. The Flames of Fellowship

The above title is used by Dale Ralph Davis in his commentary on Daniel as he discusses the events described in Daniel 3:19-30. While he is not certain that the "fourth man" in the flames was a preincarnate appearance of Jesus, he does see the miracle of their deliverance as "a sample of the way Christ preserves his people but not a guarantee of his dramatic deliverance in every case."

When the writer of Hebrews is describing the various accomplishments of those who chose to walk by faith, he refers to those who "quenched the violence of fire" (Hebrews 11:34). Most likely he is alluding to the account of Shadrach, Meshach, and Abednego. Even so, some Christians who lived in the first century (the time during which the writer of Hebrews lived) experienced being burned alive during persecution instigated by the emperor Nero (reigned AD 54–68). The apostle Peter may have been referring to such persecution when he wrote of being "tried with fire" (1 Peter 1:7) and of the "fiery trial" (4:12).

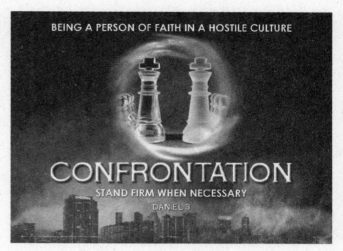

Visual for Lesson 7. *Contrast this visual with Matthew 17:24-27 as your learners wrestle with the decision of when to confront and when not to.*

Yet we do not read any accounts of Nero witnessing (as did Nebuchadnezzar) someone escaping from the fire unscathed. Nor do we know of any instances where someone similar to the "fourth man" appeared alongside someone for rescue as the flames burned the person alive.

We can be assured from Scripture, however, that the Lord is always present with His people. That is true whether seen or not, whether "the flames of fellowship" are literal or not (compare Isaiah 43:2). One should note that the inspired writer speaks of those who by faith "quenched the *violence* of fire" (Hebrews 11:34). Whatever flames one may experience while living in a broken, sin-cursed world, their *violence* is abated because of the presence of the Lord. Davis is right when he notes that no matter what fires we face—in operating rooms, funeral parlors, or empty houses— "the Fourth Man can always find his people."

B. Prayer

Father, the account of Shadrach, Meshach, and Abednego is so well known that it is easy to lose our sense of wonder at the bold faith these men demonstrated. Renew our wonder! And may we draw strength from acknowledging Your presence with us in every circumstance, whether calm or chaotic. We pray in Jesus' name, amen.

C. Thought to Remember

Our Father never abandons us.

INVOLVEMENT LEARNING

Enhance your lesson with KJV Bible Student *(from your curriculum supplier) and the reproducible activity page (at www.standardlesson.com or in the back of the* KJV Standard Lesson Commentary Deluxe Edition*).*

Into the Lesson

Ask students to reveal how recently they have watched the 1939 movie *The Wizard of Oz*. Then say, "Let's see how good your memory is. Would someone describe the scene where Dorothy meets the lion for the first time?" The description should include Dorothy's initial reaction and what finally makes her spring into action. (The answer is that when the lion goes after Toto, Dorothy acts to save him.) Invite volunteers to talk about times when they've stepped in and stood up for someone.

Alternative. Distribute copies of the "Between a Rock and a Hard Place" activity from the reproducible page, which you can download. Have students discuss in small groups or as a class.

After either activity, say, "We all struggle with doing the right thing—when to speak up and when to shut up. Sometimes we don't even know what the 'right' thing is! It can be the same when it comes to our faith. As much as we love God, there are times when we may face derision, isolation, or worse for standing up for Him. Three captives in a foreign land give us a great example of refusing to compromise in the face of unthinkable consequences. Let's see what they have to teach us."

Into the Word

Divide the class into three groups, giving each group a pen or pencil and some paper. Assign each group one of the following Scripture passages: Daniel 3:13-18; 3:19-23; 3:26-28. Have groups read their assigned text and then work together to retell the events using only questions. For example, for the first passage: Why did King Nebuchadnezzar bring Shadrach, Meshach, and Abednego before him? Why wouldn't they bow before the image he created? What will happen if they are thrown into the furnace? Will their God save them?

Allow groups to work for several minutes, offering assistance as needed. When groups have fin-ished, ask a volunteer from each group to read its question-based summary to the class.

Option: Have groups use the question-based format to present each Scripture passage as a short skit, in which the characters speak only in questions. Say, "There are many questions in this account, but Shadrach, Meshach, and Abednego needed only one answer: *God is able.*"

Introduce further discussion as you say, "Shadrach, Meshach, and Abednego faced a decision: either bow to the image King Nebuchadnezzar had built or be burned to death in a furnace. These men were well aware of God's command against worshipping other gods. What do you think was going through their minds as they pondered this choice?" As discussion winds down, ask which of those questions would likely also go through the mind of a Christian facing martyrdom today.

Invite a volunteer to read aloud Daniel 3:28. Make a transition by saying, "Sometimes Christians are challenged to endure great trials because of their convictions. Let's take a look at Christians who have faced and are facing the difficulty of such challenges."

Into Life

Tell students about www.prisoneralert.com, a site created by The Voice of the Martyrs. As a homework assignment, challenge learners to use this site later to send a message of encouragement to a believer who is imprisoned because of his or her faith. *Option:* Demonstrate the site for the class if Internet connectivity is available in your learning space. Offer the opportunity to write messages while the class is meeting. (This is preferable to a homework assignment.)

Alternative. Distribute copies of the "All Around the World" activity from the reproducible page. Have students use smartphones to research and report on the persecution of Christians in each country.

A Prayer for an Obedient Faith

DEVOTIONAL READING: Psalm 130
BACKGROUND SCRIPTURE: Daniel 9:1-19

DANIEL 9:4-8, 15-19

4 And I prayed unto the LORD my God, and made my confession, and said, O Lord, the great and dreadful God, keeping the covenant and mercy to them that love him, and to them that keep his commandments;

5 We have sinned, and have committed iniquity, and have done wickedly, and have rebelled, even by departing from thy precepts and from thy judgments:

6 Neither have we hearkened unto thy servants the prophets, which spake in thy name to our kings, our princes, and our fathers, and to all the people of the land.

7 O Lord, righteousness belongeth unto thee, but unto us confusion of faces, as at this day; to the men of Judah, and to the inhabitants of Jerusalem, and unto all Israel, that are near, and that are far off, through all the countries whither thou hast driven them, because of their trespass that they have trespassed against thee.

8 O Lord, to us belongeth confusion of face, to our kings, to our princes, and to our fathers, because we have sinned against thee.

· · · · · · · · · · · · · · · ·

15 And now, O Lord our God, that hast brought thy people forth out of the land of Egypt with a mighty hand, and hast gotten thee renown, as at this day; we have sinned, we have done wickedly.

16 O Lord, according to all thy righteousness, I beseech thee, let thine anger and thy fury be turned away from thy city Jerusalem, thy holy mountain: because for our sins, and for the iniquities of our fathers, Jerusalem and thy people are become a reproach to all that are about us.

17 Now therefore, O our God, hear the prayer of thy servant, and his supplications, and cause thy face to shine upon thy sanctuary that is desolate, for the Lord's sake.

18 O my God, incline thine ear, and hear; open thine eyes, and behold our desolations, and the city which is called by thy name: for we do not present our supplications before thee for our righteousnesses, but for thy great mercies.

19 O Lord, hear; O Lord, forgive; O Lord, hearken and do; defer not, for thine own sake, O my God: for thy city and thy people are called by thy name.

KEY VERSE

O Lord, hear; O Lord, forgive; O Lord, hearken and do; defer not, for thine own sake, O my God: for thy city and thy people are called by thy name. —**Daniel 9:19**

FAITH IN ACTION

Unit 2: A Living Faith in God
LESSONS 6–9

LESSON AIMS

After participating in this lesson, each learner will be able to:

1. Summarize the content of Daniel's prayer in today's text.

2. Explain how this prayer can serve as a model for Christians today.

3. Write out a prayer of confession and repentance based on Daniel's prayer and use it each day this week. (Report on its impact at the next gathering of the group.)

LESSON OUTLINE

Introduction

A. When Direction Is Needed

We all go through crossroads moments—times we know that life will change because of decisions we have made or are making. Here are common bits of advice for those at crossroads moments.

To newlyweds: Never go to bed angry.

To parents of a newborn: Live to be the kind of person you will want your child to marry.

To first-time homeowners: Don't ignore home maintenance.

To new drivers: The car you drive can be one of the deadliest machines ever invented.

To the teen leaving for college: Don't give up what you want most for what you want now.

These words of advice may seem trite, but they are important. At certain points of our lives, we must know who we are, what we have got ourselves into, and where to turn for help. We know what it is like to reach a crossroads moment. When such a moment comes, we know that life may change dramatically. Daniel's decision at a crossroads moment has much to teach us.

B. Lesson Background

After the incident of the fiery furnace (last week's lesson), Shadrach, Meshach, and Abednego no longer appear in the book of Daniel. The spotlight turns on Daniel himself to demonstrate unwavering faith and godly courage in pagan surroundings.

Much happens in the book of Daniel between last week's lesson from chapter 3 and this week's lesson from chapter 9. In Daniel 4, the book's namesake interpreted a dream for King Nebuchadnezzar, one with an ominous, alarming message of coming judgment on that ruler. In chapter 5, Daniel interpreted the famous "handwriting on the wall" for the terrified King Belshazzar. That message too was one of pending doom; indeed, Daniel's words came to pass that very night (5:30, 31).

Chapter 6 is the well-known account of Daniel in the lions' den. Daniel 7–12 records a series of dreams and visions granted to Daniel about things to come. Daniel's prayer of chapter 9, located among these, is the subject of today's lesson.

I. People's Sins
(DANIEL 9:4-8)

Daniel offered the prayer of today's text "in the first year of Darius the son of Ahasuerus" (Daniel 9:1; compare 5:31; 11:1). That was about 538 BC. Since Daniel was taken to Babylon in 605 BC (1:1), this means that he has been on foreign soil for nearly 70 years. He has become an old man.

While Daniel 9:1 tells us of the earthly ruler in power at the time, the verse that follows affirms that the heavenly ruler, the Lord, remains very much in control. That verse also records Daniel's recognition that Jerusalem's desolation was to last 70 years, according to Jeremiah 29:10. This means the captivity of Daniel's people is nearing its end.

This awareness stirs the elderly man of God to offer the profound prayer of our lesson. The heartfelt sincerity of the prayer is seen in Daniel 9:3 with the mention of Daniel's fasting, sackcloth, and ashes.

A. Rebellion (vv. 4, 5)

4a. And I prayed unto the LORD my God, and made my confession, and said, O Lord, the great and dreadful God.

Daniel's address of the Lord as *my God* should not be bypassed too quickly. Consider how much Daniel had learned to trust the Lord during all the turmoil in his life and pressures to conform to the surrounding pagan culture. For nearly 70 years, the Lord had repeatedly shown himself faithful. Daniel can truly, genuinely call Him *my God*.

We may normally think of the word *confession* in terms of an admission of wrongdoing. But here at the very beginning of his prayer, Daniel does not confess sins. Rather, he acknowledges important truths about his God.

Today we associate the word *dreadful* with a negative meaning (a dreadful day or dreadful weather). But in this context the word speaks to a sense of reverence we should have toward God. Just because He is a personal God (*my* God) does not mean that He can be approached casually or flippantly. Daniel knows this.

4b. Keeping the covenant and mercy to them that love him, and to them that keep his commandments.

While Daniel has acknowledged the Lord as his God, he is also keenly aware that the Lord is close to many others as well—specifically those *that love him* and *keep his commandments*. Daniel's language echoes that of Moses in Deuteronomy 7:9, 12. Much later, Solomon used this same language during his eloquent prayer at the dedication of the temple (1 Kings 8:22, 23). That temple had been destroyed by the Babylonians, the same people who took Daniel and his friends into captivity. But the Lord's faithfulness to *covenant and mercy* is not subject to such treatment.

> **What Do You Think?**
> How should remembering God's character shape how we talk to God about our sins?
> *Talking Points for Your Discussion*
> - With reference to His holiness
> - With reference to His love
> - With reference to His faithful consistency

5a. We have sinned, and have committed iniquity, and have done wickedly, and have rebelled.

After exalting the Lord for His majesty and faithfulness, Daniel now begins to confess the brazen unfaithfulness of the people. He starts by piling up the four phrases we see here, actions that are similar in meaning. This is the only place in the Old Testament where all four occur (in

HOW TO SAY IT

Abednego	Uh-*bed*-nee-go.
Ahasuerus	Uh-haz-you-*ee*-rus.
Babylon	*Bab*-uh-lun.
Babylonians	Bab-ih-*low*-nee-unz.
Belshazzar	Bel-*shazz*-er.
Cyrus	*Sigh*-russ.
Darius	Duh-*rye*-us.
Judah	*Joo*-duh.
Lamentations	Lam-en-*tay*-shunz.
Meshach	*Me*-shack.
Moriah	Mo-*rye*-uh.
Nebuchadnezzar	*Neb*-yuh-kud-***nez***-er.
Shadrach	*Shay*-drack or *Shad*-rack.
Sinai	*Sigh*-nye or *Sigh*-nay-eye.

Hebrew) in the same verse. (Coming close with three of the four are 1 Kings 8:47; 2 Chronicles 6:37; and Psalm 106:6.)

By the use of the first-person *we,* Daniel counts himself among the guilty. We may wonder why Daniel should include himself among the sinners or take part of the blame for what has happened. But those who know the Lord and His character most intimately, as Daniel clearly does, are painfully aware of their own unworthiness. Those most self-aware of their own spiritual poverty cannot help but pray the prayer of the publican: "God be merciful to me a sinner" (Luke 18:13).

5b. Even by departing from thy precepts and from thy judgments.

Although technical distinctions can be made between *precepts* and *judgments,* Daniel uses them together in a whole-picture way. God had set His standards firmly in place, whether one is talking about precepts, judgments, statutes (2 Kings 17:37), or laws (Nehemiah 9:13). Those standards have not changed, and the people are guilty of *departing* from them due to all the actions just mentioned in the previous half-verse. That is why they are in exile.

◆ *A Difficult Admission* ◆

Marion Jones was a superstar track and field athlete who won five medals at the 2000 Summer Olympics. But she was stripped of those medals after admitting to steroid use. In her public confession, she accepted full responsibility and blamed no one but herself. She spent six months in prison for lying to investigators.

Daniel did not mince words when it came to confessing the sins of God's people. It's interesting to note that he includes himself in the confession by using first-person *we.* His prayer of corporate confession pulls no punches regarding the people's sins.

After her time in prison, Marion Jones established a nonprofit organization called Take a Break. It's dedicated to getting young people to step back and think about the potential life-altering consequences of their decisions. Secular culture's term for this is "reinventing" oneself. Christianity has a different description: producing "fruits worthy of repentance" (Luke 3:8).　　　　—D. C. S.

B. Deafness (v. 6)

6. Neither have we hearkened unto thy servants the prophets, which spake in thy name to our kings, our princes, and our fathers, and to all the people of the land.

God had warned the people time and again of the judgment that awaited should they turn away from Him. To issue such warnings was the primary duty of *the prophets.* The prophet Ezekiel had been called specifically to be a "watchman" (Ezekiel 3:16-21; 33:1-9), sounding the alarm and warning of coming doom. But in one way or another, all the prophets were tasked to do so.

Yet who has listened? When the leaders of the people (the *kings* and the *princes*) have no desire to hear what the Lord has to say, judgment cannot be far behind. See 2 Chronicles 36:16 for a summary of how God's messengers have been treated.

C. Shame (vv. 7, 8)

7. O Lord, righteousness belongeth unto thee, but unto us confusion of faces, as at this day; to the men of Judah, and to the inhabitants of Jerusalem, and unto all Israel, that are near, and that are far off, through all the countries whither thou hast driven them, because of their trespass that they have trespassed against thee.

Again Daniel contrasts the Lord's *righteousness* with the sin of His people. The phrase *confusion of faces* highlights the visible, public shame that they have brought upon themselves *because of their trespass.* Jeremiah notes that God's people had lost their ability to blush in shame for their wrongdoing. The people have gladly, proudly flaunted their disobedience (Jeremiah 6:15; 8:12).

Since they have not voluntarily exhibited shame associated with repentance, they now involuntarily exhibit shame associated with captivity. No one is exempt from divine judgment. People throughout the lands of *Judah* and *Israel* suffer their respective exiles. Although politically divided for about 400 years by the time noted in Daniel 9:1, the 12 tribes of Israel share a common rebellion against God. Thus they share a common fate.

8. O Lord, to us belongeth confusion of face, to our kings, to our princes, and to our fathers, because we have sinned against thee.

This repeat of leadership culpability and shame serves to emphasize the problem.

♦   *WHEN LEADERS FAIL*   ♦

In 2015, the leadership of a certain church determined that they had treated one of their members unbiblically. The member had decided to separate from her husband after he confessed involvement with illegal pornography. She felt she needed to separate to keep her children safe. But church leaders had insisted that she extend grace to her husband and keep living with him while the problem was addressed. Shortly thereafter, however, they realized their error and sought to rectify the situation through their own repentance and confession.

The distress of Daniel and his people was traceable, in large part, to their leaders. They had set the bad examples of idolatry and spiritual complacency (example: Jeremiah 44:16, 17). Therefore, Daniel confessed to the Lord the sins of such leaders.

The humble actions of the penitent church leaders removed obstacles along the woman's path to healing. As Daniel confessed the sins of leaders, he "owned" those sins as his. Did those sinful leaders themselves ever do the same? Do ours?—D. C. S.

II. God's Holiness
(DANIEL 9:15, 16)

In Daniel 9:9-14 (not in today's lesson text), Daniel continues to call attention to the wide chasm that exists between God's faithfulness and the people's rebellion. God has not pulled any surprises on the people in bringing judgment. To the contrary, He warned them through the Law of Moses (9:13) and later through the prophets (9:10). But the people disobeyed anyway (9:14).

A. Holy in Power (v. 15)

15. And now, O Lord our God, that hast brought thy people forth out of the land of Egypt with a mighty hand, and hast gotten thee renown, as at this day; we have sinned, we have done wickedly.

Having spoken of "my God" at the outset of the prayer, Daniel now uses the inclusive *our God*. In so doing, Daniel turns the focus to God's actions in history on behalf of His people, specifically the exodus from *Egypt*.

That event was foundational for Israel's existence as a nation. The exodus had brought the Lord *renown*, or fame, far greater than it was possible for any other so-called god to obtain. The Israelites were to promote that renown by living in obedience to Him and thus being a witness to the pagan peoples around them (Deuteronomy 4:5-8). But repeated sinfulness had brought shame, not fame, to themselves and to the Lord's name.

> *What Do You Think?*
> What steps can we take to ensure that we thank God regularly for past rescues?
> *Talking Points for Your Discussion*
> - In corporate worship
> - In private prayers and devotions
> - Other

B. Holy in Mercy (v. 16)

16. O Lord, according to all thy righteousness, I beseech thee, let thine anger and thy fury be turned away from thy city Jerusalem, thy holy mountain: because for our sins, and for the iniquities of our fathers, Jerusalem and thy people are become a reproach to all that are about us.

Daniel now pleads with the Lord to continue to act in a manner consistent with His *righteousness*. God's righteous character includes not only judgment against sin but also when that judgment has run its course, when "enough is enough." In that regard, Daniel begs that the Lord's *anger* and *fury be turned away from . . . Jerusalem.*

When Solomon prayed at the dedication of the temple, he voiced desire that "all people of the earth may know thy name . . . as do thy people Israel; and that they may know that this house . . . is called by thy name" (1 Kings 8:43). But the *sins* and *iniquities* of God's people made them (and the temple) a *reproach* to the surrounding peoples. The Lord had warned Solomon of this after the temple was dedicated (9:6-9).

III. Daniel's Request

(DANIEL 9:17-19)

Daniel is nearly three-quarters through his prayer before he starts making requests.

A. For Worship Renewal (v. 17)

17. Now therefore, O our God, hear the prayer of thy servant, and his supplications, and cause thy face to shine upon thy sanctuary that is desolate, for the Lord's sake.

Daniel's request echoes the blessing in Numbers 6:22-27 that was to be issued by the high priest Aaron and his sons. The time of the "desolations of Jerusalem" is nearing its end (Daniel 9:2). Renewal of the *sanctuary that is desolate* will mean worship renewal. As Daniel recognizes this, he prays for it *for the Lord's sake.* The next two verses expand on this.

> *What Do You Think?*
> What positive changes might result if Christians started to appeal to God to act for the sake of His reputation? Why?
> *Talking Points for Your Discussion*
> - Regarding interactions with fellow believers
> - Regarding interactions with unbelievers

B. For National Renewal (vv. 18, 19)

18. O my God, incline thine ear, and hear; open thine eyes, and behold our desolations, and the city which is called by thy name: for we do not present our supplications before thee for our righteousnesses, but for thy great mercies.

Daniel asks for God's full attention to the plight of His despondent people. The basis of Daniel's plea cannot rest upon the *righteousnesses* of the people, since they have none. He knows full well that the only hope for God's people rests in the Lord's *great mercies.* The words of Lamentations 3:22, 23 acknowledge this profound truth: "It is of the Lord's mercies that we are not consumed, because his compassions fail not. They are new every morning: great is thy faithfulness." To reverse the *desolations* of the people and of *the city which is called by [God's] name* will be consistent with God's merciful character.

19. O Lord, hear; O Lord, forgive; O Lord, hearken and do; defer not, for thine own sake, O my God: for thy city and thy people are called by thy name.

Daniel concludes his fervent prayer with a staccato of impassioned appeals to the Lord. These appeals can have only one basis: God's *own sake* and *name.* Having just spoken of the Lord's "renown" (Daniel 9:15), achieved through deliverance of His people from bondage in Egypt, Daniel pleads, in effect, for a second exodus. When the Lord accomplishes this, the "great evil" that has befallen Jerusalem (9:12) will be reversed; everyone will know that such a reversal could happen only by the mercies of God.

> *What Do You Think?*
> What should we do when God doesn't seem to be answering our prayers?
> *Talking Points for Your Discussion*
> - Regarding something yet to happen
> - Regarding something that has already happened

One wonders what Daniel's posture is as he utters this intense prayer. The Scripture does not tell us. It is not hard to picture the aged saint falling to his creaking knees as he pleads with the Lord on behalf of himself and his countrymen in captivity. As his prayer reaches the especially earnest conclusion in the verse before us, perhaps Daniel falls prostrate to acknowledge total submission to the Lord and complete dependence upon Him to answer the prayer.

Within the next year or so after Daniel offers this prayer (based on the date given in Daniel 9:1), the Persian ruler Cyrus the Great issued his decree allowing the Jews who desired to do so to return home (2 Chronicles 36:22, 23). We do not read of Daniel returning to his homeland; most likely both his age and his administrative responsibilities precluded him from doing so.

However, given the date cited in Daniel 10:1 (the third year of Cyrus, which would be 536 BC), Daniel lives to see the Lord answer the prayer and keep His word regarding the 70 years. We do not read of any prayer Daniel offers when the return of the captives happens, but we can be certain that he praises the Lord—with a prayer that is just as sincere and passionate as the one we have studied today.

Conclusion

A. Priorities in Prayer

Daniel's prayer should prompt us to ask ourselves, "Do we pray like that today? Are our prayers that earnest, that sensitive to the sin and wrongdoing in our lives and to our dependence on the mercy of God?" We may be very keenly aware of the perversion in our culture, but Daniel's prayer says absolutely nothing about what is going on in Persian society. His focus is on his people's desperate need for the forgiveness that God alone can provide. But note carefully that Daniel spends much more time *acknowledging* than *asking*. Do we pray that way?

Much insight can also be gained by examining the prayer life of Paul. We are not given in Scripture the specific contents of his prayers, but we can sense what his priorities in prayer were by reading the references to prayer. As we do, we find a heavy emphasis on spiritual matters, very similar to the matters that comprised the prayer of Daniel. There was a fervent desire for the recipients of a given epistle to grow in their knowledge of Jesus and to be more aware of the spiritual blessings that accompany that knowledge.

Illustrations of this may be seen in Ephesians 1:15-23; 3:14-21; Philippians 1:9-11; Colossians 1:9-14; and 2 Thessalonians 1:11, 12. There is

Visual for Lesson 8. *Point to this visual as you ask learners how a Christian's supplications (requests) can become more like Daniel's.*

really very little in these Scriptures about physical or material concerns, which usually make up the primary topic of prayer times or prayer lists in most churches.

This is not to say that praying for physical or material needs should not be encouraged (see James 5:14, 15). Certainly God cares about every aspect of our lives (compare Philippians 4:6). But if we are honest, we must admit our clear shortcomings in failing to address on a consistent basis the kinds of issues that formed the very core of passionate pray-ers like Daniel and Paul.

We have noted that Daniel was moved to prayer by reading and understanding the Word of God that had been spoken through the prophet Jeremiah (Daniel 9:2). May reading the Scriptures today, specifically a prayer such as Daniel's, stir us to reexamine and revitalize our own priorities in prayer.

B. Prayer

Father, when we read a prayer such as Daniel's, we recognize how our own prayer priorities are so mixed up. Help us remember that we are students continually enrolled in the school of prayer. Teach us to pray with the passion and priorities of Daniel! We pray this in Jesus' name. Amen.

C. Thought to Remember
Take the first steps of important journeys on your knees.

INVOLVEMENT LEARNING

Enhance your lesson with KJV Bible Student *(from your curriculum supplier) and the reproducible activity page (at www.standardlesson.com or in the back of the* KJV Standard Lesson Commentary Deluxe Edition).

Into the Lesson

Across the top of the board, write the following five phrases:

To the graduate / To the first-time homeowner
To the expectant parent / To the newlyweds
To one whose parent is dying

Distribute self-stick notes and pens or pencils. Instruct students to write on **separate** pieces of paper a few words of advice to the five hypothetical people listed.

When students have finished writing, collect the notes and read each one aloud. Let students decide to whom the advice was written; post it under that header. Have the author of the note confirm or correct the decision.

Ask students to name other major events that can affect lives forever. Transition into the Bible story by saying, "We know what it is like to reach a figurative crossroads moment in our lives. We know that from that moment forward, our lives will change dramatically. Let's see what Daniel did when facing such a crossroads moment."

Into the Word

Prior to class, write one letter from each of the following three words on index cards so you end up with 22 cards: *Confess / Recognize / Appeal*. Mix up the cards, keeping the letters of each word together in three piles. Read Daniel 9:1-3 aloud to set the stage. Form students into three groups and provide the following: **Group 1**—Daniel 9:4-8: card pile with letters of the word *confess*. **Group 2** —Daniel 9:15, 16: card pile with letters of the word *recognize*. **Group 3**—Daniel 9:17-19: card pile with letters of the word *appeal*.

Ask groups to work quickly to see who can unscramble their word the fastest, based on the assigned text. Caution that the unscrambled word may not match the lesson outline.

Ask a member of Group 1 to read its passage and state what the unscrambled word is. Wrap up

the ensuing discussion by saying, "Daniel begins his prayer by confessing the sin of the people. He doesn't make excuses, blame someone else, or whine about how mean God is. He takes ownership." Have students look through the verses and call out confirmations.

Ask Groups 2 and 3 to do the same in turn. Wrap up the discussion of verses 15, 16 by saying "Daniel recognizes who God is and what He's done for His people." Have students confirm by calling out examples. Conclude Group 3's discussion as you say, "After acknowledging the sins of the people and the righteousness of God, Daniel chose to appeal to God's mercy." Have students look through the verses and confirm. Then read the Lord's Prayer in Matthew 6 and the Pharisee's prayer in Luke 18:11, 12. Compare and contrast all three prayers in terms of the words *confess, recognize*, and *appeal*.

Alternative. Read aloud Daniel 9:1-19. Then distribute copies of the "Mark My Words" activity from the reproducible page, which you can download. Have students work individually or in small groups to make corrections to Daniel's prayer.

After either activity, talk about the reasons people pray. Make a transition by saying, "One reason people *should* pray is to have release from feelings of shame that result from sin."

Into Life

Ask for volunteers to tell of obstacles and distractions that keep them from having an ideal prayer life. Then ask each person to give three words that describe his or her prayer time. Say, "In the week ahead, let's strive to emulate Daniel's prayer by adjusting our three-word description to become the three words *confess, recognize*, and *appeal* that describe Daniel's prayer."

Alternative. Distribute copies of the "By Definition" activity from the reproducible page. Allow students to work on this activity individually.

A STRONG FAITH

DEVOTIONAL READING: Revelation 1:9-18
BACKGROUND SCRIPTURE: Daniel 10, 11

DANIEL 10:10-19

10 And, behold, an hand touched me, which set me upon my knees and upon the palms of my hands.

11 And he said unto me, O Daniel, a man greatly beloved, understand the words that I speak unto thee, and stand upright: for unto thee am I now sent. And when he had spoken this word unto me, I stood trembling.

12 Then said he unto me, Fear not, Daniel: for from the first day that thou didst set thine heart to understand, and to chasten thyself before thy God, thy words were heard, and I am come for thy words.

13 But the prince of the kingdom of Persia withstood me one and twenty days: but, lo, Michael, one of the chief princes, came to help me; and I remained there with the kings of Persia.

14 Now I am come to make thee understand what shall befall thy people in the latter days: for yet the vision is for many days.

15 And when he had spoken such words unto me, I set my face toward the ground, and I became dumb.

16 And, behold, one like the similitude of the sons of men touched my lips: then I opened my mouth, and spake, and said unto him that stood before me, O my lord, by the vision my sorrows are turned upon me, and I have retained no strength.

17 For how can the servant of this my lord talk with this my lord? for as for me, straightway there remained no strength in me, neither is there breath left in me.

18 Then there came again and touched me one like the appearance of a man, and he strengthened me,

19 And said, O man greatly beloved, fear not: peace be unto thee, be strong, yea, be strong. And when he had spoken unto me, I was strengthened, and said, Let my lord speak; for thou hast strengthened me.

KEY VERSE

O man greatly beloved, fear not: peace be unto thee, be strong, yea, be strong. And when he had spoken unto me, I was strengthened, and said, Let my lord speak; for thou hast strengthened me. —**Daniel 10:19**

Graphic: Ingram Publishing / Getty Images / Thinkstock

AFAITH IN ACTION

Unit 2: A Living Faith in God
LESSONS 6–9

LESSON AIMS

After participating in this lesson, each learner will be able to:

1. Summarize Daniel's encounter with the heavenly messenger.

2. Explain the difference that faith in the Lord makes when facing an uncertain future.

3. Quote one or more Scripture passages that provide a personal sense of God's presence and assurance during times when the future looks uncertain.

LESSON OUTLINE

Introduction

A. What Are the Odds?

The question above pops to mind when something unusual happens or when we consider taking a risk. For many situations, an actuary has already calculated the odds. For example, the odds of being hit by lightning in any given year is about 1 in 960,000. Those with a fear of flying may be relieved to know that the odds of a person dying in a plane crash are only 1 in 8,000. Nature lovers can be confident that the odds of dying from contact with a venomous plant or animal is about 1 in 42,000.

Some odds are comforting. But at other times circumstances of life cause us to feel as if the odds are stacked against us and we can't go on. Daniel's faith gave him strength in uncertain times for himself and for his nation.

B. Lesson Background

Last week's study covered Daniel's fervent prayer of repentance on behalf of himself, his captive people, and his homeland in Judah. The verses immediately following (Daniel 9:20-27) record a response to Daniel by the angel Gabriel while Daniel was praying. Gabriel said he had come to give Daniel understanding regarding what lay ahead for God's people. The prophecy of the seventy weeks follows. It includes descriptions of some of the Messiah's achievements, though persistent questions remain regarding how to interpret details of the prophecy.

Daniel 10:1 introduces a chronological note: "In the third year of Cyrus king of Persia a thing was revealed unto Daniel." This was the year 537 or 536 BC, two or three years after the aforementioned prayer (see Daniel 9:1). The exact nature of the revelation to Daniel is not provided in the text, although verse 1 goes on to say that "the thing was true, but the time appointed was long." In addition Daniel "had understanding of the vision." Whatever this consisted of, Daniel records a period of "three full weeks" during which he mourned and suspended his daily routine of eating and grooming (Daniel 10:2, 3). We do not know the reason for Daniel's mourning.

Daniel 10:4 then describes a vision that Daniel had "by the side of the great river, which is Hiddekel." (Hiddekel appears to be another designation of the Tigris River.) An unidentified but spectacular, powerful figure appeared to him. While the figure is not identified, some suggest he may be the angel Gabriel, in keeping with other visions (Daniel 8:16; 9:21). The men with Daniel on this occasion did not see the vision but fled in terror nonetheless (10:7; compare Acts 9:7; 22:9).

The bewildered Daniel eventually fell into a "deep sleep" as the unidentified individual spoke (Daniel 10:9). This is the point at which our printed text begins.

I. Faith Relieves Fear
(Daniel 10:10, 11)
A. Touched by an Angel (v. 10)

10. And, behold, an hand touched me, which set me upon my knees and upon the palms of my hands.

We do not know how long Daniel remains in his "deep sleep" with his "face toward the ground" as the verse before this one describes (Daniel 10:9). Listening to a voice had led to the sleep, and now the touch of a hand results in the opposite. He awakens to the point of being on all fours (compare Revelation 1:17). We can compare this with what happens to the prophet Ezekiel in Ezekiel 2:2. He is a contemporary of Daniel; Ezekiel's ministry is carried out among the captives in exile, whereas Daniel remains at the royal court in a more official capacity. We do not know whether the two men ever met.

HOW TO SAY IT

Babylonian	Bab-ih-*low*-nee-un.
Cyrus	*Sigh*-russ.
Ephesians	Ee-*fee*-zhunz.
Ezekiel	Ee-*zeek*-ee-ul or Ee-*zeek*-yul.
Gabriel	*Gay*-bree-ul.
Gideon	*Gid*-e-un (*G* as in *get*).
Hiddekel	*Hid*-eh-kell.
Jeremiah	Jair-uh-*my*-uh.
Persia	*Per*-zhuh.

B. Commanded to Listen (v. 11)

11. And he said unto me, O Daniel, a man greatly beloved, understand the words that I speak unto thee, and stand upright: for unto thee am I now sent. And when he had spoken this word unto me, I stood trembling.

When a heavenly messenger appears to someone, a word of commendation may be spoken first (examples: Judges 6:11, 12; Luke 1:26-28). That happens here as well, and this is not the first time a heavenly messenger has called Daniel *a man greatly beloved* (see Daniel 9:21-23).

In order for Daniel to be able to *understand the words* that will be spoken to him, he must be fully awake; that may be why he is directed to *stand upright*. In other cases, such a command from a heavenly messenger is accompanied by a hint of disapproval or impatience (see Joshua 7:10; Jeremiah 1:17; Acts 12:6, 7; 22:14-16). That is not the case here (compare Ezekiel 1:28–2:2).

Even without hearing any words or tone of admonishment, Daniel is able to stand only with trembling. He also had been in a "deep sleep" earlier before standing, but at that time Gabriel touched him and set him in an upright position (Daniel 8:16-18). After Gabriel spoke to him then, he had "fainted, and was sick certain days" (8:27). Will the words he is about to hear have a similar effect? One can understand why Daniel is trembling at this point!

◆ *Times of Trembling* ◆

A church group was traveling to a retreat. The driver, weary from the long hours, suddenly yelled, "Look, there is a refrigerator box breaking apart and flying in the air." A passenger said, "No, there's an accident ahead. It's a van."

The driver slammed on the brakes. Members of the church group were the first to reach the mangled van and a destroyed car, which had a family inside. The group quickly understood the situation, but felt inadequate to help due to lack of first-aid training. They didn't even have a bandage. Fear began to take hold.

One of the group reminded the others that "perfect love casteth out fear" (1 John 4:18). Immediately everyone prayed for the strength to serve and love those in need. Fears were put aside in order to do what was necessary. Each began to meet the needs of the injured. One of the group flagged down an 18-wheeler, which happened to be driven by a trained emergency medical technician. The Lord had provided.

As we encounter the unexpected situations of life, may our trust in the Lord help us put aside our fears so we can face our trials with courage. Daniel's God is our God. As God responded and strengthened Daniel, so also God will strengthen us for His tasks. —V. S.

> **What Do You Think?**
> What steps can you take to ensure that your memory of God's love will be a source of strength during a difficult time?
> *Talking Points for Your Discussion*
> - In times of physical suffering
> - In times of spiritual suffering
> - Other

II. Faith Welcomes the Future
(Daniel 10:12-14)
A. God Reveals (v. 12)

12. Then said he unto me, Fear not, Daniel: for from the first day that thou didst set thine heart to understand, and to chasten thyself before thy God, thy words were heard, and I am come for thy words.

Along with or in place of words of commendation, the words *fear not* are sometimes spoken by a heavenly messenger to the recipient (examples: Judges 6:23; Luke 1:13, 30). As this messenger speaks of the *first day* that Daniel set his *heart to understand,* perhaps the reference is to the series of dreams and visions Daniel has been given. These go back to the beginning of chapter 7, and each one recorded in chapters 7 and 8 have caused him great distress (Daniel 7:15, 28; 8:27).

It is also possible that the messenger's words in the verse before us describe Daniel's response to the angel Gabriel's message in Daniel 9:21-27. Daniel's act of chastening himself would then refer to his three-week period of mourning and

his denying himself certain food and drink and portions of his daily care (10:2, 3). Daniel's prayer in chapter 9 may be the words to which the messenger is now responding, or possibly the reference may be to prayers that Daniel offered during his three weeks of mourning.

Perhaps most important to note from this verse is the description of Daniel's spiritual condition: he has *set* his *heart* to understand God's ways. Seventy years of captivity in a foreign land have not affected the state of Daniel's heart or made him bitter toward God. His heart is as firmly committed to the Lord as it had been when he and his friends had first set foot on Babylonian soil. The Hebrew behind the word *chasten* is also translated "humbled" in Psalm 35:13, and that is the sense here. What could be more important than humbling oneself before God as one works to understand His ways?

> **What Do You Think?**
> What are some ways we can help each other remain spiritually constant during hard times?
> *Talking Points for Your Discussion*
> - When plans are frustrated
> - When weariness threatens
> - When doubts arise
> - When escapism tempts

B. Powers Resist (vv. 13, 14)

13a. But the prince of the kingdom of Persia withstood me one and twenty days.

Since a heavenly messenger is speaking these words, one gets the impression that *the prince of the kingdom of Persia* is a spiritual being who stands opposed to the work to be carried out through the Lord's messengers. Thus he may be seen as representing Satan as he attempts to thwart God's holy purposes. The New Testament uses the phrases "prince of the power of the air" (Ephesians 2:2) and "prince of this world" (John 12:31; 14:30; 16:11) to describe Satan.

This half-verse may therefore be describing the kind of spiritual warfare that Paul outlines in Ephesians 6:10-18. It is noteworthy that the *one and twenty days* are equivalent to the three weeks of Daniel's mourning (Daniel 10:2). The struggle pictured in the present verse is the reason for the delay in answering Daniel's prayer.

13b. But, lo, Michael, one of the chief princes, came to help me.

Gabriel and Michael are angelic beings designated by name in Scripture (see also Revelation 9:11). Michael is mentioned also in Daniel 10:21, where he is described as Daniel's "prince," and in 12:1 as the defender and deliverer of God's people during a time of great trouble.

In the New Testament, Michael is called "the archangel" in Jude 9, where he is described as "contending with the devil . . . about the body of Moses." Michael and his angels fight and win a war in Heaven against the dragon (Satan) and his angels (Revelation 12:7-9). It appears that whenever Michael is mentioned in Scripture by name, he is engaged in some kind of intense conflict. So it is in the present verse.

We further note that Jesus' return will be announced "with the voice of the archangel" (1 Thessalonians 4:16). We presume this archangel to be Michael, although his name is not used.

13c. And I remained there with the kings of Persia.

We can only speculate as to what this detainment involved. Perhaps it reflects the struggles that the exiles who have returned home are confronting in their efforts to rebuild the temple and reestablish themselves in their homeland (Ezra 4:1-5). Are satanic elements (referring to Satan's use of various individuals or circumstances) at work to counter God's plan for His people? Is that why Michael has been dispatched to help the messenger speaking with Daniel? We cannot be certain.

> *What Do You Think?*
> In what ways can acknowledging spiritual warfare affect how we endure hard times?
> *Talking Points for Your Discussion*
> - Regarding our perspective on purpose
> - Regarding our perspectives on friend and foe
> - Regarding our perspective on resources
> - Other

14. Now I am come to make thee understand what shall befall thy people in the latter days: for yet the vision is for many days.

It's one thing to know *what* will happen; but it's another thing to know the timing, the *when* of it. What is being revealed to Daniel will not be fulfilled *for many days*. This most likely alludes to what Daniel is about to be told in chapters 11 and 12 (not in today's text).

III. Faith Receives Strength
(DANIEL 10:15-19)
A. No Strength Within (vv. 15-17)

15. And when he had spoken such words unto me, I set my face toward the ground, and I became dumb.

Daniel's reaction to *such words* is similar to that of the earlier vision in Daniel 10:9. One can understand his reaction. He has already been given an array of visions and dreams that have left him an emotional and physical wreck.

Daniel is an elderly man at this point; this may contribute to a lack of stamina for all of this. Yet here in chapter 10, a heavenly messenger has thus far said, in essence, "But wait—there's more!" No wonder Daniel can only turn his *face toward the ground* as he becomes speechless (*dumb*).

16. And, behold, one like the similitude of the sons of men touched my lips: then I opened my mouth, and spake, and said unto him that stood before me, O my lord, by the vision my sorrows are turned upon me, and I have retained no strength.

Having been reduced to speechlessness, *one like the similitude of the sons of men* (apparently another angelic being) comes to the rescue. This is the fourth of five instances recorded of Daniel's being touched by a heavenly being (compare Daniel 8:18; 9:21; 10:10, 18). The fact that this touch occurs on Daniel's lips echoes Isaiah 6:6, 7 and Jeremiah 1:9). This enables Daniel to speak, whereupon he immediately confesses his extreme weakness. His use of the term *my lord* is not to be understood that he sees the one touching him as being deity. Rather, it is a polite term of respect for the being's exalted status (compare Daniel 1:10).

17. For how can the servant of this my lord talk with this my lord? for as for me, straightway there remained no strength in me, neither is there breath left in me.

We get the impression that Daniel speaks these words while literally gasping for air. He remains more than a little unnerved by what he has been privileged to see and hear! But he is still aware of his status: he is merely a servant to the being with whom he converses. In acknowledging his weakness, it is as if Daniel is pleading for a second touch in order to obtain additional strength. And that is indeed what he receives (next verse).

B. Strength from Above (vv. 18, 19)

18. Then there came again and touched me one like the appearance of a man, and he strengthened me.

Once more Daniel receives a strengthening touch. The *one like the appearance of a man* may be the same being who touched him earlier. Various passages speak of the spiritual hand of the Lord strengthening individuals (examples: Ezra 7:28; Nehemiah 2:18). The verse before us, however, speaks of strength via physical touch from a heavenly being acting on God's authority.

19. And said, O man greatly beloved, fear not: peace be unto thee, be strong, yea, be strong. And when he had spoken unto me, I was strengthened, and said, Let my lord speak; for thou hast strengthened me.

Interestingly, Daniel's request for strength is not so that he might question the angelic being. Rather, Daniel has desired strength so that he might be able to listen, as evident in his request *let my lord speak.*

Part (most?) of the strength Daniel receives must be due to the reaffirmation that he is *greatly*

beloved (compare Daniel 10:11, above). Sometimes we too find ourselves in a state of needing calm assurance from the Lord that we are not alone, that He is still in control, and that He will supply whatever we lack. At other times we may find ourselves in a position of being the channel or conduit of the Lord's strength to someone who needs it. Such is the privilege of bearing one another's burdens (Galatians 6:2).

◆ ENCOURAGING MESSAGE ◆

Eva, our church's eldest senior at nearly 100 years of age, struggles with physical weakness. But what she lacks in physical strength she makes up for in strong Christian love. Her wisdom and ability to share her Christian message knits the community together in love (Colossians 2:2). She is particularly good at alleviating the fears of mothers whose sons and daughters in the military are deployed.

When Faith's son Kevin was deployed to Iraq, Eva reminded her of when at age 2 he walked up to the choir, carrying a hymnal, to sing with them. "What a courageous toddler!" Eva exclaimed. They laughed and reminisced of the congregation's waiting each week thereafter to see the little one run up to join the choir. "We wouldn't have had it any other way," Eva added.

"Faith," Eva's encouragement continued, "you are the courageous mom who raised Kevin. We know God hears our prayers. He answered the first time you ever mentioned Kevin's courage in a prayer."

We can be God's hands and feet in imitating this message of Daniel 10. We can set others at ease, tell them what we appreciate about them, and give them assurance that their prayers are heard. Recipients of such a message can say, as Daniel did, that the Lord has strengthened them.

—V. S.

Conclusion

A. Bible Complacency

The availability of the Bible in the Western world today is mind-boggling. Just the sheer number of editions is impressive in an "embarrassment of riches" kind of way. For print editions, one can choose from various bindings, print size, color coding, etc. For electronic versions, Bibles are available for all the major software platforms in terms of "apps" (short for "applications"). These allow one to have the text ready to read within seconds on a smartphone or tablet. Anyone with such a device can have the Bible alongside them while they are walking, running, or working.

Such an availability of Scripture is indeed a blessing, but it can also produce some less-than-desirable attitudes. It is easy for us who live in Western democracies to become complacent and take for granted what we are privileged to possess. With that complacency can come a decline in the passion for spending time in the Bible. Technology, while providing ready access to the Bible, can result in less memorization of Scripture or of hiding the Word in one's heart (Psalm 119:11). The heart then becomes more vulnerable to being filled with unholy content.

B. Bible Cost

The cure for complacency is to remember and appreciate the high price that has been paid in order for us to have the access to the Bible that we do. We can read in church history of individuals who paid with their lives so that the Scriptures might be available to everyone.

The struggle to communicate God's Word traces back ultimately to individuals such as Daniel. His experience in today's text tells us something else about the process and struggle by which our Bible has come into being. His reception of God's Word through the visions and dreams that

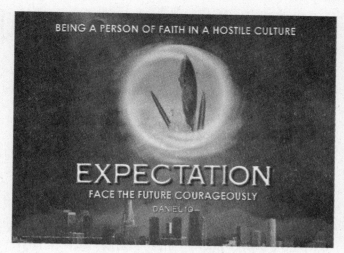

Visual for Lesson 9. *Start a discussion by pointing to this visual as you ask learners how the imperative statement relates to the picture above it.*

begin in chapter 7 left him, an elderly man, nearly unable to function. He was not a passive, unresponsive instrument who robotically received whatever God wanted him to record. Knowledge of God's Word, which eventually became written Scripture, came at a price to Daniel.

Many of us who are reading this lesson material are doing so in comfortable surroundings—at home or in the room where our class or small group meets. If the weather outside is cold, our meeting place is probably well heated. We may be relaxing in a padded chair with a cup of coffee in front of us. We hardly think of "trembling" during our encounters with the Word of God—trembling that Daniel actually experienced.

Let us never forget the price that so many individuals, including the inspired authors of Scripture, paid so that we may have and read the Bible. May we, like Daniel, set our hearts to understand and humble ourselves before God so that His Word may accomplish all that He desires of us.

B. Prayer

Heavenly Father, forgive us for the times we take Your Word for granted! May we be Your instruments today to take the Word to those who lack it. We pray this in Jesus' name. Amen.

C. Thought to Remember

Ministry success is a matter
of faith.

INVOLVEMENT LEARNING

Enhance your lesson with KJV Bible Student *(from your curriculum supplier) and the reproducible activity page (at www.standardlesson.com or in the back of the* KJV Standard Lesson Commentary Deluxe Edition*).*

Into the Lesson

Prior to class, search online for videos about Team Hoyt and select one to show.

Begin by saying, "Rick Hoyt was born with cerebral palsy. He has spent his life in a wheelchair. At the age of 15, he asked his father if they could run a race together. Dick Hoyt was 36 years old and was not a runner, but he agreed. After that race, Rick told his dad, 'When I'm running, it feels like I'm not handicapped.' Since then, they've participated in more than 70 marathons and 6 Iron Man triathlons. They even ran and biked across the U.S. Today they are known as Team Hoyt." Show the video of your choice.

Alternative. Distribute pens and copies of the "Oddly Enough" activity from the reproducible page, which you can download. Have students complete the activity individually. Discuss responses and give correct answers.

After either activity say, "Sometimes circumstances cause us to feel as if the odds are stacked against us and we can't go on. Daniel's faith was a key element in having strength in uncertain times for him and for his nation."

Into the Word

Write the following on separate slips of paper:

> *a doting grandmother*
> *a 5-year-old child*
> *a football coach*
> *an opera singer*
> *a cowboy*
> *a robot*

Fold the slips and put them in a bowl. Say, "Last week we studied one of Daniel's prayers. Today we'll see how Daniel found strength in prayer and from the angel sent by God to encourage him and answer his prayer."

Divide students into three groups, assigning each group one of the following passages: Daniel 10:10, 11; 10:12-14; 10:15-19. Say, "The angel appeared to Daniel to relay an important message. Each of these texts is part of that message."

Let each group draw a slip of paper and convey the message from its assigned text in the voice of that person. (For example, for verses 10 and 11, a football coach might say, "Daniel! Get your head in the game! Do you know how many people want to be in your shoes right now? I've got something important to say, and you'd better pay attention! Now stand up and listen up!")

Have groups prepare their messages. Then read each Scripture text and allow the appropriate group to share its dramatized version. Afterward say, "We had some fun sharing the angel's message from different perspectives. As silly as our attempts might seem, this message was a serious one—one Daniel and his people desperately needed to hear. Daniel needed not only the message, but also the strength to hear it." (If time allows, you can have groups draw second strips and enact.)

Option. Divide students into two groups, providing paper and pencils. Ask one group to skim some of the Psalms and note specific verses relating to strength. Ask the other group to skim Isaiah and do the same thing. Allow students to work for several minutes and then read their selected verses to the rest of the class. Say, "Throughout history, Christians have depended on God to strengthen their faith. So can we!"

Into Life

Encourage students to talk about times in their lives when they've looked to God for strength. Then read the following verses and challenge them to choose one on which to meditate this week: Isaiah 40:31; Psalm 31:24; Philippians 4:13.

Alternative. Distribute pens and copies of the "Give Me Strength" activity from the reproducible page. Have students complete the activity individually or in small groups.

Faith Without Works is Dead

DEVOTIONAL READING: Psalm 143
BACKGROUND SCRIPTURE: James 2:14-26

JAMES 2:14-26

14 What doth it profit, my brethren, though a man say he hath faith, and have not works? can faith save him?

15 If a brother or sister be naked, and destitute of daily food,

16 And one of you say unto them, Depart in peace, be ye warmed and filled; notwithstanding ye give them not those things which are needful to the body; what doth it profit?

17 Even so faith, if it hath not works, is dead, being alone.

18 Yea, a man may say, Thou hast faith, and I have works: shew me thy faith without thy works, and I will shew thee my faith by my works.

19 Thou believest that there is one God; thou doest well: the devils also believe, and tremble.

20 But wilt thou know, O vain man, that faith without works is dead?

21 Was not Abraham our father justified by works, when he had offered Isaac his son upon the altar?

22 Seest thou how faith wrought with his works, and by works was faith made perfect?

23 And the scripture was fulfilled which saith, Abraham believed God, and it was imputed unto him for righteousness: and he was called the Friend of God.

24 Ye see then how that by works a man is justified, and not by faith only.

25 Likewise also was not Rahab the harlot justified by works, when she had received the messengers, and had sent them out another way?

26 For as the body without the spirit is dead, so faith without works is dead also.

KEY VERSE

Faith, if it hath not works, is dead, being alone. —**James 2:17**

Faith in Action

Lesson Aims

After participating in this lesson, each learner will be able to:

1. Summarize the relationship between faith and works.

2. Explain why obedience is a necessary component to a life of faith.

3. Identify an area where actions do not follow faith in his or her life and make a plan for change.

Lesson Outline

Introduction
A. Flipping and Flopping
B. Lesson Background
I. Useless Piety (James 2:14-16)
A. Severe Need (vv. 14, 15)
B. Empty Sentiment (v. 16)
II. Empty Profession (James 2:17-19)
A. Evidence in the Actions (vv. 17, 18)
   Basis of Faith
B. Dread of Demons (v. 19)
III. Faithful Action (James 2:20-26)
A. Case Study 1: Abraham (vv. 20-24)
   Result of Faith
B. Case Study 2: Rahab (vv. 25, 26)
Conclusion
A. Works of Law vs. Works of Faith
B. Prayer
C. Thought to Remember

Introduction

A. Flipping and Flopping

When politicians change their positions on a topic, opponents are quick to deride the change as being *a flip-flop*. This derogatory label is not new, being traced back to the 1880s.

The issue at hand was U. S. President Grover Cleveland's compromise with the United Kingdom on fishing rights in the waters off Canada. This signaled a change in promised policy and outraged New England states that depended on the fishing industry.

A fallout of this political concession was a *New York Tribune* writer's calling of President Cleveland's action a "fisheries flip-flop." The phrase was probably a play on words in bringing to mind the way fish flip and flop on a boat deck. The phrase caught on, and since that time the flip-flopping charge has been made against countless leaders.

People know that talk is cheap and that actions speak louder than words. People are suspicious of those who say one thing today, but act in another way tomorrow. James has quite a bit to say about ensuring that professions of faith are matched by accompanying action consistently.

B. Lesson Background

The author identifies himself as James, "a servant of God and of the Lord Jesus Christ" (James 1:1). This clearly makes him a Christian leader, but which of the several men named James in the early church is he?

Two of the original 12 apostles of Jesus are named James. The James who was the brother of John was murdered by Herod quite early in the history of the church, too early for him to have been the author of our book (Matthew 10:2; Acts 12:1, 2). The other James, the son of Alphaeus (Matthew 10:3), is a possibility, but his lack of mention in the New Testament aside from lists of the 12 apostles makes him unlikely as the author of the book under consideration.

Most likely is the James who was a son of Mary and Joseph, thus a half-brother of Jesus (Mark 6:3). While this James did not believe in Jesus during his ministry (John 7:5), he did become a believer after Jesus' ascension (Acts 1:14). Paul records that Jesus made a special appearance to James after the resurrection, a person carefully distinguished from the 12 apostles in description (1 Corinthians 15:5-7). James was a prominent leader in the Jerusalem church in its early days (Acts 15:13; Galatians 1:19).

Based on the fact that the letter is addressed to "the twelve tribes which are scattered abroad" (James 1:1), the intended audience is Christians of Jewish background. If "scattered abroad" refers to the scattering of Stephen's martyrdom, then the intended recipients are in Judea and Samaria (Acts 8:1) as well as Phenice (Phoenicia), Cyprus, and Syrian Antioch (11:19). If "scattered abroad" is not linked to that persecution, then the intended recipients may live in the farther environs of the Roman Empire (John 7:35).

The first-century Jewish historian Josephus records that this James was martyred in the early AD 60s. Therefore we date the book to no later than AD 62. The combination of addressees, date, and content reflects the mid–first-century concerns of Jewish Christians who grappled with the place of the beloved Law of Moses in their lives. James, a Jewish Christian himself, was not afraid to teach that keeping the law is a good thing in certain circumstances (see James 2:8).

The tendency to try earning God's favor through keeping the law still held much appeal to Christians from a Jewish background. But Jesus, Paul, and others had shown that salvation could not be earned. Therefore, the place of obedience to God's commands was perplexing. Was there a place for good works that did not fall back into the Jewish system of keeping the old covenant law to please God? This is the issue that James addressed; it is an issue that resonates yet today.

I. Useless Piety
(JAMES 2:14-16)
A. Severe Need (vv. 14, 15)

14. What doth it profit, my brethren, though a man say he hath faith, and have not works? can faith save him?

James's style is often to ask questions and then bring us to his answer. Here he asks the same question in two ways. Combined, the foundational question he poses is this: Is the person who claims to have faith but has no good works going to be saved from God's condemning judgment?

In the church today, the question might be asked this way: Is faith without works saving faith? This partially misses what James is asking, however, for an underlying question is this: Is faith without works faith at all?

15. If a brother or sister be naked, and destitute of daily food.

Rather than answer immediately, James gives an example that highlights the question, and this is not merely hypothetical. It is a real-world example his readers face or have faced. Imagine someone in the congregation lacks clothing or food. What should you do? Note: the word *naked* does not necessarily mean without any clothing whatsoever. Rather, it can imply insufficient clothing to stay warm in cold weather.

B. Empty Sentiment (v. 16)

16. And one of you say unto them, Depart in peace, be ye warmed and filled; notwithstanding ye give them not those things which are needful to the body; what doth it profit?

Rather than offering physical help, clothing, and/or food, the person in James's scenario gives a blessing and tells the needy brothers and sisters to be on their way. The answer is, "God bless you and leave me alone." Does this do any good? Does a blessing of *peace* make the destitute person warmer or less hungry?

HOW TO SAY IT

Alphaeus	Al-*fee*-us.
Cyprus	*Sigh*-prus.
Herod	*Hair*-ud.
Jericho	*Jair*-ih-co.
Judea	Joo-*dee*-uh.
Phenice	Fih-*nye*-see.
Phoenicia	Fuh-*nish*-uh.
Rahab	*Ray*-hab.
Sodom	*Sod*-um.
Syrian Antioch	*Sear*-ee-un *An*-tih-ock.

Such a response is in keeping with the theory that a person of faith does not need good works. The answer is obvious then. If people who claim to have faith fail to help a needy brother or sister, then something is wrong with their faith.

II. Empty Profession
(JAMES 2:17-19)

A. Evidence in the Actions (vv. 17, 18)

17. Even so faith, if it hath not works, is dead, being alone.

This verse renders James's verdict on faith that lacks compassionate actions: it *is dead*. This is a strong statement, a condemning statement. It means there is no life, no validity to this claim to faith. Faith *alone,* divorced from actions, is hollow and empty. A lack of love for the needy is in conflict with a claim to love God, for God loves the poor and cares for those in need (see Isaiah 3:14, 15). This is not merely a Christian idea, but is taught in the Law of Moses (see Deuteronomy 15:11). Christians of Jewish background in James's day have a strong tradition of helping the unfortunate; ignoring the poor is offensive.

What Do You Think?
What questions could we ask ourselves that would reveal dead or dying faith in our lives?
Talking Points for Your Discussion
- To expose lack of action
- To expose lack of compassion
- To expose wrong priorities
- To expose a wayward heart

18. Yea, a man may say, Thou hast faith, and I have works: shew me thy faith without thy works, and I will shew thee my faith by my works.

James shifts to the other end of the argument: the person who values good *works* over claims to *faith*. This person seems tired of those who tout their faith but have nothing to show for it. He might say, "You can talk about your faith all day, but if you have no works, you have nothing to show me. I'm not even going to talk about faith! Just look at my good works! Forget about faith."

James comes back at this second position with a refusal to separate the two. He starts with faith and then moves to works, saying his claim to faith is more than words. It is demonstrated by his actions. He has backed up his talking with a life of caring about the poor, a life of feeding and clothing those in need. Faith and works are not in conflict. They are partners.

◆ *BASIS OF FAITH* ◆

A friend received devastating news: she had an aggressive form of cancer. She left the doctor's office in shock but started treatment immediately on her physician's advice. She suffered through months of surgery, chemotherapy, and rehabilitation, all while holding to the hope that she would recover and live a normal life. She believed her doctor when he told her that the best chance she had was to follow his instructions and receive the treatments. Even though she lost her hair and felt even worse from the medication, she followed the regimen faithfully.

When treatments ended, the doctor pronounced her free of cancer—and she was. She celebrated with friends and family. She trusted her doctor because of the evidence of his expertise, and that trust proved justified. Notice the sequence: evidence of expertise generated trust, which in turn resulted in the faith to follow the expert's counsel, even through the worst of the pain. Faith in God works similarly. God's track record of authority, power, expertise, etc., convinces us to trust Him. That trust results in faith. Then we act according to that faith. Our behavior, the way we live, then becomes evidence of our faith—evidence for all to see.   —L. M. W.

What Do You Think?
How do we commit to doing good works as a visible example to others without slipping into legalism or pride?
Talking Points for Your Discussion
- When others praise us
- When others criticize our motives
- Matthew 5:14-16 in relation to 6:1-4
- Other

B. Dread of Demons (v. 19)

19. Thou believest that there is one God; thou doest well: the devils also believe, and tremble.

James now moves to a topic at the heart of Jewish identity: the belief in *one God*. This is the foundation of what it means to be a Jew (see Deuteronomy 6:4; Isaiah 44:6). The Romans and the Greeks of James's day believe in many gods and goddesses, but the Jews refuse to compromise in this area. The Christians follow this, also believing in a single God (see Galatians 3:20).

But mere recognition that there is only one God is not enough. James uses an extreme example in pointing out that even *the devils also believe* this. Presumably these evil spirits have insights into the spiritual world beyond anything a human being can envision. Demons are not fooled by those who imagine many gods. The demons know better, and in their perverted demonic hearts it causes them to *tremble,* for they know they are on the wrong side. And demonic recognition of or belief in one God does not mean they serve Him. James knows for a fact that demons work in direct opposition to God and His plans. To bring it back to the earlier points, no demon cares about a person in need of clothing or food. They have no good works, only evil.

This is a word of caution for us today. Both Jews and Muslims believe in only one God. But that bare belief is not enough. In James's narrower context, one-God faith must be accompanied by godly actions, a demonstration of one's faith. In the wider context of the New Testament as a whole, faith in one God must include faith in God's Son, Jesus Christ, and in His saving sacrifice for human sins (2 Timothy 3:15).

> *What Do You Think?*
> How can an analysis of sin serve as a diagnostic tool of a person's relationship with God?
> *Talking Points for Your Discussion*
> - Regarding sins of commission
> - Regarding sins of omission
> - Regarding sin as a thermometer (reflects reality) vs. sin as a thermostat (changes reality)

III. Faithful Action
(JAMES 2:20-26)

A. Case Study 1: Abraham (vv. 20-24)

20. But wilt thou know, O vain man, that faith without works is dead?

James has stated his case: claims of faith without the evidence of good deeds make for a dead, empty faith. Now he moves to prove his case by giving some examples that his Jewish-Christian readers will appreciate.

21, 22. Was not Abraham our father justified by works, when he had offered Isaac his son upon the altar? Seest thou how faith wrought with his works, and by works was faith made perfect?

James's first example is that of the greatest of ancestors, namely *Abraham* and his willingness to obey the Lord's demand that he sacrifice *Isaac his son* (Genesis 22:1-18). This was a test of Abraham's faith, a test he passed because he feared the Lord and withheld nothing from Him (22:12).

When we read that Abraham was *justified by works,* we should not understand this as equivalent to and therefore in conflict to the idea that we are justified by faith. James is using *justified* (or being considered righteous) in the sense of "proven true." Abraham's actions were motivated by his deep convictions. Abraham believed that if he killed his son, God could somehow bring him back from the dead and therefore fulfill the promise to make Abraham's descendants a great nation (Hebrews 11:19). Abraham's trust in God made it possible for him to obey God even in the most challenging of circumstances we can imagine.

◆ *RESULT OF FAITH* ◆

A Christian aid worker struck up a conversation with a Muslim refugee from Syria who was making his way to the relative safety of Turkey. As they got to know one another, the Muslim asked the Christian what made him want to work with refugees. This opened the door to speak of faith in Jesus and the importance of demonstrating the love of Christ by caring for those in need. The Muslim man replied that he had heard of Jesus and had even read parts of the Gospels about Him.

"Maybe you can help me," he continued. "For the past 90 nights, I've had the same dream. In my dream, a man wearing white clothes and bathed in light comes to me, and every night he tells me that he loves me. Who is this man?" The Christian took out his Bible and read a description of Jesus.

"That's him!" the Muslim refugee exclaimed. "That's the man in my dream!" The Christian then explained that Jesus was pursuing the man because He loved him. The man professed Christ that day.

There is good reason to wonder whether Jesus actually appeared to the man in dreams (see 2 Corinthians 11:14; 1 Thessalonians 5:21; 1 John 4:1-3; etc.). But rather than focus on a potential problem, the Christian seized an opportunity. Faith had led the Christian to that part of the world, and one result of that faith stood right before him: a new believer in Christ. As James asked, "Seest thou . . . by works was faith made perfect?" Can the same connection be drawn between your own faith and works? —L. M. W.

23. And the scripture was fulfilled which saith, Abraham believed God, and it was imputed unto him for righteousness: and he was called the Friend of God.

Even before the testing of Abraham's faith with the Isaac episode, God recognized that man's great faith (Genesis 15:6, a verse James quotes). Abraham's relationship with God was based on his willingness to do things because of his trust in the Lord. He was willing to travel to a foreign land in obedience to God's direction (12:1-4). He was willing to entrust his nephew into the Lord's hands when God destroyed the city of Sodom (18:16-33). He was willing to try one more time with his elderly wife when the Lord told him she would become pregnant and he would finally have his long-awaited son (21:1, 2).

Abraham's faith and obedience led to his remarkable designation as *the Friend of God* (see Isaiah 41:8). Abraham is not referred to as "the obedient servant of God." He is not "the one who did what God told him." He is called the Friend of God! Faith is descriptive of a relationship with God, not a transaction.

What Do You Think?
Under what circumstances, if any, could someone today be seen as a "friend of God"?
Talking Points for Your Discussion
- Considering the connection between the terms *friend* and *righteousness*
- Considering the biblical rarity of that designation (2 Chronicles 20:7; Isaiah 41:8)
- Considering the opposite in James 4:4; etc.

24. Ye see then how that by works a man is justified, and not by faith only.

James is not implying that only works are required for justification. To do so would be a victory for those Jews who promote keeping the law as the pathway to salvation. James never minimizes or discounts the importance of faith. Therefore, we need to take this verse in concert with what James has already said and not in isolation. His overall point is that true faith will cause correct behavior. Good works are not the condition of saving fellowship with God, they are the result. Good works demonstrate true faith, and it is by this necessary combination that we are *justified*.

B. Case Study 2: Rahab (vv. 25, 26)

25. Likewise also was not Rahab the harlot justified by works, when she had received the messengers, and had sent them out another way?

James's second historical example is more obscure. Rahab was a prostitute in Jericho, and she assisted the men whom Joshua dispatched to evaluate the city. She hid the spies and thus saved their lives as well as the lives of her family (see Joshua 6:23-25). This was an act of faith, for she believed that Israel and its God were stronger than Jericho and its pagan gods and walls (Joshua 2:11). Rahab is mentioned by the author of Hebrews as one who acted in faith (Hebrews 11:31). She also is in the genealogy of Jesus (Matthew 1:5).

In some ways, the example of Rahab is more to the point of James's concerns than Abraham's. Rahab's actions in safeguarding the spies includes giving them lodging (Joshua 2:1) and, doubtlessly, food. She was the one who saw others in need and offered assistance, a perfect example of faith demonstrated by deeds of concern for the well-being of those in need (compare James 2:15, 16).

26. For as the body without the spirit is dead, so faith without works is dead also.

James's final example is an analogy. A *body without the spirit* is the most basic understanding of death. The people of James's day believe that a person's last breath releases the spirit and therefore is the dividing line between life and death. To "breath your last breath" means you have died (compare Job 34:14). When one's spirit departs, all that is left is lifeless, decomposing flesh.

James's point, then, is that works are what enliven faith. Deeds of compassion and obedience to God turn words of allegiance into actions of trust and commitment. Others will judge our faithfulness by our life, but we may do this too. Do we really believe what we say? Let us look at our own lives to find the answer. Reading James demands self-evaluation.

> *What Do You Think?*
> What are some ways to resist becoming weary (Galatians 6:9) in helping others?
> *Talking Points for Your Discussion*
> • In advance, before weariness sets in
> • Recognizing "compassion fatigue" as it begins to take hold

Conclusion

A. Works of Law vs. Works of Faith

Much unfortunate confusion has surrounded the alleged conflict between Paul's denunciation of the value of works and James's insistence on the essential role of works in the life of the Christian. As James sees it, it is never a matter of either faith or works, but faith that results in works. James attacks the common self-deception that *what you do* can be separated from *what you believe.*

Careful study shows that Paul and James are not in conflict, but are talking about works in different frames of reference. Paul's battle is against those who believe keeping the Jewish law is the ticket to salvation (see Romans 3:28; Galatians 2:16). He, an expert in the law, rails against dependence on

Visual for Lesson 10. *Start a discussion by asking "How can we make this a reality?" as you work through the stanza line by line.*

keeping the law ("works of the law") without the step of faith in Jesus Christ. Paul's contention is that this is futile, for no one can ever keep the law perfectly and earn salvation.

James, on the other hand, is fighting for the proper place of works in the life of the believer. Claims of faith need to be proven by the evidence of one's life. Compassionate actions should be evident after we come to faith in Christ.

Even so, works of the law and works of faith can look remarkably similar, so it might be helpful to visualize the difference. If we understand faith in Christ as the doorway to salvation, then we see the value of works in the contexts of both Paul and James. Before we walk through the doorway of faith in Christ, works will not save (Paul's argument); after we walk through the doorway of faith in Christ, then works are the evidence of commitment to God and His ways (James's argument). The difference is in the purpose: we can never be saved by good works, but we cannot be saved without them.

B. Prayer

Father, we truly believe You are the one and only God. May this belief be much more than words. You proved faithful by Your actions; may we do so as well. In Jesus' name we pray. Amen.

C. Thought to Remember

Faith's fitness requires exercise.

INVOLVEMENT LEARNING

Enhance your lesson with KJV Bible Student *(from your curriculum supplier) and the reproducible activity page (at www.standardlesson.com or in the back of the* KJV Standard Lesson Commentary Deluxe Edition*).*

Into the Lesson

Before class, give each of four volunteers a penny. Tell them that in this activity, they will be asked for their penny. Tell one to respond, "You can have my penny." All others are to respond, "I hope you find a penny."

To begin class have the volunteers sit at the front of the classroom with open palms displaying the pennies. Choose one volunteer from the rest of the class to say "I need a penny" to each penny-holder. Each should respond as you previously instructed.

After the demonstration, point out that while each volunteer seemed to be offering their penny by holding it in an open palm, not everyone's words matched that action!

Alternative. Distribute copies of the "Worthy of Trust?" activity from the reproducible page, which you can download. Allow learners a few minutes to work in pairs on the activity.

Transition to Bible study by saying, "People know that talk is cheap and that actions speak louder than words. People are suspicious of those whose walk does not match their talk! James agrees, saying that our professions of faith must be matched by accompanying action."

Into the Word

Divide the board into two columns, one designated *Faith Without Works (James 2:14-20, 26)* and the other *Faith That Results in Works (James 2:21-25)*. Read together the lesson text to look for who James says displays the kind of faith in either column and what that type of faith looks like. As responses are given, list them under the appropriate column heading on the board. Below are probable responses.

Faith Without Works: benefits no one (v. 14) / doesn't help with physical needs (vv. 15, 16) / is dead (v. 17) / is no better than the faith of demons (v. 19) / is like a corpse (v. 26).

Faith That Results in Works: reflects the obedient faith of Abraham (v. 21) / is a complete and perfect faith (v. 22) / shows friendship with God (v. 23) / is the kind of faith by which God justifies us (v. 24) / is like the countercultural faith of Rahab (v. 25).

Dig deeper by saying, "We know that a faith without works is a dead faith, but what about works without faith?" Guide the conversation toward the fact that works alone don't have the power to save us. Draw on the points made in the commentary's Conclusion as necessary.

Say, "James isn't telling us that we must rely on our works to be right with God. Rather, he's explaining that a healthy faith will produce visible signs of itself. A living faith produces works; and when we trust God enough to perform works, we grow and nurture our faith in the process."

Into Life

Write vertically on the board the word *FAITH*. After saying, "A healthy faith produces visible signs in the form of works," divide learners into four groups and have each create an acrostic that uses the letters in the word *FAITH* to list some of the visible signs of faith.

Possible responses include but are not limited to: F—fearlessness, financial generosity, fellowship; A—aid, assisting those in need; I—instigating change, inspiring the weary, interceding in prayer; T—trusting God with your money and time, thankfulness; H—helping, having a generous spirit.

Alternative. Distribute copies of the "Living Faith" activity from the reproducible page. Have the class spend a few minutes completing the activity in pairs. Invite volunteers to share responses with the class.

As learners depart, say, "To have a living, healthy faith, we must use our actions in addition to our words. Let's commit to demonstrating our faith throughout the week!"

A DISCIPLINED FAITH

DEVOTIONAL READING: Psalm 34:1-14
BACKGROUND SCRIPTURE: James 3:1-12

JAMES 3:1-12

1 My brethren, be not many masters, knowing that we shall receive the greater condemnation.

2 For in many things we offend all. If any man offend not in word, the same is a perfect man, and able also to bridle the whole body.

3 Behold, we put bits in the horses' mouths, that they may obey us; and we turn about their whole body.

4 Behold also the ships, which though they be so great, and are driven of fierce winds, yet are they turned about with a very small helm, whithersoever the governor listeth.

5 Even so the tongue is a little member, and boasteth great things. Behold, how great a matter a little fire kindleth!

6 And the tongue is a fire, a world of iniquity: so is the tongue among our members, that it defileth the whole body, and setteth on fire the course of nature; and it is set on fire of hell.

7 For every kind of beasts, and of birds, and of serpents, and of things in the sea, is tamed, and hath been tamed of mankind:

8 But the tongue can no man tame; it is an unruly evil, full of deadly poison.

9 Therewith bless we God, even the Father; and therewith curse we men, which are made after the similitude of God.

10 Out of the same mouth proceedeth blessing and cursing. My brethren, these things ought not so to be.

11 Doth a fountain send forth at the same place sweet water and bitter?

12 Can the fig tree, my brethren, bear olive berries? either a vine, figs? so can no fountain both yield salt water and fresh.

KEY VERSE

The tongue can no man tame; it is an unruly evil, full of deadly poison. —James 3:8

FAITH IN ACTION

Unit 3: Self-Controlled, Upright, and Godly Faith

LESSONS 10–13

LESSON AIMS

After participating in this lesson, each learner will be able to:

1. List James's metaphors about speech.

2. Explain one or more of those metaphors in light of a personal experience.

3. Identify a specific problem in his or her life regarding harmful speech and write a prayer for God's help in correcting it.

LESSON OUTLINE

Introduction
    A. Chemistry, Character, or Something Else?
    B. Lesson Background
I. Lack of Control (JAMES 3:1-5a)
    A. Issue of Qualification (vv. 1, 2)
    B. Issue of Relative Size (vv. 3-5a)
      Weighing Our Words
II. Result of Failure (JAMES 3:5b-8)
    A. It Burns (vv. 5b, 6)
      Open Mouth, Insert Foot
    B. It Poisons (vv. 7, 8)
III. Lack of Consistency (JAMES 3:9-12)
    A. Problem Observed (vv. 9, 10)
    B. Problem Illustrated (vv. 11, 12)
Conclusion
    A. Think Twice Before Hitting "Send"
    B. Prayer
    C. Thought to Remember

Introduction

A. Chemistry, Character, or Something Else?

Since the turn of the twenty-first century, more and more advocates of the "It's not your character; it's your chemistry" school of thought have emerged. This is the next round of the old "nurture vs. nature" debate, also known as "environment vs. heredity." The question is why we behave as we do. One side says behavior is learned (this is the character/nurture/environment side). The other says behavior is hardwired from birth (this is the chemistry/nature/heredity side).

This issue has profound implications. For example, researchers on the chemistry side of the debate argue that most addictions are caused by a deficiency in dopamine, a natural "feel-good" brain chemical. Therefore the preferred treatment, they say, is to change one's chemistry rather than build one's character.

The issue is complicated, and there is evidence for each position in various contexts. But the idea that behavioral issues do not stem from a lack of learned self-control tends to lessen responsibility for doing or saying what we should not. But James points to another, deeper cause.

B. Lesson Background

The background to last week's lesson applies to this one as well, so that information need not be repeated here. But since today's lesson draws heavily on figures of speech, some background information in that regard is in order.

Figures of speech add interest and excitement to writing, and chief among these are metaphors. A metaphor takes an idea and imposes it on an unrelated but familiar idea to help explain the qualities of the original. An example from the ancient world is the assertion "Achilles is a lion." This does not mean the Greek hero literally had a shaggy reddish-orange mane, sharp claws, large teeth and walked on all fours. It means, rather, that Achilles was a brave, courageous warrior in battle.

Metaphors abound in our speech, so much so that we don't always notice them. Rather than refer to a particular car's color as "gray," we might say it is "battleship gray." This does not mean the car has any of the size or armament of a war-ship. The use of the word *battleship* as a metaphor for a shade of gray helps us visualize how the car appears: it is neither nearly black nor nearly white (two possibilities for gray). An emotional element is also present, as *battleship gray* suggests drabness.

James uses a variety of word pictures, including metaphor. These are drawn from life experiences shared with his readers. This style of writing is vivid, and James chose his figurative language carefully to help the readers better understand the urgency and importance of his topic.

I. Lack of Control
(JAMES 3:1-5a)
A. Issue of Qualification (vv. 1, 2)

1. My brethren, be not many masters, knowing that we shall receive the greater condemnation.

Masters is used here in the sense of teachers—think of a schoolmaster. Thus James is addressing the topic of teachers. With the use of *we* he includes himself in this group.

James warns that the role of teacher should be considered soberly, because teachers are under great scrutiny; the Greek behind the word *condemnation* is also translated "judgment" in various places (example: 1 Peter 4:17), and that is the sense here. We see the importance of the word *greater* when we realize that teachers' thoughts and ideas are made public. Good teachers are not simply relayers of correct information, they are also interpreters.

Teachers in the first-century church had two primary responsibilities. First, they were to teach the fundamentals of the Christian faith (Jude 3); these were truths they had learned from other teachers (2 Timothy 2:2). Second, they were to interpret the Old Testament Scriptures from a Christian perspective (Acts 17:2). Since James

HOW TO SAY IT

Achilles	Uh-*kih*-leez.
Corinthians	Ko-*rin*-thee-unz (*th* as in *thin*).
Ecclesiastes	Ik-*leez*-ee-*as*-teez.
Gehenna	Geh-*hen*-uh (*G* as in *get*).
Molech	*Mo*-leck.

wrote in a time when teachers did not have all the New Testament (because not all its book were yet written and compiled), the teaching function was especially subject to error and misinterpretation.

The teaching function in the church today is easier in one sense: we have the completed New Testament. But the era of the Information Age makes the teaching function more difficult in another sense: faster communication means faster communication of error and ridicule. That fact may tempt us to embrace an old saying attributed to Abraham Lincoln: "Better to remain silent and be thought a fool than to speak out and remove all doubt."

This humorous but cynical view should not intimidate Christian teachers into silence. The church needs the spiritually mature to open their mouths and impart godly teaching and wisdom to others. But be forewarned: you will be judged by God.

2. For in many things we offend all. If any man offend not in word, the same is a perfect man, and able also to bridle the whole body.

The twice-used word *offend*, also translated "stumbled" in Romans 11:11, gives us a word picture of careless use of the tongue (*in word*). The phrase *we offend all* does not mean "we offend everyone"; rather, it means all of us stumble in using speech that offends. The person who is never guilty of verbal miscues does not exist. The hypothetical person who achieves perfection in speech would, by extension, be able to control every aspect of his or her life. That is, he or she is able *to bridle the whole body*. James uses a word picture: a bridled horse is a controlled horse. The Greek verb translated *to bridle* also occurs in James 1:26, where it is translated similarly.

B. Issue of Relative Size (vv. 3-5a)

3. Behold, we put bits in the horses' mouths, that they may obey us; and we turn about their whole body.

A bridle usually includes a bit, a metal device inserted into the mouth of a horse. The bit results in uncomfortable pressure, causing the horse to respond to the pressure of the reins attached to the bridle. If the rider pulls back on both reins, the horse will slow until the pressure from the reins is released. If the rider pulls the right rein, the trained horse will turn right until the pressure from the bit is relieved.

This is an amazing thing for James, that a metal bit that fits in one's hand can control such a large animal! The analogy is how the human tongue (the symbol of speech for James) has an influence out of proportion to its size.

4. Behold also the ships, which though they be so great, and are driven of fierce winds, yet are they turned about with a very small helm, whithersoever the governor listeth.

The next metaphor is drawn from the world of sailing ships. Such vessels may be large and strong, able to withstand the pressure of mighty winds. Despite this bulk, the ship can be turned by *a very small helm*. This steering mechanism of ancient ships is something like a large oar fastened to the side of a ship. If the end of the steering oar is pushed to the right by *the governor* (helmsman), the ship goes to the right and vice versa.

Like the bridle and bit illustration, the point is that a small device can turn a mighty ship. With the tiny tongue, a small lapse in judgment that is spoken can have an enormous influence on one's life or the lives of others.

◆ *Weighing Our Words* ◆

One trip to the pediatrician involved my daughter at the tender age of 13. Girls at that age think a lot about appearance, a problematic issue in the development of self-image. Because of a rapid growth spurt that year, it seemed that every bit of food my daughter ate went to getting taller. As a result, she appeared almost skeletal.

At one point in the exam, the doctor said to her, "Your weight is much higher than most girls your age." As the doctor paused, my daughter looked at me with large eyes.

Dismayed that the doctor would say something that would be taken so wrong by a teenage girl, I exclaimed, "Yes, but that's because she is much taller than most girls her age. Look at her! She's so thin, she almost looks unhealthy!"

"Oh yes, of course. I was going to say that," the doctor added. Unfortunately, the damage was

done. For several months after that, my daughter asked me if she really was overweight like the doctor said, and she examined herself daily for extra pounds. We might say that the pediatrician's words carried weight.

What we say can affect others for months or years to come. That's just as true today as it was in the first century AD. —L. M. W.

5a. Even so the tongue is a little member, and boasteth great things.

James personifies *the tongue* as a pint-size fellow who makes boasts far out of proportion to his size (compare Psalm 73:8, 9). But we know it is not a little muscle in the mouth that is making ill-advised boasts, it is the person who owns this tongue. The tongue is only a tool for boasting; vain claims of glory start in a person's heart and mind.

> *What Do You Think?*
> What safeguards can we adopt to protect friendships from the negative effects of boasting?
> *Talking Points for Your Discussion*
> - In terms of attitudes
> - In terms of prayer
> - In distinguishing between godly and ungodly boasting (2 Corinthians 10:12-18; etc.)
> - Considering the warning of Psalm 12:3, 4

II. Result of Failure
(James 3:5b-8)
A. It Burns (vv. 5b, 6)

5b. Behold, how great a matter a little fire kindleth!

James moves to another metaphor: the phenomenon of *fire*. Big fires start as small fires. We know that a single spark can result in a fire that burns down a forest. Likewise, a few unwise words spoken carelessly can cause permanent, life-changing damage. Reputations—either those of the ones speaking or those of the ones being spoken about—can be ruined. Most of us have had the experience of changing our opinion of someone after hearing unwise words spoken in an unguarded moment.

6. And the tongue is a fire, a world of iniquity: so is the tongue among our members, that it defileth the whole body, and setteth on fire the course of nature; and it is set on fire of hell.

What is implied in the previous verse is explicit here: the uncontrolled tongue not only causes widespread external damage, it also ends up being suicidal. James pictures this self-destruction as being a life *on fire,* a life that is fueled by the *fire of hell.* The word *hell* translates the Greek word *Gehenna,* which itself derives from the Old Testament's *Hinnom.* This is the name of a valley used to burn garbage in James's day; it is located just south of Jerusalem.

Traced further back, this valley gained a terrible reputation because of babies burned there in sacrifice to the false god Molech (see 2 Kings 23:10; Jeremiah 32:35). It was seen as a place of fire, and *Gehenna* becomes a metaphor for the eternal fire of the last judgment, the implication here. The person who ignores the need to maintain control over his or her speech is risking eternity. This is serious business.

We should stress before moving on that James's figurative, metaphorical use of *Gehenna* is much stronger than a literalistic understanding would be. The latter sense would see *Gehenna* as referring only to the valley outside Jerusalem, not to the place of eternal destruction into which both body and soul can be cast (Matthew 10:28).

◆ OPEN MOUTH, INSERT FOOT ◆

I was about 17 when it happened. I had known my friend Leah (name changed) my whole life. We had done many things together, and I considered her one of my best friends.

In youth group one night, Leah wanted to know how it was possible for people who had been married for 20 years suddenly to claim they had "fallen out of love." In youthful overconfidence I smugly replied, "They must not have been in love to start with, because people don't just fall out of love. Love is a commitment." I remember Leah's hurt expression, and I saw one of the leaders take her aside afterward to talk. I wondered what was up.

A few weeks later, I found out that her parents were divorcing after 20 years of marriage. Recalling my unsympathetic words, I felt terrible. I apologized to her right away; she forgave me and graciously acknowledged that I didn't know what was going on. Even so, my arrogant words must have stung.

Leah and I grew apart after that, in part because of what I had said. As James says, "the tongue is a fire." It can incinerate relationships. —L. M. W.

B. It Poisons (vv. 7, 8)

7. For every kind of beasts, and of birds, and of serpents, and of things in the sea, is tamed, and hath been tamed of mankind.

James now begins a comparison from another setting: that of humanity's taming of various creatures. He divides these into four categories: land animals, birds, serpents (or reptiles in general, translated "creeping things" in Acts 10:12; 11:6; Romans 1:23), and sea creatures. By *tamed* James does not mean that humans have made pets or farm animals out of all these creatures (compare Job 41:1-5). The idea of taming is closer to the command of Genesis 1:28 for humankind to "have dominion over" all creatures. In blunt terms, this means there is no creature that humans have not been able to conquer and kill. Humans exercise dominion over all earthly creatures, whether for good or bad.

8. But the tongue can no man tame; it is an unruly evil, full of deadly poison.

Animals can be tamed, but can the tongue? No one truly brings his or her tongue into full submission. As we ponder this, we should be careful not to take this verse out of context. It would be wrong to conclude, "James says no one can tame the tongue, so why even try? It is a futile waste of time." Those who accept that argument should read the previous verses again. Although no one is able to keep his or her tongue perfectly controlled, we must make the effort since uncontrolled speech destroys. James's word-picture of *deadly poison* brings to mind Psalm 140:3: "[Violent men] have sharpened their tongues like a serpent; adders' poison is under their lips" (compare Romans 3:13).

> **What Do You Think?**
> What counsel would you offer someone who is looking for help to tame his or her tongue?
> *Talking Points for Your Discussion*
> - In terms of spiritual disciplines to practice
> - In terms of friendships to cultivate and avoid
> - In terms of biblically sound resources
> - Other

III. Lack of Consistency
(JAMES 3:9-12)
A. Problem Observed (vv. 9, 10)

9, 10. Therewith bless we God, even the Father; and therewith curse we men, which are made after the similitude of God. Out of the same mouth proceedeth blessing and cursing. My brethren, these things ought not so to be.

Having used many comparisons to show the destructive power of the tongue, James now turns to the paradoxical nature of much of our speech. We have only one mouth, and we use it both to *bless* God (prayer and praise) and to *curse* others. This makes no sense! It makes sense to use our tongues to praise God. But after doing so, why would we then use *the same mouth* to curse people, who are made in the likeness of God (Genesis 1:26, 27; 5:1; 9:6)? Because of that likeness or *similitude*, cursing people is perilously close to cursing God himself!

We might apply this to a modern situation this way: How can we use the same social media both to post messages of witness for Christ and personal attacks against those who rub us the wrong way? The bottom line is that we cannot successfully live this double life. Mouths that easily bless

God should also offer godly and encouraging words to others. We must have consistency in our speech and let it be controlled by the impulse to use our words to praise and bless the Lord.

> **What Do You Think?**
> What specific steps can we take to uphold the image of God in others when we're tempted to vilify them instead?
> *Talking Points for Your Discussion*
> - Regarding those of differing political views
> - Regarding those of differing doctrinal views
> - Regarding those who have vilified us
> - Other

B. Problem Illustrated (vv. 11, 12)

11, 12. Doth a fountain send forth at the same place sweet water and bitter? Can the fig tree, my brethren, bear olive berries? either a vine, figs? so can no fountain both yield salt water and fresh.

James ends this section with a flurry of word pictures. These illustrate the inconsistency of praising God and then abusing others with the same mouth. In this, he continues the lessons of the creation account in Genesis 1. There, the author notes the nature of created plant life to be that everything reproduces according to its kind (1:11, 12). The fruit a plant bears reveals its inner nature, since fig trees do not produce olives and grapevines do not produce figs.

We have no trouble whatsoever declaring what is and is not an olive tree, what is and is not a grapevine, etc. The reason we have no problem in this regard is that we know for certainly that this morning's olive tree will not become this afternoon's grapevine. But we humans do something directly contrary to this model when we hear a person praising God on Sunday, and then cursing his boss and coworkers on Monday. What is that person's true nature?

The illogic of this inconsistency is reinforced by the bookends that begin verse 11 and conclude verse 12: comparisons with the quality of spring water. In James's territory, the area around Jerusalem, springs or natural fountains of water are highly prized, for they provide a year-round water supply. Not all springs are of the same quality, though. Some are brackish or salty. Others are fresh, sometimes referred to as *sweet water*. But the quality at any given location does not change minute to minute. A salty spring consistently yields a brackish, unsatisfying product; the fresh spring consistently produces potable water. Our speech should be like the latter, not only in its refreshing nature, but also consistently so.

The logic of James's argument is airtight: we must not settle for mixed patterns of good and evil in our talk. Speak well of others. Speak consistently well. This will improve relationships in the church and encourage your own heart.

> *What Do You Think?*
> How do you go about using your tongue in a
>   way that you would want others to emulate?
> *Talking Points for Your Discussion*
> ▪ When around unbelievers
> ▪ When around fellow believers

Conclusion

A. Think Twice Before Hitting "Send"

At the beginning of my ministry, a wise associate and friend told me that when I wanted to unload on someone verbally out of frustration, I should write that person a letter. Then I should put the letter in my desk for several days. After that, it would be best to destroy the letter and move on. In my hotheaded youthful days, I actually did this several times. To put it as a double negative, I have never regretted not sending those hurtful letters!

Today I am more likely to rehearse a conversation I want to have with a thorn-in-the-flesh person I think I need to confront. These conversations often happen in my car as I drive alone. They are often quite loud and intense, but once I have said my piece to my ever-listening automobile, I am done and can move on. I'm not sure if James would fully approve of either practice, but they have often kept my tongue from uttering hurtful and malicious words.

Visual for Lesson 11. *Start a discussion by pointing to this visual as you ask, "How have you found this to be true personally?"*

Social media postings cause great problems for many today. Hot-tempered messages result in lost jobs and irreconcilable breaches in relationships. An often repeated word of advice is "think twice before you hit 'send.'" When you rethink the fiery, flaming posting, think strongly about hitting "delete" instead of "send." You may be controlling your fingers rather than your tongue, but I think James would approve.

On a scale from 1 to 10, how do you rate on how well you have tamed your tongue? This further counsel from wise Solomon may help:

> Be not rash with thy mouth, and let not thine heart be hasty to utter any thing before God: for God is in heaven, and thou upon earth: therefore let thy words be few (Ecclesiastes 5:2).

We will never regret harsh or hurtful words if they are never spoken.

B. Prayer

Father, we claim You as Lord of our lives, but too often we withhold one area from Your control. We have hurt others, disappointed You, and embarrassed ourselves in our speech. Give us the strength and wisdom to control our tongues so that You are pleased with every word we say, type, or text. In Jesus' name we pray. Amen.

C. Thought to Remember

Problems of the tongue are
problems of the heart.

INVOLVEMENT LEARNING

Enhance your lesson with KJV Bible Student (from your curriculum supplier) and the reproducible activity page (at www.standardlesson.com or in the back of the KJV Standard Lesson Commentary Deluxe Edition).

Into the Lesson

As class begins, ask learners to participate in a short game of Simon Says. After a few rounds, say, "This is a simple children's game, but we know that doing the right thing is not always so easy. In real life, self-control gets a little trickier."

Ask volunteers to share examples of things they might have a hard time making themselves do. *(Possible responses: housework, exercise, etc.)* Be prepared with an example or two of your own. Then ask volunteers to share examples of things they might have a hard time resisting. *(Possible responses: unhealthy foods, certain luxury expenses, etc.)*

Alternative. Distribute copies of the "What's Your Excuse?" activity from the reproducible page, which you can download. Have students work individually or in small groups.

Follow either exercise by saying, "We usually want to do right, but far too often we do or say what we should not. Does the problem lie more in the area of failing to learn self-control, or is it more an issue of how we're 'wired'?" Use this discussion and the lesson Introduction as a transition.

Into the Word

Divide the class into three groups, giving each group pen and paper and one of the writing assignments below. Groups are to read their assigned portions of today's text and answer questions as they believe James would. Do not distribute the anticipated responses, which are in italics.

Group 1—James 3:1-5a

Dear James: I want to serve the Lord as a teacher. I really have my life together and would be a great Christian leader. What do you think?

Be careful! Presenting yourself as a perfect person is an invitation for others to point out where you are not. A perfect person has perfectly controlled behavior. Let's look at behavior that only you can control —your speech. I have yet to meet anyone who is not tripped up by his or her own words now and then.

Group 2—James 3:5b-8

Dear James: My life slogan is "Sticks and stones can break bones, but words will never hurt me." Not bad, huh?

Not bad—TERRIBLE! Words poison relationships, topple governments, and destroy people from the inside out. History is often witness to the fact that it is words that lead to "sticks and stones."

Group 3—James 3:9-12

Dear James: I love Jesus through and through, but people at work don't get it. How can I get them to see the real me?

Maybe they ARE seeing the real you! Think about it. How much "Jesus talk" does it take to counteract those angry words to a colleague or that bit of gossip you passed along? Just as an apple tree can only produce apples, the one controlled by the Spirit does not spew ungodly words. Concentrate on who controls you, not on how good you think you are!

Allow groups to report after they have completed their responses.

Alternative. Distribute copies of the "Control" activity from the reproducible page, which you can download. Allow learners several minutes to work in groups of two or three. Then invite volunteers to share their discoveries, jotting findings on the board.

Into Life

Write this question on the board:

Where should we start in our attempts to control our tongues as God would have us?

After a few minutes of small-group discussion, ask volunteers to share thoughts with the class. *(Primary response you are after: problems with the tongue begin in the heart.)*

Close by saying, "As James says, no one is capable of controlling his or her words perfectly. But that's still the goal to shoot for." Close with the prayer on page 207.

FAITHFUL DISCIPLES

DEVOTIONAL READING: 1 Peter 1:3-9; 4:7-11
BACKGROUND SCRIPTURE: Acts 9:36-43

ACTS 9:36-43

36 Now there was at Joppa a certain disciple named Tabitha, which by interpretation is called Dorcas: this woman was full of good works and almsdeeds which she did.

37 And it came to pass in those days, that she was sick, and died: whom when they had washed, they laid her in an upper chamber.

38 And forasmuch as Lydda was nigh to Joppa, and the disciples had heard that Peter was there, they sent unto him two men, desiring him that he would not delay to come to them.

39 Then Peter arose and went with them. When he was come,

they brought him into the upper chamber: and all the widows stood by him weeping, and shewing the coats and garments which Dorcas made, while she was with them.

40 But Peter put them all forth, and kneeled down, and prayed; and turning him to the body said, Tabitha, arise. And she opened her eyes: and when she saw Peter, she sat up.

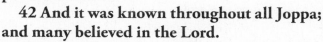

41 And he gave her his hand, and lifted her up, and when he had called the saints and widows, presented her alive.

42 And it was known throughout all Joppa; and many believed in the Lord.

43 And it came to pass, that he tarried many days in Joppa with one Simon a tanner.

KEY VERSE

Peter put them all forth, and kneeled down, and prayed; and turning him to the body said, Tabitha, arise. And she opened her eyes: and when she saw Peter, she sat up. —**Acts 9:40**

Faith in Action

LESSON AIMS

After participating in this lesson, each learner will be able to:

1. Identify the legacy of Dorcas.

2. Explain the interplay between sorrow and faith on the part of the friends of Dorcas.

3. Express appropriate ways for Christians to react to the death of a beloved fellow Christian.

LESSON OUTLINE

Introduction

A. Call the Expert

Many court cases rely on the testimony of expert witnesses. Because of their education, training, skill, and/or experience, these individuals provide specialized knowledge in a particular subject area. For example, a forensic psychologist may be called to discuss a murder suspect's mental state, a handwriting expert may testify in a forgery case, or a medical expert may offer testimony in a malpractice case.

Such experts are sometimes referred to as "hired guns" or "go-to guys." These monikers are descriptive of their roles: they are the people to whom one turns in times of legal trouble. Peter was a go-to guy of a different sort in the first-century church—an expert who could address an issue of life and death.

B. Lesson Background

Today's lesson takes place in the first decade of the church, sometime in the AD 30s. The death of Stephen (Acts 7) caused a scattering of Jerusalem church members (8:1). One of them, Philip, traveled to Samaria where he had success in preaching the gospel (8:5-8, 12). The 12 apostles were still in Jerusalem, and of those Peter and John made the trip to Samaria to assist Philip and confirm his work (8:14). There Peter had a dramatic encounter with a sorcerer named Simon, a man who attempted to buy the power of the Holy Spirit (8:18, 19). After rebuking Simon, Peter and John returned to Jerusalem, preaching in villages along the way (8:25).

Sometime after this, Peter went to Lydda, a village about 25 miles northwest of Jerusalem, to visit believers (Acts 9:32). There he healed a paralytic named Aeneas, causing many in the village and others nearby to turn to the Lord (9:33-35).

In today's lesson, Peter ended up in the seaside city of Joppa (modern Jaffa), 12 miles to the northwest of Lydda. Joppa was a walled seaport city built on a small ridge that jutted into the Mediterranean Sea. Its tiny harbor was the closest natural anchorage to Jerusalem, causing the city to become a bustling port by the time of Solomon (see 2 Chronicles 2:16). Allotted to the tribe of Dan (Joshua 19:40, 46), Joppa was the seaport to which Jonah fled to hire passage to a distant place in his attempt to escape God's call to preach to Nineveh (Jonah 1:3). Joppa was a Jewish city, and it had an established church of Christians of Jewish background. This thriving seaport is the setting for today's lesson.

I. Asking the Impossible
(ACTS 9:36-38)
A. Terrible Loss (vv. 36, 37)

36a. Now there was at Joppa a certain disciple named Tabitha, which by interpretation is called Dorcas.

The term *disciple* is common in the New Testament as a designation for a follower of Jesus, occurring dozens of times (examples: Acts 9:10; 16:1; 21:16). But here is the only time the word is used with a feminine form, much like we distinguish "actor" from "actress."

The names by which this *certain disciple* is known are noted at the outset of the account. *Tabitha* is the Hebrew or Aramaic version of her name; in Greek it is *Dorcas*. Both refer to the small, graceful antelope known as the gazelle.

The two names are used interchangeably in the account (see Acts 9:39, 40), indicating she is known to answer to both (this lesson will use the name Dorcas). Whether either indicates her given name or is the moniker accorded to her because of her graceful life, we are not told.

36b. This woman was full of good works and almsdeeds which she did.

Dorcas has standing within the Joppa church because of her acts of compassion. Her reputation may even be established among unbelievers. She both does good deeds and provides relief for the poor in various ways (*almsdeeds*). This may indicate she is a woman of some means, although we are not told the source of her income.

Her active life gives the impression of someone who is younger rather than older. Since she has a special concern for the widows of her community (Acts 9:39, below), some think that she is a widow herself. That idea tends to work against

the theory above that she is a woman of some means, since widows are generally poor. Both ideas are speculative in any case. What is not in doubt is that she is a fixture in Joppa, an example for the entire community. Both Christians and Jews admire such a person.

> *What Do You Think?*
> What one thing can you do this week to add to a godly reputation?
> *Talking Points for Your Discussion*
> - In building a legacy for meeting physical needs
> - In building a legacy for meeting spiritual needs
> - Considering Matthew 5:14-16 in relation to Matthew 6:1-4

37a. And it came to pass in those days, that she was sick, and died.

The tragic death of Dorcas begins with little detail or emotion. (The emotion comes later.) Her death from an illness seems to have been a quick process, not that of a lingering condition. There are no hospitals, so Dorcas would have been cared for by her friends. Her death most likely occurred in her own home.

37b. Whom when they had washed, they laid her in an upper chamber.

After Dorcas dies, her female friends do the normal things in preparation for burial. Probably still in her own home, her body is washed and laid out in an upstairs room. If this indicates a delay in burial, it may be because her sudden death has not allowed time to prepare a tomb. On the other hand, it may be that her friends hesitate to put the body in a grave if they anticipate she might live again. Do we see evidence of audacious faith?

The *upper chamber* image occurs elsewhere in Acts as locations for the church to meet (see Acts 1:13; 20:8; compare Luke 22:12). The readers may be intended to understand that this is the meeting place for the Joppa congregation and that Dorcas hosted this church in her home. If this bit of speculation is true, then her passing becomes even more devastating for these disciples, for their house of worship has become a place of death.

Visual for Lesson 12. *Point to the 20 images as you ask, "Under what circumstances would you expect a church leader to be a 'first responder'? Why?"*

B. Desperate Request (v. 38)

38. And forasmuch as Lydda was nigh to Joppa, and the disciples had heard that Peter was there, they sent unto him two men, desiring him that he would not delay to come to them.

The news of Peter's presence in Lydda, 12 miles away, catches the attention of the congregation in Joppa (see the Lesson Background). With a 24-mile round trip ahead of them and time being of the essence, we assume that the *two men* dispatched to Lydda are those most physically able to get there and back in the quickest time possible.

Best speed is probably a walking rate of three miles per hour with rest stops minimized. That means four hours to Lydda and four hours back to Joppa. This can be done in one period of daylight.

But wait—why the hurry? Dorcas is already dead! One factor for the haste is likely that of decomposition. Because a decaying corpse soon begins to smell, interment of the body follows quickly in this time and place. Embalming is not practiced by the Jews of the first century (contrast Genesis 50:1-3, 26). Another factor for the haste, less likely but still possible, may be the ancient Jewish belief that the souls of the dead hover near their bodies for three days, after which time the souls depart.

Do the Christians in Joppa want Peter to come quickly to perform a resurrection before a certain amount of time passes? Do they want him to come quickly so he can console the grieving before a burial must take place? Neither is stated. The only thing that seems beyond doubt is that time is of the essence for whatever Peter is expected to do.

◆ DESTINATION FAITH ◆

A 62-year-old neurosurgeon walked more than six miles in a snowstorm to save a man who had suffered a traumatic brain injury. The massive storm had shut down roads, making even traveling on foot treacherous. But when a hospital contacted Dr. Zenko Hrynkiw, he went immediately.

He started out driving, but couldn't get far because of snowdrifts. Wearing only a light jacket, scrubs, and slip-ons, he continued on foot in subfreezing temperatures. He fell a few times, helped some stranded motorists, warmed up in an ambulance, and made it to the hospital in good health. The patient, barely alive, responded well to the surgery and began to recover.

Dorcas was dead. But that did not deter two men from dashing off to find Peter. No mention is made of the weather conditions, but a 24-mile walking trip in any weather is exhausting, especially with the pressure to hurry on one's mind. The power of faith drove them on.

Faith brings a knowing, a knowing that is from God. When circumstances, conditions, and people say *no*, it is faith that says *yes, there is hope; keep on going*. How far are we willing to travel in faith to minister to someone physically or materially? Weather conditions are more endurable and miles feel shorter with faith as our fuel.   —S. K.

II. Witnessing the Incredible
(ACTS 9:39-43)

A. Loss Mourned (v. 39)

39a. Then Peter arose and went with them. When he was come, they brought him into the upper chamber.

The men from Joppa are persuasive! The timing of all we see in this verse is unstated, but a reasonable conjecture is possible. If Dorcas died during the night, her friends would have prepared her body the next morning. Concurrently, the messengers would have gone to Lydda and returned with Peter the same day. Thus it is entirely possible that Peter is in *the upper chamber* within 24 hours of the death.

39b. And all the widows stood by him weeping, and shewing the coats and garments which Dorcas made, while she was with them.

In the upper chamber, Peter finds a vigil being kept by the widows of the church. The designation *all the widows* means there are at least three, since two would be designated by the word *both* (example: Luke 1:6). This is an emotionally charged scene. No spoken words are recorded from the widows. Perhaps their profound grief renders them unable to talk. They are *weeping* without embarrassment in front of this guest. If this has been going on for eight hours or more (see comments on Acts 9:38), they must be exhausted!

What Do You Think?
In what ways can you help your church improve its grief support ministry?
Talking Points for Your Discussion
- In a visibly available capacity
- In a behind-the-scenes capacity

With no explanatory words recorded, the grief-stricken women show Peter the clothes made for them by Dorcas. Have they brought these in a pre-planned manner specifically to show to Peter? Or are they merely wearing them as part of their necessary attire? Either way, the items of clothing are visual evidence of Dorcas's "good works and almsdeeds" (Acts 9:36b, above). Most widows of the time are in a precarious financial position as evidenced by their numerous mentions in the Bible in contexts of vulnerability and need (examples: Acts 6:1; James 1:27).

Some students dig into the Greek underneath the translations *coats* and *garments* to figure out exactly what kinds of clothing Dorcas made for the widows. This is probably a dead-end street due to the general nature of the words. Wherever we see these two words together, however, they seem to speak to the entirety of one's clothing, or nearly so (compare Matthew 5:40; Luke 6:29; and John 19:23). Dorcas seems to have been a versatile seamstress! But the widows do not weep for loss of a clothing supplier. They are moved by the death of one who loved them in word and deed.

B. Loss Reversed (vv. 40, 41)

40a. But Peter put them all forth, and kneeled down, and prayed.

Peter seems to spend little if any time comforting the widows. Instead, he seems to use Jesus' procedure in the raising of Jairus's daughter in Mark 5:35-43 as something of a model. Jesus established an atmosphere of semiprivacy and relative quiet (5:37, 40); Peter establishes complete privacy (*put them all forth*), and the concurrent reduction in noise level will help him focus. He knows he must pray as hard as he has ever prayed, for he has no personal power or healing skills that will help Dorcas (compare Acts 3:12).

After the room is cleared, Peter assumes a posture suitable for fervent prayer: on his knees (the other passages that mention kneeling with praying in the same verse are 1 Kings 8:54; Daniel 6:10; Luke 22:41; Acts 20:36; 21:5).

What Do You Think?
How do you navigate the tension between expecting God to intervene and realizing that He might not?
Talking Points for Your Discussion
- Regarding doubt (James 1:6)
- Regarding personal risk (Esther 4:16)
- Regarding the possibility that God wants to intervene through you (Ezekiel 22:30)
- Other

40b. And turning him to the body said, Tabitha, arise.

After praying to God, it is time to talk directly to Dorcas, also known as Tabitha (Acts 9:36, above). Peter's imperative *Tabitha, arise* may be compared with Jesus' "Talitha cumi" and the accompanying interpretation "Damsel, I say unto thee, arise" regarding Jairus's daughter (Mark 5:41). Is it just a coincidence that there is only one letter difference between the words *Tabitha* and *Talitha* in either English or the underlying Greek transliterations? Is it just a coincidence that the second words spoken by Jesus and Peter mean the same thing? Peter is not uttering a magic incantation. But he may indeed be following Jesus' pattern.

◆ TIME SENSITIVITY ◆

First responders such as firefighters and paramedics show up at the incident scene and go right to work. Everyone stays out of their way. The clock is ticking. Their work is time sensitive.

Such was the case with Peter's emergency run from Lydda to Joppa. But Dorcas was already dead! So, why the hurry? The commentary on Acts 9:38 provides plausible reasons, but the text itself is silent on the issue.

Whatever the reason, those involved realized that time was of the essence. Everything up to one particular point screamed *hurry! hurry! hurry!* The particular point where Peter slowed down was when he knelt and prayed. Peter did not rush right in and say "Tabitha, arise." Peter's faith allowed him to wait on God for the right moment to raise Dorcas back to life.

The phrase *time is of the essence* is familiar. When we hear it, we usually think that something needs to get moving or keep moving before too much time passes. Life-and-death situations usually call for haste, and exceptions are rare (compare John 11:6). But could we use that same phrase to remind us that some things require a certain amount of time and cannot be rushed? Prayer often fits in that category. It too can fall in the category of being time sensitive. But not in the way culture usually uses that term. —S. K.

40c, 41. And she opened her eyes: and when she saw Peter, she sat up. And he gave her his hand, and lifted her up, and when he had called the saints and widows, presented her alive.

The resurrections of Jairus's daughter and Dorcas both involve taking the person by the hand and immediate physical movement on the part of the resurrected (compare Mark 5:41, 42; Luke 8:54, 55). Peter assists Dorcas in standing up. For a moment, it is just the two of them in the room. We easily imagine them both speechless at what has just happened. Peter recovers quickly and presents her alive to those waiting. Dorcas lives!

The tears of the widows probably continue, but now they are tears of joy.

C. New Births Result (vv. 42, 43)

42. And it was known throughout all Joppa; and many believed in the Lord.

There is a great bonus here for the church: many new believers *in the Lord.* God uses signs and wonders in the book of Acts to bring people to faith—the faith that leads to eternal life (see Acts 2:43; 8:6; 14:3; 15:12). Without this intended result, there wouldn't be any lasting point in performing resurrections.

There is also a great contrast here between the character of Peter and someone like Simon the sorcerer from Samaria. Simon's desire to have the power to bestow the Holy Spirit came from selfish motives (Acts 8:18, 19). Peter claims no honor for himself. He is Christ's servant, willing to go where he is called and giving all the glory to God. On an earlier occasion he specifically disavowed having healing power of his own (3:12-16); Paul and Barnabas will do likewise later (14:11-18). Bad things happen when people seek glory that is not theirs to have (12:21-23; 13:11).

What Do You Think?
What can your church do to capture the attention of the community for God's glory?
Talking Points for Your Discussion
- Considering your church's strengths
- Considering your own spiritual giftedness
- Considering community demographics

43. And it came to pass, that he tarried many days in Joppa with one Simon a tanner.

We easily imagine Peter receiving many offers for lodging, given what has just happened! He chooses to stay with someone who has a Jewish name but not a Jewish occupation. Tanners are frowned upon by Jews who are scrupulous in obeying the Law of Moses. The reason is that tanners deal in dead animal parts (skins) that are ceremonially unclean (Leviticus 11).

For Peter to accept an offer to stay at the house of one of the grateful widows would create a morally dubious appearance in addition to being financially burdensome to the one hosting him. Simon is likely a prosperous person given that he is able to accommodate Peter *many days in Joppa*. Peter's lengthy association with an "unclean" Jew undoubtedly raises eyebrows, but no outright criticism is recorded (contrast Acts 11:1-3).

> *What Do You Think?*
> What are some steps to take to neutralize unjust criticism of our actions?
> *Talking Points for Your Discussion*
> - To forestall criticism before it occurs
> - To respond to criticism after it occurs
> - Considering Ezra 8:24-34; Acts 11:1-18; 2 Corinthians 8:20, 21; 1 Peter 2:12; etc.

Conclusion

A. Living Legacies

Here's a one-question test: What legacy of Dorcas remained after she died? If you answered "clothing she made for widows," we invite you to try again! Dorcas's legacy was more than clothing. When she died, her legacy was grateful people who had been objects of her kindness and for whom she had modeled the love of Christ.

Each widow was a living legacy. She had taught them by her life how to care for others less fortunate than themselves. She had given them an example to cherish. Peter brought Dorcas back from death, but eventually she died again. When that happened, her legacy was no doubt similar if not enhanced.

What sort of legacy will you leave? Perhaps you are thinking mainly in terms of money you have designated in your will for a Christian cause or organization. Before trying to build your entire legacy that way, consider two points: (1) that's not what Dorcas did, and (2) "The man who leaves money to charity in his will is only giving away what no longer belongs to him." The quote is from Voltaire; although he was certainly no friend of Christianity, there is some wisdom in his observation.

Our primary legacies will be the people we are influencing now for Christ, people who will remain to do the work of God's kingdom after we are dead and gone. How will people remember you? Are you a workaholic who never has time for others, or are you someone who can always be counted on to stop and help? Will your memory be of one who loved money the most or who loved people the most? Are you a self-giving parent, or do you model "me first" to your children? Most importantly, will you leave behind a legacy of faith?

B. Legacy of Evil

Domitian became Emperor of Rome in AD 81. His tendency was to grab more and more power for himself. His pretentious ways were seen clearly when he required visitors to his royal court to address him as "My Lord and God Domitian." Eventually, the Roman Senate could stand no more, and Domitian was assassinated. In a remarkable move, the Senate then voted a *damnatio memoriae* (condemnation of memory) against Domitian. His legacy became that of a hated tyrant.

May we leave legacies like Dorcas rather than Domitian!

C. Prayer

Father, forgive us for not attending to the work of Your kingdom as You desire. Remind us that the legacy we leave will be that of people we have served in the name of Christ. Indeed, it is in His name we pray and no other. Amen.

D. Thought to Remember

Let us build our living legacies as we answer the calls of those in crisis.

HOW TO SAY IT

Aeneas	Ee-*nee*-us.
Domitian	Duh-*mish*-un.
Jairus	*Jye*-rus or *Jay*-ih-rus.
Joppa	*Jop*-uh.
Lydda	*Lid*-uh.
Nineveh	*Nin*-uh-vuh.
Samaria	Suh-*mare*-ee-uh.
Tabitha	*Tab*-ih-thuh.
Talitha cumi (Aramaic)	Tuh-*lee*-thuh *koo*-me.

INVOLVEMENT LEARNING

Enhance your lesson with KJV Bible Student *(from your curriculum supplier) and the reproducible activity page (at www.standardlesson.com or in the back of the* KJV Standard Lesson Commentary Deluxe Edition*).*

Into the Lesson

To begin class, choose three to five volunteers for a game of "Two Hits and a Miss." Instruct volunteers to spend a minute or two thinking about two things they're good at or know a lot about and one thing they've never done or aren't good at doing. Have volunteers state these three items in any order and allow the rest of the class to guess which skill they do not have (by a show of hands).

Alternative. Distribute copies of the "Who You Gonna Call?" activity from the reproducible page, which you can download. Have learners compete to see who can complete the activity first.

Follow either activity by saying, "They are called go-to guys. They are the people to whom we turn in times of trouble. Today we will look at someone who was a go-to guy in the early church, and what happened when people turned to him."

Into the Word

Divide learners into three groups: a *Tabitha* group, a *Peter* group, and a *believers in Joppa* group. Have groups read together the lesson text (Acts 9:36-43) and write three to five interview questions about what happened with the person/people their group is named for.

Some examples might be:

To Tabitha—Describe your relationships with others in your community.

To Peter—How did you feel when the people of Joppa told you about Tabitha?

To believers in Joppa—What did you think Peter could do in this extreme situation?

When groups are ready, have two volunteers from each perform their interview for the full class. Use the commentary to fill in any gaps or correct any misconceptions after each performance. When all groups have presented, draw learners into a full-class discussion by posing the question, "What does it say about Peter that the disciples sent for him when they heard he was near?" If necessary, guide the conversation toward the fact that, when it came to faith and miracles, Peter had become somewhat of a go-to guy.

Ask, "Does this story remind you of any other stories in the Bible?" Allow learners time to think and answer, but be prepared to cite the story of Lazarus's resurrection (John 11:1-45), the healing of the bleeding woman in the crowd (Luke 8:43-48), and the resurrection of the little girl (Luke 8:49-56).

When these other stories have been referenced, probe deeper by saying, "All these other stories centered around Jesus. What does it say about Peter that the disciples called on him in a time of need, as people had done to Jesus?"

Use the discussion to draw attention to the fact that, through his faith, Peter became an effective representation of Jesus, the ultimate go-to guy.

Into Life

Write on the board or display at the front of the room these words: *Finances / Prayer / Words / Time.* Have learners work in pairs or groups of three to answer the question, "What would it take to represent Jesus effectively with each of these personal resources?"

Allow several minutes for discussion; then ask a volunteer from each group to share their findings. Jot answers on the board as you go.

Alternative. Distribute copies of the "Be Like" activity from the reproducible page. Have learners spend several minutes completing the activity in groups of three.

Finish class by saying, "Jesus is the ultimate go-to guy, and the more like Him we become, the more often we will be able to bring a godly influence into difficult situations. This week, let's practice daily faithful uses of our words, time, money, and prayer to become better representatives of Jesus!"

The Good Fight of Faith

Devotional Reading: 1 Thessalonians 2:17–3:10
Background Scripture: 1 Timothy 6:11-21

1 Timothy 6:11-21

11 But thou, O man of God, flee these things; and follow after righteousness, godliness, faith, love, patience, meekness.

12 Fight the good fight of faith, lay hold on eternal life, whereunto thou art also called, and hast professed a good profession before many witnesses.

13 I give thee charge in the sight of God, who quickeneth all things, and before Christ Jesus, who before Pontius Pilate witnessed a good confession;

14 That thou keep this commandment without spot, unrebukeable, until the appearing of our Lord Jesus Christ:

15 Which in his times he shall shew, who is the blessed and only Potentate, the King of kings, and Lord of lords;

16 Who only hath immortality, dwelling in the light which no man can approach unto; whom no man hath seen, nor can see: to whom be honour and power everlasting. Amen.

17 Charge them that are rich in this world, that they be not highminded, nor trust in uncertain riches, but in the living God, who giveth us richly all things to enjoy;

18 That they do good, that they be rich in good works, ready to distribute, willing to communicate;

19 Laying up in store for themselves a good foundation against the time to come, that they may lay hold on eternal life.

20 O Timothy, keep that which is committed to thy trust, avoiding profane and vain babblings, and oppositions of science falsely so called:

21 Which some professing have erred concerning the faith. Grace be with thee. Amen.

Key Verse

Fight the good fight of faith, lay hold on eternal life, whereunto thou art also called, and hast professed a good profession before many witnesses. —**1 Timothy 6:12**

AFaith in Action

Unit 3: Self-Controlled, Upright, and Godly Faith

Lessons 10–13

LESSON AIMS

After participating in this lesson, each learner will be able to:

1. List the attitudes and actions Paul encouraged Timothy to maintain as a minister.

2. Explain the long-range view of lifetime faithful behavior.

3. Give a specific example how one's faith will influence his or her actions in the week ahead.

LESSON OUTLINE

Introduction

A. The Fight of Faith

In the 1990s, evangelical leaders such as Carl F. H. Henry (1913–2003) began talking about something called the "culture war." Faithful church members were pictured as battling secular forces bent on destroying Christian influence. The battlegrounds for the culture war were seen to be places such as public schools, marriage license bureaus, and courtrooms. These battles were often overtly political.

In Paul's day, no one would have taken such an outlook. Christians were a tiny minority of the population of the Roman world and had little voice or influence in culture as a whole. The "fight of faith" was not the church against the secular world. Rather, it was the battle waged within the life of each believer. The question for each Christian was, "Will I remain faithful until the end?" (compare Revelation 2:10).

In today's lesson, Paul addresses this topic with Timothy, his son in the faith. The culture may have changed over the centuries since then, but our internal fight of faith is not much different. We too must remain faithful and endure.

B. Lesson Background

The relationship between Paul and Timothy began on Paul's second missionary journey. Paul found young Timothy in Lystra (Acts 16:1) and recruited him as a missionary associate. Timothy became trusted and competent in that regard. He is mentioned seven times in the book of Acts and seventeen times in the letters of Paul, making him one of the most important church leaders in the New Testament. Six of Paul's epistles list Timothy in the opening greeting, which is a tribute to Timothy's influence.

Paul wrote two letters to Timothy while Timothy was ministering to the church in Ephesus. He had been left there by Paul to deal with some false teachers (see 1 Timothy 1:3). First and Second Timothy are among the last of Paul's letters, being written in the mid-60s AD, some 15 years after Paul and Timothy first joined forces. Timothy is perhaps 30–35 years old by this time, still a young man in Paul's eyes; but he is given responsibility for a highly influential church.

Timothy had credibility because of his association with Paul, but that went only so far. Timothy needed to show to the Ephesians that he was wise and capable in his own right. He would have been instructing and correcting men and women older than he. That is why it was so important that he demonstrate a consistent and faithful life, one above reproach in every aspect (see 1 Timothy 4:15, 16). He was called to set an example to all the Ephesian Christians despite his relative youth (4:12). Paul knew this would be difficult, so he advised Timothy to be a "good soldier" for Jesus Christ, willing to endure great hardship (2 Timothy 2:3).

I. Preparing for Battle
(1 Timothy 6:11-16)
A. What to Pursue (v. 11)

11. But thou, O man of God, flee these things; and follow after righteousness, godliness, faith, love, patience, meekness.

These things are those Paul addresses in verses 9, 10, centered on the temptations and failings coming from the "love of money" (1 Timothy 6:10). Paul strongly advises Timothy to watch for the lure of using his ministry position as a leverage to become rich. He tells Timothy that "godliness with contentment is great gain" (1 Timothy 6:6).

The Greek word translated *flee* means more than "run away"; it implies running and seeking safety (examples: Matthew 2:13; 10:23). Timothy is a man of God, not a man of money. He must follow a different path, one that pursues the qualities of a person devoted to God. Paul gives Timothy a list of six qualities that should become a priority for him. First, he must follow *righteousness*. In this context, Paul means Timothy must know the right thing to do and then do it. Sec-

HOW TO SAY IT

Ephesus	*Ef*-uh-sus.
Iconium	Eye-*ko*-nee-um.
Lystra	*Liss*-truh.
Pontius Pilate	*Pon*-shus or *Pon*-ti-us *Pie*-lut.

ond, he must pursue *godliness*. In this letter, this is the practice of proper reverence for God and the things of God. Paul teaches Timothy that the exercise of godliness is even more important than exercise for the body, though he does approve of the latter (1 Timothy 4:7, 8).

Third, Timothy is encouraged to follow *faith*. This will be the theme of some of his later advice, the need to trust in God fully for all things (v. 17, below). Fourth, he should run after *love*, the spirit of compassion that motivates one to care for others more than oneself. Ministry lacking in love is empty and doomed to failure. Fifth, Timothy must find *patience* in his task. One who reads 1 and 2 Timothy cannot help but realize how frustrating his situation must have been at times. He was surely challenged as an outsider, a meddling kid who had no right to correct his Ephesian elders. Successful ministry walks a line between patience and impatience, but the minister who is always impatient will find his people have no patience with him.

Meekness, last item on the list, is a misunderstood and underappreciated quality today. Modern culture celebrates and rewards brash, overbearing personalities in many ways (sometimes even in ministry). Meekness is not weakness. It is the willingness to handle others with care. It is cultivating a ministry of care rather than intimidation.

> *What Do You Think?*
> What would have to happen for you to follow the six listed virtues more closely?
> *Talking Points for Your Discussion*
> - In terms of positive prompts to add
> - In terms of negative influences to avoid

◆ FLEE OR FOLLOW? ◆

For nearly a decade I had the privilege of serving as dean of junior high week at a church camp in Indiana. Bible classes, chapel services, and vespers were part of our daily routine. So was recreation. One of the most popular games the students played during this time was Capture the Flag. Groups of students were assigned territories and given colored armbands to identify their teams. Each team received a flag and was instructed to place it in a protected area. Students on the opposing team were to sneak in and steal their opponents' flag without being caught. The students whose task was to capture the flag spent a great deal of time fleeing from their opponents. If you got caught trying to capture a flag, you wound up in "prison." On the other hand, a group that found and captured its opponents' flag spent a great deal of time following, making sure the captured flag—and the student who carried it—arrived safely in their home territory. Winning was a matter of knowing when to flee and when to follow.

Paul wanted Timothy to know when to flee and when to follow. Being a Christian and a leader required that Timothy turn away from greed and personal gain and pursue a life marked by godly characteristics. He was to live a life controlled by the Spirit.

Is something in your life keeping you from following Jesus? If so, identify it and pursue the qualities that lead to faithfulness and obedience.

—S. M.

B. What to Remember (v. 12)

12. Fight the good fight of faith, lay hold on eternal life, whereunto thou art also called, and hast professed a good profession before many witnesses.

The Greek word translated *fight* is the term from which we get the English word *agonize*. It does not refer to fighting in a military sense, but to struggling, or making strong effort. Paul includes significant motivation to Timothy in his fight of faith. First, he should remember that he is called to eternal life. Second, he should never forget his *good profession,* his confession of faith.

This harkens back to Timothy's initial encounter with Paul in Lystra. Paul found Timothy as a young disciple, one who had been raised in the faith by his mother and grandmother (2 Timothy 1:5). He was already well respected for his faith by the church in Lystra as well as the church in nearby Iconium (Acts 16:2). The public testimony of Timothy's faith in Christ had been heard many times by *many witnesses.* Now is not the time to nullify this confession of faith by rash

and ungodly actions. Much in Ephesus is riding on the purity and consistency of Timothy's life.

> **What Do You Think?**
> What would full application of this verse to your life look like?
> *Talking Points for Your Discussion*
> - In your use of time
> - In your spiritual disciplines
> - In your friendships
> - Other

◆ FOR THE LONG HAUL ◆

My father was a noble man. He was an elder in the church, a teacher, a preacher, a tireless worker, a successful businessman, and a philanthropist. He worked for years as a welder and pipefitter before he and my mother purchased and operated a nursing home in our hometown. Of all the qualities that made my dad my hero, one stands out among the rest. Having sat under my father's teaching and preaching hundreds of times, I can say without hesitation that every biblical principle I heard him expound in the classroom or from the pulpit, I watched him live out daily in our home. He had that kind of character, that kind of consistency, that kind of heart. I knew early on that as far as the Christian life was concerned, my dad was in it for the long haul.

Paul wanted Timothy to grasp the long-range view of faithful behavior. He wanted to show him the value of fighting the good fight, of laying hold on eternal life, and of persevering until Christ returned. Life is full of surprises—and disappointments. Often the disappointments tempt us to give in and give up in our pursuit of holiness and faithfulness. But there is good reason to remain steadfast. One day the faithful will stand before the Lord and hear Him say, "Well done, good and faithful servant" (Matthew 25:23). Those words will make every hardship and every painful moment seem like distant memories. And we will be with the Lord forever.

Are you tempted to give up? Do you want to throw in the towel? Before you do, think about what you'll gain by remaining faithful. —S. M.

C. Whom to Imitate (vv. 13-16)

13. I give thee charge in the sight of God, who quickeneth all things, and before Christ Jesus, who before Pontius Pilate witnessed a good confession.

Paul expands on the idea of a *good confession* by pointing Timothy to God himself. God is the one who *quickeneth all things,* meaning God is the source of life for every living thing (see the words of Hannah in 1 Samuel 2:6). This highlights the all-powerful nature of God. What could be more powerful than the authority over life and death?

Visual for Lessons 2 & 13. *Point to this question as you ask, "How do we know what's worth fighting for and what is not when it comes to the gospel?"*

> **What Do You Think?**
> What are some ways to remind ourselves frequently that God is the ultimate source of life?
> *Talking Points for Your Discussion*
> - By using inanimate objects
> - With regard to living things
> - With regard to personal experiences
> - Other

Paul also notes the importance of *a good confession* that *Christ Jesus* made before Pontius Pilate. All four Gospels record Pilate's asking Jesus, "Art thou the King of the Jews?" (Matthew 27:11; Mark 15:2; Luke 23:3; John 18:33). In all the accounts Jesus acknowledges the truth of Pilate's statement, with John's record providing the most extensive exchange between the two (John 18:33-38; 19:8-11). Even in the face of the threat of death, Jesus gave the right answer. Paul challenges Timothy that even if his life is threatened in Ephesus, he must always confess the truth about Jesus; for God is his ultimate judge.

14. That thou keep this commandment without spot, unrebukable, until the appearing of our Lord Jesus Christ.

Timothy may have several decades of life and ministry ahead. From Paul's perspective, this may be cut short by the return of *our Lord Jesus Christ,* his appearing in power and glory. But it should not be cut short by Timothy's denial of his Christian faith, whether by word or deed. For him to be effective in difficult times, his witness must be *without spot,* characterized by no careless words or actions. It must be *unrebukable,* so

pure that no one can find a charge against this young man.

Like Timothy, we too must strive for purity in what we teach and consistency in how we live. And this must be for a lifetime, not a season! We never retire from being Christians. We must be "faithful unto death" (Revelation 2:10). If Christ comes before we die, we will be ready. If He does not, we will die with no regrets, having fought the good fight of faith until the end (2 Timothy 4:7).

15. Which in his times he shall shew, who is the blessed and only Potentate, the King of kings, and Lord of lords.

Paul loves the promise of the second coming of Christ, and so he takes the opportunity to say more about it. We learn, first, that Christ will come *in his times,* not according to a humanly devised schedule. Why have some tried to predict this date? We should be content with the promise of His return and relinquish all control over calculating the date.

Second, no one will misunderstand who Christ is when He returns. He will be praised by every living creature (see Philippians 2:10, 11). He will be revealed as *the blessed and only Potentate,* a term that emphasizes power. Paul expands on this by designating Christ as *the King of kings, and Lord of lords.* This is similar to the title accorded Christ in Revelation 19:16, a dramatic designation indicating that the returned Christ will have immediately recognized authority over all the rulers of the earth.

16. Who only hath immortality, dwelling in the light which no man can approach unto; whom no man hath seen, nor can see: to whom be honor and power everlasting. Amen.

Third, we understand the nature of Christ in this period of awaiting His return. He has *immortality,* literally "non-deadness." Christ has the preeminence when it comes to victory over death, for He was the first to rise from death to live forever (1 Corinthians 15:20). Given that He dwells *in the light which no man can approach unto,* we cannot even imagine coming into His presence. Even so, "We know that, when he shall appear, we shall be like him; for we shall see him as he is" (1 John 3:2).

Paul ends this section with a doxology, a word of praise to Christ. The ending *Amen* means "truly." To his Lord, Paul gives recognition of ultimate and eternal *honor and power.* Paul does not need to wait until the return of Christ to say these words. He says them now, and this reality undergirds his commitment to ministry and to maintaining a witness of purity in word and deed.

II. Enlisting Allies
(1 Timothy 6:17-19)
A. Uncertain Wealth (v. 17)

17. Charge them that are rich in this world, that they be not highminded, nor trust in uncertain riches, but in the living God, who giveth us richly all things to enjoy.

Having climbed the heights of praising Christ and contemplating His nature and return, Paul brings Timothy back to the task before him. Paul has specific advice for teaching those who are *rich in this world*, perhaps referring to wealthier church members, although the teaching applies to unbelievers as well. It is worth noting that Paul does not condemn the rich for being rich. He does advise Timothy to teach those who are prosperous that they must be godly in use of money.

First, the rich must place their faith in God, not in themselves (being *highminded*). Rich people, especially self-made ones, have many reasons to trust their own judgment and abilities. There is a time and place for this in the business world, but even the most successful businessman needs to trust the Lord. Second, the rich must not place their faith in their money. The worst thing that can happen to a person of affluence is to think, "I have plenty of money; I don't need God." Jesus' parable of the rich fool illustrates the folly in this false faith, for he was so consumed by his wealth that he was unprepared for death (Luke 12:20).

Third, the wealthy must remember that God is the ultimate source of all good things. There are rewards for hard work, to be sure. God, however, is the Creator and Sustainer of the world. Farmers do not cause their crops to grow. Miners do not put minerals in the earth. Businessmen do not create people who become customers. All wealth depends upon the provision of God. Those who trust in money are rewarded with devastation when there is a stock market crash or the economy turns sour.

B. Eternal Riches (vv. 18, 19)

18. That they do good, that they be rich in good works, ready to distribute, willing to communicate.

The rich should be taught to be *rich in good works,* as should any Christian. Wealth that counts is a bank account of good deeds rather than bags of gold. Those with wealth should be generous with it, *willing to communicate* (or share) with those in need. This is true wealth and is both satisfying to the person and pleasing to God.

19. Laying up in store for themselves a good foundation against the time to come, that they may lay hold on eternal life.

The time to come that Paul has in mind might be a near future of economic distress or it might be the time of Christ's return. At any rate, one who has shared his wealth and strengthened the church community will always have a more secure future. Ultimately, this includes *eternal life,* the future that the rich fool in Jesus' parable did not consider.

In giving this advice to Timothy, Paul is not teaching that salvation can be earned. Good works are not tallied for the Day of Judgment. When rich people act with generosity, they are caring for their own souls. They are not buying friends or God's favor. They are building a strong *foundation* of faith in their own lives. They are learning to trust God, and in doing this they are winning in the fight of faith, the battle within.

III. Eyeing the Prize
(1 Timothy 6:20, 21)
A. Know Your Mission (v. 20)

20. O Timothy, keep that which is committed to thy trust, avoiding profane and vain babblings, and oppositions of science falsely so called.

That which is committed in *trust* to Timothy is a body of sound doctrine (compare Titus 2:1). All kinds of *profane and vain* viewpoints surround Timothy, threatening to pollute the gospel message. We are careful to note that the word *science* as used here means "knowledge" in a broad sense. What many accept as true and factual is often merely superstition, etc. Timothy's teaching must result in changed lives and be exemplified by his own conduct.

> *What Do You Think?*
> How will you make sure that what you value most is what God values most?
> *Talking Points for Your Discussion*
> - In how you initially Identify what God values
> - In making plans for periodic reassessment

B. Keep on Track (v. 21)

21. Which some professing have erred concerning the faith. Grace be with thee. Amen.

Paul ends with a warning: false beliefs result in false doctrine (errors *concerning the faith*). Having a great mind is no guarantee against abandoning

essential gospel truths. This is not a condemnation of careful study of doctrine. There are things of the faith that are hard to understand (2 Peter 3:16), and diligent investigation can help build one's faith. But we must always rely on the basics. Paul does not want to see a young minister like Timothy shipwreck his faith (1 Timothy 1:19). He finishes with a blessing of grace for Timothy, trusting that he will find his counsel helpful and follow it.

Conclusion
A. False Trust in Wealth

A friend of mine who was connected to big-time sports told me of a well-known former basketball player who was completely broke. This man had made over $150 million in his career. He was not only broke, but was a broken person. His trust had been in his own abilities and his wealth, and now he had neither.

Let's admit that the church and its members need money to operate. We are naïve to think otherwise, but money must not control everything. The "good fight of faith" can often be a battle against personal greed and selfishness. Do we trust in money more than God? Or are we blameless in this area? Will we trust that God will provide the opportunities and money we need? These are some of the most crucial questions we can ask ourselves, especially if we are in positions of leadership in our congregations. We must be both careful with the money with which we are entrusted and thankful to God for His provision. When we do this, we are fighting the good fight with a winning strategy.

B. Prayer

Father, when times are tough, You are with us. When we are discouraged, You are with us. When others run away, You remain. May we be like Paul, who finished faithful. We pray this in the name of Jesus our Savior. Amen.

C. Thought to Remember

"We have met the enemy and he is us."
—Cartoonist Walt Kelly (1913–1973)

INVOLVEMENT LEARNING

Enhance your lesson with KJV Bible Student *(from your curriculum supplier) and the reproducible activity page (at www.standardlesson.com or in the back of the* KJV Standard Lesson Commentary Deluxe Edition*).*

Into the Lesson

Begin class by asking your group to respond by a show of hands whether they would make the effort to retrieve the following: a penny they dropped in the street, their doggie bag left at their restaurant table, $50 they left at their bank counter, $50 left in a burning building.

Briefly discuss why they would make the effort in some situations but not in others. Allow them to come to the conclusion that not all the items are worth the time, effort, or danger involved in retrieving them.

Alternative. Distribute copies of the "Priorities" activity from the reproducible page, which you can download. Allow group members a minute or two to complete the activity. Then have the class compare their rankings. Note that one would expend great effort to fulfill top priorities, which is not true of those things one places a lower value on.

Follow either activity by saying, "Priorities are important. We face conflicts every day, and each time we must decide what to do. Some problems, arguments, or disagreements are insignificant, and so we ignore them. But what about those things worth fighting about?"

Into the Word

Say, "While it can be tricky figuring out priorities, as Christians we have a lot of guidance in the Bible about such matters, including in today's lesson."

Divide the class in half. Assign one half to be the *Toward* group and the other half to be the *Away From* group. Have the groups read together the entire lesson text (1 Timothy 6:11-21); then discuss the actions and behaviors Paul says Timothy should go toward or turn away from (as determined by each group's designation).

After several minutes of discussion, ask the groups to turn their conclusions into simple bullet points. Have the *Toward* group list the actions and beliefs we should pursue and the *Away From* group list the actions and beliefs we should distance ourselves from.

When groups are ready, have a volunteer from each read their listed actions and behaviors.

Alternative. Distribute copies of the "Tactics, Allies, Spoils" activity from the reproducible page. Have learners spend several minutes completing the activity in groups of three.

After either activity, probe deeper by having learners discuss in pairs the following questions: What is Paul's message about what our priorities as Christians should be? In light of everything Paul instructs Timothy to do and not do, what specifically does Paul mean when he says, "fight the good fight" in verse 12?

After several minutes, invite pairs to report their thoughts to the whole class. Use the ensuing discussion to draw attention to the fact that Paul primarily focuses on the attitudes, behaviors, and mind-sets that we Christians should exhibit: that we should pursue "righteousness, godliness, faith, love, patience, [and] meekness" (v. 11) over wealth and worldly riches (vv. 17, 18) and that, in this battle, we create allies by guiding others toward the same eternal life (v. 19).

Into Life

Write on the board or display at the front of the room the two headings "The Good Fight" and "God's Good Peace." Have pairs brainstorm three practical ways to "fight the good fight" and three ways to "bring God's peace"; then craft a poem incorporating these methods.

Allow volunteers to share with the class. Wrap up by saying, "This week let's not only take all of Paul's wisdom about godly priorities to heart, but let's also pray for discernment to distinguish between those situations when we should fight the good fight and those when we should be ministers of God's peace!"

ACKNOWLEDGING GOD

Special Features

Lessons

Unit 1: Follow in My Ways

Unit 2: All Glory and Honor

Unit 3: Give Praise to God

QUARTERLY QUIZ

Use these questions as a pretest or as a review. The answers are on page iv of This Quarter in the Word.

Lesson 1

1. To what land did the Lord tell Abraham to take his son, Isaac, and sacrifice him? (Syria, Nod, Moriah?) *Genesis 22:2*

2. Abraham took three things to the place of offering: wood, fire, and _____. *Genesis 22:6*

Lesson 2

1. Praying to the Lord, Solomon mentioned the name of his father, _____. *2 Chronicles 6:15*

2. What did God promise to put in/on the temple? (His name, His seal, His blessing?) *2 Chronicles 6:20*

Lesson 3

1. The _____ of the Lord filled the temple of Solomon. *2 Chronicles 7:1*

2. While dedicating the temple, Solomon sacrificed over 100,000 animals. T/F. *2 Chronicles 7:5*

Lesson 4

1. In answering the Israelites' prayer, the Lord promised to heal their ____. *2 Chronicles 7:13, 14*

2. God promised that the temple in Jerusalem would never be destroyed. T/F. *2 Chronicles 7:20, 21*

Lesson 5

1. The women brought _____ to the tomb of Jesus on Sunday morning. *Luke 24:1*

2. The apostles believed the women's report about the empty tomb. T/F. *Luke 24:9-11*

Lesson 6

1. After the resurrection, Peter decided to do what? (go fishing, hunt, sleep?) *John 21:3*

2. Jesus cooked breakfast for the disciples. T/F. *John 21:9-13*

Lesson 7

1. Jesus told Peter to feed His _____. *John 21:15-17*

2. Jesus predicted that Peter's death would do what? (unify the church, cause panic, glorify God?) *John 21:19*

Lesson 8

1. In John's vision, he sees a door in Heaven that is _____. *Revelation 4:1*

2. How many elders are seated around the throne of God? (4, 12, 24?) *Revelation 4:4*

Lesson 9

1. When the risen Christ enters the scene in Heaven, He appears as a _____ that has been slain. *Revelation 5:6*

2. At least some residents of Heaven will play a harp. T/F. *Revelation 5:8*

Lesson 10

1. If we sow sparingly, we will reap _____. *2 Corinthians 9:6*

2. What sort of giver does the Lord love? (generous, consistent, cheerful?) *2 Corinthians 9:7*

Lesson 11

1. A "drink offering" consisted of what? (water, wine, blood?) *Leviticus 23:13*

2. When the people of Israel harvested, they were to clean the field of all produce. T/F. *Leviticus 23:22*

Lesson 12

1. During the year of Sabbath rest, there was to be no planting or pruning. T/F. *Leviticus 25:4*

2. The Lord commanded the people of Israel to observe a _____ every 50 years. *Leviticus 25:10*

Lesson 13

1. As the writer of Psalm 34 sought the Lord, he was delivered from his _____. *Psalm 34:4*

2. Christ can help us when we are tempted because he was also tempted. T/F. *Hebrews 2:18*

QUARTER AT A GLANCE

by Douglas Redford

MOST OF US are familiar with the child's mealtime prayer, "God is great, God is good; let us thank Him for our food." That prayer expresses a truth that is worth remembering and honoring in adulthood as well as childhood: God is indeed great. That greatness is on display in the studies of the upcoming quarter.

Sacred Space

Unit 1 begins with a lesson from Genesis 22, which records Abraham's willingness to offer his son Isaac as a burnt offering. When Isaac questioned where the lamb for such an offering was, his father, with the faith that became his trademark, replied, "God will provide himself a lamb for a burnt offering" (Genesis 22:8). And God did indeed provide a substitute, sparing Isaac.

Certainly worth noting is the fact that the very place where this incident occurred (Mount Moriah) became the site of the magnificent temple built by King Solomon (2 Chronicles 3:1). The events surrounding its dedication are the focus of lessons 2–4. Lesson 2 examines a portion of Solomon's prayer highlighting the greatness of God: "O Lord God of Israel, there is no God like thee in the heaven, nor in the earth" (2 Chronicles 6:14). Lesson 3 describes how both Solomon and the people responded to God's glorious presence in the temple with worship. In lesson 4 the Lord encourages Solomon and the people to honor His greatness with faithful obedience. With this comes the solemn warning that disobedience will bring tragic consequences. God is indeed great, but His greatness is not something to trivialize.

Sovereign Savior

The lessons of Unit 2 are all drawn from the New Testament. This unit includes the lesson for Easter Sunday (lesson 5), taken from the Gospel of Luke. In lessons 6 and 7, from John's Gospel, the risen Lord appears to some of His disciples by the lake and challenges Peter (who had denied Jesus) to a life of service that would include a humiliating death, yet one that would glorify God. John closes this account (and his Gospel) with a ringing testimony to the greatness of Jesus: the world could not contain all the books chronicling His wondrous acts (John 21:25).

Jesus' greatness is further magnified by John through what he witnesses and records in the book of Revelation, from which lessons 8 and 9 are drawn. The texts (from chapters 4 and 5) describe John's vision of divine majesty in the throne room of Heaven.

Servant's Spirit

The final unit draws from both Old and New Testaments to encourage students to respond to God in a manner befitting His greatness. Both of the texts for lesson 10, from Exodus (describing the gifts given for the tabernacle) and 2 Corinthians, highlight the importance of the heart in one's giving to the Lord's work. Lessons 11 and 12 are taken from Leviticus and focus on, respectively, the Feast of Firstfruits and the observance of both the Sabbath Year and the Year of Jubilee. The title of lesson 12, "Remembering with Joy,"

> *"O magnify the Lord with me, and let us exalt his name together" (Psalm 34:3).*

calls our attention to the fact that Old Testament religious practices were not intended to be times of grudging compliance to God's commands; they celebrated the gifts of a great and gracious God.

The final lesson, combining texts from Psalm 34 and Hebrews 2, emphasizes the blessing of a restored relationship with our great God. All followers of the Lord are called to a lifestyle characterized by praise. "O magnify the Lord with me, and let us exalt his name together" (Psalm 34:3).

GET THE SETTING

A COMPARISON OF worship practices in the Old and New Testaments reveals two elements that undergird both biblical and pagan worship. First, worship has one or more objects, either real or imagined beings. Second, worship ascribes worthiness to the real or imagined being(s) as the worshipper adopts an appropriate posture (among other things) that is consistent with the ascription of worthiness.

While many practices or processes of worship are rooted in cultural or time-bound expressions, these two exhibit a timeless continuity throughout the Bible and cultures. Regardless of specific practices and expressions of worship, these two do not change.

The Object of Worship

The use of the word *object* here does not intend to strip God of His personal and intimate nature. Rather, *object* is a grammatical term, indicating a person or thing that receives the acts and intentions of one's worship.

Pagans had many so-called gods, but God insisted from the outset that He was the only one (Deuteronomy 4:35). He required that He must be the only object or recipient of worship. Indeed, it is the first of the Ten Commandments: "Thou shalt have no other gods before me" (Exodus 20:3). This is a commandment that bore repeating: "Thou shalt worship no other god" (34:14). When the Israelites substituted fictitious gods for the true God as objects of worship, disaster followed (see Deuteronomy 4:3; Jeremiah 1:16; etc.).

God's expectation is no less pronounced in the New Testament. Throughout the book of Revelation, He is the only valid recipient of worship; and He ultimately punishes those who worship anything or anyone else (Revelation 13:4-8; 14:9-11). Twice John falls at the feet of his angelic guide in worship, and both times the angel corrects him (19:10; 22:8, 9).

Peter did likewise when Cornelius attempted to worship him (Acts 10:25, 26), as did Paul and Barnabas in response to the people of Lystra (14:15). To desire to have an object of worship is common to humanity. To pick the wrong object is, sadly, just as common. God alone is worthy of worship.

The Posture of the Worshipper

Postures of obeisance on the part of the worshipper are found frequently in the Bible. Common in this regard is bowing in reverence and submission. Dozens of passages connect bowing with worship, both to pagan gods and to the one true God. The earliest biblical record of this connection is found in the time of Abraham, about 2000 BC (Genesis 24:26, 48, and 52).

Moving to the time of Moses and the exodus in about 1447 BC, we see the elders bow and worship (Exodus 4:31). When Moses tells the Israelites to celebrate the Passover as a lasting ordinance, the people bow and worship in response (12:27). When Solomon dedicates the temple in about 950 BC, the Israelites bow and worship after the glory of God fills the temple (2 Chronicles 7:3). The people bow and worship when Ezra opens the book of the law and blesses the Lord in about 443 BC (Nehemiah 8:6).

Similar worship postures are found in the New Testament. The wise men bow down before Jesus in Matthew 2:11. John observes the 24 elders in Heaven falling down and worshipping God in Revelation 4:10; 5:14; 7:11; 11:16; and 19:4. The list goes on.

Bowing is a posture of sincere deference. But when we see bowing in contexts of warnings and sinful actions (Leviticus 26:1; Numbers 25:2; Joshua 23:7; Judges 2:12), we realize that a posture of sincere deference must have a proper object. That object is Jesus. Matthew 4:9, 10 still applies! Is it time to reconsider our postures of worship so our allegiance is clearly to Him alone?

THIS QUARTER IN THE WORD

For convenience, you can remove this page, fold it in half, and keep it in your Bible.

Answers to the Quarterly Quiz on page 226

Lesson 1—1. Moriah. 2. a knife. **Lesson 2**—1. David. 2. His name. **Lesson 3**—1. glory. 2. true. **Lesson 4**—1. land. 2. false. **Lesson 5**—1. spices. 2. false. **Lesson 6**—1. go fishing. 2. true. **Lesson 7**—1. lambs/sheep. 2. glorify God. **Lesson 8**—1. open. 2. 24. **Lesson 9**—1. Lamb. 2. true. **Lesson 10**—1. sparingly. 2. cheerful. **Lesson 11**—1. wine. 2. false. **Lesson 12**—1. true. 2. jubile (jubilee). **Lesson 13**—1. fears. 2. true.

History of the Temple

SITE OF TEMPLE

Abraham sent to Moriah to sacrifice Isaac	Genesis 22
David buys the site for the temple from Araunah (Ornan) at Moriah	2 Samuel 24:18-25; 1 Chronicles 21:18-28

FIRST TEMPLE

Temple built and dedicated by Solomon	1 Kings 7, 8; 2 Chronicles 2–7
Temple destroyed by Nebuchadnezzar	2 Kings 25; 2 Chronicles 36:15-21; Jeremiah 52

SECOND TEMPLE

Temple rebuilt by Zerubbabel	Ezra 3:7–6:15
Temple remodeled by Herod the Great	John 2:20
Temple destroyed by Romans	Matthew 24:2; Mark 13:2; Luke 21:6

LIVING TEMPLE

Jesus' body	John 2:18-21
The church	1 Corinthians 3:16; 2 Corinthians 6:16; 1 Peter 2:5
Heavenly temple	Hebrews 9:23, 24; Revelation 21:22

TEACHING BIBLE CONTENT

Teacher Tips by Jim Eichenberger

THE PRECEDING Teacher Tips article (page 120, Winter quarter) compared an introduction of a Bible lesson with a lifeguard pulling a struggling swimmer to shore. Our job as teachers is to jump into our students' world rather than to offer advice from a distance.

Let's continue that analogy. Once someone is rescued from the deep of misunderstanding and led to the solid ground of Scripture, it is time to help the student get his or her bearings as to the nature of this ground now stood upon. This calls for the teacher to switch roles from that of lifeguard to tour guide as a lesson moves from introduction to Bible study.

Review the Itinerary

Imagine yourself as a tourist in Rome. Rather than wandering about haphazardly, you might first sit down with a guide. That guide might trace the day's route to start at the Colosseum, proceeding then to the Roman Forum to Capitoline Hill to the Pantheon to the Trevi Fountain, and ending at the Spanish Steps. With that overview in mind, you would start your event-filled day.

It is helpful for a Bible lesson to have a similar itinerary. Such an itinerary would help the Bible study be a guided tour rather than a disconnected series of Scripture attractions. Each lesson in this commentary has an itinerary; it takes the form of the lesson's passage outline.

Since we've just imagined a hypothetical tour of Rome, let's extend the tour to Paul's letter to the Romans. In preparing to teach a lesson on Romans 3:9-20, you may find the main points of the passage to be outlined this way:

    I. Humanity's Problem (v. 9)

    II. Scripture's Declarations (vv. 10-18)

    III. Law's Result (vv. 19, 20).

To get this outline in front of students, you as teacher could write the outline on the board, distribute handouts that include it, or draw learners'

attention to the student book, where it's printed. Regardless of format, a look at the itinerary helps the learner get off on the right foot in his or her tour through a Bible passage.

Explain the Culture

Trips to unfamiliar cities expose naïve travelers to cultural land mines. But a good tour guide knows where those land mines are and how to avoid them. For example, a tour guide in Rome might point out that citizens of the city have different expectations about "personal space," so don't be surprised if you are crowded and jostled a bit! Every lesson in this commentary features a Lesson Background designed to bring clarity regarding the nature of the tour. Make use of it!

Stay on the Main Roads

A tour guide in Rome no doubt has a favorite restaurant. But the guide would not be effective if the entire tour consisted of visits to it! A Bible tour guide can make a similar mistake. For example, when teaching Romans 1:18-32, it's all too easy to allow the condemnation of same-sex relationships in verses 26 and 27 to dominate as the teacher takes extended side trips through Genesis 19, Leviticus 18, 1 Corinthians 6, and 1 Timothy 1. By the time the class is over, the other verses in the passage may be left virtually untouched.

The verse-by-verse commentary in your hands helps to keep this from happening. While additional supporting Scriptures will be noted at times, the teacher is encouraged to keep moving so students will understand the lesson passage as a whole. Brief side trips are fine for support. But lengthy ones deserve a lesson all their own.

Rome is a big city. The Bible is a big book. In both cases, a good guide plans the most efficient use of limited time. The various tools and verse-by-verse path in this commentary will help you do just that as you lead students on engaging tours.

THE LORD WILL PROVIDE

DEVOTIONAL READING: Psalm 20
BACKGROUND SCRIPTURE: Genesis 22

GENESIS 22:1-3, 6-14

1 And it came to pass after these things, that God did tempt Abraham, and said unto him, Abraham: and he said, Behold, here I am.

2 And he said, Take now thy son, thine only son Isaac, whom thou lovest, and get thee into the land of Moriah; and offer him there for a burnt offering upon one of the mountains which I will tell thee of.

3 And Abraham rose up early in the morning, and saddled his ass, and took two of his young men with him, and Isaac his son, and clave the wood for the burnt offering, and rose up, and went unto the place of which God had told him.

· ·

6 And Abraham took the wood of the burnt offering, and laid it upon Isaac his son; and he took the fire in his hand, and a knife; and they went both of them together.

7 And Isaac spake unto Abraham his father, and said, My father: and he said, Here am I, my son. And he said, Behold the fire and the wood: but where is the lamb for a burnt offering?

8 And Abraham said, My son, God will provide himself a lamb for a burnt offering: so they went both of them together.

9 And they came to the place which God had told him of; and Abraham built an altar there, and laid the wood in order, and bound Isaac his son, and laid him on the altar upon the wood.

10 And Abraham stretched forth his hand, and took the knife to slay his son.

11 And the angel of the LORD called unto him out of heaven, and said, Abraham, Abraham: and he said, Here am I.

12 And he said, Lay not thine hand upon the lad, neither do thou any thing unto him: for now I know that thou fearest God, seeing thou hast not withheld thy son, thine only son from me.

13 And Abraham lifted up his eyes, and looked, and behold behind him a ram caught in a thicket by his horns: and Abraham went and took the ram, and offered him up for a burnt offering in the stead of his son.

14 And Abraham called the name of that place Jehovahjireh: as it is said to this day, In the mount of the LORD it shall be seen.

KEY VERSE

Abraham said, My son, God will provide himself a lamb for a burnt offering: so they went both of them together. —**Genesis 22:8**

ACKNOWLEDGING GOD

Unit 1: Follow in My Ways

LESSONS 1–4

LESSON AIMS

After participating in this lesson, each learner will be able to:

1. Describe the events surrounding Abraham's near sacrifice of Isaac.

2. Explain the implications for Abraham of obeying God's command to sacrifice Isaac.

3. Write a prayer of trust in God's continued provision.

LESSON OUTLINE

Introduction

A. God Will Fight for Us

Most people don't know what to make of the wars of the Old Testament. People frequently ask me how God's people can go from killing tens of thousands of people in the Old Testament to loving and evangelizing all people in the New Testament. Part of my response is to remind people that God does more of the fighting in the Old Testament than do His people.

Lately, however, I am beginning to hear a common response to that statement. People often reply, "I am sure that the Israelites believed that God was fighting for them, but all ancient peoples believed that. Why should we think that God's people were any different?" This is a great question, and the Bible has a great answer.

What other nation had no standing army? What other nation spurned strategic military alliances? What other nation refused to acquire the latest military technology from Egypt (chariots and horses)? The Israelites took none of these items into battle when they took possession of the promised land under the leadership of Joshua.

It is one thing for a nation to claim that God fights for them, but quite another to make zero provisions for national security. It is true that many ancient nations claimed that their gods fought for them. But only Israel dared to march around an enemy city multiple times, blow trumpets, shout loudly, and wait for the walls to collapse.

It is one thing to say that we trust God, but another thing to place our own future completely in God's hands. In today's passage, Abraham is given an opportunity to do this. Because he rose to the occasion, he is a model of faith for us all.

B. Lesson Background

While the Scriptures recognize Abraham as a man of faith (Genesis 15:6; Romans 4:16-22; Galatians 3:6-9; Hebrews 11:8-12, 17-19), his was by no means a perfect faith. He demonstrated great faith in leaving his home in Ur (Genesis 12:1-4). But by the end of the same chapter, he was telling his wife, Sarah, to lie and say she was his sister in order to save his own skin (12:10-20).

Later when Sarah failed to conceive, Abraham impregnated her maidservant Hagar rather than seek the Lord's will. This created serious tension in Abraham's household (Genesis 16:1-6). After God made clear that Sarah would give him a son, Abraham handed her over to a pagan king (20:1-18), failing once again to trust God.

Despite all this, God remained faithful to Abraham and Sarah. He delivered them from several powerful kings. He watched over the circumstances involving Lot, Hagar, and Ishmael (Hagar's son). And God provided the son of promise for whom Abraham and Sarah had been waiting: Isaac.

Still, by the time we get to Genesis 22, we are left wondering whether God would grow impatient. Abraham was a man of spiritual highs and lows. His faith was strong, but inconsistent. The reader is left wondering who the real Abraham is. Perhaps Abraham was wondering the same thing. Was he still the man of great faith who left Ur behind to go to an unknown land? Or had years of wandering taken their toll on his faith?

I. God Tests Abraham
(GENESIS 22:1-3)
A. God's Request (vv. 1, 2)

1. And it came to pass after these things, that God did tempt Abraham, and said unto him, Abraham: and he said, Behold, here I am.

When we use the word *tempt* today, we often associate it with leading someone astray or enticing him or her to do something sinful. This is clearly not what God is doing with Abraham. James 1:13 makes clear that God does not tempt anyone to sin.

The Hebrew underneath the translation *tempt* is also translated "prove" in numerous instances (examples Exodus 16:4; 20:20), and that is the sense here. The idea is that of proving the worth of something by testing. Hebrews 11:17 supports this in saying that Abraham "was tried." We can be sure that God is testing Abraham for the man's own good.

This verse also introduces a phrase found three times in this chapter: *Here I am* (or "Here am I").

Though the phrase itself is not extraordinary, its repetition draws special attention to three crucial moments when Abraham responds to being addressed. The other two references are in Genesis 22:7, 11.

> **What Do You Think?**
> In what ways does God test a believer's obedience today?
> *Talking Points for Your Discussion*
> - Regarding tests involving other believers
> - Regarding tests involving unbelievers
> - Regarding tests known only to God and the one being tested
> - Other

2a. And he said, Take now thy son, thine only son Isaac, whom thou lovest, and get thee into the land of Moriah.

God's request of Abraham is startling in at least three ways. First, it is odd that God identifies *Isaac* as Abraham's *only son*. We know that Abraham's firstborn son is actually Ishmael. The fact that he has been born of Sarah's maidservant does not make him any less the son of Abraham. Centuries later, four of Jacob's twelve sons—who became the 12 tribes of Israel—will be born to the maidservants of Jacob's wives (Genesis 35:25, 26).

The explanation for this curiosity lies in Genesis 21. There we see that conflict within the family results in Abraham's sending Hagar and Ishmael away. Though God continues to look after Ishmael as he grows up (21:20), he is no longer Abraham's responsibility.

Moriah is mentioned elsewhere in the Bible only in 2 Chronicles 3:1. That passage informs us that many centuries later Israel's King Solomon would build the temple on Mount Moriah in Jerusalem.

2b. And offer him there for a burnt offering upon one of the mountains which I will tell thee of.

Second, it is odd that God asks Abraham to perform child sacrifice. Not only does this violate all modern sensibilities, but God makes clear throughout the Old Testament that He vehemently opposes this practice (Leviticus 18:21;

20:2-5; 2 Kings 16:2, 3; Jeremiah 32:35). From Abraham's perspective, however, the practice in and of itself may not seem so odd. Some of the false gods of his time are worshipped this way. In addition, Abraham does not know as much about God as we do, having all of Scripture at our disposal. We should remember that the giving of the law through Moses, which will prohibit child sacrifice, won't happen for five centuries or so.

This leads to the third startling aspect of this passage: that God asks Abraham to sacrifice the child of the promise. This is undoubtedly what Abraham finds most disturbing. His whole relationship with God is built around the promise that God will make him into a great nation with countless descendants (Genesis 12:1-3). For a barren woman well past the years of childbearing to have borne a son has already been a great miracle. Now God is asking Abraham to kill this special son! Abraham is not only giving up someone he loves, he is also cutting off the only way he sees possible to beget offspring.

> **What Do You Think?**
> In what ways have you grown spiritually from occasions when you realized that obedience to God would derail your expectations? Why?
>
> *Talking Points for Your Discussion*
> - On occasions when you obeyed anyway
> - On occasions when you disobeyed

◆ THE VALUE OF TESTING ◆

In 1921, traffic fatalities in the United States occurred at the rate of 24.09 deaths per million miles traveled. In 2014, the rate had dropped to 1.08 fatalities per million miles traveled. What made the difference? Stated simply: better cars.

The National Highway Traffic Safety Administration began doing crash tests in 1979. We've all seen those tests on TV or the Internet, with the cars crumpling under various types of impacts and the crash-test dummies flailing about. As car makers began responding to government regulations based on these tests, seat belts, air bags, and better car construction have resulted in drastic reductions in fatalities and serious injuries.

Abraham didn't know whether he had enough faith to follow God's leading until he was tested. That's the purpose of testing: to discover strengths and weaknesses. Trust in God helps us build on the former and minimize the effects of the latter, even if we don't understand at the moment why we are being tested. Should we look forward to testing or dread it?   —C. R. B.

B. Abraham's Response (v. 3)

3. And Abraham rose up early in the morning, and saddled his ass, and took two of his young men with him, and Isaac his son, and clave the wood for the burnt offering, and rose up, and went unto the place of which God had told him.

We are not told that Abraham says anything in response to God's command. His actions speak for him as he rises *early* the next day to begin the trip. The three-day journey (Genesis 22:4, not in today's text) requires that *two of his young* male servants be brought along. Abraham probably needs the help for handling the logistics of food, clothing, bedding, and pack animals that are needed for the trip.

The place of which God had told him is Moriah of the previous verse. Abraham has been directed to sacrifice his son in the same place where priests will later offer Israel's legitimate sacrifices to God. Mount Moriah is either the same place or very near to it where God will offer His only Son, Jesus, as a sacrifice for sin.

II. Abraham Trusts God
(GENESIS 22:6-10)
A. Isaac's Question (vv. 6, 7)

6. And Abraham took the wood of the burnt offering, and laid it upon Isaac his son; and he took the fire in his hand, and a knife; and they went both of them together.

Genesis 22:4, 5, not in today's text, tell us that the four travelers have arrived at the destination. The parallel with Jesus is even stronger here: as Jesus will carry His own cross to Golgotha, Isaac is asked to carry *the wood* on which he is to be slain. Since Abraham has directed the two servants to remain some distance away (Genesis 22:5), they are not available to carry the wood.

This detail also tells us that Isaac is old enough to carry the required amount of wood. He is also old enough to understand that a burnt offering requires a lamb (see the next verse). Beyond that, the Scriptures do not provide further clues as to Isaac's age. For Abraham to take *the fire in his hand* likely means that he carries the necessary materials (perhaps some coals in a container) to ignite the fire for the burnt offering.

7. And Isaac spake unto Abraham his father, and said, My father: and he said, Here am I, my son. And he said, Behold the fire and the wood: but where is the lamb for a burnt offering?

At last we hear from Isaac, and his address draws the second of the three *Here am I* (or "Here I am") responses in today's text. Isaac's question is to be expected. He and his father have all the elements for a sacrificial offering except for the sacrificial animal itself.

The description of Isaac speaking *unto Abraham his father* by saying *My father* may seem unnecessarily wordy at first glance. But the intent may be to highlight the drama in the father-son relationship and interaction. Using our "sanctified imaginations," we might presume an attitude of excitement behind Isaac's question *where is the lamb for the burnt offering?* as he presumes this to be a special father-son outing, maybe even a feast for just the two of them. On the flip side, we easily imagine a somber tone in Abraham's address of Isaac as *my son.*

HOW TO SAY IT

Abimelech	Uh-*bim*-eh-lek.
Golgotha	*Gahl*-guh-thuh.
Hagar	*Hay*-gar.
Ishmael	*Ish*-may-el.
Israelites	*Iz*-ray-el-ites.
Jehovahjireh	Jeh-*ho*-vuh-*jye*-ruh.
Moriah	Mo-*rye*-uh.
Pharaoh	*Fair*-o or *Fay*-roe.
Ur	Er.

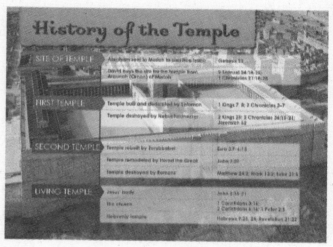

Visual for Lesson 1. *Keep this chart posted to help your learners hone their "temple alertness" across the lessons.*

B. Abraham's Answer (v. 8)

8. And Abraham said, My son, God will provide himself a lamb for a burnt offering: so they went both of them together.

Does Abraham really believe that God will provide *a lamb for a burnt offering?* Hebrews 11:19 offers helpful commentary in stating that Abraham was willing to sacrifice his son because he believed that God could bring him back from the dead. Previously, when telling his servants to stay behind, Abraham had added, "I and the lad will go yonder and worship, and come again to you" (Genesis 22:5). Abraham seems to expect God to intervene in some way on his son's behalf.

C. Abraham's Action (vv. 9, 10)

9. And they came to the place which God had told him of; and Abraham built an altar there, and laid the wood in order, and bound Isaac his son, and laid him on the altar upon the wood.

The altar Abraham builds may be no more than a simple pile of rocks. *The wood* goes on top of the rocks, and the offering goes on top of the wood—it's that simple. For Abraham to bind *Isaac his son* may not be a simple matter, however, if the lad resists. But the text gives no indication that he does.

10. And Abraham stretched forth his hand, and took the knife to slay his son.

No spoken words are recorded, but it's easy to conjecture what is going through the minds of both father and son. The level of Isaac's terror is probably matched by the level of Abraham's anguish. Only God's intervention can stop things now.

> *What Do You Think?*
> What action steps can you take to grow your faith in terms of sacrificial boldness?
> *Talking Points for Your Discussion*
> - Considering the example of someone you know
> - Considering the example of biblical characters
> - Considering your own personality traits
> - With regard to spiritual disciplines
> - Other

III. God Spares Isaac
(Genesis 22:11-14)

A. Angel's Announcement (vv. 11, 12)

11. And the angel of the Lord called unto him out of heaven, and said, Abraham, Abraham: and he said, Here am I.

For the third and final time in this story, Abraham responds, *Here am I* when addressed. This is the climax of the story. Abraham is interrupted just as he is about to carry out the sacrifice commanded of him. The two-fold calling of *Abraham, Abraham* carries a sense of urgency.

In verse 1, God spoke to Abraham. But here *the angel of the Lord* speaks to him. It is possible that God was speaking through an angel in verse 1 as well. Or perhaps in both verses, God takes the form of an angel in order to address Abraham rather than appoint a separate heavenly being to carry out His bidding.

The scene is similar to what later occurs at the burning bush with Moses. There the angel of the Lord appears to Moses "in a flame of fire out of the midst of a bush" (Exodus 3:2), but then God is said to be the one who calls to Moses from the bush (3:4). It is clear that the angel represents divine authority.

◆ *Where Are You?* ◆

Malaysia Airlines Flight 370 disappeared on March 8, 2014. The last voice contact came less than an hour after takeoff. Radar showed the plane deviating from its flight plan soon afterward. Satellite tracking eventually revealed that the flight headed southwest over the Indian Ocean. Nearly a year and a half later, pieces of debris from the plane began to appear. As of this writing, though, the plane has yet to be found.

Flight 370's disappearance has led to various theories about the cause. Was it an act of terrorism? Did the pilot intentionally change the flight path and crash the plane into the ocean? The cockpit's failure to respond to a multitude of "Where are you?" requests may indicate the latter.

When God and Isaac each called to Abraham, that man declared his presence by saying, "Here am I." He had not deviated from where he was expected to be. Whether the situation involves family, friends, work, or our relationship with God, when we are called upon to be wholly present, the only satisfactory answer is "Here I am," when "here" is the appropriate place to be. It's a matter of integrity and responsibility. But ultimately, it's a matter of being accountable to those whom we love and who love us, especially God.

—C. R. B.

12. And he said, Lay not thine hand upon the lad, neither do thou any thing unto him: for now I know that thou fearest God, seeing thou hast not withheld thy son, thine only son from me.

These words tell us that Abraham has indeed passed the test that God has set before him. In essence, God has asked him, "Do you trust me and me alone to fulfill my promises to you? Are you willing to give up all control and place your entire future into my hands?" The answer to both questions is a resounding *yes*!

No other feat could demonstrate with such certainty Abraham's faith in God alone to fulfill His promise. Isaac is not merely his only son; Isaac is Abraham's only chance at securing his own future. In raising the knife, Abraham boldly declares his conviction that God is his only hope. With that unspoken confession of faith, he receives his son back, as though from the dead (Hebrews 11:19).

We should not misinterpret the phrase *thou fearest*. God is not glad that Abraham is afraid of him. Rather, fear is another way to express worship. It signifies that Abraham understands that his son and thus his future belong to God. Abraham's obedience echoes David's later testimony of the Lord: "For as the heaven is high above the earth, so great is his mercy toward them that fear him" (Psalm 103:11).

Clearly, God's will is the driving force in Abraham's life. God is his ultimate motivation. This is the heart of true worship. God values obedience over sacrifice (1 Samuel 15:22).

> **What Do You Think?**
> How should the lifestyle of one who fears God differ from that of one who does not?
> *Talking Points for Your Discussion*
> - In terms of what others can perceive
> - In terms of what is known only between God and the God-fearer

B. Abraham's Acknowledgment (vv. 13, 14)

13. And Abraham lifted up his eyes, and looked, and behold behind him a ram caught in a thicket by his horns: and Abraham went and took the ram, and offered him up for a burnt offering in the stead of his son.

To Abraham's delight, his own words then come to pass. God does indeed provide the animal to be sacrificed. The mention of Abraham's *eyes* is important, given what occurs in the following verse.

14. And Abraham called the name of that place Jehovahjireh: as it is said to this day, In the mount of the LORD it shall be seen.

God has faithfully provided for Abraham. As a result, the man names the location *Jehovahjireh*, which means "God sees to it," which is another way of saying "God provides." Abraham fully understands that the one true God always see to it that His people are provided for.

It is worth noting that Abraham does not name the place "Isaac is spared" or "a father is relieved." This whole account has been about God's faithfulness and whether Abraham truly believes that God will keep His promises. Indeed God is faithful, and Abraham truly believes.

> **What Do You Think?**
> How have you reacted on those occasions when God sent a "substitute provision" your way?
> *Talking Points for Your Discussion*
> - When the substitute was a person
> - When the substitute was a tangible, material asset
> - Other

Conclusion

A. God Still Fights for Us

God kept His promise to Abraham and made him into a great nation. But that promise has now been superseded by the gospel of Jesus Christ. God no longer has to fight wars for His people to possess and protect a special promised territory. All territories are special to Him.

Yet God's people are still in a real fight. Various powers, both human and supernatural, wage war against us. They tempt us to compromise our faith. They invite us to trust in our own strength. Like Abraham, we must trust God and God alone to provide for all our needs. We must live in light of His promises to us. We must go into battle equipped with His armor (Ephesians 6:10-18). and Through Him we will indeed triumph!

B. Prayer

Mighty God, we trust in Your strength. Alone we are weak. Our best plans always seem to fail. Give us the courage to put our faith in You alone. We ask this in Jesus' name. Amen.

C. Thought to Remember

God always provides, but not always in ways we expect.

VISUALS FOR THESE LESSONS

The visual pictured in each lesson (example: page 237) is a small reproduction of a large, full-color poster included in the *Adult Resources* packet for the Spring Quarter. That packet also contains the very useful *Presentation Tools* CD for teacher use. Order No. 3629118 from your supplier.

INVOLVEMENT LEARNING

Enhance your lesson with KJV Bible Student *(from your curriculum supplier) and the reproducible activity page (at www.standardlesson.com or in the back of the* KJV Standard Lesson Commentary Deluxe Edition*).*

Into the Lesson

Give each person two slips of paper and a pen. Have each student write an adjective on one slip of paper and a noun on the other. Ask students to fold their slips of paper and place them in separate piles of adjectives and nouns. When everyone is finished, ask a volunteer to pull a slip from each pile and say, "There is nothing in this world I love more than my [adjective] [noun]."

Depending on class size and time available, allow several or everyone to take a turn. You should hear some pretty interesting combinations! Afterward, ask students to tell how they would really fill in those blanks. Take the opportunity to share your own response as well.

Transition into the Bible study by saying, "We all have cherished possessions and relationships. While we may claim to love God above all, how would we react if we were convinced that God wanted us to sacrifice that which we truly cherished? Abraham found himself in that position. Let's see what happened."

Into the Word

Invite a volunteer to read aloud Genesis 22:1-3, 6-14. Then divide students into three groups, giving each group paper, a pen, and one of the following assignments.

Group 1—Write a soliloquy in which Abraham describes what was going through his mind during his three-day journey. The commentary's observations on Hebrews 11:17, 19 (pages 235, 237, and 238) might prove helpful.

Group 2—List comparisons between Isaac and Jesus. Some additional Scriptures to consider are 2 Chronicles 3:1; John 19:17; and 1 John 4:10.

Group 3—Imagine that before Abraham left with Isaac, he told his wife what God had asked him to do. Write diary entries from Sarah's perspective to reflect her thoughts during the period that Abraham and Isaac were gone. Part of those

entries may be reflections on the situations surrounding Isaac's birth (Genesis 18:1-15).

Alternative. Distribute copies of the "That's an Order!" activity from the reproducible page, which you can download. Have students work individually or in small groups to put the events from today's text in chronological order.

After either activity, pose the following questions for discussion (one at a time, not all at once):

What was God's purpose in calling for this sacrifice?

Had you been Abraham, what would your initial reaction have been?

What do you imagine Abraham said to himself in order to move past that reaction and obey?

How was Isaac's response to his father's instructions similar to Abraham's response to God's?

How did things turn out at a time when God required you to give up something?

Wrap up this segment by saying, "People are reluctant to make personal sacrifices unless they can see a clear reason for doing so. By being willing to offer his son without being given the reason, Abraham set an example that God can be trusted to have the reason."

Into Life

Write *God Provides* and *God Sees to It* on the board. Say, "These are two ways of expressing the meaning of Jehovahjireh. It was Abraham's name for the spot where he went to sacrifice his son and where God provided the ram. When was a time God provided for you in a remarkable way?" Allow students to respond freely, but don't put anyone on the spot to answer. Pray together, thanking God for His gracious provision.

Alternative. Distribute copies of the "God Will Provide" activity from the reproducible page. Have students work individually or in small groups. They are to read the Scriptures there and think about how they need greater faith in "our God who provides" relative to their present circumstances.

THERE IS NO GOD LIKE YOU

DEVOTIONAL READING: Psalm 132
BACKGROUND SCRIPTURE: 2 Chronicles 6:1-21

2 CHRONICLES 6:12-21

12 And he stood before the altar of the LORD in the presence of all the congregation of Israel, and spread forth his hands:

13 For Solomon had made a brasen scaffold, of five cubits long, and five cubits broad, and three cubits high, and had set it in the midst of the court: and upon it he stood, and kneeled down upon his knees before all the congregation of Israel, and spread forth his hands toward heaven.

14 And said, O LORD God of Israel, there is no God like thee in the heaven, nor in the earth; which keepest covenant, and shewest mercy unto thy servants, that walk before thee with all their hearts:

15 Thou which hast kept with thy servant David my father that which thou hast promised him; and spakest with thy mouth, and hast fulfilled it with thine hand, as it is this day.

16 Now therefore, O LORD God of Israel, keep with thy servant David my father that which thou hast promised him, saying, There shall not fail thee a man in my sight to sit upon the throne of Israel; yet so that thy children take heed to their way to walk in my law, as thou hast walked before me.

17 Now then, O LORD God of Israel, let thy word be verified, which thou hast spoken unto thy servant David.

18 But will God in very deed dwell with men on the earth? behold, heaven and the heaven of heavens cannot contain thee; how much less this house which I have built!

19 Have respect therefore to the prayer of thy servant, and to his supplication, O LORD my God, to hearken unto the cry and the prayer which thy servant prayeth before thee:

20 That thine eyes may be open upon this house day and night, upon the place whereof thou hast said that thou wouldest put thy name there; to hearken unto the prayer which thy servant prayeth toward this place.

21 Hearken therefore unto the supplications of thy servant, and of thy people Israel, which they shall make toward this place: hear thou from thy dwelling place, even from heaven; and when thou hearest, forgive.

KEY VERSE

Thou which hast kept with thy servant David my father that which thou hast promised him; and spakest with thy mouth, and hast fulfilled it with thine hand, as it is this day. —**2 Chronicles 6:15**

ACKNOWLEDGING GOD

Unit 1: Follow in My Ways

LESSONS 1–4

LESSON AIMS

After participating in this lesson, each learner will be able to:

1. Recount what Solomon said concerning the Lord's character and faithfulness in keeping promises.

2. Explain how Solomon's prayer can serve as a model for the Christian's prayer life.

3. List scriptural promises that God has kept to him or her.

LESSON OUTLINE

Introduction
  A. Big Sandals to Fill
  B. Lesson Background
 I. Solomon's Preparation (2 CHRONICLES 6: 12, 13)
  A. Place (vv. 12, 13a)
  B. Posture (v. 13b)
II. Solomon's Prayer (2 CHRONICLES 6:14-21)
  A. Sovereign God (v. 14)
  B. Sacred Promises (vv. 15-17)
  C. Small House (v. 18)
    Of Architecture and Attitudes
  D. Sincere Plea (vv. 19-21)
    The Need to Ask
Conclusion
  A. Solomon's God Is Our God
  B. Prayer
  C. Thought to Remember

Introduction

A. Big Sandals to Fill

When someone who has been in a leadership position steps down after many years, the next person in the position often faces a daunting task. This is seen in sports, when a coach of a certain team resigns or retires after being in charge of that team for many years. Perhaps in the process the coach has become something of a legend and has led the team to several championships. That's often referred to as a "tough act to follow" or having "big shoes to fill."

Consider the position that Solomon was in when he became king of Israel. David, his father, was a man after God's own heart (1 Samuel 13:14; Acts 13:22). This is not to say that David was perfect (as the events involving Bathsheba and Uriah reveal). But the general direction of David's life was one well pleasing to God, and he had gained the admiration and respect of the entire nation. How does one follow such an individual who has set the bar so high?

It is certainly to Solomon's credit that he possessed a sense of unworthiness to fill his father's shoes (or sandals): "I am but a little child: I know not how to go out or come in" (1 Kings 3:7). Then came Solomon's request of the Lord for "an understanding heart to judge thy people, that I may discern between good and bad" (3:9). Thus Solomon recognized an important truth: the key to following in his father's footsteps was to follow his father's God.

B. Lesson Background

One of Solomon's primary tasks as king of Israel was to finish a project his father had prepared for: building a temple to the Lord. This was something that David himself had sincerely desired to accomplish. But God did not permit David to fulfill his desire, telling him in 1 Chronicles 22:8, "Thou shalt not build an house unto my name, because thou hast shed much blood upon the earth in my sight." David did, however, provide valuable assistance and resources so that Solomon would have a head start in completing the massive building project (22:5).

Today's lesson from 2 Chronicles 6 records a portion of the dedication ceremony for the finished temple over which Solomon presided. As the ceremony began, the king "blessed the whole congregation of Israel: and all the congregation of Israel stood" (2 Chronicles 6:3). He then called attention to the Lord's fulfillment of His promise to David that his son, Solomon, would reign in his place and would build a house for the Lord (6:10). The Lord acknowledged that David "didst well that it was in [his] heart" to build such a house (6:8), but that was not the Lord's intention. Solomon understood that the completed temple was not a personal accomplishment for him as much as it was the keeping of a divine promise. The king was merely an instrument in the hands of the master builder.

The temple's arrangement was similar to that of the tabernacle in that there were three main parts: the Most Holy Place (or Holy of Holies), the Holy Place, and the outer courtyard (Exodus 26, 27). Prior to the ceremony of dedication, the priests had carried the ark of the covenant into the Most Holy Place (2 Chronicles 5:7). After they had done so, the temple was filled with a cloud signifying the presence of the Lord. So overwhelming was this presence that "the priests could not stand to minister by reason of the cloud: for the glory of the Lord had filled the house of God" (5:14).

I. Solomon's Preparation
(2 CHRONICLES 6:12, 13)
A. Place (vv. 12, 13a)

12a. And he stood before the altar of the LORD in the presence of all the congregation of Israel.

The altar of the Lord before which Solomon stands is the "altar of brass" (2 Chronicles 4:1). This altar is to be used for the daily sacrifices as well as the various offerings and sacrifices brought by the people. Since this altar is situated in the outer courtyard, Solomon is able to stand *in the presence of all the congregation of Israel.* This altar is not to be confused with the golden altar of incense, which is set within the Holy Place as described in Exodus 30:1-6.

12b. And spread forth his hands.

This gesture is noted elsewhere in Scripture when an individual calls upon the Lord in prayer (Ezra 9:5; Psalm 88:9; 143:6; 1 Timothy 2:8). Some suggest that the posture resembles that of a young child raising his or her arms to a parent. Solomon may be king of Israel, but he still seems to recognize his status as a "little child" (1 Kings 3:7) in need of his Father's guidance.

13a. For Solomon had made a brasen scaffold, of five cubits long, and five cubits broad, and three cubits high, and had set it in the midst of the court: and upon it he stood.

This verse adds a detail to the parallel account in 1 Kings 8:22-30. The reason for a *scaffold* is quite practical: it allows Solomon to be visible to those gathered (compare Nehemiah 8:1-5). With a cubit being about 18 inches, its horizontal dimensions compute to about seven and a half feet *long* and *broad,* with vertical dimension of about four and a half feet. We assume this edifice to be temporary.

B. Posture (v. 13b)

13b. And kneeled down upon his knees before all the congregation of Israel, and spread forth his hands toward heaven.

The king adopts a posture of obeisance as he prepares to address the Lord in prayer. The position for prayer we see here is also found elsewhere in Scripture; one instance is in Psalm 95:6: "O come, let us worship and bow down: let us kneel before the Lord our maker." It should be noted that this psalm is attributed to David, according to the quotation found in Hebrews 4:7. Perhaps Solomon can think of no better way to approach God in prayer than that which David recommended!

> *What Do You Think?*
> In what ways might one's physical posture in prayer reflect one's attitude toward God?
> *Talking Points for Your Discussion*
> - Considering looking up vs. looking down (Matthew 14:19; Luke 18:13)
> - Considering lying prostrate vs. kneeling vs. standing (Joshua 7:6; Daniel 6:10; Luke 18:13)
> - Other

II. Solomon's Prayer
(2 Chronicles 6:14-21)
A. Sovereign God (v. 14)

14a. And said, O LORD God of Israel, there is no God like thee in the heaven, nor in the earth.

Solomon begins his prayer with an acknowledgment of the Lord's uniqueness. Those outside of God's covenant people worship many gods in Solomon's time and continue to do so today. But the king's declaration remains just as true today as when originally uttered: *there is no God like thee.*

14b. Which keepest covenant.

One way the Lord demonstrates His uniqueness is by dealing with people on the basis of *covenant*. That the Lord God of Israel desires a close covenant relationship with people is foreign to other religious mind-sets. Solomon has already recognized the covenant God made with Israel (see 2 Chronicles 6:11) and with David (6:10).

What Do You Think?

What decisions do Christians make differently when their belief that God keeps His covenant promises grows?

Talking Points for Your Discussion
- Regarding financial priorities
- Regarding witness to unbelievers
- Regarding changes in what is viewed as risky
- Other

14c. And shewest mercy unto thy servants, that walk before thee with all their hearts.

This acknowledgment highlights an important ingredient of that covenant. The covenants that God makes with individuals require certain conditions to be met by the parties to the covenant. God's part is to show *mercy*; the people's part is to obey God *with all their hearts* as they do as God commands (Deuteronomy 7:12-14; compare Mark 12:30). Although he was not perfect, a good example of the latter is David (next verse).

B. Sacred Promises (vv. 15-17)

15a. Thou which hast kept with thy servant David my father that which thou hast promised him.

The example of God's faithfulness that hits closest to home for Solomon concerns *David*, his *father*. The record of God's covenant with David is found in 2 Samuel 7. The intended result of the covenant is stated with the Lord's promise in verse 16: "thine house and thy kingdom shall be established for ever before thee: thy throne shall be established for ever."

Imperfect King David faced severe consequences for his adultery and related sins (2 Samuel 12:10-19). Nevertheless (and this is Solomon's emphasis), the Lord continued to honor His covenant with David. A key reason God did so with David and not with David's predecessor on the throne, Saul, was because David's repentance was deeply sincere (2 Samuel 12:13; Psalm 51) while Saul's repentance seemed hollow (1 Samuel 13:8-14; 15:10-31).

15b. And spakest with thy mouth, and hast fulfilled it with thine hand, as it is this day.

Solomon's description of God's commitment to keeping His word is noteworthy. The one true God both speaks and acts. The gods of other peoples and nations can do neither (compare Numbers 23:19; Jeremiah 10:5; etc.).

What Do You Think?

What can we do to be more mindful of the long history of God's faithfulness? Why is it important to do so?

Talking Points for Your Discussion
- In worship contexts
- In small group contexts
- In family contexts
- During alone times
- Other

---

16. Now therefore, O LORD God of Israel, keep with thy servant David my father that which thou hast promised him, saying, There shall not fail thee a man in my sight to sit upon the throne of Israel; yet so that thy children take heed to their way to walk in my law, as thou hast walked before me.

Here we see again the combination of the Lord's covenant faithfulness and the expected response of obedience. Regarding the former, Solomon reiterates the Lord's intent to keep His promise to David of *a man . . . to sit upon the throne of Israel* (again, compare 2 Samuel 7:16). Ultimately that covenant promise is fulfilled in Jesus, a descendant of David (see Matthew 1:6-17; Luke 1:30-33; Acts 2:29-32; etc.).

But participation in that promise by individual *children* (descendants) of David is dependent on their living in obedience to the *law* of the Lord as David himself had *walked*. If they fail to do so, they will be subject to the Lord's discipline.

Sadly, this is exactly what will happen to Solomon himself. When he grows old, he will allow his many wives to lure him into worshipping their gods. As a consequence, the Lord will inform him that his kingdom will be divided (1 Kings 11:9-13). But the promise made to David will remain intact (compare Psalm 89:20-37).

17. Now then, O Lord God of Israel, let thy word be verified, which thou hast spoken unto thy servant David.

Solomon recognizes that the primary impetus in God's *word* being *verified*, or proven true, is God himself. People do serve as instruments in carrying out His plans and purposes, but ultimately it is God who must see to it that those plans and purposes are accomplished.

What Do You Think?

> If God were to remind you to bring to fruition a promise that you have made, what promise would that be? Why?

Talking Points for Your Discussion

- Regarding a promise to Him
- Regarding a promise to someone else
- Regarding a promise made to yourself

C. Small House (v. 18)

18. But will God in very deed dwell with men on the earth? Behold, heaven and the heaven of heavens cannot contain thee; how much less this house which I have built!

Here Solomon expresses awareness of the sacred mystery surrounding the temple. God has indeed promised to place His name in this structure (2 Chronicles 6:20); however, His people must not conclude from this that God can somehow be limited to that structure. In fact, it is absurd to think that the Creator of *heaven* and *earth* and all the vastness that exists within them could ever be confined to any earthly dwelling (compare 2 Chronicles 2:6; Isaiah 66:1 [quoted in Acts 7:48-50]; Acts 17:24, 25). He will put His name there, which is another way of stating that His presence will dwell in the temple. This is represented by the presence of the ark of the covenant (see the Lesson Background).

Sadly, God's people will eventually associate His presence with the temple to the degree that it will become a kind of good-luck charm (Jeremiah 7:4). They will come to trust in it more than in the Lord himself. Isaiah will remind the people of his day that the place where God truly desires to dwell is with the person "that is of a contrite and humble spirit" (Isaiah 57:15; compare 66:2). That is no less true today (Matthew 5:3, 4; Luke 18:13, 14; 1 Peter 5:5, 6; etc.).

◆ *Of Architecture and Attitudes* ◆

Recent decades have seen Christians engaged in so-called worship wars. Some battles have been over architecture. Should a church building "look like a church"? Is it a good idea to worship in a rented strip mall location among secular businesses? Or should Christians worship in homes as they did in New Testament times? One cartoon showed two men looking up at a basketball goal that had a stained-glass backboard as one remarked to the other that it was a compromise between "traditional" and "multipurpose."

For the Israelites of Old Testament times, the decision was easy because God had already made it. He is the one who specified how the tabernacle was to be constructed and furnished (Exodus 25:8–27:21; 39:42, 43). He is the one who specified it to be the only place for proper worship (Deuteronomy 12:5-14). In building the temple, Solomon followed the pattern for the tabernacle in an upscale way.

Which is more important to God: the style and location of the building where we worship, or how we view fellow believers whose choice of worship style and location differs from ours? —C. R. B.

D. Sincere Plea (vv. 19-21)

19. Have respect therefore to the prayer of thy servant, and to his supplication, O LORD my God, to hearken unto the cry and the prayer which thy servant prayeth before thee.

Is Solomon stunned by what he has just acknowledged about the one He is addressing? How can he request anything of God, let alone be speaking to Him? Humbly the king confesses his status as a mere *servant* (twice) and asks that the Lord *have respect* to his *prayer* and *to his supplication* and *hearken* to his *cry*. Solomon knows who the real king of Israel is and how dependent even he is on His provision.

20. That thine eyes may be open upon this house day and night, upon the place whereof thou hast said that thou wouldest put thy name there; to hearken unto the prayer which thy servant prayeth toward this place.

Solomon also recognizes that his own need for the Lord's help and mercy can occur any time— *day* or *night*. He asks that the Lord's *eyes may be open* and that He *hearken unto the prayer* that Solomon offers *toward this* temple. Solomon knows that his allegiance must not be to a building, but only to the God who has placed His *name there* and is committed to His covenant people.

21. Hearken therefore unto the supplications of thy servant, and of thy people Israel, which they shall make toward this place: hear thou from thy dwelling place, even from heaven; and when thou hearest, forgive.

In pleading not only that his prayers be heard but also those of the *people Israel*, Solomon contrasts *this place* (the temple) with the Lord's *dwelling place, even . . . heaven*. In doing so, he again affirms that the true residence of the Lord is in Heaven. It can never be in a temple such as the one Solomon is dedicating, as magnificent as it may be.

The last line of the verse seems to presuppose that the reason someone would be praying *toward this place* would be for forgiveness of sin. That is indeed the greatest need of human beings, even that of kings as wise as Solomon! The most meaningful prayer anyone can voice is a plea for forgiveness. Such a request is repeated within the remainder of Solomon's eloquent dedicatory prayer (2 Chronicles 6:25, 27, 30, 39).

The God of Israel must not be treated as though He were some kind of genie who automatically provides whatever His people demand. He is the holy God of Heaven, the one whose splendor and majesty have earlier filled the temple to the degree that the priests were unable to enter and render their service.

◆ THE NEED TO ASK ◆

A true story involves a couple we'll call Mary and Joe. They married too young, and probably not for the best of reasons. A child soon came; then Mary was pregnant again. During that pregnancy, Joe had an affair and left. Alcohol became an overpowering factor. He married again . . . and again.

One night after the third marriage failed, Joe held a bottle in one hand and a gun in the other. He prayed, "God, I can't go on like this. If you are there, please forgive and help me." Joe went to a Bible study where he met a woman who introduced him to Jesus. His new life in Christ gave him the power to overcome his addiction. He also found the strength to seek forgiveness from Mary (now a Christian herself) and their teenage children. When they responded positively over the phone, Joe drove 1,000 miles to ask forgiveness in person. That was decades ago; today their relationships with Christ bind them in forgiving love.

A strange story? Perhaps. But forgiveness is how God deals with us, loving us and giving us the strength to do the same. Solomon's life experience taught him that God is gracious and forgiving. But we do well to remember two things: (1) it's better not to do things for which one needs forgiveness, and (2) God's forgiveness has its limits.

—C. R. B.

Conclusion

A. Solomon's God Is Our God

As we consider the portion of Solomon's prayer recorded in today's text, we have noted its primary themes. These are (1) God's fulfillment of His covenant promises to David and (2) Solomon's acknowledgment of the temple in Jerusalem as the place where He would put His name. It was a visual reminder of God's desire to hear the prayers of His covenant people Israel. But how does such a prayer apply to Christians?

It is important to note the manner in which Solomon begins his prayer: "O Lord God of Israel, there is no God like thee in the heaven, nor in the earth" (2 Chronicles 6:14). Those words can be prayed with the utmost confidence by any follower of Jesus today. The enduring truth is that there is no god like the God of the Bible.

This God is the one who has revealed himself to fallen, lost humanity in the person of Jesus Christ. As Hebrews 1:2 tells us, God "in these last days [has] spoken unto us by his Son." Jesus is the superior and final revelation of God; despite the "many roads to Heaven" heresy that continues to deceive people, if anyone rejects Him as Savior, that person rejects all hope of salvation and eternal life (John 3:36; 14:6).

God is also still in the covenant-keeping business. The covenant Solomon alluded to in his prayer was mainly the covenant God made with David; the new covenant established by Jesus fulfills that promise to David. God still requires of us, as He did of those under previous covenants, that we walk before the Lord "with all [our] hearts" (2 Chronicles 6:14). Paul uses similar terminology when he tells Christians to "walk worthy of the vocation wherewith ye are called" (Ephesians 4:1).

We can also be certain that God will keep His promises to us as He did with David, a point noted by Solomon in his prayer (2 Chronicles 6:15). Paul declared that "all the promises of God

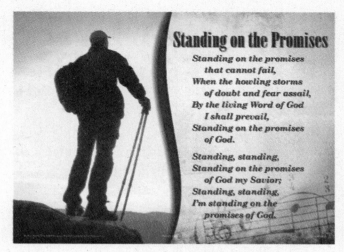

Visual for Lessons 2 & 13. *Post this visual before class begins. Use it to introduce any of the questions on pages 244 and 245.*

in [Christ] are yea, and in him Amen, unto the glory of God by us" (2 Corinthians 1:20). What God has spoken by His mouth He will carry out with His hand, as Solomon affirmed in 2 Chronicles 6:15. God continues to speak throughout the rest of Scripture, and His words and actions are as dependable for us as they were for Solomon. His God is indeed our God.

B. Prayer

Father, we praise You as the covenant-keeping God of mercy. We thank You for the mercy offered through the new covenant established by Jesus' blood. May we walk before You daily with all our hearts. We pray in Jesus' name. Amen.

C. Thought to Remember

God will keep both His promises and those who faithfully walk with Him.

HOW TO SAY IT

Ahaz	*Ay*-haz.
Bathsheba	Bath-*she*-buh.
Corinthians	Ko-*rin*-thee-unz (*th* as in *thin*).
Ephesians	Ee-*fee*-zhunz.
Ezra	*Ez*-ruh.
Isaac	*Eye*-zuk.
Isaiah	Eye-*zay*-uh.
Solomon	*Sol*-o-mun.
Uriah	Yu-*rye*-uh.

INVOLVEMENT LEARNING

Enhance your lesson with KJV Bible Student *(from your curriculum supplier) and the reproducible activity page (at www.standardlesson.com or in the back of the* KJV Standard Lesson Commentary Deluxe Edition*).*

Into the Lesson

Distribute a variety of magazines. Have students search through them to find examples of ads promising outlandish results. (For example: "Lose 20 pounds in 30 days!" "Earn a 6-figure salary while working one day a week!" or "Miracle cream makes you look and feel half your age!") Write the promises from the ads on the board. Read through each headline and talk about which are even remotely possible. Erase those that are not. Invite students to talk about times they've been deceived by (or avoided deception of) unrealistic promises.

Alternative: Distribute copies of the "Promises Made, Promises Broken" activity from the reproducible page, which you can download. Have students work individually or in small groups to match each United States president with a promise made and broken.

After either activity, transition to Bible study by saying, "People want to know that others will keep their word. Sadly, experience has taught us that such is not always the case. At the temple dedication, Solomon thanked the Lord for keeping His promises to Israel."

Into the Word

You will need three cardboard boxes for this activity. No specific size is needed, and they don't have to be identical. But you do need to be able to stack them on top of each other. You will also need a marker.

Invite volunteers to read aloud 2 Chronicles 6:1-11. Ask students to name the promises God made and kept to His people. Say, "The people of Israel had seen God keep His promises since the day He led them out of slavery in Egypt. This would become the foundation for their growing faith."

Have someone read aloud verses 12-15. Ask students to describe the promise mentioned in those verses. Write the word *STRUCTURE* in large let-

ters on a box, and place the box on the floor or on a table. Ask, "Why was this temple STRUCTURE important to the people of Israel?"

Ask someone to read aloud verses 16, 17. Have students describe the promise mentioned. Write the word *REIGN* in large letters on a second box, and stack it on top of the first. Ask, "Why was the REIGN of David's descendants important to the people of Israel?"

Invite someone to read aloud verses 18-21. Let students describe the promise in these verses. Write the word *PRESENCE* in large letters on a third box, and stack it on top of the second. Ask, "Why was God's continued PRESENCE important to the people of Israel?"

Refer to the stack of boxes and say, "As God kept His promises, the people's faith grew. Their trust grew. Their expectations grew. The building of the temple wasn't about a physical building. It was about a building of relationship, a building of trust, a building of a future."

Alternative: Read 2 Chronicles 6:1-21. Distribute copies of the "Scripture Scramble" activity from the reproducible page, which you can download. Have students work individually or in small groups to unscramble words from the text and review the account.

Into Life

Say, "People want to know that others will keep their word. How can they respond to a fulfilled promise? At the temple dedication, Solomon thanked the Lord for keeping His promises. We can too."

Distribute paper and pens. Ask class members to create an acrostic using the word *PROMISES*. Each letter should be included in a promise from God (examples: "**P**eace I give to you," "I will give you **R**est").

Allow class members to share their completed work before closing the session.

THE PEOPLE GAVE THANKS TO GOD

DEVOTIONAL READING: Psalm 138
BACKGROUND SCRIPTURE: 2 Chronicles 7:1-11

2 CHRONICLES 7:1-9

1 Now when Solomon had made an end of praying, the fire came down from heaven, and consumed the burnt offering and the sacrifices; and the glory of the LORD filled the house.

2 And the priests could not enter into the house of the LORD, because the glory of the LORD had filled the LORD's house.

3 And when all the children of Israel saw how the fire came down, and the glory of the LORD upon the house, they bowed themselves with their faces to the ground upon the pavement, and worshipped, and praised the LORD, saying, For he is good; for his mercy endureth for ever.

4 Then the king and all the people offered sacrifices before the LORD.

5 And king Solomon offered a sacrifice of twenty and two thousand oxen, and an hundred and twenty thousand sheep: so the king and all the people dedicated the house of God.

6 And the priests waited on their offices: the Levites also with instruments of musick of the LORD, which David the king had made to praise the LORD, because his mercy endureth for ever, when David praised by their ministry; and the priests sounded trumpets before them, and all Israel stood.

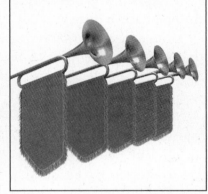

7 Moreover Solomon hallowed the middle of the court that was before the house of the LORD: for there he offered burnt offerings, and the fat of the peace offerings, because the brasen altar which Solomon had made was not able to receive the burnt offerings, and the meat offerings, and the fat.

8 Also at the same time Solomon kept the feast seven days, and all Israel with him, a very great congregation, from the entering in of Hamath unto the river of Egypt.

9 And in the eighth day they made a solemn assembly: for they kept the dedication of the altar seven days, and the feast seven days.

KEY VERSE

When all the children of Israel saw how the fire came down, and the glory of the LORD upon the house, they bowed themselves with their faces to the ground upon the pavement, and worshipped, and praised the LORD, saying, For he is good; for his mercy endureth for ever. —**2 Chronicles 7:3**

Graphic: Model-la / iStock / Thinkstock

ACKNOWLEDGING GOD

Unit 1: Follow in My Ways
LESSONS 1–4

LESSON AIMS

After participating in this lesson, each learner will be able to:

1. Describe God's response to Solomon's prayer of dedication at the temple and how Solomon and the people gave thanks to God.

2. Explain why giving thanks to God receives the emphasis it does in today's passage.

3. Suggest one specific way to make giving thanks a consistent part of his or her daily walk.

LESSON OUTLINE

Introduction

A. The "Write" Advice

When our son graduated from college in June of 2011, the school's president addressed the class as was customary. The content was pretty typical fare for a graduation speech, and I couldn't tell you much of what he said that day. But I have never forgotten one piece of advice the president offered those graduates: they should write a thank-you note to each person who gave them a graduation present.

He went on to emphasize the need for *handwritten* notes. He urged the graduates not to send thank-you cards having preprinted messages; graduates should instead write personal messages of thanks, no matter how small the gift. To my recollection, I have not heard such advice in any other graduation ceremony I have attended before or since.

A prominent reminder to God's people throughout Scripture is to be thankful. The Psalms include many such exhortations (Psalm 95:2; 100:4; 116:17), as does the New Testament (Ephesians 5:20; Philippians 4:6; Colossians 2:7). As Paul told the Thessalonians, "In every thing give thanks: for this is the will of God in Christ Jesus concerning you" (1 Thessalonians 5:18).

In today's lesson we see the important role that giving thanks played in celebrating the dedication of Solomon's temple. The nation of Israel observed not just a day of thanksgiving (as is commonly done in countries such as the United States and Canada) but a celebration that spanned two weeks (2 Chronicles 7:8-10)!

B. Lesson Background

The background for last week's lesson on Solomon's dedicatory prayer also applies to this week's lesson, so that information need not be repeated here. The conclusion to Solomon's eloquent prayer, which immediately precedes today's lesson text, is of such power that its wording is also closely reflected in a psalm:

> Arise, O Lord, into thy rest; thou, and the ark of thy strength. Let thy priests be clothed with righteousness; and let thy saints shout for joy.

For thy servant David's sake turn not away the face of thine anointed. —Psalm 132:8-10

Now therefore arise, O Lord God, into thy resting place, thou, and the ark of thy strength: let thy priests, O Lord God, be clothed with salvation, and let thy saints rejoice in goodness. O Lord God, turn not away the face of thine anointed: remember the mercies of David thy servant. —2 Chronicles 6:41, 42

I. Fire from God
(2 CHRONICLES 7:1-3)
A. Glory Comes Down (vv. 1, 2)

1a. Now when Solomon had made an end of praying, the fire came down from heaven, and consumed the burnt offering and the sacrifices.

Solomon had concluded his dedicatory prayer with the plea that the Lord would "arise" and come into His "resting place" (see above). The immediately ensuing *fire . . . from heaven* is dramatic evidence that the Lord is pleased with the sentiment.

As the ark of the covenant was brought into the temple, so many sacrifices had been offered that it became impossible to keep track of their number (2 Chronicles 5:5, 6). What is *consumed* after the completion of Solomon's prayer is apparently whatever remains on the altar at this point. The scene reminds us somewhat of the confrontation that occurs later between Elijah and the prophets of Baal on Mount Carmel (see 1 Kings 18:38). Similar demonstrations of heavenly fire associated

HOW TO SAY IT

Asaph	*Ay*-saff.
Baal	*Bay*-ul.
Elijah	Ee-*lye*-juh.
Ephesians	Ee-*fee*-zhunz.
Hamath	*Hay*-muth.
Levites	*Lee*-vites.
Leviticus	Leh-*vit*-ih-kus.
Orontes	Awe-*rahnt*-eez.
Philippians	Fih-*lip*-ee-unz.
tabernacle	**tab**-burr-*nah*-kul.
Thessalonians	*Thess*-uh-**lo**-nee-unz (*th* as in *thin*).

with an altar had also accompanied the dedication of the tabernacle (Leviticus 9:23, 24) and David's offering prepared on a threshing floor to stop a pestilence (plague) sent upon the people of Israel (1 Chronicles 21:14-27). In each case, fire signifies God's acceptance of the offerings given. So it is with the fire that consumes Solomon's sacrifices.

1b. And the glory of the LORD filled the house.

The phrasing here is virtually identical to that found in 2 Chronicles 5:14 (see the Lesson Background of lesson 2, page 243). It also echoes what took place when the assembling of the tabernacle was completed (Exodus 40:34, 35). God's blessing upon and approval of Solomon's temple is obvious to all present.

> *What Do You Think?*
> As a congregation, how can we know when our sensing of God presence is genuine?
> *Talking Points for Your Discussion*
> - Regarding His love
> - Regarding His correction
> - Other

2. And the priests could not enter into the house of the LORD, because the glory of the LORD had filled the LORD's house.

This too is exactly what transpired at the completion of the tabernacle. On that occasion Moses was not able to enter that structure because of the overwhelming presence of *the glory of the Lord.* Neither could *the priests* conduct their ministry when the ark of the covenant was brought into the temple due to the overwhelming nature of the sacred presence (2 Chronicles 5:14).

B. People Bow Down (v. 3)

3a. And when all the children of Israel saw how the fire came down, and the glory of the LORD upon the house, they bowed themselves with their faces to the ground upon the pavement, and worshipped, and praised the LORD.

The immediate response of *all the children of Israel* befits such a display of Heaven-sent power. This response also calls to mind the people's reaction at the dedication of the tabernacle when fire came forth and consumed the sacrifices on the altar (Leviticus 9:24). A similar outpouring of praise will occur much later following the descent of heavenly fire in answer to Elijah's prayer on Mount Carmel (1 Kings 18:39).

3b. Saying, For he is good; for his mercy endureth for ever.

The words the people utter in praise were also voiced when the ark of the covenant was placed within the temple (2 Chronicles 5:13). This refrain is in fact an integral part of Israelite worship within the Old Testament record. "David delivered first this psalm [which included this refrain] to thank the Lord into the hand of Asaph and his brethren" for use as part of the worship ceremony that accompanied bringing the ark of the covenant into Jerusalem (1 Chronicles 16:7, 34). That the refrain became a kind of worship standard is indicated later in 1 Chronicles 16 where a list of names is included, designating those responsible for various matters of temple worship. Verse 41 records that all these individuals were chosen "to give thanks to the Lord, because his mercy endureth for ever."

This refrain is also found in Psalms 100, 106, 107, 118, and 136. Each of the latter's 26 verses concludes with the refrain. Furthermore, when the prophet Jeremiah pictures the return of God's people to Jerusalem from captivity, he describes them using these very words in celebrating their return (Jeremiah 33:10, 11). And when God's people do return and lay the foundation of the second temple, the words of this refrain form part of their grateful worship (Ezra 3:10, 11). All in all, this refrain occurs about 40 times in the Old Testament.

> *What Do You Think?*
> What changes might we experience by being more mindful of God's goodness, mercy, and love? Why?
> *Talking Points for Your Discussion*
> - In our families
> - In our churches
> - In our workplace
> - Personally

II. Worship by People
(2 Chronicles 7:4-6)
A. Their Sacrifices (vv. 4, 5)

4. Then the king and all the people offered sacrifices before the LORD.

Now come the actions of worship that follow the posture and words of worship of the previous verse. It should be highlighted that both *king* and *people* take part in this. In other nations of the ancient Near East, the king is commonly viewed as a deity to whom worship is offered. Solomon understands his proper place in this ceremony; he is just as much a worshipper as any member of the common people.

5. And king Solomon offered a sacrifice of twenty and two thousand oxen, and a hundred and twenty thousand sheep: so the king and all the people dedicated the house of God.

When the ark of the covenant had been carried into the temple, so many sheep and oxen were sacrificed that it was impossible to keep count (2 Chronicles 5:6). Numbers of animals *offered* in the current instance are given, and the figures are staggering to consider. The sacrifice of 22,000 *oxen* and 120,000 *sheep* dwarfs those of later reform celebrations in 2 Chronicles 29:32; 30:24; 35:7-9.

> *What Do You Think?*
> What steps can we take to better express our reverence and thanks to God?
> *Talking Points for Your Discussion*
> - In worship
> - In prayers
> - In conversation
> - Other

Some claim that such numbers cannot be taken literally, estimating that the slaughter of 142,000 animals would require 20 sacrifices per minute for 10 hours a day for 12 straight days. So the figures are said to reflect an enormous number but need not be considered an actual, literal count. However, see comments on verse 7, below.

Later the Lord appears to Solomon and tells him, "I have heard thy prayer, and have chosen this place to myself for a house of sacrifice" (2 Chronicles 7:12; see lesson 4). The temple's function as a "house of sacrifice" is certainly being fulfilled on this memorable dedication ceremony!

◆ How Much Is "Too Much"? ◆

"The biggest party on earth" is how the Shah of Iran described the gala he had planned for 1971. The party was to celebrate the 2,500th anniversary of the founding of the Persian Empire by Cyrus the Great (note Ezra 1:2). Ecstatic because of his role in the event, the Shah designated himself *Shahanshah*—"King of Kings."

In October 1971, the world's political elite came to Iran to observe the Shah's attempt to show how his reign replicated the greatness of the ancient kingdom. A colossal tent city made of silk was erected for the occasion. Eighteen tons of food and as many as 25,000 bottles of wine and liquor were flown in. Six hundred guests dined for more than five hours. It was a truly grand occasion, the epitome of *excess*. But the Shah found himself in exile a few years later, replaced by an Islamic dictatorship. The excesses of his lifestyle played a significant part in bringing him down.

The abundance of sacrifices Solomon brought to the temple dedication can be seen in a different light: they were intended to glorify God for His goodness to Israel. These sacrifices constituted the epitome of true worship. They were offered to exalt a gracious God whose "mercy endureth for ever." Is that why you give back to the Lord?—C. R. B.

B. Their Music (v. 6)

6. And the priests waited on their offices: the Levites also with instruments of musick of the LORD, which David the king had made to praise the LORD, because his mercy endureth for ever, when David praised by their ministry; and the priests sounded trumpets before them, and all Israel stood.

Worship through music is an integral part of the ceremony. The mention of *David* is noteworthy. Even though David was not permitted to build the temple, he was allowed to contribute "abundantly" to the project (1 Chronicles 22:5). Part of that preparation was organizing the ministry of worship through music, which was something very close to David's heart. Second Samuel 23:1 refers to him as "the sweet psalmist of Israel." On use of the refrain *his mercy endureth for ever*, see comments on 2 Chronicles 7:3, above.

The fact that *David the king had made* certain *instruments of musick* to use in worship and that he *praised by their ministry* fits well with his own status as a musician (see 1 Samuel 16:23; 2 Samuel 6:5). These skills form the backdrop of David's expertise in organizing the music ministry during his reign (1 Chronicles 16:4-7; 25:1-7).

> *What Do You Think?*
> What are some ways we can ascribe worthiness to God?
> *Talking Points for Your Discussion*
> ▪ In good times
> ▪ In hard times

III. Further Actions
(2 Chronicles 7:7-9)
A. Many Offerings (v. 7)

7. Moreover Solomon hallowed the middle of the court that was before the house of the LORD: for there he offered burnt offerings, and the fat of the peace offerings, because the brasen altar which Solomon had made was not able to receive the burnt offerings, and the meat offerings, and the fat.

Here we see how the numbers of 2 Chronicles 7:5 can be taken literally: Solomon has *hallowed* (dedicated) additional sacred space for the various sacrifices of the occasion. In addition, the entire ceremony of dedication lasts two weeks (see further on 7:9). Thus, while the task of offering the sacrifices requires a significant effort from the priests and Levites present, the numbers of the sacrificial animals do not need to be interpreted in any way other than literally.

The types of offerings noted reflect the totality of the people's worship and devotion to the Lord. Usually *burnt offerings* (described in Leviticus 1) address issues of sin or of dedication to the Lord. The term *meat offerings* represents the grain offerings, with the word *meat* describing the choice part of the grain as opposed to the worthless chaff; compare Leviticus 2:14; Isaiah 62:8). These offerings symbolize thanksgiving, and the regulations for presenting them are found in Leviticus 2. *Peace offerings* are the only offerings in which a portion may be eaten by the worshipper and the priest (Leviticus 3; 7:11-18); the *fat* of such offerings is to be presented only to the Lord (3:16, 17).

The phrase *the brasen altar which Solomon had made* is not to be understood as indicating that the king has dreamed up his own ad hoc addition to the temple furnishings. This altar was part of the original design for the tabernacle (the precursor to the temple), as noted in Exodus 27:1-8; 38:1-7. Solomon *made* this altar in the sense that he authorized its size be scaled up to match the larger size of the temple (2 Chronicles 4:1). Even given its larger size, however, it is *not able to receive the* various *offerings*, so numerous are they.

B. Many Worshippers (vv. 8, 9)

8. Also at the same time Solomon kept the feast seven days, and all Israel with him, a very great congregation, from the entering in of Hamath unto the river of Egypt.

The *feast* alluded to here is the Feast of Booths, or Tabernacles (also known as Ingathering). We know this because of the reference in 2 Chronicles 7:10 to "the seventh month," which is the month when this feast is to be observed for a period of *seven days* (Leviticus 23:33-36, 39-43; compare 2 Chronicles 5:3). Its purpose is to recognize the harvest provided by the Lord. Thus, the dedication of the temple (for which the people are gathered to give thanks) occurs adjacent to a feast already on the Israelite calendar, a feast already set aside for giving thanks to God.

The sense of unity and support for Solomon's undertaking is clear from both the number of worshippers and the distances they travel: *from the entering in of Hamath unto the river of Egypt.* Hamath is a city located in upper Syria on the Orontes River. The *river of Egypt* most likely refers to the stream of water known as the Wadi el Arish, which is situated on the southwestern border of Palestine and flows into the Mediterranean Sea.

These boundaries are significant in that they reflect God's intention as to the territory that His people should possess (Numbers 34:5-8). Hamath designates the northernmost point; the Wadi el Arish marks the southernmost point. The people gathered on this day could celebrate not only the achievement of building a temple but also the building of a great nation in fulfillment of the promise to Abraham (Genesis 12:1-3; 1 Kings 4:21, 24). Neither could have happened without the Lord's blessing.

◆ A KING ABOVE ALL OTHERS ◆

Over two dozen nations today require their heads of state to belong to a particular religion. Several other nations have religious requirements for their ceremonial monarchs. For example, Queen Elizabeth II's role in that regard is "Supreme Governor of the Church of England and Defender of the Faith" for the British Commonwealth of Nations.

These traditions can be traced to biblical times. Solomon, king of Israel, is an example. So are the Herods of the New Testament. Centuries later, King Henry VIII of England demonstrated how a monarch may provide questionable spiritual leadership. Henry's maneuverings to be granted a divorce resulted in his receiving one from a religious authority that he himself had created—not the best of spiritual examples for his people.

Solomon, by contrast, did set an appropriate example as he led in worship of the Lord. However, the history of God's people in the Old Testament demonstrates that no matter how devout leaders may be, we do well not to place too much faith in them. Saul, David, Solomon, and their successors prove the point. In Jesus we have a king who will never lead us astray. Although we are to honor earthly authorities (1 Peter 2:17), our ultimate allegiance must be only to Him.

—C. R. B.

9. And in the eighth day they made a solemn assembly: for they kept the dedication of the altar seven days, and the feast seven days.

The Law of Moses stipulates that the Feast of Tabernacles lasts *seven days*, beginning the fifteenth day of the seventh month (Leviticus 23:33, 34). Since the people are sent home on the twenty-third day of this month (2 Chronicles 7:10), the dedication of the temple lasts seven days followed by the seven-day observance of the Feast of Tabernacles.

The *solemn assembly* on the *eighth day* concludes both the gathering for the dedication of the temple and the Feast of Tabernacles (Leviticus 23:36b; Numbers 29:35-38). That the *dedication of the altar* is specifically noted is perhaps in keeping with the temple's purpose as a sacred place for sacrifices to be offered (2 Chronicles 7:12).

Verse 10, though not in our lesson text, describes the conclusion of what must have been an uplifting time of praise and worship. The people leave "glad and merry in heart for the goodness that the Lord had shewed unto David, and to Solomon, and to Israel his people." Once more the important role of David is highlighted. What has transpired on this momentous day marks the fulfillment of part of God's covenant with David. Both his son Solomon and the entire nation of Israel are the beneficiaries of God's faithfulness, and they acknowledge that truth as they depart from this memorable celebration to return home.

Conclusion

A. *Semper Gratus*

Many will recognize the words *Semper Fidelis* as the motto of the United States Marine Corps. The phrase means "always faithful" and highlights the unwavering devotion to duty and country that those in the Marines have exhibited consistently throughout their history. In thinking about the theme of today's lesson, perhaps the phrase *Semper*

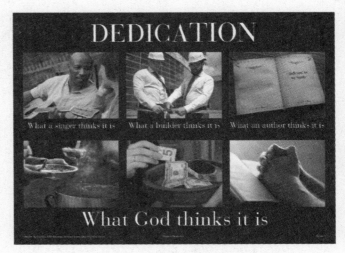

Visual for Lesson 3. *Point to the various images as you ask, "What are the different senses of the words* dedication *and* dedicated?

Gratus, meaning "always grateful," is appropriate. This is a motto for Christians to live by in recognition of God's mercy. Of that mercy we can say, as the worshippers at the temple dedication proclaimed, it "endureth for ever." It doesn't hurt to note again Paul's exhortation "in every thing give thanks" (1 Thessalonians 5:18).

We should keep in mind that those words came from someone whose surroundings were often less than comfortable or carefree. Earlier in that same epistle, Paul referred to the suffering and shameful treatment that he and his companions had experienced while preaching the gospel (1 Thessalonians 2:1, 2). He even writes of Christians being "appointed" for such treatment (3:3).

Yet Paul did not allow such situations to shake his spirit or cloud his view of the Lord's mercy to him. His motto could have been *Semper Gratus*. May it be ours as well.

B. Prayer

Father, may our worship include every part of our lives—thoughts, words, deeds, and will. Help us to live as thankful people in the midst of a broken and often cynical world. Let us dedicate anew, with no less resolve and sincerity than Solomon, the temples of our bodies to Your service. In Jesus' name we pray. Amen.

C. Thought to Remember

Give thanks and live thanks—daily.

INVOLVEMENT LEARNING

Enhance your lesson with KJV Bible Student *(from your curriculum supplier) and the reproducible activity page (at www.standardlesson.com or in the back of the* KJV Standard Lesson Commentary Deluxe Edition*).*

Into the Lesson

Write the word *DEDICATION* on the board. Then divide the class into two groups, giving each a paper and a pen. At your signal, groups should use the letters in the word *DEDICATION* to create as many different words as they can (*edict*, *noted*, *code*, etc.). Allow several minutes for groups to work. Let groups read their lists, crossing out words that have been duplicated by the other team. The group with the most unique words wins. Talk about what dedication means (as related to reaching a goal) and then about what a ceremonial dedication symbolizes.

Alternative. Make one copy of the "To the One I Love" activity from the reproducible page, which you can download. Have class members decide which of the dedications found there come from actual books. Discuss the purpose of book dedications and other ceremonial tributes.

After either activity say, "We like to celebrate when a project is completed. Can those celebrations be times of worship? As Solomon and the people of Israel dedicated the temple, they did just that."

Into the Word

Lead into the Bible study by saying, "Solomon had finished building the temple, where God's people would worship. God had promised to live among His people in this special place—and Solomon trusted in that promise." Invite a volunteer to read aloud Solomon's prayer in 2 Chronicles 6:41, 42.

Read aloud 2 Chronicles 7:1. Say, "When Solomon finished praying, God sent fire from Heaven as a sign that He was keeping His promise." Divide students into three groups, giving each group a sheet of paper and a marker. Assign one of the following passages to each group: verses 2, 3; verses 4-7; verses 8, 9. Challenge each group to read its passage and create a sign that summarizes its message. (For example, a group could summarize verses 2, 3 by creating a "Do Not Enter" sign to reflect the fact that the priests could not enter the temple because it was filled with the glory of the Lord. A group could summarize verses 4-7 by creating a "Yield" sign to reflect the sacrifices that Solomon and the people surrendered to God. A group could summarize verses 8, 9 by creating a "Festival Parking Only" sign to reflect the celebrations that occurred.) Guide groups as needed and encourage them to be creative!

Option. If laptop computers are available, allow groups to design their signs using PowerPoint or other software.

After several minutes, ask each group to read aloud its passage and explain its sign to the class. Invite volunteers to suggest ideas for other possible signs, and briefly discuss each passage. Focus on the reverent worship, generous sacrifice, and eager celebration that marked the temple dedication.

Conclude by saying, "People celebrate things that are important to them. How can their celebrations become a form of worship? As they dedicated the temple, Solomon and the people worshipped the Lord by bowing on their knees, making burnt offerings, playing music, and praying. We can honor and thank God during important times in our lives as well."

Into Life

Challenge students to think of something they would like to dedicate to God (their lives, their families, your congregation, etc.). As a group, discuss a potential dedication service: How could worship be incorporated? What offering(s) could be given? What song(s) could be played or sung? What would be prayed?

Alternative. Make copies of the "My Dedication" activity from the reproducible page. Let students work individually to finish the sentences and make private dedications to God.

KEEP MY STATUTES AND ORDINANCES

DEVOTIONAL READING: Isaiah 58:6-12
BACKGROUND SCRIPTURE: 2 Chronicles 7:12-22

2 CHRONICLES 7:12-22

12 And the LORD appeared to Solomon by night, and said unto him, I have heard thy prayer, and have chosen this place to myself for an house of sacrifice.

13 If I shut up heaven that there be no rain, or if I command the locusts to devour the land, or if I send pestilence among my people;

14 If my people, which are called by my name, shall humble themselves, and pray, and seek my face, and turn from their wicked ways; then will I hear from heaven, and will forgive their sin, and will heal their land.

15 Now mine eyes shall be open, and mine ears attent unto the prayer that is made in this place.

16 For now have I chosen and sanctified this house, that my name may be there for ever: and mine eyes and mine heart shall be there perpetually.

17 And as for thee, if thou wilt walk before me, as David thy father walked, and do according to all that I have commanded thee, and shalt observe my statutes and my judgments;

18 Then will I stablish the throne of thy kingdom, according as I have covenanted with David thy father, saying, There shall not fail thee a man to be ruler in Israel.

19 But if ye turn away, and forsake my statutes and my commandments, which I have set before you, and shall go and serve other gods, and worship them;

20 Then will I pluck them up by the roots out of my land which I have given them; and this house, which I have sanctified for my name, will I cast out of my sight, and will make it to be a proverb and a byword among all nations.

21 And this house, which is high, shall be an astonishment to every one that passeth by it; so that he shall say, Why hath the LORD done thus unto this land, and unto this house?

22 And it shall be answered, Because they forsook the LORD God of their fathers, which brought them forth out of the land of Egypt, and laid hold on other gods, and worshipped them, and served them: therefore hath he brought all this evil upon them.

KEY VERSE

If my people, which are called by my name, shall humble themselves, and pray, and seek my face, and turn from their wicked ways; then will I hear from heaven, and will forgive their sin, and will heal their land.
—2 Chronicles 7:14

ACKNOWLEDGING GOD

Unit 1: Follow in My Ways

LESSONS 1–4

LESSON AIMS

After participating in this lesson, each learner will be able to:

1. Summarize the promises of both blessing and discipline that the Lord spoke to Solomon.

2. Tell how these promises serve to both encourage and warn Christians today.

3. Keep a journal during the coming week in which to record times of blessing and discipline from the Lord, along with lessons learned from these experiences.

LESSON OUTLINE

Introduction
  A. Good House "Keeping"
  B. Lesson Background
I. Promised Blessings (2 CHRONICLES 7:12-18)
  A. For the Temple (v. 12)
    Our Place of Sacrifice
  B. For the People (vv. 13-16)
  C. For Solomon (vv. 17, 18)
II. Promised Discipline (2 CHRONICLES 7:19-22)
  A. Against the People (vv. 19, 20a)
  B. Against the Temple (vv. 20b-22)
    Cause and Effect
Conclusion
  A. Words for Today?
  B. Prayer
  C. Thought to Remember

Introduction

A. Good House "Keeping"

My wife is a big fan of the TV programs that feature homes undergoing a major renovation. Some use the term *makeover* to describe the sweeping changes made to a house. When the project is complete, the "before and after" contrasts are amazing to see.

The previous two lessons covered the dedication ceremony of the newly completed temple in Jerusalem. Today's lesson follows with a solemn warning from the Lord to Solomon that disobedience would result in what we might call a reverse makeover to that structure. The "before and after" contrast would be amazing in a bewildering way. How could something so unthinkable happen? A structure dedicated to God meant nothing if the people themselves were not dedicated to being God's people. What was true in Solomon's time is no less true today.

B. Lesson Background

Between the final verse of last week's lesson treatment and the first verse of this week's is the single verse 2 Chronicles 7:11: "Thus Solomon finished the house of the Lord, and the king's house: and all that came into Solomon's heart to make in the house of the Lord, and in his own house, he prosperously effected." Yes, Solomon's accomplishment was indeed impressive (see the temple dimensions in chapter 3 and the temple furnishings in chapter 4). Further, the people whom he ruled were "glad and merry in heart for the goodness that the Lord had shewed unto David, and to Solomon, and to Israel his people" (7:10).

Perhaps the king was tempted to rest on his laurels at that point, satisfied with his record. But God desired far more from Solomon and from the Israelites than the mere construction of a building. God wanted what He has always wanted from His people, be they kings or commoners: obedience. Not even a temple as magnificent as the one Solomon had just completed could substitute for that.

As today's text opens, the year would have been sometime after 950 BC. Parallel in content to today's lesson text is 1 Kings 9:1-9.

I. Promised Blessings

(2 CHRONICLES 7:12-18)

A. For the Temple (v. 12)

12. And the LORD appeared to Solomon by night, and said unto him, I have heard thy prayer, and have chosen this place to myself for a house of sacrifice.

This is the second time *the Lord* has *appeared to Solomon by night.* Perhaps God does this deliberately in order to call Solomon's mind back to the first time, when the Lord said, "Ask what I shall give thee" (2 Chronicles 1:7). In response, Solomon had requested "wisdom and knowledge" for ruling (1:10). The Lord was pleased with this response and promised Solomon that and much more (1:11, 12).

The Lord deems it important to affirm that He has *heard* Solomon's *prayer* (see lesson 2). Even so, the first decision that the Lord says he has made was not in Solomon's prayer requests: to choose *this place* (the temple) *for a house of sacrifice.* Solomon indeed sacrificed many animals during the dedication ceremony (2 Chronicles 7:5) and made many requests in his prayer of dedication (6:12-42). But for the temple to be known as *a house of sacrifice* was not explicitly one of those requests. God's declaration calls to mind Moses' words in Deuteronomy 12:5, 6 regarding a chosen place of sacrifice. Now, some five centuries later, the Lord is announcing that such a chosen site exists, and it is Solomon's temple.

What Do You Think?

How did an experience of God's answer to a prayer shape your attitude toward future prayers?

Talking Points for Your Discussion

- When the answer was a long time coming
- When the answer came quickly

◆ OUR PLACE OF SACRIFICE ◆

Most religions have their holy places. For Hindus, it's the Ganges River in India. Japan's Mount Fuji is sacred to the Shinto and Buddhist religions. Muslims consider the Sacred Mosque in Mecca, Saudi Arabia, a holy site. Jews think of Jerusalem as their holy city, since it's the place where Solomon dedicated the first temple to God.

Within the wider scope of the Christian faith, there is no consensus. Some think of Jerusalem as a special place, "more holy" than others. Others focus on Rome and the Vatican. Still others think of the church building where they worship each Sunday as a place in which God is especially near. Some even refer to the room where they worship as a "sanctuary."

We must keep in mind that the New Testament affirms that God does not live in temples made with human hands (Acts 7:48, 49 [quoting Isaiah 66:1, 2]; 17:24). Christians are themselves God's temple, individually and collectively as the body of Christ—the church. His Spirit lives within us (Romans 8:9; 1 Corinthians 3:16, 17; 6:19). It's even fair to say that the "house of sacrifice" of which Solomon was told has transferred in concept to Christians personally. As you read Romans 12:1 in this regard, how will you apply it in the week ahead?　　　　　—C. R. B.

B. For His People (vv. 13-16)

13. If I shut up heaven that there be no rain, or if I command the locusts to devour the land, or if I send pestilence among my people.

By contrast, the language of the three negative situations here are all reflected in the language of Solomon's dedicatory prayer (2 Chronicles 6:26-28). Solomon has noted the cause for God's needing to take such action: sin (6:26). The outcomes of famine (due to *no rain* or *locusts*) and *pestilence* are mentioned within the curses pronounced by Moses when he warned the Israelites of how they

HOW TO SAY IT

Ahab	*Ay*-hab.
Assyrians	Uh-*sear*-e-unz.
Babylonians	Bab-ih-*low*-nee-unz.
Deuteronomy	Due-ter-*ahn*-uh-me.
Elijah	Ee-*lye*-juh.
Jerusalem	Juh-*roo*-suh-lem.
Moriah	Mo-*rye*-uh.
Nineveh	*Nin*-uh-vuh.

would be disciplined should they turn away from God (Deuteronomy 11:17; 28:21, 38).

14a. If my people, which are called by my name, shall humble themselves, and pray, and seek my face, and turn from their wicked ways.

The conditional *if* statement here introduces reasons why the deadly conditions of verse 13 need not be permanent. With the Lord there is and will be hope! Again, this reflects the contents of Solomon's earlier prayer. After describing the withholding of rain because of the people's sin, Solomon prayed, "If they pray toward this place, and confess thy name, and turn from their sin, when thou dost afflict them; then hear thou from heaven, and forgive the sin of thy servants, and of thy people Israel" (2 Chronicles 6:26, 27). God's disciplinary action must be recognized as such by His people, and they must respond to it in the way directed by the Lord in the verse before us. The steps of repentance are four in number:

First, the wayward people are to *humble themselves.* Scripture contains ample warnings and examples about the danger of pride (Proverbs 16:18; Daniel 4:28-33; James 4:6). Humility acknowledges one's need for God and dependence on Him (2 Chronicles 12:6; Isaiah 57:15; 1 Peter 5:6).

Second is to *pray.* Prayer is a must, especially when turning away from sin, as is the case here. One may consider David's earnest prayer of repentance in Psalm 51 and the simple yet heartfelt plea of the publican in Jesus' parable: "God be merciful to me a sinner" (Luke 18:13).

To *seek* the Lord's *face* implies a desire for the closest kind of relationship. David expressed such a longing in Psalm 27:8. Jeremiah gave this promise to God's wayward people: "Ye shall seek me, and find me, when ye shall search for me with all your heart" (Jeremiah 29:13).

It will do no good to take the first three steps without taking the fourth: sinners must *turn from their wicked ways.* Words of contrition must be followed up by actions that match. To turn from one's sinful ways is precisely what the biblical teaching about repentance means: to do an "about face," reversing the course of one's conduct. The process embodied by the terms used in this verse indicates a total surrender to God.

14b. Then will I hear from heaven, and will forgive their sin, and will heal their land.

God's response to such determination is total as well. Forgiveness of *sin* will go hand in hand with healing of the *land.* This suggests a reversal of whatever conditions have been part of God's disciplinary action. If rain has been withheld, it will now fall freely. The effects of any locust plague or any pestilence will be replaced by the provision of God's blessings (compare Exodus 15:26).

15. Now mine eyes shall be open, and mine ears attent unto the prayer that is made in this place.

As Solomon neared the end of his dedicatory prayer, he implored, "Now, my God, let, I beseech thee, thine eyes be open, and let thine ears be attent unto the prayer that is made in this place" (2 Chronicles 6:40). The Lord indicates His intention to do just that!

16. For now have I chosen and sanctified this house, that my name may be there for ever: and mine eyes and mine heart shall be there perpetually.

The language of this verse indicates the fullness of God's identification with the temple. The fact that the Lord has *sanctified this house* (the temple) implies its being set apart for a divine purpose. In further accordance with Solomon's request, the Lord also promises to attach His *name* in the temple (2 Chronicles 6:20; compare Deuteronomy 12:11). Although God states that His *name*, *eyes*, and *heart* will be there *for ever* and *perpetually*, the promise is not unconditional, as we shall see.

C. For Solomon (vv. 17, 18)

17. And as for thee, if thou wilt walk before me, as David thy father walked, and do according to all that I have commanded thee, and shalt observe my statutes and my judgments.

Now the Lord's message transitions from a focus on temple and people to Solomon himself. The message begins with another conditional if-statement that focuses on behavior. That behavior is stated in terms of David's walk as an example for Solomon to follow. The evidence of a right walk will be seen in obedience to God's *statutes* and *judgments*. Clearly, Solomon's responsibility before the Lord is not fulfilled simply because the temple is completed!

To walk as David walked does not imply perfection, for David was certainly no perfect man. But the overall direction of his life was pleasing to God, who calls him "a man after mine own heart" (Acts 13:22). When David was confronted about his sinful behavior, he acknowledged his guilt without reservation (2 Samuel 12:13; Psalm 51).

What Do You Think?
Do the requirements for walking before God differ from person to person? Why, or why not?
Talking Points for Your Discussion
- In terms of spiritual disciplines (personal Bible study, prayer, etc.)
- In terms of personality characteristics (extravert vs. introvert, etc.)
- In terms of age
- Other

18. Then will I stablish the throne of thy kingdom, according as I have covenanted with David thy father, saying, There shall not fail thee a man to be ruler in Israel.

We expect an if-statement to be followed by a then-statement, and that is certainly the case here. The promise made to David in 2 Samuel 7:13, 16 can be Solomon's as well. As David lay dying, he had voiced this same promise, along with the challenge of the previous verse, to Solomon (1 Kings 2:1-4).

II. Promised Discipline
(2 Chronicles 7:19-22)

A. Against the People (vv. 19, 20a)

19. But if ye turn away, and forsake my statutes and my commandments, which I have set before you, and shall go and serve other gods, and worship them.

The pronouns *ye* and *you* in this verse are plural in the Hebrew text. Thus the warnings in the verses that follow apply to "my people" of 2 Chronicles 7:13, 14, above). But Solomon himself must still take these cautions personally; as the leader of God's people, he is responsible to set the example of observing the Lord's *statutes* and *commandments*.

More specifically, the primary warning given in this segment of the text concerns idolatry—the decision to *go and serve other gods, and worship them*. This violates the very first of the Ten Commandments. The prohibition against other gods is first because it is foundational to keeping the other nine.

20a. Then will I pluck them up by the roots out of my land which I have given them.

The consequences of forsaking the Lord and following other gods will be disastrous. If God's people reverse their loyalty to Him and turn from Him, then He will reverse His loyalty to them and turn from them.

This eventually happens during the time of the divided monarchy. Israel (the northern kingdom) is conquered by the Assyrians, and later Judah (the southern kingdom) is conquered by the Babylonians (2 Kings 17, 25).

B. Against the Temple (vv. 20b-22)

20b. And this house, which I have sanctified for my name, will I cast out of my sight,

and will make it to be a proverb and a byword among all nations.

Disaster will also befall *this house*, Solomon's temple. Instead of the Lord's eyes being on the temple (2 Chronicles 7:16, above), He promises to cast it *out of* His *sight*. This passage clearly shows (as does the entirety of Scripture) the two sides of God's promises. Yes, He will bless those who turn to Him in sincere repentance (as described earlier in 7:14); but those who turn from Him and reject His commandments will experience His judgment.

We tend to associate the word *proverb* with the contents of the book of Proverbs. While the word can describe wise, practical advice, it is also used to refer to other kinds of sayings. These include the scornful words to be directed toward the temple once it has been cast out of the Lord's sight. The Hebrew term translated *byword* carries the idea of a taunt (compare Deuteronomy 28:37; Jeremiah 24:9). Such terms reflect the complete reversal in status that Solomon's temple will experience. Instead of being treated with reverence as a sacred place, it will be viewed with abject contempt.

21. And this house, which is high, shall be an astonishment to every one that passeth by it; so that he shall say, Why hath the Lord done thus unto this land, and unto this house?

The temple in Jerusalem is intended to be a place where God's people can joyfully anticipate gathering for worship. This especially includes the annual pilgrimage feasts (see Leviticus 23; Deuteronomy 16; etc.).

But instead of being awestruck at the sight of the renowned temple, passers-by will be stunned to see it lying in ruins. Ancient peoples often think of deity as responsible for the condition of the local temple and of the surrounding territory where the worshippers live. Given that belief, the question *Why hath the Lord done thus unto this land, and unto this house?* is bound to arise.

22. And it shall be answered, Because they forsook the Lord God of their fathers, which brought them forth out of the land of Egypt, and laid hold on other gods, and worshipped them, and served them: therefore hath he brought all this evil upon them.

In the case of Israel, the destruction of the temple will not reflect poorly on the Lord; it will reflect poorly on His people who will have forsaken Him. The reference to the people's deliverance from bondage in Egypt is important to note; it suggests that they will have forgotten their history, their roots. They will have forgotten that no other people have a history like theirs because no other people have a God who can do the wonders that only He is capable of.

The word *evil* does not refer to a moral evil, which God does not inflict (James 1:13). Rather, it refers to the physical disaster that eventually befalls both the northern and southern kingdoms as a result of God's judgment. That will happen because the people will have *worshipped* and *served* other gods instead of the God who delivered them from bondage and established His covenant with them. They will have no one but themselves to blame for their sad state.

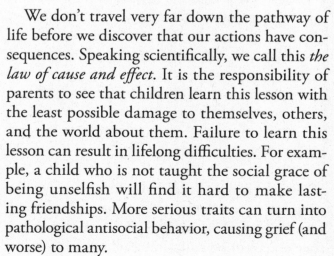

What Do You Think?
What lessons did you learn from observing someone become a cautionary tale because of disobeying God?
Talking Points for Your Discussion
- Regarding the personal impact of sin
- Regarding the impact of sin on others
- Regarding the character of God
- Regarding the response of God's people
- Other

◆ *CAUSE AND EFFECT* ◆

We don't travel very far down the pathway of life before we discover that our actions have consequences. Speaking scientifically, we call this *the law of cause and effect*. It is the responsibility of parents to see that children learn this lesson with the least possible damage to themselves, others, and the world about them. Failure to learn this lesson can result in lifelong difficulties. For example, a child who is not taught the social grace of being unselfish will find it hard to make lasting friendships. More serious traits can turn into pathological antisocial behavior, causing grief (and worse) to many.

Societies and nations can also suffer from a failure to learn the law of cause and effect. America still feels the damaging societal effects of enslaving human beings as lessons of equal treatment are learned, forgotten, relearned, forgotten again, etc.

God repeatedly warned the Israelites that their actions would have consequences. In the excitement of dedicating the temple, the people reaffirmed their allegiance to God (2 Chronicles 7:3-6. But euphoria has a tendency to be fleeting, and the God's warnings were eventually forgotten.

Even so, God was patient. He withheld His judgment for centuries. But His promise to destroy the temple because of the people's idolatry eventually became reality.

It's been said that there are two ways to learn: (1) by *wisdom* (which is learning from the mistakes of others) and (2) by *experience* (which is learning from our own mistakes). Which way will you choose? See 1 Corinthians 10:1-13.

—C. R. B.

Conclusion

A. Words for Today?

The words of 2 Chronicles 7:14 include a very special promise from God to Solomon following the completion and dedication of the temple in Jerusalem. The verse reads, "If my people, which are called by my name, shall humble themselves, and pray, and seek my face, and turn from their wicked ways; then will I hear from heaven, and will forgive their sin, and will heal their land."

Over the years many Christians, particularly in the United States, have quoted this verse in appealing for nationwide repentance and revival. Critics claim that such a view is taking the verse out of its original context since the term "my people" refers to Old Testament Israel, with which God had a special covenant relationship. No nation today, the critics claim, has the right to quote and apply this verse. Some say that it is a bit arrogant for any nation to claim to be "God's people."

While it is true that the words of this verse are addressed specifically to Old Testament Israel, does that mean it's wrong to apply the principle and the promise of the verse to any other nation

Visual for Lesson 4. *Start a discussion by pointing to this visual as you ask, "Are any important choices missing? If so, what are they?"*

in history? One of the foundational teachings of Scripture is that God is willing to forgive any individual or nation turning to Him in true repentance (compare Luke 24:47; Revelation 21:24; etc.).

One of the lessons Jeremiah learned from his visit to the potter's house was that God blesses or disciplines a nation or kingdom (implying any nation or kingdom) because of the choices its people make (Jeremiah 18:1-10). Jonah's experience in Nineveh revealed that non-Israelites would be shown mercy if they demonstrated genuine repentance—and they did.

Rather than focus too closely on trying to identify "my people," it is probably preferable to focus on bringing as many individuals as possible to the place where they can address the Lord as "my God." That place is the forgiveness available only in Jesus.

B. Prayer

Father, we recognize that what You challenged Your people to do in Solomon's day is what You challenge us to do now: humble ourselves, pray, seek Your face, and turn from evil ways. Help us to give heed to both Your warning and Your promise of blessing. We pray in Jesus' name. Amen.

C. Thought to Remember

God's law of harvest has not been revoked: we still reap what we sow.

INVOLVEMENT LEARNING

Enhance your lesson with KJV Bible Student *(from your curriculum supplier) and the reproducible activity page (at www.standardlesson.com or in the back of the* KJV Standard Lesson Commentary Deluxe Edition*).*

Into the Lesson

Open class by inviting students to recall funny videos they have seen of people trying to do or accomplish something but failing. (Option: bring a video clip of you yourself enduring such an outcome.) Jot a brief note on the board about each situation mentioned. After you have several responses, go back through the list and discuss how each failure could have been avoided.

Alternative. Distribute pens and copies of the "Secret of My Success" activity, which you can download. Have students work individually or in small groups to match each quote with the correct celebrity.

After either activity say, "We want to live successful lives. But what lifestyle gives us the best chance of enjoying prosperity and avoiding catastrophe? God answered that very question during the reign of King Solomon."

Into the Word

Option: begin this segment by distributing handouts (you create) of a matching quiz. Down the left side have names of various household products; down the right side have brief instructions for using those products, instructions you have copied from the products' labels. Allow one minute for students to complete the quiz individually.

After you call time, go over the answers as a class; expect some intentionally humorous mismatches. Then say, "Solomon built a temple, and God kept His promise to dwell among His people there. But God had some clear instructions to help the Israelites be successful in their relationship with Him."

Divide students into three groups, assigning each group one of the following segments from 2 Chronicles 7: verses 12-16; verses 17, 18; and verses 19-22. Give each group several index cards and two pens or markers of different colors. Tell each group to read through its assigned passage, using one color of pen to write every if-statement on a separate index card (example: if my people humble themselves).

Following that, each group should use the other color of pen to write every then-statement on a separate index card (example: then will I hear from heaven).

When students have finished, read through the entire text together. As you do, have groups present their index cards, putting the if-statements into one pile and the then-statements into another. Afterward, count the cards in each pile. Say, "God was very clear about what He expected from Solomon and the rest of the Israelites. And God was very clear about how He would respond to their actions. There was no 'secret' to success. God gave clear instructions. The 'secret' was obedience. But it's not always easy to obey. Is it?"

Invite students to talk about times in their lives when it was (or still is) difficult to obey God. Ask for volunteers to talk about the consequences of their disobedience or the rewards of their obedience, but don't put anyone on the spot. Offer examples from your own life as well.

Into Life

Say, "Living a truly successful life requires people to sacrifice their own desires and thoughts. God told Solomon that if he did not follow the statutes and ordinances given to him, then calamity would come upon the people and the temple would be abandoned. But He also offered them hope and healing, as He also offers us." Read aloud 2 Chronicles 7:14 and challenge students to summarize it (either aloud or silently) in reference to their own lives.

Alternative: Review the text together. Distribute copies of the "Sum Up Success" activity. Have students work individually to complete biblical formulas for success based on today's lesson text.

HE HAS RISEN

DEVOTIONAL READING: Luke 24:36-49
BACKGROUND SCRIPTURE: Luke 24:1-35

LUKE 24:1-12, 30-35

1 Now upon the first day of the week, very early in the morning, they came unto the sepulchre, bringing the spices which they had prepared, and certain others with them.

2 And they found the stone rolled away from the sepulchre.

3 And they entered in, and found not the body of the Lord Jesus.

4 And it came to pass, as they were much perplexed thereabout, behold, two men stood by them in shining garments:

5 And as they were afraid, and bowed down their faces to the earth, they said unto them, Why seek ye the living among the dead?

6 He is not here, but is risen: remember how he spake unto you when he was yet in Galilee,

7 Saying, The Son of man must be delivered into the hands of sinful men, and be crucified, and the third day rise again.

8 And they remembered his words,

9 And returned from the sepulchre, and told all these things unto the eleven, and to all the rest.

10 It was Mary Magdalene and Joanna, and Mary the mother of James, and other women that were with them, which told these things unto the apostles.

11 And their words seemed to them as idle tales, and they believed them not.

12 Then arose Peter, and ran unto the sepulchre; and stooping down, he beheld the linen clothes laid by themselves, and departed, wondering in himself at that which was come to pass.

. . . .

30 And it came to pass, as he sat at meat with them, he took bread, and blessed it, and brake, and gave to them.

31 And their eyes were opened, and they knew him; and he vanished out of their sight.

32 And they said one to another, Did not our heart burn within us, while he talked with us by the way, and while he opened to us the scriptures?

33 And they rose up the same hour, and returned to Jerusalem, and found the eleven gathered together, and them that were with them,

34 Saying, The Lord is risen indeed, and hath appeared to Simon.

35 And they told what things were done in the way, and how he was known of them in breaking of bread.

KEY VERSE

The Lord is risen indeed, and hath appeared to Simon. —**Luke 24:34**

Acknowledging God

Unit 2: All Glory and Honor

Lessons 5–9

Lesson Aims

After participating in this lesson, each learner will be able to:

1. Restate the mystery of Jesus' missing body and the resolution of that mystery.

2. Explain why the women's preparation was unnecessary.

3. Offer a prayer of thanksgiving that God keeps His promises.

Lesson Outline

Introduction
  A. An Enduring Proverb
  B. Lesson Background
I. Witness of the Women (Luke 24:1-12)
  A. Prepared with Spices (v. 1)
  B. Unprepared for the Scene (vv. 2, 3)
  C. Angelic Explanation (vv. 4-8)
     Because I Promised
  D. Apostolic Disbelief (vv. 9-12)
II. Epiphany at Emmaus (Luke 24:30-35)
  A. Instant Awareness (vv. 30-32)
  B. Return to Jerusalem (v. 33)
  C. Resurrection Confirmed (vv. 34, 35)
     Disappearance
Conclusion
  A. Remembering the Risen Lord
  B. Prayer
  C. Thought to Remember

Introduction

A. An Enduring Proverb

How do we find the strength to go on during the most difficult of times? We might wish we were the victim of a mere April Fool's Day joke, only to realize our problems are quite real!

Many find encouragement from a proverb of English theologian and historian Thomas Fuller (1608–1661). In his *A Pisgah-Sight of Palestine and the Confines Thereof*, Fuller wrote, "It is always darkest just before the Day dawneth." Two centuries later, Irish songwriter Samuel Lover remarked that this saying had become proverbial "amongst the Irish peasantry to inspire hope under adverse circumstances." Today the same words are used by therapists, self-help gurus, and motivational speakers. "Don't give up," is their message. "Better times are ahead!"

We all have experienced dark times that we thought would never end—yet they did end! The crucifixion of Jesus was such a dark time, but it was dispelled by the brightness of the resurrection.

B. Lesson Background

Luke 23:54 is clear that Jesus was crucified and buried on the day of preparation, the day before the Sabbath (see also Matthew 27:62; Mark 15:42; John 19:14, 31, 42). Luke 23:56 further indicates that the women prepared "spices and ointments" on the day of preparation so as not to violate the Sabbath. Mark 16:1 states the spices were for anointing Jesus' body, and John 19:39, 40 demonstrates the Jews' burial custom of wrapping a body in linen clothes and spices. This was not an easy task, at least in the case of Jesus, as John 19:39 reveals use of about 100 Roman pounds (about 75 modern pounds) of myrrh and aloes.

I. Witness of the Women

(Luke 24:1-12)

The focus in Luke 24 on the witness of certain women has Luke 23:50-56 as its point of departure. What follows presupposes that the women knew the location of the sepulchre; indeed they did, because they had watched Joseph of

Arimathaea place Jesus' body there (compare Matthew 27:61). The same is not said of any of the remaining eleven apostles, although at least two of them seem to know exactly where the sepulchre is (John 20:3, 4).

A. Prepared with Spices (v. 1)

1. Now upon the first day of the week, very early in the morning, they came unto the sepulchre, bringing the spices which they had prepared, and certain others with them.

The first day of the week is Sunday; the day of preparation (Friday) and the Sabbath (Saturday) are past. *They* refers to the women from Luke 23:55, 56. Combining the observation that it is now *very early in the morning* with a sunset-to-sunset understanding of transition from one day to the next (Luke 23:54) leaves no doubt that this is the third day (compare Matthew 16:21; 17:22, 23; 20:17-19). Regarding *the spices which they had prepared,* see the Lesson Background.

B. Unprepared for the Scene (vv. 2, 3)

2. And they found the stone rolled away from the sepulchre.

Archaeologists have uncovered hundreds of tombs within three miles of Jerusalem. Many have stones that can be *rolled away* like the one mentioned here. Mark 16:4 records that the stone over Jesus' sepulchre was "very great." And since limestone weighs about 170 pounds per cubic foot, even a stone of moderate size means substantial weight. If the stone is three feet in diameter and one foot thick, then the resulting volume of seven cubic feet computes to a weight of about 1,200 pounds. A stone four feet across would weigh over a ton.

3. And they entered in, and found not the body of the Lord Jesus.

Jesus' missing body is the central, dramatic element of Luke 24. Luke stresses this as he builds to the climax of his Gospel in order to establish that Jesus' body is missing for a reason.

C. Angelic Explanation (vv. 4-8)

4, 5. And it came to pass, as they were much perplexed thereabout, behold, two men stood by them in shining garments. And as they were afraid, and bowed down their faces to the earth, they said unto them, Why seek ye the living among the dead?

The women's confusion about the missing body doesn't last long as it gives way to fear. The *two men* who elicit the fear are expressly identified as angels in Luke 24:23 (see also John 20:12). Matthew 28:2 and Mark 16:5 mention just one angel, likely because the focus is on the speaker only.

Fear at the appearance of an angel is apparent in the writings of Luke (Luke 1:11, 12, 29; 2:9; Acts 10:3, 4). In other appearances, angels tell people not to fear. But here there is no such admonition. The women's response of bowing appears to be instinctual. Abraham reacted the same way to the three men in Genesis 18:2, as did Lot regarding the two angels in Genesis 19:1. Bowing also seems to be a common act of respect for authority in the ancient Near East, as seen in Genesis 33:3; 42:6; and Ruth 2:10.

The angel's concluding question is valid but incomprehensible to the women. The women have not yet seen Jesus alive, and they do not expect to. Even so, a hint to the mystery of the missing body is embedded in the angel's question.

> *What Do You Think?*
> How can we ensure we relate to Jesus as living Lord and not as a long-dead historical figure?
> *Talking Points for Your Discussion*
> - In the form and content of our prayers
> - In how we talk about Him
> - Considering the degree to which we keep His commandments (John 14:15, 21)
> - Other

6. He is not here, but is risen: remember how he spake unto you when he was yet in Galilee.

The angels state the most important fact in all of history when they declare the reason for the absence of Jesus' body—that He *is risen.* Then the angels give the women a command: to *remember* the words of Jesus while He was still with them *in Galilee.* These verses form the beginning of a poetic sandwich using the word *remember.*

We can note in passing the curious fact that Jesus' enemies remember His prediction of rising from the dead (Matthew 27:62, 63) but His followers do not!

◆ BECAUSE I PROMISED ◆

A friend and his wife celebrated their 50th wedding anniversary not long ago. The husband admitted in a touching tribute that their years together had not been without struggle. "Marriage has been hard sometimes—much harder than we expected," he said. Despite the difficulties they experienced, they stayed together. "After one extended difficult patch, I asked my wife why she stayed. I didn't like her answer: 'Because I promised.' I thought she'd say something about my charm or my being a good guy under it all. But it was nothing about me—it was about the promise. On our wedding day she said she would."

Reading this, I thought about the times in my own marriage when things have been less than what I thought they'd be. During those times, I often remembered the day I stood before all my family and friends, before God, and before my husband and promised to love him even when it was hard. That promise we made holds us together. It trickles down to our children, who live under the umbrella of that bond. As my friend so aptly put it, "Keeping a promise requires more of us—it makes us better. And receiving a promise is a gift. It brings a priceless sense of security."

God promised that a Savior would come, and God kept that promise. Then Jesus promised that He would rise again, and He did. Is it not glorious to serve a promise-keeping God?

—L. M. W.

HOW TO SAY IT

Arimathaea	*Air*-uh-muh-***thee***-uh (*th* as in *thin*).
Emmaus	Em-*may*-us.
Galilee	*Gal*-uh-lee.
Magdalene	*Mag*-duh-leen or Mag-duh-*lee*-nee.
Pharisee	*Fair*-ih-see.
sepulchre	*sep*-ul-kur.

7. Saying, The Son of man must be delivered into the hands of sinful men, and be crucified, and the third day rise again.

This verse is the center of the verbal sandwich begun in verse 6. The angels remind the women of the words of Jesus that they should not have forgotten in the first place. These, the most critical of Jesus' words, have been lost to conscious thought —possibly because Jesus' followers did not wish to believe them (compare Matthew 16:21, 22).

8. And they remembered his words.

This is the conclusion of the verbal sandwich begun in verse 6. The sequence says something. The first encounter on this the third day is not between the risen Jesus and the women. Rather, the first encounter is with angels who bear an imperative to remember *his words*. We do well to apply this imperative to our lives daily!

> **What Do You Think?**
> How do lives focused on the resurrection differ from those that are not?
> *Talking Points for Your Discussion*
> - Regarding outlook on sin
> - Regarding outlook on suffering
> - Regarding outlook on salvation
> - Other

D. Apostolic Disbelief (vv. 9-12)

9. And returned from the sepulchre, and told all these things unto the eleven, and to all the rest.

The return of the women to Jerusalem echoes their previous return in Luke 23:56, but this time the reason is quite the opposite! Instead of preparing spices to anoint the dead body of Jesus, they return with the message of the live body of Jesus. Mention of *the eleven* highlights the fact that these are "the twelve" of Luke 22:47 minus Judas the betrayer.

10, 11. It was Mary Magdalene, and Joanna, and Mary the mother of James, and other women that were with them, which told these things unto the apostles. And their words seemed to them as idle tales, and they believed them not.

Luke indicates there are at least five women involved, with three being named. *Mary Magdalene* is recorded by the Gospels as being present at the crucifixion of Jesus, at His burial, and at the empty tomb early Sunday morning. She was delivered from demon possession by Jesus, which helps us understand her devotion to Him (Luke 8:2). *Joanna* is the wife of an official in the household of Herod, the king of Galilee (8:3).

Mary the mother of James is further defined as being "the mother of James and Joses" in Matthew 27:56. This may be Matthew's way of referring to Mary, the mother of Jesus, for she had sons named James and Joses (Mark 6:3). It would be odd, however, that Jesus' mother would not be identified as such at this point rather than by the names of two of Jesus' half-brothers (compare Acts 1:14). So it is more likely that the Mary in view here is a different woman from Galilee.

In any case, these women are followers of Jesus. But that is not enough to make their account of the empty tomb credible to the rest. Instead, those gathered (including *the apostles*) dismiss their story *as idle tales* (compare Acts 12:14, 15). We can imagine the disappointment and hurt these faithful women must feel at not being believed.

What Do You Think?
How can we prepare to respond to those who struggle to believe in the resurrection?
Talking Points for Your Discussion
- Regarding awareness of presuppostions (Acts 17:31, 32; 23:6-8; 26:8; etc.)
- Regarding context of the interaction (Acts 2:22-36; 10:34-43; 13:14-41; etc.)
- Regarding our demeanor when challenged
- Other

---

12. Then arose Peter, and ran unto the sepulchre; and stooping down, he beheld the linen clothes laid by themselves, and departed, wondering in himself at that which was come to pass.

This section of the account began with the women returning to the eleven apostles, but it ends with a focus on only one of them: *Peter*. The biblical record is clear that he is a key figure

among the apostles, and especially in the resurrection accounts. In Mark 16:7 the angel specifically instructs the women to tell Peter that Jesus is going to Galilee and the apostles will see Him there. The fact that he is *wondering in himself at that which was come to pass* indicates that he needs a reminder of Jesus' words just as much as the women did.

II. Epiphany at Emmaus
(LUKE 24:30-35)

Luke 24:13-29 sets the stage for the next segment. Jesus has appeared unrecognized to two disciples on the road from Jerusalem to Emmaus. The nature of the conversation and the fading of daylight impels the two to invite the incognito Jesus to remain with them. But before everyone turns in for the night, a meal is shared.

A. Instant Awareness (vv. 30-32)

30. And it came to pass, as he sat at meat with them, he took bread, and blessed it, and brake, and gave to them.

Contexts of meals, eating, and drinking are important vehicles for portraying kingdom truths in Luke's Gospel (examples: Luke 5:27-39; 7:36-50). Mealtimes in this Gospel are dramatic and suspenseful. Concerning the case at hand, the drama has been building since 24:13, with the climax now unfolding.

The similarity between Jesus' actions in this verse and His earlier actions in Luke 22:19 are intriguing. There Jesus "took bread, and gave thanks, and brake it, and gave unto them" in instituting the Lord's Supper. Does Jesus intend the current situation to be a reminder of the previous?

Three factors suggest the answer is no. First, Jesus has said that He "will not any more eat thereof, until it be fulfilled in the kingdom of God" (Luke 22:16). Second, no cup is mentioned (compare 22:17, 20). Third, the blessing and breaking of bread was not something unique to the last supper (see Matthew 14:19).

31. And their eyes were opened, and they knew him; and he vanished out of their sight.

On the other hand, some students say that a certain link with the Lord's Supper is suggested by the fact that Jesus' dining companions are able to recognize Him as soon as Jesus gives them bread, recalling that Luke 22:19 has Jesus distributing bread as He says, "This is my body which is given for you: this do in remembrance of me." Up to this point in Luke 24, Jesus' body has been missing or otherwise kept from being recognized. This is the point in Luke's resurrection account where that changes.

An interplay of physical and spiritual blindness may also be intended by Luke. Jesus' two hosts for the meal are men whose eyes have been "holden that they should not know him" (Luke 24:16); concurrently, they had received a tongue lashing from Jesus, who called them "fools, and slow of heart to believe" (24:25). The suggested connection is that the lifting of their spiritual blindness (see 24:32, next) had to happen before they were able to recognize Jesus physically.

The gospel message includes Jesus' proclaiming "recovering of sight to the blind" (Luke 4:18). This is not limited to those who are physically unable to see. It also (and more importantly) addresses the need of those who lack spiritual awareness.

32. And they said one to another, Did not our heart burn within us, while he talked with us by the way, and while he opened to us the scriptures?

The expression of *heart burn* here does not refer to indigestion, but rather to a sense of longing or excitement that comes while learning truth. We should notice the sequence: (1) the correcting of deficient understanding of the Scripture while on the road to Emmaus was accompanied by burning hearts; (2) that correction in turn has led to the ability to recognize Jesus; and now (3) the two disciples comprehend the connection between (1) and (2).

What Do You Think?
How can we maintain hunger for God's Word?
Talking Points for Your Discussion
- Regarding positive thoughts and behaviors to reinforce
- Regarding negative thoughts and behaviors to eliminate

B. Return to Jerusalem (v. 33)

33. And they rose up the same hour, and returned to Jerusalem, and found the eleven gathered together, and them that were with them.

The general designation "two of them" in Luke 24:13 leaves open the possibility that the one who is unnamed (see 24:18) is an apostle if 24:13 is read as a direct continuation of 24:9-12. That possibility is negated by the fact that these two men find *the eleven gathered together* in *Jerusalem*.

The action of and reporting by the two men bears similarities to those of the women in Luke 24:9. Although "the day is far spent" (24:29), they have the light of the nearly full moon by which to walk, since the Feast of Passover, recently completed, occurs during full moon. They cannot wait until morning to share their experience. So they scurry the seven miles (24:13) back to Jerusalem.

C. Resurrection Confirmed (vv. 34, 35)

34. Saying, The Lord is risen indeed, and hath appeared to Simon.

The men return to Jerusalem only to hear from the eleven and the others what they now already believe and have experienced, that *the Lord is risen indeed*. This is the focus of all accounts in Luke 24 and the central idea of what is commonly called Easter today. Statement parallels in Luke 24 form a certain long-standing Easter tradition in churches. In 24:9, the women pass along the angelic claim that the Jesus is risen; now some or all those in Jerusalem affirm *the Lord is risen indeed*. In many services today, a worship leader will declare, "He is risen," to which the congregation responds, "He is risen indeed!"

Those gathered also confirm that the Lord has *appeared to Simon*. This is Peter's other name (see Luke 5:8; 6:14); he also is known as Cephas (John 1:42). But wait—why isn't this described here? When Peter last appears in Luke 24:12, the Lord has not appeared to him. Now we read that He has. Is something missing?

The short answer is no. Like all careful historians, Luke chooses what to include and what not to (compare John 21:25). Each Gospel makes its unique contribution of detail.

◆ *DISAPPEARANCE* ◆

In the early days of the United States, rugged settlers braved the unknown to explore beyond the Appalachian Mountains. One such was James Harrod, who trapped and traded in what would later become Kentucky. Eventually, he helped found a settlement in 1774 that became known as Harrodsburg.

Over the years, Harrod married and had a family. He became involved in politics and farming and grew wealthy. He also used his skills to help the military periodically.

But Harrod became increasingly solitary, sometimes taking long trips into the wilderness alone. He disappeared on one such trip, leaving behind a wife, daughter, and stepson. His family searched for him, and many theories regarding his disappearance evolved.

Some people said they saw him alive and that he even told them he planned to return home eventually. Some said he went back to a secret wife and family in the wilderness. Others said he had been killed by Indians. His daughter claimed a fellow hunter had murdered him and hidden the body. But no body was ever discovered, and all trails eventually went cold.

James Harrod lived a life of distinction, but when he disappeared, he did not return. The life Jesus lived was more distinctive by far, He did return from the grave, and He promised to return again from Heaven. His resurrection proves Him to be more than just a unique leader—far more.

—L. M. W.

35. And they told what things were done in the way, and how he was known of them in breaking of bread.

Visual for Lesson 5. *Start a discussion by pointing to this visual as you ask, "How does this fact affect the way you live daily? How should it?"*

This verse serves as a transition to Jesus' appearance in verse 36. It also is a summary statement of all that has happened to the two men from Luke 24:13 until now. Jesus' body was missing from the tomb, but found when *he was known of them in breaking of bread*, with bread perhaps serving to represent Jesus' body—the main focus of the drama of Luke 24. He is risen!

Conclusion
A. Remembering the Risen Lord

Although many Christians say "He is risen" to one another only at Easter, there are some churches where Christians greet each other regularly with "He is risen!" This practice reminds them that the body of Jesus is missing from the tomb for a reason: because He is risen now and forever. This should be remembered daily, not just at Easter. The resurrection of Christ has daily implications, consisting of both blessings and responsibilities, for all believers.

B. Prayer

Father, thank You for keeping Your promises by raising Jesus from the dead! Help us to trust You more because You are trustworthy. We pray in Jesus' name. Amen.

C. Thought to Remember
No darkness can overshadow the Son.

INVOLVEMENT LEARNING

Enhance your lesson with KJV Bible Student (from your curriculum supplier) and the reproducible activity page (at www.standardlesson.com or in the back of the KJV Standard Lesson Commentary Deluxe Edition).

Into the Lesson

Begin today's lesson by playing a version of the game Two Truths and a Lie. Give each person paper and a pen. Students are to write three bad things that happened in their lives. Two should be true; one should be made up. (For example: *I was fired from my job for sleeping; I recently had a root canal; I grew up feeling stupid.* Two of these statements must be true; the other will be fictitious.) Have each person read his or her statements and let the class guess which one is the lie by a show of hands.

Alternative: Distribute pens and copies of the "Mystery Message" activity on the reproducible page, which you can download. Have students work individually to solve the puzzle.

After either activity say, "We have all experienced dark times that we thought would never end—yet they did end! The crucifixion of Jesus was such a dark time, but it was dispelled by the brightness of the resurrection."

Into the Word

Divide the class into three groups. Supply each group with pen and paper and one of the following assignments. They will read portions of today's text and write a newspaper headline and subhead for those texts. Two sample HEADLINES and *Subheads* for each group follow.

Group 1—Luke 24:1-8
UNBELIEVABLE!
  Heavenly messengers say Jesus has risen

EMPTY TOMB MYSTERY
  Witnesses perplexed about missing body

Group 2—Luke 24:9-12
DIVINE OR DELUDED?
  Jesus' followers skeptical of resurrection report

GRAVE CLOTHES FOUND
  But Jesus' body still missing

Group 3—Luke 24:30-35
DINNER GUEST DISAPPEARS!
  Is this evidence that Jesus lives?

RESURRECTION EVIDENCE GROWS?
  Some claim fulfillment of prophecy

Option: Research the events of Christ's resurrection as recorded here and elsewhere in Scripture. Compare and contrast the accounts to get a broader picture of what took place. You may want to point to these:
  Appearance to 2 (Luke 24:13-32)
  Appearance to 10 (John 20:19-24)
  Appearance to 11 (Matthew 28:16-20)
  Appearance to 500 (1 Corinthians 15:6)
  Appearance to 1 woman (John 20:11-18)
  Appearance to 1 persecutor (Acts 9:1-5)
Alternative: Distribute pens and copies of the "Scripture or Supposition?" activity. Have students work individually or in small groups to determine which statements are Scripture facts and which are things we infer from Scripture.

After either activity say, "People often question the promises of their leaders. Can they have assurance in the midst of doubt? In the breaking of bread and making himself known to His disciples, the risen Christ kept His promises—to His followers then and now."

Into Life

Option: Discuss the resurrection scene from *The Passion of the Christ.*

Give each person a plastic egg, several slips of paper, and a pen. Challenge students to complete the following statement in as many ways as they can, writing each response on a separate slip of paper and placing it inside the egg: "Because Jesus lives, I . . ."

Allow students to take the eggs home, and encourage them to share their responses with their families this week.

THE RISEN LORD APPEARS

DEVOTIONAL READING: Psalm 19:7-10; 119:105-112
BACKGROUND SCRIPTURE: John 21:1-14

JOHN 21:1-14

1 After these things Jesus shewed himself again to the disciples at the sea of Tiberias; and on this wise shewed he himself.

2 There were together Simon Peter, and Thomas called Didymus, and Nathanael of Cana in Galilee, and the sons of Zebedee, and two other of his disciples.

3 Simon Peter saith unto them, I go a fishing. They say unto him, We also go with thee. They went forth, and entered into a ship immediately; and that night they caught nothing.

4 But when the morning was now come, Jesus stood on the shore: but the disciples knew not that it was Jesus.

5 Then Jesus saith unto them, Children, have ye any meat? They answered him, No.

6 And he said unto them, Cast the net on the right side of the ship, and ye shall find. They cast therefore, and now they were not able to draw it for the multitude of fishes.

7 Therefore that disciple whom Jesus loved saith unto Peter, It is the Lord. Now when Simon Peter heard that it was the Lord, he girt his fisher's coat unto him, (for he was naked,) and did cast himself into the sea.

8 And the other disciples came in a little ship; (for they were not far from land, but as it were two hundred cubits,) dragging the net with fishes.

9 As soon then as they were come to land, they saw a fire of coals there, and fish laid thereon, and bread.

10 Jesus saith unto them, Bring of the fish which ye have now caught.

11 Simon Peter went up, and drew the net to land full of great fishes, an hundred and fifty and three: and for all there were so many, yet was not the net broken.

12 Jesus saith unto them, Come and dine. And none of the disciples durst ask him, Who art thou? knowing that it was the Lord.

13 Jesus then cometh, and taketh bread, and giveth them, and fish likewise.

14 This is now the third time that Jesus shewed himself to his disciples, after that he was risen from the dead.

KEY VERSE

Jesus saith unto them, Come and dine. And none of the disciples durst ask him, Who art thou? knowing that it was the Lord. —**John 21:12**

ACKNOWLEDGING GOD

Unit 2: All Glory and Honor
LESSONS 5–9

LESSON AIMS

After participating in this lesson, each learner will be able to:

1. Recount the story of Jesus' appearance at the Sea of Galilee following His resurrection.

2. Identify elements of the story that reveal Jesus' constant provision for His followers.

3. Write a prayer of commitment to trust in Jesus' provision under all circumstances.

LESSON OUTLINE

Introduction
  A. No Job Too Big or Too Small
  B. Lesson Background
 I. Unhappy Result (JOHN 21:1-4)
  A. Fishermen at Work (vv. 1-3)
  B. Figure on the Shore (v. 4)
 II. Unforeseen Provision (JOHN 21:5-8)
  A. Specific Command (vv. 5, 6a)
  B. Surprising Result (v. 6b)
    Inconvenient Fishing
  C. Sudden Realization (vv. 7, 8)
 III. Unexpected Meal (JOHN 21:9-14)
  A. Food Shared (vv. 9-13)
    What We Need, When We Need It
  B. Faith Strengthened (v. 14)
Conclusion
  A. Presence and Provision
  B. Prayer
  C. Thought to Remember

Introduction

A. No Job Too Big or Too Small

One of the most widely used business slogans is "No job is too big or too small." Business people of all kinds want potential customers to hire them regardless of the circumstances. Is there so much to be done that you cannot even think where to begin? Call us! Is your task so small you cannot imagine someone bothering with it? Call us! But in fact, however, some jobs *are* too big or too small. How absurd to call a plumber to drain a large swamp or an exterminator to swat one fly.

Christians sometimes rule out certain matters as too big or too small for God. The evil and suffering of the world may seem so big that some may not believe that God can do much about it. Death is universal, the terror of human existence, the penalty for sin (Genesis 2:17). Some believe that God cannot overcome it. Meanwhile, our day-to-day needs may seem so trivial that we hesitate to "bother" God with them.

Today's text reminds us that for God no matter is too big or small. The apostle John's account of Jesus, raised from the dead and meeting His disciples by the Sea of Galilee, is a profound reminder that by Jesus' death and resurrection God is transforming our world to become what He always intended it to be and is overcoming the sin and death that infect our lives. In this story, Jesus surprises His disciples with a morning meal, a simple gesture that underlines His promise always to provide what they need.

B. Lesson Background

Today's text is the first part of an extended narrative detailing one of Jesus' appearances following His resurrection, an account recorded only by John. As the text opens, John has already recounted events from the day of the resurrection itself. Mary Magdalene, finding Jesus' tomb empty, told Simon Peter and "the other disciple" (apparently John himself) that Jesus' body had been taken (John 20:1, 2). The two rushed to the tomb to see for themselves (20:3-10). Then Jesus appeared to Mary, confirming that He was indeed raised from the dead (20:11-18).

Later that same day, the "first day of the week," Jesus appeared to His disciples in a locked room (John 20:19-23). He appeared to them again a week later, that time addressing Thomas, who had been absent before. That man needed and received personal, tangible evidence that Jesus really was alive (20:24-28).

The appearance to Thomas is, in certain ways, the climax of John's Gospel in light of Jesus' statement, "Because thou hast seen me, thou hast believed: blessed are they that have not seen, and yet have believed" (John 20:29). John then immediately informs us of the "many other signs" (miracles) that Jesus performed (20:30). These comprise the fabric of this Gospel. Understanding the meaning of these signs, readers can put their faith in the risen Jesus whom they have not seen (20:31).

That purpose statement could be a good place for this Gospel to conclude. But there is yet a bit of unfinished business with the apostles in general and Peter in particular.

I. Unhappy Result
(JOHN 21:1-4)
A. Fishermen at Work (vv. 1-3)

1. After these things Jesus shewed himself again to the disciples at the sea of Tiberias; and on this wise shewed he himself.

We come to the final post-resurrection appearance of Jesus that is recorded in the Gospel of John. The general description *after these things* refers to the unspecified amount of time between the previous appearances in and near Jerusalem and the one that takes place *at the sea of Tiberias,*

HOW TO SAY IT

Deuteronomy	Due-ter-*ahn*-uh-me.
Didymus	*Did*-uh-mus.
Galilee	*Gal*-uh-lee.
Magdalene	*Mag*-duh-leen or Mag-duh-*lee*-nee.
Nathanael	Nuh-*than*-yull (*th* as in *thin*).
Nazareth	*Naz*-uh-reth.
Tiberias	Tie-*beer*-ee-us.
Zebedee	*Zeb*-eh-dee.

which is another name for the Sea of Galilee (John 6:1; compare Luke 5:1).

This body of water is a large freshwater lake of about sixty-four square miles. It is the dominant feature of the region where Jesus grew up and conducted much of His ministry. It was was along the shore of this lake that Jesus called His first disciples (Matthew 4:18-22). Those disciples were eyewitnesses of the miracles Jesus performed in the area, including four involving the lake itself: the calming the storm (Matthew 8:23-27; Mark 4:37-41; Luke 8:22-25), the first catch of fish (Luke 5:1-7); walking on the water (Matthew 14:25; Mark 6:48-51; John 6:16-21), and a coin in a fish's mouth (Matthew 17:27).

With Passover and the Feast of Unleavened Bread now complete (John 19:14), some of the disciples have arrived back in this familiar territory (see Mark 14:28; 16:7). The walking distance from Jerusalem is about 70 miles.

2. There were together Simon Peter, and Thomas called Didymus, and Nathanael of Cana in Galilee, and the sons of Zebedee, and two other of his disciples.

Seven men other than Jesus are present: three are named, two are unnamed but identifiable, and *two other of his disciples* who are unidentifiable. The mention first of *Simon Peter* is fully consistent with his name appearing first in the listings of the twelve in Matthew 10:2-4; Mark 3:16-19; Luke 6:13-16; and Acts 1:13. It is not uncommon in the New Testament for people to be known by more than one name, and Peter is one of those (compare John 1:42). *Thomas called Didymus* is another; the Aramaic word *Thomas* and the Greek word *Didymus* both mean "twin." Popularly known today as "doubting Thomas" (see the Lesson Background), he is a man of courage (see John 11:16).

Nathanael of Cana in Galilee is mentioned toward the beginning of John's Gospel, when Peter and others first encounter Jesus (John 1:35-42). When confronted with Jesus' divine power, he exclaimed that Jesus was truly God's promised king of Israel (v. 49). Cana is the site of Jesus' first miracle (2:1-11), undoubtedly witnessed by Nathanael. One theory is that Nathanael is another name for Bartholomew (Mark 3:18). If that theory is correct, then Nathanael is one of the original 12 apostles.

The sons of Zebedee are James and John. Along with Peter and his brother Andrew, they are among the fishermen whom Jesus had called to follow Him (Mark 1:16-20). With Peter they were invited as witnesses to Jesus' raising of a dead girl (5:35-43), Jesus' transfiguration (9:2-8), and His prayers in Gethsemane before His death (14:32-42).

James and John are not named in John's Gospel and are mentioned explicitly only in the account before us. An ancient and widely affirmed explanation for this is that John is the author of this account, elsewhere humbly calling himself the "disciple whom Jesus loved" to emphasize that his place in the story comes only because of Jesus' gracious love (John 13:23; 19:26; 21:7).

3. Simon Peter saith unto them, I go a fishing. They say unto him, We also go with thee. They went forth, and entered into a ship immediately; and that night they caught nothing.

Some have interpreted Peter's announcement to be an expression of impatience or despair, a sign that he is returning to the old way of life from which Jesus had called him. But the text does not support this as the sole or even the best interpretation. Peter may simply be hungry, or he may want to retain a means of self-support, not knowing what the Lord intends for him personally. The others decide to join him. Fishing is generally done at *night*, when fish are nearer the water's surface and so that fish can be sold fresh the next morning. But as was the case previously, he fishes all night without a catch (Luke 5:5).

B. Figure on the Shore (v. 4)

4. But when the morning was now come, Jesus stood on the shore: but the disciples knew not that it was Jesus.

Some readers find it implausible that the disciples do not recognize Jesus. But dim light and long distance surely account for this fact. Further, the disciples may not be expecting to see the risen Jesus in this particular setting. In Luke 24:16, part of another account of a resurrection appearance, Jesus seems deliberately to prevent His identity from being known. That may also be the case here.

II. Unforeseen Provision
(JOHN 21:5-8)
A. Specific Command (vv. 5, 6a)

5. Then Jesus saith unto them, Children, have ye any meat? They answered him, No.

Jesus calls out as an older man might speak to friends for whom he is concerned. Notably, the Greek text indicates that Jesus already anticipates the answer to His question: "You do not have any fish, do you?" The fishermen, undoubtedly tired and hungry from a night of repeatedly casting their nets, acknowledge that they do not.

6a. And he said unto them, Cast the net on the right side of the ship, and ye shall find.

Now Jesus speaks as much more than just a sympathetic onlooker. His instructions are specific, as they were in Luke 5:4. There the fishermen were to "launch out into the deep"; here they are to *cast the net on the right side of the ship*.

B. Surprising Result (v. 6b)

6b. They cast therefore, and now they were not able to draw it for the multitude of fishes.

The result is immediate and overwhelming as zero fish are replaced by a *multitude of fishes* (numbered in John 21:11 as 153). This outcome closely resembles what happened when Jesus previously challenged Peter to let down his nets one more time after an unproductive night (Luke 5:4-7).

> *What Do You Think?*
> In what ways can this verse encourage believers today?
> *Talking Points for Your Discussion*
> - In how we see past and current situations in light of each other
> - In how we anticipate the future

◆ *INCONVENIENT FISHING* ◆

A young Muslim man left his home in central Asia to study at a university in the U.S. Before classes even began, he suffered a brain aneurysm that almost took his life. He survived the aneurysm, but needed several surgeries over the course of the next year.

A friend from his hometown who was living in the U.S. cared for him. A local church heard about his plight and chipped in to help with the staggering medical bills. High school students from the church visited and helped him learn English. The young Muslim could have been ignored by Christians. Instead, Christians became Jesus' hands and feet in providing the care he needed.

We fulfill the Great Commission (Matthew 28:19, 20) as we become "fishers of men" (4:19). But not all "fish" are easy catches. The success of those fishing in John 21:6 came after they had caught nothing all night. They had only blistered hands and sore muscles to show for their efforts. When advised to "cast the net on the right side of the ship," everything in their experience probably said that such an action would be pointless. But they obeyed in faith, and a magnificent catch of fish was their reward.

The young Muslim man began learning about Jesus as Christians met his needs. Will he be captured permanently in the net of God's love in Christ? We pray so, but ultimately it's up to the man himself. Our task is to cast the net as the Savior desires. Will you be ready to do so, even at the most inconvenient times when you're the most worn out?   —L. M. W.

C. Sudden Realization (vv. 7, 8)

7. Therefore that disciple whom Jesus loved saith unto Peter, It is the Lord. Now when Simon Peter heard that it was the Lord, he girt his fisher's coat unto him, (for he was naked,) and did cast himself into the sea.

The *disciple whom Jesus loved* is, by traditional reckoning, the apostle John, author of this Gospel. He is the first to realize that the one who has just provided a huge catch of fish can only be the one who has command of the forces of nature. His declaration *It is the Lord* is the basis for Peter's spontaneous act of swimming and wading to shore to meet the Lord.

This personality difference is also seen in John 20. "The other disciple, whom Jesus loved" (20:2) had rushed with Peter to Jesus' tomb after Mary Magdalene's report. Peter was the first to enter the tomb although he had arrived second (20:3-

Visual for Lesson 6. *As you discuss John 21:7, point to this visual as you ask, "What first caused you to recognize Jesus for who He is?"*

7). Eventually "that other disciple" overcame his caution and also entered the tomb, where "he saw, and believed" (20:8); Peter's state of belief is left unrecorded. It seems in both cases that John is the one with greater insight while Peter is the one with greater propensity to act.

What Peter does first upon hearing *It is the Lord* may be confusing, since it can seem that he puts on more clothes before jumping *into the sea*! We should probably understand that he has been lightly clothed in a smock worn by fishermen (the word translated *naked* can mean "lightly clothed"), but that the garment is loose around his body. To *girt* this garment is to secure it close to his body so it does not interfere with swimming or wading.

> *What Do You Think?*
>   What can we do to ensure a consistently genuine witness in the presence of fellow believers?
> *Talking Points for Your Discussion*
>   • When gathered for Bible study
>   • When gathered for prayer
>   • When gathered for worship
>   • When participating in service projects
>   • Other

8. And the other disciples came in a little ship; (for they were not far from land, but as it were two hundred cubits,) dragging the net with fishes.

The distance to shore is not so great that Peter cannot swim to shore. (*Two hundred cubits* is about a hundred yards.) The close proximity to the shore also helped the six other disciples cooperate to drag the net to shore, as they may have been unable to empty its contents into the bottom of the boat as was the usual practice. The Lord's provision is abundant, yet within their capacity to receive it.

III. Unexpected Meal
(JOHN 21:9-14)
A. Food Shared (vv. 9-13)

9. As soon then as they were come to land, they saw a fire of coals there, and fish laid thereon, and bread.

Those who come in from fishing for their breakfast would not expect someone on shore to have a breakfast of cooked fish ready for them! That is all the more so when considering that *a fire of coals* requires considerable time to heat fully. But the Lord who directed the fish to the fishermen's net is also the Lord who fed the hungry multitudes with a scant amount of bread and fish (John 6:1-15). He is able to provide for His people in both large and small ways that astonish.

10. Jesus saith unto them, Bring of the fish which ye have now caught.

The disciples may be in something of a state of shock at this point. People in such a state may wonder what to do next. Jesus has the answer.

11. Simon Peter went up, and drew the net to land full of great fishes, a hundred and fifty and three: and for all there were so many, yet was not the net broken.

We may wonder how far *Simon Peter* makes it toward Jesus before turning back to help with *the net . . . full of great fishes*. The text does not say. However, the text does specify the number of fish and further implies that the net should break under the weight and volume of so many but does not. Readers also wonder about the significance of the specific number 153. Perhaps the reason for its inclusion is to highlight the impact of the miracle.

Jesus has called His disciples to be "fishers of men" (Matthew 4:18, 19). He has told them that as the Father had sent Him, so He was sending them (John 17:18; 20:21). But how can this undistinguished band, so often marked by weak faith and failure, undertake such a task? The miraculous catch of fish points to the answer. By themselves, these men are inadequate. But empowered by the Spirit of Christ (16:7-11), they will do great things (14:12-14). Abiding in Jesus, relying on His provision, they will bear much fruit (15:1-11).

What Do You Think?
How did a time of God's unexpected provision prepare you for future service?
Talking Points for Your Discussion
- Regarding a provision of finances
- Regarding a provision of emotional support
- Regarding a provision of Bible understanding
- Other

12. Jesus saith unto them, Come and dine. And none of the disciples durst ask him, Who art thou? knowing that it was the Lord.

The Lord is host of this feast, and all present are His welcome guests. Gone is the doubt that had plagued Thomas and others. All recognize their host as the sovereign Lord who commands the elements and the creatures that dwell in them. He is the one who was dead but is now gloriously alive again. They will testify with confidence about Him, bringing multitudes and generations who have not seen to believe in what they have seen.

What Do You Think?
How would things change were we to acknowledge Christ as host and center of mealtimes?
Talking Points for Your Discussion
- Regarding mealtime conversations
- Regarding mealtime priorities
- Regarding dinner invitations
- Other

13. Jesus then cometh, and taketh bread, and giveth them, and fish likewise.

Jesus' actions are described in a manner that highlights the meal as His gracious provision for

His followers. As He did with the multitude, He distributes the *bread* and *fish* himself (John 6:11). It is a simple meal, one typical for the times, but also an abundant meal, with plenty for everyone.

◆ WHAT WE NEED, WHEN WE NEED IT ◆

As a child growing up in Zimbabwe, Isaac saw the graves of American missionaries who had died bringing the gospel to his people. He decided to be a missionary to the U.S. in gratitude to those who had sacrificed for him.

He was accepted to attend a seminary in America, but he needed visas. When he took his paperwork to the American embassy, he discovered that they would give visas to him and his wife, but not to their children. Not wanting to move without them, he declined the offer and went home.

The next day he sensed a divine pull to return to the embassy, even though he had no appointment. As Isaac sat down with the official who had interviewed him the day before, the ambassador walked in, looked at Isaac, and told the interviewer to give Isaac whatever he wanted. Isaac walked out with visas for himself, his wife, and their children!

Today, Isaac continues to take steps in faith, and God continues to provide. Isaac doesn't know where the funds for each step will come from, but God never lets him down. Sometimes God provides for us in big ways (John 21:11), sometimes in small (21:13). But faith to follow the Lord's leading must come first (21:6). Is lack of faith a challenge for you?
—L. M. W.

B. Faith Strengthened (v. 14)

14. This is now the third time that Jesus shewed himself to his disciples, after that he was risen from the dead.

The enumeration *the third time* counts the appearances in John 20:19-23 and 20:24-29 as the first and second of Jesus' post-resurrection appearances, respectively, *to his disciples*. But wait—what about the appearance to Mary Magdalene in John 20:11-18? Has John gotten his count wrong?

The answer is *no*, and the key lies in the phrase *to his disciples*. The word *disciples* is plural, whereas Jesus' appearance to Mary Magdalene represents an encounter with an individual. Further, the accounts by other Bible writers record additional appearances, including the mention of an appearance to Peter individualy.

Jesus' resurrection was no illusion, no mere visionary experience in the minds and hearts of His followers. It was an unexpected, life-transforming event in real space and time. It altered the flow of history as it fulfilled the most important promises of God. The resurrection accounts of John and the others demonstrate how real and powerful was and is the resurrection of Jesus.

What Do You Think?
How would you describe the reality and power of Jesus' resurrection in your life?
Talking Points for Your Discussion
- In terms of how it affects your relationships with fellow believers
- In terms of how it affects your relationships with unbelievers

---

Conclusion

A. Presence and Provision

Christ's presence with and provision for Christians are constant. Whether our lives are easy, hard, or somewhere in between, He is with us. Whether our faith feels strong, shaken, or somewhere in between, He never fails or forsakes us.

Jesus is not present in the flesh as He was for the disciples. But as He rules from Heaven and empowers by His Spirit, He is no less present with us than He was with them. Are we ready to acknowledge these facts, ready to receive what He gives, and ready to testify to His constant provision?

B. Prayer

Father, may we acknowledge daily that You are with us, providing for our every need and empowering us to fulfill Your every task. May Your rule in the world find an anchor in our hearts. We pray in Jesus' name. Amen.

C. Thought to Remember

Jesus provides, now and forevermore.

INVOLVEMENT LEARNING

Enhance your lesson with KJV Bible Student (from your curriculum supplier) and the reproducible activity page (at www.standardlesson.com or in the back of the KJV Standard Lesson Commentary Deluxe Edition).

Into the Lesson

Give each person a sheet of paper and a pen. Challenge them to look back over their lives and create a line graph depicting three highs and three lows they've experienced. Have them label significant events and give approximate years when those things took place (examples: graduating from school, joining the military, birth of a child, loss of a parent, career change). Prepare a graph of your own before class. Have learners work quickly.

Ask for volunteers to share a low point, but don't put anyone on the spot. Be prepared to share one of your own. Discuss emotions experienced at those points, whether the volunteer was tempted to give up, and what kept him or her going.

Alternative. Distribute copies of the "Famous Failures" activity from the reproducible page, which you can download. Have students complete it in small groups.

After either activity, transition to the Bible lesson by saying, "Sometimes life seems painful, unproductive, or even humdrum. Though Peter may have doubted his value as a follower and representative of Jesus, this appearance of the risen Lord would have dispelled those thoughts."

Into the Word

Divide the class into three groups. Supply each group with a marker, sheets of paper, and one of the following assignments. Groups are to read portions of today's text and create "thought bubbles" to explore potential thoughts of the people in that text. Some possible responses follow.

Group 1—John 21:1-5
Peter: *I'm not sure what the future holds, so I'm going to clear my head by going fishing.*
Disciples: *What else do we have to do? Let's go with Peter!*

Group 2—John 21:6-9
Disciples when told where to cast their nets:
Who is that who thinks he knows our business?

The "disciple whom Jesus loved" (John):
Nobody could do this but Jesus!

Group 3—John 21:10-14
Jesus: *They still need to believe that I have risen.*
Any disciple: *Somebody should say something, but it won't be me!*

After groups have created two or three thought bubbles each, work through the lesson text as a class. First, have a member of Group 1 read verses 1-5 slowly. At appropriate points, have group members hold up a thought bubble. Explore the possible mind-sets of Peter and the other disciples regarding their uncertainty about what the future held.

Repeat this process with Group 2 and verses 6-9. Compare and contrast the text with the similar situation in Luke 5:1-11.

Repeat this process with Group 3 and verses 10-14. Note that the disciples' full understanding of the implications of the resurrection was still incomplete and would remain so at least until the ascension (use Acts 1:6 as evidence for incomplete understanding). Point out that eating a meal with the disciples proved that Jesus was not a ghost or vision (compare Luke 24:39-43).

After this activity, ask, "When feeling lost, where do people find purpose and direction? The disciples discovered (and had to rediscover) that Jesus was the one who could provide both."

Into Life

Ask students to review the graphs created at the beginning of the lesson, if you used that activity. Invite them to discuss times when they sensed the presence of God strongly and how that presence affected them.

Alternative: Distribute copies of the "Forever Faithful" activity. Have students work individually or in small groups to personalize Scriptures that describe the faithfulness of our Lord. After either activity, have students write prayers of commitment to trust in Jesus' provision always.

FOLLOW ME

DEVOTIONAL READING: Matthew 10:5-15
BACKGROUND SCRIPTURE: John 21:15-25

JOHN 21:15-25

15 So when they had dined, Jesus saith to Simon Peter, Simon, son of Jonas, lovest thou me more than these? He saith unto him, Yea, Lord; thou knowest that I love thee. He saith unto him, Feed my lambs.

16 He saith to him again the second time, Simon, son of Jonas, lovest thou me? He saith unto him, Yea, Lord; thou knowest that I love thee. He saith unto him, Feed my sheep.

17 He saith unto him the third time, Simon, son of Jonas, lovest thou me? Peter was grieved because he said unto him the third time, Lovest thou me? And he said unto him, Lord, thou knowest all things; thou knowest that I love thee. Jesus saith unto him, Feed my sheep.

18 Verily, verily, I say unto thee, When thou wast young, thou girdest thyself, and walkedst whither thou wouldest: but when thou shalt be old, thou shalt stretch forth thy hands, and another shall gird thee, and carry thee whither thou wouldest not.

19 This spake he, signifying by what death he should glorify God. And when he had spoken this, he saith unto him, Follow me.

20 Then Peter, turning about, seeth the disciple whom Jesus loved following; which also leaned on his breast at supper, and said, Lord, which is he that betrayeth thee?

21 Peter seeing him saith to Jesus, Lord, and what shall this man do?

22 Jesus saith unto him, If I will that he tarry till I come, what is that to thee? follow thou me.

23 Then went this saying abroad among the brethren, that that disciple should not die: yet Jesus said not unto him, He shall not die; but, If I will that he tarry till I come, what is that to thee?

24 This is the disciple which testifieth of these things, and wrote these things: and we know that his testimony is true.

25 And there are also many other things which Jesus did, the which, if they should be written every one, I suppose that even the world itself could not contain the books that should be written. Amen.

KEY VERSE

Simon, son of Jonas, lovest thou me more than these? He saith unto him, Yea, Lord; thou knowest that I love thee. He saith unto him, Feed my lambs. —**John 21:15**

Acknowledging God

Unit 2: All Glory and Honor

Lessons 5–9

Lesson Aims

After participating in this lesson, each learner will be able to:

1. Summarize the conversation between the risen Jesus and Peter at the Sea of Galilee.

2. Explain the relationship between loving Jesus and imitating His gracious love and service.

3. Demonstrate the gracious, self-sacrificial love of Jesus in one or more situations in the week ahead.

Lesson Outline

Introduction
  A. The Comeback Kid
  B. Lesson Background: Synonyms
  C. Lesson Background: Shepherds
 I. Repeated Exchange (John 21:15-17)
  A. First (v. 15)
  B. Second (v. 16)
    Called to Sacrifice
  C. Third (v. 17)
 II. Solemn Prophecy (John 21:18, 19)
  A. Unwelcome News (v. 18)
  B. Warm Invitation (v. 19)
 III. Refocused Challenge (John 21:20-22)
  A. Wrong Focus (vv. 20, 21)
  B. Right Focus (v. 22)
    The English Chinese Man
 IV. Witness's Declaration (John 21:23-25)
  A. False Rumor (v. 23)
  B. True Testimony (vv. 24, 25)
Conclusion
  A. Rising to the Challenge
  B. Prayer
  C. Thought to Remember

Introduction

A. The Comeback Kid

Most football fans will recognize the name Joe Montana. Montana was a star quarterback for the University of Notre Dame during the late 1970s. He then played professional football, spending most of his career with the San Francisco 49ers. He won four Super Bowls with the 49ers and was named Most Valuable Player in three of those games. He became known as the Comeback Kid because of his reputation for leading his team from behind to some dramatic victories. He guided his teams to 31 come-from-behind triumphs during his professional career.

Simon Peter was a broken man following his denial of Jesus; he "wept bitterly" at having done so (Matthew 26:75). We can only imagine how often his thoughts tormented him in the aftermath of Jesus' crucifixion. But the resurrected Jesus offered Peter the opportunity to make a "comeback." Accepting that opportunity meant leaving remorse and shame behind as he entered a place of renewed service to the Master. Jesus' words of restoration and His challenge of service to Peter have something to teach us yet today.

B. Lesson Background: Synonyms

Today's lesson considers the final 11 verses of John's Gospel. The immediate background is the 14 verses of John 21:1-14, which was last week's lesson. A further item of background to consider in relation to this week's text specifically is a caution in how we interpret the Gospel writer's use of synonyms and near synonyms.

Noticing that the writer used two Greek words that are translated "love," two translated "sheep," two for the care given to sheep, and two for "know," readers over the years have tried to determine what point John was making by using different words. But there is scant evidence that John intended anything significant by this variety.

For example, when considering the Gospel of John as a whole, we see the different Greek verbs translated "love" used interchangeably in John 3:35; 5:20; 11:5, 36. It is therefore more likely that John used different words stylistically, perhaps to avoid monotonous repetition. We do the same thing by using words like *cat* and *feline* interchangeably. We may also think of *welcoming* and *hospitable*; *automobile* and *car*; *desire* and *want*; etc.

C. Lesson Background: Shepherds

The image of a shepherd caring for sheep is central to our text. This was an image very close to the experience of biblical people, drawing as it does on a common occupation. The Old Testament uses sheep and shepherd to picture the relationship between God and His people, most notably in Psalm 23. The relationship between God's people and their leaders, especially the king, was portrayed in similar terms. Israel could be described as sheep with no shepherd (Numbers 27:15-17; 1 Kings 22:17), and wicked leaders of the people were characterized as bad shepherds (Jeremiah 23:1-4; 50:6; Ezekiel 34:1-10).

The picture of sheep without a shepherd is also used of the people in Jesus' day (Matthew 9:36). Jesus described himself as "the good shepherd" (John 10:11), contrasting himself with those "thieves and robbers" who had no concern for the welfare of the sheep (10:8-10). Jesus went beyond what an ordinary shepherd would do, even giving His own life for the sake of His sheep (10:11, 17, 18). His exchange with Peter in today's text should be understood against this backdrop.

I. Repeated Exchange

(JOHN 21:15-17)

A. First (v. 15)

15a. So when they had dined, Jesus saith to Simon Peter, Simon, son of Jonas, lovest thou me more than these?

The *they* are the seven of John 21:2 plus Jesus (see last week's lesson). The shared meal eventually gives way to a one-on-one conversation between Jesus and Peter. Jesus addresses Peter formally, using his given name *Simon* and the name of his father, which functions like a surname does today.

Jesus' question creates its own question for the reader: What does the word *these* refer to? Does *more than these* mean, "Do you love me more than

these nets and boats, than your old life of fishing?" Does it mean, "Do you love me more than you love these other people?" Or does it mean, "Do you love me more than these other people love me?" An answer is impossible to gain from what the text says. We may conclude that Jesus means *these* as a general point of reference: "Do you love me supremely, most of all?"

15b. He saith unto him, Yea, Lord; thou knowest that I love thee.

Peter's answer is strongly affirmative, but worded in an interesting way. Before Jesus' death, Peter expressed bold confidence that he was willing to give his own life for Jesus' sake. But Jesus countered that Peter would in fact deny Him three times before the rooster crowed (John 13:37, 38). Jesus knew better than Peter what was in Peter's heart. Now Peter acknowledges Jesus' awareness of his inner life. Peter's statement of love for Jesus is also a confession that he no longer has anything to hide from his Lord.

15c. He saith unto him, Feed my lambs.

Jesus then challenges Peter to act on the love that he proclaims. As the Good Shepherd, Jesus has laid down His life for the sheep (John 10:15). If Peter loves Jesus, he will live in the same way, protecting and providing for God's people as Jesus' under-shepherd. It is most interesting that in Peter's first epistle, he charges elders to serve as nurturing, protecting shepherds under the supreme shepherd, Jesus (1 Peter 5:1-4).

What Do You Think?
What diagnostic questions can we ask to ensure lesser loves do not displace love for Jesus?
Talking Points for Your Discussion
- Regarding finances and possessions
- Regarding time and leisure
- Regarding passions and priorities
- Other

B. Second (v. 16)

16. He saith to him again the second time, Simon, son of Jonas, lovest thou me? He saith unto him, Yea, Lord; thou knowest that I love thee. He saith unto him, Feed my sheep.

With only slight variation, the exchange is repeated: question, answer, challenge. We imagine that Peter is puzzled to be asked a question he has already answered! Once more, however, he expresses his *love* for Jesus; and Jesus responds with a challenge similar to the first: *Feed my sheep*.

> **What Do You Think?**
> In what ways can you personally accept the challenge to feed Jesus' sheep?
>
> *Talking Points for Your Discussion*
> - Identifying aspects of the challenge that applied only to apostles, if any
> - Concerning aspects of the challenge that apply only to church leaders, if any
> - Concerning aspects of the challenge that apply to all Christians

◆ CALLED TO SACRIFICE ◆

Ann and her family moved to a developing country to live for nine months. While ministering there, they experienced the economic devastation of the culture. Basic necessities were in short supply. She washed clothes by hand, cooked meals without proper ingredients, and endured frequent power outages. When the time to leave came, Ann left happily, ready to be back in her own home.

After their return, however, Ann noticed that part of her husband's heart remained back in their host country. He sensed that God was opening the door for them to return, calling them back to feed God's sheep there. Ann, however, did not want to return to a place of such hardship. Yet her husband's sense of God's calling only grew. Finally, she agreed, and they moved back, remaining for several years.

The apostle Peter was married (Matthew 8:14). His wife's reaction to his calling to feed God's sheep is not recorded in Scripture. Perhaps her decision was a bit like Ann's. "I realized that I could insist on my way, and my husband would relent," Ann said. "But I'd live knowing that I had kept him from doing what God wanted him to do. Now I'm glad I didn't." Everyone has a sacrifice to make, and each person's sacrifice is different. What's yours?　　　　　—L. M. W.

C. Third (v. 17)

17a. He saith unto him the third time, Simon, son of Jona, lovest thou me? Peter was grieved because he said unto him the third time, Lovest thou me?

If this were a court of law, Peter's defense attorney might object "Asked and answered! Move on!" For Peter to be *grieved* at this repetition is understandable. Does Jesus doubt his answer? Is Jesus questioning his loyalty? Or is Peter's distress the result of seeing a connection between these three exchanges and his three denials of Jesus (John 18:15-18, 25-27)?

17b. And he said unto him, Lord, thou knowest all things; thou knowest that I love thee.

Peter expands on his previous responses by confessing not just that Jesus knows his inner thoughts but that He knows *all things*. Jesus' knowledge is not just exceptional. It is the kind of knowledge that God alone has. John has previously stated that Jesus knew what was inside a person (John 2:25).

17c. Jesus saith unto him, Feed my sheep.

For a third time Jesus repeats the command that flows out of Peter's confession of supreme love. The challenge is unchanged: Peter is to put his love into action as he leads God's people, with Jesus as his example of the good shepherd.

The scope of Jesus' grace is demonstrated by this repeated exchange. Without prior warning or explanation, Jesus has given Peter the opportunity to declare openly three times what he had denied three times during Jesus' trials. But Jesus is not finished with Peter.

> **What Do You Think?**
> How has an experience of a "second chance" from God shaped you? How should it?
>
> *Talking Points for Your Discussion*
> - Regarding attitude changes
> - Regarding priority adjustments
> - Regarding relationships
> - Other

II. Solemn Prophecy

(John 21:18, 19)

A. Unwelcome News (v. 18)

18a. Verily, verily, I say unto thee.

The expression *verily, verily* is a favorite of John's, occurring 25 times in his Gospel but never in the Gospels of Matthew, Mark, and Luke. It emphasizes the absolute certainty of what follows. Jesus used the same expression when he warned Peter of his coming denial (John 13:38). Now Jesus uses it to preface a different kind of warning.

18b. When thou wast young, thou girdedst thyself, and walkedst whither thou wouldest: but when thou shalt be old, thou shalt stretch forth thy hands, and another shall gird thee, and carry thee whither thou wouldest not.

Grown, able-bodied people, especially the *young*, tend to be independent—they usually are willing and able to do things for themselves, things such as dressing themselves (*girdest thyself*). This has characterized Peter's life to this point.

But in the future, Jesus declares, when Peter is *old*, he will not tie his own garment but will instead be tied up and led against his will. This is an unmistakable prophetic warning that Peter will be arrested and bound, his hands stretched out as a prisoner who will be taken to wherever his captors desire, as Jesus was (John 18:12, 13).

Jesus has told His followers that if the world has hated Him, the world will also hate them (John 15:18-21; 16:1-4). That warning is now personalized to Peter. Peter's life will reflect his Lord's. But though Jesus' words are solemn, they are not hopeless.

B. Warm Invitation (v. 19)

19a. This spake he, signifying by what death he should glorify God.

John removes any doubt about the meaning of Jesus' words: they predict Peter's arrest and execution. But this is no mere tragedy. Peter's *death* will *glorify God*. Jesus has previously spoken of His own death in just this way (John 12:23-28). This means that those who follow Him must be prepared to do so at the cost of their lives. It is in giving one's life that one truly receives life from God (12:25, 26). Peter's looming imprisonment and death are not a sentence of doom but a call to embrace the greatest purpose for which one can live life: to glorify God.

19b. And when he had spoken this, he saith unto him, Follow me.

As John's explanation ends, Jesus' words resume. He ends the prophetic warning with the command *follow me*. Peter was among the first to follow Jesus because of the testimony of John the Baptist and Peter's brother, Andrew (John 1:35-42). Now Jesus calls him to follow with a new perspective, understanding all the implications.

A very ancient tradition tells us that Peter indeed goes on to die a martyr's death as a prisoner in Rome. Some expressions of that tradition say that he was crucified, but by Peter's request he was crucified upside down so that his death would not too closely resemble the Lord's. It is clear that Peter will indeed do what he had earlier claimed: "I will lay down my life for thy sake" (John 13:37).

> **What Do You Think?**
> In what ways does Peter's reinstatement serve and not serve as a model for reinstatements to Christian service today?
> *Talking Points for Your Discussion*
> - Considering how forgiveness and consequences do and do not interrelate
> - Considering uniqueness of the apostles' roles
> - Considering the nature of the offense
> - Other

III. Refocused Challenge

(John 21:20-22)

A. Wrong Focus (vv. 20, 21)

20. Then Peter, turning about, seeth the disciple whom Jesus loved following; which also leaned on his breast at supper, and said, Lord, which is he that betrayeth thee?

Perhaps overwhelmed with the hard words that Jesus has just shared with him, Peter attempts to change the subject. Following behind Peter and Jesus at this moment is *the disciple whom Jesus loved*, traditionally understood as John, the author of this Gospel. The verse further makes reference to the fact that when the disciples were gathered in the upper room before Jesus' death, Peter had asked John to find out from Jesus the identity of Jesus' betrayer (John 13:23-26).

21. Peter seeing him saith to Jesus, Lord, and what shall this man do?

Having earlier asked John to pose a question to Jesus about another disciple, Peter now asks Jesus directly about John. If Peter will be arrested and killed, will his friend John as well? If both are followers of Jesus, hated by the world that hated Him, will they both suffer the same fate?

Peter's question may be motivated by fear, jealousy, uncertainty, or curiosity. The text does not reveal his state of mind. But it surely expresses faith in Jesus as the one who can supply the answer.

B. Right Focus (v. 22)

22. Jesus saith unto him, If I will that he tarry till I come, what is that to thee? follow thou me.

Jesus' reply refocuses Peter's thoughts on what Jesus has just charged him to do. What might happen in the future to others is not Peter's concern. It will not change Peter's situation, and it will in no way change the fulfillment of the Lord's promise to abide with His followers through the ongoing presence of the Holy Spirit (John 16:33).

Jesus has already spoken to His disciples about departing from the earth and returning someday (John 14:1-3). The furthest point to which a person's death might be delayed is Jesus' return. That time is unknown to any but God the Father (Matthew 24:36). So to put the other disciple's future out of Peter's reach, Jesus' rhetorical question has the effect of declaring that even if that disciple lives until Jesus comes, it is not Peter's concern. A Christian's focus is not to be on the future of fellow believers, but their own faithfulness.

Thus Jesus tells Peter a second time to *follow . . . me*. Peter's primary focus is to be on his response to the Lord's leading. To follow Jesus means not pursuing irrelevant matters (compare 1 Timothy 4:7; Titus 3:9) but rather serving as a shepherd cares for his sheep.

What Do You Think?
How do we walk the line between meeting the needs of others (feeding sheep) while not allowing their callings to distract us from ours?
Talking Points for Your Discussion
- When the feeding involves physical concerns
- When the feeding involves spiritual concerns

◆ *THE ENGLISH CHINESE MAN* ◆

In 1853, at the age of 21, Hudson Taylor became a missionary to China. Believing that the other missionaries spent too much time with Europeans and did not relate well with the Chinese people, Taylor began to dress in Chinese clothes and grew a long ponytail in imitation of Chinese men. His fellow missionaries disdained his attempts, but he maintained a good rapport with the Chinese people he loved so much.

At that time, foreigners were permitted to live only in coastal cities. But Taylor believed that all the Chinese needed to know about Jesus, so he began a movement to send missionaries inland, to more remote and dangerous regions. Despite criticism, he continued to recruit people for the work of his mission organization, China Inland Mission (now known as Overseas Missionary Fellowship).

Taylor struggled with depression in feeling the crushing need for missionaries, eventually suffering a physical and mental breakdown. But by then he had recruited hundreds of missionaries. His influence continues, as many believers study his life and become missionaries as well. Does that mean you should too? Not necessarily. The fact that Jesus had different plans for Peter and John is worth noting.   —L. M. W.

IV. Witness's Declaration
(JOHN 21:23-25)
A. False Rumor (v. 23)

23. Then went this saying abroad among the brethren, that that disciple should not die: yet Jesus said not unto him, He shall not die; but, If I will that he tarry till I come, what is that to thee?

Here the direct narration of the story ends, and reflection from John the author begins. There's an old saying among preachers that "anything you say that *can* be misunderstood, *will* be misunderstood." That seems to be the case here. Jesus' words to Peter are remembered and passed along. But somewhere along the line, an interpretation develops that Jesus promised *that that disciple* (John) would remain alive until Jesus returned. John points out that this is a false inference.

How interesting that the rumor that spreads from Jesus' declaration is much like Peter's own question: it reflects a concern to know about another person's future. By reminding readers of Jesus' true intent, John also reminds us of that to which all disciples of Jesus must give full attention: we are to focus on Him and His task for us.

B. True Testimony (vv. 24, 25)

24. This is the disciple which testifieth of these things, and wrote these things: and we know that his testimony is true.

Now the reflection widens in scope. The *disciple* of whom Peter inquired is the one who tells the story we have just read. Indeed, he is the source of the entire record in this Gospel. It is *his testimony* of what he has witnessed, in both signs and sayings. The testimony includes many things, including the vital fact that Jesus is Word become flesh (John 1:14). Amazing as this is, the testimony about it *is true*. John interrupted the narrative once before to make a statement of truthfulness (19:35). Now he does so again.

25. And there are also many other things which Jesus did, the which, if they should be written every one, I suppose that even the world itself could not contain the books that should be written. Amen.

After Thomas's confession of Jesus, John reminds the reader that Jesus performed "many other signs" not recorded in his Gospel (John 20:30). Now he makes a similar statement, emphasizing the magnitude of what Jesus did. As an eyewitness to Jesus' ministry, John realizes that he must be selective in his material; he can't record everything. But what John does provide in his record is sufficient to bring any reader to faith

Visual for Lesson 7. *Point to this visual as you ask, "How is the commission in John 21:15 like and unlike the one in Matthew 28:19, 20?"*

in Jesus. Indeed, that is the stated purpose of this Gospel (20:31).

Conclusion
A. Rising to the Challenge

Jesus' words to Peter are both reassuring and unsettling. They reassure us that anyone, even one who denies knowing Jesus, can be restored to fellowship with the Lord by His gracious forgiveness. But they are unsettling because they remind us of the opposition to the gospel. John experienced that opposition personally through his exile on the island of Patmos. There he wrote the Book of Revelation, describing himself as "your brother, and companion in tribulation" (Revelation 1:9).

Our response to Jesus' words to Peter needs to be what Peter's was: to rise to the challenge to follow Jesus and feed His sheep. Martyrdom may not be in our future. But giving our lives sacrificially in service to Jesus must still be the theme of our lives.

B. Prayer

Father, we belong to You only by Your grace, granted to us by Your Son's willing death on our behalf. Empower us, Lord, to follow Him and to feed His flock. We pray in Jesus' name. Amen.

C. Thought to Remember
Feed the flock while following the shepherd.

INVOLVEMENT LEARNING

Enhance your lesson with KJV Bible Student (from your curriculum supplier) and the reproducible activity page (at www.standardlesson.com or in the back of the KJV Standard Lesson Commentary Deluxe Edition).

Into the Lesson

Briefly discuss the missions your church supports. Talk about what each does and how your church supports it (financially, through prayer, etc.). Then move to a broader discussion, asking students to talk about what non-political causes they support personally or as a family. (Support doesn't have to be monetary. It could involve volunteer work, donating items, etc.) Have students explain why they support each cause and how they became involved.

Finally, invite students to talk about causes they want to support in the future. These could include existing groups or ideas for new causes students would like to champion. Discuss the reasons that these causes are so important to students, and the long-term implications they have.

Alternative: Distribute pens and copies of the "Go Fund Whom?" activity, which you can download. Have students work individually to determine which real-life causes they might support. Ask volunteers to explain why they would or would not support each cause.

After either activity say, "Popular causes give people a purpose in life—at least for a while. The disciples of Jesus, on the other hand, were enlisted in a cause that gave them eternal purpose."

Into the Word

Write the following incorrectly copied verses from today's lesson text on the board:

After they finished preaching, Jesus asked Simon Peter, "Lovest thou me more than thy family?" Peter replied, "Lord; thou believest that I love thee." Jesus shouted, "Feed my lambs."

Jesus avoided him again [saying], "Simon, obeyest thou me?" Peter sang, "Lord; thou forgettest that I obey thee." Jesus said, "Feed my dog."

A third time Jesus asked, "Simon, followest thou me?" Peter was annoyed and said, "Lord, thou knowest most things; thou knowest that I follow thee." Jesus said to Peter, "Herd my sheep."

This is the disciple which read about these things, and wrote these things: and we know that his testimony is hard to believe.

And this is a complete list of things which Jesus did.

Slowly read John 21:15-25 together as a class. Have the class make corrections to the miscopied verses on the board as needed.

Alternative: Distribute copies of the "Go Follow Him" activity. Have students work in small groups to unscramble key principles from the text.

After either activity, wrap up by saying, "Peter learned a lot about following Jesus after their breakfast! Jesus restored Peter, who had denied Him, by giving him a mission ('feed my sheep') and a direction ('follow me'). John reflected on all this by writing an accurate account of Jesus' ministry, yet certainly not all of it. When we take Jesus' "follow thou me" personally, what does that involve?" Allow free discussion.

Into Life

Begin by reading aloud Psalm 23. As you do so, encourage students to list the different ways that the shepherd in this psalm cares for his sheep. List them on the board.

Read aloud John 21:15. Then say, "Jesus calls Peter and all disciples to show their love for Him by taking care of His sheep. But as we do so, it is important that our hearts are in the right place. It is important that we not only know *what* to do as believers, but also that we know *why* we do those things."

Distribute paper and pens or pencils. Challenge each student to write two or three sentences on why he or she is a follower of Jesus. Allow one minute to work, then invite volunteers to read their reflections for the group.

THE LORD GOD ALMIGHTY

DEVOTIONAL READING: Revelation 19:1-8
BACKGROUND SCRIPTURE: Revelation 4

REVELATION 4:1-6, 8-11

1 After this I looked, and, behold, a door was opened in heaven: and the first voice which I heard was as it were of a trumpet talking with me; which said, Come up hither, and I will shew thee things which must be hereafter.

2 And immediately I was in the spirit: and, behold, a throne was set in heaven, and one sat on the throne.

3 And he that sat was to look upon like a jasper and a sardine stone: and there was a rainbow round about the throne, in sight like unto an emerald.

4 And round about the throne were four and twenty seats: and upon the seats I saw four and twenty elders sitting, clothed in white raiment; and they had on their heads crowns of gold.

5 And out of the throne proceeded lightnings and thunderings and voices: and there were seven lamps of fire burning before the throne, which are the seven Spirits of God.

6 And before the throne there was a sea of glass like unto crystal: and in the midst of the throne, and round about the throne, were four beasts full of eyes before and behind.

8 And the four beasts had each of them six wings about him; and they were full of eyes within: and they rest not day and night, saying, Holy, holy, holy, Lord God Almighty, which was, and is, and is to come.

9 And when those beasts give glory and honour and thanks to him that sat on the throne, who liveth for ever and ever,

10 The four and twenty elders fall down before him that sat on the throne, and worship him that liveth for ever and ever, and cast their crowns before the throne, saying,

11 Thou art worthy, O Lord, to receive glory and honour and power: for thou hast created all things, and for thy pleasure they are and were created.

KEY VERSE

Thou art worthy, O Lord, to receive glory and honour and power: for thou hast created all things, and for thy pleasure they are and were created. —**Revelation 4:11**

ACKNOWLEDGING GOD

Unit 2: All Glory and Honor

LESSONS 5–9

LESSON AIMS

After participating in this lesson, each learner will be able to:

1. Describe the content of John's vision in Revelation 4.

2. Explain the worship reality behind the text's symbols.

3. Specify one way to enhance his or her own approach to worship.

LESSON OUTLINE

Introduction

A. Thrones

The Royal Throne of Nepal is behind glass in the palace in Katmandu, for the palace is now a museum. The royal family of Nepal was massacred in 2001 and replaced by a constitutional government. The throne remains a symbol of the monarchy's once-revered status. Some see a risk in its preservation, for any restoration-of-monarchy movement in Nepal would likely want to use this throne for seating a new king. Thus it may be considered both a national treasure and a threat to democracy at the same time.

Today's lesson pictures Heaven in terms of a royal throne room. The one seated on the throne is the king of Heaven and earth. The ones allowed access into the throne room have a certain derivative honor based on their proximity. John's vision of this scene is overwhelming for him—almost indescribable. Yet he does his best to explain what he sees, and we are thereby rewarded when we consider his words.

B. Lesson Background

Many theories exist as to how Revelation should be interpreted. Some believe it is prophetic of future events, primarily those of the end times. Others think it presents a panorama of church history. Some believe Revelation is symbolically speaking of people and events from the first century, mainly those linked with the Roman Empire. Still others think that Revelation is entirely symbolic, a story that portrays the timeless struggle of good versus evil.

Whatever one's view, there are some important details about Revelation that should be kept in mind while studying the book. One concerns the historical setting of the book. The apostle John was exiled on the barren island of Patmos in the Aegean Sea because of his unwavering loyalty to Jesus (Revelation 1:9). Patmos was situated about 50 miles southwest of Ephesus, off the coast of modern Turkey. Ephesus was likely the city from which John was exiled. The church at Ephesus is the first of the seven churches addressed by Jesus in Revelation 1:11; 2:1–3:22.

The most probable time of writing is AD 90–96. It is remarkable that this elderly man was seen as such a threat to the Roman Empire that he would be banished in his 80s or 90s! He must have been a tireless and effective preacher.

In addition, we should remember that the book of Revelation is narrative, a story told by a narrator. This does not mean it is a fictional story. Much factual history is written in narrative style. John tells what he experiences: marvelous divine visions given to him in exile by Christ. The best way to read Revelation, then, is as a story with various scenes in which the content is connected. The primary overall message of the book is that despite how intense the opposition to God's people may be, in the end they triumph and evil is vanquished for eternity.

As today's lesson begins, John has already described himself "in the Spirit on the Lord's day" (Revelation 1:10). He then experienced a marvelous vision of "one like unto the Son of man" (1:12-16) just before receiving Jesus' messages to the seven churches in chapters 2 and 3. Chapter 4 opens up a new dimension of John's experiences.

I. Vision of Heaven
(Revelation 4:1, 2)
A. Open Door (v. 1)

1. After this I looked, and, behold, a door was opened in heaven: and the first voice which I heard was as it were of a trumpet talking with me; which said, Come up hither, and I will shew thee things which must be hereafter.

The Scriptures describe *heaven* as a place located above the earth, behind a covering described as

HOW TO SAY IT

Aegean	Ih-*jee*-un.
Chebar	*Kee*-bar.
Ephesus	*Ef*-uh-sus.
Ezekiel	Ee-*zeek*-ee-ul or Ee-*zeek*-yul.
ex nihilo (Latin)	eks **nee**-huh-*low*.
omnipotence	ahm-*ni*-puh-tents.
omniscience	ahm-*ni*-shuntz.
Patmos	*Pat*-muss.

the "firmament" (Genesis 1:7, 17; Ezekiel 1:26). This covering blocks any direct view of Heaven, so access requires Heaven to be *opened* (as in Luke 3:21). In John's vision, he is looking up into the sky; and he sees what appears to be an open *door*, an entry into Heaven itself.

This glimpse is marvelous all by itself, but John's account does not end there. John hears a *trumpet*-like voice inviting him to *come up*. This is identified as *the first voice*, therefore that of the risen Christ who previously spoke in a trumpet-like voice and then gave John the messages for the seven churches of Asia (Revelation 1:10, 11). The voice beckons John to join the speaker in Heaven. The speaker promises to reveal more *things* to the apostle, events that have yet to happen.

B. Majestic Throne (v. 2)

2. And immediately I was in the spirit: and, behold, a throne was set in heaven, and one sat on the throne.

In the Spirit as in Revelation 1:10, John's vision places him *in heaven* itself, and the first thing he sees is *a throne*. This probably means he is in a large room, for this would be the normal location for a throne.

Most people today don't think of thrones as possessing much significance. They are in museums, appearing to be little more than ornate and impractical chairs, inferior to our comfortable recliners. But in Bible times, thrones were more than expensive chairs for kings. Palaces had elaborate throne rooms that served as audience halls. The king would enter with pomp and ceremony (compare Acts 25:23). The throne was the king's seat of authority, recognized as such by all.

The phrase "the throne" could serve as a metaphor for the one who was authorized to sit on it (Genesis 41:40). Judgments issued from the throne were absolute. The throne was synonymous with royal power, and such is the case here.

The throne John sees is occupied. This indicates that the royal court of Heaven is in session; and the King has taken His seat. Something dramatic is about to happen, and we can imagine the anticipation John feels at his opportunity to witness it.

<table>
<tr><td>

What Do You Think?

What further steps can we take to conduct ourselves in light of the fact that God is King?

Talking Points for Your Discussion
- Regarding ways that others can see
- Regarding ways that others cannot see

</td></tr>
</table>

II. Arrangement of Heaven
(REVELATION 4:3-6a)
A. On the Throne (v. 3)

3a. And he that sat was to look upon like a jasper and a sardine stone.

We are to understand that the one on the throne is God, the King of Heaven. John can offer only comparisons to describe the scene before him. *Jasper* is a red stone that can be polished highly and is prized for its beauty. A *sardine stone* is also red in appearance. The imagery John uses to capture the radiance of God is that of precious jewels in all their brilliance.

3b. And there was a rainbow round about the throne, in sight like unto an emerald.

As is characteristic of the visions of John, he sees something familiar and different at the same time, something both known and gloriously unknown. The *rainbow round about the throne* is not the familiar multicolored kind. Rather, it reminds John of *an emerald* in having a brilliant shade of green. This is like no throne John has ever seen!

◆ THE CROWN JEWELS ◆

The famed Tower of London protects the crown jewels, the national treasures of the United Kingdom monarchy. The centuries-old collection features the Queen Mother's Crown, glistening with 2,800 diamonds. The dazzling display in the Jewel House is adorned with an impressive array of emeralds, rubies, and sapphires for the royal regalia, still in use today by Her Majesty for notable national ceremonies.

Assuredly these crown jewels rank as one of the world's most spectacular displays of beauty and brilliance. Yet, as John implies, the majesty of the King of kings far outshines any gemstone

ever seen. The glorious luster emanating from God and around His throne amazed John. No natural or man-made jewel will ever measure up to the stunning wonder of God and our eternal home.

While we may never see a resplendent storehouse of royal jewels this side of eternity, God reminds us that we are to focus our hearts on the "treasures in heaven" (Matthew 6:19-21). The true sovereign of all creation commands the attention and adoration of every living being. Jesus Christ is *the* crown jewel of our relationship with God. If we are able now to "worship the Lord in the beauty of holiness" (1 Chronicles 16:29), think how magnificent worship in heaven will be!   —B. J. L.

B. Around the Throne (v. 4)

4. And round about the throne were four and twenty seats: and upon the seats I saw four and twenty elders sitting, clothed in white raiment; and they had on their heads crowns of gold.

Twenty-four occupied *seats* now catch John's attention. In the Greek text, the word used for these chairs is the same word used for the throne of God. Since other Greek words for "places to sit" are available for John to use (see Matthew 21:12; 23:2), this can indicate that the occupants have a degree of royalty of their own. They surround the main throne, but are clearly lower in status and less glorious.

Although those who occupy the 24 thrones are wearing golden *crowns,* they are not called kings or princes. Instead, they are *elders,* a term used for leaders in the church or synagogue. The fact that they are religious rulers rather than political authorities is indicated by their *white raiment,* a sign of faith more than royalty. White robes identify the saved of the church in Heaven (Revelation 6:11; 7:13, 14).

The unexplained number 24 has been the subject of much debate. The book of Revelation often uses numbers in a symbolic way, letting them stand for certain people or objects. Generally speaking, the number 12 represents the people of God. This includes the 12 tribes of 12,000 each (Revelation 7:5-8) and the various references to 12 found in the description of the New Jerusalem (21:12, 14, 16, 21; 22:2).

The number 24, being double the number 12, may represent the people of God from both the Old and New Testaments. Israel, the covenant people of the Old Testament, was comprised of 12 tribes (Exodus 24:4; compare Revelation 21:12). The covenant people of the New Testament, Christians, are linked with the 12 apostles (Luke 6:13; compare Revelation 21:14), who comprise the foundation of the church (Ephesians 2:20). Jesus himself combines the idea of 12 tribes with 12 apostles in His description of the future (Matthew 19:28; Luke 22:30).

The 24 elders are not named nor is their function explained. But they do have an unforgettable role a few verses later.

> **What Do You Think?**
> When a church comes to view itself as people of the King, how should its members conduct themselves, individually and collectively?
> *Talking Points for Your Discussion*
> - In worship
> - In ministry priorities
> - In ministry leadership
> - Other

C. From the Throne (v. 5)

5a. And out of the throne proceeded lightnings and thunderings and voices.

The *lightnings and thunderings* John experiences find something of a parallel in the occasion when God descended upon Mount Sinai before the Israelites (Exodus 19:16-19). These details add to the splendor of the throne and the one seated upon it.

5b. And there were seven lamps of fire burning before the throne, which are the seven Spirits of God.

A more orderly type of lighting is positioned in the area *before the throne. Seven* is another important number in Revelation, signifying completeness or perfection. For example, the seven churches of Revelation indicate congregations known to John, but also symbolize the entirety of the church on earth.

John helps us with the symbolism here. The reference to *seven Spirits* does not require us to understand divisions or multiplicity in the Holy Spirit, but gives the sense of perfection and wholeness (as in Revelation 1:4). We see evidence and activity of the Holy Spirit on the earth among the people of the church, but in Heaven is the fullness of the Holy Spirit found.

> **What Do You Think?**
> What steps can we take to identify and eliminate things that work against the activity of the Holy Spirit in the here and now?
> *Talking Points for Your Discussion*
> - In terms of sin against the Spirit (Matthew 12:31, 32)
> - In terms of resistance to the Spirit (Acts 7:51)
> - In terms of what grieves the Spirit (Ephesians 4:30)
> - In terms of what quenches the Spirit (1 Thessalonians 5:19)

D. Before the Throne (v. 6a)

6a. And before the throne there was a sea of glass like unto crystal.

John's eyes move beyond the seven lamps to what looks like a large body of water. To most readers, this suggests an outdoor venue, but more likely it simply reflects the immensity and grandeur of the heavenly throne room.

The sea's characteristic *glass like unto crystal* can be subdivided into two parts: the glass aspect and the crystal aspect. Glass is a common material today, but is a luxury item in John's world. Yet the description *sea of glass* is not intended to emphasize the abundance of a costly thing. The emphasis, rather, is on the smooth calmness of the sea. The sea's being *like unto crystal,* for its part, emphasizes purity and transparency (Ezekiel 1:22; compare Revelation 15:2; 21:18).

III. Action in Heaven
(REVELATION 4:6b, 8-11)
A. Beasts Worship (vv. 6b, 8, 9)

6b. And in the midst of the throne, and round about the throne, were four beasts full of eyes before and behind.

John's attention returns to the throne, and he describes *four* creatures nearby. *Beasts* is a generic description that implies that while they may have human or angelic characteristics, they are not quite humans or angels. This sight is reminiscent of the four creatures seen by Ezekiel in his vision by the River Chebar (Ezekiel 1:3, 5; 10:15).

The number 4 is significant. In Revelation, it is the symbolic number of the entirety of the earth and its inhabitants (compare Revelation 7:1). Combining the creatures' multitudes of eyes with the number 4 indicates that these beasts are watching the entire earth; nothing is hidden from them. They symbolize the all-knowing nature of the Lord, or His omniscience.

> *What Do You Think?*
> How would we live differently were we to accept fully the fact of God's omniscience? How do we get there?
> *Talking Points for Your Discussion*
> - Regarding observable behavior
> - Regarding thought processes
> - Regarding relationships
> - Other

8a. And the four beasts had each of them six wings about him; and they were full of eyes within: and they rest not day and night, saying, Holy, holy, holy, Lord God Almighty.

Like the six-winged creatures of Isaiah's vision (Isaiah 6:2), the beasts here declare God's holiness. But it is not enough to say God is holy; He is *holy, holy, holy* (6:3)—absolutely pure. We cannot emphasize God's holiness too much; there is always more to this than we can imagine.

The title *Almighty* emphasizes God's omnipotence; He is all-powerful. The Greek behind this title occurs 10 times in the New Testament, nine of which are in Revelation. References to God's all-powerful nature are even more frequent in the Old Testament, with different words in the original language translated "Lord God of hosts" (2 Samuel 5:10), "God Almighty" (Exodus 6:3), or variations thereof. The Hebrew inscription around the picture of the cross on page 289 is from Isaiah 6:3: "Holy, holy, holy, is the Lord of hosts."

8b. Which was, and is, and is to come.

God is eternal—there is no beginning or end either to His omniscience, His holiness, His omnipotence, or He himself (compare Revelation 1:4, 8).

9. And when those beasts give glory and honour and thanks to him that sat on the throne, who liveth for ever and ever.

The fact that the beasts lead in worship indicates they are intelligent, speaking beings. Worship for them consists of the praise words of *glory and honour and thanks,* all directed to the one seated *on the throne.* Accompanying these words of worship is another expression of the Lord's eternal nature: He lives *for ever and ever.*

B. Elders Worship (vv. 10, 11)

10. The four and twenty elders fall down before him that sat on the throne, and worship him that liveth for ever and ever, and cast their crowns before the throne, saying.

The action returns to the 24 elders, who now rise from their thrones and *fall down* in the classic posture of *worship.* This is the first of several times these elders will do so (Revelation 5:8, 14; 7:11; 11:16; 19:4).

The elders engage in an additional act of reverence as they *cast their crowns* at the foot of the *throne.* This is one of the most unforgettable scenes in the Bible and should challenge us to cast ourselves in service before the Lord. It also emphasizes a central teaching of Revelation, that worship is for God alone and not for any other being or entity (Revelation 22:8, 9).

> *What Do You Think?*
> On a scale from 1 (most important) to 4, how would you rank-order the talking points below for enabling you to cast yourself in service before God? Why?
> *Talking Points for Your Discussion*
> - Considering the examples others have set
> - Considering how you have benefited from the service of others
> - Considering how others may benefit from your service
> - Considering passion in worship

11a. Thou art worthy, O Lord, to receive glory and honour and power.

The words of the elders offer a concise lesson on the nature of worship. Worship means "to ascribe worthiness." The elders acknowledge God's worthiness by saying that He alone should receive humanity's expressions of *glory and honour and power*. The reason for this comes next.

11b. For thou hast created all things, and for thy pleasure they are and were created.

The elders offer a rationale for this expression of worship: the identity of God as the Creator of *all things*. We rightly praise God as our Redeemer, but we should not forget that before He was Redeemer, He was the Creator. The contenders for power, whether the Roman emperors of John's day or the dreadful beasts who come later in Revelation, have no power to create *ex nihilo* ("from nothing") as God does. When we begin to grasp the omniscience, the holiness, the eternality, and the omnipotence of the Lord, worship is the only reasonable response.

◆ *WORTHY OF ALL PRAISE* ◆

California's Silicon Valley is the mecca of the world's technology giants. It's where science fiction meets science fact. The result is the next generation of mind-stretching innovations. Start-ups press to be the investment of venture capitalists, while the established powerhouses jockey to stay ahead of the wannabes.

Yet Silicon Valley's stellar lineup does not hold a solar-powered candle to Heaven and the everlasting Creator, who is worthy of all glory, honor, and power. As much as we honor inventors and innovators, the Lord God Almighty is the impetus behind human creativity.

As we marvel at human discoveries and inventions, we must keep a clear view of the originator of everything. Scripture tells us that our Creator designed the seas, land, birds, animals, and humans for His pleasure and His glory (Colossians 1:16). God's imagination and ingenuity far surpass any blueprint by human engineers and developers. To our "holy, holy, holy, Lord God Almighty" (Revelation 4:8) be the highest recognition, respect, and reverence. —B. J. L.

Visual for Lesson 8. *As you discuss Revelation 4:8, ask, "What consequences are there for not grasping the profound nature of God's holiness?"*

Conclusion
A. Qualities of God

The Bible consistently teaches qualities of God that highlight the immeasurable distance between Him and human beings. God is all-knowing (omniscient), for nothing is hidden from Him (Jeremiah 23:24). God is eternal, living and reigning forever (Psalm 146:10). God is holy, unstained by any unrighteousness or blemish of sin (Habakkuk 1:13). God is the Almighty (omnipotent), the all-powerful one, far above any human authority or spiritual power (1 Timothy 6:15, 16).

Revelation has much to teach us about worship and about the nature of God. In our desire to understand the prophetic message of the book, we sometimes miss these additional insights. The more we know about God, the more we are compelled to worship Him and the more genuine our worship becomes. Let us worship God in His holiness, His power, His eternality, and His knowledge. Let us worship the Lord God Almighty.

B. Prayer

Lord God Almighty, Heaven and earth are full of Your glory. May You reign forever in all creation and in our hearts. In the name of Jesus, by whom all things are created, we pray. Amen.

C. Thought to Remember

Almighty God alone is worthy of worship.

INVOLVEMENT LEARNING

Enhance your lesson with KJV Bible Student *(from your curriculum supplier) and the reproducible activity page (at www.standardlesson.com or in the back of the* KJV Standard Lesson Commentary Deluxe Edition*).*

Into the Lesson

Choose a funny topic about which students can make their own "Top 5 List" (examples: birthday gifts for Bigfoot, veggie ice cream flavors, reasons to bathe, names for Chihuahuas). Give each person a sheet of paper and a pen. Have students write up a list, with 5 being the lowest-ranked item and 1 being the highest. Allow one minute, then let volunteers read aloud their lists. (If you have a large number of volunteers have students read only their top one or two.)

If outlandish topics seem like too much for your group, you can opt to have students make more traditional lists (TV shows, musical groups, etc.).

Alternative: Distribute copies of the "Once the Best" activity from the reproducible page, which you can download. Make this a whole-class activity in which members choose an answer by a show of hands.

After either activity, move into the Bible study by saying, "We all have seen lists of best restaurants, movies, books, etc. But how long does something remain number one? The Bible tells us about the one who is truly the best of the best!"

Into the Word

Have students work together to create a drawing based on Revelation 4. Before class, hang or lay out a large sheet of mural paper and have markers available. If you are unable to provide mural paper, bring sheets of white paper and let students make individual drawings.

Read aloud Revelation 4:1-6, 8-11—pausing often to allow students to draw the images described (throne, rainbow, crowns, lightning, etc.). Be supportive and encouraging, as most people aren't natural artists, and some things described are like nothing they've ever seen. After drawings are complete, thank students, and read verse 11 again.

Ask students to give examples of people who received something they didn't earn (examples: someone awarded an honorary doctorate degree, a lottery winner). Discuss why some people may resent such a recipient and/or the gifts or honors received. Counter that discussion by talking about people who have worked very hard to be where they are today. Ask, "Why do we respect the latter more?" Connect the discussion with the lesson text by comparing and contrasting the respect we have for hard workers with the praise and glory we give to God. Some questions you can pose are (1) "What types of words do we use to praise Him? (2) "Why is He worthy of worship?"

Option. Sing or play a hymn or song about God's holiness (such as "I Bowed on My Knees and Cried Holy," "Holy, Holy, Holy," or "Holy Is the Lord God Almighty"). Pay special attention to the lyrics and the reasons why God is being glorified.

Alternative. Distribute pens and copies of the "In Other Words" activity on the reproducible page. Have students work individually to match the correct words from Revelation 4 with their definitions. Call time in one minute.

After either activity say, "People often wonder to whom they should give ultimate allegiance. Who deserves to be worshipped and praised? Revelation teaches that God alone is worthy of all praise, wonder, and awe."

Into Life

Read aloud Exodus 20:3. Distribute wooden craft sticks and pens. Remind students that in Bible times people built altars to worship their gods. On each craft stick, have students write something that they are tempted to put before God. Discuss why each "something" is, in essence, a false god. Have students stack the sticks to make an altar of sorts, then challenge students to plan to remove them from their lives. Talk about practical steps to make that happen.

BLESSING, GLORY, HONOR FOREVER

DEVOTIONAL READING: Philippians 2:1-11
BACKGROUND SCRIPTURE: Revelation 5:6-14

REVELATION 5:6-14

6 And I beheld, and, lo, in the midst of the throne and of the four beasts, and in the midst of the elders, stood a Lamb as it had been slain, having seven horns and seven eyes, which are the seven Spirits of God sent forth into all the earth.

7 And he came and took the book out of the right hand of him that sat upon the throne.

8 And when he had taken the book, the four beasts and four and twenty elders fell down before the Lamb, having every one of them harps, and golden vials full of odours, which are the prayers of saints.

9 And they sung a new song, saying, Thou art worthy to take the book, and to open the seals thereof: for thou wast slain, and hast redeemed us to God by thy blood out of every kindred, and tongue, and people, and nation;

10 And hast made us unto our God kings and priests: and we shall reign on the earth.

11 And I beheld, and I heard the voice of many angels round about the throne and the beasts and the elders: and the number of them was ten thousand times ten thousand, and thousands of thousands;

12 Saying with a loud voice, Worthy is the Lamb that was slain to receive power, and riches, and wisdom, and strength, and honour, and glory, and blessing.

13 And every creature which is in heaven, and on the earth, and under the earth, and such as are in the sea, and all that are in them, heard I saying, Blessing, and honour, and glory, and power, be unto him that sitteth upon the throne, and unto the Lamb for ever and ever.

14 And the four beasts said, Amen. And the four and twenty elders fell down and worshipped him that liveth for ever and ever.

KEY VERSE

Worthy is the Lamb that was slain to receive power, and riches, and wisdom, and strength, and honour, and glory, and blessing. —**Revelation 5:12**

ACKNOWLEDGING GOD

Unit 2: All Glory and Honor
LESSONS 5–9

LESSON AIMS

After participating in this lesson, each learner will be able to:

1. Describe the makeup of the expanding numbers of worshippers in Heaven.

2. Explain why the Lamb is worthy of worship.

3. Specify how his or her church can better fulfill the calling of Christians to be "kings and priests."

LESSON OUTLINE

Introduction
  A. Destiny or Deity?
  B. Lesson Background
I. Seeing the Lamb (REVELATION 5:6-8)
  A. Standing in the Midst (v. 6)
  B. Taking the Scroll (vv. 7, 8)
    Who Holds the Future?
II. Singing a New Song (REVELATION 5:9, 10)
  A. Worthy Lamb (v. 9)
    The Diverse Church United
  B. Exalted Followers (v. 10)
III. Worshipping with Hosts (REVELATION 5:11-14)
  A. Countless Angels (vv. 11, 12)
  B. Countless Creatures (v. 13)
  C. Additional Praise (v. 14)
Conclusion
  A. God's Position
  B. Humanity's Obligation
  C. Prayer
  D. Thought to Remember

Introduction

A. Destiny or Deity?

Many religious beliefs feature a strong sense of destiny, of divine control over the lives of humans. In the Greek mythological world of Mount Olympus, familiar to the first readers of Revelation, this was personified by the three goddesses of fate: one who spins the thread of life, one who allots the number of life's days, and one who cuts the thread of life at the time of death. The Greeks and Romans also believed in Fortuna, the goddess who determined a person's destiny, whether prosperous or disastrous.

The Bible presents God as sovereign; He declares, "My counsel shall stand, and I will do all my pleasure" (Isaiah 46:10). God's plans are not to be thwarted, for He has the power to carry out His will in all things (Proverbs 19:21). Yet God allows humans to devise and carry out their own plans for life, reserving for himself the final say on the outcomes (Proverbs 16:9). Unlike the capricious and unpredictable actions of the goddesses of fate or Fortuna, the Lord's will works with human wills for God's desired outcomes. These outcomes are always and utterly consistent with God's unchanging nature.

Today's lesson considers the ultimate outcome that God ensures will happen. In chapters 4 and 5 of Revelation, John sees the Lord seated on His heavenly throne. In God's hand is a scroll sealed with seven seals; the opening of this scroll reveals the future, the events "which must be hereafter" (Revelation 4:1, last week's lesson).

B. Lesson Background

Revelation 4 begins John's vision of the throne room of Heaven. John describes its majestic features and residents, including the "beasts" who lead worship and the elders who bow in worship. The chapter ends with a song praising the worthiness of the Lord God to receive worship. This is based on God's being the creator and sustainer of all things. Chapter 5 begins with John's observation of a new detail: in the hand of the one seated on the throne (God) is an unusual scroll, unusual for two reasons.

First, it has writing on both sides, which is not the standard practice. The scroll is likely made of treated animal skins. With such scrolls it was much easier to write on the "flesh" side than the "hair" side. Writing on both sides gives the impression of the scroll overflowing with important information.

Second, the scroll has seven seals instead of the usual one seal. These are wax seals affixed by God himself. They can be broken only by one who has the proper authority. Consequently, a search throughout Heaven attempts to find one worthy to open this scroll. Initially, no one with suitable authority is found.

This disappoints John, and we are told that his disappointment moves him to tears (Revelation 5:4). John wants, even needs, to know what the words of the scroll reveal. He understands that this is why he has been granted access to Heaven, for the scroll will reveal what will take place on earth (4:1). Something seems wrong, even in Heaven, and John's sadness overwhelms him.

But all is not lost. One of the elders from the group near the throne tells John not to weep. The one who can break the seals, open the scroll, and reveal its secrets is arriving. This is the conquering Lion of Judah (Revelation 5:5), Jesus, but He is also the Lamb; and His appearance begins our lesson for this week.

I. Seeing the Lamb
(Revelation 5:6-8)
A. Standing in the Midst (v. 6)

6a. And I beheld, and, lo, in the midst of the throne and of the four beasts, and in the midst of the elders, stood a Lamb as it had been slain.

The four beasts and *the elders* are nothing new to John at this point (see last week's lesson). But the figure *in the midst of the throne and . . . in the midst of the elders* is new. This newcomer is at the center of everything, the focus of Heaven and its residents. John's description of this figure contains important symbolic truth.

First, the figure is that of *a Lamb*, a favored sacrificial animal in biblical teaching. Readers are reminded of the words of John the Baptist:

"Behold the Lamb of God!" (John 1:29, 36; compare 1 Peter 1:18, 19).

Second, John includes the puzzling detail that the Lamb looks as if *it had been slain*. This does not mean that the Lamb exhibits a deathly pallor, but that it has evidence of a horrendous wound. It is the kind of wound that no living creature should have survived. The Lamb is not dead, though, or else the entire episode would make no sense. This is John's way of saying that the Lamb had been dead but is now alive again—a reference to the resurrected Christ.

6b. Having seven horns and seven eyes, which are the seven Spirits of God sent forth into all the earth.

The description of the Lamb combines the number *seven* (the symbol of perfection or completeness; see Revelation 15:1, 8) with *horns* (the symbol of power; see Daniel 8:7-9) and *eyes* (the symbol of divine knowledge; 2 Chronicles 16:9). The Lamb has perfect and undisputed power. This is not a meek baby sheep, but the mighty, conquering Lamb of God.

Like the multi-eyed creatures near the throne who serve as God's witnesses of everything on the earth (Revelation 4:6, last week's lesson), the seven-eyed Lamb also has personal knowledge of everything. This is because of the Lamb's close ties to the *seven Spirits of God*, which (as noted in last week's study) is this book's way of presenting the Holy Spirit (Revelation 1:4; 4:5). The fact that the Spirit is *sent forth into all the earth* calls to mind Jesus' promise to send the Holy Spirit (John 15:26).

> *What Do You Think?*
> What would life be like if Jesus were the touchstone of all your thoughts?
> *Talking Points for Your Discussion*
> - In business contexts
> - In family contexts
> - In your entertainment choices
> - Other

B. Taking the Scroll (vv. 7, 8)

7. And he came and took the book out of the right hand of him that sat upon the throne.

No doubt all present, including John, watch in amazement as the Lamb does an audacious thing: He takes *the book out of the right hand* of God! This is not an act of thievery or usurpation, however, for God has been waiting for the Lamb. The scroll and its decrees are prepared for the Lamb, and only He can break the seals and open the scroll.

8a. And when he had taken the book, the four beasts and four and twenty elders fell down before the Lamb.

The transfer of the scroll allows the worship of Heaven to resume, but now *the four beasts and four and twenty elders* are bowing *before the Lamb*. This is not to recognize a transfer of power that somehow diminishes the authority of the one on the throne. Rather, it is a recognition of the Lamb's authority and His unity with the one on the throne. (Regarding the nature of the beasts, the elders, and the numbers associated with them, see comments on Revelation 4:4, 6 in last week's lesson.)

8b. Having every one of them harps, and golden vials full of odours, which are the prayers of saints.

Following the transfer of the scroll, new details unfold before John's eyes. The *elders*, who previously had cast their crowns when they fell in worship before the throne (Revelation 4:10, last week's lesson), now have *harps* that they presumably use for playing worship music.

Further, they all hold *vials full of odours*, which is symbolic of *the prayers of saints*. This is one of the few places in Revelation where symbolic language is explained—and for that we are grateful. The aroma likely comes from incense, which is later linked with prayer when the seventh seal is opened (Revelation 8:3). Because smoke from incense rises and creates a pleasing aroma, incense has come to symbolize prayers rising to God (Psalm 141:2).

HOW TO SAY IT

Alpha	*Al*-fa.
Ephesus	*Ef*-uh-sus.
Fortuna	*Fawr-too*-nuh.
Judah	*Joo*-duh.
Nostradamus	*Noss*-truh-**daw**-muss.
Omega	O-*may*-guh or O-*mee*-guh.

Many have heard the name Nostradamus. Although he was born in 1503, his followers claim this man predicted future events, including World War II, the atomic bomb, the assassination of John F. Kennedy, the moon landings, and the 9/11 terror attacks. Nostradamus's followers continue to pore over his quatrains—his collection of four-line prophecies—in an attempt to figure out what else the French astrologer seems to have successfully predicted.

Nostradamus wasn't received as kindly by his contemporaries, however. Some of his critics claimed he used sleep deprivation and hallucinogenic drugs to put himself into an altered state. Others labeled him incompetent because of his unorthodox methodology.

Nostradamus's continued popularity points to human anxiety and curiosity about the future, especially regarding the end times. But Revelation 5 reminds us that our future is in the hands of the worthy Lamb. When the Lamb took the scroll, its contents became secondary to the rightful worship of the one holding it. Much more important than knowing the future is knowing the one who holds our future.   —L. G. S.

II. Singing a New Song
(REVELATION 5:9, 10)
A. Worthy Lamb (v. 9)

9a. And they sung a new song.

Worship of the Lamb includes singing. What the elders sing is not an old favorite but *a new song*. Revelation 14:3 is similar, but there it is the 144,000 redeemed who sing rather than the elders. Of the other seven occurrences of the word *new* in Revelation, all are actions of God (2:17; 3:12 [twice]; 21:1 [twice], 2, 5).

9b. Saying, Thou art worthy to take the book, and to open the seals thereof: for thou wast slain, and hast redeemed us to God by thy blood.

The song John hears acknowledges the worthiness of the Lamb and therefore the appropriateness of offering Him worship (contrast Revelation 19:10; 22:8, 9). The fact that the Lamb is eligible to be worshipped goes hand in hand with the fact that He is eligible *to take the book, and to open the seals thereof.* Because He was *slain,* people are *redeemed . . . to God,* sin's price having been paid by the Lamb's shed *blood* (see Romans 3:25). Yet He is the living Lamb, the one who has conquered death. This is a great victory indeed (1 Corinthians 15:55)! Could there be anyone more worthy to break the seals on the scroll than the Lamb?

9c. Out of every kindred, and tongue, and people, and nation.

The elders' song recognizes those who have been redeemed as being a marvelously diverse lot. The diversity is fourfold in nature, as the redeemed come from every family group (*kindred*), every language group (*tongue*), every cultural group (*people*), and every ethnic group (*nation*). This heavenly mix encompasses all the people of the world, symbolically represented by the number four (compare Isaiah 11:12; Revelation 7:1). It is a mix that should characterize the church on earth.

What Do You Think?
    What steps can a church take to achieve the
        diversity seen in Revelation 5:9?
Talking Points for Your Discussion
    ▪ Steps for ministers and elders to take
    ▪ Steps for leaders of midsize groups (Sunday
        school classes, etc.) to take
    ▪ Steps for leaders of small groups to take
    ▪ Other

◆ *THE DIVERSE CHURCH UNITED* ◆

Dr. Martin Luther King's famous "I Have a Dream Speech" rightly challenged the conscience of a country divided by racism. His vision for racial equality was rooted in his understanding of the Scriptures. For King, the uneven terrain of Isaiah 40:3-5 represented the decades of racial injustice that fueled and was fueled by segregation.

King's dream wasn't wishful thinking or idle hope. He challenged his audience to participate in leveling "the mountain of despair." A nation changed its laws and began to repent of its racism as a result (with a ways yet to go).

King's dream of racial equality was preceded by John's vision of a multinational, multiethnic redeemed people of God who are unified in their praise to Him. Having read of that heavenly outcome, the question then becomes one of what we should be doing to bring it about. What are we doing to have a church on earth that is as unified in its diversity as the redeemed people of God in John's vision?   —L. G. S.

B. Exalted Followers (v. 10)

10. And hast made us unto our God kings and priests: and we shall reign on the earth.

Another consequence of Christ's redeeming, sacrificial death is the elevated status of this purchased people. They (*we*) have now become *kings and priests,* which are offices representative of significant authority. The Greek word rendered *kings* is also translated "kingdom" in many places (examples: Matthew 5:20; John 3:3, 5), and that may be the sense here.

In either case, believers are given an astonishing and humbling responsibility: to *reign on the earth.* Entrusted to deliver the saving message of the gospel, Christians are appointed by God to extend His rule to every nation. In that way we have become kings who assist the great king and invite others to become part of the kingdom that is "not of this world" (John 18:36).

III. Worshipping with Hosts
(REVELATION 5:11-14)
A. Countless Angels (vv. 11, 12)

11. And I beheld, and I heard the voice of many angels round about the throne and the beasts and the elders: and the number of them was ten thousand times ten thousand, and thousands of thousands.

The chorus is taken up by another group that surrounds the throne as *many angels* join *the beasts and the elders.* John does not attempt to count them; there are far too many. If we take the Greek word translated *ten thousand* and change the Greek letters to English letters that sound the same (a procedure known as transliteration), we end up with the English word *myriad.*

12. Saying with a loud voice, Worthy is the Lamb that was slain to receive power, and riches, and wisdom, and strength, and honour, and glory, and blessing.

This majestic choir proclaims what we might call the second stanza of the new song. It too acknowledges the worthiness of *the Lamb that was slain*, and therefore the appropriateness of worshipping Him. New is this stanza's recognition of the Lamb's worthiness *to receive* the sevenfold listing of *power* (ability), *riches* (wealth), *wisdom* (knowledge and how to use it), *strength* (might), *honour* (esteem), *glory* (splendor), *and blessing* (praise). These attributes include every possible qualification for worthiness (compare Revelation 4:11; 7:12):

> *What Do You Think?*
> How can you help your church proclaim Jesus
> "with a loud voice" in a figurative sense?
> *Talking Points for Your Discussion*
> • When opposition is strong
> • When opposition is low or nonexistent

B. Countless Creatures (v. 13)

13. And every creature which is in heaven, and on the earth, and under the earth, and such as are in the sea, and all that are in them, heard I saying, Blessing, and honour, and glory, and power, be unto him that sitteth upon the throne, and unto the Lamb for ever and ever.

John's view includes all creatures in every conceivable location. This includes all other heavenly creatures, all creatures *on the earth,* all creatures *under the earth* (perhaps the dead or whatever exists beneath the physical surface of the earth; compare Philippians 2:10, 11), and all creatures *in the sea.* This leaves out no one or thing. Again we see a grouping of four, the number representing the entirety of the earth.

This is a magnificent moment, a picture of all the universe joined in praise. This is as it should be. There are no holdouts, no protesters. Later, Revelation 22:15 presents us some who are excluded from the presence of God, but for now there is a unanimous voice of praise.

The perfect list of seven attributes in the earlier new song has been condensed to four: *blessing, honour, glory,* and *power.* The fourfold nature of this version is appropriate for the creatures of the world in their entirety. The list is similar to the original song of God's worthiness in Revelation 4:11 with one key difference: this time worship is directed to *the Lamb.* This is not the worship of a second deity, but an affirmation of the unity of Christ with the one seated on the throne.

> *What Do You Think?*
> What safeguards can we put in place to keep
> our worship Christ-centered?
> *Talking Points for Your Discussion*
> • Regarding safeguards that lead up to worship
> • Regarding safeguards to enact during worship

C. Additional Praise (v. 14)

14a. And the four beasts said, Amen.

John's attention is drawn back to *the four beasts.* What he sees and hears in this half-verse and the next is a repeat of Revelation 4:9, 10. The *Amen* voiced by the beasts is derived from a Hebrew word that means, "It is true" or "It is correct." Nothing is out of place in the scene.

14b. And the four and twenty elders fell down and worshipped him that liveth for ever and ever.

The "amen" of the beasts is followed by a physical act from *the four and twenty elders* as they repeat their posture of worship (Revelation 4:10, 11). The Lamb is the one who was dead but now *liveth for ever and ever.* By His resurrection He has unlocked the prison house of death and released God's people from death's power (1:18). He is truly the worthy one, and we cannot worship Him enough.

> *What Do You Think?*
> What steps can you take to ensure that what
> others see in you affirms the truths of what
> you sing and pray?
> *Talking Points for Your Discussion*
> • When in the presence of unbelievers
> • When in the presence of believers

Conclusion

A. God's Position

Our world is filled with awards. Sports teams keep trophy shops busy with orders. The roster of award shows on television includes the Oscars, Emmys, Tonys, Grammys, and Golden Globes. We have halls of fame for football players, rock bands, rodeo winners, etc. Schools hand out certificates frequently for all manner of achievements. Hollywood has its Walk of Fame. All compete for our attention, whether as spectators to admire achievements of others or as potential candidates to be recognized.

Acknowledging achievements is a good thing in and of itself. We must be careful, however, to distinguish proper from improper applause both given to and accepted from our fellow human beings. A primary lesson of Revelation is that God alone is worthy of receiving worship. God alone must be glorified (compare Acts 12:21-23; 14:11-18).

Revelation shows us that Christ, the Lamb of God, is also worthy of worshipful praise and glory. We may not understand fully the relationship within the Trinity of God the Father, God the Son, and God the Holy Spirit. All three are important in Revelation, but there is no essential division between the three. They are one God. Worship in Heaven is given to the one on the throne and to the Lamb, and this is the same worship.

At the beginning of Revelation, "the Lord . . . the Almighty" describes himself as "Alpha and Omega (Revelation 1:8). At the end of Revelation, Jesus describes himself in the same way (22:13). There is no separation. May all glory be given to the one seated on the throne and to the Lamb forever and ever.

B. Humanity's Obligation

When God established His covenant with the Israelites at Mount Sinai, He called them to be "a kingdom of priests" (Exodus 19:6). Now, under the new covenant, Christians carry out that role as "a royal priesthood" (1 Peter 2:9).

Unlike under the old covenant, however, our priestly sacrifices do not consist of animals. Rather, our sacrifices are spiritual in nature (1 Peter 2:5); and our priesthood involves being living sacrifices (Romans 12:1). In that light, we are to "offer the sacrifice of praise to God continually, that is, the fruit of our lips giving thanks to his name" (Hebrews 13:15). Worship must never be about us. Worship, whether corporate or individual, should have an audience of one: the Lord himself.

The thanks that we offer can include gratitude that our eternal destiny does not rest on decisions made by three goddesses on Mount Olympus or any other fickle and unpredictable deity. The one true God is utterly consistent, always faithful to His promises, whether those promises involve positive or negative outcomes for people in various contexts. When we first read the book of Revelation, we may be astounded and even terrified of its imagery; but terror gives way to relief as we realize that in the end it is God who wins. Our choice concerns which side we want to be on. But that's really no choice at all, is it?

B. Prayer

Lord God, may we give our worship to no other. May all glory and honor be given to You. May we join our voices with Your worshippers from all over the world to sing Your praises forever. In the name of Your Son, amen.

C. Thought to Remember

The Lamb is worthy of our worship.

Visual for Lesson 9. *In discussing Revelation 5:9, point to this visual and ask, "How does this text's lamb imagery connect with the lion imagery of 5:5?"*

INVOLVEMENT LEARNING

Enhance your lesson with KJV Bible Student *(from your curriculum supplier) and the reproducible activity page (at www.standardlesson.com or in the back of the* KJV Standard Lesson Commentary Deluxe Edition*).*

Into the Lesson

Bring to class some employment ads from the newspaper or Internet. Begin the discussion by asking each person to describe his or her current (or most recent) job. Briefly talk about the job's responsibilities and what he or she enjoys most about it.

Then divide students into small groups and give each group an ad, some paper, and a pen. Have each group choose one person to be the employer. Other students will be various job seekers. Groups will role-play job interviews, in which the applicants draw from their own life experiences in order to impress the employer. Encourage students to be creative as they think about experiences that might prove relevant to each job.

Alternative: Distribute pens and copies of the "Help for Hire" activity, which you can download. Have students work individually to rank the jobs described and then name things that might qualify them for their top pick.

After either activity say, "When applying for a job, we list accomplishments that might impress a potential employer. Today we will talk of one who has the greatest résumé ever."

Into the Word

Divide the class into three groups. Supply each group with pen and paper and one of the following assignments. Groups will read portions of today's text from Revelation 5 and convert the images about Jesus' qualities into straightforward language for whole-class discussion. Sample responses are in italics.

Group 1—Slain Lamb (vv. 6-8)

Jesus is qualified to sit on the throne because of who He is and what He has done. He gave himself up to be sacrificed, yet He lives again! He has power that no other has. He has insight not available to any mortal. Only He is worthy to take the scroll from the hand of God.

Group 2—Universal Redeemer (vv. 9, 10)

Lambs were sacrificed by the people of Israel to atone for their sins. But Jesus did more!

The effect of His sacrifice went far beyond Israel. He paid the price for people throughout the world! Humans, created to be with God and to have dominion over the world, can be what God intends because of what Jesus did.

Group 3—Eternal God (vv. 11-14)

Jesus demonstrated that He was more than human and even more than an angel. He received praise in Heaven that is reserved only for the eternal, living God. And with good reason: that is exactly who He is!

Alternative. Distribute pens and copies of "Savior of All" activity. Have students work in pairs or small groups to discuss each of these verses in relation to Revelation 5:6-14.

After either activity say, "The Lamb of God is worthy of our praise forever. However, people find it difficult to find a source of allegiance that is permanent and lasting. Why is that? What response do they give when they find this lasting allegiance? Let's find out how Jesus compares with other figures in world religions."

Into Life

Write the following on the board:

Muslims—*believe that God sent Muhammad as the last of the prophets to finalize the word of God.*

Buddhists—*believe that Gautama Buddha was an enlightened teacher who shared his insights to help people end their suffering through the elimination of ignorance and craving.*

Hindus—*may believe that one of their gods (Vishnu) would take human form (an avatar) occasionally to guide people back to the right path.*

Close class by comparing these religious figures with Jesus. Ask, "Considering what Jesus accomplished that the others did not, how does this affect your calling in Revelation 5:10?

GIVING FROM A GENEROUS HEART

DEVOTIONAL READING: Psalm 112
BACKGROUND SCRIPTURE: Exodus 25:1-7; 35:4-29;
Leviticus 27:30-33; 2 Corinthians 9:6-8

EXODUS 35:20-29

20 And all the congregation of the children of Israel departed from the presence of Moses.

21 And they came, every one whose heart stirred him up, and every one whom his spirit made willing, and they brought the LORD's offering to the work of the tabernacle of the congregation, and for all his service, and for the holy garments.

22 And they came, both men and women, as many as were willing hearted, and brought bracelets, and earrings, and rings, and tablets, all jewels of gold: and every man that offered offered an offering of gold unto the LORD.

23 And every man, with whom was found blue, and purple, and scarlet, and fine linen, and goats' hair, and red skins of rams, and badgers' skins, brought them.

24 Every one that did offer an offering of silver and brass brought the LORD 's offering: and every man, with whom was found shittim wood for any work of the service, brought it.

25 And all the women that were wise hearted did spin with their hands, and brought that which they had spun, both of blue, and of purple, and of scarlet, and of fine linen.

26 And all the women whose heart stirred them up in wisdom spun goats' hair.

27 And the rulers brought onyx stones, and stones to be set, for the ephod, and for the breastplate;

28 And spice, and oil for the light, and for the anointing oil, and for the sweet incense.

29 The children of Israel brought a willing offering unto the LORD, every man and woman, whose heart made them willing to bring for all manner of work, which the LORD had commanded to be made by the hand of Moses.

2 CORINTHIANS 9:6-8

6 But this I say, He which soweth sparingly shall reap also sparingly; and he which soweth bountifully shall reap also bountifully.

7 Every man according as he purposeth in his heart, so let him give; not grudgingly, or of necessity: for God loveth a cheerful giver.

8 And God is able to make all grace abound toward you; that ye, always having all sufficiency in all things, may abound to every good work.

KEY VERSE

This I say, He which soweth sparingly shall reap also sparingly; and he which soweth bountifully shall reap also bountifully. —**2 Corinthians 9:6**

ACKNOWLEDGING GOD

Unit 3: Give Praise to God
LESSONS 10–13

LESSON AIMS

After participating in this lesson, each learner will be able to:

1. Recall how the Israelites demonstrated generosity in funding the tabernacle's construction.

2. Compare and contrast the Old and New Testament texts in today's study with regard to giving.

3. Identify one way that he or she can better express generosity in giving and make a plan to do so.

LESSON OUTLINE

Introduction
    A. "Giving While Living"
    B. Lesson Background
 I. Old Covenant Giving (Exodus 35:20-29)
    A. Willing Givers (vv. 20-22a)
    B. Valuable Gifts (vv. 22b-28)
       Hearts Moved
    C. Obedient Givers (v. 29)
II. New Covenant Giving (2 Corinthians 9:6-8)
    A. Law of the Harvest (v. 6)
       Sowing for Hope
    B. Decision of the Giver (v. 7a)
    C. Love of God (v. 7b)
    D. Ability of God (v. 8)
Conclusion
    A. Common Factor
    B. Prayer
    C. Thought to Remember

Introduction

A. "Giving While Living"

In 2012, Chuck Feeney made a remarkable and highly publicized announcement: he had decided to stop giving. That marked the end of a 30-year campaign to give away the large majority of his considerable fortune. The son of Irish-American immigrants, Feeney was born during the Great Depression and served as a radio operator in the U.S. Air Force during the Korean conflict (1950–1953). To make extra money, he started a small side business selling duty-free alcohol to American soldiers; by 1960, at the beginning of the travel boom, Feeney had begun to build an international empire of duty-free shops.

But in 1984, Feeney changed course, deciding to give rather than receive. After selling his share in his company, he established a foundation to promote global education, public health, care for the elderly, and peace efforts. Feeney's foundation closed in 2016 after fulfilling its objective of distributing $8 billion (U.S. currency).

In many ways, this low-key approach reflects the biblical perspective. Feeney's foundation used the slogan "Giving While Living" to summarize his view that people should not simply amass wealth to leave to their heirs, but instead use what they have to do good while they are alive and well. God consistently calls us to give while living, viewing the financial resources we have as assets to be used for His purposes.

B. Lesson Background

The exodus from Egypt and the receiving of the law at Sinai marked the beginning of the nation of Israel. We should remember Abraham's descendants had lived in Egypt for many generations, and over time they had become quite familiar with the religious views of their Egyptian overlords. Perhaps for this reason, the first two of the Ten Commandments stressed that God's people were not to worship like the Egyptians, who believed in many gods. The Israelites were to serve no gods other than the only true God and were not permitted to make idols or other physical representations of Him (Exodus 20:1-6).

To further assist in the religious reeducation of the people, God commanded Moses to construct a sanctuary, a national center of worship. That large, semiportable tent-complex came to be called *the tabernacle* (Exodus 25:8, 9; 26:1). Significantly, God did not miraculously provide the construction materials for the project. Instead, He called for an offering "of every man that giveth it willingly with his heart" (25:2). That challenge takes us to the result.

I. Old Covenant Giving

(Exodus 35:20-29)

The Old Testament passage of our lesson takes us into a whole-community assembly of the Israelites at Mount Sinai, with Moses in charge. He has just finished specifying in some detail the material needed for construction of the tabernacle, its furnishings, and the nature of the garments to be worn by priests (Exodus 35:4-19).

A. Willing Givers (vv. 20-22a)

20, 21. And all the congregation of the children of Israel departed from the presence of Moses. And they came, every one whose heart stirred him up, and every one whom his spirit made willing, and they brought the LORD's offering to the work of the tabernacle of the congregation, and for all his service, and for the holy garments.

These two verses and the next set the tone for the remainder of the passage. Two points are particularly notable. First, all those who give do so willingly, as they are moved in their hearts. This theme is repeated several times to emphasize not only the personal commitment of individuals but also the spirit of national unity that emerges around the project (Exodus 35:22, 29; 36:2, 3).

Second, the people's response addresses all areas of God's instructions given through Moses regarding construction of the tabernacle proper (see Exodus 36:8-38), its furnishings (*for all his service*; see 37:1–38:8; etc.), and the priestly *holy garments* (see 39:1-31).

22a. And they came, both men and women, as many as were willing hearted.

Another theme that runs throughout this passage is that contributors are not limited to a select group since *both men and women* give (compare 1 Chronicles 29:1-9). God's call does not go out only to the wealthy but to everyone. The people respond as their hearts move them.

B. Valuable Gifts (vv. 22b-28)

22b. And brought bracelets, and earrings, and rings, and tablets, all jewels of gold: and every man that offered offered an offering of gold unto the LORD.

God has instructed that many of the fixtures and furnishings in the tabernacle are to be gold-plated, while the priestly garments are to be gold-embroidered and covered with precious gems (examples: Exodus 25:11-13, 24-28, 38-40; 26:6; 28:11-28). Such costly materials call attention to the majesty of God and symbolize the significance and the sacred privilege of worship.

> **What Do You Think?**
> How do we decide when "going first class" on church furnishings is worth the extra cost?
> *Talking Points for Your Discussion*
> - Considering beauty and functionality
> - Considering life-cycle cost
> - In handling designated gifts
> - Considering interest on borrowing to do so
> - Considering ministry opportunities lost by doing so

We may find it surprising that the Israelites, who had left Egypt as slaves, are able to provide the necessary gold and gems primarily through donations of personal jewelry. But God had made a way for the Israelites to give, even before they realized it would be necessary to do so. When God first appeared to Moses in the burning bush to announce delivery of the Israelites from slavery, He also promised to "give this people favour in the sight of the Egyptians" so that "when ye go [out of Egypt], ye shall not go empty" (Exodus 3:21). The Hebrew women were to acquire "jewels of silver, and jewels of gold, and raiment" from the Egyptians just before the exodus, with the result that the Hebrews would "spoil the Egyptians" by escaping with their personal goods (Exodus 3:22)!

These instructions were followed (Exodus 11:2, 3; 12:35, 36), and the Israelites left Egypt with a substantial amount of gold, silver, and precious gems. Now, having experienced God's deliverance in crossing the Red Sea, the people realize that this plunder was not for their personal benefit, but for the good of the people as a whole. Thus they willingly contribute as God, through Moses, requests.

◆ HEARTS MOVED ◆

Bill and Melinda Gates, one of the wealthiest couples in the world, established the Bill and Melinda Gates Foundation in 2000. Through it the couple has given billions of their own dollars to, among other things, improve health and well-being in developing countries. The couple knows that not all of their projects will be successful. But they continue to try because they have a heart to "help all people live healthy, productive lives."

To have a heart that is willing is where true giving begins, as today's text makes clear. That willingness is founded in realizing that one is involved in something greater than self. Bill and Melinda Gates give so people have the best chance possible to live their best lives. The Israelites were generous in constructing something that would help everyone in their community lift eyes to God: the tabernacle.

What thing bigger than yourself motivates you to give? Perhaps you know of children whose only daily meal is provided in school. Perhaps you see homeless people living in deplorable conditions. People are often more receptive to the gospel when their physical needs are met. Not having the wealth of Bill and Melinda Gates is no excuse for not giving. See Luke 21:1-4.   —S. K.

23a. And every man, with whom was found blue, and purple, and scarlet, and fine linen.

The word *every* stresses again the broad participation in the special offering. The precious fabrics mentioned here include various colors of cloth. Such fabrics are an expensive commodity in the ancient world, where all fabrics are hand-dyed (compare Proverbs 31:22; Acts 16:14). Dyes are produced from natural elements, usually shellfish harvested from the Mediterranean Sea.

Fine linen refers to a bright white, high-quality Egyptian cloth spun from flax fibers. Extant samples recovered from ancient Egyptian tombs are so finely woven that they resemble silk in appearance and texture. The *blue, and purple, and scarlet, and fine linen* will be used to make the hanging curtains of the tabernacle (Exodus 26:31, 32) as well as priestly garments (39:1, 2).

23b. And goats' hair, and red skins of rams, and badgers' skins, brought them.

Use for the material we see here is found in Exodus 26:14; 36:14, 19. *Red skins of rams* are created by tanning and dyeing, producing a look and texture similar to modern Moroccan leather.

24a. Every one that did offer an offering of silver and brass brought the Lord's offering.

Many of the tabernacle's fixtures are to be fashioned from *silver* or *brass* (Exodus 26:11, 19-21; 27:2, 3, 6, 10, 11, 17-19). Such material is likely obtained by melting down jewelry and other household items that the Israelites acquired from the Egyptians.

24b. And every man, with whom was found shittim wood for any work of the service, brought it.

Shittim wood refers to what is now called *acacia*, a thorny tree common in the Sinai Peninsula. No doubt the Israelites harvest this locally. Acacia is an exceptionally durable building material, harder than oak and highly resistant to wood-boring insects. Perhaps for this reason, the wooden sections of the tabernacle itself and all its furnishings, including the altar and the ark of the covenant, are

HOW TO SAY IT

acacia	uh-*kay*-shuh.
Goshen	*Go*-shen.
Judea	Joo-*dee*-uh.
Macedonia	Mass-eh-*doe*-nee-uh.
Shittim	Shih-*teem*.
Sinai	*Sigh*-nye or *Sigh*-nay-eye.
tabernacle	***tab***-burr-*nah*-kul.
Thummim	*Thum*-im (*th* as in *thin*).
Urim	*You*-rim.

to be made of shittim wood (see Exodus 25:10, 23, 28; 26:15-30, 32; 27:1, 6-8).

25. And all the women that were wise hearted did spin with their hands, and brought that which they had spun, both of blue, and of purple, and of scarlet, and of fine linen.

Wise hearted refers not to intellectual wisdom but rather to technical skill, in this case the skill of weaving (see Exodus 28:3). The larger flow of the passage suggests that men, who work primarily outside the home and have oversight of flocks and fields, bring natural resources (lumber, skins, dyes) to their wives and daughters, who in turn work to produce the needed fabrics. The overall impression is that entire families are involved in responding to the call to give.

26. And all the women whose heart stirred them up in wisdom spun goats' hair.

The fabric mentioned here is doubtless obtained from the Hebrews' herds of long-haired goats. These produce a coarse, black cloth often used for making tents (such as the tabernacle will be).

> *What Do You Think?*
> What steps can you take to serve God generously with your talents?
> *Talking Points for Your Discussion*
> - Regarding talents that don't seem to have much spiritual applicability
> - When time is tight
> - When your church isn't sure how to make use of your talents
> - Other

27. And the rulers brought onyx stones, and stones to be set, for the ephod, and for the breastplate.

Not surprisingly the leaders of the people, being generally wealthier, provide the more costly items that others might not easily obtain. *The ephod* and *the breastplate* are garments worn by the high priest during his service in the tabernacle. The ephod is a large vest worn as an outer garment; *onyx stones* engraved with the names of the twelve tribes of Israel are attached to the shoulders of the vest to serve as a symbol of the people when the high priest appears before the Lord (Exodus 25:7; 28:6-14).

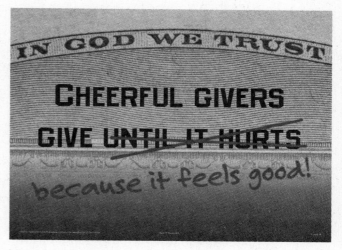

Visual for Lesson 10. *Start a discussion by pointing to this visual as you ask, "Why are both of these sentiments biblically deficient?"*

The *breastplate* is a woven garment worn over the ephod and is also mounted with twelve precious stones in gold settings, one for each of the tribes. The breastplate contains pockets that hold the Urim and Thummim, which are used to determine the Lord's will on serious matters (Exodus 28:15-30).

28. And spice, and oil for the light, and for the anointing oil, and for the sweet incense.

Specific amounts and kinds of *spice* will be used along with olive *oil* to create *the anointing oil*. The recipe for preparing this is found in Exodus 30:22-25; its use—and penalty for misuse—is specified in 30:26-33.

Oil for the light refers to another use for olive oil: that being fuel for the flame of the tabernacle's lampstand (Exodus 27:20, 21; 35:14; 39:37). Burning of *the sweet incense* will happen concurrently with tending to the lamps (30:7). As with the anointing oil, instructions for creating and using this incense are provided (30:34-36); the penalty for misuse is identically severe (30:37, 38). Doubtless God intends that this unique scent will communicate a special sense of His presence to the Israelites in their worship.

C. Obedient Givers (v. 29)

29a. The children of Israel brought a willing offering unto the LORD, every man and woman, whose heart made them willing to bring for all manner of work.

This verse summarizes the persistent theme of the passage. First emphasized is the involvement of *every man and woman* in this undertaking. One senses that people at every social level contribute to ensure that God's house is completed as planned.

29b. Which the LORD had commanded to be made by the hand of Moses.

Also noted is that the master plan for this tabernacle is not of human origin; it has been *commanded* by *the Lord*, to be supervised by *Moses*. That leader will eventually inspect the finished effort and bless the people for having done as the Lord commanded (Exodus 39:43).

> *What Do You Think?*
>   What steps can we take to remind ourselves
>   that all good things come from God?
> *Talking Points for Your Discussion*
> ▪ Regarding helpful Scriptures to memorize
> ▪ Considering prayer patterns that should change
> ▪ Considering how doing so serves as a witness

II. New Covenant Giving
(2 Corinthians 9:6-8)

About 15 centuries pass as we reach the New Testament passage of today's lesson. The apostle Paul is on his third missionary journey as he pauses to write to his beloved Corinthians. As today's text opens, he has just reported on the generous financial gifts that the churches of Macedonia have sent to help meet the needs of Christians in Judea/Jerusalem who are suffering severely (2 Corinthians 8:1-15).

Assuming that the Corinthians will follow suit, Paul plans to send several of his associates to collect their contributions to this worthy cause (2 Corinthians 8:16–9:5).

A. Law of the Harvest (v. 6)

6. But this I say, He which soweth sparingly shall reap also sparingly; and he which soweth bountifully shall reap also bountifully.

Paul uses a common-sense principle from the world of agriculture to illustrate a spiritual truth.

The person who sows few seeds will get little yield, whereas those who invest more aggressively will gain a larger and more profitable harvest.

Applied to the situation at hand, those who give generously to help others in need will receive a larger reward than those who give less. This verse is not promising that those who give to others will necessarily receive a financial bonus in return; Paul's own experiences, which he recounts in some detail in 2 Corinthians 11 and 12, prove that God does not operate that way. There's a fine line to walk here. We must not doubt that our giving will be rewarded, but we must not give with the attitude that God "owes" us something as we tap our foot impatiently waiting for the blessing to show up.

◆   *Sowing for Hope*   ◆

Born to a teenage mother and living in the worst parts of town, basketball superstar LeBron James is grateful for his great fortune. So he is giving back. Drafted into the NBA right out of high school in 2003, LeBron founded the LeBron James Family Foundation in 2004 to help single parents and their children who are in need.

LeBron has also donated $41 million to pay college tuition for 1,100 youth in Ohio. Those who enroll in his "I Promise" program at the University of Akron will be eligible to receive this scholarship. LeBron states that the young people are "the reason I do what I do. These students have big dreams, and I'm happy to do everything I can to help them get there." He notes that many African-American children can only dream of attending college because of the expense. The more LeBron earns, the more he gives to provide hope to many for a better life. He is sowing into lives generously and will reap generously the joy of helping improve lives.

It is often said that we get out what we put in. Athletes become superstars by constant practice. Great inventors spend countless hours creating new products. Great chefs suffer many failures on their way to prepare food as no one else does. Sowing involves risk. But so does failure to sow. See Jesus' parables about servants entrusted with resources (Matthew 25:14-30; Luke 19:11-27).   —S. K.

B. Decision of the Giver (v. 7a)

7a. Every man according as he purposeth in his heart, so let him give; not grudgingly, or of necessity.

Paul's counsel to potential givers echoes the attitude of the actual givers who supported the construction of the tabernacle. That giving was "willing hearted" (Exodus 35:22), and Paul insists that true giving must come from the *heart*. To give from the heart is the opposite of giving *grudgingly* (example: "I'd rather keep the money, but I guess I'll give") or *of necessity* (example: "It's my duty to give a certain percentage").

C. Love of God (v. 7b)

7b. For God loveth a cheerful giver.

This statement does not suggest that we earn God's love by giving, of course. It simply communicates that God is pleased when His people give out of a genuine desire to do so, rather than from a sense of obligation.

> *What Do You Think?*
> How do you make sure that your attitude about giving honors the Lord?
> *Talking Points for Your Discussion*
> - During lean times
> - During bountiful times

D. Ability of God (v. 8)

8. And God is able to make all grace abound toward you; that ye, always having all sufficiency in all things, may abound to every good work.

This verse indirectly addresses the unspoken thought that often lies behind contemplated acts of generosity: "If I give away what I have, what will happen if I myself need it back someday?" Paul's answer shows that the question is misguided. God owns everything, is concerned about all His people, and shows abundant *grace* to those who follow Him.

This being the case, we can be confident that He will always supply what we need. As Paul writes elsewhere, "My God shall supply all your need according to his riches in glory by Christ Jesus" (Philippians 4:19). Our future need might even by met by those whose needs we meet now (see 2 Corinthians 8:13-15)!

> *What Do You Think?*
> How do these passages impact you?
> *Talking Points for Your Discussion*
> - Regarding how they affirm your attitude and practice of giving
> - Regarding how they challenge or correct you

Conclusion

A. Common Factor

The challenges of Moses to the Israelites and of Paul to the Corinthians were for different reasons. The Israelites were challenged to give to construct a place of worship by which they, the givers, would benefit. The end result could be seen and touched as a physical reminder of God's presence. By contrast, the Corinthians were challenged to give to meet the needs of people they had never seen and might never see.

Although the anticipated outcomes of the two giving plans were different, they shared a common factor: willingness—actual on the part of the Israelites; anticipated on the part of the Corinthians. When we find ourselves faced with an important and valid opportunity to give to meet a need, we should examine our attitude before we examine our bank account (2 Corinthians 8:12). A good place to start to test for a proper giving attitude is to recall the ultimate example of having a willingness to give: Jesus. "Though he was rich, yet for your sakes he became poor, that ye through his poverty might be rich" (8:9).

B. Prayer

Heavenly Father, sometimes it's hard to let go of what we have in order to help others. Teach us to trust You enough to give cheerfully. We pray this in the name of Jesus, who gave His all for us. Amen.

C. Thought to Remember

A proper attitude about giving trumps the size of the gift.

INVOLVEMENT LEARNING

Enhance your lesson with KJV Bible Student (from your curriculum supplier) and the reproducible activity page (at www.standardlesson.com or in the back of the KJV Standard Lesson Commentary Deluxe Edition).

Into the Lesson

Divide students into small groups, giving each group a poster board and some markers. (If poster board is not available, paper will do.) Challenge groups to think of an outlandish, made-up charity organization and then design a fund-raising poster to promote it. Have them come up with a name for the organization, a catchy slogan, and some statistics or success stories that support their efforts.

If students need an example, you can mention "The Human Fund" from the TV series *Seinfeld* or "Support the Rabid" from the TV series *The Office,* etc.

Alternative. Distribute pens and copies of the "Real or Really Not?" from the reproducible page, which you can download. Have students work individually to determine which charities are "real" and which are "really not."

After either activity say, "There are a lot of great organizations that would like our financial support as well as fake ones to avoid. We want to be good stewards in our generosity, but what principles help us express that generosity? The Bible gives us important insights about that."

Into the Word

Bring to class a handful of beans and a pan of soil. (If you can't bring these items, use coins to represent beans.) Give two volunteers an equal amount of beans. Ask one volunteer to plant three beans in the soil and keep the rest. Ask the other volunteer to plant all the beans he was given. Then ask, "How valuable are the beans that were left unplanted? Who will reap the bigger harvest based on what was sown? Who is better off in the long run?"

Read aloud 2 Corinthians 9:6-8. Discuss the principles for giving in this text. Frame the discussion in terms of how much to give, how to give, and why give.

Then read aloud Exodus 35:20-29. Discuss how this incident reflects the principles Paul gave to the church in Corinth. Who gave, what did they give, and why?

Have students skim the text and name things that God's people gave, including things other than money. Then give each student three index cards and a pen. Have students think about the gifts they have to offer. On one card have students write a gift they can give to God that involves TIME. On another card have them write a gift that involves their TALENT or abilities. On the last card have them write a gift that involves money or other earthly TREASURE.

When students are finished, have them put the cards in order according to how happy they would be to give each gift. Challenge them to use the cards over the next three months and give each gift to God with a cheerful heart.

Alternative: Distribute pens and copies of the "Cheerful Givers?" activity from the reproducible page. Assign each character and text to a small group. Have each group read its text and answer the questions that follow.

Into Life

Make a transition by writing these two commands on the board:

Give until it hurts
Give because it feels good

Divide the class into two groups. Have one group name reasons to "give until it hurts"; have the other group name reasons to "give because it feels good." After allowing a few minutes discussion, bring groups together to share their ideas.

Talk about whether or not it is possible to do both, or whether the concepts are contradictory. Finally, be prepared to tell, if no one else does, why neither is the best motive for giving from a biblical perspective (since both are based on feelings).

BRINGING FIRSTFRUITS

DEVOTIONAL READING: Ephesians 4:25–5:2
BACKGROUND SCRIPTURE: Leviticus 2:14; 23:9-22

LEVITICUS 2:14

14 And if thou offer a meat offering of thy firstfruits unto the LORD, thou shalt offer for the meat offering of thy firstfruits green ears of corn dried by the fire, even corn beaten out of full ears.

LEVITICUS 23:9-14, 22

9 And the LORD spake unto Moses, saying,

10 Speak unto the children of Israel, and say unto them, When ye be come into the land which I give unto you, and shall reap the harvest thereof, then ye shall bring a sheaf of the firstfruits of your harvest unto the priest:

11 And he shall wave the sheaf before the LORD, to be accepted for you: on the morrow after the sabbath the priest shall wave it.

12 And ye shall offer that day when ye wave the sheaf an he lamb without blemish of the first year for a burnt offering unto the LORD.

13 And the meat offering thereof shall be two tenth deals of fine flour mingled with oil, an offering made by fire unto the LORD for a sweet savour: and the drink offering thereof shall be of wine, the fourth part of an hin.

14 And ye shall eat neither bread, nor parched corn, nor green ears, until the selfsame day that ye have brought an offering unto your God: it shall be a statute for ever throughout your generations in all your dwellings.

. . . .

22 And when ye reap the harvest of your land, thou shalt not make clean riddance of the corners of thy field when thou reapest, neither shalt thou gather any gleaning of thy harvest: thou shalt leave them unto the poor, and to the stranger: I am the LORD your God.

KEY VERSE

Speak unto the children of Israel, and say unto them, When ye be come into the land which I give unto you, and shall reap the harvest thereof, then ye shall bring a sheaf of the firstfruits of your harvest unto the priest. —**Leviticus 23:10**

ACKNOWLEDGING GOD

Unit 3: Give Praise to God

LESSON AIMS

After participating in this lesson, each learner will be able to:

1. Describe the firstfruits offering and its purpose.

2. Relate the firstfruits concept to the new covenant.

3. Adjust one behavior in order to live biblically as a firstfruit.

LESSON OUTLINE

Introduction

A. Marking Time by God's Calendar

Cultures have different ways and traditions of marking time. In contemporary Western culture, January 1 is significant. It serves the official purpose of marking the beginning of the year and the unofficial purpose of reminding people that "the holiday season" is over.

The months of November and December are the important months in the holiday season, especially for the retail industry. Unofficial special days such as Black Friday (the day after Thanksgiving) and Cyber Monday three days later have become cultural staples for bargain hunters. But modern culture changes quickly. Recent years have seen Brown Thursday added to the unofficial calendar of retail merchandising.

Cultures not only mark time differently with regard to specific calendar dates but also in terms of seasons. Some cultures have only two seasons: rainy and dry. For those of us who experience four seasons, spring is the season of new life, with Easter a fitting holiday in that regard as we celebrate the resurrection of Jesus.

For the ancient Israelites, the first and seventh months were particularly important. As agrarian people, their existence was closely tied to their crops. Their major celebrations revolved around gratitude to God for what He had done for them in the past and how He was sustaining them in the present. Today's lesson focuses on one such celebration.

B. Lesson Background

The beginning of the Jewish year is called *Rosh Hashanah*. This phrase appears in the Hebrew Bible only in Ezekiel 40:1, and scholars debate what exactly it is referring to in that passage.

The Jews ultimately ended up with two calendars. The religious calendar began with the month of Abib (Exodus 12:2; 13:4), also called Nisan (Esther 3:7). On the civil calendar, the month called Ethanim (1 Kings 8:2), later known as Tishri, serves that purpose; that is six months after the beginning of the religious new year. *Rosh Hashanah* begins the civil new year.

Most important on either calendar were the three annual pilgrimage feasts: the Feast of Unleavened Bread (combined with Passover), the Feast of Harvest, and the Feast of Ingathering (Exodus 23:14-17). The first and third of these are weeklong observances. Between them is the single-day Feast of Ingathering that is also called the Feast of Weeks, Feast of Harvest, or Day of Firstfruits (see Exodus 23:16a; 34:22a; Leviticus 23:15-21; Numbers 28:26-31; Deuteronomy 16:9-12, 16). This is the subject of today's lesson.

The Feast of Weeks designation points to seven weeks of grain harvest. On day 50, the day that is seen to conclude this harvest, the Israelites celebrate Pentecost, a later designation that reflects the number 50.

The correspondence between agrarian-based holidays and God's saving acts on behalf of His people were not mere coincidence. God acted powerfully to create a people and settle them in the promised land. The Israelites were to recognize that their presence in the land was a gift. The land really belonged to God, and He allowed the people to dwell there by His gracious provision. But as today's text opens, the people were not there yet. The setting of today's text is, rather, the encampment at Mount Sinai, where the Lord gave His law to Moses for the people (see Leviticus 27:34).

I. Preparing Firstfruits
(LEVITICUS 2:14)

14. And if thou offer a meat offering of thy firstfruits unto the LORD, thou shalt offer for the meat offering of thy firstfruits green ears of corn dried by the fire, even corn beaten out of full ears.

There are many kinds of *firstfruits* that can be offered *unto the Lord*. One must be sure to read the entirety of the verse before us to understand what a *meat offering* includes. In the *King James Version,* the word *meat* can refer to anything edible, food in general. We see that in the case at hand as the word *meat* refers to *green ears of corn* (compare Isaiah 62:8). The word *corn,* for its part, is a generic word for any kind of grain.

Thus the offering described here is a grain offering. Grains cannot be ground into flour suitable for baking until the moisture is removed; hence the need for the grain's being *dried by the fire* (compare Leviticus 23:17).

II. Offering Firstfruits
(LEVITICUS 23:9-14)
A. Presentation (vv. 9-13)

9, 10a. And the LORD spake unto Moses, saying, Speak unto the children of Israel, and say unto them, When ye be come into the land which I give unto you.

Having left Egypt by God's design and protection, they need instructions regarding how to conduct themselves in *the land* He is going to give them. Since the land is ultimately His, it must be cared for according to those instructions.

10b. And shall reap the harvest thereof, then ye shall bring a sheaf of the firstfruits of your harvest unto the priest.

To bring *a sheaf of the firstfruits* of the harvest is a requirement, not an option or a guideline. Firstfruits, as the name implies, consist of the very first portion of the crop to be harvested. It is the part that the farmer is most excited about because it serves as a sort of sign or down payment of the full crop to come. It assures the farmer that all

HOW TO SAY IT

Aaronic	Air-*ahn*-ik.
Abib	*Ay*-bib.
Baal	*Bay*-ul.
Canaan	*Kay*-nun.
Corinthians	Ko-*rin*-thee-unz (*th* as in *thin*).
Deuteronomy	Due-ter-*ahn*-uh-me.
Ethanim	*Eth*-uh-nim.
Ezekiel	Ee-*zeek*-ee-ul or Ee-*zeek*-yul.
Jordan	*Jor*-dun.
Leviticus	Leh-*vit*-ih-kus.
Nisan	*Nye*-san.
Rosh Hashanah	Rawsh Huh-*shuh*-nuh.
Sinai	*Sigh*-nye or *Sigh*-nay-eye.
tabernacle	**tah**-burr-*nah*-kul.
Tishri	*Tish*-ree.

Visual for Lesson 11. *Start a discussion by pointing to this visual and asking, "How exactly do we balance these three with one another?"*

his hard work of tilling, planting, and watering is beginning to pay off.

Most likely the crop harvested in view is barley, which ripens before wheat (compare Ruth 1:22; 2:23.) But here some additional details are provided about the offering that are not found in our earlier passage. *A sheaf* is a small bundle or armful. Of that portion, only a small amount is offered directly to God by being burned up. The majority of it goes to the priests to be eaten (see Leviticus 2:1-3). The Aaronic priests depend on the offerings of the people for their livelihood since their devotion to working in the tabernacle keeps them from being able to reap regular harvests like everyone else (Numbers 18:8-24).

Providing for the priests is important, but it is not the primary reason for the firstfruits offering. It is more vital that the Israelites take time to recognize that it is God who is blessing them by His grace; they have not earned it (Deuteronomy 9:5, 6). They must never forget that He, not fictitious fertility gods such as Baal, is the source of all they will enjoy in the promised land. After a firstfruits offering is made, the Israelites will be free to enjoy the remainder of the harvest.

But what proportion of the people's harvest is to constitute the firstfruits offering? A specific proportion is not mentioned at this point, perhaps because the very nature of a firstfruits offering means that a specific proportion cannot be calculated. That is, one wouldn't know how to apply a

proportional calculation until after the entire crop is harvested.

Even so, passages such as Leviticus 27:30; Numbers 18:21-29; 2 Chronicles 31:5; and Nehemiah 10:35-37; 12:44 seem to suggest that a tithe (10 percent) is intended at some point. It's safe to conclude in any case that God does not want the people to give a set portion legalistically, as if making a mortgage payment. They are not to be thinking, "Here's Your cut, God." Instead, their attitude should be, "I'm giving the first part in faith that there will be plenty of the remainder to meet my needs."

11. And he shall wave the sheaf before the LORD, to be accepted for you: on the morrow after the sabbath the priest shall wave it.

After receiving a firstfruits offering, the priest elevates it above his head to make clear that it is dedicated to God. The people believe that God's blessing will result (Proverbs 3:9, 10; Ezekiel 44:30).

> *What Do You Think?*
> What visual aids can you build into routines to remind you to be grateful for God's provision?
> *Talking Points for Your Discussion*
> - Regarding regular, daily routines (meals, etc.)
> - Regarding irregular, occasional routines (holidays, etc.)
> - Other

Historically, Jews have been divided over when this offering is to occur. Exactly what does *on the morrow after the sabbath* mean? Some students point out that Leviticus 23:15, 16a demonstrates a definite connection between the Feast of Unleavened Bread and the Day of Firstfruits. God's instructions show that an event within one feast is used to determine the timing of a feast that is to follow. Since Passover is discussed in the preceding section of Leviticus 23:4-8, *the sabbath* in the verse before us refers to a Passover Sabbath.

Others point out, however, that Leviticus 23:9 begins a new section. So rather than pointing back to the Passover Sabbath, it points to the first Sabbath of the actual harvest. Under this proposal, the Day of Firstfruits in 23:9-14 is a different observance than the Feast of Weeks in 23:15-21.

Ultimately, it's more important to come to grips with the meaning and significance of the Day of Firstfruits than the day of its observance.

12. And ye shall offer that day when ye wave the sheaf an he lamb without blemish of the first year for a burnt offering unto the LORD.

Israel's offerings often involve a series of steps. The second step of this offering is that of a year-old *lamb*. It is important that this lamb be *without blemish* because the one giving the offering is identifying with the offering. It is a way of saying to God that the worshipper is giving his best to Him, not just the best of the flock but also the best of himself.

In contrast with the Passover observance, which looks to the past in celebration of God's deliverance, the Day of Firstfruits looks to the future. Firstfruits are offered on the first day of the week (v. 11, just considered), the beginning of the workweek after the Sabbath day of rest. The very designation "firstfruits" implies there's more fruit to follow, and that includes not only the grain offering just discussed, but also an abundance of livestock. Thus the worshipper need not fear giving the "best first" of his livestock—God always has more to provide!

Burnt offerings are unique in that they are turned completely into smoke. They are not cooked for human consumption, but burned up so that the smoke ascends to God. Though God sometimes acknowledges the pleasing aroma of offerings (see v. 13, next), He does not need the food (Psalm 50:12, 13). These offerings are about what Israel needs: the people need to keep God first by returning to Him the first of the blessings that they have received from Him. They owe their abundance to their gracious heavenly provider. Should they forget that, they will begin to drift from the life God has called them to live.

What Do You Think?

How do you ensure that you're offering God your best?

Talking Points for Your Discussion

- In preparing your heart for worship
- In preparing to participate in a Bible class
- Other

13a. And the meat offering thereof shall be two tenth deals of fine flour mingled with oil, an offering made by fire unto the LORD for a sweet savour.

To mix the grain offering (see comments on Leviticus 2:14, above) with *fine flour* and *oil* constitutes the third step of the firstfruits offering. *Two tenth deals* computes to about 6.2 quarts; this amount of flour weighs about 6.6 pounds. This is twice the normal amount of flour used for grain offerings (see Leviticus 6:20; Numbers 28:13). Olive oil is produced by the hard work of crushing and grinding.

13b. And the drink offering thereof shall be of wine, the fourth part of a hin.

The drink offering is step four. This signifies a joyous occasion. *The fourth part of a hin* computes to 41.4 fluid ounces or 1.22 liters. Drink offerings are also described in Exodus 29:38-42.

B. Proper Time (v. 14)

14. And ye shall eat neither bread, nor parched corn, nor green ears, until the selfsame day that ye have brought an offering unto your God: it shall be a statute for ever throughout your generations in all your dwellings.

For the offering to fulfill its intended function, the Israelites must not eat of any produce of the promised land until the firstfruits offering is given to God. To eat of the produce before offering the firstfruits to God is to indicate that the food is theirs to do with as they wish. But since the whole purpose of the offering is to focus on God as the provider, it is more than appropriate that the Israelites acknowledge Him properly before they begin to indulge themselves.

◆ PUT HIM FIRST ◆

Rick Warren often teaches about the importance of putting God first when it comes to personal finances. The author of *The Purpose-Driven Life* explains that in whatever area of your life you desire God's blessing, you put Him first in that area.

"You want God to bless your business? Put him first in your business. You want God to bless your marriage? Put him first in your marriage. You want God to bless your time? Put him first in your time. You want God to bless your finances? Put him first in your finances."

The prescribed offering of firstfruits served to remind the ancient Israelites that the Lord was the one who could be trusted to provide secondfruits, thirdfruits, fourthfruits, etc., after the firstfruits were given to Him. The people were to focus first on God, not themselves.

And so it is with Christians. Regular giving is not optional (1 Corinthians 16:2), and that is a good thing because each gift requires us to focus on the one who ultimately receives the gift: God. But the primary firstfruit He desires is us ourselves. See James 1:18.   —D. C. S.

> *What Do You Think?*
>   How will you apply the firstfruits principle today?
>
> *Talking Points for Your Discussion*
>   - Regarding firstfruits of your time
>   - Regarding firstfruits of your talents (abilities and spiritual gifts)
>   - Regarding firstfruits of your treasure (money and other tangible resources)

III. Sharing Blessings

(Leviticus 23:22)

22. And when ye reap the harvest of your land, thou shalt not make clean riddance of the corners of thy field when thou reapest, neither shalt thou gather any gleaning of thy harvest: thou shalt leave them unto the poor, and to the stranger: I am the Lord your God.

God does not generously give to the Israelites so they can stingily hoard His gifts and focus on themselves. The firstfruits offering is one way to keep them from doing so. The verse before us is another.

Sharing takes various forms for the Israelites. Here, God requires His people to underharvest their fields intentionally. They must leave a portion of the harvest in the fields *unto the poor*.

This command may be difficult for many Israelites to obey. Famines are not unknown (Genesis

12:10; 1 Kings 18:2; Acts 11:28; etc.), and hoarding is a temptation (Luke 12:18, 19). Some will want to harvest every bit of grain and store all they can for the future. This seems the smart and responsible thing to do.

Yet God disapproves of this. He wants His people to share selflessly. So He requires those who have been blessed to leave some of the blessing behind for others to reap and enjoy. Ruth, a Moabite widow, is perhaps the most prominent example of this procedure in operation (Ruth 2:1-3), and she ends up as an ancestor of Jesus (Matthew 1:5). What an impact!

God promises to bless those who share with the needy as He commands (Deuteronomy 24:19). So the Israelites face a choice. They can do the frugal thing by harvesting every square inch of their fields, or they can obey God and trusting Him to provide for their needs. Life as God's people has always been a life of faith day in and day out.

> *What Do You Think?*
>   How can we apply Leviticus 23:22 today without violating 2 Thessalonians 3:10?
>
> *Talking Points for Your Discussion*
>   - In personal helping situations
>   - While serving on a benevolence committee
>   - Other

◆ *"Gleaning" Today* ◆

A ministry in Atlanta practices a modern form of the law of gleaning, allowing low-income parents to obtain toys for their children at Christmas by charging only half the retail price. Bob Lupton, the initiator of Pride for Parents, used to have wealthier families buy extra presents for free distribution.

The youngsters were excited to get the toys, and mothers were gracious but subdued. But if the father was home when the toys were delivered, he'd disappear out of embarrassment. Lupton's revised plan enabled parents to "glean" from the "fields" of others and maintain the dignity of providing for their children in the process. As Lupton explained, "What we found was, parents would rather work and pay for the toys that would bring joy to their kids on Christmas, much more so than standing in the free toy line with their proof of poverty."

Since Jesus reminded us that the poor will always be among us (John 12:8), we will always have multiple opportunities to help them. The challenge is to do this in a way that fosters a sense of dignity and not dependency for those receiving help. What would have to happen for you to embrace rather than ignore these opportunities?

—D. C. S.

Conclusion

A. Firstfruit Facts

The Jewish people were under the boot of the Roman Empire when Christ came. Many Jews were living in the promised land, although it didn't feel like it (Acts 1:6). Many other Jews were scattered throughout the Roman Empire (James 1:1). Since taxes were paid to a pagan government in both cases, the Jews undoubtedly felt as if they were paying rent to Rome wherever they lived. How can one pay firstfruits to God when that which would constitute such an offering goes to Rome?

Jesus did not reverse this. He did nothing to regain control of Canaan for His people. Instead, He died for their sins and sent them to live among all nations as witnesses to His kingdom. Wherever Christians live, we are resident aliens or exiles on foreign soil (1 Peter 1:1). That is indeed God's will as it lines up with the Great Commission (Matthew 28:19, 20), but firstfruits giving can be difficult when secular governments take so much in taxes right off the top.

Monetary giving is important, and the New Testament has principles for so doing (Matthew 6:1-4; 1 Corinthians 16:2; 2 Corinthians 9:6, 7; etc.). There are indeed certain parallels between old and new covenant expectations for giving, but we should not press these too far since the old law is nailed to the cross (Colossians 2:14). Still, the firstfruits concept should be deeply meaningful to Christians. Christ is designated as "firstfruits" (1 Corinthians 15:20, 23). As a result of Christ's redeeming work, we "have the firstfruits of the Spirit" (Romans 8:23). The result is that we ourselves have become "a kind of firstfruits" (James 1:18; compare Revelation 14:4).

B. Firstfruit Application

But what does it mean to be "a kind of firstfruits"? Linking together the New Testament passages just mentioned leads to the conclusion that our witness is to center on representing the newness of life we have in Christ. Do others see the good result of Christ's redemptive work in us, or do they see something else? Are we being salty salt, bright light, a city on a hill, and stars shining in the universe? When people look at us, do they catch a glimpse of the good news of God's salvation?

Usually we think of the firstfruits of the Israelites' flocks and crops being offered to God. But reversing the direction of the offering is Jeremiah 2:3: "Israel was holiness unto the Lord, and the firstfruits of his increase." The significance of this is in the very next line: "all that devour him shall offend; evil shall come upon them." If such could be said about God's old covenant people, is His love and protection for us any less?

> **What Do You Think?**
> In what ways would your life change were you to live consistently as a firstfruit of God's new creation?
> *Talking Points for Your Discussion*
> - In ways visible to others
> - In ways visible only to God

C. Prayer

Faithful God, You have always given Your best. And still we struggle to give back to You. We are tempted to hold back. We are tempted to store up treasures on this earth. We are then tempted to keep everything to ourselves. Lord, we need You to save us from our self-deception so we may live as Your firstfruit witnesses to the world. We pray this in Jesus' name. Amen.

D. Thought to Remember

Live as firstfruits.

INVOLVEMENT LEARNING

Enhance your lesson with KJV Bible Student *(from your curriculum supplier) and the reproducible activity page (at www.standardlesson.com or in the back of the* KJV Standard Lesson Commentary Deluxe Edition*).*

Into the Lesson

Write each of the following on a separate index card: *medical bill, rent/mortgage, cable/satellite TV, charity pledge, phone, credit card, insurance, utilities.* Lay the cards facedown on a table. Then ask a volunteer to turn over two of the cards and read them aloud. Ask the volunteer to imagine having enough money to pay only one of the two bills. Which would it be?

After answer and explanation, turn the cards back over and mix. Ask another volunteer to do the same thing. Continue until everyone has had the opportunity to participate, but don't let this drag out.

Lead into the Bible lesson by saying, "Life is a matter of priorities, isn't it? The Bible tells us how to recognize what our priorities should be."

Into the Word

Say, "Firstfruits was a Jewish feast to celebrate the gift of God's provision. Let's learn more about it and what it means to us."

Ask a volunteer to read aloud Leviticus 2:14; 23:9-13. As the Scripture is being read, blow up a balloon, tie it, and write the word PRIORITIZE on it with a felt-tip pen. Say, "God commanded the Israelites to bring Him offerings immediately after reaping the first of the harvest He would provide. How should these offerings have helped the Israelites keep their priorities straight?"

Ask another volunteer to read aloud Leviticus 23:14. As it is being read, blow up another balloon, tie it, and write the word PARTAKE on the balloon. Then ask, "What requirement had to be met before the Israelites were permitted to partake of the food from the harvest? Why?"

Ask a final volunteer to read aloud Leviticus 23:22. As it is being read, blow up another balloon, tie it, and write the word PROVIDE on the balloon. Ask, "After God had been given His portion, and after the Israelites had met (not exceeded) their own needs, for whom were they to provide? How?"

Option. Discuss the following New Testament references to firstfruits and the symbolism therein: Romans 8:23; 1 Corinthians 15:20; James 1:18. Expected observations on the latter two references are that firstfruits are part of the "crops" of God's people and the "farmer" is God. Be sure to note, if no one else does, that firstfruit in the Old Testament primarily refers to agricultural bounty, with Jeremiah 2:3 being an exception. Use the commentary to explore how that passage relates to Christians as firstfruits.

Alternative. Distribute pens and copies of the "Firstfruits Fill-In" activity from the reproducible page, which you can download. Have students work in small groups to complete the verses.

After either activity say, "Let's take this a bit further by exploring the significance in not just *giving* firstfruits, but also in *being* firstfruits."

Into Life

Give each student three slips of paper. Ask students to write a single word on each that describes their reasons for giving of themselves to God. Collect the slips, shuffle them to ensure anonymity, and read them aloud. Discuss the most common words listed (possible responses are *feeling, command, gratitude,* etc.). Challenge students to pray about their giving of themselves for Christ's work in the week ahead.

Alternative 1. Tie or hold together the balloons from the Into the Word segment. Challenge students to apply today's Scriptures to modern times as you ask, "What would it look like to give God your firstfruits today in terms of these three words?"

Alternative 2. Distribute copies of the "My Giving to God" activity from the reproducible page. Have students work individually to reflect on their giving.

REMEMBERING WITH JOY

DEVOTIONAL READING: Psalm 50:1-15
BACKGROUND SCRIPTURE: Leviticus 25

LEVITICUS 25:1-12

1 And the LORD spake unto Moses in mount Sinai, saying,

2 Speak unto the children of Israel, and say unto them, When ye come into the land which I give you, then shall the land keep a sabbath unto the LORD.

3 Six years thou shalt sow thy field, and six years thou shalt prune thy vineyard, and gather in the fruit thereof;

4 But in the seventh year shall be a sabbath of rest unto the land, a sabbath for the LORD: thou shalt neither sow thy field, nor prune thy vineyard.

5 That which groweth of its own accord of thy harvest thou shalt not reap, neither gather the grapes of thy vine undressed: for it is a year of rest unto the land.

6 And the sabbath of the land shall be meat for you; for thee, and for thy servant, and for thy maid, and for thy hired servant, and for thy stranger that sojourneth with thee.

7 And for thy cattle, and for the beast that are in thy land, shall all the increase thereof be meat.

8 And thou shalt number seven sabbaths of years unto thee, seven times seven years; and the space of the seven sabbaths of years shall be unto thee forty and nine years.

9 Then shalt thou cause the trumpet of the jubile to sound on the tenth day of the seventh month, in the day of atonement shall ye make the trumpet sound throughout all your land.

10 And ye shall hallow the fiftieth year, and proclaim liberty throughout all the land unto all the inhabitants thereof: it shall be a jubile unto you; and ye shall return every man unto his possession, and ye shall return every man unto his family.

11 A jubile shall that fiftieth year be unto you: ye shall not sow, neither reap that which groweth of itself in it, nor gather the grapes in it of thy vine undressed.

12 For it is the jubile; it shall be holy unto you: ye shall eat the increase thereof out of the field.

KEY VERSE

Ye shall hallow the fiftieth year, and proclaim liberty throughout all the land unto all the inhabitants thereof: it shall be a jubile unto you; and ye shall return every man unto his possession, and ye shall return every man unto his family. —**Leviticus 25:10**

ACKNOWLEDGING GOD

Unit 3: Give Praise to God

LESSONS 10–13

LESSON AIMS

After participating in this lesson, each learner will be able to:

1. Summarize the nature of the rest the land was to receive during the Sabbath Year and the Year of Jubilee.

2. Explain the spiritual principles that these laws were meant to instill.

3. Identify one way he or she can proclaim the "Year of Jubilee" that Jesus has ushered in and make a plan to do so.

LESSON OUTLINE

Introduction
    A. Living by Faith
    B. Lesson Background
 I. Sabbath Year (LEVITICUS 25:1-7)
    A. Principle Stated (vv. 1, 2)
    B. Details Specified (vv. 3-5)
       Give the Land a Break!
    C. Results Promised (vv. 6, 7)
II. Year of Jubilee (LEVITICUS 25:8-12)
    A. Counting Sevens (v. 8)
    B. Sounding Trumpets (v. 9)
    C. Proclaiming Liberty (v. 10)
       Living as Reconciled People
    D. Observing Jubilee (vv. 11, 12)
Conclusion
    A. Old Testament Jubilee
    B. New Testament Jubilee
    C. Prayer
    D. Thought to Remember

Introduction

A. Living by Faith

When we think about living by faith, we generally consider that to be a religious concept, meaning that one who lives by faith is trusting in God. But the fact is that *everyone* lives by faith, even the person who is not religious in the least!

Why do we get on airplanes? Because we have faith that the pilot has the proper skills to get us to our destination safely. How do we know that the pound of hamburger we purchase at the store is indeed (1) a pound and (2) hamburger? Because we have faith that the grocer is dealing with us honestly. Why do we entrust a package to a delivery person? Once again, we are taking a step of faith. Devout Christians, strident atheists, and everyone in between takes such steps of faith. This is faith based on evidence; it is not blind faith.

But imagine a world in which we could trust no one else because there was no evidence upon which to base that trust. How demoralizing that would be! Every action we took during any given day would be subject to incredible risk.

In truth, none of us lives totally on our own. To survive in society, we must have a certain level of faith in the competence of others. This sometimes involves risk. Many portions of the Law of Moses challenged the Israelites to exercise a measure of trust and risk. But the basis of the Israelites' actions was rooted first and foremost in their trust in God.

B. Lesson Background

Often the various regulations found within the Law of Moses are placed in three categories: *civil* (those that helped maintain an orderly society), *ceremonial* (those dealing with how God's covenant people were to express their worship to Him), and *moral* (those dealing with right living). Whereas the first two groups applied only to Old Testament Israel (though there may still be general principles of conduct to be drawn from them), the moral laws continue to serve as standards of right and wrong behavior.

Today's passage from Leviticus 25 falls primarily within the ceremonial category, since it concerns certain religious observances that do not apply to Christians (see Colossians 2:14-17), specifically the Sabbath Year and the Year of Jubilee. These topics also have civil ramifications as well, since obedience to them was intended to help build a just society.

But if the specific commandments of today's text no longer apply, then why bother studying them? The answer is hinted at above: because they speak to principles of conduct that are important yet today.

I. Sabbath Year
(LEVITICUS 25:1-7)
A. Principle Stated (vv. 1, 2)

1. And the LORD spake unto Moses in mount Sinai, saying.

There are dozens of references in the book of Leviticus that record *the Lord* speaking *unto Moses*. This is direct word-revelation: God communicating with humans (in distinction from general revelation that is affirmed in, for example, Psalm 19:1-4).

The Israelites gathered at *mount Sinai* in the third month after leaving Egypt (Exodus 19:1). The people encamp here for a little less than a year (Numbers 10:11, 12) in order to receive God's law.

2. Speak unto the children of Israel, and say unto them, When ye come into the land which I give you, then shall the land keep a sabbath unto the LORD.

HOW TO SAY IT

Canaan	*Kay*-nun.
Deuteronomy	Due-ter-*ahn*-uh-me.
Isaiah	Eye-*zay*-uh.
Israelites	*Iz*-ray-el-ites.
Levites	*Lee*-vites.
Levitical	Leh-*vit*-ih-kul.
Leviticus	Leh-*vit*-ih-kus.
Nazareth	*Naz*-uh-reth.
Sinai	*Sigh*-nye or *Sigh*-nay-eye.
synagogue	*sin*-uh-gog.
Thessalonians	*Thess*-uh-**lo**-nee-unz (*th* as in *thin*).

The most important feature of the promised land that lies ahead is that it will be God's gift. His covenant people, *the children of Israel*, will not be able to claim they have earned it (Deuteronomy 9:6). They will be stewards of God's grant, not owners who are entitled.

At this point, the Israelites have already received the Ten Commandments, the fourth being that of keeping the Sabbath (see Exodus 20:8-11). The importance of this commandment is underlined by the fact that it is the longest of the 10. It is to be obeyed by every person in Israel, including non-Israelites who live among the covenant people. Even animals are to be given a rest.

In the verse before us we have reached the point of *wait—there's more!* as the command regarding Sabbath is to be applied to *the land* as well.

> **What Do You Think?**
> As you personalize the Sabbath principle, how will you know when you've gotten the proper amount of rest?
> *Talking Points for Your Discussion*
> - Considering tell-tale signs of inadequate rest
> - Considering tell-tale signs of too much rest

B. Details Specified (vv. 3-5)

3, 4. Six years thou shalt sow thy field, and six years thou shalt prune thy vineyard, and gather in the fruit thereof; but in the seventh year shall be a sabbath of rest unto the land, a sabbath for the LORD: thou shalt neither sow thy field, nor prune thy vineyard.

The *sabbath of rest unto the land* operates on a principle similar to that which undergirds the Sabbath Day: just as the people are to work for six days and rest on the seventh, the land is to be sown and its produce reaped for *six years . . . but in the seventh year* neither sowing nor reaping is to done. From a productivity standpoint, we know that it is good to let farmland lie fallow for a time or to rotate crops. But the focus of this legislation is spiritual: this period *of rest unto the land* is *for the Lord*.

The timetable to be observed with this law is similar to the laws concerning both debts and servants. In the Sabbath Year, debts are to be canceled (some suggest "suspended") in the case of loans made to Israelites (Deuteronomy 15:1-6). The law also states that a Hebrew servant is to serve for six years, then in the seventh year he or she is to be set free (15:12).

◆ GIVE THE LAND A BREAK! ◆

A 2013 report by the Economics of Land Degradation (ELD) Initiative indicates that not giving the agricultural land breaks from growing crops or forests has consequences. Erosion increases, soil quality declines, and the capacity of the land to yield crops goes down.

Farmers are discovering they can double the amount of crops a parcel of land yields by allowing it to lie fallow for a few years. Such a practice has the potential of doubling the amount of livestock the land can support. ELD researchers estimate that if some form of resting the land were practiced worldwide, the crop yield could potentially increase by 2.5 billion tons annually.

The ancient Israelites did not have access to ELD research. They had something better: God. They could either honor His desire in faith or trust their own instincts. We face the same choice in countless ways daily, don't we?　　—L. G. S.

5. That which groweth of its own accord of thy harvest thou shalt not reap, neither gather the grapes of thy vine undressed: for it is a year of rest unto the land.

The Sabbath law of rest applies, not only to what the people intentionally sow and harvest, but also to any edible substance that grows on its own. Thus the entire land is given the opportunity to rest, not just the part the people have farmed.

What Do You Think?
How will you deal with obstacles to build seasons of rest into your life?
Talking Points for Your Discussion
- Regarding practical obstacles
- Regarding cultural obstacles
- Regarding psychological obstacles
- Other

C. Results Promised (vv. 6, 7)

6, 7. And the sabbath of the land shall be meat for you; for thee, and for thy servant, and for thy maid, and for thy hired servant, and for thy stranger that sojourneth with thee, and for thy cattle, and for the beast that are in thy land, shall all the increase thereof be meat.

Although no harvesting or reaping occurs during *the sabbath of the land,* enough food will be available during that entire year. (We noted in comments on Leviticus 2:14 in lesson 11 that *meat* often refers to food in general.) The people need not fear, for God promises that there will be adequate food for all, whether Israelite, non-Israelite, or animal.

One wonders how the land is to provide food when the people are not allowed to eat what normally is sown and reaped (Leviticus 25:4, above) or reap what grew apart from any cultivation (25:5, above). The answer may lie in distinguishing between harvesting and simply living off the land. The key concept of "harvesting" is gathering the crop for storage. During the sabbatical year people can collect food from the field for use at that time. The people are to live much like the poor among them, who are permitted during the seventh year to take whatever they wish from the land (Exodus 23:11).

Later in Leviticus 25, the Lord offers additional assurance in anticipation of the people's concern for having enough to eat during the Sabbath Year. He says, "I will command my blessing upon you in the sixth year [that is, the year before the Sabbath Year], and it shall bring forth fruit for three years" (Leviticus 25:21). The land will experience its rest in the seventh year, the people will sow new crops in the eighth year, and then the ninth year will be the next year during which crops are harvested (25:22).

Such laws as these are grounded in a key truth that bears repeating: the promised land is the Lord's. His people must trust that He, as its ultimate caretaker, will ensure that it produces exactly what the people and the animals need. Of course, the stated blessings and provisions hinge on the people's faithful obedience to the Lord as Leviticus 25:18, 19 make quite clear.

II. Year of Jubilee
(LEVITICUS 25:8-12)
A. Counting Sevens (v. 8)

8. And thou shalt number seven sabbaths of years unto thee, seven times seven years; and the space of the seven sabbaths of years shall be unto thee forty and nine years.

This is another one of those *wait—there's more!* moments. In addition to the Sabbath Year that occurs every seventh year, God has another requirement. This one involves counting off seven cycles of sabbath years to determine the passage of *forty and nine years.* The reason why is given next.

B. Sounding Trumpets (v. 9)

9. Then shalt thou cause the trumpet of the jubile to sound on the tenth day of the seventh month, in the day of atonement shall ye make the trumpet sound throughout all your land.

Given the importance of the seventh day and year, it is not surprising that the *seventh month* (late September and early October) is also special. The first day of this month is commemorated as a day of rest and offerings (Leviticus 23:24, 25). The people cease working *on the tenth day* and celebrate *the day of atonement* (23:27-31). The details of its observance are outlined in Leviticus 16. This particular day is also described as "a sabbath of rest" (23:32). On the fifteenth day of the seventh month, the people cease work at the start of the seven-day Feast of Tabernacles (23:34).

The tenth day also heralds the arrival of the *jubile* (modern spelling adds another *e* at the end). The Hebrew word being translated appears to be derived from a word translated "rams' horns" in Joshua 6:4. The word translated *trumpet* here is different, although still referring to a ram's horn.

Just who is to sound the trumpet is not stated. Since it is to be sounded *throughout all your land,* it may be the duty of the priests or Levites who will be assigned territory among the people of Israel (see Joshua 21).

C. Proclaiming Liberty (v. 10)

10a. And ye shall hallow the fiftieth year, and proclaim liberty throughout all the land

Visual for Lesson 12. *Point to this visual as you ask, "Under what conditions does God expect us to apply the Jubilee principle today, if any? Why?"*

unto all the inhabitants thereof: it shall be a jubile unto you.

Our word *holiday* derives from the phrase *holy day,* but in many cases we have kept the celebration part while not retaining the holiness aspect. The Israelites are not to miss the latter. The liberty to be proclaimed *throughout all the land unto all the inhabitants thereof* every *fiftieth year* is certainly cause for celebration. But the people must also be sure to *hallow* that year, meaning to set it aside as a holy year. Exactly what the terms *liberty* and *hallow* include are next explained.

10b. And ye shall return every man unto his possession.

This is to be the result of the proclamation of liberty. The word *possession* refers to one's ancestral property within the promised land. A scenario is described in Leviticus 25:25-28 in which an Israelite sells property because of his impoverished state. When the Year of Jubilee arrives, the property reverts back to its original owner, who is allowed to *return* to it. Leviticus 25:14, 15 establishes how this is fair to those who must give the land back.

10c. And ye shall return every man unto his family.

In some cases, an impoverished Israelite may sell himself into servitude to another Israelite, as Leviticus 25:39-43 describes. That person is to be given freedom to *return . . . unto his family* in the Year of Jubilee. Every fiftieth year is, in effect, an opportunity to start over.

The Israelites are thus being encouraged to see their land and their fellow Israelites as God sees them. Land is not something to be acquired and hoarded for selfish purposes, and people are not to be used as a means for promoting one's own personal status or comfort. In all of this the Israelites are to remember their former status in Egypt (Leviticus 25:38, 42, 55) and treat others with the compassion and mercy that God showed them when He brought them out of that bondage.

The announcement of the Year of Jubilee on the same day that the Day of Atonement is observed is not mere coincidence. God wants His covenant people to understand that on the same day that reconciliation with Him is carried out, a kind of reconciliation among people is to happen as well every 50 years. As the people are restored with God spiritually, those who have been separated from their homes due to personal setbacks are to be restored to their families and their property. Thus reconciliation with God is to be demonstrated in a very practical, tangible manner.

> *What Do You Think?*
> What steps can we take to become known as people of reconciliation?
> *Talking Points for Your Discussion*
> - When relational debt is outstanding
> - When sin debt is outstanding
> - When monetary debt is outstanding
> - When deficits of justice abound

◆ *LIVING AS RECONCILED PEOPLE* ◆

In modern times, there is perhaps no greater example of practicing reconciliation than that of Nelson Mandela. Mandela spent 27 years in prison for his role in resisting the South African government and its commitment to racial apartheid. Instead of emerging from prison embittered against his captors, he displayed an unflagging commitment to unify a nation that had been divided by years of institutionalized racism.

Mandela eventually became the first black president of South Africa. In that role he created the Truth and Reconciliation Commission, which

provided amnesty to anyone who had committed a politically motivated human rights violation during the apartheid era. Neither side of the conflict was exempt from being called to stand before these public hearings. Part of the plan's genius was that amnesty would be granted only to those who fully disclosed their crimes. This model of restorative justice created the possibility for forgiveness between a people hopelessly divided.

The Day of Atonement offered reconciliation between a holy God and His sinful people. The Year of Jubilee, which was proclaimed on the Day of Atonement, encouraged the people to think of a kind of reconciliation with fellow Israelites by allowing them to return to ancestral property and family. God's people were thus taught to think of reconciliation not just as a matter of their personal relationship with the Lord but also in terms of how others were treated. The spiritual and the practical were thus closely linked together. So it should also be for God's people today. —L. G. S.

D. Observing Jubilee (vv. 11, 12)

11, 12. A jubile shall that fiftieth year be unto you: ye shall not sow, neither reap that which groweth of itself in it, nor gather the grapes in it of thy vine undressed. For it is the jubile; it shall be holy unto you: ye shall eat the increase thereof out of the field.

The laws concerning sowing and reaping to be followed during the Year of Jubilee are similar to those that accompany the Sabbath Year (Leviticus 25:5). A question arises as to whether the Year of Jubilee is the same as the seventh Sabbath Year within a given cycle or is an additional year. If the latter, the result is two consecutive years of neither sowing nor reaping.

Leviticus 25:20-22 appears to say that God's promises to provide enough abundance in the sixth year that the people's needs will be met through the seventh, eighth, and ninth years. But that text specifies sowing during the eighth year. Since (1) the year on which the Year of Jubilee falls is an eighth year and (2) sowing is forbidden on a jubilee year (25:11), then (3) it appears that the seventh Sabbath Year in the cycle is also a Year of Jubilee. The *fiftieth year* may have been the same as the forty-ninth year by counting both the first and last years of the cycle.

The primary purpose of legislation such as that in today's text is not agricultural or economic, although there are indeed benefits to be had along those lines. Rather, the primary purpose is spiritual. God's people are being encouraged to place their faith in the Lord and to trust Him as the giver of the land to provide for His people.

> **What Do You Think?**
> How will your neighbors see your life change as you rely more and more on God's provision?
> *Talking Points for Your Discussion*
> - In your approach to generosity
> - In contentment
> - In family life
> - Other

Sadly, what follows in the Old Testament record is the account of a people who repeatedly disobey God's commands. When the people of the southern kingdom of Judah are taken into exile, 2 Chronicles 36:21 states the land enjoyed Sabbath rests while lying desolate—rests presumably denied before the exile by the disobedience of God's people.

Conclusion

A. Old Testament Jubilee

Did the Israelites ever practice jubilee as a nation? We don't have any firm evidence that they did (Isaiah 37:30 is a possible reference to jubilee ideas). Although the generation that followed Moses rebelled against God (Judges 2:10-13), the lack of reference to jubilee in the historical narratives of the Old Testament does not mean that jubilee was not practiced. That would be an argument from silence. We simply do not know.

Yet we know that the prophets appealed to the jubilee ideal figuratively with reference to the coming kingdom of God. An example is Isaiah 61:1, where the Hebrew word translated *liberty* is the same word translated as *liberty* in Leviticus 25:10 (the only other places where this word is used are Jeremiah 34:8, 15, 17; Ezekiel 46:17).

B. New Testament Jubilee

When one considers what the Year of Jubilee signified for God's people in the Old Testament, it is not difficult to see a reference to a new jubilee in Jesus' declared intent "to preach deliverance to the captives, . . . to set at liberty them that are bruised" as He quoted from Isaiah 61 in Luke 4:18.

Jesus is the one who has made it possible for human beings, separated from God because of sin, to come home, to return to where we belong—with the Lord. The "liberty" of this jubilee is the freedom from sin that Jesus brought about by defeating the devil and releasing us from bondage to him (see Hebrews 2:14, 15).

The jubilee that Jesus inaugurated at His first coming will reach its ultimate fulfillment and consummation when He returns. At that time a trumpet will sound (1 Thessalonians 4:16; compare Leviticus 25:9), and all Christians will be gloriously and finally liberated from the curse and the brokenness of sin—to dwell with our rightful owner in His home forever.

A jubilee for eternity!

> **What Do You Think?**
> What steps can you take to help your fellow Christians live more fully as beneficiaries of Jesus' jubilee?
> *Talking Points for Your Discussion*
> - In congregational worship settings
> - In Bible class settings
> - In fellowship settings
> - Other

C. Prayer

Our Father, we acknowledge that true freedom comes only when we follow Your commandments. Help us to treat Your Word as the ultimate authority, to follow Your Son as Lord, and to depend on Your Spirit for the power to live holy lives before the world. We pray in the name of the one who set us free. Amen.

D. Thought to Remember

View people and possessions as God does.

INVOLVEMENT LEARNING

Enhance your lesson with KJV Bible Student *(from your curriculum supplier) and the reproducible activity page (at www.standardlesson.com or in the back of the* KJV Standard Lesson Commentary Deluxe Edition*).*

Into the Lesson

Distribute handouts (you prepare) of the poem below, which is "No Man Is an Island," by John Donne (1573–1631).

No man is an island entire of itself; every man is a piece of the continent, a part of the main; if a clod be washed away by the sea, Europe is the less, as well as if a promontory were, as well as any manner of thy friends or of thine own were; any man's death diminishes me, because I am involved in mankind. And therefore never send to know for whom the bell tolls; it tolls for thee.

Invite a volunteer to read the poem aloud, and then write on the board, "No man is an island." Talk about what this statement means, and challenge students to give examples from their own lives when they have seen this to be true.

Alternative. Distribute copies of the "Who Would I Trust?" activity from the reproducible page, which you can download. Have students work individually to decide whom to trust in various situations. Afterward, read each statement and let volunteers share the names they listed.

After either activity say, "None of us lives totally on our own. To flourish, we must show trust in others, trust that sometimes involves risk. One key part of the Jewish law demonstrates this type of trust and risk."

Into the Word

Say: "Putting one's trust in God is not a mere mental exercise. It is following God's commands, even when those commands seem to violate common sense or endanger one's well-being. God's commands to observe a periodic Sabbath Year and a Year of Jubilee fall into that category."

Divide the class into three groups. The groups should read their assigned Bible texts and come up with objections that may have been voiced by the people of Israel concerning those commands. (Possible objections are listed in italics.)

Group 1—Leviticus 25:1-5
Why does land need rest anyway? It's just dirt!
It's my property; I'll do what I want with it!
Isn't this just promoting laziness? Why should someone who is willing to work sacrifice a year of income?

Group 2—Leviticus 25:6, 7, 20-22
What will keep me from starving if the land does not produce enough food in these special years?
Faith in God is fine, but shouldn't I take responsibility to provide for myself and my family?
If there is a food shortage in one of these special years, why should I give some of the food to my servants and animals?

Group 3—Leviticus 25:8-12, 23, 24
These people are my servants because they owed me money. I am supposed to forgive that debt? How unfair!
Wait a minute. I worked hard to buy more land to provide for my security and to pass it on to my children. I am supposed to give up what I worked a lifetime to earn?
What I worked for is mine. No one has the right to tell me to give it away!

After groups have finished, allow them to share their findings and objections. Point out how controversial these commands are. Yet by following them, the Israelites would have grown in their trust for God as well as their compassion for their countrymen who had difficult years.

Into Life

Challenge students to talk about ways they could celebrate a type of jubilee year in their own lives. Distribute lengths of streamers and have students write on the streamers different words or Bible verses that remind them to trust and thank the Lord.

Alternative. Distribute copies of the "Remember and Rest" activity for students to complete.

REJOICING IN RESTORATION

DEVOTIONAL READING: Hebrews 7:20-28
BACKGROUND SCRIPTURE: Leviticus 16; Psalm 34; Hebrews 2:5-18

PSALM 34:1-10

A Psalm of David, when he changed his behaviour before Abimelech; who drove him away, and he departed.

1 I will bless the LORD at all times: his praise shall continually be in my mouth.

2 My soul shall make her boast in the LORD: the humble shall hear thereof, and be glad.

3 O magnify the LORD with me, and let us exalt his name together.

4 I sought the LORD, and he heard me, and delivered me from all my fears.

5 They looked unto him, and were lightened: and their faces were not ashamed.

6 This poor man cried, and the LORD heard him, and saved him out of all his troubles.

7 The angel of the LORD encampeth round about them that fear him, and delivereth them.

8 O taste and see that the LORD is good: blessed is the man that trusteth in him.

9 O fear the LORD, ye his saints: for there is no want to them that fear him.

10 The young lions do lack, and suffer hunger: but they that seek the LORD shall not want any good thing.

HEBREWS 2:17, 18

17 Wherefore in all things it behoved him to be made like unto his brethren, that he might be a merciful and faithful high priest in things pertaining to God, to make reconciliation for the sins of the people.

18 For in that he himself hath suffered being tempted, he is able to succour them that are tempted.

KEY VERSE

O taste and see that the LORD is good: blessed is the man that trusteth in him. —**Psalm 34:8**

Photo: rawpixel LTD / iStock / Thinkstock

ACKNOWLEDGING GOD

Unit 3: Give Praise to God

LESSONS 10–13

LESSON AIMS

After participating in this lesson, each learner will be able to:

1. Describe the connection between Psalm 34 and Hebrews 2:17, 18.

2. Give examples of God's desire and ability to provide for His people.

3. Encourage one person in the week ahead who feels as though God doesn't care about his or her suffering.

LESSON OUTLINE

Introduction
    A. Father of the Afflicted
    B. Lesson Background: Psalm 34
    C. Lesson Background: Hebrews
 I. Call to Praise (PSALM 34:1-3)
 A. Personal (vv. 1, 2)
        At All Times
 B. Public (v. 3)
 II. Caring God (PSALM 34:4-10)
 A. God Delivers (vv. 4-7)
 B. God Provides (vv. 8-10)
 III. Compassionate Savior (HEBREWS 2:17, 18)
 A. He Relates to Us (v. 17)
 B. He Supports Us (v. 18)
        One Who Can Relate
Conclusion
    A. Son of David
    B. Prayer
    C. Thought to Remember

Introduction

A. Father of the Afflicted

A Christian girl soaks her pillow with tears. Her prom date drives away with another girl who won't refuse him. An unemployed father hangs his head in shame. Christmas won't seem so merry because he refused to lie for the good of his company. A faithful family spends another night in the shelter. Speaking publicly about one's Christian faith is not welcomed in their village.

The apostle Paul referred to himself and the other apostles in very unflattering terms, as "the filth of the world" (1 Corinthians 4:13). Through the years, many followers of Jesus have felt much the same. They stuck to their faith whether popular or not. They have proclaimed Christ unswervingly even when it led to abandonment, poverty, and homelessness. This world does not claim them. It does not appreciate their integrity and commitment to purity and truth. But God claims them. He recognizes them as His children, for He is the father of the afflicted.

In the midst of rejection and scornful treatment from the world, it can be hard to sense God's parental love. We are more likely to feel anger and resentment. In times like these, we can know that the pain is only temporary. We are encouraged by those who have been there and persevered. We can use examples like David and Jesus, who faced affliction, experienced God's favor, and left behind a powerful witness and testimony.

B. Lesson Background: Psalm 34

Psalm 34, one of many written by David, is an alphabetic acrostic poem. This means that each verse begins with a letter of the Hebrew alphabet, in consecutive order. In English this would mean beginning the first verse with A and beginning the last verse with Z. There are 22 letters in the Hebrew alphabet, thus there are 22 verses in Psalm 34. A more elaborate acrostic is Psalm 119. Its first 8 verses begin with the first letter of the Hebrew alphabet, the second set of 8 verses begin with the second letter, and so on until all 22 letters are used 8 times for a total of 176 verses in the psalm.

Some psalms include a heading that provides the setting. Psalm 34 has such a heading. It mentions a time in David's life "when he changed his behaviour before Abimelech; who drove him away, and he departed." This account is in 1 Samuel 21:10-15, when David was fleeing from jealous King Saul, who wanted to kill him. David came to the territory of the king of Gath, but his reputation for killing "ten thousands" of Philistines had preceded him. To avoid suspicion, David acted as if he were insane. The king berated his servants for bringing such a man into his presence, and David was allowed to leave. It was a time of great distress for David, one when he desperately needed God's help.

The contents of Psalm 34 do not fit neatly into any one category. The first 10 verses contain elements of an individual thanksgiving hymn. The remaining verses contain strong wisdom elements. The verses in our printed text fall within the thanksgiving section.

C. Lesson Background: Hebrews

The two verses from Hebrews come from a different setting altogether. The book of Hebrews was written to Christians from a Jewish background who were suffering their own version of rejection: being ostracized for choosing to follow Jesus as Messiah. The pressure to return to Judaism was intense.

The writer, who is not named in the book, urges them not to do so, lest they abandon all they have received in Christ (example: Hebrews 10:32-39). This is why the word *better* occurs so often (13 times) in Hebrews: the writer is trying to persuade his readers that what Christ provides through the new covenant is much better than what the old covenant was able to provide. The portion of our printed text from Hebrews 2 is part of the writer's case for why Jesus is the better (in fact the perfect) high priest.

I. Call to Praise
(Psalms 34:1-3)
A. Personal (vv. 1, 2)

1. I will bless the Lord at all times: his praise shall continually be in my mouth.

First to note here is the defining characteristic of Hebrew poetry: *parallelism*. This means making a statement and then repeating the thought in slightly different words. We should not understand the author to be talking about two different topics. The action of the first half of the verse is the same action in the second half.

David maintains that he has chosen to adopt a posture of continual *praise* to the Lord. David is not claiming that he lives in a nonstop state of praise. Rather, he is emphasizing that situations of distress and despair (such as the one described in the psalm's heading) are occasions when God should be blessed and not discarded. This is a powerful thing for a man on the run to say. He is not singing this song from a padded pew in a beautiful sanctuary. He sings a song of praise when others would be tempted to curse their enemies and feel sorry for themselves. David strives to exalt God at all times—even the worst of times.

> *What Do You Think?*
> What would our neighbors notice about us if we were committed to praising God at all times?
> *Talking Points for Your Discussion*
> - In speech and demeanor when times are good
> - In speech and demeanor when times are hard

HOW TO SAY IT

Abimelech	Uh-*bim*-eh-lek.
Corinthians	Ko-*rin*-thee-unz (*th* as in *thin*).
Gath	Gath (*a* as in *bath*).
Gethsemane	Geth-*sem*-uh-nee (*G* as in *get*).
Herod	*Hair*-ud.
Judaism	*Joo*-duh-izz-um or *Joo*-day-izz-um.
Philistine	Fuh-*liss*-teen or *Fill*-us-teen.
Sinai	*Sigh*-nye or *Sigh*-nay-eye.

◆ *At All Times* ◆

The lead singer of the popular Christian band Casting Crowns heard back from his doctor after a routine visit for heartburn. Apparently the tests discovered a cancerous tumor on his kidney. After the initial shock, Mark Hall's deeply ingrained faith in Christ kicked in. "My feelings kept slamming up against something solid in me, and that was the roots of my faith. The fact that I've been in the Word for years. The fact that I've been following Jesus for years, and the roots of my faith were reminding me: God is who He says He is."

Though on the run from King Saul, David likewise found the ability to praise God despite his circumstances. To be determined to "bless the Lord at all times" is not denial or escapism; rather, this is the normal response of someone who has been grounded in the Lord and knows that God will be faithful, regardless of difficulties.

When was the last time you praised God while you were in a difficult situation?   —D. C. S.

2. My soul shall make her boast in the LORD: the humble shall hear thereof, and be glad.

David eventually escapes his perilous surroundings, but he doesn't dwell on his own ingenuity. Instead he directs all glory to God. In addition, he does not keep his rescue to himself. He wants others to know about it. This verse therefore introduces another party who will be present throughout the verses to follow.

The plural Hebrew word translated *humble* appears also in singular form in verse 6, below. There it is translated "poor"; see commentary on that verse.

B. Public (v. 3)

3. O magnify the LORD with me, and let us exalt his name together.

More parallelism presents itself as David invites others to join him in praising the Lord. The word *magnify* appears numerous times in the psalms, and that word causes us to think of magnification or enlargement. Of course, we cannot do anything to "enlarge" God's status. Neither can we *exalt his name* in the sense of lifting it any higher than it already is.

What we can do, however, is magnify God and exalt His name in the sense of changing our perspective. Our perspective must always be that He is the transcendent, eternal Creator, Redeemer, and Ruler—and we are not.

II. Caring God
(PSALM 34:4-10)
A. God Delivers (vv. 4-7)
4a. I sought the LORD, and he heard me.

We begin to see in this verse a repeated poetic pattern. David began this psalm by speaking of himself. Then in verse 3, just considered, he addresses an audience (which may be his band of 400 followers noted in 1 Samuel 22:2). This is evidence of the psalm's being a communal invitation rather than an individual meditation.

Again the psalmist shares his own testimony and indirectly invites his audience to seek God. The Lord is responsive when His people seek Him out (Jeremiah 29:13).

4b. And delivered me from all my fears.

David doesn't list specific fears. But judging from the psalm's superscription, we may surmise that he feared being killed either by King Saul or King Abimelech (see the Lesson Background).

David probably knows of the times when Abraham and Isaac felt threatened by a Philistine king, so both spoke to him deceptively (Genesis 20:2; 26:7). They were found out, but God protected them nonetheless. David has had good reason to fear; yet he has had even better reason not to fear: God can deliver him. And He has done so.

5. They looked unto him, and were lightened: and their faces were not ashamed.

Although God "maketh his sun to rise on the evil and on the good, and sendeth rain on the just and on the unjust" (Matthew 5:45), He is especially interested in providing for all of His faithful ones. Abraham and Isaac revealed character flaws in speaking deceptively. God knew what was going on, of course (see Genesis 20:3-7), but He was merciful.

God's people have hope as long as they look *unto him*. That hope is not rooted in their own worthiness, but in the worth that God attributes to them. Though disdained by the world, they have no reason to be *ashamed*. By contrast, David prays in Psalm 40:14 that those who intend to harm him "be ashamed and confounded together."

6. This poor man cried, and the LORD heard him, and saved him out of all his troubles.

This verse may seem redundant in light of verse 4. One suggestion is that its function is to maintain the acrostic structure of the psalm as a whole (see the Lesson Background).

Even so, there seems to be one point of additional emphasis. Notice that the verse begins with the specific *this poor man*. That means David is talking about himself, thus identifying with the poverty of his audience. The word *poor* is the singular version of the plural word translated "humble" in verse 2, above. David himself is from a lowly background. He was watching his father's sheep when the prophet Samuel came to Bethlehem seeking one of Jesse's sons to anoint as the next king of Israel (1 Samuel 16:11). No one considered David, the youngest, as a possible candidate. No one, that is, except God.

7. The angel of the LORD encampeth round about them that fear him, and delivereth them.

The language of this verse presumes a more military context. *The angel of the Lord* forms a protective perimeter around those who *fear* God. *Fear* is a term of reverence and respect for God. The passage is reminiscent of Joshua 5:13-15 where Joshua encounters the captain of the Lord's army. Joshua wants to know whose side the angel is on. The angel refuses to pick sides; God's angel simply fights for or against whomever God says. If we

want God to fight for us, we must fear Him. Only then can we be confident that He will deliver us. The Lord's protection may not take a visible form (compare 2 Kings 6:15-17), but it is there.

B. God Provides (vv. 8-10)

8. O taste and see that the LORD is good: blessed is the man that trusteth in him.

In verse 3, above, David has invited listeners to join in magnifying the Lord. Now he invites them to enter into a personal relationship of trust in God and to experience Him firsthand.

If life is likened to a choice of banquets, we can picture several hosts who beckon us to eat at their respective tables. Some offer us wealth and privilege. Others offer us friendship in idolatry. Those meals may please our palate for a brief moment, but in the end they make us sick. David invites us to eat at the Lord's table, for only He truly satisfies. Peter uses similar language when he encourages believers to crave the milk of God's Word, "if so be ye have tasted that the Lord is gracious" (1 Peter 2:2, 3; contrast Hebrews 6:4-6).

The state of being *blessed* that is experienced by those who trust God is one of sustained satisfaction and contentment. The Psalms begin with this same word (Psalm 1:1).

9. O fear the LORD, ye his saints: for there is no want to them that fear him.

Proverbs 9:10 teaches that "the *fear* of the Lord is the beginning of wisdom." Fearing God includes believing that what He says is true. When He says that certain actions will yield certain negative consequences, we must believe Him. In other words, we should fear what God says we should fear.

Corresponding with that is the understanding that we should not fear what God says we should not fear. There are many commands throughout Scripture that instruct us in that regard (example: Matthew 10:28). If we live as God desires, we have nothing to fear because He created us and knows what is in our best interests. He knows all our needs and will provide for them (compare Matthew 6:25-34).

10. The young lions do lack, and suffer hunger: but they that seek the LORD shall not want any good thing.

David in his day knows as well as we do in ours that lions stand at the top of the land-animal food chain. They are quite skilled at acquiring food, and David has had personal experience in protecting sheep from them (1 Samuel 17:34-37). They are extremely self-sufficient. But they can and do *suffer hunger* at times in spite of that self-sufficiency. Yet in David's experience, those who *seek the Lord* will lack for nothing they need. David said the same thing more famously in Psalm 23:1: "The Lord is my shepherd; I shall not want."

What Do You Think?
What life-lessons have you learned about God's provision?

Talking Points for Your Discussion
- In regard to your faith
- In regard to God's character
- In regard to your fellow believers
- Other

III. Compassionate Savior
(Hebrews 2:17, 18)
A. He Relates to Us (v. 17)

17. Wherefore in all things it behoved him to be made like unto his brethren, that he might be a merciful and faithful high priest in things pertaining to God, to make reconciliation for the sins of the people.

Psalm 34 focuses on God's desire and ability to provide for those in need. David experienced this and eagerly invites his followers to trust the Lord in a similar fashion. But one might reasonably ask how God can know what we really need since He himself has never needed anything (Psalm 50:9-13). One might respond by pointing out that since God created us, of course He knows what we need. As a car designer knows what it takes to keep an automobile running, so also God knows what we need to flourish.

Even so, it is particularly reasonable to ask how God knows what it is like to suffer oppression. No one can oppress God. His greatest enemies tremble before Him. He may know what our bodies need on a biological level, but how can He relate to us on an emotional level? How could He identify with being afflicted?

The author of Hebrews provides a most convincing reply. When God became flesh in Jesus, He entered personally into all the frailty of human existence. In the flesh, He suffered hunger, poverty, neglect, betrayal, torture, and a horrendous death. What God knew to be true as the all-knowing God, He experienced as a vulnerable human.

That experience qualified Jesus to be the perfect *high priest* to mediate between humanity and God. Like us, He experienced temptation; unlike us, He remained *faithful* and did not sin (Hebrews 4:15). Thus Jesus could become the perfect sacrifice for our sins, unlike the high priests of the old covenant, who had to offer sacrifices for their own sins (7:26, 27).

God then raised Jesus from the dead. Now, having ascended into Heaven, Jesus intercedes on our behalf (Hebrews 7:25). Though our sin separates us from God, Jesus has provided *reconciliation* with God by taking the punishment for our sins upon himself at the cross.

What Do You Think?
How should a Christian's life change when becoming fully convinced that Jesus is the merciful and faithful high priest?

Talking Points for Your Discussion
- Regarding prayer interactions with God
- Regarding interactions with other believers
- Regarding interactions with unbelievers

B. He Supports Us (v. 18)

18. For in that he himself hath suffered being tempted, he is able to succour them that are tempted.

Some might suggest that Jesus cannot relate to our spiritual poverty because He himself never sinned. The writer of Hebrews disagrees with this kind of reasoning. One does not have to sin to relate to sinners. It is enough that Jesus was "in all points tempted like as we are" (Hebrews 4:15). He faced a period of severe temptation following His baptism (Matthew 3:13–4:11). The spiritual warfare that occurred during that experience must have been intense to a degree we cannot fathom. Jesus also wrestled in Gethsemane with carrying out the Father's plan for Him to drink the bitter cup of suffering just ahead. But Jesus fully surrendered to His Father's will (Matthew 26:39).

By overcoming temptation, Jesus became someone who is able to *succour* (help) those who are *tempted*. That, of course, includes us all.

◆　ONE WHO CAN RELATE　◆

Jordan Rogers has a responsible position as a brand manager at a company that produces athletic apparel. But his ability to perform at this level wouldn't have been possible without Christ's intervention over the power of heroin. In an "I Am Second" video, Jordan shares how Christ helped him overcome the temptation of a raging drug habit, resulting in 13 years of sobriety.

Jordan first experimented with heroin at age 15, and by the time he was in his early 20s he was a full-blown addict. In reference to his ever-worsening addiction, Jordan says, "I had this black hole in my soul and just wanted to change the way I felt." His attempted solution was to get high in as many new and different ways as possible.

Jordan hit rock bottom when he found himself in a jail cell. There he thought to himself, "This is not what I was made for. I absolutely deserve to be here, but I don't belong here." As two of his cell mates argued over a roll of toilet paper, Jordan cried out to God: "Whoever You are, whatever You are . . . I need help."

God is able to come alongside and help those who are being tempted (1 Corinthians 10:13). The Lord used a mentor who entered Jordan's life, showed him the love of Christ, and helped him find recovery and freedom from temptation. Remember: the Jesus you take to someone this week is the Jesus who suffered the temptations that the one you help does.　　　　—D. C. S.

Conclusion

A. Son of David

From a genealogical perspective, Jesus was clearly a descendant of David. We can trace his ancestry using the genealogies of Matthew 1

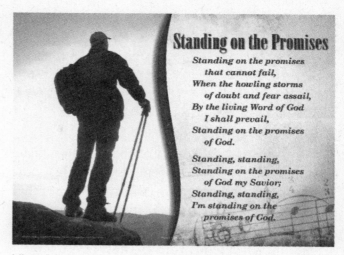

Standing on the Promises

Standing on the promises
that cannot fail,
When the howling storms
of doubt and fear assail,
By the living Word of God
I shall prevail,
Standing on the promises
of God.

Standing, standing,
Standing on the promises
of God my Savior;
Standing, standing,
I'm standing on the
promises of God.

Visual for Lessons 2 & 13. *Point to this visual as you ask, "Which verse of today's lesson reflects these thoughts most closely? Why?"*

and Luke 3. But when we read Hebrews alongside Psalm 34, we see Jesus linked with David in a different way. David suffered oppression. He had to escape the wrath of one, possibly two, jealous kings. Not only did he trust God for deliverance, but he encouraged others to do the same.

Jesus too faced oppression. The paranoid King Herod tried to kill the infant Jesus. Religious and secular authorities eventually succeeded in putting Him to death. But Jesus was not someone who obsessed about the injustices surrounding His trial and execution. Rather, He used His experience to identify with us in the many forms of affliction that beset us in a fallen world. His perfect example of faithfulness even in the face of death encourages us to hold fast. Though the world may appear to get the best of us, the God who vindicated Jesus by raising Him from the grave will raise us too; and we will reign victorious with Him!

B. Prayer

Heavenly Father, we are humbled by Your concern for us. We are so small in the grand scheme of things! Yet You love us beyond our ability to comprehend. We thank You for delivering us from the evil that surrounds us and the evil that lies within us. We pray in Jesus' name. Amen.

C. Thought to Remember

"Taste and see that the Lord is good."
　　　　　　　　　　—Psalm 34:8

INVOLVEMENT LEARNING

Enhance your lesson with KJV Bible Student *(from your curriculum supplier) and the reproducible activity page (at www.standardlesson.com or in the back of the* KJV Standard Lesson Commentary Deluxe Edition*).*

Into the Lesson

Bring a small collection of tools to class. Pass them around and ask students to describe a purpose for each. Discuss things in your homes that need fixing; talk about what tools you would use to fix them. Invite students to give examples of home-improvement projects they are currently undertaking, as well as fix-it situations gone wrong.

Option. Before class, research clips from the TV show *Home Improvement* that feature a main character fixing (or attempting to fix) something. Describe it as a lead-in to the above.

Alternative. Distribute pens and copies of the "Get a Fix" activity from the reproducible page, which you can download. Have students work individually to match words containing FIX with their correct definitions. (You can place the copies in chairs for learners to begin working on as they arrive.)

After either alternative say, "We may fix broken appliances and broken furniture, but how do we fix broken lives? The Bible has the answer."

Into the Word

Divide the class into three groups. Give each group a pen, paper, and a prepared index card with a single word and a Scripture reference:

Group 1—Deliverance (Psalm 34:1-6)
Group 2—Provision (Psalm 34:7-10)
Group 3—Reconciliation (Hebrews 2:17, 18)

Groups are to do the following:

1. Define their word. 2. Give an example of a person performing that function. 3. Tell how their Scripture text defines God or Jesus as one who performs that function.

Here are possible responses:

Group 1

1. *Deliverance* is to release, rescue, or liberate from an unfavorable situation.

2. Example: A firefighter rescues someone from a burning building.

3. God delivers those who trust Him from fear, shame, and troubles.

Group 2

1. *Provision* is to meet or supply a need.

2. Example: A church or community food pantry helps feed homeless people.

3. God protects His people by providing for their needs.

Group 3

1. *Reconciliation* is to bring about peace between estranged or warring parties.

2. Example: A marriage counselor helps a couple work out their differences.

3. Jesus interceded for sinners by placing himself in the path of God's wrath. Jesus did so as He took the penalty for our sins upon himself at the cross. His task of intercessory reconciliation included remaining sinless while being tempted as we are in all ways.

After groups have completed their research, ask them to share their findings with the class. When they have done so, say, "Fixing our state as broken human beings is not as easy as repairing an appliance or a piece of furniture. But God took steps to see that we are removed and shielded from everlasting danger and that the penalty for our sins is paid."

Into Life

Write this statement on the board: *God repairs the irreparable.* Invite students to react to the statement; jot responses on the board. Push deeper by requesting respondents to explain their reactions and to support their explanations with examples.

Alternative. Distribute pens and copies of the "You Can Say That Again!" activity from the reproducible page. Have students work in small groups to say the same thing in a new way.

JUSTICE IN THE NEW TESTAMENT

Special Features

Lessons

Unit 1: God Is Just and Merciful

Unit 2: Jesus Calls for Justice and Mercy

Unit 3: Paul Teaches About New Life in Christ

QUARTERLY QUIZ

Use these questions as a pretest or as a review. The answers are on page iv of This Quarter in the Word.

Lesson 1

1. Who ate the shewbread intended only for the priests? (Joshua, Saul, David?) *Matthew 12:3, 4*

2. The man in the synagogue suffered from what? (withered hand, blindness, leprosy?) *Matthew 12:9, 10*

Lesson 2

1. In one of Jesus' parables, a man's _____ sowed tares (weeds) in the wheat. *Matthew 13:25*

2. Jesus described the mustard seed as the greatest of all seeds. T/F. *Matthew 13:31, 32*

Lesson 3

1. Some Pharisees accused Jesus' disciples of not praying before eating. T/F. *Matthew 15:2*

2. The Pharisees circumvented the command to honor parents. T/F. *Matthew 15:4-6*

Lesson 4

1. Lazarus was carried by the _____ to Abraham. *Luke 16:22*

2. The rich man wanted Lazarus to warn whom? (his wife, friends, brothers?) *Luke 16:27, 28*

Lesson 5

1. Peter offered to forgive a person who sinned against him _____ times. *Matthew 18:21*

2. A man in Jesus' parable was forgiven a debt but refused to forgive another's debt of the same amount. T/F. *Matthew 18:23-30*

Lesson 6

1. Jesus said that the scribes and Pharisees sit in _____ seat. *Matthew 23:2*

2. Jesus said the Pharisees were blind. T/F. *Matthew 23:24*

Lesson 7

1. The parable of the unjust judge teaches that we should always pray. T/F. *Luke 18:1*

2. Jesus asked, "When the Son of man cometh, shall he find _____ on the earth?" *Luke 18:8*

Lesson 8

1. Jesus said everyone who seeks to enter the gate of God's kingdom will be able to. T/F. *Luke 13:24*

2. Jesus said His listeners would see Abraham, Isaac, Jacob, and all the _____ in the kingdom of God. *Luke 13:28*

Lesson 9

1. In the banquet parable, those invited are told, "Come; for all things are now _____." *Luke 14:17*

2. One invited guest said he couldn't come because he had just got married. T/F. *Luke 14:20*

Lesson 10

1. Paul says that God's goodness leads us to _____. *Romans 2:4*

2. The unrepentant are storing up _____ against themselves. *Romans 2:5*

Lesson 11

1. Paul spoke of giving in terms of _____. (obligation, grace, obedience?) *2 Corinthians 8:7*

2. Though Jesus was _____, yet for our sakes He became _____. *2 Corinthians 8:9*

Lesson 12

1. Paul tells us to _____ those who persecute us. *Romans 12:14*

2. To show mercy to one's enemy is to heap _____ of fire on his head. *Romans 12:20*

Lesson 13

1. Paul says that the _____ of the Lord should rule in our hearts. *Colossians 3:15*

2. Christians should teach and admonish each other through singing. T/F. *Colossians 3:16*

QUARTER AT A GLANCE

Through the years, some have claimed that the two testaments of the Bible portray two very different Gods: an Old Testament God of intense wrath and judgment in contrast with a New Testament God of love, grace, and compassion—demonstrated through the life and ministry of Jesus.

Such a view is totally disproven by an examination of each testament. The words *love* and *mercy* are not missing from the Old Testament, as a Bible concordance readily demonstrates. At the same time, God's judgment and justice permeate the New Testament; and justice is the theme of this quarter. God's righteous judgment will one day be visited on all people everywhere, and He requires justice from His people in their dealings with others.

Teachings of Jesus

The lessons of units 1 and 2 emphasize Jesus' desire that people be treated with the mercy that was often denied them. That denial came about because of social standing or because of the twisted priorities of those who claimed to be godly. The wide chasm between the viewpoints of the religious leaders and Jesus is illustrated by the confrontations recorded in lessons 1 and 3. It will also be clear from the Scripture text of lesson 6, taken from Jesus' denunciation of the scribes and Pharisees in Matthew 23.

Jesus clearly taught that a Day of Judgment is included in God's timetable. This is seen in His parable of the tares (weeds), covered in lesson 2, and then dramatically conveyed in the account of Lazarus and the rich man, presented in lesson 4. Jesus' parable of the widow and the unjust judge, lesson 7, teaches us that patience is required of those who may at times be troubled by God's apparent slowness to act. He will indeed "avenge his own elect" (Luke 18:7) at His appointed time. In the meantime, we should never lose sight of how much mercy God has shown to us. The parable of the unforgiving servant, lesson 5, is a cautionary tale of a man unwilling to extend to a fellow servant the same mercy that he himself had been granted.

Within these lessons, attitudes of pride and self-righteousness are exposed for the dangers they pose. In lesson 8, a smug complacency is seen in those who assume they already "have their ticket punched" to the kingdom of God. They will be very surprised, says Jesus, to find themselves on the outside looking in. A similar attitude is condemned in the parable of the great dinner, lesson 9. Those who treat spiritual matters with a "take it or leave it" attitude will find their names omitted from the guest list.

Paul's Teaching

The same combination of concern for living justly now while being aware of God's future judgment is seen in the third unit of studies, drawn from Paul's letters. Paul warns Christians that they should not presume to don their judicial robes, especially when they are guilty of the same sins for which they are condemning others. God will judge all people with "no respect of persons" (Romans 2:11, lesson 10).

> **God requires justice from His people in their dealings with others.**

The remaining three lessons challenge Christians to faithful giving and living. In today's world, so marked by intense strife and division, Paul's exhortations provide timeless and practical guidelines that should be the trademarks of followers of Jesus. The final verse of the final lesson, Colossians 3:17, provides a fitting finish: "Whatsoever ye do in word or deed, do all in the name of the Lord Jesus, giving thanks to God . . . the Father by him."

• 339 •

GET THE SETTING

by Tom Thatcher

OUR LESSONS this quarter focus on justice, a key attribute of God that believers must emulate. The word for this concept in the Greek New Testament is often translated "righteousness" in reference to God (see Romans 3:21-26), to what believers receive through faith (see 4:3-11), and to the godly attribute that Christians must exhibit (see 6:13-19).

Justice is a prominent theme in the Old Testament, and the New Testament significantly expands this concept by connecting justice with the work of Christ and the Christian lifestyle. The Bible touches on each of four classical subcategories of justice.

Distributive Justice

This is economic fairness, the principle that individuals should receive what is due them. A classic expression is Moses' command to pay workers fairly and not delay their compensation (Leviticus 19:13; Deuteronomy 24:14, 15; compare James 5:4). On the other hand, Paul states that those who will not work should not eat (2 Thessalonians 3:10)—it would be unjust for people who have not earned their keep to take from those who have. At the same time, hardworking individuals may be victims of misfortune or oppression; and both Old and New Testaments call on God's people to help them (Leviticus 19:9, 10; Matthew 5:42; 6:1-4; 2 Corinthians 8:1-15 [lesson 11]).

Procedural Justice

This refers to due process, or fairness, in the application of rules. This principle is emphasized in the commands to treat foreigners, widows, and orphans—individuals with no legal status—justly (Exodus 22:21-23; Leviticus 19:33, 34; Deuteronomy 10:17-19). Failure to live by this principle, and the exploitation of vulnerable people that results, is often cited by the prophets as a cause of God's judgment on Israel (Isaiah 1:23; Jeremiah 22:3-5; Eze-

kiel 22:6, 7). Concern for due process also underlies the teachings of Jesus and Paul regarding church discipline (Matthew 18:15-20; 1 Timothy 5:17-20). Jesus was denied due process (Acts 8:33); Paul did his best to ensure that he himself wasn't (16:37, 38; 22:25-29). God shows no favoritism, and neither should we (Exodus 23:3; James 2:1-9).

Restorative Justice

This refers to punishments that require an offender to make restitution. There were no jails in ancient Israel; instead, criminals were expected to repay damages. Exodus 22:1-15 describes a number of situations in which those who caused loss of property through theft or negligence were required to compensate the victim with an equal or greater amount. This distinctive system was part of the fabric of the first century as well (Luke 12:58, 59; 18:3-5 [lesson 7]; 19:8).

Retributive Justice

This is punishment for its own sake, penalties levied proportionate to the crime. Retributive justice is summarized by the "eye for an eye" principle (Exodus 21:23-25; Deuteronomy 19:21). Jesus mentioned this principle not to set it aside but to prevent its use as a reason to retaliate personally (Matthew 5:38-42). The New Testament affirms retributive justice to be a valid function of government (Romans 13:4, 5).

Retributive justice is also God's response to unrepentant sinners (Jeremiah 5:3; Colossians 3:25; Romans 2:5; 6:23; Revelation 16:8-11). We are not to retaliate when wronged, but to leave it to God (Deuteronomy 32:35; Romans 12:17-19 [lesson 12]; Hebrews 10:30). Jesus is our way to escape God's wrath because Jesus bore the penalty on our behalf through His death (Romans 8:1-4; 2 Corinthians 5:17-21). The experience of such mercy should inspire us to extend forgiveness to those who have wronged us (Matthew 18:23-35 [lesson 5]).

THIS QUARTER IN THE WORD

For convenience, you can remove this page, fold it in half, and keep it in your Bible.

Answers to the Quarterly Quiz on page 338

Lesson 1—1. David. 2. withered hand. **Lesson 2**—1. enemy. 2. false. **Lesson 3**—1. false. 2. true. **Lesson 4**—1. angels. 2. brothers. **Lesson 5**—1. seven. 2. false. **Lesson 6**—1. Moses'. 2. true. **Lesson 7**—1. true. 2. faith. **Lesson 8**—1. false. 2. prophets. **Lesson 9**—1. ready. 2. true. **Lesson 10**—1. repentance. 2. wrath. **Lesson 11**—1. grace. 2. rich, poor. **Lesson 12**—1. bless. 2. coals. **Lesson 13**—1. peace. 2. true.

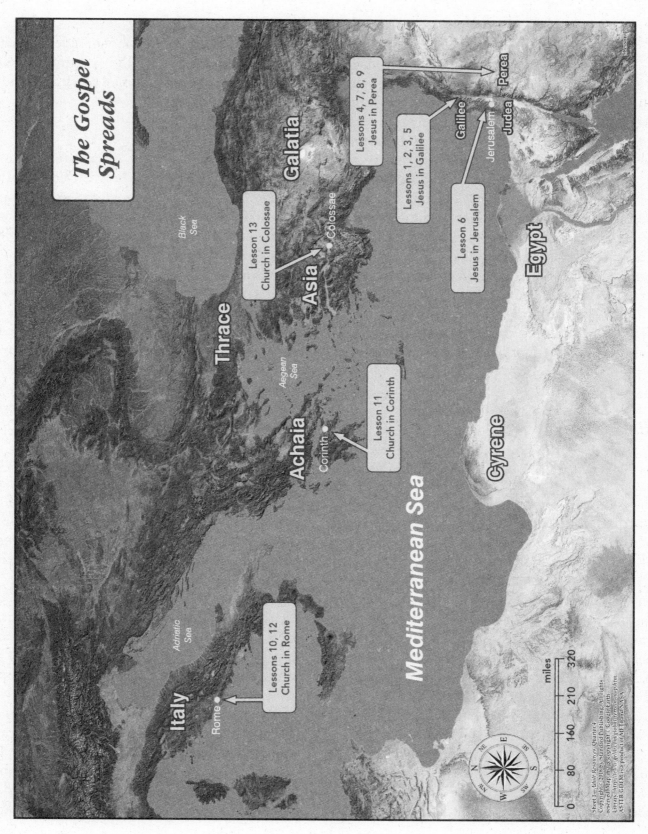

The Gospel Spreads

Black Sea

Galatia

Lessons 4, 7, 8, 9
Jesus in Perea

Perea

Lessons 1, 2, 3, 5
Jesus in Galilee

Galilee

Lesson 13
Church in Colossae

Colossae

Asia

Lesson 6
Jesus in Jerusalem

Jerusalem

Judea

Thrace

Egypt

Aegean Sea

Achaia

Lesson 11
Church in Corinth

Corinth

Cyrene

Mediterranean Sea

Adriatic Sea

Lessons 10, 12
Church in Rome

Italy

Rome

miles

0   80   160   210   320

N   NE   E   SE   S   SW   W   NW

APPLYING BIBLE CONTENT

Teacher Tips by Jim Eichenberger

THE TWO PRECEDING teacher tips articles compare the introduction of a Bible lesson with (1) a lifeguard pulling a struggling swimmer to shore and (2) the teaching of the Bible lesson as leading a tour in an unfamiliar land. Let's continue to explore those analogies.

Some popular tourist locations post signs saying, "If you lived here, you would be home by now!" A visit to some places inspires a desire to become a permanent resident. Turning "visitors" into "naturalized citizens" is also the goal of the final step in a good Bible lesson. Once students acknowledge the winds and waves that batter them and tour the landscape of the kingdom of God, the next step is for them to affirm or reaffirm their citizenship there. Note that there are no native-born citizens of God's kingdom. Each of us is born with a bent toward sin that makes us citizens of the world (John 8:23; etc.).

Principles

In becoming a naturalized citizen of the U.S., a person needs to be familiar with American civics. This includes a certain level of knowledge of the country's founding documents. Valid understanding of those documents begins with asking what their words and phrases meant to the authors of the documents. The same is true of Bible study.

As we ponder what a Bible author intended in any given text, we keep in mind that application is distinct from Bible study itself. In Bible study, the teacher leads students in understanding the original author's intended meaning. Once that is established, the application question is "What does this passage signify *for you*?" Some have described the two elements of meaning and application as "What's so?" and "So what?"

While there is one meaning in Bible passages, there may be more than one way to live out that meaning in a person's life. In every lesson of this commentary are five "What Do You Think?" questions. These do not ask the students what the Bible text means. Rather, they ask students to take the principles of the kingdom of Heaven and live them out.

Patriots

A person applying for citizenship also needs to know about some of the great heroes of that nation. We learn by example, and examining the lives of great citizens shows us how to be great citizens ourselves. The same is true when teaching how to apply the Bible to life.

It is not just the notable figures of the Bible and church history who are to be considered, however. Bible principles can be demonstrated in the lives of both the famous and the obscure in the here and now. Many of the verbal illustrations in this commentary's lessons are case studies of these, challenging students to ponder how things turn out when Bible standards are accepted or rejected today.

Pledges

The goal of someone seeking citizenship is to take the oath of citizenship. That oath contains a lot of action words—what the oath-taker pledges to do. Every Bible lesson should challenge students in a similar way—to pledge to demonstrate something learned, in a concrete way (see the third lesson aim in every lesson here). A closing prayer can be more than a formality; it can be a sincere pledge to make a small life-change. Simple object lessons or quiet periods of self-evaluation and reflection can also accomplish this important step.

By following the plan in this series of articles, a teacher can help students resist the culture in which they live, learn great Bible truths, and put those truths into practice daily. But we remember that teaching is much more than telling—it's also being a role model for applying Bible truths.

JUSTICE AND SABBATH LAWS

DEVOTIONAL READING: Psalm 10
BACKGROUND SCRIPTURE: Matthew 12:1-14

MATTHEW 12:1-14

1 At that time Jesus went on the sabbath day through the corn; and his disciples were an hungred, and began to pluck the ears of corn, and to eat.

2 But when the Pharisees saw it, they said unto him, Behold, thy disciples do that which is not lawful to do upon the sabbath day.

3 But he said unto them, Have ye not read what David did, when he was an hungred, and they that were with him;

4 How he entered into the house of God, and did eat the shewbread, which was not lawful for him to eat, neither for them which were with him, but only for the priests?

5 Or have ye not read in the law, how that on the sabbath days the priests in the temple profane the sabbath, and are blameless?

6 But I say unto you, That in this place is one greater than the temple.

7 But if ye had known what this meaneth, I will have mercy, and not sacrifice, ye would not have condemned the guiltless.

8 For the Son of man is Lord even of the sabbath day.

9 And when he was departed thence, he went into their synagogue:

10 And, behold, there was a man which had his hand withered. And they asked him, saying, Is it lawful to heal on the sabbath days? that they might accuse him.

11 And he said unto them, What man shall there be among you, that shall have one sheep, and if it fall into a pit on the sabbath day, will he not lay hold on it, and lift it out?

12 How much then is a man better than a sheep? Wherefore it is lawful to do well on the sabbath days.

13 Then saith he to the man, Stretch forth thine hand. And he stretched it forth; and it was restored whole, like as the other.

14 Then the Pharisees went out, and held a council against him, how they might destroy him.

KEY VERSE

If ye had known what this meaneth, I will have mercy, and not sacrifice, ye would not have condemned the guiltless. —Matthew 12:7

Justice in the New Testament

Unit 1: God Is Just and Merciful

Lessons 1–4

Lesson Aims

After participating in this lesson, each learner will be able to:

1. Summarize the incidents in today's text and Jesus' response in each case.

2. Explain why mercy trumps sacrifice.

3. Plan a merciful act toward a specific person in the week ahead.

Lesson Outline

Introduction

A. The Best Rest

Someone has said it to you, probably more than once. You have heard it from friends and family when you have worked hard for a long time, when you have been under great stress, or when you have been ill: "You need to get some rest."

Humans are divinely designed to need rest. Our bodies and minds are attuned to the rhythms of days and seasons, thriving on a blend of productive work and peaceful rest.

But as with so many other matters, we resist what we need. There always seems to be more work than there is time to do it. Something clamors for our attention at every moment. We lie awake thinking about what needs to be done. We worry that we have forgotten something important.

Our text today deals with the true rest that God gives His people through Jesus.

B. Lesson Background

Our text comes from the Gospel of Matthew, near the middle of its narration of Jesus' life, death, and resurrection. Having presented himself in teaching and action as having authority belonging only to God (Matthew 5–9), Jesus encountered both opposition and belief. The religious leaders, for their part, opposed Him at nearly every turn. Even so, many chose to follow Jesus, believing God was about to fulfill His ancient promises to restore Israel. Of special focus in the latter group are the 12 disciples, called by Jesus and sent out to represent Him in teaching and action (10:1-8).

In the discourse that comes just before our text, Jesus invited those who were tired and needy to find rest in Him (Matthew 11:28-30). For Israel, the concept of rest was closely associated with two of God's provisions: the Sabbath Day and the promised land (Exodus 20:8-11; Deuteronomy 12:10; 25:19; Joshua 1:13-15). In effect, Jesus declared that He fulfilled the promises that God had made through these divine institutions.

But that claim was challenged. We see that especially in today's text, where Jesus dealt with a controversy concerning what He and His disciples were doing on the Sabbath. The Law of Moses described the Sabbath as a day of rest from work. It celebrated God's resting from His acts of creation and His liberating Israel from slavery in Egypt (Exodus 20:8-11; Deuteronomy 5:15). But the law never clearly defined what constituted "work."

For the Pharisees, that was a question to be settled with great care. From sources outside the New Testament, we learn that the Pharisees began as a movement opposed to what they saw as corrupt leadership in the temple. They hoped that God would restore His blessing to Israel if Israel began to observe God's neglected law.

To that end, they sought to "build a fence" around the law. That is, they imagined every circumstance in which the law might come into play and devised strict responses to those situations. The person who followed their teachings would, as a result, not even come close to violating the law. Among these teachings were strict regulations about the Sabbath. Not even small, effortless deeds of "work" were to be done.

How would Pharisees, so strict in their interpretation of the Sabbath and so powerful in their influence over others, respond to Jesus' claims to bring the Sabbath's promised rest of Matthew 11:28-30?

I. Law and Temple
(MATTHEW 12:1-5)
A. David in the Temple (vv. 1-4)

1. At that time Jesus went on the sabbath day through the corn; and his disciples were an hungred, and began to pluck the ears of corn, and to eat.

The scene is set as *Jesus . . . and his disciples* pass through a field of grain. (*Corn* in the *King James Version* refers to any grain; wheat and barley are common in this time and place, but corn in the sense of maize is unknown.) The Law of Moses allows a hungry traveler to take a modest amount of grain from a farmer's field to eat immediately (Deuteronomy 23:24, 25), and that is what the disciples are doing. God gave Israel such laws so that His people would be generous in response to God's generosity (15:12-14). So the plucking of grain is

not a controversial matter in and of itself. (Mark 2:23 and Luke 6:1 begin parallel accounts.)

2. But when the Pharisees saw it, they said unto him, Behold, thy disciples do that which is not lawful to do upon the sabbath day.

The problem with the disciples' action is that it is being done *upon the sabbath day*. According to the interpretation of the *Pharisees*, what the *disciples* are doing amounts to three kinds of work: reaping (plucking the grain), threshing (rubbing the grain to separate kernel from husk), and winnowing (blowing the husks away from the grain). It does not matter that their actions are simple and easy, expending little energy. They have transgressed the "fence" around the Sabbath law.

These Pharisees have no official position from which to stop the disciples' actions. They do not occupy any governmental or religious office, but they do have powerful influence. They do not confront Jesus' disciples, but Jesus himself. They hold Him, as the teacher, responsible for His followers' actions. They perceive Jesus as a rival, so they seek to discredit Him for not correcting His disciples' mistake.

> **What Do You Think?**
> How were you shaped by an experience of being judged though a lens of legalism?
> *Talking Points for Your Discussion*
> - Regarding your own use of such a lens
> - Regarding presuppositions
> - In terms of response
> - Other

◆ HAVE HAT, NO SERVICE ◆

He looked like a typical teenager. It was the first time we had seen him in church, and he appeared to be by himself. He came in and sat down, and it was obvious that he was out of his element.

We'll never know why he came, but we do know why he left. He left because of his baseball cap. During the song service, a deacon sitting behind the boy leaned forward and demanded rather gruffly, "Please remove your hat."

The boy did not comply, so during the preacher's prayer a few minutes later, the deacon leaned

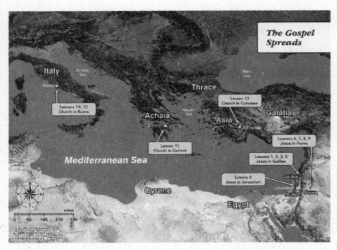

Visual for Lesson 1. *Keep this map posted through-out the quarter to give your learners a geographical perspective.*

forward again and whispered, "I said, remove your hat!" The teen turned around and pleaded, "I really don't want to take off my cap. Maybe I should just leave."

"You don't need to leave. Just take off that hat!"

After the boy turned back around, the deacon reached forward and snatched off his hat and dropped it into his lap. "That wasn't so hard, was it?" That was when everyone near the spectacle noticed the ashy paleness of the teen's bald head and the nasty scar that stretched across it. The teen jammed the baseball cap back on his disfigured head and got up and left. The preacher was just beginning his sermon, which was titled "The Love of Christ."

We don't know who that boy was. We will probably never know him. He might have been blessed by hearing a message about the love of Christ. It's a sermon we all need to hear, but most of all to apply. Don't let human traditions get in the way of the message of Christ's love.   —C. T.

3. But he said unto them, Have ye not read what David did, when he was an hungred, and they that were with him?

Jesus begins His response by summarizing a story from 1 Samuel 20:1–21:6. *David* had been a member of King Saul's court, but Saul had become jealous of David's popularity and success. Warned to flee for his life, David became a fugitive in desperate need of food.

4. How he entered into the house of God, and did eat the shewbread, which was not lawful for him to eat, neither for them which were with him, but only for the priests?

The house of God that David entered was the tabernacle—the tent that served as Israel's center of worship before Solomon built the temple. Asking the high priest for food, David was told that the only food available was the bread ritually placed in the tabernacle as an offering to God. No one was permitted to eat that bread except *the priests* (Leviticus 24:5-9). Yet the high priest gave the bread to David.

The high priest's reasons for giving the bread were apparently twofold. David's life was in danger, so the high priest acted to save his life. And David's anointing by Samuel to be king was likely known, even though Saul still occupied the office (1 Samuel 16:1-13). The high priest acted in submission to God's chosen.

B. Priests in the Temple (v. 5)

5. Or have ye not read in the law, how that on the sabbath days the priests in the temple profane the sabbath, and are blameless?

Jesus then appeals to another part of Israel's Scriptures. The Law of Moses explicitly requires priests to offer sacrifices on the Sabbath, first in the tabernacle and then in the temple that superseded it (Numbers 28:9, 10). Jesus sarcastically uses the deliberately harsh expression *profane* to describe their action. By the Pharisees' definition, this work would reduce the holy Sabbath to an ordinary day. Yet the Law of Moses commands sacrifice on the Sabbath, and so the priests who perform the sacrifice must be without guilt.

> ### What Do You Think?
> Where do you draw the line regarding what you will and won't do on a day of rest? Why?
> *Talking Points for Your Discussion*
> - In terms of physical activity
> - In terms of mental activity
> - Considering Proverbs 6:10, 11; Matthew 11:28; 26:45; Mark 6:31; John 9:4; Hebrews 4:9, 10; 6:11, 12; 10:25

II. Sabbath and Messiah

(MATTHEW 12:6-8)

A. Greater Law (vv. 6, 7)

6. But I say unto you, That in this place is one greater than the temple.

As Jesus' authority is greater than that of David, so He is *greater than the temple*. This statement, like many others that Jesus makes, no doubt shocks the religious leaders and others. To be allowed to have a temple is a gift from God. The temple was built according to His design for sacrifices and rituals instituted by God. To claim standing greater than the temple's standing is to claim the authority of God himself.

7. But if ye had known what this meaneth, I will have mercy, and not sacrifice, ye would not have condemned the guiltless.

The regulations that allow plucking grain in order to satisfy hunger are expressions of God's *mercy* (see comments on verse 1, above). This practice is an expression of God's loving generosity. His people live in the land He has given them because of that generosity. So they are obliged to be similarly generous to one another.

Jesus quotes from Hosea 6:6 to make this point. The prophet Hosea had warned God's people centuries before that their love for God was weak and erratic. They relied on sacrifice in the temple to express their devotion to God, but they practiced violence and theft day by day. True devotion to God must be expressed with His degree of mercy. These Pharisees, however, are using the Sabbath to enforce a devotion to God that has no place for mercy.

The Pharisees may not acknowledge it, but Jesus stands before them as the ultimate expression of God's mercy. He is God as a human being, living among sinful humans, eventually to die as the innocent one in place of the guilty. When the

HOW TO SAY IT

Babylonian	Bab-ih-*low*-nee-un.
Hosea	Ho-*zay*-uh.
Leviticus	Leh-*vit*-ih-kus.
Pharisees	*Fair*-ih-seez.

Pharisees ignore Him while enforcing their view of the Law of Moses, they are ignoring the mercy of God in its greatest demonstration.

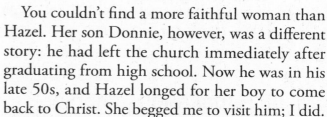

What Do You Think?

How can you help your church improve its extensions of mercy?

Talking Points for Your Discussion

- In physical, material terms
- In spiritual terms
- As the material needs interrelate with the spiritual

◆ FOR LACK OF TRACK SHOES ◆

You couldn't find a more faithful woman than Hazel. Her son Donnie, however, was a different story: he had left the church immediately after graduating from high school. Now he was in his late 50s, and Hazel longed for her boy to come back to Christ. She begged me to visit him; I did.

"Would you mind telling me why you stopped attending church?" I asked Donnie.

"In high school I was a good distance runner. I even broke our league's mile record. But I ran every race in my clodhoppers, the same shoes I wore to school—the only pair of shoes I owned. I asked Mom and Dad for a pair of track shoes, but they said we couldn't afford them. I reminded them of the flour canister in the cupboard. Every payday Dad would put money in there. I asked if we could use that money."

"'Oh no!' they said. 'That's the Lord's money. We made a pledge to the church. We can't use it for anything else.' I went to the state meet, ran in my old shoes, and lost," Donnie continued sadly. "Track shoes would have made a difference."

Not knowing what to say, I responded, "I'm sorry, Donnie." With misty eyes Donnie concluded, "I decided that if the God who owns the entire universe needed money more than I needed track shoes, He isn't much of a God."

I enjoyed my visits with Donnie and prayed for him often, but he never said yes to Jesus as far as I know. I could conclude here with "the moral of the story," but I think you know what it is.

—C. T.

B. Greater Authority (v. 8)

8. For the Son of man is Lord even of the sabbath day.

Jesus' divine authority is summed up in this statement. The phrase *Son of man* echoes Daniel 7:1-14. In the prophet's vision, "beasts" representing kingdoms opposed to God's people are overcome by "one like the Son of man." To Him God gives authority to rule forever. Jesus claims to be that very figure, having come into the world with authority that belongs only to God. (By contrast, the dozens of references to the prophet Ezekiel as "Son of man" highlight his mortality.)

The Sabbath was a gift of God's mercy for people who needed rest. Jesus declares himself *Lord* of that gift. As God's divine Son, He exercises full authority over God's Sabbath. The rest that He gives accomplishes what Sabbath promises.

III. Ritual and Humanity
(MATTHEW 12:9-14)
A. Trick Question (vv. 9, 10)

9. And when he was departed thence, he went into their synagogue.

Matthew records another incident that occurs on this particular Sabbath Day. The *synagogue* is the traditional gathering place for Jewish believers on the Sabbath. Apparently the concept of the synagogue was established during the Babylonian captivity, when the people no longer had access to the temple. Faithful Jews would gather on the Sabbath to read Scripture and pray together.

Jesus is found often in the synagogues in the Gospels. But they prove to be places of controversy, as Jesus makes claims and performs actions to which the religious leaders object.

10a. And, behold, there was a man which had his hand withered.

In this synagogue meeting Jesus encounters a man with a disability. The term *withered* suggests that his hand appears shrunken, like a plant that has dried up. The man has little or no ability to use this hand and probably not his arm.

10b. And they asked him, saying, Is it lawful to heal on the sabbath days? that they might accuse him.

Jesus' opponents see this as an opportunity to discredit Him. He has healed people before (Matthew 4:24; 8:16, 17; 9:1-7, 18-35), but will He "work" in a way that breaks the Sabbath law by healing the man? They once more illustrate that they don't comprehend the priority of mercy.

B. Bold Response (vv. 11-14)

11. And he said unto them, What man shall there be among you, that shall have one sheep, and if it fall into a pit on the sabbath day, will he not lay hold on it, and lift it out?

Jesus responds to His opponents with a question of His own. They take for granted that an act of mercy on the Sabbath is a violation of the Law of Moses. But Jesus points out the inconsistency in their own practice.

Longstanding Jewish tradition allows a shepherd with a *sheep* in distress on the Sabbath to do what is necessary to rescue the animal. Oddly, many Jewish teachers of the day (like these in the synagogue with Jesus) do not allow acts of mercy toward other people.

> *What Do You Think?*
> What safeguards can be implemented to ensure that a Scripture discussion sheds "light" and not "heat"?
>
> *Talking Points for Your Discussion*
> - In terms of predefined safeguards, which everyone knows in advance
> - In terms of impromptu safeguards, enacted on the spot

12. How much then is a man better than a sheep? Wherefore it is lawful to do well on the sabbath days.

Arguing from the lesser to the greater, Jesus implies that humans are more worthy of mercy than livestock. How can a person who knows God apply the law of the Sabbath to treat a fellow human as less than an animal? The practice of Jesus' opponents refutes their position.

But Jesus' point is broader than just this comparison. *It is lawful to do well* for others *on the sabbath days* because the Sabbath is a gift from the generous God to His people in need. Israel had labored many years as slaves in Egypt. The Sabbath was God's blessing of rest to those who had known no rest (Deuteronomy 5:15). Acts of goodness and mercy are not forbidden on such a day. In fact, they may be even more appropriate because of what the Sabbath celebrates.

> **What Do You Think?**
> What accessibility boundaries do you need to establish so you don't overextend yourself in being available to help others?
> *Talking Points for Your Discussion*
> ▪ In matters of time
> ▪ In matters of money

13. Then saith he to the man, Stretch forth thine hand. And he stretched it forth; and it was restored whole, like as the other.

Jesus proceeds to demonstrate the point He has just made. As He commands the man to place his afflicted *hand* where all can see, the hand is fully *restored*. This is no temporary or partial healing, for the formerly withered hand is as strong as the man's *other* hand.

Jesus' previous assertion about mercy on the Sabbath is more than just sound reasoning. It has now become authoritative. Jesus has the power to restore life to the lifeless, including this man's withered hand. Such power belongs only to the God who has granted Israel the Sabbath as His gift commemorating His creation of the world and as His gift of freedom to captive Israel. Such power identifies the "Lord of the Sabbath," the one who has come to give true rest to suffering humanity. He authoritatively interprets the Sabbath. He fulfills the Sabbath's promise of rest.

14. Then the Pharisees went out, and held a council against him, how they might destroy him.

Jesus has faced opposition since early in His ministry (Matthew 9:3, 11; 11:19). He has warned His disciples that they will face the same (10:16-25, 34-39). Now *the Pharisees*, repeatedly put to shame by Jesus' responses to their objections, conspire to kill Him. In sad irony, those who outwardly profess to honor God's law the most now secretly plan murder.

What comes of their plot? In every later controversy, Jesus still gets the best of His opponents. Eventually He warns His disciples that when He goes to Jerusalem, He will be arrested by the religious authorities, then handed over to the Romans to be crucified—only to be raised again to life (Matthew 16:21; 17:12, 22, 23; 20:18, 19; 26:2).

Jesus will surrender himself when approached by soldiers (Matthew 26:45-56). He will make no defense when on trial (26:57-68; 27:11-26). Jesus dies not because of His enemies' power but because of His willing self-surrender. The Lord of the Sabbath is also the Lord of life and death. The Lord who restores life to a lifeless hand will make life possible for everyone by giving away His own life.

Conclusion

A. No Longer Sick and Tired

People today often complain that they are tired. Ironically, we enjoy more laborsaving devices than people in the past could even imagine! Yet we seem to find ourselves worn out all the time.

Perhaps we are tired because we look for rest in the wrong places. Leisure and recreation have their place. But true rest can be found only from the Christ who made us and redeemed us. He makes us whole. He gives us life. He grants us rest even in the midst of trouble.

B. Prayer

Lord, we cast our cares on You. We cast our lives on You. Make us whole. Give us Your peace. Grant us rest. And make us the instruments of Your peace and rest for others. We pray in Jesus' name. Amen.

C. Thought to Remember

Jesus gives us rest in a weary world.

VISUALS FOR THESE LESSONS

The visual pictured in each lesson (example: page 348) is a small reproduction of a large, full-color poster included in the *Adult Resources* packet for the Summer Quarter. That packet also contains the very useful *Presentation Tools* CD for teacher use. Order No. 4629118 from your supplier.

INVOLVEMENT LEARNING

Enhance your lesson with KJV Bible Student *(from your curriculum supplier) and the reproducible activity page (at www.standardlesson.com or in the back of the* KJV Standard Lesson Commentary Deluxe Edition*).*

Into the Lesson

Before class, write the following situations on separate index cards. Do not include the italicized answers. (1) A judge gives people who play their car stereos too loudly the sentence of *(listening to blaring music—such as Barry Manilow—for one hour).* (2) In addition to a $100,000 fine, a judge sentenced a slumlord who owned 40 run-down properties to *(six months of house arrest in one of the units).* (3) The mother who received a ticket because her 6-year-old son kept unbuckling his seat belt asked for the judge's help. He *(sentenced the boy to a seatbelt safety class specially designed for the child).*

Divide students into small groups and hand a card to each group. Say, "Read the situation on your card and decide what punishment you would give." Allow time for groups to reveal the sentence they came up with. Review the judges' actual sentences. Then say, "It seems these judges had the accused in mind when handing out just the right sentence. The Pharisees of Jesus' day, on the other hand, didn't seem to have much concern regarding how their interpretation of Sabbath laws would affect people. We'll see what Jesus has to say about this."

Alternative. Distribute copies of the "Strange Sunday Laws" activity from the reproducible page, which you can download. After students finish working on this individually, say, "The Pharisees also had some strange and strict laws related to their Sabbath. We'll find out what Jesus had to say when they tried to shame Him and His disciples for not keeping their laws."

Into the Word

Ask two students to read Matthew 12:1-14 aloud. Assign half of your class to represent the Pharisees' beliefs and the other half to represent Jesus' teaching. Have each group select a spokesperson. Distribute copies of the following list, and ask the groups to decide how the Pharisees or Jesus would respond. (1) The disciples walk through a field and eat grain.

(2) David asks for bread reserved for priests. (3) The temple is more important than anything except God himself. (4) Mercy is more important than sacrifice. (5) Healing on a Sabbath violates the prohibition of work on that day (Exodus 20:10).

Alternative. Give each student a copy of the "How Do They Compare?" activity from the reproducible page. Have students work in pairs.

After either of the above activities, lead a class discussion with the following questions. Anticipated responses are italicized.

1. How did the Pharisees' beliefs on Sabbath observance reveal their imperfect understanding of the Sabbath law? *Their added traditions had the effect of minimizing the importance of mercy.*

2. What were Jesus' corrections of the Pharisees regarding what was important when observing the Sabbath? *Mercy predominated when David accepted bread reserved for priests to feed his hungry men. Also, priests who work to perform sacrifices on the Sabbath are guiltless for doing so. Jesus also pointed out the inconsistency of allowing the rescue of lost sheep on the Sabbath while disallowing merciful acts toward people.*

3. How was the fact of Jesus' greater importance than the temple relevant to the Sabbath discussion? *His claim to be greater than the temple is a claim to deity. As such, He was the one who had the authoritative interpretation of how to observe the Sabbath.*

Into Life

Say, "The Pharisees got it wrong by emphasizing their traditions over the needs of the people. If a visitor did either of the following, how should we handle it?" Allow time for comments as you present these scenarios: (1) a guest comes to church dressed inappropriately; (2) parents keep their very young and noisy children with them in the main service rather than taking them to age-appropriate classes.

Encourage students to take special note of visitors and find one person to whom they can show a kind and merciful welcome.

PARABLES OF GOD'S JUST KINGDOM

DEVOTIONAL READING: Psalm 78:1-8
BACKGROUND SCRIPTURE: Matthew 13:24-43

MATTHEW 13:24-33

24 Another parable put he forth unto them, saying, The kingdom of heaven is likened unto a man which sowed good seed in his field:

25 But while men slept, his enemy came and sowed tares among the wheat, and went his way.

26 But when the blade was sprung up, and brought forth fruit, then appeared the tares also.

27 So the servants of the householder came and said unto him, Sir, didst not thou sow good seed in thy field? from whence then hath it tares?

28 He said unto them, An enemy hath done this. The servants said unto him, Wilt thou then that we go and gather them up?

29 But he said, Nay; lest while ye gather up the tares, ye root up also the wheat with them.

30 Let both grow together until the harvest: and in the time

of harvest I will say to the reapers, Gather ye together first the tares, and bind them in bundles to burn them: but gather the wheat into my barn.

31 Another parable put he forth unto them, saying, The kingdom of heaven is like to a grain of mustard seed, which a man took, and sowed in his field:

32 Which indeed is the least of all seeds: but when it is grown, it is the greatest among herbs, and becometh a tree, so that the birds of the air come and lodge in the branches thereof.

33 Another parable spake he unto them; The kingdom of heaven is like unto leaven, which a woman took, and hid in three measures of meal, till the whole was leavened.

KEY VERSE

Let both grow together until the harvest: and in the time of harvest I will say to the reapers, Gather ye together first the tares, and bind them in bundles to burn them: but gather the wheat into my barn. —**Matthew 13:30**

Justice in the New Testament

Unit 1: God Is Just and Merciful

Lessons 1–4

Lesson Aims

After participating in this lesson, each learner will be able to:

1. Identify the central idea about God's kingdom in the lesson's three parables.

2. Contrast Jesus' understanding of God's kingdom with the misunderstandings commonly held by Jews of the first century AD.

3. Tell which parable of the three is most challenging to him or her and explain why.

Lesson Outline

Introduction

A. A Different Kind of Riddle

Most of us enjoy the challenge of a good riddle. The best riddles challenge our minds to solve a problem of language and logic. They can prove hard to solve but are also hard to forget. We may puzzle over them for days trying to solve them. When we discover or learn the answer, the best riddles surprise us. We realize that they have exposed our assumptions, our normal ways of thinking. These riddles challenge us to consider how often we may miss the truth because we assume something that is not true.

Jesus is known for having taught in parables, a form of speech much like a riddle. Although His parables used commonly understood images and everyday events, they forced listeners to rethink their understanding of how God was working in the world. The parables combined familiar details with the demand for serious reflection.

Today's text is a selection from a much longer discourse that consists mostly of parables. The lessons Jesus taught in these parables challenged widely held (mis)conceptions of how God was to bring about His kingdom.

B. Lesson Background

Parables are prominent in Jesus' teaching in the Gospels of Matthew, Mark, and Luke. The term *parable* translates a Greek word that indicates a saying or story implying a comparison. Jesus' parables always involved such comparisons. The key to their interpretation is observing the comparison that Jesus intended. That intent is signaled by the details of the parable, its context, any explanation that Jesus offered, and the parable's role in His wider teaching.

Each parable in today's text begins with some form of the phrase "The kingdom of heaven is like." The term refers to the fulfillment of God's promise to reverse the course of human life, establishing His reign in place of the tyrannous, selfish reign of sin and death. It is a kingdom, as Jesus later told Pilate, that "is not of this world" (John 18:36).

For Jesus' audience, God's promise of a future kingdom had a strongly nationalistic focus. Many in Jesus' day expected God's promised kingdom to bring about the defeat of Israel's enemies, meaning the pagan empires that had ruled God's people for generations (compare Acts 1:6). God's kingdom, in other words, was expected to be a political and military kingdom like any other, only one ruled righteously and in submission to God.

> *What Do You Think?*
> How do we avoid errors regarding allegiances to God's kingdom and to earthly nations?
>
> *Talking Points for Your Discussion*
> - Regarding errors that see such allegiances as completely compatible
> - Regarding errors that see such allegiances as completely incompatible

One way Jesus challenged this expectation was through parables. These gave a very different vision of God's promised kingdom. The sudden, decisive action of a powerful military ruler was not Jesus' picture. He used instead comparisons to farming, which involves patience, trust, and the passing of time. Rather than depict dramatic, obvious events that would capture the world's attention, He spoke of subtle but powerful processes that were hard to see except by the eye of faith.

Earlier in the context of today's passage from Matthew 13, Jesus had delivered and explained a parable about a man sowing seed in a field. The message of the kingdom of God is not something that yields instant, universal success. Rather, it often seems unsuccessful at first, as people respond without persistent faith to the good news of the kingdom. For those ready to hear and heed, Jesus explained His teaching. For others, the seeming difficulty of the message itself seemed to turn them away from belief. God's kingdom, Jesus taught, would divide people. Such divisions are apparent in the parables of our text as well.

HOW TO SAY IT

Corinthians	Ko-*rin*-thee-unz (*th* as in *thin*).
Galatians	Guh-*lay*-shunz.
Leviticus	Leh-*vit*-ih-kus.

I. Parable of the Tares
(Matthew 13:24-30)
A. Secret Sabotage (vv. 24, 25)

24. Another parable put he forth unto them, saying, The kingdom of heaven is likened unto a man which sowed good seed in his field.

This parable seems, at first glance, to be like the previous one in that both involve the sowing of seed. But the similarity is superficial. Here it is the *seed* that is *good;* in Matthew 13:8 it is the ground that is good. Other differences present themselves as well.

Jesus' contemporaries are familiar with agricultural terminology. Seed is spread by hand as a farmer walks through a field. With a sack of seed over his shoulder, he sows seed over cultivated ground—ground prepared to receive it. Seed is typically sown in the autumn, in anticipation of the winter rains that allow it to flourish. Wheat and barley are the staple grains planted in this way.

25. But while men slept, his enemy came and sowed tares among the wheat, and went his way.

An *enemy* of the farmer now appears in the story, attempting to do him harm. *Tares* translates a Greek word that refers to a kind of weed that looks very much like wheat until it matures. These are not just weeds that threaten the growth of the crop. These are weeds easily confused with the crop itself. Removing them will be very difficult. But early in the story, the farmer and his workers do not recognize what has happened. The enemy conceals his act by doing it while everyone sleeps.

B. Damage Discovered (vv. 26-28)

26. But when the blade was sprung up, and brought forth fruit, then appeared the tares also.

As the plants begin to grow, the difference between the wheat and the weeds begins to become apparent. At first the two kinds of plants seem identical, but their differences become more apparent with time. Eventually the workers discern that their field is infested with weeds.

27. So the servants of the householder came and said unto him, Sir, didst not thou sow good seed in thy field? from whence then hath it tares?

As Jesus tells the story, *the servants* do not inform the master, *the householder,* about the weeds in so many words. Rather, they ask how the situation has arisen. They know that their master is a good farmer who saw to it that *good seed* has been sown. The servants are at a loss to explain the weeds. But they assume that their master understands, so they ask him.

28. He said unto them, An enemy hath done this. The servants said unto him, Wilt thou then that we go and gather them up?

The master's response is clear and decisive. He knows that only someone with malicious intent could have sown the weeds among the wheat.

The servants' response is in line with conventional wisdom: weeds must be dealt with immediately. Every hour they live they draw water, sunlight, and nutrients away from the good plants. Surely the master will agree that the weeds must be dealt with immediately!

C. Temporary Coexistence (vv. 29, 30a)

29, 30a. But he said, Nay; lest while ye gather up the tares, ye root up also the wheat with them. Let both grow together until the harvest.

The master's reply is very different from what the servants expect. He will not have the weeds removed immediately. He wants to protect the good plants from being uprooted in the weeding process. Because the weeds and *wheat* are growing so close together, weeding is bound to cause collateral damage.

> *What Do You Think?*
> How does our proximity to worldly weeds of sin affect the safeguards we adopt against them?
> *Talking Points for Your Discussion*
> - Individual vs. communal safeguards against unholy lifestyles
> - Individual vs. communal safeguards against ungodly definitions of success
> - Other

In the larger context, this is the second parable of Jesus that tells a story of seed and harvest (see Matthew 13:3-9). Jesus subsequently explains both parables to His disciples (13:18-23, 36-43). These explanations make clear that Jesus is not offering advice about agriculture but challenging His hearers to begin thinking differently about God's kingdom.

Many in Jesus' audience expect that when God's king brings God's kingdom into the world, both evil and evildoers will be judged and eliminated immediately. But Jesus tells a very different story. The inbreaking of God's kingdom and the final judgment on evil are separated by an interval of time. During that interval, the people of the kingdom live alongside evildoers. A separation will indeed come, but only at *the harvest.*

◆ WEEDS TO WHOM? ◆

Joe and Bonnie missed their former neighbors. The Heinrichs had sold their house and moved into a long-term care facility. They had been the best of neighbors! Joe and Bonnie were sad to lose their compassionate Christian friends.

The new neighbors were quite different. Joe and Bonnie didn't know their names, but they did know that they were rowdy beer drinkers. The peace and quiet of the neighborhood was now shattered by loud music, loud voices, and cars without mufflers, squealing in and out at all hours of the night.

Because they were offended, Joe and Bonnie made no effort to get to know their new neighbors. They prayed that God would intervene and help them get rid of their "headache." But one Sunday morning as the two were walking to their car, Bibles in hand, something incredible happened: the lady next door said, "Hello." A brief conversation took place, cut short since Joe and Bonnie were headed for church. "Maybe you'd like to come with us sometime," Bonnie said offhandedly as she slid into the car seat.

The next week the new neighbors were at Sunday worship. They were guests of Joe and Bonnie, who learned to trust God's ability to transform lives. Those we see as "weeds" to be removed immediately may be viewed differently by God. —C. T.

D. Eternal Separation (v. 30b)

30b. And in the time of harvest I will say to the reapers, Gather ye together first the tares, and bind them in bundles to burn them: but gather the wheat into my barn.

Those who carry out the *harvest* will follow the distinctive instructions we see here. The instructions are stated not only in terms of the final dispositions of *the tares* and *the wheat*, but also of a certain sequence.

When requested by His disciples to do so, Jesus later identifies the elements of the parable this way (Matthew 13:37-39):

the sower of good seed → the Son of man
the field → the world
good seed → the children of the kingdom
the tares → the children of the wicked one
the enemy → the devil
the harvest → the end of the world
the reapers → the angels

Jesus closes His explanation, as He did the earlier parable of the sower, by saying that the one who has ears must hear what He says (Matthew 13:9, 43). These are solemn warnings to listeners to think carefully about Jesus' teaching and to act on it wisely. The warnings echo words from the prophet Isaiah that Jesus quoted in the earlier context regarding those who hear God's Word but do not understand, and those who see but do not perceive (13:14). This spiritual deafness and blindness is traced to problems of the heart (13:15). Destruction awaits them (13:41, 42).

By contrast, those who follow Jesus and listen with willing hearts will discern the truth of God's kingdom. They are the ones who receive the fullness of God's blessing as they heed the message (Matthew 13:16, 17, 43). Even so, Jesus' followers must expect to work in a field where weeds and wheat grow together until the harvest. We can expect to be surrounded continually by evil. We can expect frustration and discouragement because of that evil. We can even expect scorn and opposition from those who do not listen to the kingdom's call. Thus we must be prepared to endure with patience as we serve in expectation of the Lord's bringing His kingdom to its fullness. When that happens, the Lord's promise is that His people will be with Him in His kingdom, where all the disappointments and heartaches of a sinful world will have no place.

II. Parable of the Mustard Seed
(Matthew 13:31, 32)
A. From Tiny Seed (vv. 31, 32a)

31, 32a. Another parable put he forth unto them, saying, The kingdom of heaven is like to a grain of mustard seed, which a man took, and sowed in his field. Which indeed is the least of all seeds.

Matthew records 10 parables of Jesus using some form of the phrase *the kingdom of heaven is like.* The parable of the sower in Matthew 13:3-23 does not use that phrase, but that parable can be added to the tally of 10 nonetheless since its phrase "the word of the kingdom" (13:19) indicates the same intent. Therefore we have come to the third of such parables in this Gospel (see also Luke 13:18, 19).

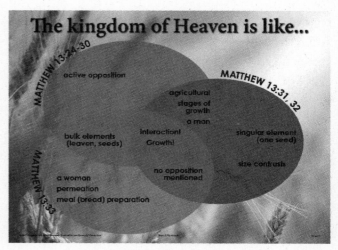

Visual for Lesson 2. *Start a discussion by pointing to this visual as you ask, "Who can explain how a Venn diagram works?"*

The imagery now shifts from sowing grain to planting *a grain of mustard seed.* The phrase *which indeed is the least of all seeds* is not intended to be a comparison with the seeds of all plants known today. Rather, it reflects the experience of Jesus' first-century audience. Such a seed measures only one to two millimeters in diameter.

Mustard is a common garden plant in the biblical world. It is grown for its seeds, which can be ground into a powder to add savory flavor to cooked dishes.

What Do You Think?

How has experiencing the fact that God's work often has humble beginnings affected you? How should it?

Talking Points for Your Discussion
- In positive situations of church growth, answered prayer, etc.
- In negative situations of church conflict, unanswered prayer, etc.

B. To Large Tree (v. 32b, c)

32b. But when it is grown, it is the greatest among herbs, and becometh a tree.

This partial verse reflects the fact that mature mustard plants are large shrubs that can grow as high as 10 or 12 feet. The mustard seed is tiny; the mustard plant is impressively tall. But over time the small, hard-to-see, seemingly insignificant seed grows to become an exceptionally tall plant. And that is the point about God's inbreaking kingdom that Jesus desires His listeners to understand. Many expect God's kingdom to enter the world suddenly and dramatically (see the Lesson Background), and they must change their thinking.

32c. So that the birds of the air come and lodge in the branches thereof.

The final phrase of the parable underlines the extent of the mustard plant's growth by noting one result. This detail may prompt us to wonder what the birds might represent.

In reading Jesus' parables, we generally should first ask not what the details represent but how each detail contributes to the main point(s) of the parable. Clearly, the birds' ability to *lodge in the branches* stresses the great size of the plant.

Another theory, however, is that Jesus is drawing a parallel with Ezekiel 17:22-24. The imagery of birds there suggests people of other nations who come to know God. It's possible that Jesus is making the same point: the kingdom of God that He brings, though humble in its beginnings, will fulfill Ezekiel's promise and make people of all nations part of God's people.

III. Parable of the Leaven
(Matthew 13:33)

33. Another parable spake he unto them; The kingdom of heaven is like unto leaven, which a woman took, and hid in three measures of meal, till the whole was leavened.

The third parable of today's lesson makes a point similar to the second. Jesus often delivers units of teaching in pairs in this Gospel (see Matthew 5:13-16; 13:44-46; 24:27, 28). Here the focus is on *leaven,* another name for yeast (Luke 13:20, 21 is parallel). This substance is added to flour to make bread dough rise.

As with the mustard seed, the details of the story contrast the smallness of something with its outsized impact or result. The words *hid in* do not indicate secretiveness on the part of the cook; rather, they underline the difficulty (if not impossibility) of seeing the yeast in the context of being initially mixed into *three measures of meal.* That is quite a large amount of flour, estimated to be enough to feed as many as 100 people when the flour is baked into bread.

Leaven is often used in the Bible as a symbol for evil that infiltrates God's people (Matthew 16:6; 1 Corinthians 5:6-8; Galatians 5:9). But it can also be associated with positive actions (Leviticus 7:13; 23:17). As always in interpreting Scripture, we must give due weight to the immediate context. The context at hand suggests a parallel between the growth of a mustard seed and the impact of a small amount of yeast.

It is often noted that this parable depicts the action of a woman, following the action of a man in the story of the mustard seed. Certainly,

Jesus is offering every member of His audience the opportunity to connect to His message about God's surprising kingdom. Everyone needs to hear the challenge that God's kingdom will operate almost unnoticed at first, but the end result will be astonishing.

> **What Do You Think?**
> What are some ways to resist un-Christian temptations of implementing change?
> *Talking Points for Your Discussion*
> - With regard to changing ethics
> - With regard to changing morals
> - With regard to changing definitions (of truth, etc.)
> - Other

◆ THE BIG IMPACT OF A LITTLE LEAVEN ◆

Molly was a beagle of average intelligence who did a very dumb thing. One morning Jane, her master, mixed up a batch of bread dough and left it on the kitchen table to rise. Then Jane went to the back of the house to do laundry. In Jane's absence, Molly somehow nudged a chair over to the table, hopped up, and gobbled down the entire batch of dough.

When Jane returned to the kitchen, her bread dough was gone! But Molly hadn't gone far. Lying on her back with legs sticking straight up in the air, Molly looked like a bratwurst that had been left on the grill too long! The poor little dog was groaning in agony from the swelling taking place in her tummy.

The small amount of yeast in the dough had created a big crisis within Molly. So an emergency trip to the veterinarian followed. Four hours and $800 later, Molly was on her way to becoming her old happy self.

Jesus' parable of the leaven describes what just a small portion of the message of His kingdom will do. When that message is received in faith and obedience, an incredible spiritual growth begins—not the harmful kind of growth Molly experienced, but the kind that leads to fullness in Christ. The good news is that Jesus' promise of spiritual fullness is still valid.
—C. T.

Conclusion
A. Wait with Patience

None of us likes having to be patient—we just don't like to wait! We all prefer to get what we need immediately. When we are victimized by injustice and evil, we want relief and vindication without delay.

The promise of God's kingdom is that God will certainly bring that relief and vindication. Our holy and just God cannot abide evil and injustice forever. His kingdom promises to defeat the devil and his works, creating a "new heavens and a new earth, wherein dwelleth righteousness" (2 Peter 3:13).

But the kingdom of God that Christ establishes does not bring about the defeat of evil all at once. The separation happens not at the beginning but at the end. For now the kingdom operates quietly, almost invisibly, like a tiny seed that grows or like yeast that makes dough rise. As that happens, the Lord calls on people to have ears that hear, to heed His call to turn to Him in repentance and receive the blessing of His mercy before it is too late.

If the full reign of God takes longer to occur than His people want, it is only to allow more people the opportunity to become subjects of the kingdom (2 Peter 3:9). Meanwhile, God supplies the strength for His people to wait faithfully, to serve faithfully, and to see the true impact of His seemingly invisible kingdom.

What part of God's future reign do you wish you could experience now? How do you see His kingdom at work as you wait? How has God enabled you to wait with patience? As we reflect on questions like these, we understand what it means to live with ears that hear Jesus' message of God's reign.

B. Prayer

Father, we long for Your rule over every part of Your world! Empower us to wait with patience and discernment, knowing that Your kingdom is present among us and will one day be complete. We pray in Jesus' name. Amen.

C. Thought to Remember
Wait patiently and work prayerfully.

INVOLVEMENT LEARNING

Enhance your lesson with KJV Bible Student *(from your curriculum supplier) and the reproducible activity page (at www.standardlesson.com or in the back of the* KJV Standard Lesson Commentary Deluxe Edition*).*

Into the Lesson

Ask students, "Have you ever experienced a misunderstanding with your GPS? What happened?" Allow people to share their stories. Then say, "At least, no one did what some tourists in Australia managed to do. Being unfamiliar with the country and relying too heavily on the GPS, which said it was leading them to a road, they managed to drive their car into the ocean."

Alternative. Distribute copies of the "What Do You Know?" activity from the reproducible page, which can be downloaded. After students finish, give the answers with explanations.

After either activity say, "Most of the misunderstandings we have are not that significant. But the vast majority of Jewish people in Jesus' day misunderstood the nature of the kingdom of God. So Jesus used parables to help correct this problem."

Into the Word

Using the Lesson Background, explain what parables are, how and why Jesus used them, and principles to observe when interpreting them; the "why" explanation should focus on Jewish expectations regarding God's promised kingdom.

Give each student a handout (you prepare) featuring one of the three assignments below. Leave appropriate space for students to write answers. Title every handout "Jesus Teaches About the Kingdom of Heaven." Form students into small groups based on the assignment received.

Assignment 1: The Jewish people of Jesus' day expected that when God's kingdom burst onto the scene, God's king would defeat Israel's enemies immediately and purge the land of evil and unbelief. Summarize the parable of the weeds (Matthew 13:24-30) and why it overturned this expectation.

Assignment 2: The Jewish people of Jesus' day expected that when God's king came, he would enter the world suddenly and sweep swiftly into power. Summarize the parable of the mustard seed (Matthew 13:31, 32) and why it contradicted this expectation.

Assignment 3: The Jewish people expected that when God's king came, his kingdom would be located in Israel. Summarize the parable of the leaven (Matthew 13:33) and explain how it contradicted the Jewish expectation.

Allow each group to report on its findings. Expected responses are as follows: *Assignment 1:* God's people can expect to be surrounded by evil and opposition. We are to endure patiently and wait expectantly for the triumphant future harvest. *Assignment 2:* Just like the mustard seed, God's kingdom starts small and unnoticed, but grows to a greatness that cannot be missed. *Assignment 3:* As leaven spreads through the bread and causes it to grow, God's kingdom will spread throughout the world and have great influence.

Into Life

Distribute handouts (you prepare) with the following simple matching test. Have the following three statements down the left side of each handout: A. The world treats the church as insignificant. B. Christians should spread God's kingdom. C. We live in a world surrounded by evil. Down the right side, have the following parable subjects listed to be matched to the statements above: 1—mustard seed; 2—tares (weeds); 3—leaven (yeast).

Distribute handouts and call for 15 seconds of silence as you challenge students to match each statement with one of the three parables. (*Answers: A1; B3; C2.*) Ask for volunteers to verbalize which of the three statements challenges them most and why.

Alternative. Distribute copies of the "What Would You Say?" activity from the reproducible page. Have students discuss how they might use Jesus' parables from today's text to respond to each person.

Jesus Teaches About Justice

DEVOTIONAL READING: Mark 7:1-13
BACKGROUND SCRIPTURE: Matthew 15:1-9; Mark 7:1-13

MATTHEW 15:1-9

1 Then came to Jesus scribes and Pharisees, which were of Jerusalem, saying,

2 Why do thy disciples transgress the tradition of the elders? for they wash not their hands when they eat bread.

3 But he answered and said unto them, Why do ye also transgress the commandment of God by your tradition?

4 For God commanded, saying, Honour thy father and mother: and, He that curseth father or mother, let him die the death.

5 But ye say, Whosoever shall say to his father or his mother, It is a gift, by whatsoever thou mightest be profited by me;

6 And honour not his father or his mother, he shall be free. Thus have ye made the commandment of God of none effect by your tradition.

7 Ye hypocrites, well did Esaias prophesy of you, saying,

8 This people draweth nigh unto me with their mouth, and honoureth me with their lips; but their heart is far from me.

9 But in vain they do worship me, teaching for doctrines the commandments of men.

KEY VERSE

This people draweth nigh unto me with their mouth, and honoureth me with their lips; but their heart is far from me. —**Matthew 15:8**

JUSTICE IN THE NEW TESTAMENT

Unit 1: God Is Just and Merciful

LESSONS 1–4

LESSON AIMS

After participating in this lesson, each learner will be able to:

1. Summarize the nature of the conflict between Jesus and the Pharisees in today's text.

2. Explain how human traditions and institutions can hinder a person from responding to God's message.

3. Identify a behavior that is based on improper motives, and make a plan for change.

LESSON OUTLINE

Introduction
    A. I Was Misquoted!
    B. Lesson Background
I. Outer Cleanliness (MATTHEW 15:1, 2)
    A. Approaching Jesus (v. 1)
    B. Accusing the Disciples (v. 2)
II. Inner Corruption (MATTHEW 15:3-9)
    A. Specific Example (vv. 3-6a)
    B. Sad Result (vv. 6b-9)
        Our Traditions or His Touch?
        Lip Service?
Conclusion
    A. Devoted to What?
    B. Prayer
    C. Thought to Remember

Introduction

A. I Was Misquoted!

Public figures sometimes find themselves defending controversial or offensive statements. Often their defense is to say, "I was misquoted." Of course, our experience with the media shows that they are in some cases right.

We who are not celebrities know the frustration of being misquoted. Parents hear their children twist their words to use against them. Angry spouses sometimes do the same. On the job, a worker claims to be following instructions while the boss insists that those instructions were misunderstood. Misquoting, misunderstanding, misremembering, or just ignoring other people's words is a common cause of conflict.

When we are misquoted and misunderstood, we want to shout, "That's not what I meant, and you should know that!" We value our words and their integrity. We become exasperated when we are misunderstood, and we become discouraged at the hard feelings that often follow.

God experiences misunderstanding as well. Some of the Bible's sternest messages are directed at those who have received God's Word but have misunderstood and misapplied it. They claim devotion to God, but their actions reveal more interest in their own will than in His.

Today's lesson features one of God's stern messages. We study it to ensure that we do not resemble the group against which it was originally directed.

B. Lesson Background

Jesus was confronted often by scribes and Pharisees during His earthly ministry. Of the four Gospels, the frequency of their mention together in Matthew is fully equal to the other three Gospels combined.

Scribes were experts in the Law of Moses and the traditions about its application. In Jesus' time, these learned men could quote large sections of Scripture and could cite the opinions of renowned experts on interpretation.

Pharisees took a distinct approach to the Law of Moses. Their movement arose about 150 years before Jesus' birth, in response to what many saw as the corruption of the high priesthood in the temple at Jerusalem. Pharisees believed that God would restore His blessing on Israel only when Israel kept God's law faithfully.

To ensure that people kept the law, the Pharisees developed many traditions that had the effect of building a fence around it. The idea was that if the traditions were followed, then a person wouldn't even come close to breaking some part of God's law. To illustrate, Pharisees might teach that to avoid taking God's name in vain (and thus violate Exodus 20:7), one should play it safe by not uttering His name under any circumstances whatsoever.

Among these add-on traditions was a custom of washing hands before meals. Today we wash hands before eating as a means of hygiene. For the Pharisees, the custom was not an issue of physical hygiene but ceremonial religious washing. The Law of Moses required priests to wash their hands and feet before performing tabernacle duties (Exodus 30:17-21). The Pharisees seem to have built a fence around this law by expecting every faithful Israelite to perform a similar ceremonial washing before every meal; this treated meals as though they were acts of worship in the temple. To eat without having performed this ceremonial washing was to eat unclean food.

While Christians today often think of Pharisees as evil because of their opposition to Jesus, in His day they were highly respected. We should also remember that not all Pharisees opposed Jesus. Nicodemus was a Pharisee who desired a private meeting with Jesus (John 3:1, 2) and later assisted in His burial (19:38-42). A number of Pharisees became Christians, though some still struggled with their understanding of the Law of Moses and its application to Christians of Gentile background (Acts 15:3-6). Most notable of the Christian Pharisees was the apostle Paul. Years after his conversion, he continued to refer to himself as a Pharisee (23:6).

I. Outer Cleanliness
(MATTHEW 15:1, 2)
A. Approaching Jesus (v. 1)

1. Then came to Jesus scribes and Pharisees, which were of Jerusalem, saying.

Jesus has had many confrontations with *scribes and Pharisees* already in this Gospel (Matthew 9:3, 11, 34; 12:2, 14, 24). In most instances their opposition to Jesus arises as He offers controversial teaching or performs a miraculous deed that defies the religious leaders' standards. Here the initiative comes from the opponents.

The fact that these men come from *Jerusalem*, the center of Israel's religious life, suggests that Jesus has drawn the attention of the nation's most important religious leaders. Ultimately He will go to Jerusalem and surrender himself to His enemies to be put to death. Here we see a glimpse of the opposition that will grow increasingly hostile toward Him.

> **What Do You Think?**
> How should you conduct yourself when in the presence of someone who thrives on religious controversy?
> *Talking Points for Your Discussion*
> - If the person challenges you while others are present
> - If the person challenges you privately
> - If the person challenges someone else

B. Accusing the Disciples (v. 2)

2. Why do thy disciples transgress the tradition of the elders? for they wash not their hands when they eat bread.

The scribes and Pharisees pose a question to Jesus, one that could be taken as a serious inquiry. But the question strongly implies accusation and

HOW TO SAY IT

Esaias	E-*zay*-us.
Gentile	*Jen*-tile.
Hosea	Ho-*zay*-uh.
Leviticus	Leh-*vit*-ih-kus.
Moses	*Mo*-zes or *Mo*-zez.
Nicodemus	*Nick*-uh-**dee**-mus.
Pharisees	*Fair*-ih-seez.

criticism. These leaders do not simply ask why Jesus' *disciples* do not wash their hands before eating or how Jesus regards the practice of handwashing. Rather, they assert that Jesus' followers have broken a certain *tradition of the elders*—the elders being godly men well versed in God's law.

Many traditions of the Pharisees in Jesus' time are a few generations old. Others are relatively new. All are constantly debated. But the Pharisees teach that their traditions had their origins in a law delivered by God to Moses by spoken word and passed on to experts in each successive generation by spoken word.

Effectively, then, the religious leaders are claiming that these traditions are oral law having authority equal to the written Law of Moses. Both the written law and the oral law have thus come from God. So the question posed to Jesus implies strong condemnation for violating not just a human tradition but a tradition of divine origin, a command of God.

> *What Do You Think?*
> How can we make sure that our church's traditions serve the intent of the Word of God and not the other way around?
>
> *Talking Points for Your Discussion*
> - Regarding worship traditions
> - Regarding holiday traditions
> - Regarding traditional times for services
> - Other

II. Inner Corruption
(Matthew 15:3-9)
A. Specific Example (vv. 3-6a)

3. But he answered and said unto them, Why do ye also transgress the commandment of God by your tradition?

Jesus' response indicts the scribes and Pharisees for breaking God's law with their traditions. These traditions are wrong, Jesus says, and not simply because they claim an authority that God did not grant them. They are wrong because they lead to the actual breaking of God's true law, as Jesus proceeds to illustrate.

> *What Do You Think?*
> Which, if either, is the bigger danger: adding to God's commandments or disregarding them? How can we avoid both extremes?
>
> *Talking Points for Your Discussion*
> - In contexts dealing with personal obligation
> - In contexts dealing with obligations of the church as a body
> - Considering Revelation 22:18, 19

4a. For God commanded, saying, Honour thy father and mother.

To demonstrate how tradition leads to the breaking of God's true law, Jesus quotes from the written law, specifically the fifth of the Ten Commandments (Exodus 20:12; Deuteronomy 5:16). To honor one's parents means more than just showing them respect and obedience. It means that as parents grow older, their children assume responsibility for their care. Aging parents cannot simply be ignored because they no longer contribute to the livelihood of the family.

4b. And, He that curseth father or mother, let him die the death.

Leviticus 20:9 is quoted. The fact that capital punishment is the responsibility of the entire community (20:2; 24:16; etc.) places great restraint on such action; the entire community and its leaders must be convinced of the guilt and the appropriateness of the punishment. It is therefore unlikely that disrespectful children often receive this severe punishment. But the fact that the law has this instruction shows the seriousness of the command to honor father and mother.

> *What Do You Think?*
> What should honoring one's parents look like in terms of witness to culture?
>
> *Talking Points for Your Discussion*
> - When we are with them in public
> - When they have needs
> - When they disappoint us
> - Considering Luke 14:26; Ephesians 6:1-3; 1 Timothy 5:4, 8; 1 Peter 2:12
> - Other

5. But ye say, Whosoever shall say to his father or his mother, It is a gift, by whatsoever thou mightest be profited by me.

Jesus now cites a tradition common among the Pharisees. Sources outside the New Testament show that the Pharisees have developed a custom by which a person can make a gift to the temple of a valuable possession, but keep the use of that possession until the owner dies.

Jesus notes how this custom provides a loophole that many exploit for their own gain. The tradition of dedicating that possession as a gift to the temple means that it cannot be used for the parents' benefit, as it belongs to the temple. But the gift remains in the custody of the giver as long as the giver lives. Therefore the giver can receive all the profit from the possession for the rest of his life.

6a. And honour not his father or his mother, he shall be free.

By following this tradition of providing a gift to the temple, a person appears to be very godly and generous. Sacrificing a valuable possession to support the worship of God seems a fine thing to do. But it can come at the price of disobeying God's direct command to love and care for one's parents. How can a person claim to honor God while dishonoring the parents through whom God brought that person into the world?

B. Sad Result (vv. 6b-9)

6b. Thus have ye made the commandment of God of none effect by your tradition.

To make God's commandment *of none effect* is to make it empty and null. Of course, the handwashing tradition that has allegedly been violated by Jesus' disciples seems much less serious. It comes at little personal cost and seems to do very little harm. Those who follow it may appear to be honoring God by treating their ordinary meals like acts of worship in the temple.

But all of these traditions distract God's people from the real focus of their devotion. Such traditions make the law hard, but righteousness easy. Additional rules are hard to remember and follow. But if a person does follow them, that person is deemed righteous.

God's law to Israel, on the other hand, is a constant reminder of the people's unrighteousness. The laws are simple, but Israel has continually abandoned them. The law points out that failure, leaving only one alternative: turning to God in repentance and seeking His merciful forgiveness.

The traditions of the elders interrupt that process. Only by confronting the law itself can the law's purpose be fulfilled and the people of God receive the blessing they falsely seek by keeping human traditions.

◆ OUR TRADITIONS OR HIS TOUCH? ◆

Mildred was very upset. Her sense of the dignity of worship had been disrupted. After 40 years of sitting in one spot in the sanctuary, she moved to the other side of the aisle. Why? Wayne, a newcomer, had the annoying habit of loudly saying "Amen!" or "Praise the Lord!" while the minister was preaching. Wayne would also raise his hands during worship time, and he was known to jump to his feet on occasion and shout "Hallelujah!"

"That kind of thing has never been done in this church before," said Mildred, "and it is totally unnecessary! The man is just trying to draw attention to himself!"

Nothing could have been further from the truth. Wayne was just an excited Christian. The preacher appreciated his affirmations. He knew that at least one person was listening! But the conflict continued to grow in Mildred's mind.

One Sunday, she finally had had enough. She confronted Wayne in the foyer. "I'll have you know that in the New Testament it is not reported one time that Jesus ever jumped to His feet and shouted 'Hallelujah!' If *He* didn't do it, then we shouldn't either!"

Wayne reflected briefly, then simply replied, "What you say may be true. Perhaps Jesus never did leap up and shout 'Hallelujah!' But I'll tell you another truth, Mildred. Every person who was ever touched by Jesus certainly did!"

Wayne worshipped as he did only because he could feel the Master's hand on him. Maybe it is time to break with some of the traditions of the church in favor of the touch of His hand.

—C. T.

7. Ye hypocrites, well did Esaias prophesy of you, saying.

Jesus' use of the term *hypocrites* for the Pharisees has become so well known that to say "hypocrite" or "Pharisee" is, for many, to say the same thing. The term *hypocrite* prior to Jesus was used for actors on the Greek stage. Actors pretend to be someone they are not. Jesus uses the term to criticize the Pharisees and scribes for their pretending to honor God with their traditions while using the traditions to disobey God's commands.

> **What Do You Think?**
> ▶ Is the familiar question "What would Jesus do?" a proper guide for determining whether to call someone a hypocrite? Why, or why not?
> *Talking Points for Your Discussion*
> ▪ When others are present
> ▪ In private

Jesus uses the word *hypocrites* to introduce a quotation from the Old Testament prophet Isaiah (*Esaias*). By saying that Isaiah had prophesied *well* about these scribes and Pharisees, Jesus is saying that the prophet's words apply just as much to Jesus' contemporaries as they did to the people of Isaiah's time centuries earlier. What had happened among God's people in Isaiah's day is now happening again during Jesus' ministry.

8. This people draweth nigh unto me with their mouth, and honoureth me with their lips; but their heart is far from me.

Jesus' quotation comes from Isaiah 29. There the prophet was addressing God's people at a time when Israel was under grave threat from a foreign power. Isaiah warned that because of Israel's unfaithfulness, God would allow pagan nations to take the people captive, exiling them from the land of promise. The chapter begins with a stark warning of invasion and destruction to come.

Then in Isaiah 29:13, where this quotation is found, the prophet gives the reason for the coming judgment. Israel, *this people* who were called as God's people, outwardly made a great show of their devotion to God. But inwardly they were far from God. They lived as if God could be bribed with offerings and sacrifices while remain-ing unaware of the thoughts and motives that lay behind the acts of devotion. As another prophet said, God desires not sacrifice but mercy (Hosea 6:6), a text that Jesus also quotes to His opponents (Matthew 9:13; 12:7; lesson 1).

◆ LIP SERVICE? ◆

Teresa of Calcutta (1910–1997), also known as Mother Teresa, is legendary for her generous work with orphans, the poor, and the terminally ill. She was constantly on the move, helping wherever she could. She fought tirelessly for the underprivileged. She raised the funds necessary to expand a growing ministry. The prize money accompanying her Nobel Peace Prize went directly to caring for the poor of Calcutta.

The world saw what she was doing and beat a path to her door. While others were asking what should be done about those poor folks in Calcutta, Teresa was doing it. Her ministry was not large at first. She took in one child off the streets—then another, and another, and another.

We do a lot of talking about what needs to happen in our churches and in our world. We call that *lip service*. Every hand would be raised if the average congregation were asked, "Who believes in evangelism?" But very few hands would be raised if the follow-up question was "How many are personally involved in evangelism?"

The outcome would likely be the same for visiting the sick and the widows. Or for praying. Or for biblical giving. It's not hard to see the trend here. Every person will quickly confess with his or her mouth those principles known to be true. But how many Christians actually practice the truths they say they believe?
—C. T.

9. But in vain they do worship me, teaching for doctrines the commandments of men.

The quotation of Isaiah continues, and now we see how appropriate this text is for addressing the issue at hand. In Jesus' time, the religious leaders have elevated traditions of their own making to an importance that supersedes even the most obvious and important of God's commandments. Those traditions provide an outward veneer of religiosity that leaves people insensitive to their need to seek and rely on God's mercy in their weakness and failure. What may have started out as a good means to an end has become a bad end in and of itself.

The result is that for both Isaiah's audience and Jesus' opponents, their worship of God is *vain*; that is, empty and meaningless. God has no use for acts of devotion that are merely outward. True devotion to God comes from the heart, in response to God's grace. It then expresses itself in sincere obedience to God's commands and in demonstrating that same grace on a daily, consistent basis.

Conclusion

A. Devoted to What?

As Jesus continued His teaching on this occasion, He told His disciples that what comes out of a person makes the person clean or unclean, not the food that goes into a person (Matthew 15:10, 11). This teaching became vitally important to the church after Jesus' resurrection.

As the gospel was shared with Gentiles, who did not keep Israel's laws of clean and unclean foods (let alone the handwashing tradition), the church struggled to maintain unity between Jewish and Gentile Christians. Jesus' teaching reminded everyone that obedience to the God who had given His Spirit to the Gentiles meant uniting with them in fellowship around the dinner table (compare Galatians 2:12, 13). All people and all foods had become clean (Mark 7:18, 19; Acts 10:9-16, 28).

Jesus' encounters with the scribes and Pharisees continued after the incident in today's text. As Jesus' death approached, He delivered a stinging rebuke of them (Matthew 23:1-36). They made a show of their devotion because they cared more about people's opinions than about honoring God. They looked righteous on the outside, but inside was spiritual filth. Most of all, the Pharisees prevented others from finding God's blessing in Jesus. By extolling themselves and their traditions, they drew people away from the one whom God had sent to make them clean inside and out. Because they claimed to be teachers of God's people but

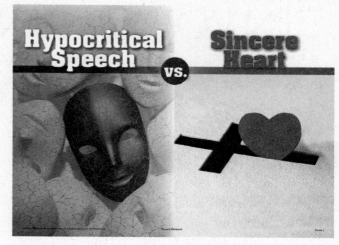

Visual for Lesson 3. *Start a discussion by pointing to this visual as you ask learners what the images represent and how to distinguish between them.*

in fact worked against God's purpose, Jesus criticized them severely.

Jesus saw in His time what Isaiah had seen in his: people who claimed to be faithful to God but whose primary devotion was to human traditions and institutions. That should make us realize how easy it is to do the same in any time and place. It is easy to point the finger of condemnation at others whom we believe to be hypocrites. But we do well to realize that the same may be true of us. Our true devotion may be not to God but to human traditions—forms of worship, rules of behavior, or teachings of our favorite preachers.

That misplaced devotion may prevent us from reckoning with our need for God's cleansing, to be made truly clean not by what people see on the outside but by what Christ does to us on the inside. Only after we are cleansed within can God's love flow out of us to a world that badly needs it.

B. Prayer

Our Father, we confess that we often rely on our own ideas instead of Your grace. Cleanse us by the blood of Christ on the inside, so that our outward deeds may reflect Your true nature and will. We pray in Jesus' name. Amen.

C. Thought to Remember

Make sure your traditions neither add to nor subtract from God's Word.

INVOLVEMENT LEARNING

Enhance your lesson with KJV Bible Student *(from your curriculum supplier) and the reproducible activity page (at www.standardlesson.com or in the back of the* KJV Standard Lesson Commentary Deluxe Edition*).*

Into the Lesson

On the board write the following words: *Job, Church Building, Gym Class, Opera.* Bring to class the following items inside a bag: sneakers, man's tie, a pair of jeans, a fancy shawl or scarf, backpack, baseball cap. Draw out one item at a time, writing its name on the board, and putting checks under each category where it *might* be appropriate. Discuss how dress codes can be very different depending on prevailing traditions. Ask students to share experiences where they or someone they know dressed in an inappropriate manner for the location.

Alternative. Distribute copies of the "Looking for Loopholes" activity from the reproducible page, which can be downloaded. Have a volunteer read the scenario aloud. Then ask for a show of hands as to which solution is correct. (It is B.)

After either activity, make the following statement: "Whether dress codes or laws are clearly stated or only implied, some people will try to find ways around them. The Pharisees were guilty of that, and Jesus called them on it in today's lesson."

Into the Word

Have students form small groups. Give each group a copy of the Lesson Background, and ask them to work through the following questions under the title "What Did the Pharisees Believe?" Do not include the answers in italics. (1) When would God restore His blessing on Israel? *(Only when the people were carefully keeping God's law.)* (2) What did the Pharisees do to help them keep the law? *(Developed a large collection of traditions as a fence around the scriptural laws.)* (3) Why was washing hands one of the traditions? *(It was similar to what was required of the priests and had the effect of making meals acts of worship.)* Discuss.

On the board write the two words *Charge* and *Countercharge.* Ask for two volunteers: one to read aloud the text from Matthew 15:1-9 and

one to read the parallel passage from Mark 7:1-13. Then ask the following questions and jot responses under *Charge.* Expected responses are in italics. "What charge did the Pharisees bring against Jesus' disciples?" *(The disciples ate without washing their hands.)* "Why were the Pharisees so upset about this issue?" *(The disciples were breaking tradition.)*

Then ask the following question and jot responses under *Countercharge.* "What four countercharges did Jesus bring against the Pharisees?" *(A—They negated the commands of God with their traditions. B—They authorized gifts to the temple that excused the givers from honoring and caring for parents. C—They were hypocrites. D—They pretended to honor God, but were more concerned with human rules.)*

Conclude by asking, "Instead of helping people keep the law, how did the traditions of the Pharisees prevent them from doing so?" Discuss.

Into Life

Then say, "The Pharisees' traditions, which were created to help people keep the law, sometimes ended up being used as loopholes for not keeping the law. But usually, the traditions were just too burdensome in going above and beyond God's stated requirements. Let's consider some questions along that line."

Form students into small groups and distribute index cards you have prepared with the following questions, one per card. "How do traditions that start with good intentions end up being harmful?" "Does the word *tradition* strike you as a negative word in and of itself? Why, or why not?" "What is the difference, if any, between the Pharisees' traditions and modern church traditions involving Christmas and Easter?"

Alternative. Distribute copies of the "Excuses, Excuses!" activity from the reproducible page. Have students pair off to discuss it.

REAPING GOD'S JUSTICE

DEVOTIONAL READING: Luke 6:20-26
BACKGROUND SCRIPTURE: Luke 16:19-31; John 5:24-30

LUKE 16:19-31

19 There was a certain rich man, which was clothed in purple and fine linen, and fared sumptuously every day:

20 And there was a certain beggar named Lazarus, which was laid at his gate, full of sores,

21 And desiring to be fed with the crumbs which fell from the rich man's table: moreover the dogs came and licked his sores.

22 And it came to pass, that the beggar died, and was carried by the angels into Abraham's bosom: the rich man also died, and was buried;

23 And in hell he lift up his eyes, being in torments, and seeth Abraham afar off, and Lazarus in his bosom.

24 And he cried and said, Father Abraham, have mercy on me, and send Lazarus, that he may dip the tip of his finger in water, and cool my tongue; for I am tormented in this flame.

25 But Abraham said, Son, remember that thou in thy lifetime receivedst thy good things, and likewise Lazarus evil things: but now he is comforted, and thou art tormented.

26 And beside all this, between us and you there is a great gulf fixed: so that they which would pass from hence to you cannot; neither can they pass to us, that would come from thence.

27 Then he said, I pray thee therefore, father, that thou wouldest send him to my father's house:

28 For I have five brethren; that he may testify unto them, lest they also come into this place of torment.

29 Abraham saith unto him, They have Moses and the prophets; let them hear them.

30 And he said, Nay, father Abraham: but if one went unto them from the dead, they will repent.

31 And he said unto him, If they hear not Moses and the prophets, neither will they be persuaded, though one rose from the dead.

KEY VERSE

Abraham said, Son, remember that thou in thy lifetime receivedst thy good things, and likewise Lazarus evil things: but now he is comforted, and thou art tormented. —**Luke 16:25**

Justice in the New Testament

Unit 1: God Is Just and Merciful

LESSONS 1–4

LESSON AIMS

After participating in this lesson, each learner will be able to:

1. Relate the primary details in Jesus' story of the rich man and Lazarus.

2. Explain what this passage teaches about caring for those who are poor materially and/or spiritually.

3. Help implement one specific improvement to his or her church's benevolence ministry.

LESSON OUTLINE

Introduction

A. *Noblesse Oblige*?

Western culture has long emphasized that those of greater wealth have a duty to be generous with those less well off. The French phrase *noblesse oblige* has been used for centuries to refer to this sense of obligation. The phrase means "nobility obliges." It expresses the idea that those with privilege are obligated to be generous with those less privileged.

We commonly hear people express this sense of obligation. They say that they must "give back" because they have been blessed beyond what they need or want. They want to "pay forward" what they have received, to show themselves grateful for their abundance.

These are virtuous impulses. We encourage them, and we admire them. But from the perspective of the gospel of Jesus, some adjustment is required. Jesus showed His followers that godly generosity springs not simply from our realization that we are abundantly blessed, but from our sense of our own need. The idea of *noblesse oblige* may permit me to think of myself inappropriately as different from the person in need. The gospel in general and today's text in particular reveal, however, that I am really in the same position as the person in need.

What Do You Think?
How can you protect yourself from the defective aspects of *noblesse oblige* thinking?
Talking Points for Your Discussion
- To avoid having a condescending attitude
- To avoid failure to sense your own need
- Other

B. Lesson Background

The story in our text comes at the end of a series of parables found in Luke 15 and 16. The series begins with the Pharisees and scribes complaining about Jesus' practice of feasting with sinners (15:1, 2). Jesus responded by telling three stories of things lost and found—a sheep, a coin, and a son. At the end of each of those three stories is a celebration that what was lost has been found. Expressed or implied in each case is comparison with the rejoicing of God and angels over sinners who repent (15:7, 10, 32). In contrast, the Pharisees and scribes failed to celebrate what God celebrated. They were indifferent to God's generous grace; they did not share God's character.

The dialogue continued with the Pharisees scoffing at more of Jesus' teaching because in their covetousness they loved money (Luke 16:14). Jesus replied that these religious leaders were trying to make themselves appear to be righteous, concealing hearts that harbored a condescending pride that is the opposite of what God values (16:15). Apparently not long afterward, Jesus told the story in our text.

Some Bible students question whether this account should be considered a parable. As evidence, they point out that in no other parable does Jesus give a name to one of the characters. Regardless of what position one holds on this question, the impact that the story was intended to have on Jesus' detractors is unmistakable (Luke 16:15).

I. Inequity in Life
(LUKE 16:19-21)
A. Living in Luxury (v. 19)

19a. There was a certain rich man, which was clothed in purple and fine linen.

The story begins with a brief description of *a certain rich man*, who is unnamed in Scripture. There is a tradition that his name is Dives. This probably comes from a Latin word for "rich," which was mistaken to be a personal name in the Middle Ages.

He is described briefly in a way that lets us know that he is substantially wealthier than all but a few others around him. In the ancient

HOW TO SAY IT

Hosea	Ho-*zay*-uh.
Lazarus	*Laz*-uh-rus.
noblesse oblige	no-*bless* uh-*bleezh*.
Pharisees	*Fair*-ih-seez.
Vitellius	Vih-*tell*-ih-us.

world, clothing of any kind is expensive because it involves time-consuming manual labor at every stage of production. People with surplus wealth, however, can afford even more expensive clothing —clothing that allows them to display their abundance publicly. *Purple* dyes are especially rare, so purple clothing is notably expensive (compare Acts 16:14; Revelation 17:4; 18:12, 16). Linen cloth is more comfortable and desirable than something made of cheaper wool, so *fine linen* is also prized and expensive (see Ezekiel 27:7).

19b. And fared sumptuously every day.

Most people in the ancient world use a majority of their income or labor to obtain subsistence-level food. But the wealthy can use their abundance for more costly, exotic food and drink. They approach their meals not as needed nourishment but as a way to indulge themselves. The rich man of this story enjoys all these benefits of his wealth. His actions bespeak an attitude of entitlement.

◆   *WHO'S ENTITLED?*   ◆

History supplies a large number of public figures noted for their demands, vices, and peculiar habits. Consider Herod the Great, the king of Judea when Jesus was born. His infamous deed of massacring infants (Matthew 2:16) is only one of his many deranged actions. He was so unpopular among his subjects that he arranged for some prominent Jewish men to be executed when the time of his own death would come, to ensure that sorrow rather than joy would be expressed! Fortunately for them, Herod's son did not carry out this order.

Or how about the Roman emperor Vitellius, who loved to eat? While feasting during his three or four daily meals, all accompanied by drunken revelry, he regularly vomited so he could eat more. Delicacies were brought from hundreds of miles to satisfy his gluttonous habits.

But the powerful and wealthy are not the only ones with demanding expectations. Just look how often the word *entitlement* is used in our culture! Most of us desire recognition and status as well. But we must be careful to reject the world's seductive pull and maintain our relationship with the one who denied His own rightful, entitled place.

In doing so, He showed us true servanthood (Mark 10:35-45; Philippians 2:5-8). —C. M. W.

B. Suffering in Squalor (vv. 20, 21)

20. And there was a certain beggar named Lazarus, which was laid at his gate, full of sores.

The second man provides a complete contrast to the first. His name, *Lazarus,* is a variation on the name Eleazer, meaning "God will help."

But God's help seems absent from his life. He is a *beggar*, unable to obtain what he needs to survive. He seems too weak to walk, so someone has to carry him to the *gate* that guards the rich man's luxurious home. His destitution is visible in every way. His body, covered in *sores*, makes him unclean and repulsive to others, and certainly in a miserable condition (compare Job 2:7, 8).

21a. And desiring to be fed with the crumbs which fell from the rich man's table.

The poor man isn't picky. All he desires are the scraps *from the rich man's table*—stuff that the rich man isn't going to eat anyway. But there is no indication that the rich man offers even that small gesture, which would cost him nothing. Lazarus is ignored, left to starve and suffer alone.

21b. Moreover the dogs came and licked his sores.

The poor man's only apparent relief ironically comes from the *dogs* that lick *his sores*. But even that is a disgraceful condition, one associated with uncleanness and the stench of extreme misery.

God has called His people Israel to be generous to the poor (Deuteronomy 15:7-11). He had generously called Israel out of Egypt and brought them into the promised land (15:15; 24:17-22). To fail to be generous in turn is to deny the generosity of God. The rich man of Jesus' story has sadly founded his identity, security, and pleasure in his wealth rather than in God's provision (see Proverbs 18:11).

◆ *WHAT WILL YOU DO?* ◆

Some time ago, I was approached by a person asking for a handout as I exited my car at a shopping center. It took me by surprise, but I managed to scrounge up a few small bills. After a lavish display of appreciation, she turned and headed toward another arriving vehicle. As I continued on my way, I noticed an onlooker sitting in a nearby vehicle. The look on his face and the shake of his head expressed his disdain at what he'd just witnessed—calling into question the poor person's genuineness and my gullibility at giving to her.

Such occasions may indeed cause us to pause and wonder about the sincerity or actual need of a person appealing to our generosity. We experience it frequently: someone holding a sign at an intersection, solicitations by phone or mail, people approaching us on the street, etc. It is easy to distrust any request if at some time we have been duped by tricksters. Also, we do not want to violate 2 Thessalonians 3:10: "If any would not work, neither should he eat."

It's tempting to use the question "What would Jesus do?" as a guide, as Charles Sheldon proposed in his 1896 classic *In His Steps*. There's a lot to be said for using that question as a model. But there is also a limitation as we realize that we cannot do everything Jesus did. He fed thousands miraculously (Matthew 14:13-21; 15:29-38). Although we cannot match that, we can all do something (Mark 9:41). One of the church's earliest benevolence efforts was tainted with wrong motives (Acts 4:32–5:11), but that didn't stop the willingness to help.   —C. M. W.

II. Justice in Death
(LUKE 16:22-26)

A. Reward and Punishment (vv. 22, 23)

22a. And it came to pass, that the beggar died, and was carried by the angels into Abraham's bosom.

Jesus chooses to depict the beggar's status after death in terms drawn from a popular Jewish conception of God's people in the afterlife. The Old Testament says remarkably little about life after death. But by Jesus' time, many Jews have developed the belief that God's faithfulness and justice mean that He must bring His people to a place of blessing beyond death.

One way of depicting this future is to draw on Old Testament passages that depict God's promised future as a great banquet (Isaiah 25:6-8; compare Luke 13:23-29). That image is present here. Because people in Jesus' time commonly eat in reclining positions gathered closely around low tables, a person at a banquet often reclines against the chest of another guest. For Lazarus to be positioned at *Abraham's bosom* echoes such a situation. This represents a complete reversal of the beggar's condition.

22b. The rich man also died, and was buried.

The rich man apparently dies at about the same time as Lazarus. We can imagine a rich person's lavish funeral and burial in a family tomb, but these mean nothing to the bigger picture of the story. The man's wealth does not spare him from the fate common to all. Despite vastly different lifestyles, the earthly outcomes of the rich man and Lazarus are one and the same: they both die.

What Do You Think?

In what ways should remembering our mortality affect how we live without becoming fatalistic?

Talking Points for Your Discussion

- Regarding use of time
- Regarding use of money
- Regarding relationships we choose to have and choose not to have
- Other

---

23. And in hell he lift up his eyes, being in torments, and seeth Abraham afar off, and Lazarus in his bosom.

The rich man's lavish burial is not reflective of his condition on the other side of the grave. Whereas he enjoyed nothing but the good life while on earth, now he is *in hell . . . in torments.* The Greek word behind the translation *hell* occurs nine other times in the New Testament; context always indicates an undesirable place—a place of abandonment or condemnation (see Matthew 11:23; 16:18; Luke 10:15; Acts 2:27, 31; Revelation 1:18; 6:8; 20:13, 14).

Perhaps the rich man's worst suffering is mental in nature as he realizes that the *afar off* distance of *Abraham* means exclusion from the blessings of God's people. His condition is now reversed from what it was before.

B. Request and Reply (vv. 24-26)

24. And he cried and said, Father Abraham, have mercy on me, and send Lazarus, that he may dip the tip of his finger in water, and cool my tongue; for I am tormented in this flame.

As the rich man speaks, we notice that he addresses not the poor man but *Abraham*, not the one he knows to be of low estate but the one who had also become rich (Genesis 13:2). The request is to *send Lazarus* as a servant to relieve his suffering, if only with the slightest drop of *water.*

Thus we see in this request a blend of newfound humility and long-established haughtiness. The rich man seems to accept the justice of his condition, asking only for the slightest relief. Yet he still speaks as one accustomed to commanding. He has more to learn.

25. But Abraham said, Son, remember that thou in thy lifetime receivedst thy good things, and likewise Lazarus evil things: but now he is comforted, and thou art tormented.

Abraham makes clear the justice of the new reality. The two men's conditions after death represent reversals of their conditions in life. The rich man had the capacity and the responsibility to see that the poor man was treated with compassion, but the rich man willfully neglected that responsibility.

So what the rich man did not do, God now does. The poor man reclines in comfort. The rich man, transported from luxury to abject misery, longs for even the tiniest drop of water that might

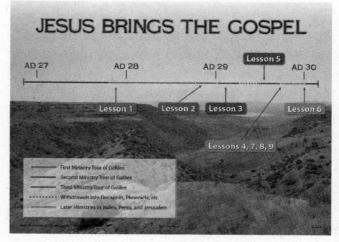

Visual for Lesson 4. *Post this visual next to the map visual for lesson 1 so learners can have the chronological perspective as well.*

come from the poor man's hand, just as the poor man, in his earthly torment, had longed for the slightest crumb from the rich man's table.

> ### What Do You Think?
> What more can our church do to help its members maintain a proper awareness of the reality of God's retributive justice?
>
> *Talking Points for Your Discussion*
> - In proactively addressing the issue before false ideas arise (see page 340)
> - In reactively addressing the issue after false ideas are already causing trouble

26. And beside all this, between us and you there is a great gulf fixed: so that they which would pass from hence to you cannot; neither can they pass to us, that would come from thence.

If verse 25 leaves any doubt regarding the permanence of the reversal, this verse removes it. While one lives on earth, crossing status lines between riches and poverty is possible. But after death there can be no going back and forth between the place of blessing and the place of punishment. The barrier in this reality is pictured as *a great gulf* that separates the two. Not only is the rich man unable to reach the company of Abraham, Lazarus cannot cross to provide relief, even if he wanted to.

The message is that the opportunity for repentance and receiving mercy remains open while life lasts. And there is no guarantee that everyone will get 70 years of life (compare Psalm 90:10). Reading today's text carefully, we realize that the rich man expresses no repentance despite his torment; a similar attitude is seen in Revelation 6:15-17.

III. Warning in Writing
(Luke 16:27-31)
A. Anguished Plea (vv. 27, 28)

27. Then he said, I pray thee therefore, father, that thou wouldest send him to my father's house.

The rich man realizes that it is too late for him to change his surroundings. So he turns his attention to others, specifically the members of his own family. Perhaps they can avoid the misery that he now experiences. Notice that the rich man does not ask that either he himself or Abraham go; rather, the rich man asks that Lazarus be sent as a servant to those who live in privilege. This presumes that Lazarus would even want to go!

28. For I have five brethren; that he may testify unto them, lest they also come into this place of torment.

The rich man's *five brethren* who remain alive are presumably as wealthy as he was. The rich man assumes that they are as unaware as he was of their need to (1) repent and (2) work for distributive justice so that those having the greatest need are provided with resources to meet those needs. Perhaps something can be done to warn them.

B. Adequate Proof (vv. 29-31)

29. Abraham saith unto him, They have Moses and the prophets; let them hear them.

Abraham's reply is terse. The man's brothers already have sufficient witness to their responsibilities, in the form of *Moses and the prophets*. In Jesus' day, the sections of the Old Testament are seen as three in number: the Law of Moses, the Prophets, and the Psalms (see Luke 24:44). The first section is the first five books of the Bible; the second consists of books bearing names of prophets as well as several historical books such as Joshua and Kings; the third includes not only the Psalms as such, but also every book not included in the other two categories.

The first two of the three divisions are sufficient for communicating God's just requirements. The man's brothers should already know what the Scripture calls them to do (Leviticus 19:10; etc.).

> ### What Do You Think?
> How can you safeguard yourself against things that interfere with your hearing God's Word?
>
> *Talking Points for Your Discussion*
> - During your initial preparations for the day
> - As you endure ungodly talk
> - In how you manage your time
> - Other

30. And he said, Nay, father Abraham: but if one went unto them from the dead, they will repent.

The rich man knows that his brothers, like him and like so many before him, do not heed the message of the law and the prophets. Living as if God has provided no witness of His will, they are as heedless of their responsibility as their late brother had been.

But the rich man hopes that a spectacular intervention will help. Perhaps if someone *from the dead* will show up to warn the brothers, then they will listen. After all, who could resist a message from a dead person who has been restored to life?

31. And he said unto him, If they hear not Moses and the prophets, neither will they be persuaded, though one rose from the dead.

The story ends abruptly with these grim words from Abraham. The rich man is informed that he has wrongly assessed what his brothers need. The witness of *Moses and the prophets* is formidable. They testify to the mighty deeds of God and their implications. They offer God's rich promises, but promises that are conditional.

To ignore the requirements of the promises is a symptom of a hard heart, of a human will that refuses to align with God's will. Even if someone were to return *from the dead*, those who do not listen to God's Word now will not listen then. Thus the story reaches its climax as it points in a veiled way to the resurrection of Jesus.

Conclusion

A. Who Were "the Needy" Then?

Jesus' opponents fancied themselves to be experts in the Law of Moses and the books of the prophets. They sought to apply those laws zealously to every aspect of life.

In that process, however, they lost sight of the God who gave the law. They became deaf and blind to His initiatives. Standing before them was the greatest of God's prophets—and more. He stood head and shoulders above Moses and the prophets. God was present in the world as He has not been before. In Jesus all the law and the prophets come to fulfillment.

Yet many Pharisees and scribes did not see this. Their love of power and wealth left them insensitive. So when Jesus rose from the dead, many still did not believe. Those who looked down on the poor could justify their attitude by misreadings of texts such as Proverbs 13:18; 20:4; 24:33, 34; etc. In ignoring the physically needy, they missed seeing the most spiritually needy: themselves.

B. Who Are "the Needy" Now?

When we see need around us, what comes to our minds? Gratitude that we are not in their situation? Memory of what it was like to be in need? A sense of annoyance? A sense of responsibility? A sense of opportunity? A mixture of these?

Jesus' story reminds us that regardless of our circumstances, we are all people in need. Before we label someone else as "needy," we first ought to see ourselves that way. We are not self-sufficient. Even as we live as responsible, productive citizens, we do not make it on our own. We depend on God for everything, especially eternal life. One day we will stand before Him either to receive that great gift or to be consigned to eternal ruin for rejecting it. Today's text offers a solemn call to listen and repent *now*, before it's too late.

> *What Do You Think?*
> If an unbeliever dismisses "before it's too late" as a scare tactic, how would you respond?
> *Talking Points for Your Discussion*
> - Responses that agree, at least partially, with the unbeliever
> - Responses that disagree with the unbeliever

C. Prayer

Gracious and loving Father, we confess that we depend completely on You for life, both present and eternal. Open our eyes to our own need. Open our hearts to the needs of others. Make us Your instruments of mercy, never growing weary in giving that reflects Your generosity. We pray this in Jesus' name. Amen.

D. Thought to Remember

To meet a needy person, look in the mirror.

INVOLVEMENT LEARNING

Enhance your lesson with KJV Bible Student (from your curriculum supplier) and the reproducible activity page (at www.standardlesson.com or in the back of the KJV Standard Lesson Commentary Deluxe Edition).

Into the Lesson

Option 1. Begin class by asking, "Can you identify the person who said this: 'It's not a coincidence that in the Scriptures, poverty is mentioned more than 2,100 times. It's not an accident. That's a lot of air time, 2,100 mentions.' Was it (a) Franklin Graham, (b) Bob Dylan, (c) Bono?" (The correct answer is Bono.) Ask, "Why do you think God's Word talks so much about the poor?"

Option 2. Ask your students, "Was there a time in your life when you considered yourself to be poor? If so, what was the hardest aspect of poverty for you?" Allow time for responses.

After either activity say, "We know that God has compassion for the poor. In today's lesson Jesus tells about a poor person who experienced a complete reversal of his situation. But it's much more than a feel-good story."

Into the Word

Option 1. Distribute copies of the "Turnabout Is Fair Play" activity from the reproducible page, which can be downloaded. Ask four of your students to read through and be prepared to act out the parts. Select your best actors for the parts of Lazarus and the Rich Man. Have a stuffed dog for Lazarus to use.

Option 2. Ask for three volunteers to read the Scripture text aloud; assign them the parts of the narrator, the rich man, and Abraham. The narrator will read all of the text except for the words actually spoken by Abraham and the rich man.

Lead a discussion of the story and its central meaning with the following statements and questions: (1) "Earlier in this chapter Jesus was talking to the Pharisees about not putting their trust in money; but the Pharisees were rich and mocked Him. How did this story help Jesus make His point clearer?" (2) "The Pharisees also looked down on all the 'little people' who weren't as righteous as they were in keeping the law. What might this story say about that?" (3) "In this story Abraham says that some would not believe 'though one rose from the dead.' In what way did this come true for the Pharisees? Why didn't they believe?"

Before class write the following statements on separate index cards: (1) "I've worked hard to earn my wealth, and I intend to use it to enjoy life." (2) "My life has been hard ever since I became a Christian, and it feels like God doesn't care about me." (3) "I just don't believe in life after death; once you're gone, it's lights out." (4) "I believe that we all go to Heaven when we die; I just don't think a loving God would condemn people to Hell." Prepare enough cards so that there is one for every two people. Have students pair off and discuss how they would respond to a person with that opinion. Ask for volunteers to share their discussion.

Into Life

Tell the following true story: "A church in Rochester, NY, became aware of the large number of people who were deaf or hard of hearing in their community who were attending the local college for the deaf. Several members worked at the college and knew sign language, so they were able to provide interpretation for worship services as well as training others to sign. Many close friendships developed between hearing and non-hearing, and many hearing-impaired people came to the Lord. In turn, they reached out to their unchurched friends. Can you think of a similar opportunity that we have in our community among the disadvantaged, disabled, or poverty stricken?" Allow time for people to discuss this and suggest ways to establish such a ministry.

Alternative. Distribute copies of the "Different Kinds of 'Poor'" activity from the reproducible page. Briefly talk about the three kinds of poverty mentioned. Then ask students to pair off and talk about which of those types of people they can best reach out to and help.

PARABLE OF THE UNFORGIVING SERVANT

DEVOTIONAL READING: Colossians 3:12-17
BACKGROUND SCRIPTURE: Matthew 18:21-35

MATTHEW 18:21-35

21 Then came Peter to him, and said, Lord, how oft shall my brother sin against me, and I forgive him? till seven times?

22 Jesus saith unto him, I say not unto thee, Until seven times: but, Until seventy times seven.

23 Therefore is the kingdom of heaven likened unto a certain king, which would take account of his servants.

24 And when he had begun to reckon, one was brought unto him, which owed him ten thousand talents.

25 But forasmuch as he had not to pay, his lord commanded him to be sold, and his wife, and children, and all that he had, and payment to be made.

26 The servant therefore fell down, and worshipped him, saying, Lord, have patience with me, and I will pay thee all.

27 Then the lord of that servant was moved with compassion, and loosed him, and forgave him the debt.

28 But the same servant went out, and found one of his fellowservants, which owed him an hundred pence: and he laid hands on him, and took him by the throat, saying, Pay me that thou owest.

29 And his fellowservant fell down at his feet, and besought him, saying, Have patience with me, and I will pay thee all.

30 And he would not: but went and cast him into prison, till he should pay the debt.

31 So when his fellowservants saw what was done, they were very sorry, and came and told unto their lord all that was done.

32 Then his lord, after that he had called him, said unto him, O thou wicked servant, I forgave thee all that debt, because thou desiredst me:

33 Shouldest not thou also have had compassion on thy fellowservant, even as I had pity on thee?

34 And his lord was wroth, and delivered him to the tormentors, till he should pay all that was due unto him.

35 So likewise shall my heavenly Father do also unto you, if ye from your hearts forgive not every one his brother their trespasses.

KEY VERSE

Shouldest not thou also have had compassion on thy fellowservant, even as I had pity on thee?
—Matthew 18:33

Justice in the New Testament

Unit 2: Jesus Calls for Justice and Mercy

LESSONS 5–9

LESSON AIMS

After participating in this lesson, each learner will be able to:

1. Summarize Jesus' parable of the unforgiving servant.

2. Compare and contrast Jesus' viewpoint on forgiveness with viewpoints of today's culture.

3. Express forgiveness to one person in the week ahead.

LESSON OUTLINE

Introduction
   A. No Limits
   B. Lesson Background
 I. Posing a Problem (MATTHEW 18:21, 22)
   A. Peter's Question (v. 21)
   B. Jesus' Answer (v. 22)
II. Presenting a Parable (MATTHEW 18:23-35)
   A. Servant's Crisis (vv. 23-25)
   B. King's Compassion (vv. 26, 27)
   C. Servant's Cruelty (vv. 28-31)
      Forgiving a Father
   D. King's Condemnation (vv. 32-34)
      Receiving Mercy, Extending Mercy
   E. Jesus' Challenge (v. 35)
Conclusion
   A. From Parable to Real Life
   B. Prayer
   C. Thought to Remember

Introduction

A. No Limits

Many car insurance companies include "accident forgiveness" in their policies. The specifics of how this concept works vary, but the foundational idea is that the insurance company will "forgive" a policyholder's first accident by not increasing his or her premiums. Some companies offer accident forgiveness as a reward for anyone who chooses to be insured by them. Some offer it to customers who have been with them for a certain length of time, etc.

At the same time, there are limits to this kind of forgiveness. Just because an insurance company forgives your at-fault accident does not mean that the points added to your driving record are removed. That part of your driving record is separate from what the insurance company can promise to do for you. Accident forgiveness does have its limitations.

In today's text, Peter asks Jesus a question about limits on forgiveness. The gist of Jesus' initial response is that there should be none. The master teacher then proceeds to tell a parable that challenges Peter (and us) to think not only of forgiving others but also of how much we have been forgiven by our heavenly Father. The measure of the latter should affect our perspective on the former.

B. Lesson Background

The parable of the unforgiving servant, which Matthew alone records, was spoken during the third year of Jesus' earthly ministry. By that time He had become much more direct in speaking to His disciples of His coming death and resurrection (Matthew 16:21; 17:12, 22, 23).

Such predictions led to Peter's ill-advised rebuke of Jesus' intentions (Matthew 16:22), a glimmer of understanding (17:13), and great sorrow (17:22, 23). Into this mix was a debate among the Twelve as to who would be the greatest in the kingdom of Heaven (18:1-5; compare Mark 9:34-37).

Immediately preceding the parable of the unforgiving servant (today's text) is Jesus' teaching about how to deal with a brother who sins against you. Jesus outlined the steps to be taken, then climaxed His teaching on this subject by highlighting the power of prayer when even two or three are gathered in His name (Matthew 18:19, 20).

Peter appears to have been especially attentive to Jesus' counsel on confronting another who has sinned. Perhaps Peter was thinking of the recent argument regarding "who should be the greatest" (Mark 9:34). One commentator speculates that Peter desires clarification about how much forgiveness Jesus expects because Peter has taken offense at one of the Twelve who has challenged Peter's worthiness to receive the "keys of the kingdom of heaven" (Matthew 16:19). This theory is indeed speculative; no evidence exists to support it.

I. Posing a Problem
(MATTHEW 18:21, 22)
A. Peter's Question (v. 21)

21. Then came Peter to him, and said, Lord, how oft shall my brother sin against me, and I forgive him? till seven times?

Peter tends to be the most vocal of the Twelve, whether it's a matter of desiring to walk on the water (Matthew 14:28-31) or objecting to Jesus' more candid description of what the future holds (16:21, 22). The question he raises with Jesus sounds almost pharisaical in nature, challenging Jesus to explain a portion of His teaching.

But Peter's motivation is different from that of the Pharisees. He is not trying to embarrass Jesus or find grounds for accusing Him of something. Peter simply wants to know the extent to which he is expected to forgive another, should that person continue to *sin against* him.

In posing the question, Peter may have in mind the Jewish teaching that states forgiveness should be granted to someone three times. If so, then Peter's question to Jesus doubles the requirement, then adds one more perhaps for good measure.

Also worth noting is how Peter phrases his question. He does not say, "If I sin against someone, how often should that person be expected to forgive me?" Forgiveness is usually a more comfortable subject to discuss if approached from the point of view of the offended person rather than that of the person who has caused the offense.

Despite any good intentions on the part of Peter, there's an element of scorekeeping here that must be dealt with.

> *What Do You Think?*
> What steps can we take to resist keeping score when it comes to extending forgiveness?
> *Talking Points for Your Discussion*
> - When wronged by a family member
> - When wronged by someone at church
> - When wronged by a stranger
> - Other

B. Jesus' Answer (v. 22)

22. Jesus saith unto him, I say not unto thee, Until seven times: but, Until seventy times seven.

Jesus' answer must leave Peter stunned and speechless (which is quite something for him!). The phrase *seventy times seven* conveys the idea that forgiveness is to be extended without limits. The number is purposely stated extremely high so that the "how oft" of Peter's question (previous verse) becomes irrelevant.

> *What Do You Think?*
> As we become willing to forgive without limits, how do we protect ourselves from being taken advantage of?
> *Talking Points for Your Discussion*
> - By family members
> - By coworkers
> - By strangers
> - Other

II. Presenting a Parable
(MATTHEW 18:23-35)
A. Servant's Crisis (vv. 23-25)

23. Therefore is the kingdom of heaven likened unto a certain king, which would take account of his servants.

Aware of what is in others' hearts, Jesus knows that more needs to be said on the subject at hand. There is another side to forgiveness that Peter seems to have overlooked (and that we sometimes do too).

As before, Jesus teaches by means of a parable. This teaching format requires work on the part of the listener. The challenge for comprehension is to match images in the parable with things and people in the real world. The Twelve usually seem not very good at doing so (see Matthew 13:36; 15:15, 16; 16:6-12).

The *servants* of this parable are unlikely to be slaves, who work for no compensation. They are probably better described as stewards or managers who have been commissioned by the *king* to invest his wealth in profitable ventures. Now the time has come for the king to *take account* of how well these individuals have done their assigned tasks. The Greek behind the translation "take account" occurs only three times in the New Testament: here, in the verse that follows (translated "reckon"), and in Matthew 25:19 (translated "reckoneth" in the parable of the talents).

The imagery of a king auditing the books should bring to mind what will happen on the Day of Judgment. That will be when "the dead, small and great, stand before God" to be "judged out of those things which were written in the books, according to their works" (Revelation 20:12; compare Matthew 12:36; Romans 2:5; 14:12; Hebrews 13:17; 1 Peter 4:1-5).

24. And when he had begun to reckon, one was brought unto him, which owed him ten thousand talents.

This day of reckoning bodes ill for one particular servant. Having been *brought* before the king, the audit reveals that the servant owes a debt of *ten thousand talents*! A talent should not be thought of in the modern sense of gifts or abilities. In Old Testament times, a talent seems to have been a unit of weight (examples: 2 Samuel 12:30; 1 Kings 10:14). In Jesus' day, a talent is also a monetary

unit, one talent being roughly equivalent to 6,000 denarii (or drachmas). A denarius is the equivalent of one day's wages (compare Matthew 20:10, where the Greek word *denarius* is translated "penny"; also 18:28, below). This servant's debt thus amounts to the pay for 6,000 workdays—times 10,000!

Nothing is said about how this servant has amassed such a debt. The point is that this is a staggering amount to owe anyone, and it is readily understood by Peter as a debt virtually impossible to pay off.

25. But forasmuch as he had not to pay, his lord commanded him to be sold, and his wife, and children, and all that he had, and payment to be made.

Jesus does not comment on the rightness or wrongness of the procedure used to satisfy the debt. What He describes is a typical way for a situation like this one to be handled at the time. There is no option to declare chapter 7 or chapter 13 bankruptcy. Instead, the servant, his family, and all their possessions are *to be sold* so *payment* can *be made*.

This suggests that all the members of the family will become slaves to someone; any income their labor generates will automatically go toward payment of the debt. For a debt of this magnitude, it is very unlikely that the king can ever fully recoup his losses. He will, however, get a portion back.

B. King's Compassion (vv. 26, 27)

26. The servant therefore fell down, and worshipped him, saying, Lord, have patience with me, and I will pay thee all.

Faced with such a dire future, *the servant* does the only thing he can do: he begs for mercy. His promise to *pay . . . all* he owes is undoubtedly sincere in intent, but next to impossible in practicality, given the size of the debt.

27. Then the lord of that servant was moved with compassion, and loosed him, and forgave him the debt.

The king's sense of *compassion* for this desperate *servant* overrules the stark requirements of justice. He forgives the man this unpayable *debt*.

HOW TO SAY IT

Colossians	Kuh-*losh*-unz.
denarii	dih-*nair*-ee or dih-*nair*-eye.
denarius	dih-*nair*-ee-us.
Ephesians	Ee-*fee*-zhunz.
pharisaical	*fair*-ih-say-ih-kul.
Pharisees	*Fair*-ih-seez.

C. Servant's Cruelty (vv. 28-31)

28. But the same servant went out, and found one of his fellowservants, which owed him an hundred pence: and he laid hands on him, and took him by the throat, saying, Pay me that thou owest.

One would think that this *servant* would rejoice and celebrate at receiving such wonderful news, as do other characters in Jesus' parables (compare Luke 15:5, 9, 32). But the parable takes an unexpected and disappointing turn.

One gets the impression that not too much time passes until the first servant comes upon one of his coworkers. The difference between the amount the first servant owed the king and the amount this second servant owes the first is just as staggering as the enormity of the first man's debt. *An hundred pence* is literally 100 denarii (see comments on verse 24, above). The second servant's debt to the first servant is practically nothing in comparison with what the first servant owed the king.

Equally as staggering is the difference between the king's treatment of the first servant and the same servant's behavior toward his fellow servant. He says nothing about requesting repayment until he first grabs the man *by the throat*—something the king did not do.

29. And his fellowservant fell down at his feet, and besought him, saying, Have patience with me, and I will pay thee all.

The response of the *fellowservant* mirrors that of the first servant's when the latter pleaded for mercy from the king (verse 26, above). One would think that when the first servant hears the plea that he himself had used, a merciful response would result.

30. And he would not: but went and cast him into prison, till he should pay the debt.

Instead, the first servant's reaction is the very opposite of how he was treated by the king. There is no compassion whatsoever in the heart of this servant, in spite of the mercy recently granted to him. The king had planned to arrange for some of his debt from the first servant to be repaid by selling him, along with his family and possessions. But the forgiven servant simply has his fellow servant thrown *into prison*.

That action puts the man in an obviously difficult position: How can he pay what he owes if he is confined to prison? Perhaps his only recourse is to hope that family members or friends will come to his aid.

◆ FORGIVING A FATHER ◆

On Father's Day in 2015, actor Oliver Hudson posted on social media a picture of himself, his sister (actress Kate Hudson), and their father with the caption "Happy Abandonment Day." Though Oliver said he was just trying to be funny, the father lashed out at his two adult children in response. But not long after that, the incident actually helped open up renewed communication between father and son, who had been estranged for 12 years.

About a year later, Kate stated that she had forgiven her father for abandoning her and her brother as children. Recognizing that her father has to live with his own issues, Kate said to the radio host who was interviewing her, "That must be painful for him. So I forgive him." She added that forgiveness is "the greatest tool" for moving forward.

Failing to extend the grace that has been given to us is one of the most spiritually damaging things we can do to ourselves. When Kate Hudson was able to enter into the heart of her father's pain, she found the ability to forgive him.

Over the course of a lifetime, we will also be presented with many opportunities either to forgive or demand restitution of some kind. We won't go wrong if we choose mercy.　—D. S.

31. So when his fellowservants saw what was done, they were very sorry, and came and told unto their lord all that was done.

The *fellowservants* can't keep quiet about what they have just seen. The one to hold the first servant accountable is the king, so it is to him they report what has happened.

D. King's Condemnation (vv. 32-34)

32, 33. Then his lord, after that he had called him, said unto him, O thou wicked servant, I forgave thee all that debt, because thou desiredst me: shouldest not thou also have had compassion on thy fellowservant, even as I had pity on thee?

The unforgiving servant finds himself facing the searing anger of the king, who addresses him as a *wicked servant*. The king presents the simple logic that should have guided the servant's attitude toward his companion: since the first servant had been forgiven *all that debt*, shouldn't he have shown similar *compassion* on his fellow debtor? Anyone who has been forgiven (especially such a large debt) should demonstrate a forgiving heart to another.

34. And his lord was wroth, and delivered him to the tormentors, till he should pay all that was due unto him.

The king's anger results in this servant's being placed in a position similar to the one in which he himself had placed the second servant. Only now the unforgiving servant's position is far worse; he is given over to be tormented or tortured until his debt is paid.

The torment is presumably done to force the servant to confess where he may have any hidden resources needed to reduce his debt. One is led to believe that the man will never know freedom again, given the size of his debt. His condition

may well be a way for Jesus to portray the eternal torment of Hell (Matthew 25:41, 46; Mark 9:43-48).

◆ RECEIVING MERCY, EXTENDING MERCY ◆

When a drug deal went bad, Bob's brother was killed by a guy named Harvey, whom Bob and his brother had known well. Vowing revenge, Bob went on the hunt for Harvey but lost track of him. Then Bob himself got into trouble with the law and went to jail. Lo and behold, Harvey ended up in the same prison.

Although by then Bob had come to Christ and let go of his vow of revenge, he still could not fully forgive. One day, in a common area for inmates, Harvey timidly asked Bob for mercy. Bob, now a forgiven man in Christ, was finally able to extend that mercy to his brother's killer.

Imagine our heavenly king's delight when Bob forgave his brother's penitent killer. These days, Bob and Harvey attend worship service together every week. Even in the most difficult of circumstances, through the power of the Holy Spirit we can find the ability to forgive our offenders—to extend the same mercy to them that God generously offered to us.　—D. S.

E. Jesus' Challenge (v. 35)

35. So likewise shall my heavenly Father do also unto you, if ye from your hearts forgive not every one his brother their trespasses.

Here Jesus states the application of the parable. Obviously much more than money is being pictured by the master teacher. Ultimately Jesus wants His audience (then and now) to get a picture of the enormity of our debt of sin before God, our heavenly king.

We, God's servants, are in a position similar to the first servant in this parable. There is no way we can repay the debt represented by our sin. Justice requires punishment; our only recourse is to beg for mercy from our king—as did the first servant of the parable.

Forgiveness is thus not merely a matter of how we treat those who have offended us. It is also a matter of how God has chosen to treat us who have offended Him. Perhaps we are taken aback by the enormity of times we must forgive. But have we considered the enormous debt of which God has forgiven us?

The importance of forgiveness is repeated elsewhere in the New Testament. In Ephesians 4:31, 32 and Colossians 3:12, 13, Christians are exhorted to forgive others based on how Christ has forgiven them. How would our daily conduct (our thoughts, our words, our actions) be affected if we kept that point of view in mind?

We must also note how Jesus instructs us to forgive from our hearts. Forgiveness is not forgiveness if it is offered insincerely. If we tell someone "I forgive you" while continuing to harbor anger and resentment, then, in a manner of speaking, we still have our hands on the throat of the person we refuse to forgive.

What Do You Think?

Without giving advice, how would you counsel a friend who is hesitant to forgive someone?

Talking Points for Your Discussion

- Considering the nature of the wrong
- Considering the nature of the relationship between the two individuals
- Considering the difference between forgiveness and consequences
- Considering the extent of forgiveness your friend has received from Jesus
- Considering repentance or lack thereof

Conclusion

A. From Parable to Real Life

Because Peter was the one who raised the question about forgiveness, it is interesting to follow up on what happened later to him concerning forgiveness. After Peter had denied Jesus three times, in spite of his bold claims that this could never happen, he wept bitter tears (Matthew 26:69-75). It is hard for us to fathom the measure of remorse Peter felt at that moment and throughout the course of that day when Jesus was crucified. Perhaps Peter resigned himself to being confined to the "prison" of his failure for the rest of his life.

Visual for Lesson 5. *Start a discussion by pointing to this visual as you ask, "If forgiveness is the key, then what is being locked or unlocked?"*

But three days later the startling news began to circulate that Jesus was alive. The message was first conveyed by the women who had come to Jesus' tomb to pay their respects, only to find no corpse there. Then came the words of an angel with a message for the women to pass along: "Go your way, tell his disciples and Peter that he goeth before you into Galilee: there shall ye see him, as he said unto you" (Mark 16:7).

This specific reference to Peter was not accidental. It was Jesus' way of letting him know that forgiveness was more than a topic to be discussed in a parable. It was real. Jesus, the king of life and death, was declaring Peter forgiven. He did not have to remain bound in the prison of failure and defeat, because Jesus did not remain bound in the prison of the grave. The King had forgiven His servant of his debt. Peter was free to go.

B. Prayer

Father, through Jesus' death and resurrection we have been released from a debt so large that no human could have paid it. Only by Your putting on flesh and blood to dwell among us and die in our place could the price be paid. And it has been! Thank You for setting us free—free from sin and now free to serve You. We pray in Jesus' name. Amen.

C. Thought to Remember

The master teacher is also the master forgiver.

INVOLVEMENT LEARNING

Enhance your lesson with KJV Bible Student *(from your curriculum supplier) and the reproducible activity page (at www.standardlesson.com or in the back of the* KJV Standard Lesson Commentary Deluxe Edition*).*

Into the Lesson

Ask for volunteers to identify one of the more significant losses in their lives that were caused by the indifference, negligence, or malice of someone else; stress that real names are not to be used. Encourage them to pick a loss where they can say, "I used to have [blank], which was very valuable to me, but because of what [not real name] said [or did], I will never have it again." Help learners identify the type of emotional reaction that they usually have whenever the memory of that loss bubbles to the surface.

Alternative 1. Ask class members to describe the challenges of forgiving those who cause significant losses to us. After several responses, say, "Now imagine that the person who caused the significant loss experienced a small aneurism that caused him or her to lose all memory of what happened. Because of this, he or she would never be able to internalize responsibility for their harmful words or actions. What would be the challenges associated with forgiving an offender who experienced this type of amnesia?"

Alternative 2. Distribute copies of the "What a Loss!" activity from the reproducible page, which can be downloaded. Say, "This activity will help you determine exactly what it is you need to forgive and if you're moving toward forgiving the people who caused the loss(es)." Remind learners if they are the one who caused the loss, then they'll need to move toward seeking forgiveness.

Into the Word

Divide the class into three groups. Each will represent a character in Jesus' parable:

Group 1—The King
Group 2—The Unforgiving Servant
Group 3—The Unforgiving Servant's Debtor

Ask learners to read Matthew 18:21-30 within their groups to identify the requests and responses of the character for which their group is named.

Expect learners to identify the following: (1) the king's request that the debt be paid in full, (2) his response of sentencing the servant and his family to be sold, (3) the unforgiving servant's request for mercy and time to pay the debt, (4) the king's response of canceling the debt, (5) the unforgiving servant's demand for payment owed to him, (6) the unforgiving servant's debtor's response of asking for mercy and time to pay the debt, and (7) the unforgiving servant's denial of that request.

Following these identifications, read the remainder of the lesson text (Matthew 18:31-35) to the class. Discuss the implications of who and what the characters and the debt represent.

Option. Prior to discussion of today's text, distribute copies of the "Get the Flow" diagram from the reproducible page. As discussion of the text proceeds from action to plea to reaction, participants can summarize the flow as indicated. Your visually oriented learners will benefit most, especially if you use a lecture format.

Into Life

Say, "As soon as the unforgiving servant saw someone who owed him something, he went after the guy with a vengeance (completely forgetting the grace that he himself had just been shown)." Ask students to make a list of people who owe them something. Say, "The debt can be of various kinds: a debt of money, a debt of an explanation owed for something that happened, a debt of an apology owed, etc."

After learners make their lists, encourage them to get the ball rolling on resolution, reconciliation, and forgiveness even if the chances of success are miniscule. End class with this strong affirmation: "As you approach these reconciliations, always keep foremost in your mind how much Christ has forgiven you and what it cost Him to do so."

JESUS CRITICIZES UNJUST LEADERS

DEVOTIONAL READING: Luke 14:7-14
BACKGROUND SCRIPTURE: Matthew 23

MATTHEW 23:1-4, 23-26

1 Then spake Jesus to the multitude, and to his disciples,

2 Saying, The scribes and the Pharisees sit in Moses' seat:

3 All therefore whatsoever they bid you observe, that observe and do; but do not ye after their works: for they say, and do not.

4 For they bind heavy burdens and grievous to be borne, and lay them on men's shoulders; but they themselves will not move them with one of their fingers.

. . . .

23 Woe unto you, scribes and Pharisees, hypocrites! for ye pay tithe of mint and anise and cummin, and have omitted the weightier matters of the law, judgment, mercy, and faith: these ought ye to have done, and not to leave the other undone.

24 Ye blind guides, which strain at a gnat, and swallow a camel.

25 Woe unto you, scribes and Pharisees, hypocrites! for ye make clean the outside of the cup and of the platter, but within they are full of extortion and excess.

26 Thou blind Pharisee, cleanse first that which is within the cup and platter, that the outside of them may be clean also.

KEY VERSES

The scribes and the Pharisees sit in Moses' seat: all therefore whatsoever they bid you observe, that observe and do; but do not ye after their works: for they say, and do not. —**Matthew 23:2, 3**

JUSTICE IN THE NEW TESTAMENT

Unit 2: Jesus Calls for Justice and Mercy

LESSONS 5–9

LESSON AIMS

After participating in this lesson, each learner will be able to:

1. List some hypocritical practices of the religious leaders of Jesus' day.

2. Contrast a hypocritical religious practice with its opposite.

3. Write a prayer of confession and repentance of a hypocritical attitude or behavior.

LESSON OUTLINE

Introduction
    A. Homes and Hearts
    B. Lesson Background
I. Warnings (MATTHEW 23:1-4)
    A. Esteemed Position (vv. 1, 2)
    B. Exploited Position (vv. 3, 4)
      Imposing Burdens on Others
II. Woes (MATTHEW 23:23-26)
    A. Regarding the Law (vv. 23, 24)
    B. Regarding the Leaders (vv. 25, 26)
      On Gullibility
Conclusion
    A. One Pharisee's Testimony
    B. Staying Heart Healthy
    C. Prayer
    D. Thought to Remember

Introduction

A. Homes and Hearts

Real-estate agents often emphasize the importance of good "curb appeal" in an effort to sell houses. That expression refers to presenting an attractive outward appearance of the house or property so that passersby will have a favorable first impression. Foliage should be well-trimmed and pruned, fencing and sidewalks should be in good repair, etc.

The intended effect is that potential buyers will want to stop and take a look inside. Needless to say, it is important that the inside be just as well-kept as the outside. But people will likely not go inside the house if the outside shows too many signs of wear and tear. The reasoning is that a poorly maintained exterior signals similar neglect on the interior whereas a well-maintained exterior points to the opposite.

The scribes and the Pharisees in Jesus' day were known for their religious "curb appeal." But in their case a well-maintained exterior did not indicate the same on the inside.

B. Lesson Background

Today's lesson from Matthew 23 covers an incident that occurred during what is often called Passion Week, the final week of Jesus' earthly life and ministry. The week began with Jesus' triumphal entry into Jerusalem (Matthew 21:1-11) and climaxed with His crucifixion and resurrection.

It is generally believed that the events recorded in Matthew 21:23–24:51 (part of which is today's text) occurred during Tuesday of Passion Week. This segment of text includes Jesus' authority being questioned by the chief priests and elders of the Jews, a series of parables, and various questions directed toward Jesus.

I. Warnings

(MATTHEW 23:1-4)

Matthew 22 concludes with a question *from* Jesus to the Pharisees, a question to which they gave no answer. Having silenced His opponents, Jesus then had some preliminary things to say to

His audience before launching a series of condemnations at the scribes and Pharisees. These men were already seeking to arrest Jesus (21:46); no doubt His words of condemnation in Matthew 23 intensified these efforts.

A. Esteemed Position (vv. 1, 2)

1. Then spake Jesus to the multitude, and to his disciples.

Jesus has been attracting a *multitude* of people throughout His ministry (Matthew 4:25; 8:1, 18; 9:8, 36; 12:15; 13:2; 15:30; 19:1, 2). Since this is the week during which Passover will be celebrated, the crowds gathered in Jerusalem are much larger than usual. Some estimate that Jerusalem's population, which generally numbers a few hundred thousand, swells to around two and a half million during Passover week. Jesus is also addressing more specifically *his disciples*.

2. Saying, The scribes and the Pharisees sit in Moses' seat.

The scribes and the Pharisees are considered the scholars in Jesus' day. To *sit in Moses' seat* describes their esteemed position; they are the expounders and interpreters of the law given by God to Moses. In the Old Testament, the scribes were at first primarily officials who kept records of various kinds in a king's administration (2 Samuel 8:15-17; 1 Kings 4:1-3; 2 Kings 12:9, 10). The office appears to take a more religious turn with Ezra, who is described as "a ready scribe in the law of Moses" (Ezra 7:6) and who was also adept at teaching the law (7:10).

The term *Pharisees* comes from a Hebrew word meaning "to separate." The Pharisees could be described as "separatists" or "separated ones." They came to be during the period between Old and New Testaments; many believe their origin may be traced to the time of the Maccabean revolt in the second century before Christ. They interpret

HOW TO SAY IT

anise	*a*-nuss (*a* as in mat).
cummin	*kuhm*-mun or *cue*-mun.
Maccabean	Mack-uh-*be*-un.
Nicodemus	*Nick*-uh-*dee*-mus.

the Law of Moses very rigidly in an attempt to protect it from being violated; their added traditions and regulations have become of equal importance with the Word of God, sometimes even serving to negate the intent of Scripture.

The Pharisees may be considered a religious "party," while the scribes hold an office. However, the majority of scribes are Pharisees. Both see Jesus as a threat to their teachings and their authority. Paul, in his staunchness as a Pharisee by the name of Saul (Philippians 3:5), will later "do many things contrary to the name of Jesus of Nazareth" (Acts 26:9).

B. Exploited Position (vv. 3, 4)

3a. All therefore whatsoever they bid you observe, that observe and do.

Jesus encourages His hearers to respect the scribes and the Pharisees' positions and their interpretation of the Law of Moses. Jesus has not come to overthrow these authorities, any more than He has come to start an uprising against Rome.

3b. But do not ye after their works: for they say, and do not.

Even so, Jesus goes on to expose the inconsistency between what the scribes and Pharisees *say* and the example that they actually set (*their works*). They do not practice what they preach. (See examples on Matthew 23:23, 25, below.)

It is worth noting that Jesus encourages His listeners not to allow the hypocrisy of the scribes and Pharisees to diminish their respect for the authority of the law. The law is still from Moses (and ultimately from God) in spite of how the scribes and Pharisees have failed to live it out.

4. For they bind heavy burdens and grievous to be borne, and lay them on men's shoulders; but they themselves will not move them with one of their fingers.

The *heavy burdens* are the many traditions that the scribes and Pharisees have instituted to guarantee faithfulness (as they see it) to the Law of Moses. But as Jesus noted during a confrontation with the scribes and Pharisees, in certain cases they "transgress the commandment of God by [their] tradition" (Matthew 15:3; see the commentary and Lesson Background to lesson 3).

At the same time, the scribes and Pharisees offer no compassion to those who struggle to keep the traditions—only contempt for those who cannot measure up to their standards. Even worse, these leaders have created clever (but in reality reprehensible) means by which they themselves can avoid keeping those same standards. In Matthew 15:1-9 (again, see lesson 3), Jesus gave an example of how this works. As a consequence, they had "made the commandment of God of none effect" (15:6). Although these leaders "sit in Moses' seat" (23:2), they certainly do not demonstrate Moses' spirit of humility, which was a distinctive part of his character (Numbers 12:3).

When one considers this kind of onerous burden created by these leaders, we can appreciate even more Jesus' invitation, recorded in Matthew 11:28-30, that ends with His words, "For my yoke is easy, and my burden is light." The one through whom grace and truth come (John 1:14) offers a freedom that is impossible to experience within the rigid, twisted system of the Jewish leaders.

◆ *Imposing Burdens on Others* ◆

Wells Fargo, one of America's largest banks, was hit with a $185 million fine for setting up bogus accounts for customers who had no idea what was happening. The bank employees who set up these accounts claimed they were forced to do so to meet quotas placed on them by upper management under threat of being fired. Apparently several of these employees had reported the pressure to an internal hotline, only to find themselves fired soon afterward for reasons supposedly unrelated to the whistle-blowing.

Wells Fargo claimed that it had fired more than 5,300 low-level and middle-management employees for these illegal and unethical practices, but federal regulators began to wonder if these workers were being blamed for implementing high-pressure tactics that had come from the highest levels in the corporation instead. Shortly after the exposure of the scandal, a $2.6 billion class-action suit was filed by many of these employees for the unrealistic expectations placed on them.

Even in our day, leaders of religious, political, and business organizations place unsustainable (even illegal) burdens on individuals. If we ever find ourselves in a position of authority, may we never require that someone carry a burden that we wouldn't gladly accept ourselves.   —D. S.

II. Woes
(Matthew 23:23-26)

Matthew 23:13 begins a series of woes pronounced by Jesus upon the scribes and Pharisees. A characteristic of these woes is Jesus' description of the religious leaders as hypocrites. In only one of the woes does Jesus not use that word, describing them instead as "blind" three times (23:16-22). The next part of our lesson text picks up with the woe that follows.

A. Regarding the Law (vv. 23, 24)

23a. Woe unto you, scribes and Pharisees, hypocrites!

The Greek word translated as *hypocrites* describes a stage actor, therefore someone who is pretending to be something he or she is not. The term is quite fitting for the *scribes and Pharisees*, whom Jesus will later describe as "whited sepulchres, which indeed appear beautiful outward, but are within full of dead men's bones, and of all uncleanness" (Matthew 23:27, not in today's text).

23b. For ye pay tithe of mint and anise and cummin, and have omitted the weightier matters of the law, judgment, mercy, and faith: these ought ye to have done, and not to leave the other undone.

Mint and anise and cummin are garden herbs used either for cooking or medicinal purposes. Tithing items such as these is not commanded in the Law of Moses, but for the religious leaders such an act gives the impression of how scrupulously they follow the law. One thinks of the Pharisee (in a parable) who proudly claimed, "I give tithes of all that I possess" (Luke 18:12).

It is noteworthy that Jesus does not criticize the tithing per se of the religious leaders. In fact, He says *these ought ye to have done*. The problem is that paying such close attention to the details of tithing garden herbs has caused these leaders to miss the *weightier* (more important) requirements of the Law of Moses. Specifically, those are *judgment, mercy, and faith*. These more crucial *matters of the law* must be given first priority, then tithing as the leaders desire to do can be done as private matters of devotion to God.

What Do You Think?

How can our church ensure it gives proper attention to the weightier matters of the gospel?

Talking Points for Your Discussion

- In the area of upreach (worship)
- In the area of outreach (evangelism and benevolence)
- In the area of inreach (spiritual growth)

Judgment here most likely refers to carrying out justice on behalf of others, not to judging right from wrong or to a formal act of judgment on another's actions. This closely relates to *mercy*, or compassion, toward those in need. *Faith* as used here most likely describes active faith supported by works, the opposite of which is dead (James 2:26).

24. Ye blind guides, which strain at a gnat, and swallow a camel.

Jesus further illustrates the hypocrisy of the scribes and Pharisees. The phrase *strain at a gnat* means "strain out a gnat." The conscientious religious leader carefully filters his drinking water through a cloth to make sure he does not swallow a gnat.

The gnat is not specifically mentioned in the list of clean and unclean creatures found in Leviticus 11. The *camel*, however, is found in Leviticus 11:4, where it is the first "unclean" creature cited. Jesus' reference to swallowing a camel is His way of pointing out how the scribes and Pharisees major in minors as they give painstaking attention to relatively less important details while they ignore the law's "weightier matters."

What Do You Think?

How can we protect our church leaders from the danger of spiritual blind spots?

Talking Points for Your Discussion

- When they invite us to do so
- When we have not been invited to do so

B. Regarding the Leaders (vv. 25, 26)

25. Woe unto you, scribes and Pharisees, hypocrites! for ye make clean the outside of the cup and of the platter, but within they are full of extortion and excess.

We come to yet another woe of the series. This condemnation is similar to Jesus' earlier description of the religious leaders' zeal to impress others with external displays of piety (Matthew 23:5-7) while being *full of extortion and excess* internally.

The word *extortion* highlights the attitude of selfishness that characterizes these religious leaders' approach to spiritual matters. *Excess* describes a certain lack of self-control (compare Luke 11:39). Jesus, who "knew what was in man" (John 2:25), sees the inside, and He is disgusted.

What Do You Think?

What steps can you take to avoid a spirituality that is oriented toward outward appearance?

Talking Points for Your Discussion

- When you think you're not at risk in this regard
- Considering the tension between needing to let your light shine (Matthew 5:14-16) and doing good deeds in private (6:1-4)

26. Thou blind Pharisee, cleanse first that which is within the cup and platter, that the outside of them may be clean also.

We do not know why Jesus at this point calls out only the Pharisees. Perhaps it is because they are the ones who are especially fastidious in their passion for the outward show of purity and piety (Mark 7:3, 4). What Jesus says here, however, describes not only the Pharisees but the human condition in general. Jesus pointed this out to His disciples following the confrontation with the scribes and Pharisees in Matthew 15:18: "But those things which proceed out of the mouth come forth from the heart; and they defile the man." Real change must happen from the inside out.

Earlier, Jesus had talked about such a transformation with Nicodemus, another Pharisee. On that occasion, Jesus described the necessary transformation in terms of being born again (John 3:3).

◆ ON GULLIBILITY ◆

Nazi Germany and the Soviet Union agreed to a nonaggression pact on August 23, 1939. The pact paved the way for Hitler's invasion of Poland a week later, thus beginning World War II.

This treaty of nonaggression, initiated by Germany, was supposed to guarantee nonbelligerence between the two countries. It contained the further promise that neither would come to the aid of the other's enemies in an armed conflict.

This caused the Soviet Union to believe that Hitler would be no threat to them. But while the Soviet guard was down, Hitler violated the treaty and invaded in 1941. The Soviets eventually pushed German forces out of their territory, but only after suffering 26 million deaths. Some historians speculate that Hitler entered into the nonaggression pact as a ruse to lull the Soviets into complacency.

There can be no nonaggression pact with Satan. Jesus did not sign a nonaggression treaty with the Pharisees. Their viewpoint was wrong, and that wrong had to be exposed lest it cause even more damage. In sending us out "as sheep in the midst of wolves," Jesus challenges us to be "wise as serpents, and harmless as doves" (Matthew 10:16). With discerning, Spirit-filled hearts, may we filter out alluring claims that are inconsistent with the revealed Word of God.   —D. S.

Conclusion

A. One Pharisee's Testimony

Let us revisit the case of Saul, the ardent Pharisee who was second to none in his hostility toward the Christian faith. After his conversion, he became, as the apostle Paul, one of the most passionate spokesmen for that same faith. What made the difference?

Certainly, the appearance of Jesus to Saul on the road to Damascus was the determining factor. But as we read Paul's later testimony, particularly in the third chapter of his letter to the Philippians, we see that something took place in his thinking and perspective. He had come to reject completely the typical set of priorities that guided a Pharisee's outlook on matters of religion.

Paul described himself as someone who, as a Pharisee, had "confidence in the flesh" (Philippians 3:4). His résumé was quite impressive in an earthly sense (3:5, 6). All the items he lists in that description he refers to as "gain to me" (3:7). They constituted what he calls "mine own righteousness" (3:9).

But Paul discovered something (and someone) far greater than his own self-made faith (which really wasn't faith at all). He calls it "the excellency of the knowledge of Christ Jesus my Lord" (Philippians 3:8). While Paul calls his righteousness obtained through the law "blameless" (3:6), law is by its very nature cold and impersonal. One cannot have a personal relationship with the law.

> **What Do You Think?**
> How do you guard against placing confidence in yourself rather than in God?
> *Talking Points for Your Discussion*
> - Steps that evaluate whether a problem exists
> - Steps that correct an identified problem
> - Steps that ensure the problem stays corrected

It was in a person (Jesus) that Paul found what the law could never provide. Among those blessings was a joy (a repeated theme in Philippians) that rigid devotion to the law (any law) is powerless to give. Gladly did Paul suffer "the loss of all things" (all the ingredients of his self-made religion) and "count them but dung, that I may win Christ" (Philippians 3:8). He was determined to move forward (3:13, 14), with his ultimate goal of seeing Jesus—not in a vision, but face-to-face in His heavenly presence (3:20).

It can be hard for us to appreciate Paul's experience fully. It may be difficult to grasp the radical nature of the decision that led him to follow Jesus and reject an upbringing and a heritage that was deeply ingrained within him. Even so, Paul's example and testimony remind us that following Jesus is worth any price we pay to do so.

B. Staying Heart Healthy

The spiritual condition of the religious leaders, as exposed by Jesus in our text, was, sadly, nothing out of the ordinary. God's people in both Old and New Testaments were always subject to the temptation to focus more on external acts of worship or devotion to God while neglecting the condition of the heart. This can be an especially serious pitfall for leaders of God's people (the focus of today's lesson title). They can become so enamored with their authority and the title they hold that they forget to give proper attention to their own spiritual condition as a model for others to emulate.

Wise King Solomon advised, "Keep thy heart with all diligence; for out of it are the issues of life" (Proverbs 4:23). Yet Solomon failed to follow his own advice and allowed his heart to turn from the Lord through the influence of his pagan wives (1 Kings 11:1-4). We too must be cautious of how we care for our hearts. We cannot just point our fingers at the Pharisees and highlight their faults, lest we too fall prey to the pride that acted like a cancer on their hearts.

Our society is very conscious these days (as it should be) about taking care of the physical heart by eating right, exercising, and getting sufficient rest. The spiritual heart, however, is for the most part ignored or viewed as one's own business. Clearly, though, the corruption and decay going on in our world spiritually and morally (and with increasing speed, it seems) cannot be good for the spiritual heart.

At the grocery store, certain foods are now marked as "heart healthy." If an individual has concerns about his or her heart, that person watches out for such a label. Wouldn't it be nice if certain items (TV shows, books, movies, music) came with a (spiritual) heart unhealthy warning

THEY BIND heavy burdens . . . and lay them on men's shoulders; but they themselves will not move them with one of their fingers.

MATTHEW 23:4, KJV

Visual for Lesson 6. *Start a discussion by pointing to this visual as you ask for examples of burdens Jesus is talking about and their modern equivalents.*

attached? What if we started watching, reading, or listening to one of these and a siren or alarm went off as if to say, "Careful, this is bad for your heart"?

The Bible is meant to serve as that kind of alarm. But it has to become a part of our spiritual heart to the point that we know it well enough (a good reason to memorize Scripture!) to call on it for guidance in times of temptation, tragedy, or other circumstances that have the potential to draw our hearts away from God.

Perhaps the words of Psalm 119:11 say it best—words that are part of the "pledge to the Bible" that is often recited by young people in Sunday school or Vacation Bible School classes: "Thy word have I hid in mine heart, that I might not sin against thee."

C. Prayer

Our Father, in the world around us is so much spiritual darkness that poses a grave threat to the health of our spiritual hearts! Help us to exercise discernment: to listen to, to watch, and to read what will keep our hearts in tune with Yours. May the source of our discernment be Your Word; may it always be the lamp to our feet and the light to our path. We pray in Jesus' name. Amen.

D. Thought to Remember

Let the great physician keep your spiritual heart healthy.

INVOLVEMENT LEARNING

Enhance your lesson with KJV Bible Student *(from your curriculum supplier) and the reproducible activity page (at www.standardlesson.com or in the back of the* KJV Standard Lesson Commentary Deluxe Edition*).*

Into the Lesson

Ask students to name some of their favorite actors and actresses and the roles they have played. Jot responses on the board. After several are listed, ask how the roles they have played contrast with their real life personalities.

Alternative. Have students role play a conversation in which they take the parts of characters whose personalities and values are completely the opposite of those of the students in real life. When the activity is over, encourage participants to talk about how hard (or how easy) it was to pretend to be someone they are actually nothing like in real life.

Make a transition by saying, "The word *hypocrite* is a Greek word that means 'actor,' one who pretends to be someone other than himself or herself. Today's lesson is about Jesus' frustration with people who put on a godly appearance, but inwardly they were much different."

Into the Word

Give each student a sheet of paper, and ask them to draw a line down the middle to create two columns. Have them head the left column *What They Were Doing* and the right column *What They Should Have Been Doing*. (*Option.* Create this yourself and distribute as handouts.)

Next, read the eight verses of lesson text, then have everyone spend no more than one minute making entries in the columns concerning what the Pharisees were actually doing and what Jesus said that they should have been doing in the last four of the eight verses.

Call for responses after exactly one minute. As students give "surface" responses, push deeper by asking for specific examples from Scripture passages that are not part of today's lesson text. An expected surface response is that the Pharisees were so focused on their own interpretation of the Law of Moses by tithing their spices that they neglected more important matters of mercy, faith, etc. Anticipate that some learners will push deeper by mentioning the handwashing of lesson 3 as a specific example of majoring in minors.

Next, draw the learners' attention back to the first four verses of the text and read them aloud. Pose this question: "Would it be fair to summarize Jesus' instructions as 'Do as they say, but not as they do'?" Be prepared to allow a silent pause of up to 15 seconds for someone to respond. Discuss implications of this instruction.

Alternative. To better grasp the practice of the Pharisees of tithing their spices, distribute copies of the "The Spices of Life" activity from the reproducible page, which can be downloaded. Bring salt and pepper shakers, as well as about ¼ cup of cinnamon and ¼ cup of sugar. As the activity begins, put ½ teaspoon of one of the spices on the big circle at the top of each of the participants' papers. Then they will try to "distribute" their spice to the other people in the class, putting a little of their spice in the appropriately labeled small circle on their activity page.

Into Life

Say, "Jesus described some of the Pharisees as dirty dishes: clean on the outside, but full of crud on the inside." Poll students for modern examples of this; stress that real names should not be used. Responses can be in terms of things rather than people themselves (example: a car that is kept meticulously clean on the outside, but the engine oil is never changed).

Alternative. Have students complete the spice matching game on the reproducible page. Allow them to score their own results. Tie this to the lesson by discussing the importance of using dishes that are clean both inside and out when preparing and serving food. Use this as an illustration of the importance of making sure our souls are clean so we can serve God with hearts free of hypocrisy.

THE WIDOW AND THE UNJUST JUDGE

DEVOTIONAL READING: Psalm 145:13b-20
BACKGROUND SCRIPTURE: Luke 18:1-8

LUKE 18:1-8

1 And he spake a parable unto them to this end, that men ought always to pray, and not to faint;

2 Saying, There was in a city a judge, which feared not God, neither regarded man:

3 And there was a widow in that city; and she came unto him, saying, Avenge me of mine adversary.

4 And he would not for a while: but afterward he said within himself, Though I fear not God, nor regard man;

5 Yet because this widow troubleth me, I will avenge her, lest by her continual coming she weary me.

6 And the Lord said, Hear what the unjust judge saith.

7 And shall not God avenge his own elect, which cry day and night unto him, though he bear long with them?

8 I tell you that he will avenge them speedily. Nevertheless when the Son of man cometh, shall he find faith on the earth?

KEY VERSE

Shall not God avenge his own elect, which cry day and night unto him? —**Luke 18:7**

JUSTICE IN THE NEW TESTAMENT

Unit 2: Jesus Calls for Justice and Mercy

LESSONS 5–9

LESSON AIMS

After participating in this lesson, each learner will be able to:

1. Retell Jesus' parable of the persistent widow and the unjust judge.

2. Explain what the parable teaches about prayer.

3. Identify a spiritually mature Christian to use as a role model for persistence in prayer.

LESSON OUTLINE

Introduction

A. Contest of Wills

As of the time of this writing, there were at least a dozen "judge shows" airing on North American television. Their popularity is traced to the launch of *The People's Court* in 1981. The formats are often the same: judges preside over certain types of cases, listen to evidence presented by each side, and issue rulings. Usually these programs last a half hour and feature two cases; thus each case is wrapped up in a little under 15 minutes.

Not so the legal drama of today's lesson! Our lesson text features instead a drawn-out process in which two people having entrenched viewpoints engage in a contest of wills. It may remind us of the old conundrum "What happens when an irresistible force meets an immovable object?" Jesus used this parable to call attention to important truths concerning our relationship with the ultimate judge, the judge of judges: Almighty God.

B. Lesson Background

Whereas last week's lesson was drawn from an incident that occurred during Passion Week, this week's study actually moves back a bit on the time line, to perhaps a couple of months before Passion Week. The text comes from a portion of Luke's Gospel that covers the ministry of Jesus in Perea. The designation *Perea* is not found in the Gospels, but it is used in records of the time to describe the territory east of the Jordan River, opposite the southern part of Samaria and most of Judea.

John 10:39-42 may indicate the beginning of Jesus' Perean ministry. Following His presence in Jerusalem at "the feast of the dedication" (10:22), He departed "beyond Jordan into the place where John at first baptized" (10:40). Luke 13:22–19:27 is that Gospel's record of Jesus' Perean ministry.

Immediately before giving the parable of today's lesson, Jesus had been addressing a question of the Pharisees concerning when the kingdom of God would come (Luke 17:20). In doing so, He issued some very solemn warnings about the future, most of them tied to His second coming. The suddenness of Jesus' return will catch many people off guard; they will be engaged in ordinary, routine activities "when the Son of man is revealed" (17:30). His return will not be a time for looking back and attempting to save anything of value, as indicated by the ominous warning, "Remember Lot's wife" (17:32). After the time frame of Jesus' teaching shifts from the future (17:20-25) to analogies between past and future (17:26-33) to the future again (17:34-37), Jesus puts the spotlight on the present with the parable that follows.

I. Parable
(LUKE 18:1-5)
A. Particular Purpose (v. 1)

1. And he spake a parable unto them to this end, that men ought always to pray, and not to faint.

After the intense instruction of Luke 17, Jesus returns to His common teaching method of using parables. The word *them* refers to Jesus' disciples, as noted in Luke 17:22. Perhaps they are taken aback by Jesus' teaching concerning His return. The analogies to lightning, the flood of Noah's day, and the destruction of Sodom in chapter 17 indicate much turmoil to come. How does one prepare?

The preparation of prayer is foundational. The word translated *not to faint* carries the idea of "be not weary," which is how the word is translated in 2 Thessalonians 3:13. It's vital not to get worn out as one prays *always*. Stay focused! The story at hand is out of the ordinary among Jesus' parables in that the purpose is stated at the outset.

◆ *YES, WE PRAY . . . BUT "ALWAYS"?* ◆

In the immediate aftermath of the 9/11 terrorist attacks, Americans spontaneously turned to God in prayer. President Bush subsequently proclaimed September 14 as a National Day of Prayer and Remembrance. Bells rang across the land at noon as churches opened their doors for memo-

HOW TO SAY IT

Micah	*My*-kuh.
Perea	Peh-*ree*-uh.
Samaria	Suh-*mare*-ee-uh.

rial services. That evening, candlelight services marked the solemn occasion.

But the change didn't hold for long. Even as the cleanup of the massive pile of rubble and human remains continued, Americans returned to everyday habits. Prayer was again tucked away like a spare tire—to be saved for use when the next calamity struck.

Tucked-away prayer is symptomatic of a tucked-away God. More than one commentator agreed with Anne Graham Lotz (Billy Graham's daughter) when she said, "For several years now Americans in a sense have shaken their fist at God and said, 'God, we want you out of our schools, our government, our business, we want you out of our marketplace.' And God, who is a gentleman . . . [has removed] his hand of blessing and protection." Whether one agrees with these thoughts or not, Jesus' instruction is still valid: we ought *always* to pray! What are we saying about our relationship with Him if we view prayer as only our "spare tire" to be used in emergencies?—C. R. B.

B. Pompous Judge (v. 2)

2. Saying, There was in a city a judge, which feared not God, neither regarded man.

The first person described has no redeeming qualities. To have no fear of God is to have no concern for God's righteous standards. Neither does this judge care about what people may think about any decision he renders. One gets the impression that he is entirely self-centered. Cold and insensitive, he lacks any degree of compassion for anyone.

This is not the kind of character that judges are to possess, according to the Law of Moses. Judges are to judge God's people "with just judgment" (Deuteronomy 16:18). They are not to "wrest," or pervert, justice (16:19). They are to show no favoritism and must not allow bribes to influence their thinking (16:19). Judging in this manner reflects the just character of the Lord himself (10:17, 18).

C. Persistent Widow (v. 3)

3. And there was a widow in that city; and she came unto him, saying, Avenge me of mine adversary.

Widows in antiquity are especially vulnerable to being mistreated or taken advantage of by unscrupulous individuals (which is often the case today as well). The Law of Moses includes several commands that widows be properly cared for and not be abused or abandoned (Exodus 22:22-24; Deuteronomy 14:28, 29; 24:17-22; 26:12, 13; 27:19). Jesus confronted the religious leaders of His day with their heartless treatment of widows, stating that they "devour widows' houses, and for a shew make long prayers" (Luke 20:47).

We are not told what this widow's *adversary* has done to her. But we keep in mind that this is a fictional story; unstated actions are unimportant. What is important is that the widow needs someone to intervene on her behalf, which she hopes this judge will do. The verb *came* in the Greek indicates a continual coming; that is, she comes repeatedly in an effort to persuade this callous judge to show a measure of concern for the law.

D. Promising Perspective (vv. 4, 5)

4, 5. And he would not for a while: but afterward he said within himself, Though I fear not God, nor regard man; yet because this widow troubleth me, I will avenge her, lest by her continual coming she weary me.

Jesus does not specify the amount of time that passes before the judge tires of the woman's persistent nagging. His decision to hear her out is not based on any change in his personal character; he still neither fears God nor has any concern for people. His reasoning is purely pragmatic: "If I help her, I'll get her off my back, and she'll quit bothering me!"

> *What Do You Think?*
> If you were to discuss persistent prayer with someone who models it, what would you want to learn regarding his or her motivations? Why?
> *Talking Points for Your Discussion*
> - Regarding intecessory prayer
> - Regarding prayers of praise and worship
> - Regarding prayers of petition
> - Regarding prayers of thanksgiving

II. Principles
(LUKE 18:6-8)
A. Affirming God's Justice (vv. 6-8a)

6, 7. And the Lord said, Hear what the unjust judge saith. And shall not God avenge his own elect, which cry day and night unto him, though he bear long with them?

Jesus does not say specifically how *the unjust judge* decides the widow's case. The implication, however, is that the judge adjudicates in the widow's favor.

Jesus' explanation of this parable should not be taken to mean that God is the equivalent of an unjust judge. God is the very essence of justice (Deuteronomy 32:4). Jesus is drawing a contrast between God and the unjust judge in arguing from the lesser to the greater: If this self-centered, unjust judge will finally agree to come to the aid of a person who persistently seeks his assistance, then will not the sovereign *God avenge his own elect* who come to Him persistently (*day and night*) in prayer? Responding to prayer is part of His nature as not only a righteous and just judge but also a compassionate heavenly Father.

> *What Do You Think?*
> How did a time of persistence in prayer result in your spiritual growth?
> *Talking Points for Your Discussion*
> - In ways unseen to others
> - In ways seen to others but personal to you
> - In ways others could see and learn from

The phrase *though he bear long with them* carries the idea of longsuffering, as the same Greek wording is translated in 1 Corinthians 13:4 and 2 Peter 3:9. It appears that Jesus is telling us that God exercises His own brand of persistent patience as He delays answering those who call on Him. There will be an opportune time to respond, but that time may not come as soon as we would like.

This speaks to the issue Jesus raises in the parable: When will God come to the defense of His people (His *elect*) who are under attack from their enemies? When will He carry out retributive justice on their behalf?

Considering again 2 Peter 3, we are told concerning "the day of the Lord" that God in His longsuffering is "not willing that any should perish, but that all should come to repentance" (3:9, 10). Paul echoes this thought in Romans 2:4. Part of God's seeming failure to come to the aid of His beleaguered, suffering people is that He is giving those enemies a period of time, an opportunity, to turn from their sinful ways and find His salvation. Thinking of your own previously lost state, aren't you glad He does?

> **What Do You Think?**
> How does (or should) God's concern for justice influence how you pray?
> *Talking Points for Your Discussion*
> - Regarding prayers for yourself
> - Regarding prayers for your church
> - Regarding prayers for your nation

8a. I tell you that he will avenge them speedily.

Jesus answers the question He has raised. In so doing, He assures His disciples (and us) that God will come to His people's defense in the proper way at the proper time. What must be kept in mind, however, is that *speedily* has to be understood according to God's timetable, not ours. Again to the apostle Peter: "One day is with the Lord as a thousand years, and a thousand years as one day" (2 Peter 3:8). The speed will occur when God determines that the time for judgment has come (compare Hebrews 10:37).

From our standpoint, God often does not act as quickly as we would like. As the prophet reminds us, "my thoughts are not your thoughts, neither are your ways my ways, saith the Lord" (Isaiah 55:8). We are to trust that He, as the righteous judge, will bring about justice in His time.

When that time comes—and come it will—it will happen in no uncertain terms. Abraham asked, during his "negotiations" with the Lord over Sodom and Gomorrah, "Shall not the Judge of all the earth do right?" (Genesis 18:25). Most assuredly He will, at the right time. His timing is always perfect (compare Galatians 4:4, 5). Waiting for that perfect timing is, of course, the hard part for us (compare Psalm 94:1-7).

B. Asking a Question (v. 8b)

8b. Nevertheless when the Son of man cometh, shall he find faith on the earth?

In the parable just told, the unjust judge is the one who is concerned about becoming worn out because of the widow's persistence. But in our time of waiting for our judge (God) to act, we are the ones who may grow weary at His seemingly delayed response to our cries for justice. This leads to the question that Jesus raises here as He concludes His parable.

The verse before us should be read in light of Jesus' teaching regarding His second coming (see the Lesson Background). The question thus is asking the disciples to consider whether their faith will be strong enough to survive the wait until Jesus returns. During that time, they (and we) may have to endure ridicule, persecution, etc. Will faith continue or collapse?

> **What Do You Think?**
> Without giving advice, how would you counsel someone who struggles in prayer waiting for God's help?
> *Talking Points for Your Discussion*
> - Considering the person's level of spiritual maturity
> - Considering the nature of the need
> - Considering appropriate and inappropriate use of Romans 8:28; etc.

Jesus' question is rhetorical. It is not a question that requires a specific answer on the spot, but rather is a challenge for self-examination and reflection. Each person listening to this parable is challenged to consider whether he or she will be judged as a person of faith. Such reflective reaction is similar to what Jesus' disciples will experience later during the last supper as each asks in turn "Lord, is it I?" (Matthew 26:20-22) when learning of the pending betrayal.

◆ WAITING FOR CHRISTMAS ◆

Do you remember how hard it was to wait for Christmas when you were a child? We are reminded of our own long-ago childhood every year as we watch the little ones in our families

Visual for Lesson 7. *Put learners in small groups to come up with more words that begin with the letter P to describe prayer.*

eagerly anticipate Christmas. Many families use a calendar to count down the days to December 25.

A certain company specializes in calendars for this purpose and claims to have 300 varieties in stock. For example, the company sells a chocolate calendar with a piece of chocolate behind the window for each day. Then there are religious calendars with Scripture verses behind each window. Those with a more secular orientation have Santas, snowmen, winter scenes, or Victorian-era art as the surprise each day. Admittedly, the last one probably would not be of much interest to the average child!

Jesus concluded His parable about the unjust judge by making a point about how we should await His return. Some Christians create "end-times calendars" with "windows" that feature clues as to how close we are to the second coming. The Lord doesn't want us to waste time trying to determine the exact timing of His return. He's more interested in what we do and how we pray during that interim, right?   —C. R. B.

Conclusion

A. Prayer in a Weary World

It is easy when reading this parable to forget, or at least fail to give attention to, the specific purpose for it. That purpose is stated in the opening verse: "that men ought always to pray, and not to faint" (Luke 18:1). We can get so caught up

in the issues of God's justice and the timing of His action on behalf of His people that we overlook the fact that this parable is meant to help us with our prayer life. Proper prayer will result in self-examination; this is much more useful than prayers of complaint regarding a perceived lack of action on God's part. A vital ingredient in maintaining the faith that Jesus mentioned at the close of the parable is steadfast, refuse-to-faint prayer.

At times prayer may seem ineffective in providing genuine solutions to the burning issues of our time. Some skeptics view prayer as a means of avoiding the hard work required to right or reverse some of the injustices in a terribly broken world. Those participating in various social programs and working hard to solve society's ills are often presented as those who are really making a difference (and in many cases, they are). People who pray, by contrast, are seen as out of touch or unwilling to get their hands dirty and tackle the problems that exist.

But that's a false either-or distinction. Certainly prayer should not be a substitute for work. God does expect His people to be salt and light (Matthew 5:13-16), to penetrate the darkness and to give more of His "seasoning" to the world as salt does to food. Part of this includes doing "justly" as the prophet tells us (Micah 6:8).

B. Justice as a Burning Issue

We recognize that justice (or rather the lack of it) is a burning issue in contemporary society. But we take care to note that the justice specifically addressed by Jesus in today's parable is that which concerns God's "elect" (Christians). The issue is their continuing to be persecuted in various ways while God does not intervene on their behalf. So, how are Christians to react to this kind of continuing injustice?

As we read Jesus' Sermon on the Mount, we see that we are not to take personal vengeance against wrongdoers; in fact, we are to seek the good of our enemies (Matthew 5:38-48). Paul's counsel in Romans 12:19-21 is consistent with this: "Dearly beloved, avenge not yourselves, but rather give place unto wrath: for it is written, Vengeance is mine; I will repay, saith the Lord" (12:19).

For many Christians today, this requirement creates great tension. This is particularly so in parts of the world where places of Christian worship are being burned to the ground and followers of Jesus (including children) are being tortured, mutilated, and killed because of their allegiance to Him. Christians see sin flourishing and wrong-doers enjoying life, apparently free to live under the radar of divine wrath. In the midst of this, the teaching that "men ought always to pray, and not to faint" can seem hollow, certainly much easier said than done.

> **What Do You Think?**
> How did you grow spiritually during a time when you prayed for God to change your circumstances, but He ended up changing you instead?
>
> *Talking Points for Your Discussion*
> - Regarding patience
> - Regarding how you view circumstances
> - Other

C. Revelation as an Insightful Help

The book of Revelation offers a proper perspective on this matter of maintaining faith under fire. As John describes the opening of the fifth of seven seals, he testifies, "I saw under the altar the souls of them that were slain for the word of God, and for the testimony which they held" (Revelation 6:9). He then notes how they cry out as they ask, "How long, O Lord, holy and true, dost thou not judge and avenge our blood on them that dwell on the earth?" (6:10).

This language calls to mind the reality behind the imagery of our lesson's parable: oppressed believers are crying out for God to judge their enemies and avenge them. They are in danger of growing "faint" in the sense of wondering *What's the use in praying? Nothing changes, so we might as well spend the time doing something else.* The "how long" question posed by both the dead and the living (see Psalm 35:17-28; Habakkuk 1:2-4; etc.) is felt profoundly.

As we read through Revelation, we see vividly portrayed the intense conflict between good and evil, between the Lord and Satan. Finally as we draw near to the book's conclusion, we read how John describes hearing a "great voice of much people in heaven" proclaiming the praises of the Lord (Revelation 19:1). A few verses later the great marriage supper of the Lamb is pictured, to which all the faithful are invited (19:7-9).

As Revelation 19 progresses, a rider on a white horse appears. "He that sat upon him was called Faithful and True, and in righteousness he doth judge and make war" (19:11). The rider is called "The Word of God" (19:13) and "hath on his vesture and on his thigh a name written, King of Kings, and Lord of Lords" (19:16). He has come to judge the nations and to carry out the wrath of Almighty God (19:15).

There is no question who this rider is: He is Jesus, coming in glory as He promised to do in today's parable. And He comes speedily, to avenge the faithful and to carry out God's holy judgment on the wicked.

The cry for vengeance will be answered, in the ultimate sense, when Satan is cast into the lake of fire (Revelation 20:10). He is the one whom Jesus came to destroy (Hebrews 2:14, 15; 1 John 3:8). Those who accept Jesus as Lord and Savior are equipped with the power of the Holy Spirit to overcome Satan's temptations and schemes (1 John 4:4).

Even so, we still feel the impact of the broken, sin-cursed world that awaits redemption (Romans 8:22, 23). That full redemption will come with the creation of the new heavens and the new earth (2 Peter 3:13; Revelation 21:1). And when that takes place, it will happen *speedily*.

May Jesus find *us* faithful when He comes.

D. Prayer

Father, we live in a time when so many voices are raised in protest, in anger, in defiance—but so few voices are raised in prayer. May we not allow the unchanging evil around us to silence our prayers. We ask this in Jesus' name. Amen.

E. Thought to Remember

Prayer is a plea
to the highest court of appeals.

INVOLVEMENT LEARNING

Enhance your lesson with KJV Bible Student (from your curriculum supplier) and the reproducible activity page (at www.standardlesson.com or in the back of the KJV Standard Lesson Commentary Deluxe Edition).

Into the Lesson

Read to the group the following quote by a famous minister:

> Nothing paralyzes our lives like the attitude that things can never change. We need to remind ourselves that God can change things. Outlook determines outcome. If we see only the problems, we will be defeated; but if we see the possibilities in the problems, we can have victory. —Warren Wiersbe

Pose the following questions for whole-class response in light of this quote. 1–Why do people get stuck thinking that there's nothing that they can do to change their situation? 2–Why does believing that God can make a difference give some people the energy to take the next, most responsible small step? 3–In what ways does God call us to participate in the change He wants to create in our lives?

After discussion say, "Today's lesson focuses on a parable that illustrates the importance of persevering with the Lord in prayer."

Into the Word

Read the eight verses of the lesson text to the class or have two volunteers take turns doing so.

Then divide the class into two groups. Group 1 will examine the parable and make a list of ways the unjust judge and God are alike. Group 2 will examine the parable and make a list of ways that the judge and God are different.

After a few minutes, bring everyone together to talk about conclusions. Ask, "Why would Jesus use a corrupt and calloused human character to help us better understand something about God?" *(Expected response: Jesus was using a lesser-to-a-greater form of logic.)*

Ask for volunteers to suggest how the parable sets the stage for Christians to understand the importance of perseverance in prayer. At some point in the discussion, give examples of two prayers: one that has been offered humbly for the thirtieth time, and one that is impatient, even though it is being offered for only the second time.

Into Life

Ask students to name a mature Christian in their lives whose prayer life is characterized by respectful persistence, especially on behalf of others. Jot each name on the board as it is mentioned.

When no further names are forthcoming, go back through the names one at a time and ask the one who offered the name to describe that person's prayer in terms of *form* (how the prayers are structured and offered) and *content* (what is actually said). Jot responses in two columns on the board.

When the list is complete, ask learners to identify common elements and how they can emulate those traits.

Option. Encourage your students to fill out the "Answers to Prayer" chart on the reproducible page, which can be downloaded. One of the goals of the chart is to give them an idea of how long they might have been praying for a particular thing—or how long God took to answer a particular prayer.

Option. If you wish to explore the lesson's subtheme of justice, distribute copies of the "The Pursuit of Justice" activity from the reproducible page. Have students identify some injustices happening to people close to them or themselves.

Encourage students to use their chart to keep track of how persistently they pray for those experiencing injustice. Draw their attention to the column they can use to describe a small step that they can take to address the injustices they've listed.

If learners need an introduction to the important distinctions among various types of justice, distribute copies of the Get the Setting article on page 340. Depending on group interest and time available, work through some of the Scripture references to clarify.

ENTERING GOD'S KINGDOM

DEVOTIONAL READING: Psalm 1

BACKGROUND SCRIPTURE: Matthew 7:15-23; Luke 13:22-30

LUKE 13:22-30

22 And he went through the cities and villages, teaching, and journeying toward Jerusalem.

23 Then said one unto him, Lord, are there few that be saved? And he said unto them,

24 Strive to enter in at the strait gate: for many, I say unto you, will seek to enter in, and shall not be able.

25 When once the master of the house is risen up, and hath shut to the door, and ye begin to stand without, and to knock at the door, saying, Lord, Lord, open unto us; and he shall answer and say unto you, I know you not whence ye are:

26 Then shall ye begin to say, We have eaten and drunk in thy presence, and thou hast taught in our streets.

27 But he shall say, I tell you, I know you not whence ye are; depart from me, all ye workers of iniquity.

28 There shall be weeping and gnashing of teeth, when ye shall see Abraham, and Isaac, and Jacob, and all the prophets, in the kingdom of God, and you yourselves thrust out.

29 And they shall come from the east, and from the west, and from the north, and from the south, and shall sit down in the kingdom of God.

30 And, behold, there are last which shall be first, and there are first which shall be last.

KEY VERSE

Strive to enter in at the strait gate: for many, I say unto you, will seek to enter in, and shall not be able.

—Luke 13:24

JUSTICE IN THE NEW TESTAMENT

Unit 2: Jesus Calls for Justice and Mercy

LESSONS 5–9

LESSON AIMS

After participating in this lesson, each learner will be able to:

1. State attitudes and actions to be practiced and avoided.

2. Explain the position reversal of the first and the last.

3. Create a written plan to resist a cultural hindrance to inclusion in the kingdom of God.

LESSON OUTLINE

Introduction

A. "Getting In" Trouble

An old joke tells of the man who, while touring through New York City, asked someone, "How do you get to Carnegie Hall?" The response: "Practice, practice, practice."

Admittance into an exclusive organization or institution is not easy. One usually has to have a certain amount of money, friends, and/or special abilities for that to happen. Take, for example, the baseball Hall of Fame. Nomination to be counted part of such an elite group must be earned. A player has to have the statistics to prove that he is worthy of belonging.

Entrance into God's kingdom (the subject of today's study) is quite a different matter! There is no way we can earn admission. Our "statistics" are dismal; Romans 3:23 states that "all have sinned, and come short of the glory of God." We can never measure up on our own.

To make it, we need help. In baseball terms, we needed a pinch hitter—someone to go to bat for us. That person is Jesus. He is "the way, the truth, and the life" (John 14:6). But He has a caution for us in today's lesson, a caution we must heed.

B. Lesson Background

Luke 13:22 (the opening verse of today's lesson text) marks the beginning of Jesus' ministry in the territory east of the Jordan River known as Perea. The Lesson Background of last week's lesson offers information on Perea, so that material need not be repeated here.

I. Concern over the Kingdom
(LUKE 13:22-24)

A. Question (vv. 22, 23a)

22. And he went through the cities and villages, teaching, and journeying toward Jerusalem.

The cities and villages mentioned here are those in Perea as Jesus proceeds southward through this region. The trip narrative *toward Jerusalem* and, ultimately, crucifixion begins in Luke 9:51. Many teaching opportunities are recorded along this journey of 10-plus chapters. As best as can be determined, Jesus has not visited Perea before now. As early as Luke 4:43, Jesus had stated, "I must preach the kingdom of God to other cities also: for therefore am I sent." That urgency still compels Him.

Steadfastness characterizes Jesus' urgency in accomplishing His mission. The centerpiece of that mission will be His sacrificial death for all humanity.

23a. Then said one unto him, Lord, are there few that be saved?

Luke's Gospel includes different occasions when it appears that individuals within Jesus' audience raise questions or make comments spontaneously. That is much as a student might do in a classroom setting today.

Sometimes the questioner desires clarification of something Jesus has said (12:41). At other times the question or statement becomes the springboard for further teaching from Jesus (10:25; 11:27, 28; 12:13-21). On still other occasions, individuals desire Jesus to comment on a current event (13:1), while others take offense at something Jesus says (11:45).

When an individual asks *Lord, are there few that be saved?*, we are not given any information as to the motive for this question. Perhaps it is asked simply out of curiosity.

In the Sermon on the Mount, Jesus spoke of "few" who will find the "narrow" way leading to life while many will follow the "broad" way to destruction (Matthew 7:13, 14). But He has also spoken of the great growth of God's kingdom, as in the parable of the mustard seed recorded just a few verses before our text (Luke 13:18, 19). So perhaps this individual is seeking some clarification from Jesus. How can it be "few" if the kingdom is to grow so spectacularly?

B. Exhortation (vv. 23b, 24)

23b. And he said unto them.

One person has asked the question; the answer is directed to *them,* implying that a group (or crowd, as is typical with Jesus) is present. The answer is crucial enough that Jesus wants more than just the questioner to hear it.

24. Strive to enter in at the strait gate: for many, I say unto you, will seek to enter in, and shall not be able.

We notice that Jesus does not answer the question with a direct yes or no as it has been posed to Him—nor is He obligated to do so. But the question is valuable in that it offers opportunity to establish a more important teaching point. The first order of business is not to inquire about how many or few will be saved; rather, the first order of business is to make certain that *we* are among those striving to be saved.

It is easy to raise questions and generate discussions over a host of religious matters. It is another thing to take such matters out of the realm of abstract ideas, make them personal, and consider their bearing on one's personal relationship with God. The result should be to know what one must do (Acts 2:37; 16:30; Titus 3:14; etc.).

The word *strive* translates a Greek word from which we get our word *agonize*. It was used in reference to Greece's athletic games in describing the kind of determined effort that is necessary to achieve victory (compare 1 Corinthians 9:24, 25, which uses the same word). Jesus is saying that a similar degree of commitment is needed to enter the kingdom. This Greek word also occurs in 1 Timothy 6:12 as both a verb and a noun, being translated "fight the good fight."

> **What Do You Think?**
> Considering that we are not saved by works, what should striving to enter the kingdom of Heaven look like?
>
> *Talking Points for Your Discussion*
> - In terms of actions of setting time and financial priorities, etc.
> - In terms of reactions to un-Christian influences that pull one away from the kingdom

Strait refers to something that is narrow; think of the Strait of Gibraltar. Thus a *strait gate* is one difficult to enter, requiring persistent effort. Jesus also refers to the "strait gate" in the Sermon on the Mount (Matthew 7:13, 14). There the emphasis seems to be on finding that gate; here the emphasis shifts to the difficulty of actually entering through it. Thus it is at this point that the question in Luke 13:23a is answered. But why will many *not be able* to enter? Jesus proceeds to elaborate.

◆ TWISTY STRAITS ◆

Slot canyons abound in the southwestern United States. Zion National Park in southwestern Utah has two well-known examples. One very difficult hike in that park—for technically proficient canyoneers only—is called The Subway. Traversing this narrow, winding canyon involves wading or swimming in water that is cold and deep, climbing over waterfalls, and scrambling over huge boulders.

Zion's larger canyon (and the one visited by the greatest number of people) is called The Narrows. The gorge has walls 1,000 feet high in places, and the Virgin River, which forms the canyon, is occasionally only 20 to 30 feet across. The hike up this canyon is most accessible to the average park visitor in the summer, when the water is at its shallowest depth and warmest temperature. That's when hundreds—sometimes thousands—of people a day hike through the water for a mile or more, drawn on from bend to bend, to see what lies around the next twist in the canyon's depths.

These canyons make for an interesting comparison with entry into the kingdom of Heaven. Jesus implies that the narrowness of the passageway to the kingdom acts as a deterrent to a majority of people who might otherwise enter it. On the other hand, it seems the difficulty involved in making one's way through narrow slot canyons is a challenge. What do you suppose draws people to the earthly Zion National Park and not to the heavenly Zion?

—C. R. B.

II. Citizens of the Kingdom
(LUKE 13:25-30)

A. Those on the Outside (vv. 25-28)

25. When once the master of the house is risen up, and hath shut to the door, and ye begin to stand without, and to knock at the door, saying, Lord, Lord, open unto us; and he shall answer and say unto you, I know you not whence ye are.

The word picture of a *house* with *the door* having been *shut* signals the end of the day. The scene depicted is similar to that of the parable of the 10 virgins (Matthew 25:10-12). In both cases, those who are still outside the house when the door is closed plead to be let in.

But the pleas in both cases are to no avail. The response *I know you not whence ye are* is quite alarming and similar to Matthew 7:23 ("I never knew you") and 25:12 ("Verily I say unto you, I know you not"). In all cases, Jesus is describing what will happen to the disobedient on the Day of Judgment. The declaration *I know not whence ye are* by *the master of the house* indicates that those on the other side of the door clearly do not belong in the kingdom of God.

26. Then shall ye begin to say, We have eaten and drunk in thy presence, and thou hast taught in our streets.

Those on the outside are stunned, perhaps a bit incensed, at the owner's words. How can the master of the house claim not to know them, given all they've done in his *presence*? This verse describes how public Jesus' ministry has been and how much He has interacted with people by sharing meals with them.

27. But he shall say, I tell you, I know you not whence ye are; depart from me, all ye workers of iniquity.

The owner repeats his denial and, echoing Psalm 6:8, adds the yet more ominous *depart from me, all ye workers of iniquity*. While there will be many who claim to know Jesus, the knowledge He is talking about is far more than just a familiarity with Him. Those on the outside knocking at the door are people who lack a sound understanding of who Jesus is and the nature of the kingdom He came to establish. They may have dined in Jesus' presence—perhaps they were even the beneficiaries of His miracles such as the feedings of thousands—but their overall commitment to matters of His kingdom is no more than superficial.

The condemnation *depart from me, all ye workers of iniquity* is quite similar to Jesus' words "depart from me, ye that work iniquity" in the Sermon on the Mount in Matthew 7:21-23. There

Jesus was describing those who on "that day" (apparently the Day of Judgment) will try to be admitted to the kingdom of Heaven by pointing to the prophecies, exorcisms, and various miracles they did in Jesus' name.

Here in Luke 13, however, Jesus says nothing specific about what those to be excluded will claim as credentials; He merely calls them *workers of iniquity.* We can discern what this means within Luke's context by looking back a few verses to Luke 12:45-47. There we find characteristics and behaviors of a condemned servant (who should know better) alongside his penalty.

In short, the one condemned is the one who does not do the will of God. Thus the message Jesus taught and preached during His Galilean ministry at the Sermon on the Mount is entirely consistent with the message now being taught and preached during His Perean ministry.

Visual for Lesson 8. *Point to this visual as you ask, "What deceptive labels does Satan put on these doors to tempt us to choose unwisely?"*

What Do You Think?

What has to happen for us to know that we are not fooling ourselves with regard to being a genuine follower of Christ?

Talking Points for Your Discussion
- Regarding the talk we talk (specifics)
- Regarding the walk we walk (specifics)
- Regarding connecting points between our talk and our walk (specifics)

◆ OUTSIDERS ◆

We've all heard stories about lifelong residents of New England, those supposedly taciturn folks who don't take well to outsiders who move into their communities. It's been said that individuals can live in the Northeast for 30 or 40 years but still not be trusted, because they "aren't from around here." Distrust of outsiders is not limited to New Englanders, however. We all have ways of describing outsiders—people not of our own "tribe," whether that definition is ethnic, regional, socioeconomic, or any other category by which we differentiate ourselves from others.

Greeks of biblical times called the rest of the world "barbarians" (compare Colossians 3:11). This apparently is from the sound "bar-bar," which

is what foreign languages supposedly sounded like to Greeks. "Country bumpkin" and "city slicker" are derogatory terms by which urban and rural people, respectively, sometimes refer to folks who live in the opposite environment. Of course, we are sadly aware of the various racial and ethnic slurs that poison society. Our view of those who differ from us is often not a positive one.

When Christ's kingdom comes in its fullest extent, some people will truly be outsiders . . . forever! It won't be because they "aren't from around here," but because they have not done the will of the heavenly Father. —C. R. B.

28. There shall be weeping and gnashing of teeth, when ye shall see Abraham, and Isaac, and Jacob, and all the prophets, in the kingdom of God, and you yourselves thrust out.

Comparing this verse with Matthew 8:11, 12, we again see absolute consistency between Jesus' teaching in His Galilean and Perean ministries. In both addresses, exclusion results in *weeping and gnashing of teeth.* Such language is associated with the outer darkness that characterizes the punishment of those who have no place *in the kingdom of God* (Matthew 22:13; 25:30).

Seeing *Abraham, and Isaac, and Jacob, and all the prophets, in the kingdom* will add to the misery of those excluded. Their position may be likened to that of the rich man who could see the beggar Lazarus with Abraham on the other side of the "great gulf" that separated the places to which they were consigned (Luke 16:19-31; see lesson 4).

Many of the Jews in Jesus' day, especially the religious leaders, assume that their natural ties to Abraham give them automatic entry into the kingdom of God (Luke 3:8; John 8:33). That they can be denied entrance to the kingdom and not be in the company of their renowned ancestors is unthinkable. The standard of judgment, however, is one's personal relationship to the Lord and faithful obedience to Him. Physical or ancestral ties mean nothing; the obedient ones make up the Lord's true family.

B. Those on the Inside (v. 29)

29. And they shall come from the east, and from the west, and from the north, and from the south, and shall sit down in the kingdom of God.

The language of coming from all points of the compass echoes Psalm 107:3. Inhabitants of *the kingdom of God* will come from everywhere! This signals the inclusion of people with no ancestral ties to Abraham (compare Matthew 8:5-12). This scene may be likened to that described in Revelation 7:9 of "a great multitude, which no man could number, of all nations, and kindreds, and people, and tongues," gathered before the throne of God in Heaven.

It is worth noting that the covenant God established with Abraham included a plan to bring all nations to Him, not to limit His blessings to certain individuals. That covenant concludes with the words "and in thee shall all families of the earth be blessed" (Genesis 12:3). In Galatians 3:8 Paul notes that with those words God "preached . . .

the gospel" to Abraham. The church now has the responsibility of continuing the fulfillment of that promise by taking the gospel to "all nations" as Jesus commissioned (Matthew 28:19, 20). To be a spiritual descendant of Abraham, not a physical descendant, is what counts (Galatians 3:29).

C. Concluding Principle (v. 30)

30. And, behold, there are last which shall be first; and there are first which shall be last.

Jesus makes this paradoxical statement elsewhere. We see it twice in the parable of the workers in the vineyard (Matthew 19:30; 20:16) as well as in His encounter with the rich young ruler (Mark 10:31).

These contexts highlight a crucial principle: those who consider themselves *first* or in a privileged position regarding the kingdom of God are in great danger of finding themselves *last*. They need to make serious changes in their thinking, and they must begin to view people through Jesus' eyes. Those whom the haughty Jewish leaders view as *last*, including publicans, harlots, and Gentiles, will find themselves at places of honor in the kingdom because they have chosen to enter on the King's terms (compare Matthew 21:31).

At this juncture we would do well to return to the question of Luke 13:23, at the beginning of our lesson text: "Are there few that be saved?" In one sense, the answer is yes; compared with the multitudes of people who have lived over the course of history, few will enter the kingdom of Heaven. In another sense, the answer is no; for many from around the world, representing a variety of nations, people groups, and languages, will be included in Jesus' kingdom.

It cannot be stressed enough that the more important issue is that each of us should "strive to enter" the kingdom (Luke 13:24) as we maintain a life of faithful obedience to the Lord. Doing so means ordering our lives around the King's priorities and viewing people as He sees them.

Conclusion

A. Thinking in Reverse

"Nice guys finish last" is an oft-used expression. But after considering Jesus' teaching in today's text, the saying could be reversed (and also modified) to read "Last people finish nice [first]." This illustrates Jesus' promise of a reversal of the way that the world often views people and situations.

The first/last reversal further illustrates the extent to which Jesus' kingdom is, as He told Pilate, "not of this world" (John 18:36). Those considered movers-and-shakers or headliners in the world's estimation do not carry such weight in the eyes of God. He is looking for those who acknowledge their spiritual poverty, the poor in spirit (Matthew 5:3), those who know they can never earn a place in the kingdom of God and do not have a sense of entitlement.

Consider what happened to the prodigal son in Jesus' classic parable. This young man arrogantly took his father's wealth and wasted it, then found himself in such desperate straits that he was relegated to feeding pigs. When he "came to him-

HOW TO SAY IT

barbarians	bar-*bare*-ee-unz.
Galilean	Gal-uh-*lee*-un.
Perea	Peh-*ree*-uh.

self" (Luke 15:17), he determined that he would return to his father and prepared what was a very humbling speech.

To the son's amazement, the father welcomed him with open arms and spared no expense in showing mercy. Here is the irony: when the son thought he was of no further value to his father (or *last* in his father's eyes), that is when he was truly ready to go home. And his father gave him *first*-class treatment, much to the chagrin of his older brother (who represents the haughty scribes and Pharisees and their disdainful attitude toward the "last" in society).

Jesus' words also have application to the work of the local congregation. Sometimes those who are more visible or vocal or up front receive the greatest attention or adulation from others. And those serving in more isolated areas (especially in more remote foreign fields) may never be appreciated here on earth for the degree of sacrifice they make for the kingdom.

However, such individuals will never be overlooked by the heavenly Father. He sees what is done "in secret" (as Jesus taught, Matthew 6:4), and those who have served in seemingly minor roles will receive an abundant reward from the Father. Nobody goes under the radar with Him.

Churches and individual Christians should evaluate their ministries to "the last" in their communities. How such ministries manifest themselves can vary depending on the location, need, resources, etc. But each of us probably has some of the "last" in our neighborhoods, schools, and workplaces—people who are used to being overlooked, scorned, or ridiculed. What can we do to be salt and light to those individuals, to treat them as "first" for a change?

B. Prayer

Father, help us not to lose our sense of needing to put forth our best effort in serving You. May we encourage one another to remain faithful servants. We pray in Jesus' name. Amen.

C. Thought to Remember
We must abide by the King's terms
to enter the kingdom.

INVOLVEMENT LEARNING

Enhance your lesson with KJV Bible Student *(from your curriculum supplier) and the reproducible activity page (at www.standardlesson.com or in the back of the* KJV Standard Lesson Commentary Deluxe Edition*).*

Into the Lesson

Announce to the class that they will be playing a game called Captain Obvious. Every time you ask one of the following questions, the answer must be proceeded by the words, "Well, Captain Obvious …"

Begin by holding up a genuine $20 bill and a $20 bill from a board game. Ask: 1–What do these two pieces of paper have in common? 2–What is the biggest difference between these two pieces of paper? 3–What would happen if you attempted to purchase something using the play money?

As a transition, say, "Today's lesson deals with counterfeits in which people place their hope for Heaven; but Jesus has something quite different in mind."

Into the Word

Read the following paragraph out loud:

During Jesus' ministry, many people in Jerusalem were counting on their biological connection with Abraham as a type of guarantee that they would be included in the kingdom of God. Many of them were convinced that as long as the temple was still standing, God would never abandon any descendant of Abraham, either in this age or the age to come. Some of the people who followed Jesus and listened to Him teach thought that this would be enough to merit eternal life. Jesus challenged these assumptions, emphasizing that what mattered was the condition of one's heart, not ancestral lineage or perceived level of "goodness."

Divide the class into two group, the *Expectations Group* and the *Reality Group*. Ask the *Expectations Group* to look at today's text and identify all the unchallenged, unspoken, or unsubstantiated expectations (based on ancestry) that Jesus describes of His opponents. Ask the *Reality Group* to identify how Jesus defined reality in terms of who will enter into the kingdom of God and who will not. Encourage students to describe how, when, and where they see this tendency at work today in supporting false expectations regarding who will be in Heaven and who won't.

Into Life

Draw learners' attention back to Luke 13:29. Ask, "What does this verse imply about surprise guests at the great feast?" (See the commentary for possible responses.) Stress that no one will be excluded on the basis of family or national origin.

Shifting perspective on Luke 13:29, say, "This verse speaks of arrivals *from* the four compass directions, but those arrivals can depend on what is happening *in* those four compass directions." Jot on the board the names of locations where Christianity is being suppressed and/or Christians are being oppressed (based on your research in advance, which you pass along during class). *Option.* Distribute copies of the map from the reproducible page, which you can download, to enhance this discussion. Encourage students to take notes on the map and use it later to prompt prayers for steadfast faith of their fellow believers the world over.

Bring the discussion back home as you say, "Praying for others is necessary and proper. But we don't want to neglect our own spiritual health in the process." Form students into small groups and challenge them to (1) identify local cultural forces that tempt Christians to take their eyes off the kingdom of God and (2) create a written plan to resist those hindrances.

After groups complete their work, reconvene for whole-class discussion. Set the tone for the discussion by quoting Psalm 73:2, 3: "But as for me, my feet were almost gone; my steps had well nigh slipped. For I was envious at the foolish, when I saw the prosperity of the wicked."

Option. Distribute copies of the "First and Last" word-search puzzle on the reproducible page. After students complete it, lead a discussion regarding relevance, or lack thereof, to entering the kingdom of God.

PARABLE OF THE GREAT DINNER

DEVOTIONAL READING: Luke 14:25-33
BACKGROUND SCRIPTURE: Luke 14:15-24

LUKE 14:15-24

15 And when one of them that sat at meat with him heard these things, he said unto him, Blessed is he that shall eat bread in the kingdom of God.

16 Then said he unto him, A certain man made a great supper, and bade many:

17 And sent his servant at supper time to say to them that were bidden, Come; for all things are now ready.

18 And they all with one consent began to make excuse. The first said unto him, I have bought a piece of ground, and I must needs go and see it: I pray thee have me excused.

19 And another said, I have bought five yoke of oxen, and I go to prove them: I pray thee have me excused.

20 And another said, I have married a wife, and therefore I cannot come.

21 So that servant came, and shewed his lord these things. Then the master of the house being angry said to his servant, Go out quickly into the streets and lanes of the city, and bring in hither the poor, and the maimed, and the halt, and the blind.

22 And the servant said, Lord, it is done as thou hast commanded, and yet there is room.

23 And the lord said unto the servant, Go out into the highways and hedges, and compel them to come in, that my house may be filled.

24 For I say unto you, That none of those men which were bidden shall taste of my supper.

KEY VERSE

Go out quickly into the streets and lanes of the city, and bring in hither the poor, and the maimed, and the halt, and the blind. —**Luke 14:21**

JUSTICE IN THE NEW TESTAMENT

Unit 2: Jesus Calls for Justice and Mercy

LESSONS 5–9

LESSON AIMS

After participating in this lesson, each learner will be able to:

1. Retell Jesus' parable of the great dinner.

2. Identify the two general categories of people who were invited to the dinner.

3. List excuses given today for refusing the invitation of Jesus, and present a response to each.

LESSON OUTLINE

Introduction

A. Jesus' Eating Habits

Some time ago a study was undertaken to address the question, "What would Jesus eat?" The study investigated common foods of Jesus' day in order to determine what was most likely a regular part of His diet. The Gospels note that Jesus ate fish and honey (Luke 24:41-43) and shared a typical Passover meal with His disciples (22:15). They also record different times when Jesus ate in homes or ate with His disciples, but no specific menu is mentioned on those occasions.

A more important issue involving Jesus' eating habits, according to the Gospels, is *whom* He ate with. These include Matthew (also known as Levi) the publican (tax collector), in whose house Jesus ate along with "a great company of publicans and of others" (Luke 5:29). He also ate with unnamed Pharisees (Luke 11:37; 14:1-24, the Scripture from which today's text is taken), with various "publicans and sinners" (Luke 15:1, 2), with Martha and Mary (Luke 10:38-42; John 12:1-3), and with His disciples (as noted above). In fact Jesus was criticized as being "gluttonous" (Luke 7:34).

Jesus' eating habits reveal His desire to reach out to all people—both the sinners who knew they were sinners and sinners such as the Pharisees whose self-righteousness blinded them to the truth about their condition.

Those habits highlight Jesus' purpose for coming into the world. As He told another publican, Zacchaeus, "For the Son of man is come to seek and to save that which was lost" (Luke 19:10).

B. Lesson Background

The parable of the great dinner in today's text comes not long after Jesus' teaching in last week's text from Luke 13. Following that section of teaching in 13:22-30, some of the Pharisees informed Jesus that He needed to vacate the territory of Perea because Herod Antipas (son of Herod the Great) wanted to kill Him (13:31).

Jesus was not fazed by this threat (which may have been fabricated by the Pharisees in order to diminish the effectiveness of Jesus' ministry). He continued to focus His attention on reaching Jerusalem and lamented over its failure throughout the years to accept the words of God's appointed messengers, some of those even being killed (Luke 13:34, 35). He knew that in just a few months, He would be among that number.

Luke 14 begins with Jesus' entering the house of "one of the chief Pharisees" for a meal on a Sabbath Day. We do not know the exact location of this house, but it can be assumed that Jesus was still in the territory of Perea (where the teaching in last week's text occurred). He was being watched closely, apparently to see if He would violate the Pharisees' standards of conduct. After healing a man in the house, Jesus rebuked the Pharisees for their hypocritical behavior (14:2-6).

Jesus then told a parable aimed at those in attendance at the meal, in order to correct their behavior of selecting prominent seats (Luke 14:10). He then spoke more directly to the man who had invited him to the dinner (14:12). Jesus challenged him to invite the rejects and the outcasts of society—those unable to return the favor. A reward for such generosity may not come in this life, but it will come in God's time: "at the resurrection of the just" (14:14). The mention of resurrection prompted a comment from one of the guests in the Pharisee's house, which is where the lesson text begins.

I. The Place
(Luke 14:15)
A. Sitting with Jesus (v. 15a)

15a. And when one of them that sat at meat with him heard these things, he said unto him.

We noted in last week's study how Luke often recounts situations when people in an audience speak up spontaneously with a question or comment directed toward Jesus. Here, following Jesus' teaching concerning proper dinner etiquette (from a spiritual standpoint), *one of* the guests in the Pharisee's house speaks up.

B. Speaking to Jesus (v. 15b)

15b. Blessed is he that shall eat bread in the kingdom of God.

The guest's comment is an interesting one. Jesus has said nothing in the house thus far spe-

cifically about *the kingdom of God.* He used the word *blessed* in verse 14 to encourage His listeners to invite to their dinners the outcasts and the neglected. Perhaps this man is trying to one-up Jesus' statement by declaring his own understanding of what blessedness means. Perhaps Jesus' teaching has made this man a bit uncomfortable since neither he nor any other Pharisee seems likely to follow Jesus' advice when planning his next dinner. So his statement may be an effort to turn the conversation in a different direction.

On the other hand, this person may be one of the few in attendance who understands what Jesus has said thus far. He seems to understand that Jesus is speaking of *the kingdom of God,* which will include a heavenly banquet (see Isaiah 25:6; Luke 13:29; Revelation 19:9). The future banquet is a symbol of God's acceptance and reward of the resurrected, righteous people. This ultimate inclusion by God is also the ultimate blessing.

II. The Parable
(Luke 14:16-24)
A. Invitation Extended (vv. 16, 17)

16. Then said he unto him, A certain man made a great supper, and bade many.

Jesus speaks this parable *unto him,* to the man who had made the previous remark. But it is certainly intended to be heard by all who are present.

That the host in this parable—who undoubtedly represents God—*bade many* should be understood in light of how such gatherings are typically planned and organized. The initial invitation to a gathering like *a great supper* amounts to being given a heads-up: be prepared! At some future time the invitation will be followed by an announcement that the supper is indeed ready. Then it will be time for the invited to come.

17. And sent his servant at supper time to say to them that were bidden, Come; for all things are now ready.

The *supper* likely takes a considerable amount of time to prepare, to accommodate the many who have been invited. Once everything is in order, a *servant* is dispatched to issue the second invitation: *Come; for all things are now ready.*

B. Invitation Rejected (vv. 18-20)

18a. And they all with one consent began to make excuse.

Amazingly (perhaps shockingly to those hearing the parable), the individuals who had earlier been invited to the supper reply with a series of excuses as to why they cannot attend. The phrase *they all with one consent* does not suggest that these people conspire to answer as they do. It means that they all offer reasons why they cannot come.

18b. The first said unto him, I have bought a piece of ground, and I must needs go and see it: I pray thee have me excused.

Two issues may be raised regarding this excuse. First, one would not buy *a piece of ground* without first going to see it and assess its value. Second, a field can be (re)examined at any time; why does it have to be done right at this moment? No doubt Jesus' audience sees through the flimsiness of this response. It's obvious that the man simply does not want to come.

19. And another said, I have bought five yoke of oxen, and I go to prove them: I pray thee have me excused.

The same critique applies to the second excuse. Why do these *oxen* have to be tested now? As was true with the piece of ground, the time to test the oxen is before the purchase, not after.

HOW TO SAY IT

Antipas	*An*-tih-pus.
Demas	*Dee*-mus.
Herod	*Hair*-ud.
Perea	Peh-*ree*-uh.
Pharisees	*Fair*-ih-seez.
Zacchaeus	Zack-*key*-us.

20. And another said, I have married a wife, and therefore I cannot come.

This third individual does not present even any semblance of politeness; there is no "I pray thee have me excused" accompanying his statement, as with the other two. All he says is *I have married a wife, and therefore I cannot come.*

But this is as poor an excuse as the previous two. Why should marriage keep one from responding to a previously given invitation? Even if this man has gotten married since the original invitation was issued, common courtesy requires that he follow through and attend the dinner once it is ready. Not to do so is to insult the host's gracious spirit.

It should be noted that these activities that are used as reasons not to attend the dinner are not wrong in and of themselves. There is nothing inherently sinful with buying a field, buying oxen, or getting married. The problem is that these three situations have become nothing more than pathetic excuses to cover the individuals' unwillingness to come to the dinner. If they really want to attend, they will come.

◆ MAKING EXCUSES ◆

Most people are pretty good at making excuses. It happens in every realm of life. Children blame misdeeds on their siblings or friends. Politicians blame their predecessors, at least during the first few years of their terms in office. Married people excuse their own contribution to the problems in their marriages. Students blame poor grades on their teachers or the subject matter. Examples are legion.

On the other hand, a lot has been said as to why we shouldn't excuse ourselves. Benjamin Franklin put it this way: "He that is good for making excuses is seldom good for anything else." J. C. Penney built a successful retail chain on this principle: "I do not believe in excuses. I believe in hard work as the prime solvent [solution] of life's problems." But as Mason Cooley observed, "Excuses change nothing, but make everyone feel better." Cooley was only partially right: we may feel better at the moment; but when the truth comes out, the game is over.

Think of the people who excused themselves from attending the feast Jesus spoke of in this parable. They each had what, at the time, might have seemed like a good reason for declining the invitation. But in the context of this invitation to God's eternal feast, they missed the chance of their lifetimes! Those who reject this invitation may think they are choosing correctly. Oh, how wrong they are! —C. R. B.

What Do You Think?
  What changes are needed for believers to make their relationship with Jesus the highest priority?
Talking Points for Your Discussion
  ▪ Considering distractions of a person's age demographic
  ▪ Considering distractions based in cultural expectations
  ▪ Considering family fissures that may result

C. Invitation Expanded (vv. 21-24)

21. So that servant came, and shewed his lord these things. Then the master of the house being angry said to his servant, Go out quickly into the streets and lanes of the city, and bring in hither the poor, and the maimed, and the halt, and the blind.

The host is understandably upset at such cavalier rejections of his invitation, especially when they are accompanied by obviously unacceptable reasons for doing so.

Although angry, *the master of the house* orders the servant to invite the village's most unfortunate: *the poor* (destitute beggars), *the maimed* (disabled due to injury), *the halt* (unable to walk), and *the blind*. These people are to be found on the main *streets*, perhaps begging, but will also live in the *lanes*, the backstreets of hovels and shacks. They are the very same groups that Jesus had encouraged those in attendance at this gathering to invite to any supper they may prepare (Luke 14:13, where "lame" is used to translate the word rendered *halt* in this verse).

We can imagine that the fatted calf is roasted, the raisin cakes are baked, the wine has been delivered, and the musicians are already playing. The feast cannot be delayed.

What Do You Think?
  How will you help your church reach out to the overlooked people in your community?
Talking Points for Your Discussion
  ▪ Regarding those with disabilities
  ▪ Regarding those with addictions
  ▪ Regarding the poverty-stricken
  ▪ Other

◆ UNEXPECTED INVITATIONS ◆

Each year, the president of the United States delivers the State of the Union address to a joint session of Congress, gathered in the House of Representatives chamber of the Capitol Building. The hall is filled for the event with "important" people. The speech is televised and seen by millions. Presidents of both parties have used the occasion to promote their programs for the nation, hoping to rally the support of the citizenry.

In more recent times, a few ordinary people who represent some element of the presidential agenda have received unexpected invitations. They are seated in a prominent place in the audience. When the president mentions them in an effort to draw sympathetic attention to the presidential agenda, TV cameras zoom in on these newly created celebrities-of-the-moment.

Much like the guests invited by the host near the end of Jesus' parable, the presidential guests are often the victims of life's injustices. However, the invited guests in the parable were not so honored to promote the host's political agenda. Instead, they were summoned to show that the Lord's desire to share His feast. But remember: those invited who dishonor the summons cannot reconsider later. —C. R. B.

22. And the servant said, Lord, it is done as thou hast commanded, and yet there is room.

Even though those in the streets and lanes of the city have not received an earlier invitation, they are more than happy to come. Perhaps, being in the condition they are in, they have never been asked to such a gathering as this. However, as *the servant* reports, *yet there is room.*

23. And the lord said unto the servant, Go out into the highways and hedges, and compel them to come in, that my house may be filled.

Now the host instructs *the servant* to extend his invitation even farther. *The highways and hedges* likely refers to the territory beyond the city limits; we might say "out in the sticks."

The appeal is not to be given halfheartedly or casually; the servant is to *compel* these residents *to come.* Perhaps this is necessary because at first those in these far-removed locations will find it hard to believe that someone in the city actually wants *them* to attend a dinner. But the host's objective is clear: he desires that his *house . . . be filled.*

> **What Do You Think?**
> What additional steps can you take to share
>   God's Word with the lost?
> *Talking Points for Your Discussion*
> - Personally
> - In cooperation with other Christians

24. For I say unto you, That none of those men which were bidden shall taste of my supper.

The ending of this parable does not turn out "happily ever after" for the original invitees. As we contrast those originally invited with those receiving the later invitations, the message of the parable becomes clear: Jesus is describing how God's invitation to His kingdom is presented first to the Jews. It is they who have received the initial invitation by means of possessing the prophecies of Jesus' coming and their position as God's covenant people. But they, for the most part, reject the kingdom as presented by Jesus. John writes, "He came unto his own, and his own received him not" (John 1:11).

Then the message of the kingdom is offered to a different group, including those scorned by groups such as the scribes and Pharisees. These outcasts are represented by the poor and physically disabled. The third group, in the highways and hedges, represents the Gentiles, those peoples and nations who are also among the lost whom Jesus came to save (Luke 19:10). They were described in last week's text as those from the four corners of the earth who will have the privilege of sitting down in the kingdom of God (13:29).

The tragic irony is that those first bidden to come to the kingdom (the Jews) are the ones who will be excluded from the dinner; however, they have no one to blame but themselves for being left out. The parable's message thus ties very closely with Jesus' statement that concluded last week's printed text: "And, behold, there are last which shall be first, and there are first which shall be last" (Luke 13:30).

> **What Do You Think?**
> How should we interact, if at all, with those who
>   accepted Christ at one point but now reject
>   Him?
> *Talking Points for Your Discussion*
> - Considering arguments for seeking them out
>   (Luke 15:4-10; etc.)
> - Considering arguments for not seeking them
>   out (Hebrews 6:4-8; etc.)

Conclusion
A. Keeping First Things First

While last week's text included the statement that the first will be last, today's study could be summarized by considering the importance of keeping first things first. There is no contradiction between the two ideas. Last week's lesson dealt with the way that God sees people and the manner in which they will be treated on the Day of Judgment; today's study concerns priorities in the lives of God's people.

The excuses offered by the three individuals in Jesus' parable reveal much about the individuals who offered them. Each excuse clearly shows that attending the dinner was not a priority for any of the three. They had something better to do. They could have made time for the dinner—if they had *wanted* to. Attendance was not high on their to-do list, if it was on there at all.

It is still true that the cares of this world and the obligations associated with it can often take priority over the things of God. This is a warning that is found throughout the Scriptures and one that today's Christian must take seriously. "Love not the world, neither the things that are in the world," writes John. "If any man love the world, the love of the Father is not in him" (1 John 2:15). James is just as direct: "Know ye not that the friendship of the world is enmity with God? whosoever therefore will be a friend of the world is the enemy of God" (James 4:4).

In the parable of the sower, Jesus described how some of the seed fell among thorns (Luke 8:7). He later explained that this represents "they, which, when they have heard, go forth, and are choked with cares and riches and pleasures of this life, and bring no fruit to perfection" (8:14). In his second letter to Timothy, Paul lamented of Demas, who "hath forsaken me, having loved this present world" (2 Timothy 4:10). Demas may not have been tempted by a field, by oxen, or by a wife, but something in the world had seized control of his heart.

B. Knowing the Times

During the change to David's leadership in ancient Israel, some who "came to David to Hebron, to turn the kingdom of Saul to him" are described as those who "had understanding of the times, to know what Israel ought to do" (1 Chronicles 12:23, 32). We live in a time when spiritual values are not promoted in any significant, meaningful way by culture. The lure of the world is very strong and begs for our attention through the various media outlets of our time. Our youth are especially the targets of these outlets and must be instructed by both the home and the church. The battle for hearts has never been more intense. Do we know the times? Having that knowledge, do we know what to do with it?

Those are important questions, and we must answer them to protect our own relationship with God first and foremost. Let's face it: we won't be much good for the kingdom of God if we're so focused on protecting others that we neglect our own spiritual well-being. While multitudes clamored for Jesus' attention, He still realized the need to be alone with the Father from time to time (Luke 5:15, 16). He realized that His apos-

Visual for Lesson 9. *Point to this visual as you say, "Physical malnutrition is easy to spot. But what are some signs of spiritual malnutrition?"*

tles needed rest (Mark 6:30-32). But rest and time alone with God go against the grain of an always-connected, 24/7 culture. Inadequate rest lowers our spiritual defenses. Consider how Satan timed his attack on Jesus: the attack came when Jesus was physically at His weakest (Matthew 4:1-11). Adequate rest makes possible the effectiveness of spiritual disciplines such as prayer, Bible study, and the supportive fellowship of other believers.

To know the times and to know what to do with that knowledge has a direct bearing on the cost of discipleship. To attend the great supper requires not only an invitation to do so, but also the willingness to pay the "opportunity cost" required to be there. From the world of economics, an opportunity cost is the "benefit that a person could have received, but gave up to take another course of action." We see opportunity cost in Mark 10:21, 28; Luke 14:33; etc. What price are you willing to pay to be at the great supper?

C. Prayer

Our Father, with gratitude we thank You for the invitation we have received to be at Your great supper! May we examine our hearts as the day approaches and destroy all excuses for not attending. We pray this in the name of Jesus, who makes the great supper possible. Amen.

D. Thought to Remember

Only the life that puts Jesus first will last.

(image contains text:)
Come, Sinners, to the Gospel Feast

Come, sinners, to the gospel feast, let every soul be Jesus' guest. Ye need not one be left behind, for God hath bid all humankind.

Come, all ye souls by sin oppressed, ye restless wanderers after rest; ye poor, and maimed, and halt, and blind, in Christ a hearty welcome find.

by Charles Wesley

INVOLVEMENT LEARNING

Enhance your lesson with KJV Bible Student *(from your curriculum supplier) and the reproducible activity page (at www.standardlesson.com or in the back of the* KJV Standard Lesson Commentary Deluxe Edition*).*

Into the Lesson

Divide the class into two groups. Ask one group to list banquets they have attended that were memorable for their delicious food, spectacular settings, interesting guests, etc. Ask the other group to compile a list of the worst excuses they've heard (or given) for not attending an event. After two minutes, call for results. After discussion, say, "Today's lesson offers what may be surprising parallels to our best meals and our worst excuses."

Alternative. Distribute copies of the "Face Value" activity from the reproducible page, which can be downloaded. Allow no more than a minute for students to match coins with values. Say, "Depending on condition, the Indian Head penny could be worth more than all the others combined. But that raises an interesting question: What determines value? And what—or whom—do we undervalue because we don't look at the larger picture?"

Into the Word

Read the lesson text aloud to the class. Then announce a closed-Bible true/false test to gauge retention. As you distribute copies of the following test (you create), assure participants that they will score and retain their own tests; you, the teacher, will not collect them. Time limit is one minute.

1. There were four rounds of invitation to the meal.
2. One excuse for not attending was that the invitee's daughter was getting married.
3. One excuse for not attending was the recent purchase of five yoke of oxen.
4. The host of the banquet personally went out to issue the third round of invitations.
5. The poor and the blind were invited during one of the rounds of invitations.
6. Substitute invitations were to be offered to those in "the streets," among other places.
(Answers: 1–F; 2–F; 3–T; 4–F; 5–T; 6–T.)

Discuss results. *Option.* Announce the test before reading the lesson text instead of after.

Alternative. After reading the text aloud, distribute copies of the "Parable Details" activity on the reproducible page. Form students into small groups to answer questions about entries as indicated. See the answer key to the reproducible page for expected responses in the second column.

Responses in the third column should be of a more personal nature than the responses in the second column, depending on class members' spiritual maturity. At a minimum, expect individuals' take-aways to include a sense of gratitude at being invited to the banquet and a realization of the need to be ready to attend when the time comes.

Option. Ask students to use their general knowledge of the Bible to state *why* the first invitees made excuses. Expect responses to include the nature of the Jewish leaders' attitude toward Jesus.

Into Life

Say, "Let's draw parallels between the excuses the first invitees made with the excuses people often make today to spurn Jesus' invitation to enter the kingdom." Jot responses on the board as students voice them. When there are no further responses, go back through the list item by item as you ask, "What would be a good way to answer this excuse?" Encourage free discussion.

Alternative. Give each student a paper plate and a marker. Say, "Take a moment to evaluate how you spend your hours outside of work and sleep. Present those activities on your plate in the form of a pie chart." Challenge students to compare their priorities with biblical priorities. Ask them how they know when they have "too much on their plate" (expect groans at the play on words). Then discuss what needs to happen to correct the problem.

After either activity, wrap up by saying, "It's no surprise that twenty-first-century priorities often crowd out kingdom priorities. Today's parable spurs us to consider our values."

GOD'S JUSTICE

DEVOTIONAL READING: Psalm 32

BACKGROUND SCRIPTURE: Romans 2:1-16

ROMANS 2:1-12

1 Therefore thou art inexcusable, O man, whosoever thou art that judgest: for wherein thou judgest another, thou condemnest thyself; for thou that judgest doest the same things.

2 But we are sure that the judgment of God is according to truth against them which commit such things.

3 And thinkest thou this, O man, that judgest them which do such things, and doest the same, that thou shalt escape the judgment of God?

4 Or despisest thou the riches of his goodness and forbearance and longsuffering; not knowing that the goodness of God leadeth thee to repentance?

5 But after thy hardness and impenitent heart treasurest up unto thyself wrath against the day of wrath and revelation of the righteous judgment of God;

6 Who will render to every man according to his deeds:

7 To them who by patient continuance in well doing seek for glory and honour and immortality, eternal life:

8 But unto them that are contentious, and do not obey the truth, but obey unrighteousness, indignation and wrath,

9 Tribulation and anguish, upon every soul of man that doeth evil, of the Jew first, and also of the Gentile;

10 But glory, honour, and peace, to every man that worketh good, to the Jew first, and also to the Gentile:

11 For there is no respect of persons with God.

12 For as many as have sinned without law shall also perish without law: and as many as have sinned in the law shall be judged by the law.

KEY VERSES

[There will be] glory, honour, and peace, to every man that worketh good, to the Jew first, and also to the Gentile: for there is no respect of persons with God. —**Romans 2:10, 11**

Justice in the New Testament

Unit 3: Paul Teaches About New Life in Christ

Lesson Aims

After participating in this lesson, each learner will be able to:

1. Summarize what today's passage says about God's judgment.

2. Explain why judging others brings God's judgment on ourselves.

3. Identify and repent of a sinful discriminatory behavior.

Lesson Outline

Introduction

A. Insiders Out

Insider trading is the buying or selling of a public company's stock by those with access to information not generally available. This is seen as unfair to other investors, and laws have been written to discourage it. Insider-trading cases involving high-profile people have been major news stories of the past two decades.

However, it seems that those who made laws forbidding insider trading were exempt from those very laws! In November 2011, the TV show *60 Minutes* aired an exposé on insider trading by members of Congress in both parties. The program cited examples of lawmakers using non-public information about pending legislation and other congressional matters to make lucrative investments. Members of Congress had exempted themselves from the very rules they had created, which jailed bankers, CEOs, and others.

After this information was disclosed, Congress took action and passed, with overwhelming support, a law to prevent this abuse. As a result, members of Congress and their staffs are no longer exempt from the insider-trading laws that apply to everyone else.

It's easy to expect more of others than we expect from ourselves. In today's lesson, Paul points out just how dangerous such an attitude can be.

B. Lesson Background

The letter to the Romans is considered by many to be Paul's greatest literary accomplishment. Are we surprised, then, to learn that he wrote it to a church in a city he had not visited? This lack of face-to-face contact, however, contributes to the book's value. Paul was not writing to a congregation that had heard him preach or teach; therefore there were no assumptions that he left some things unsaid, thinking that the readers already knew his views on a topic. This is of great benefit to us, the modern readers, because we have had no face-to-face contact with Paul either.

Reading Romans carefully gives us the best single picture of what Paul taught to first-century Christians on a wide range of topics, including the origin and consequences of sin, God's plan for justifying sinners by Christ's atoning death, the role of the Holy Spirit in the life of the believer, the comforting promise of never being separated from the love of God, the problem of the unbelief of the people of Israel, and many other matters.

Paul wrote Romans at the end of his third missionary journey. Acts gives fewer details concerning this trip compared with the first two, but it does mention that Paul spent three months in Greece (Acts 20:2, 3); the specific Greek city was likely Corinth, located in the province of Achaia. Romans 16:1 mentions someone from Cenchrea (Corinth's port city), who seems to be the delivery person for the letter. All this puts the dating of the letter in AD 57 or 58.

I. Human Judge
(ROMANS 2:1-4)
A. Acting with Hypocrisy (v. 1)

1. Therefore thou art inexcusable, O man, whosoever thou art that judgest: for wherein thou judgest another, thou condemnest thyself; for thou that judgest doest the same things.

The opening *therefore* connects what follows with Paul's discourse on God's wrath against sinners in Romans 1:18-32. The strong accusation that follows (*thou art inexcusable*) is thus not a gentle prodding to do better, but a sweeping condemnation. There are no mitigating factors to the crime, no insanity plea, no attacking the credibility of witnesses, no procedural mistakes by the police. You are guilty, plain and simple.

The Greek word translated *inexcusable* occurs also in Romans 1:20, where Paul describes those who are "without excuse" in failing to acknowledge the reality of God. Here, however, his focus has shifted from unbelieving, idolatrous pagans to those among his readers who might consider themselves to be somewhat godly and righteous, especially Jews (whom he will address specifically in Romans 2:17). What is Paul's purpose for shifting his focus in this way?

If we look at Romans 1, Paul's condemnation of the God-deniers is summed up when he says that they worship created things rather than the Creator (1:25). This is a fatal mistake and has led to all sorts of sinful activities, and Paul lists some of those. Such is the background for his accusation in the verse before us. Paul is leading toward the universal statement that "all have sinned" (3:23). For Paul, both riotously wicked Gentiles and respectable law-loving Jews are in the same category: sinners.

Therefore, his conclusion is that those who judge others as more sinful than themselves are condemning themselves with such judgments. We do *the same things*, meaning we engage in sin. We cannot say, "That guy is an 8 on the sin scale and I'm only a 3." It doesn't work that way. We are all sinners according to the judgment of our sinless, holy God.

> *What Do You Think?*
> How do you ensure that you are not guilty of the same shortcomings that you note in others?
> *Talking Points for Your Discussion*
> - Regarding people you know personally
> - Regarding high-profile public figures
> - Regarding those in groups different from yours

B. Awaiting an Exemption (vv. 2, 3)

2. But we are sure that the judgment of God is according to truth against them which commit such things.

Such things include the catalog of sins listed in Romans 1:29-31, the most extensive list found in Paul's writings. This list is not intended to be exhaustive, as shown by Paul's language, since he says "such" things rather than "these very" things.

Romans 1 outlines why sin is rampant among those who have turned from God. Why, then, does sin continue among those who claim to be serving God? For Paul, the second category includes non-Christian Jews as well as some within the church. Paul's logic here is inescapable. Sins are committed when we ignore or fail to take seriously the reality that *the judgment of God is according to truth.* By this Paul means that God is the eternal and absolute judge for all men and women, and that God's standards of judgment are also eternal and absolute.

3. And thinkest thou this, O man, that judgest them which do such things, and doest the same, that thou shalt escape the judgment of God?

Paul's relentless argument continues, destroying any pretense that less sinful people have the privilege of condemning more sinful people. Consider the illustration of a husband who cheats on his wife only once and a husband who has cheated weekly over the course of five years of marriage. Both are adulterers; both are sinners. And no sinner can *escape the judgment of God*. Every person reading Paul's words fits in this category.

◆ *PROJECTION* ◆

Most of us can point to behavior in other people that we find sinful, even reprehensible. Ironically, we often are guilty—to some degree—of the same sins we find so evil in others. Psychologists have a word for this: it's called projection. Our criticism of others is often an expression of the guilt we feel for our own sins—a guilt we find uncomfortable acknowledging as a part of our own being.

The subject of our projection may be something as benign as a characteristic that a parent has modeled for us. For example, a child may be angered by a parent's criticism and yet exhibit the same trait in his or her attitude toward the parent.

For the Jews, it had to do with a more serious charge. They saw in the behavior of Gentiles a whole catalog of sins they found to be gross and blameworthy. But Paul has words for them (and for us): they deserved the judgment they placed on the Gentiles for their sinful behavior. They might argue that the Gentiles' sins of the flesh were of a different sort than their own sins of the heart and mind, but in God's eyes there is no difference: sin is sin.

Thus, in condemning others for not living up to God's standards, we, like the Jews, are saying we deserve the same censure. But it is through the death of Christ, which paid the penalty for sin, that God is able to "project" His righteousness on us. Hallelujah!

—C. R. B.

C. Avoiding Repentance (v. 4)

4. Or despisest thou the riches of his goodness and forbearance and longsuffering; not knowing that the goodness of God leadeth thee to repentance?

If we label the inexcusable people of Romans 1 as "God-deniers," then the inexcusable of chapter 2 would be the "sin-deniers." By seeing sinfulness in comparative rather than absolute terms, they deny its consequences.

Having shown that the sin-deniers will be judged and condemned as will the God-deniers, Paul now intensifies his withering assault: sin-deniers are missing the graciousness of God. This points to the great paradox in understanding our relationship with God. If we understand God as only a judge demanding penalty for sin, we lose sight of God as a loving Father who provides a way out of our sinful dilemma. To rest on the hope that our sins are less serious than that of others amounts to despising the graciousness of God.

But why are God's judgments not immediate? Why does He not punish sins immediately? The answer lies in Paul's characterization of God's grace in terms of *goodness, forbearance,* and *long-*

suffering. The old saying "Justice delayed is justice denied" does not apply. God is patient and wants all sinners to come *to repentance* (compare 2 Peter 3:9).

II. Heavenly Judge
(Romans 2:5-12)
A. No Exceptions (vv. 5-10)

5. But after thy hardness and impenitent heart treasurest up unto thyself wrath against the day of wrath and revelation of the righteous judgment of God.

Having briefly touched on the graciousness of God, Paul returns to God as judge. The phrasing *hardness and impenitent heart* may make us think of hardening of the arteries. But Paul is not talking about a medical condition. Nor is he talking about an emotional condition, which we might call cold-heartedness. Hardness of heart is a spiritual condition, a common biblical metaphor for the person who refuses to repent (John 12:40; etc.).

Refusal to repent and receive God's grace is willful. It is the opposite of receiving "the riches of his goodness" (Romans 2:4). Instead, it chooses the "treasure" of God's wrath. This is not the sort of wealth that any reasonable person would wish! The wrath of God may be delayed, but it will be revealed on *the day of wrath*, or what we commonly think of as Judgment Day (compare John 12:48; Acts 17:31; 2 Peter 3:7).

6. Who will render to every man according to his deeds.

This verse expresses a thought found throughout the Bible (examples: Psalm 62:12; Proverbs 24:12; Jeremiah 17:10; Matthew 16:27; 2 Corinthians 5:10; Revelation 22:12). But the thought is easy to misinterpret if not seen in the light of the entire New Testament witness. The misinterpretation is that we can work our way into Heaven if we pile up enough good deeds. But sin cannot

HOW TO SAY IT

Achaia	Uh-*kay*-uh.
Cenchrea	*Sen*-kree-uh.
Corinth	*Kor*-inth.

be canceled out by our works. As Paul will clarify in Romans 3:10, no one is righteous. We are not saved by works (Ephesians 2:8, 9). Even so, the nature of our works indicates the nature of our faith (James 2:14-26). With the significance of works understood in that sense, there are two possible outcomes.

7. To them who by patient continuance in well doing seek for glory and honour and immortality, eternal life.

On the Day of Judgment, God will reward those whose faith has resulted in deeds that please Him; it is they who will be given *eternal life*. But *patient continuance* is a key. This carries the idea of endurance and/or persistence in various contexts, which Paul uses frequently (examples: Romans 5:3; 8:25; 15:4, 5; 2 Thessalonians 1:4).

> *What Do You Think?*
> What approach helps you most to maintain the lifestyle of patience and persistence described here? Why?
> *Talking Points for Your Discussion*
> - Advantages and drawbacks of mentoring
> - Advantages and drawbacks of having an accountability partner
> - Advantages and drawbacks of going it alone with spiritual disciplines
> - Other

8, 9. But unto them that are contentious, and do not obey the truth, but obey unrighteousness, indignation and wrath, tribulation and anguish, upon every soul of man that doeth evil, of the Jew first, and also of the Gentile.

The righteous judgment of God upon sinners is universal (*Jew* and *Gentile*), and Paul views sin through four lenses here. The first lens is the word *contentious*. The Greek term behind this (as used also in 2 Corinthians 12:20; Galatians 5:20; Philippians 1:16; 2:3; and James 3:14, 16) refers to self-absorbed people whose me-first attitude is a source of strife in the church.

The second is failure to *obey the truth*. This wording might be surprising to some, because we usually think of truth as something to be accepted or believed. For Paul, more is required. Unless acceptance of God's truth results in godly actions, it is just words. Unless we act on the truths of the faith, we remain in sin.

Obey unrighteousness, the third lens through which Paul sees sin, is the flip side of the second (2 Thessalonians 2:12 is similarly so). To choose to obey unrighteousness is to knowingly defy God, to turn one's back on the Creator of the universe. This is the "vain . . . imaginations" that Paul explained and condemned earlier (Romans 1:21).

The fourth entry is that way Paul defines sinful persons: they *doeth evil.* Some today claim that evil is subjective. One man's good is another man's evil, they say; therefore we should avoid such moral judgments. Paul could not disagree more. The four components together depict a person who fights me-first battles, spurns God's patterns of right behavior, and chooses to do things that God has forbidden. That is evil behavior.

10. But glory, honour, and peace, to every man that worketh good, to the Jew first, and also to the Gentile.

The first and second halves of this verse are nearly mirror images of the first and second halves, respectively, of verse 9. Thus does Paul link his points together. But the apparent cause and effect connection between *glory, honour, and peace* and *worketh good* seems to point again toward the concept of "works righteousness."

To the comments on verse 6, above, in this regard, we can mention two theories of note. One theory is that Paul is speaking only hypothetically: those whose good works add up to a score of 100 percent and whose sin is zero earn the rewards listed. But since all have sinned (Romans 3:23), this is only a theoretical possibility. The second theory is that Paul is specifically thinking of Christians, the nature of their good works being an indicator of the presence of saving faith.

The phrase *to the Jew first, and also to the Gentile* and its near twin in verse 9, above, seem to reveal at least part of Paul's intent: he is establishing what the standard of God's judgment will not be. That judgment will not be on the basis of religious heritage or ancestry. Paul may be establishing more than this, but he is not establishing less. This fact can undergird either of the two theories.

B. No Favoritism (vv. 11, 12)

11. For there is no respect of persons with God.

This verse forms one of two bookends of a subsection of Paul's thought. The other bookend is Romans 2:6, and the complicated interlinking of Paul's thoughts are made clearer by a diagram:

A¹–God will judge everyone fairly ....(v. 6)
  B¹–Well doers receive eternal life............(v. 7)
    C¹–Evildoers   suffer wrath.............(v. 8)

    C²–Wrath   for evildoers.............(v. 9)
  B²–Glory for workers of good...............(v. 10)
A²–God doesn't play favorites....................(v. 11)

The most important points occur at the outer edges, the bookends—but it's actually just a single point from two perspectives. Paul opened this subsection of thought by discussing God's impartial judgment (A¹) applied in a positive sense (B¹), then in a negative sense (C¹). He then reversed the pattern by moving from the application of judgment in a negative sense (C²) to its application in a positive sense (B²) to repeat the point of Romans 2:6 in the verse before us (A²).

We should clarify that the phrase *no respect of persons* does not mean that God lacks respect for us as individuals. It means, rather, that all humans are equal in the sight of God when it comes to sin and salvation. Regarding access to salvation, God does not base His judgments on people's biological or ethnic distinctions (Galatians 3:28). Jews are not privileged in this way. The Jewish law will be no defense for Jews on the Day of Judgment, for they have not kept it perfectly (Acts 7:53). All Jews, like all Gentiles, are sinners in the eyes of God.

What Do You Think?
What have you found to be most helpful in avoiding the ancient Jews' error of seeing themselves as part of a favored religious elite? Why?
Talking Points for Your Discussion
- Favorite Scriptures that help
- Spiritual disciplines that help
- Positive role models that help
- Other

The year 2016 was marked by a very large number of shootings in the United States involving police and black citizens. No part of the country seemed to be safe from the violence. Sometimes the citizens were the ones shot, and sometimes it was the police. Sometimes the response to shootings by police was rioting, sometimes sniper shots that killed police officers, and sometimes peaceful demonstrations. Many protesters thought that the police valued the lives of certain people less than the lives of others.

Each side in the public debate marshaled statistics to support its case. And each side had its partisans who were all too quick to see the other side as the villains. Both sides called for equality under the law, but just how that equality was to be defined and manifested was a point of disagreement.

We should be grateful that God judges people without looking at the superficial elements that bias human judgments. His unbiased evaluations apply not only to the final Day of Judgment, but also to day-to-day life (example: 1 Samuel 16:7). Jesus seeks disciples from every nation and race "in whom is no guile" (John 1:47), followers whose uniform is nothing more or less than "the whole armour of God" (Ephesians 6:11). Can you help recruit some today?　　　—C. R. B.

12. For as many as have sinned without law shall also perish without law: and as many as have sinned in the law shall be judged by the law.

In the end, Jews and Gentiles both come under the same judgment: they are sinners. Paul later teaches that the great value of the Jewish law is to define sin more clearly (Romans 7:7). We see the expectations of God quite clearly. But this is not a consoling factor, for everyone who expects to be judged by this law will be found guilty. Those without access to the Jewish law (the vast majority of the Roman world) will still be judged and condemned as sinners "because that which may be known of God is manifest in them" (1:19). All are under the power of sin (3:9). Without Jesus, there is no hope.

Visual for Lesson 10. *Ask learners what Scriptures they would add next to Romans 2:9-11 on this gavel to reflect the theme of the depiction.*

Conclusion
A. Not Trivial

God's system of judgment is perfectly just: if we do not sin, we will be judged as righteous. But our sin means we deserve God's judgment of death. We may think it unfair that a single sin could cancel a lifetime of righteous choices, but we know that is never the case. We are not good people with trivial sin problems. We are sinners who are sometimes coated with a thin veneer of righteous appearance. The sinful part of us is dense and deep, and we do not have to scratch the surface very hard to uncover it. This sin has brought alienation from God and threat of a harsh judgment for eternity.

This is not Paul's last word, however. The great good news of Paul is that we can be forgiven and restored to a proper relationship with God. That relationship is not based on our merits, but on faith in Jesus Christ, who paid our sin penalty.

B. Prayer

Father God, help us not to forget the offense that sin is to You! Help us long for Your holiness, trusting You to count us righteous through faith in Your Son. We pray this in His name. Amen.

C. Thought to Remember

God's law is a mirror in which we see our flaws, not a club with which to punish others for theirs.

INVOLVEMENT LEARNING

Enhance your lesson with KJV Bible Student *(from your curriculum supplier) and the reproducible activity page (at www.standardlesson.com or in the back of the* KJV Standard Lesson Commentary Deluxe Edition*).*

Into the Lesson

Ask the class to define *blind ambition* (expected response: when the drive to succeed comes at the expense of everything else). Ask, "What are some historical examples of blind ambition?" (Many responses are possible, including Bernie Madoff and Richard Nixon). Discuss the disaster these people brought on others and themselves.

Say, "Today we're not going to take on the big guns of blind ambition. We'll start small with just our own attitudes that might blind us to justice."

Alternative. Distribute copies of the "Blind Justice" photo from the reproducible page, which can be downloaded. Ask, "Who is this?" (Expected response: a representation of the ancient Roman goddess of justice—Justitia, or Lady Justice). "What do her sword, scales, and blindfold symbolize?" (Expected responses: the sword symbolizes law; the scales symbolize equity; the blindfold symbolizes impartiality).

Say, "The idea of 'blind justice' is a good one in terms of eliminating favoritism by being blind to everything but the evidence in an earthly courtroom. But God needs no blindfold to judge impartially."

Into the Word

Make photocopies of the Scripture from the first page of the lesson. Give each student a copy, along with two colored pencils. Have them go through the text and circle negative words and phrases in one color and positive words and phrases in the other. (*Option.* Rather than having students do this individually, you can use small groups.)

Have groups or individuals summarize their discoveries. Move to whole-class discussion as you ask, "Do you see how the negative terms are linked—with sinful actions bringing harsh consequences?" Affirm valid observations and clarify misconceptions. Then ask, "And do you see how the positive terms link blessings with selfless behavior?" Again, affirm valid observations and clarify misconceptions.

Alternative. Distribute copies of the "Truths and Consequences" activity from the reproducible page. Work through the text as a class, identifying the truths of what some people do and the consequences of those actions. (Some possible responses: Passing judgment on others results in condemnation in return. / Stubborn and unrepentant hearts invite God's wrath. / Persistence in doing good invites God's gift of eternal life. / Rejecting truth and following evil has no good end. See the answer key at the end of the quarter's reproducible pages for a comprehensive list of expected responses.)

After either alternative, conclude this section by saying, "It's easy to spot 'bad guys' and their bad behavior. But let's remember that Paul points a finger at 'good guys' with a stern warning: everyone is guilty. We have all broken God's law. That's why we need grace."

After pausing for reactions and discussion, continue by pointing out that the lesson text also reveals a critical truth about God: he does not show favoritism. No one will be judged on the basis of religious heritage or ethnic ancestry. The consequence of that truth is that his judgment is right.

Into Life

Say, "On a scale of 1 to 10—1 being a Madoff-type of blind ambition and 10 being Jesus' selfless ambition and service to humankind—how would you rate yourself? No matter how we rate ourselves, we are all guilty sinners. But if just the people in this room could love God and others a notch more and self a notch less, can you imagine what difference that would make?"

Give participants a chance to respond, but don't put anyone on the spot. Point out that the church of millions today began small, with a core group of only about 120 (Acts 1:15), led by flawed apostles.

GIVING JUSTLY

DEVOTIONAL READING: Proverbs 3:9, 10, 13-20, 27, 28
BACKGROUND SCRIPTURE: 2 Corinthians 8, 9

2 CORINTHIANS 8:7-15

7 Therefore, as ye abound in every thing, in faith, and utterance, and knowledge, and in all diligence, and in your love to us, see that ye abound in this grace also.

8 I speak not by commandment, but by occasion of the forwardness of others, and to prove the sincerity of your love.

9 For ye know the grace of our Lord Jesus Christ, that, though he was rich, yet for your sakes he became poor, that ye through his poverty might be rich.

10 And herein I give my advice: for this is expedient for you, who have begun before, not only to do, but also to be forward a year ago.

11 Now therefore perform the doing of it; that as there was a readiness to will, so there may be a performance also out of that which ye have.

12 For if there be first a willing mind, it is accepted according to that a man hath, and not according to that he hath not.

13 For I mean not that other men be eased, and ye burdened:

14 But by an equality, that now at this time your abundance may be a supply for their want, that their abundance also may be a supply for your want: that there may be equality:

15 As it is written, He that had gathered much had nothing over; and he that had gathered little had no lack.

KEY VERSE

Ye know the grace of our Lord Jesus Christ, that, though he was rich, yet for your sakes he became poor, that ye through his poverty might be rich. —**2 Corinthians 8:9**

JUSTICE IN THE NEW TESTAMENT

Unit 3: Paul Teaches About New Life in Christ

LESSONS 10–13

LESSON AIMS

After participating in this lesson, each learner will be able to:

1. Identify the circumstances of the offering Paul anticipated receiving from the Corinthian church.

2. Explain how Paul's use of Exodus 16:18 supports his argument regarding sharing through giving.

3. Perform an act of material kindness toward someone in the week ahead.

LESSON OUTLINE

Introduction

A. Robin Hood Justice

The exploits of Robin Hood and his Merry Men in Sherwood Forest have long entertained imaginations. Numerous film versions have been made of the Robin Hood saga, including remakes of the story on an asteroid, among gangsters in Chicago, and in an animated version in which the hero is a talking fox.

Central to the Robin Hood legend is his role as a "social bandit" or "heroic outlaw," as expressed in the description that he "robbed from the rich to give to the poor." In Robin Hood's world, the rich are wealthy because of severe taxation, exploitative labor practices, and/or downright dishonesty. The poor are hard-working and honest, but suffer poverty because of oppression from the rich.

Robin Hood is therefore a hero to the poor (for whom he provides money and goods) and a villain to the rich (from whom he steals). His thievery is justified because of the positive things he does with his stolen wealth.

With some allowance for motive (Proverbs 6:30, 31), the Bible never condones stealing, however. The eighth commandment, "Thou shalt not steal" (Exodus 20:15), is applied consistently. The Scriptures also have harsh words for wealthy people who oppress the poor, which may be a form of stealing (Proverbs 22:16; Amos 5:11, 12; James 2:6, 7).

Is there a better way to correct economic inequity than to resort to Robin Hood's methods? Is robbing the rich the only way to relieve the poor? Within the church, Paul teaches another way. It neither steals from the rich nor ignores the desperate plight of the poor. This is the subject of today's lesson.

B. Lesson Background

The travels of the apostle Paul gave him bases of operation in several cities of the Roman Empire in the mid–first century AD. He was a native of the commercial hub of Tarsus and studied in Jerusalem (Acts 22:3). He became a leader in the early Christian center of Antioch (11:25, 26). He founded churches in important Greek cities such as Philippi (16:11-40), Corinth (18:1-18), and Ephesus (19:1-41). He served as a bridge between the Greek/Gentile world and the Jewish world in the first-century church.

The latter was clearly evident in Paul's role in the project we often refer to as the Jerusalem collection or the offering for the poor saints in Judea. Paul and Barnabas visited Jerusalem around AD 51 to help decide whether circumcision would be required of Gentile Christians (Acts 15:1-29; Galatians 2:1-10). They left the city assured that Gentiles did not need to be circumcised and with the responsibility to "remember the poor" (Galatians 2:10). This was more than just a request to be charitable. There seems to have been an expectation that Paul would be asking his network of churches to give money for the economic relief of suffering Christians in and around Jerusalem.

This relief project is mentioned several times in the New Testament. In Paul's first letter to the Corinthian church (written about AD 56), Paul instructed the Corinthians to make weekly contributions to the fund so that it would be ready when he visited. They were also to select men who would accompany him in taking the offering to Jerusalem (1 Corinthians 16:1-4).

The collection of this gift provides the backdrop for Paul's teachings on Christian stewardship that are found in 2 Corinthians 8 and 9. Paul wrote 2 Corinthians about a year after writing 1 Corinthians, thus around AD 57. This indicates that the Jerusalem relief project was a plan spread over several years, for Paul did not arrive in Jerusalem until AD 58.

In 2 Corinthians 8:1-6, which immediately precedes today's lesson text, Paul informed his readers of some details of this relief offering for the poor Christians of Judea. The offering from the Macedonian churches was complete, which likely includes the cities of Philippi, Thessalonica, and Berea (see Acts 16:12; 17:1, 13). The generous results of the collection effort encouraged Paul. Titus was coming to Corinth as Paul's envoy to help the Corinthians complete their part of the relief mission (2 Corinthians 8:6).

I. Excellent Giving
(2 Corinthians 8:7-9)
A. Corinthians' Goal (vv. 7, 8)

7a. Therefore, as ye abound in every thing, in faith.

Paul commends the Corinthians for five specific qualities. To *abound . . . in faith* indicates they continue to be strong believers in spite of the various controversies within the church.

7b. And utterance, and knowledge.

To excel in *utterance* refers to the quality and fidelity of the preaching and teaching ministry. Paul's commendation of the Corinthians' *knowledge* refers to their growth in doctrine as gained from Paul, Apollos, and others (compare 1 Corinthians 3:2, 6). A connection between the two characteristics is easy to see since a person utters what he or she knows (compare 1 Corinthians 1:5).

7c. And in all diligence.

Diligence is a quality we may not tend to associate with the Corinthians as we read of their besetting problems. But Paul uses the Greek word translated *diligence* also in 2 Corinthians 7:11 to refer to the church's "carefulness." The picture is that of a congregation emerging from controversy and being stronger for it.

7d. And in your love to us.

The word *us* refers to Paul and Titus in this fifth of the five commendations. At times the relationship between Paul and the Corinthians has been strained (examples: 1 Corinthians 4:18-21; 2 Corinthians 1:23–2:5; 6:11-13; 10:10; 12:19-21). Relationships can be repaired when there is an underlying foundation of love and respect for one another. When love is lacking, even small disagreements can be fanned into flames of church warfare.

HOW TO SAY IT

Antioch	*An*-tee-ock.
Apollos	Uh-*pahl*-us.
Berea	Buh-*ree*-uh.
Caesarea	Sess-uh-*ree*-uh.
Macedonian	Mass-eh-*doe*-nee-un.
Philippi	Fih-*lip*-pie or *Fil*-ih-pie.
Tarsus	*Tar*-sus.
Thessalonica	*Thess*-uh-lo-**nye**-kuh (*th* as in *thin*).

7e. See that ye abound in this grace also.

Paul desires that along with the five qualities just noted the Corinthians should strive to *abound* in a sixth: the *grace* of giving for the relief of the suffering of others. Although the word *giving* does not occur here, the words *this grace* refer back to "the same grace also" in 2 Corinthians 8:6, which in turn refers to the giving program of 8:1-5.

Churches still need a multifaceted foundation to become most effective and generous in their grace of giving. This is especially true of giving for purposes outside the congregation's local needs. A church with a shaky foundation in the five qualities noted for Corinth may find it difficult to fund even the local monthly costs of building maintenance and staff salaries.

8. I speak not by commandment, but by occasion of the forwardness of others, and to prove the sincerity of your love.

Paul is not issuing a command for the Corinthians to collect money for this offering. Christian giving should be a joy, not a duty; a privilege, not an obligation. Paul's point is that the Corinthians and other churches have agreed to support this project. To keep this promise is not a test of fellowship, but a demonstration of the *sincerity* of the Corinthians' *love*. The Greek word translated "diligence" in the previous verse occurs again here, this time translated *forwardness*, with the same meaning. The *prove* idea is reflected again in the concluding verse of this chapter.

◆ *THE GIVING PLEDGE* ◆

Noted businessman and investor Warren Buffett challenged his employees to predict the winners of the 2016 college basketball championship tournament. Any employee who guessed every correct pick in the first two rounds would win $1 million a year—for life! No one accomplished that feat, but two employees split the consolation prize of $100,000 for making the most correct picks in the first two rounds.

A few years earlier, Buffett had joined Bill and Melinda Gates in a more significant challenge: they called on the world's billionaires to give more than half their wealth to philanthropic causes. As of June 2016, 154 individuals or families from 16 countries had joined the Giving Pledge, as the agreement was called. The causes they support are wide-ranging, with urban renewal, global economic opportunities for women, environmental issues, and scientific advancement among others.

We may be tempted to think that billionaires like them can afford to give all that money, but not us—we're too strapped to give very much money away. Would the apostle Paul be impressed with that line of thinking? The benevolent cause to which he refers involved unwealthy Christians whose hearts were touched by the needs of Christians who were even worse off than they were (2 Corinthians 8:1-4). This situation challenges us continually, does it not?   —C. R. B.

B. Jesus' Example (v. 9)

9. For ye know the grace of our Lord Jesus Christ, that, though he was rich, yet for your sakes he became poor, that ye through his poverty might be rich.

Paul sometimes points to himself as an example (1 Corinthians 11:1; Philippians 3:17), but not here. Christ's willingness to leave His heavenly home and come to earth to live among men and women was an act of great humility (Philippians 2:6-8). Paul does not see Christ's sacrifice as being limited to the cross. It began with His becoming human, the Word of God taking on flesh (John 1:14). Jesus was born to a simple peasant couple and grew up in an obscure Galilean town. His was never a life of luxury (Luke 9:58).

This creates a great and wonderful paradox for Paul. Christ's humility and *poverty* make His followers spiritually *rich*. With Christ taking human form and dying for human sins, those who have accepted Him have become sons and daughters of God, and fellow heirs with Christ (Romans 8:17; Titus 3:7). Paul sees that true wealth is found in the blessings of grace and salvation that God has provided for us in Christ (Ephesians 1:7; 2:7).

> *What Do You Think?*
> How does your giving to Christian causes and organizations differ from your giving to secular causes? How should it?
> *Talking Points for Your Discussion*
> - In times of immediate crisis
> - In terms of motive
> - In terms of delayed giving via pledges
> - Other

II. Freewill Giving
(2 Corinthians 8:10, 11)
A. Well Begun (v. 10)

10. And herein I give my advice: for this is expedient for you, who have begun before, not only to do, but also to be forward a year ago.

The reminder to the Corinthians of their spiritual wealth leads Paul to give them strong *advice* concerning what they should do to finish the offering for those in need in the Jerusalem church. Paul begins this by reminding them that *a year ago* they were *forward* in this project, meaning they were among the first to give. Now they should complete the offering and send it on its way.

B. Get It Done (v. 11)

11. Now therefore perform the doing of it; that as there was a readiness to will, so there may be a performance also out of that which ye have.

Churches and other Christian organizations often launch building campaigns or other projects in which financial pledges are received for future giving. Sometimes a project lingers without being completed for several months or even years. These projects are good endeavors, but they can become discouraging if not completed.

Rather than push the Corinthians for a specific amount, Paul tells them to do their best to collect

what they can and move on. Remember: giving should be motivated by love, not guilt.

> *What Do You Think?*
> How do you stay motivated to keep giving?
> *Talking Points for Your Discussion*
> - When finances are tight
> - When tempted to divert a regular offering to buy a luxury item
> - Other

◆ FOLLOW-THROUGH ◆

Follow-through is stressed by coaches in many sports. Good coaches know that the most effective motion is one that doesn't stop when the bat or club strikes the ball or when objects leave the hand.

Follow-through counts in other areas of life also. A prime example is how well children do in school. The University of Chicago Consortium on School Research reports that three factors affect success in school. The first is a student's belief that hard work can bring improvement. Second, a student must have confidence that he or she belongs in school and can thrive in that setting.

Finally, the student must believe that what one does in school is valuable and relevant to life. Educators have found that students who don't have these attitudes aren't likely to succeed. In other words, these values help the student to "follow through" when school is difficult.

Paul's counsel for his readers to follow through and make good their commitments is his counsel to us as well. Satan will try to defeat efforts to follow through (compare Nehemiah 4:6-11). But follow-through is too vital to let him win.

—C. R. B.

III. Equitable Giving
(2 Corinthians 8:12-15)
A. Willing and Able (v. 12)

12. For if there be first a willing mind, it is accepted according to that a man hath, and not according to that he hath not.

Two elements must be present for money to be given: (1) there must be willingness to give and

(2) there must be ability to give. If a person is willing to give but not able, then no giving occurs. If a person is able to give but not willing, then no giving occurs.

Both elements of willingness and ability have been addressed in verse 11, but Paul senses that more needs to be said about ability. Assuming that *a willing mind* desires to give, that willingness results in the acceptability of a contribution that comes from available resources (compare Mark 12:43, 44). There is no guilt trip here (compare 2 Corinthians 9:7). No potential giver is expected to think of what he "should" give, then make up any shortfall by borrowing money. The readers are not expected to give money they don't have. While there is room for faith and growth in giving, it is irresponsible for church leaders to push people to give beyond their means.

B. Relief and Burden (vv. 13-15)

13. For I mean not that other men be eased, and ye burdened.

Paul also wants the Corinthians to know that no recipient of the gift will end up living a life of ease due to this offering. This is a matter of helping supply others' needs, not aiding them in becoming wealthy.

Likewise today, it is improper to ask church members to give to support extravagant lifestyles for their leaders. The televangelist scandals of decades past still stand as somber reminders of the dangers in this area.

14. But by an equality, that now at this time your abundance may be a supply for their want, that their abundance also may be a supply for your want: that there may be equality.

The two instances of the word *equality* are easy to misinterpret, and we must ask the question, "Equality in terms of what?" As always, it is context that determines: Paul is discussing how churches are to handle issues of dire need.

The equality he pushes for is equality in terms of meeting basic subsistence needs. People in one area may be experiencing a good economy, a bountiful harvest, etc., while people in another location live near the starvation level because of drought, war, etc. Such disparity may be regional, as it is

in this situation between churches in Greece and churches in the Jerusalem area. When such a need and a corresponding abundance are known, the needy can be helped.

Should this situation be reversed in subsequent years, the helpers may become the helped. The Corinthians who offer help now may be the ones in need later. We must be ready both to give and to receive, depending on the need. Relief offerings can be one-time projects, such as the one with which Paul and the Corinthians are involved. There can also be ongoing efforts by congregations to support food banks and clothing closets for the needy. All in all, we should not understand Paul to be calling for exact equality of wealth, resulting in neither wealthy nor poor people in the church.

> **What Do You Think?**
> How would you deal with the challenges of depending on someone else's generosity?
> *Talking Points for Your Discussion*
> - When making your need known
> - In receiving the gift
> - In maintaining the relationship
> - Other

15. As it is written, He that had gathered much had nothing over; and he that had gathered little had no lack.

Paul concludes this section by quoting Exodus 16:18, a verse drawn from the wilderness experience of the nation of Israel. The lesson the verse gives is related to the miraculous provision of manna for the people of Israel. Exodus 16 shows that there were many rules associated with the manna. There was no value in gathering extra to save, for it would spoil. The exception was gathering an extra amount on the day before the Sabbath. No one was allowed to hoard a surplus. When all was gathered, everyone had just enough.

Paul challenges his readers then and now to learn from Israel's example. Just as the Israelites had to exercise faith in God in their gathering of manna, so it is when we give offerings for the poor. Many of us do not have substantial reserves of money. We give and have faith that God will provide for our future needs.

<table>
</table>

What Do You Think?

How do you establish the dividing line between unbiblical hoarding and reasonable savings for future needs?

Talking Points for Your Discussion

- Regarding short-term emergency or "rainy day" savings
- Regarding long-term retirement savings or investing

Visual for Lesson 11. *Pass this poster around class and invite learners to write on it their responses to the question it poses. Discuss results.*

Conclusion

A. Their Examples

Frank Houghton (1894–1972) was a missionary in China. During the persecution of Christians there in the 1930s, he wrote a beautiful Christmas song titled "Thou Who Wast Rich Beyond All Splendor" to encourage his fellow missionaries. Its two opening lines are drawn directly from our lesson's key verse, 2 Corinthians 8:9. Houghton and his fellow missionaries had given up much to preach the gospel to the Chinese, but he reminded them that the example of Christ surpassed by far anything they could ever have done.

Houghton is just one example of a long line of individuals who gave up much for the sake of Christ. This line stretches all the way back to the New Testament, beginning with Peter, who had a fishing business (Matthew 19:27). Paul himself was a highly educated rabbi who came from a family wealthy enough to send him from Tarsus to Jerusalem for schooling (Acts 22:3). Yet he adopted the vocation of an itinerant missionary who had to live hand to mouth at times (Philippians 4:12). The examples they set for giving includes martyrdom by some.

B. Our Obligation

Churches and individual Christians should help relieve suffering for two reasons. First, it's a biblical requirement to do so (1 John 3:17; etc.). In the Old Testament, assistance to the needy was seen as reflecting God's compassion toward them (Psalm 140:12; Jeremiah 22:16). For His people to go through the actions of worship while ignoring the genuine needs of destitute people around them made their worship a sham and an insult to God (Isaiah 1:10-17).

Second, and less obvious, the giving of aid can help free the giver of selfishness, greed, and prejudice against those in need. And we probably have more of a fortune than we think, from which we can give. Consider this conclusion by Pew Research Center, published July 9, 2015:

> The U.S. stands head and shoulders above the rest of the world [in terms of income]. More than half (56%) of Americans were high income by the global standard. . . . Another 32% were upper-middle income. In other words, almost nine-in-ten Americans had a standard of living that was above the global middle-income standard.

Most of us *do* have extra dollars; it just takes planning and sacrifice to free them up. It might be as simple as one less cup of coffee a week or as complicated as downsizing a home to make cash available. But the first question is, do we care?

C. Prayer

Heavenly Father, may we look for opportunities to share with those in need of the bounty You have entrusted to us. May we be people who love others as You would have us to love them. We pray this in the name of Jesus. Amen.

D. Thought to Remember

Measure generosity as God does.

INVOLVEMENT LEARNING

Enhance your lesson with KJV Bible Student *(from your curriculum supplier) and the reproducible activity page (at www.standardlesson.com or in the back of the* KJV Standard Lesson Commentary Deluxe Edition*).*

Into the Lesson

Write this statement on the board: "Unless we share our wealth, we will share their poverty." Ask, "In what ways can this statement come true for a church or for individual Christians who are aware of others in dire need but do nothing to help?"

Jot responses on the board. Try to keep the discussion from becoming political with regard to what governments should do; keep it focused on the church. Anticipate that your more astute learners will voice the issue of spiritual poverty that results from and/or in failure to help relieve a known physical need.

Say, "In Matthew 26:11, Jesus told His disciples that the poor would always be with them. But He did not intend that truth to be used as an excuse to do nothing. Today's lesson examines principles for responding to situations of dire need among fellow believers."

Into the Word

Ask, "As you hear the lesson text read, be alert for differences between Christian and secular philosophies and methods of crisis response." Read 2 Corinthians 8:7-15 to the class, then call for reflections on those differences (expected responses, stated in terms of the Christian system's superiority, may include grounding in love for Christ and his church; eternal significance; connection with sharing the gospel; reasonable expectations [no guilt trip]; future reciprocity; fulfillment of God's promise to supply needs).

Jot all responses on the board. Work through them individually, asking for the respondent to clarify where necessary.

Alternative. Form learners into groups and distribute copies of the "Mission: Money" tour map activity from the reproducible page, which can be downloaded. Say, "While Paul was evangelizing areas of Asia and Europe, he was also helping desperately poor Christians." Instruct groups to follow the instructions on the map, tracing Paul's mission and following the money. After groups reconvene for whole-class discussion, ask students to ponder out loud the scope of one man's response to one area's need. (*Option.* On a world map, make your own "Mission: Money" map, drawing lines from your church to places you've sent assistance; discuss.)

Into Life

Write on the board the following statement from the commentary in two lines:

*Christ's humility and poverty
make His followers spiritually rich.*

Form students into small groups to discuss the following questions (write the questions on the board). *Option.* Distribute to the small groups handouts on which you have reproduced both the statement above and the questions below.

1–How is the first line related to the second line?
2–What is the relationship between spiritual riches and willing generosity?

After 10 minutes, have groups share conclusions in whole-class discussion. Brainstorm ways for spiritual riches to result in one act of intentional generosity as a class and/or as individuals in the week ahead.

Option or Alternative. Give each student a copy of the "Case Studies" activity from the reproducible page. Begin by naming a few benevolence ministries of your church, such as food pantry, Operation Christmas Child, Compassion International, and/or IDES disaster relief. Allow one minute for each student to write a similar case study; they should not put their names on them. Collect the stories, shuffle, and redistribute so students can read case studies that are not their own. As time permits, ask volunteers to read aloud. Conclude with the prayer on page 431.

LOVING AND JUST BEHAVIOR

DEVOTIONAL READING: Matthew 5:38-48
BACKGROUND SCRIPTURE: Romans 12:9-21

ROMANS 12:9-21

9 Let love be without dissimulation. Abhor that which is evil; cleave to that which is good.

10 Be kindly affectioned one to another with brotherly love; in honour preferring one another;

11 Not slothful in business; fervent in spirit; serving the Lord;

12 Rejoicing in hope; patient in tribulation; continuing instant in prayer;

13 Distributing to the necessity of saints; given to hospitality.

14 Bless them which persecute you: bless, and curse not.

15 Rejoice with them that do rejoice, and weep with them that weep.

16 Be of the same mind one toward another. Mind not high things, but condescend to men of low estate. Be not wise in your own conceits.

17 Recompense to no man evil for evil. Provide things honest in the sight of all men.

18 If it be possible, as much as lieth in you, live peaceably with all men.

19 Dearly beloved, avenge not yourselves, but rather give place unto wrath: for it is written, Vengeance is mine; I will repay, saith the Lord.

20 Therefore if thine enemy hunger, feed him; if he thirst, give him drink: for in so doing thou shalt heap coals of fire on his head.

21 Be not overcome of evil, but overcome evil with good.

KEY VERSE

Let love be without dissimulation. Abhor that which is evil; cleave to that which is good. —**Romans 12:9**

JUSTICE IN THE NEW TESTAMENT

Unit 3: Paul Teaches About New Life in Christ

LESSONS 10–13

LESSON AIMS

After participating in this lesson, each learner will be able to:

1. Give three examples (drawn from the teaching in today's text) of overcoming evil with good.

2. Explain why God reserves vengeance for himself.

3. Correct a behavior in light of the loving and just standards stressed by Paul.

LESSON OUTLINE

Introduction

A. The Wrong Seems Strong

It is easy to despair over the prevalence of evil. One result of expanded media coverage is that we seem to get extensive coverage of an endless parade of tragedies from all over the world. The stories range from cruelty to kittens to beheadings of Christians. Media outlets never seem to tire of presenting the latest in human depravity, so much so that we can become numb to its significance.

While we might imagine we have entered a new age of tragedy, the truth is that we have been in it for a long time. Maltbie Babcock, a nineteenth-century minister, knew this all too well. He and his wife, Katherine, had two sons, but both died as infants. Babcock found solace in taking long walks in nature and in writing poetry. These two came together in a public way when one of his poems was published and set to music after his death. The combination became the beloved hymn "This Is My Father's World." Often recognized for its appreciation of God's creation, the lyrics also draw an important conclusion in stating "that though the wrong seems oft so strong, God is the ruler yet."

We only escape the results of sin and evil when we get to Heaven. Even so, the apostle Paul, like Babcock, encourages us not to sink into despair. Evil will not prevail in the end. In our lesson this week, we see Paul address the problem of evil in a direct and practical manner.

B. Lesson Background

The ancient Greek philosophers pondered questions of morality in their writings. In their discussions, they considered categories of *virtue* and *vice*. The authors of the Bible provided their own teachings on these subjects. The Greek word for *virtue* occurs five times in the New Testament: Philippians 4:8; 1 Peter 2:9; 2 Peter 1:3, 5 (twice). The translation is "virtue" in four out of five instances; the sole exception is 1 Peter 2:9, which translates "praises."

The philosopher Plato, writing 400 years before the New Testament authors, believed in four cardinal virtues: prudence, justice, temperance, and courage. These four were still held in esteem in the city of Rome in the century before Paul wrote Romans. This is clear from the writings of the Roman statesman Cicero (106–43 BC). We also find them in Wisdom of Solomon 8:7, a Jewish writing of the period: "If a man love righteousness her labours are virtues: for she teacheth temperance and prudence, justice and fortitude."

For Paul, virtue was more than just a philosophical matter. Today's lesson looks at a passage in Romans in which the apostle becomes intensely practical. Romans 12 begins with Paul calling followers of Jesus to be "transformed by the renewing of your mind" (12:2). Transformed to what? What does a transformed life look like?

The first 11 chapters of Romans are filled with wonderful but heavy doctrinal instruction. With chapter 12, Paul turns his attention squarely to the practical side of living the Christian life. The teachings in chapter 12, especially in the portion found in our printed text, are almost like proverbs: brief, self-contained statements. Many are similar to Jesus' teachings as found in the Sermon on the Mount.

I. Relating with Fellow Believers
(Romans 12:9-13)

A. Loving Behavior (vv. 9, 10)

9a. Let love be without dissimulation.

Paul begins this section primarily discussing behaviors between Christians within the fellowship of the church. Paul's first virtuous teaching serves to define loving behavior among Christians. The original word translated *without dissimulation* is rendered elsewhere as "unfeigned" (sincere), and that is the sense here (2 Corinthians 6:6; 1 Timothy 1:5). This includes both speech and actions. We should not say we love when we don't. We should not act like we love when we don't. The

HOW TO SAY IT

Apollos	Uh-*pahl*-us.
Cicero	*Si*-suh-row.
Corinthians	Ko-*rin*-thee-unz (*th* as in *thin*).
Deuteronomy	Due-ter-*ahn*-uh-me.

solution, however, is not to quit talking about love or merely acting as if one loves. It is to love truly, to overcome barriers of resentment or distrust and love from the heart.

9b. Abhor that which is evil; cleave to that which is good.

Lest we think the previous line means that we ignore virtue or vice in others, Paul's second virtuous teaching presents two actions regarding our interpersonal approach. This pair of commands does not focus on individuals themselves but on things they may do. It is the basis for the oft-quoted advice that we must "love the sinner but hate the sin" (although we realize that God sometimes hates both; see Proverbs 3:32; 11:20; 12:22; 16:5). Our love for others does not mean we encourage their sinful behaviors.

10. Be kindly affectioned one to another with brotherly love; in honour preferring one another.

Paul's third set of virtuous teaching employs the Greek word that William Penn used in naming the first capital city of his Pennsylvania colony: Philadelphia, the city of *brotherly love*. We are to care for our Christian brothers and sisters with great affection. We are friends with our fellow Christians, but friends who are willing to make sacrifices for each other (as a parent would do for a son or daughter). We are to love each other deeply with the type of love a brother or sister would have for a sibling.

This is demonstrated when we quash our natural selfishness and elevate the needs of others over our own, *preferring one another*. Many Bible students are aware of the dozens of "one another" passages in the New Testament. Paul writes just over half of these. Imagine a community where every person is more concerned about the needs of others than his or her own! When we put others first, we honor them.

When election campaigns heat up, pay attention to how candidates talk to and about their opponents. If the typical pattern occurs, candidates appearing together will shake hands and exchange smiles. But then they will launch into vicious attacks on the other's positions—and sometimes their persons!

U.S. presidential campaigns serve as examples. When two candidates are together in social settings, they appear fairly civil toward one another. However, their debates are characterized by scathing attacks on each other's integrity more than by a serious discussion of the issues that face the nation at the time.

People may disagree over whether the behavior of political candidates merely reflect the divided (and divisive) temperament of the nation or, on the other hand, fuel it. There is probably truth on both sides of that argument.

Regardless, the question for us as Christians is whether our own attitudes and behavior are any better than those of the world at large. Are *we* hypocritical? Do *we* hate what is evil and hold fast to what is good? Are *we* patient with those who disagree with us? Whatever the situation, whether in personal interactions with Christians or unbelievers, or in those tense moments that sometimes occur in the fellowship of the church, do we exhibit a godly spirit?   —C. R. B.

B. Just Behavior (vv. 11-13)
11a. Not slothful in business.

In quick order, Paul offers eight brief descriptions of the life of virtue. All eight consist of an "in _____" category (although the word *in* is not explicitly used in every case), along with a command related to this category. *Slothful* has the sense of carelessness, even sloppiness. The Greek word behind the translation *business* is also translated "diligence" elsewhere, and that is the sense here (as in Romans 12:8 and 2 Corinthians 8:7). Rather than speaking of his readers' business activities, Paul is directing their attention to those qualities that are important in their relationships within the church. Christians should not treat their responsibilities to others with carelessness or neglect.

11b. Fervent in spirit.

This refers to a self-motivated excitement about living the kind of spiritual life that relentlessly seeks God. Acts 18:25 uses a similar phrase of Apollos.

What Do You Think?
How do you keep your spiritual passion high?
Talking Points for Your Discussion
- When discouragement starts to set in
- When complacency starts to set in
- When a Christian support system is absent
- Other

11c. Serving the Lord.

When our desire to serve others grows weak, we should remember that we serve our Lord when we meet the needs of others (Matthew 25:40).

12a. Rejoicing in hope.

The gospel offers *hope* in ways no other religion does. The church should be a place of joy and hope, even in the midst of tragic circumstances. We need never doubt God's love for us or that He is in control of our lives.

12b. Patient in tribulation.

Christians are not promised that their lives will be without trouble and free of worry—quite the opposite! (See Matthew 10:22; John 15:18; etc.) There are times when our faith must carry us through, when we must wait on the Lord (Isaiah 40:30, 31; Micah 7:7). Ignoring problems does not make them go away, but sometimes patient, hopeful endurance that is supported by others is the only answer we have.

12c. Continuing instant in prayer.

The Greek behind this unusual phrase is almost identical to that in Colossians 4:2a, and the translation "continue in prayer" there is the sense here (compare Acts 1:14). To have patience in the midst of trouble does not mean we are inactive. We bring our needs, both spiritual and physical, before the throne of God in our prayers.

Remember that Paul is writing in the context of the church as a whole. While we should have times of private prayer, a healthy and committed church will have members praying for each other in an informed way. Sometimes just knowing that others are praying for you brings comfort.

13a. Distributing to the necessity of saints.

The idea here is that of mutual sharing based on need (see 2 Corinthians 8:14, last week's lesson). It describes tangible actions such as taking care of needs for food, clothing, or shelter.

This is part of the joyful fellowship of the church. We are encouraged in knowing that others in the fellowship care about us. They wait on the Lord with us. They pray for us. And they step up when we need help in managing the day-to-day pressures of living, such as providing for our families (compare Acts 2:42-47; 4:32-37; 6:1-6).

13b. Given to hospitality.

This means much more than being willing to have friends over to watch the big game. It means opening our homes to those going through trying circumstances, who need a place to stay or a meal (compare 1 Peter 4:9; 3 John 6-8). Even church members may at times need temporary housing.

All of these admonitions follow the idea of the more fortunate helping the less fortunate. Since the biblical idea of justice includes relief of the plight of the poor, the church is acting justly when it behaves this way (Micah 6:8). While Paul is primarily focused on relationships within the church in this section, he does nothing to forbid or discourage acts of compassion outside the body of Christ. The relationships outside the church are the focus of the next section.

> *What Do You Think?*
> In what ways can you be a role model in extending hospitality?
> *Talking Points for Your Discussion*
> - In light of scriptural directives (1 Timothy 3:2; Titus 1:8; 1 Peter 4:9; 3 John 6-8)
> - In light of current possibilities and challenges

II. Independent Exhortations
(ROMANS 12:14-16)
A. Empathetic Behavior (vv. 14, 15)

14. Bless them which persecute you: bless, and curse not.

Historical evidence tells us that the church in Rome is suffering persecution at this point, but not from the Roman government. That affliction will begin about 10 years after Paul writes this letter. The persecutors at this time come from the non-Christian Jewish community. They target Jews who have left the synagogue for the church and who believe that Jesus is indeed the Messiah. Such persecution likely presents itself in social and economic ostracism: those Jews who choose to follow Jesus find themselves shunned.

When troubled by another person, our first impulse might be simply to endure, to weather the storm. Another reaction might be to return aggression with aggression, cursing the other and striking back. Paul disallows both responses. When attacked unjustly, he calls his readers to *bless* their persecutors. We don't fight fire with fire. We respond with love and grace, in a manner consistent with Jesus' teaching (Matthew 5:43, 44).

> *What Do You Think?*
> In practical terms, what could it look like to bless someone who is consistently aggressive toward you?
> *Talking Points for Your Discussion*
> - When it's a coworker
> - When it's a neighbor
> - When it's a family member
> - Other

15. Rejoice with them that do rejoice, and weep with them that weep.

Paul shifts the focus back to connections between Christians in speaking about the nature of Christians' interdependence. Shared joy seems to multiply; shared sorrow seems to lighten the burden (compare 1 Corinthians 12:26).

B. Humble Behavior (v. 16)

16a. Be of the same mind one toward another.

This is another of Paul's "one another" passages; there are about 30 of them across all his letters. This particular one is fronted by one of the apostle's hot-button issues: being unified in thought. The challenge to *be of the same mind* reverberates across his letters (see Romans 15:5; 1 Corinthians 1:10; 2 Corinthians 13:11; Philippians 2:2, 5; 4:2; compare Ephesians 4:13; 1 Timothy 6:3-5). Being able to "rejoice with them that do rejoice,

Visual for Lessons 12 & 13. *Challenge learners to sum up the 14 entries on the left with a single word, then do the same with the 22 entries on the right.*

and weep with them that weep" (just considered) is prerequisite to being of the same mind.

But we caution that the need for unity in thought should not be interpreted to mean that church members are to be absolutely uniform in their thinking. There is room in the church for differing opinions on certain issues (examples: Romans 14; 1 Corinthians 8). The call is to have a shared attitude that springs from a transformed mind (Romans 12:2).

16b. Mind not high things, but condescend to men of low estate.

The enemy of unity is pride (Philippians 2:2-4). Thinking of oneself too highly will hinder, if not prevent altogether, relationships with those *of low estate* (compare Romans 12:3).

16c. Be not wise in your own conceits.

Those guilty in this area become blind to the possibility that their viewpoint may be wrong (see Romans 11:25). No one wants to be around an arrogant person. Proverbs 3:7 connects a lack of conceit with fear of the Lord.

III. Relating with Unbelievers
(ROMANS 12:17-21)
A. Peaceful Behavior (vv. 17, 18)
17a. Recompense to no man evil for evil.

We do not take justice into our own hands when we are wronged, because it is not our prerogative to do so (Proverbs 20:22; 24:29). We are

to respond to unjust treatment with kindness—a consistent teaching of the New Testament (Luke 6:28; 1 Thessalonians 5:15; 1 Peter 3:9). Paul has more to say on this subject two verses below.

17b. Provide things honest in the sight of all men.

The opposite of evil is *things honest*. Our standard is always to act with unmistakable integrity and compassion (see also 2 Corinthians 8:21). This is an important witness to the unbelieving world.

18. If it be possible, as much as lieth in you, live peaceably with all men.

Here's how we can measure our progress in achieving the high standards at issue: the measure is the degree to which we are able to *live peaceably with all men*. Are you a troublemaker or a peacemaker? Do your actions provoke tense situations or calm them? Are you the person whom no one wants to cross because of your reputation for meanness, or are you one whom others trust and admire? We cannot control the behavior of others, but we can influence them by our lives of kindness, patience, forgiveness, and love (compare 2 Corinthians 13:11; 1 Thessalonians 5:13).

> *What Do You Think?*
> What techniques have you used to attempt to de-escalate a conflict with unbelievers?
> *Talking Points for Your Discussion*
> - Techniques that have worked
> - Techniques that had no effect
> - Techniques that backfired, making things worse

B. Compassionate Behavior (vv. 19-21)

19. Dearly beloved, avenge not yourselves, but rather give place unto wrath: for it is written, Vengeance is mine; I will repay, saith the Lord.

The taking of personal revenge is forbidden because of the nature of God himself. Paul quotes Deuteronomy 32:35 to assure his readers that injustice will not go unpunished (this verse is also quoted in Hebrews 10:30). There is a time and *place* for God's *wrath*. There will be repayment from the Lord himself for evil done to the people of God. God reserves *vengeance* to himself.

20. Therefore if thine enemy hunger, feed him; if he thirst, give him drink: for in so doing thou shalt heap coals of fire on his head.

Paul continues to address proper behavior toward antagonists by quoting Proverbs 25:21, 22a. Jesus' teaching on love for enemies (Matthew 5:44; Luke 6:27) forms the basis for Paul's thoughts here, and the verses from Proverbs reflect this.

What Paul and the author of Proverbs mean by the phrase *heap coals of fire on his head* is not entirely certain. Figurative uses of "coals" and "fire" in the Old Testament are connected with God's judgment (Psalm 18:8; 140:10; etc.). If this is the connection, then unrepentant enemies will suffer the vengeance of Romans 12:19, just considered. The hoped-for repentance may come about from feelings of shame when the actions of evildoers are met with acts of kindness.

◆ *RESPONDING TO INDIRECT PERSECUTION* ◆

One could make a case that America was at one time a "Christian nation," if defined broadly enough. But various court decisions in the 1960s and 1970s have caused that designation to fall into disuse. These cultural shifts resulted in some Christians' referring to themselves as "persecuted." But this is, at best (worst?), what we might call indirect persecution, since it does not involve loss of livelihood, torture, and/or martyrdom that Christians have faced and are facing.

Decades after the 1970s, we experience the secularizing winds' blowing ever stronger. An example is a certain bill that was working its way through the California legislature a couple of years ago. Among other things, it outlawed so-called discrimination in any Christian college that received government aid for students: there should be no moral behavior codes for students; no doctrinal standards for their professors; no religious content in nonreligious courses; etc.

There may be no direct persecution in such legislation, but there is abundant indirect persecution in that the result is that the truths of the Bible in general and the gospel in particular are ever more marginalized. How do we put Romans 12:20 into practice in such a context?　　　—C. R. B.

21. Be not overcome of evil, but overcome evil with good.

A two-step process is in view here. Step 1, resisting successfully being *overcome of evil,* is indeed a major victory! But wars are not won merely by being good at defense. There is also the absolutely vital nature of Step 2, *overcome evil with good.*

We see the good and do the good, thereby joining our Lord as the one who overcomes the world (John 16:33). Evil will not prevail, nor will the evil one, Satan (1 John 2:13, 14). At the final judgment, we will see the vengeance and justice of God prevail. The Bible promises it!

Conclusion
A. Overcoming Evil

A prevailing message in most cultures is that "might makes right." Usually *might* refers to physical power and intimidation, but it may also describe economic power. The richest person often has lawyers who know how to win court judgments. *Might* can also be political power.

"Might makes right" is not Paul's position. His position flips the phrase around: "right makes might." When Christians do right things, the mighty power of God is behind them. God is in control, and His justice will prevail. To say that the good will overcome the evil is to say that God will overcome evil.

These are comforting thoughts for those who suffer affliction and injustice in a sin-broken world. We both depend on God and pursue His agenda for repairing the brokenness, using His principles and Jesus' teachings. This is part of what it means to represent the kingdom "not of this world" (John 18:36).

B. Prayer

Lord God, may we respond with love, not hate, to people who oppose You. May we demonstrate patience, not anger. May we be like Your Son, who asked forgiveness for those who crucified Him. We pray this in His name. Amen.

C. Thought to Remember
Do good to those who *aren't* good.

INVOLVEMENT LEARNING

Enhance your lesson with KJV Bible Student *(from your curriculum supplier) and the reproducible activity page (at www.standardlesson.com or in the back of the* KJV Standard Lesson Commentary Deluxe Edition*).*

Into the Lesson

Ask, "When you were sick as a child, how did your parents bring you comfort?" Responses may include blankets, soup, snuggling, etc. Continue: "Today we'll work through a list of instructions to help sick relationships. Christians are sometimes accused of being all about crusty old rules. But let's delve into directives that show otherwise."

Alternative. Distribute copies of the "Shirt and Shoes Required" activity from the reproducible page, which can be downloaded. Form students into groups with the task of adding to the list of seemingly nit-picky rules. Have them state why such rules exist.

Say, "Here's another rule, from a tea station on a Chinese passenger train:

> Walk steadily and slowly to the boiled water and pour it not too full as this can be scalding you or other passengers when the train is shaking and braking to get back to your seat.

"The writer needs a little help with English, but we get the point: don't overfill cups of boiling liquid. Rules are everywhere. We'll find today's list refreshingly concise and universally important."

Into the Word

Cut out at least 30 paper squares (about 5" to a side) in a variety of colors. Give several squares and marking pens to students formed into groups. Say, "We're making a patchwork quilt. We'll summarize instructions in the text, using no more than three words per instruction."

Give an example by reading aloud the first verse of the text then saying "You might write *love sincerely* on one square, *hate evil* on another, and *cling to good* on the third." Divide the remaining 12 verses among the groups. Mount finished squares on the wall to form a patchwork "quilt."

Possible entries on the remaining squares: live like family, prefer each other (v. 10); don't be lazy, be passionate, serve the Lord (v. 11); rejoice in hope, be patient, pray always (v. 12); be generous, practice hospitality (v. 13); bless your enemies, don't curse persecutors (v. 14); share joy, share grief (v. 15); think alike, avoid snobbery, help the lowly, avoid conceit (v. 16); don't retaliate, show honesty (v. 17); be peace-loving (v. 18); don't seek revenge, let God judge (v. 19); care for enemies (v. 20); be an overcomer (v. 21).

Alternative. Distribute copies of "The Good News Post" activity from the reproducible page and follow the instructions.

Into Life

If you made the "quilt," say, "Imagine a life where everyone lives according to these descriptions, yourself included. Imagine a workplace where everyone is patient and passionate to serve. Imagine a home where joys and griefs are shared. This quilt reflects how the Holy Spirit guides us into love." Let students take quilt squares home, especially squares that speak to heart-work needed.

Alternative. Ask, "If you hear a person say, 'It's not about rules; it's about relationship,' what would that person be referring to?" Jot answers on the board. Then ask the follow-up question: "Were you ever in a relationship with a person who followed no rules—no code of conduct, no respect for the law, no consideration of your feelings?" (Note: show of hands only; do not allow stories to delay the segment.) Continue: "Such relationships range from painful to impossible. Granted, our faith is absolutely in the Lord, not the law. *But our rules of engagement require daily attention.*"

Write the immediately preceding statement on the board and challenge students to reword it so it is more in line with the directives studied in today's lesson (possible responses: My relationship with Christ sets my rules. / My Ruler guides my relationships. / It is about rules and the Ruler who made them). Ask whether any student has changed his or her mind regarding the usefulness of rules.

PRACTICING JUSTICE

DEVOTIONAL READING: Romans 8:1-11
BACKGROUND SCRIPTURE: Ephesians 4:25–5:2; Colossians 3:1-17

COLOSSIANS 3:5-17

5 Mortify therefore your members which are upon the earth; fornication, uncleanness, inordinate affection, evil concupiscence, and covetousness, which is idolatry:

6 For which things' sake the wrath of God cometh on the children of disobedience:

7 In the which ye also walked some time, when ye lived in them.

8 But now ye also put off all these; anger, wrath, malice, blasphemy, filthy communication out of your mouth.

9 Lie not one to another, seeing that ye have put off the old man with his deeds;

10 And have put on the new man, which is renewed in knowledge after the image of him that created him:

11 Where there is neither Greek nor Jew, circumcision nor uncircumcision, Barbarian, Scythian, bond nor free: but Christ is all, and in all.

12 Put on therefore, as the elect of God, holy and beloved, bowels of mercies, kindness, humbleness of mind, meekness, longsuffering;

13 Forbearing one another, and forgiving one another, if any man have a quarrel against any: even as Christ forgave you, so also do ye.

14 And above all these things put on charity, which is the bond of perfectness.

15 And let the peace of God rule in your hearts, to the which also ye are called in one body; and be ye thankful.

16 Let the word of Christ dwell in you richly in all wisdom; teaching and admonishing one another in psalms and hymns and spiritual songs, singing with grace in your hearts to the Lord.

17 And whatsoever ye do in word or deed, do all in the name of the Lord Jesus, giving thanks to God and the Father by him.

KEY VERSE

Put on therefore, as the elect of God, holy and beloved, bowels of mercies, kindness, humbleness of mind, meekness, longsuffering. —**Colossians 3:12**

Photo: kieferpix / iStock / Thinkstock

Justice in the New Testament

Unit 3: Paul Teaches About New Life in Christ

LESSONS 10–13

LESSON AIMS

After participating in this lesson, each learner will be able to:

1. Identify several imperatives of godly behavior.

2. Explain what it means to put off the old self and put on the new.

3. Write a prayer asking God's help in eliminating a besetting sin from the old life.

LESSON OUTLINE

Introduction

A. Agents of Change

Often in classic TV or movie Westerns, a new sheriff comes into a corrupt locale and proceeds to "clean things up." A twentieth-century true version of the story is found in the life of Sheriff Buford Pusser (1937–1974).

In the late 1950s, Pusser moved from his childhood home in McNairy County, Tennessee, to earn a living as a local wrestler in Chicago under the name "Buford the Bull." Pusser returned home in 1962 after marrying. He then became police chief of Adamsville, Tennessee, a position his father once held.

After the sheriff of McNairy County was killed in an auto accident, Pusser was elected to that position. Despite being the youngest sheriff in Tennessee's history, Pusser promptly began trying to eliminate organized crime in his county. His one-man war on moonshine, prostitution, and gambling along the Tennessee-Mississippi state line became legendary. The 1973 movie *Walking Tall* was based on Pusser's story. The film spawned sequels, a series, and a remake.

There is much that is corrupt with our world. But how can we make a difference when problems seem overwhelming? Paul tells us how to be a true agent of change in our world.

B. Lesson Background

The letter to the Colossians is one of the four "prison epistles," letters written by Paul while under arrest in Rome. The other three are Ephesians, Philippians, and Philemon. The letter we call 2 Timothy was also written by Paul while imprisoned (later), but that letter is grouped with the pastoral epistles. We estimate that Paul wrote the four prison epistles about the year AD 63.

The letter under consideration was addressed to the church in Colosse. That town was situated on the Lycus River in southwest Asia Minor (modern Turkey) on an important commercial highway. The church was made up primarily of Gentiles.

The book of Acts does not mention Paul's being in Colosse, but we believe that Philemon (the recipient of a letter from Paul that bears his name) lived there. This is because Onesimus, the slave whom Paul sent back to Philemon (Philemon 10-12), lived in Colosse for he is mentioned in Colossians 4:9 as "one of" the Colossians.

We find powerful doctrinal content in the first two chapters of Colossians, given by Paul to combat false teaching in the church. He refers to this as "philosophy" (Colossians 2:8), and it seems to have included false teaching about the nature of Christ.

As he often does in his letters, Paul follows the opening doctrinal section with practical teachings on how to live out these great truths. Coming to chapter 3, Paul twice encourages his readers to focus on things above (Colossians 3:1, 2). This means that their behavior should be according to God's standards, not earthly standards. They should conduct themselves in expectations of Christ's return (3:4). This is a way of exhorting them not to be engaged in activities that would embarrass themselves if their Lord made a sudden appearance. This brings us to today's text.

I. Put Off
(COLOSSIANS 3:5-9)

A. Ending Sinful Actions (vv. 5-7)

5a. Mortify therefore your members which are upon the earth.

If the Lord Jesus could return at any time, how should we then live? A focus on "things above" (Colossians 3:1, 2) will lead us to *mortify* (put to death) the *members* that keep our attention *upon the earth*. This means putting to death the sinful elements of our lives that separate us from God and make us unprepared for Christ's return (compare Matthew 5:29, 30). Paul teaches elsewhere about putting the old life to death and beginning the new life in Christ (Romans 6:1-7). Being for-

HOW TO SAY IT

Barbarians	Bar-*bare*-ee-unz.
Colosse	Ko-*lahss*-ee.
Colossians	Kuh-*losh*-unz.
Onesimus	O-*ness*-ih-muss.
Philemon	Fih-*lee*-mun or Fye-*lee*-mun.
Scythians	*Sith*-ee-unz.

given of our sins is not a justification for continuing in them (6:1, 2).

5b. Fornication, uncleanness, inordinate affection, evil concupiscence, and covetousness, which is idolatry.

Lest the readers misunderstand what must be given the death sentence, Paul lists five examples. The first is *fornication*. Paul and the other writers of the Bible consistently limit sexual activity to the relations between a man and a woman married to each other. All other sexual activity is seen as fornication (compare 1 Corinthians 6:18).

The words that follow are related to this prohibition of fornication. *Uncleanness* in this context is not about personal hygiene, but sexual misbehavior. *Inordinate affection* characterizes sexual desires not in keeping with God's standards. This is similar to *evil concupiscence*, an expression using another word for "desire" or "passion." These are both the inclinations and actions of sexual immorality, and both should be put to death if we are to be ready to meet Christ.

> **What Do You Think?**
> What practical steps help you stay morally pure in a sexually saturated culture?
> *Talking Points for Your Discussion*
> - When confronted with cultural redefinitions of morality
> - When in the presence of people whose moral boundaries are unbiblical
> - Other

The last item, *covetousness*, may seem misplaced in a list oriented toward sexual immorality; we may immediately think of the tenth commandment. However, not coveting a neighbor's wife is part of that commandment (Exodus 20:17; Deuteronomy 5:21). Such coveting can lead to sexual sin, as it did with David (2 Samuel 11).

Paul summarizes his teaching by equating covetousness with *idolatry* (compare Ephesians 5:5). The biblical concept of idolatry is more than the worship of statues of other gods. In the first century AD, worship involving idols often includes immoral sexual activity; but there is more than this here. At its core, idolatry occurs when we allow anything to displace God as the proper recipient of our worship. Covetousness disregards God and His proper place in our hearts, and this is never clearer than in the commission of sexual sin in deliberate violation of God's intent for our lives.

6, 7. For which things' sake the wrath of God cometh on the children of disobedience: in the which ye also walked some time, when ye lived in them.

Paul's list of sexually oriented sins is familiar to the Colossians on a personal level. They have *walked* in this kind of sin, which is similar to have *lived in* it. The word *walk* is used commonly as a metaphor in the Bible to indicate the way people live their lives, the life choices they make (examples: Deuteronomy 10:12; John 8:12; 1 John 1:6, 7).

Paul's warning is dire: disregard for God and His standards of holiness promises a frightful outcome at the return of the Lord. That outcome is to be subject to *the wrath of God*. His judgmental anger will fall on the unrepentant, *the children of disobedience,* who defiantly and consistently disobey His standards.

Many Christians do not like to talk or think about the wrath of God, preferring to dwell on His love. But God's anger, which is never arbitrary or capricious, is real. Human sin calls it forth.

B. Leaving the Past Behind (vv. 8, 9)

8, 9. But now ye also put off all these; anger, wrath, malice, blasphemy, filthy communication out of your mouth. Lie not one to another, seeing that ye have put off the old man with his deeds.

This list focuses on our attitudes and actions toward others. To drive home his conviction that these belong to the old life and not to the new, Paul commences to use one of his most powerful metaphors: that of taking off and/or putting on garments (compare Romans 13:12; Galatians 3:27; Ephesians 4:22-24). He depicts Christians "wearing" their deeds as clothing, meaning they are public for all to see. We shed filthy garments of dishonor when we eliminate particular sins from our lives.

The first two items on the list, *anger* and *wrath,* might seem ironic since Paul has just warned

of the impending wrath of God on unrepentant sinners. Here, however, Paul is condemning human anger that seeks to harm others. Anger as such is not a sin; it is a God-given emotion. But anger born of a desire for revenge is indeed sinful. The third item, *malice,* reinforces the distinction between God's righteous wrath and our self-serving anger.

> **What Do You Think?**
> How do you keep anger from crossing the line from justified (Mark 3:5) to sinful (James 1:19, 20)?
> *Talking Points for Your Discussion*
> - Prior to anger arising
> - While you are angry

Paul ends with three sinful deeds of the mouth. *Blasphemy* is deliberate disrespect in speech and is often applied to speech against God. It is a particularly grievous sin that the Jews of Paul's day believe worthy of the death penalty (John 10:33). On a human level, though, such strong disrespectful language amounts to malicious defamation, something often the product of angry words.

This is followed by two other types of sinful talk, *filthy communication* and lying to others. With public discourse becoming coarser by the day, we can become numb to obscenity and profanity. If we're not vigilant, that numbness can lead to participation. It is unfortunate that some Christians, even church leaders, do not hold themselves to a higher standard in this area.

The prohibition against lying calls to mind the ninth commandment (Exodus 20:16). At its core, lying is deception intended to achieve our own selfish ends. Deception and selfishness are foundational to our old self and must have no part in our new life.

Paul's summary of leaving this ungodly behavior behind uses his metaphor of taking off clothing. We have discarded (*put off*) the robe of *the old man,* the selfish sinful person, as signified by discarding our sinful *deeds*. We do this deliberately and intentionally, just as we would take off a winter jacket when we come into the house.

II. Put On

(COLOSSIANS 3:10-14)

A. New Creature (vv. 10, 11)

10, 11. And have put on the new man, which is renewed in knowledge after the image of him that created him: where there is neither Greek nor Jew, circumcision nor uncircumcision, Barbarian, Scythian, bond nor free: but Christ is all, and in all.

In Paul's imagery, we don't stand naked after disrobing from our sinful behaviors. We replace the discards with the proper clothing, *the new man*, because we are being restored to *the image* in which we were *created*, the image of God (Genesis 1:26, 27). Ultimately this is the image of Christ, God's Son (Romans 8:29). From a behavior standpoint, we should look a lot like Jesus. This also involves a *knowledge* renewal, changed thinking in regard to sin.

The universal application of the image of Christ finds expression in Paul's description of Him as being *all, and in all*. This is further defined by the three inclusive contrasts that precede that sweeping statement. In Paul's world one is either a *Greek* (Gentile) or a *Jew*, either circumcised or not, either *bond* (slave) or *free*. All of humanity is thus included; all are eligible to be clothed with the image of Christ.

Paul uses two other categories. Barbarians are non-Greek speakers considered uncultured and barely civilized. Scythians live on the north shore of the Black Sea and are considered to be extremely backward, the ultimate barbarians of the ancient world. Paul is not putting these groups down. Rather, he is telling the Colossians (who think of themselves as educated, cultured Greeks) that donning the image of Christ is possible even for those on the lowest rung of the culture ladder.

◆ WHAT'S A PICTURE WORTH? ◆

"A picture is worth a thousand words"—or so we used to think! Before the days of digital imagery, faking a picture to make it seem real required much skill and time, plus a darkroom equipped for the task. Today all it requires is a computer and proper software such as Photoshop. The right software enables digital manipulation to the heart's content: people can be added and removed from scenes, day can be changed to night—the list is endless.

You've probably received an e-mail with a subject line that suggests the photographer was on hand at just the right moment to take a striking photo. Chances are, the "right moment" was the moment at the computer when the one editing the photo combined pieces from two or more photos to create the desired effect. A common example from calendars is a spectacular picture of a rising full moon in which the moon fills a much larger portion of the sky than it ever does in reality. So nowadays a picture may be worth only one word: *fake* or *manipulated*.

The question for each and every Christian is, "Does the image of Christ I present to the world reflect reality, or is it a fake?" A highly manipulated image that we put together for Sunday services or Monday work will eventually be seen for what it truly represents: hypocrisy. Don't go there.

—C. R. B.

B. New Wardrobe (vv. 12-14)

12. Put on therefore, as the elect of God, holy and beloved, bowels of mercies, kindness, humbleness of mind, meekness, longsuffering.

Paul begins to specify seven qualities that are to be *put on*, but first he defines his audience. *The elect of God* are the Christians, further defined as *holy and beloved*. God's love makes salvation possible (John 3:16). When we accept His Son according to the biblical plan of salvation, we become set apart in purity (holy) from sinful humanity even as we continue to live among unrepentant people. In the pattern of Christ, we are not of the world (17:14, 16). The new garments we wear to reflect this reality should be evident for all to see.

The phrase *bowels of mercies* indicates a strong feeling of compassion for others; we usually call this a response of the heart, but we sometimes say we feel something "in the gut." *Kindness* likewise indicates a positive, generous, gracious response to others' needs. *Humbleness of mind* and *meekness* both stress adopting a position of lowliness, seeking to serve others instead of asserting one's own rights or privileges. *Longsuffering* indicates the willingness to wait as long as it takes for others to make the right response, just as God waited for us to respond to Him (Ephesians 4:32). Such "clothing" as this surely identifies a person as belonging to Christ.

> ### What Do You Think?
> In practical terms, what does it look like to have put on the attributes of which Paul speaks?
>
> *Talking Points for Your Discussion*
> - When interacting with fellow believers
> - When interacting with unbelievers
> - When interacting with total strangers whose spiritual status is unknown to you

13. Forbearing one another, and forgiving one another, if any man have a quarrel against any: even as Christ forgave you, so also do ye.

Paul's sixth category of Christlike clothing is particularly applicable when a *quarrel* takes place within the church. *Forbearing one another* means we don't give up on our relationships. A vital aspect of that is *forgiving one another*. When a quarrel looms, we don't have to win. We can derail a church fight before it begins if we practice mutual forbearance and forgiveness.

Paul includes a humbling reminder of our prime example: *Christ*. Those who clothe themselves with Christ should not forget the great forgiveness that Jesus has bestowed on all of us. This reminder should make our quibbles seem vanishingly petty by comparison.

14. And above all these things put on charity, which is the bond of perfectness.

Paul ends his list of Christ-clothing with the one that ties it all together: *charity* (in modern English, *love*; Romans 13:8, 10). The phrase *above all these things* is striking in that it views charity/love as a topcoat, to be put on over all else. This *bond of perfectness* is the ultimate unifier for the body of Christ. Let us love one another as Christ has loved us (John 13:34).

◆ *WIT VERSUS WISDOM* ◆

Who among us doesn't secretly admire the wit that enables some people to come up with sponta-neous, clever retorts? On a certain occasion, Winston Churchill was purportedly speaking with Lady Nancy Astor, a longtime political enemy, when she said to him, "If you were my husband, I'd put poison in your tea." Churchill's response was, "Madam, if you were my wife, I'd drink it."

Much as we might admire the ease that some people have with witty retorts, the wisdom of Scripture urges a different approach. A put-down won't succeed in building up, but compassion and forgiveness will.
—C. R. B.

III. Put Forth
(COLOSSIANS 3:15-17)
A. With Jesus' Power (vv. 15, 16)

15. And let the peace of God rule in your hearts, to the which also ye are called in one body; and be ye thankful.

The loving church will be a peaceful church, and for this we should be *thankful*. This has not been engineered by our brilliance but by following the example of Christ and conforming to His image (Romans 8:29).

If we live with love, forgiveness, and patience for others, our hearts will be filled with *the peace of God*. We are part of *one body*, the organization whose head loved its future constituents so much that He died for them (Ephesians 5:23-25).

> ### What Do You Think?
> Does one focus on having inner peace to be able to exhibit love and forgiveness to others, or does one exhibit love and forgiveness to others so inner peace will result?
>
> *Talking Points for Your Discussion*
> - Considering situational issues
> - Considering scriptural guidance (Proverbs 12:20; 14:30; Matthew 15:18, 19; Luke 6:45; Romans 14:19; Galatians 5:22; Ephesians 4:1-3; 2 Timothy 2:22)

16. Let the word of Christ dwell in you richly in all wisdom; teaching and admonishing one another in psalms and hymns and spiritual songs, singing with grace in your hearts to the Lord.

Paul finishes this section with specific qualities that characterize the peaceful church. First, *the word of Christ* must find a home in the hearts of believers. There should be an eagerness to learn the ways of God. This is a path of *wisdom*, knowing God's plan for living and then choosing to live that way.

Paul then offers a mechanism for implementing this imperative: *teaching* (primary instruction) and *admonishing* (encouragement to follow the instruction). A highly effective but often underused method of doing both is through the words of the songs we sing together in the context of worship. There are technical distinctions among *psalms and hymns and spiritual songs*, but it's their cumulative effect that interests Paul. The songs we sing together will find their way into our hearts in powerful and memorable ways, often coming to mind later. Therefore, we should sing what we believe and believe what we sing.

B. In Jesus' Name (v. 17)

17. And whatsoever ye do in word or deed, do all in the name of the Lord Jesus, giving thanks to God and the Father by him.

Paul's final words in this section call us to harmonize our words and our deeds, our talk and our actions. This harmonization happens when both are in accordance with what *the name of the Lord Jesus* signifies (Matthew 18:5, 20; etc.). We are to say and do what He would have us say and do.

Jesus' message is for everyone. All are invited to come to Him (Matthew 11:28-30). We can be His ambassadors for kindness, for hope, and for justice in our communities, but above all we are His ambassadors for eternal life in Heaven. For such a privilege let us be thankful, and may our actions express this gratitude *to God* through His Son Jesus Christ.

What Do You Think?
What steps can you take to ensure that your efforts are always in the name of Jesus?
Talking Points for Your Discussion
- Regarding what you say (speech patterns)
- Regarding what you do (behavior patterns)

Visual for Lessons 12 & 13. *Point to this visual as you ask, "Which entry on the left exerts the strongest pull on a Christian to return to the old way? Why?"*

Conclusion

A. Just Thinking

Righteousness means doing the right thing. It is closely tied to the biblical understanding of justice: wanting to see the right thing done from God's perspective and according to His Word. The one who loves justice is the person who wants to see the right thing done for others.

But sin stands in the way of that happening. Sin comes in two categories: acts of commission and acts of omission. God becomes angry not only when His commandments are actively broken but also when people fail to do what they should. When we commit unrighteous acts, we sin by commission; when we can correct an injustice we see but fail to act, we sin by omission. Both dishonor the name of the Lord Jesus. Both discredit what Paul says we have put on.

B. Prayer

Lord God, may Your Word dwell richly in our hearts, so much so that we are increasingly conformed to the image of Your Son. Make us ever aware that what we have put off has no further place in our lives, and what we have put on must be honored. In Jesus' name we pray. Amen.

C. Thought to Remember

We can only bring change to the extent that we let God change us.

INVOLVEMENT LEARNING

Enhance your lesson with KJV Bible Student *(from your curriculum supplier) and the reproducible activity page (at www.standardlesson.com or in the back of the* KJV Standard Lesson Commentary Deluxe Edition*).*

Into the Lesson

Bring three outfits to class: one that you might wear to an office, one that you'd wear at a more formal gathering (wedding, etc.), and one that you'd wear to a workout at the gym. (*Alternative.* For simplicity, search for images online and print them out instead.) Display each outfit and have class members offer several suggestions as to where each set of clothes might be worn.

Alternative. Distribute copies of the "Puzzled" activity from the reproducible page, which can be downloaded. Have learners work in pairs to discover a verse from today's study that speaks to elements of spiritual attire to discard.

After completing either activity, lead into the Bible study by saying, "The way someone dresses can tell a lot about that person. Sometimes we can guess a person's occupation, or even where he or she might be headed. We have spiritual clothing as well. And how we dress ourselves spiritually speaks volumes about us and where we are headed."

Into the Word

Divide the class into three groups. Assign one group verses 5-9 of the lesson text, another group verses 10-14, and the third group verses 15-17. Instruct groups to (1) list character traits in their passages, (2) identify what impact those traits would have on someone's relationship with God, and (3) identify what positive or negative impact those traits could have on other people.

After several minutes have groups share their findings. Lead a discussion about the impact that reemergence of the old self can have on Christian unity. Then discuss how the new life has the opposite effect.

Option. Use the "Sounds Like / Looks Like" exercise from the reproducible page, which can be downloaded. Decide whether to do the activity in small groups or to stay together. If you stay together, ask for a volunteer to choose one of Paul's imperatives. When it is voiced, ask the class, "If you had only your sense of hearing, what would it sound like for someone to practice that virtue?" Jot answers in the left column. Then ask, "If you only had your sense of vision, how would you know someone was practicing that virtue? What would it look like?" Jot answers in the right column. Repeat as time allows.

Alternative. Instead of allowing volunteers to choose which of Paul's imperatives to discuss as above, you can either (1) make the choices yourself or (2) go down the list in the order Paul wrote them.

Into Life

Create a time of quiet reflection. Set the mood by playing meditative worship music in the background. Explain that you are giving your class a few minutes to reflect quietly on which of the negative attributes of the old self they most continue to wrestle with. Have them write that attribute on a slip of paper (assure students that you will not collect what they write). Point out that Paul's list wasn't intended to be comprehensive. For those who don't see their besetting sin on the list, encourage them to write in what seems most applicable.

Next, have learners meditate on who may be negatively affected by the besetting sin just written. Encourage learners to feel free to use symbols to protect privacy. Again, assure learners that you will not collect their written notes.

Finally, instruct students to look at Paul's imperatives that contribute to putting on the new self and choose one to work on in the week ahead. Have them write down one practical way they will live out that imperative this week; suggest they affix the note in a location where it will be seen daily as a reminder. Close with the prayer from page 447.